Text, Copyright © 2004, Linda Lacour Hobar

ISBN-10: 1-892427-06-0
ISBN-13: 978-1-892427-06-9
First Edition

Printed in the United States of America

Bright Ideas Press
Dover, Delaware

www.BrightIdeasPress.com
1.877.492.8081

15 14 13 12 11 10   24 23 22 21 20

PRODUCTION CREDITS
Kathryn Dix: project management/editing; Ivy Ulrich-Bonk: page layout; Christy Shaffer: cover design; Tyler H. Hogan: outline maps; Penny Baker and Evelyn Podsiadlo: proofreading.

PHOTO CREDITS
Athletes in Action Media: p. 156. **Steve Bisagno:** pp. 157, 177, 283 (farmer), 410, 414 (temple). **Jim Blackburn:** pp. 431 (2), 432. **Erin Briscoe:** p. 250 (piggy bank). **Stephen Burak:** p. 409.
Sue Gile: pp. 114 (castle), 120 (church), 136, 195 (church), 274, 275, 338. **Emily Harkey:** pp. 32, 39, 88 (from the collection of the Museum of Biblical Archaeology, Columbus, Ohio). **Ryan Harkey:** pp. 140, 183, 188, 263, 376, 470. **Kathy Harl:** pp. 255, 256. **Mary Harl:** p. 306 (2). **Tim Harrison:** p. 315. **Heather Hobar:** pp. 130, 216, 223 (rune stone), 227 (Eastern church), 262, 277 (2), 284, 358 (2). *Photo Credits continued on page 714.*

ILLUSTRATION CREDITS
Treanne Schutt: Dedication cross.
Amy Pak: From *History Through the Ages: Resurrection to Revolution,* Copyright © 2003 Amy Pak, Home School in the Woods, and *History Through the Ages: Creation to Christ,* Copyright © 2003 Amy Pak, Home School in the Woods, the following illustrations were used by permission.

Quarter 1: pp. 8, 12, 15, 23, 27 (2), 28, 29 (2), 30, 31, 32, 40, 43, 46, 55, 58, 60, 65, 68, 73, 81, 83, 86, 94, 97, 99. *Illustration Credits continued on page 714.*

I sincerely dedicate this book to my husband, Ron,
who still makes me laugh after twenty years of marriage.

That their hearts may be encouraged, being knit together in love,
and attaining to all riches of the full assurance of understanding,
to the knowledge of the **mystery** *of God, both of the Father and of Christ,*
in whom are hidden all the treasures of wisdom and knowledge.

(Colossians 2: 2 - 3)

ACKNOWLEDGMENTS

I'm not attending an awards ceremony. But if I were, I would take out a folded piece of paper with the following names on it to acknowledge and thank them for contributing to *The Mystery of History*.

First, I acknowledge that apart from the grace of my dear Lord and Savior, Jesus Christ, there would be no *Mystery of History*. "For the gifts and the calling of God are irrevocable." (Romans 11:29) Thank you, Lord, for wooing me with your Word and for finding use of me, a weak and weary vessel.

Next, I thank my ever-loving "flam-i-ly" (pet name) for extending such grace to me over these years. You are still my most cherished legacy.

I thank Bob and Maggie Hogan for their labor of love as my publishers *and* as my dear friends. Thank you, Maggie, for making me laugh despite how terribly long it has taken me to finish this book.

I am incredibly indebted to my editor, Kathy Dix. Apart from you, this work would still be a mess. Thank you for pouring your giftedness into this — and doing it so pleasantly.

Many thanks to my historical editor, Pastor Reed Depace, for sharing your knowledge of Christian history. You are like the "chaplain" of this team, giving encouragement when needed and contributing a wealth of theology.

I thank Ivy Ulrich-Bonk for your expertise in making these pages come to life as you painstakingly arrange every letter and exclamation point of this book (of which there are many)!

I am delighted to thank Amy Pak for her beautiful artistry. Your sketches breathe new life into people who are no longer with us and they suspend events in time that might otherwise be forgotten.

I thank my own dear husband, Ron Hobar, for the many, *many* hours he toiled as my photo editor. Your tedious perfectionism is greatly appreciated. I couldn't trust anyone else with your job.

I am grateful to Shawne Bolam for contributing her love of quality literature by compiling the extensive book list. We will all benefit.

I thank Tyler Hogan for customizing each and every map to fit my challenging needs.

I thank my daughter, Heather Hobar, for her tedious help in compiling the index and organizing my detail work. I'm glad you "like" it too.

I thank Sherri Shores for her compilation of the materials list. It will help teachers spend more time teaching and less time scrambling.

I thank Joanne Nolte and Lori Blum for providing me with some creative activity ideas when my own ran dry.

I offer much gratitude to the test families who waded through my rough drafts and helped me shape this curriculum so it would better meet your needs.

I thank the many dear homeschool teachers on the Yahoo group who have kept my spirits lifted through their words of encouragement, ideas, and resources. The experiences with this material that you share continue to inspire me!

I appreciate all the kind words from students, whose newfound enthusiasm for history makes my efforts worthwhile.

Finally, and of great importance, I thank the dear friends, and those of you whom I've never met, who have prayed for my family and me over the past few years through many trials. "Therefore we also, since we are surrounded by so great a cloud of witnesses, let us lay aside every weight, and the sin which so easily ensnares us, and let us run with endurance the race that is set before us, looking unto Jesus, the author and finisher of our faith." (Hebrews 12:1–2a) Your prayers and presence in my life do make a difference. To God be the glory!

CONTENTS

Preface xiii
Letters to the Students xiv
Letter to the Teacher xvii
A Classical Approach to Education xxv
Memory Cards xxvii
Wall of Fame Timeline Suggestions xxx
The X File: Tips on Grading xxxviii
Grade Record xli

SEMESTER I
THE EARLY CHURCH • 1

QUARTER 1 — The Fire Ignites: c. A.D. 33 to 476   3

Around the World • 3

WEEK 1 / Pretest **7**
  Lesson 1: **PENTECOST and the First Followers of Jesus**   **8**
      (**c. A.D. 33** and following)*
    Activities   10
  Lesson 2: **"Saul, Who Also Is Called Paul"** (c. A.D. 35)   **11**
    Activities   13
  Lesson 3: **Paul's Missionary Journeys** (c. A.D. 46–66)   **14**
    Activities   17
    Review 1: Lessons 1–3   19
    Week 1: Exercise   21

WEEK 2 / Pretest **22**
  Lesson 4: **Nero** (A.D. 37–68)   **23**
    Activities   26
  Lesson 5: **Martyrs of the Early Church** (c. A.D. 64–257)   **27**
    Activities   30
  Lesson 6: **Josephus** (A.D. 66)   **31**
    Activities   33
    Review 2: Lessons 4–6   35
    Week 2: Quiz   36

WEEK 3 / Pretest **38**
  Lesson 7: **Masada** (A.D. 66–73)   **39**
    Activities   41
  Lesson 8: **The Dead Sea Scrolls** (c. 100 B.C.–c. A.D. 75)   **42**
    Activities   44

*All lesson titles in bold caps and dates in bold are key events and dates to memorize. There are 12 key items in this volume.

Lesson 9: **The Buried City of Pompeii** (A.D. 79)   **45**

    Activities   47

    Review 3: Lessons 7–9   49

    Week 3: Exercise   50

WEEK 4 / Pretest **52**

    Lesson 10: **Bar-Kokhba** (A.D. 135)   **53**

        Activities   56

    Lesson 11: **The Apostles' Creed** (A.D. 2nd–7th Centuries)   **57**

        Activities   59

    Lesson 12: **St. Valentine** (A.D. 269)   **59**

        Activities   61

        Review 4: Lessons 10–12   62

        Week 4: Quiz   63

WEEK 5 / Pretest **64**

    Lesson 13: **Diocletian Divides the Roman Empire** (A.D. 284–305)   **65**

        Activities   66

    Lesson 14: **Constantine I and the EDICT OF MILAN (313)***   **67**

        Activities   69

    Lesson 15: **The Golden Age of India** (c. 320–500)   **71**

        Activities   74

        Review 5: Lessons 13–15   76

        Week 5: Exercise   78

WEEK 6 / Pretest **79**

    Lesson 16: **The Maya** (c. 350–900)   **80**

        Activities   82

    Lesson 17: **St. Augustine of Hippo** (354–430)   **83**

        Activities   85

    Lesson 18: **The Holy Bible and the Vulgate by Jerome** (382–405)   **86**

        Activities   88

        Review 6: Lessons 16–18   90

        Week 6: Quiz   92

WEEK 7 / Pretest **93**

    Lesson 19: **St. Patrick, Missionary to Ireland** (c. 389–461)   **94**

        Activities   96

    Lesson 20: **Attila the Hun** (434–453)   **96**

        Activities   98

    Lesson 21: **FALL OF THE WESTERN ROMAN EMPIRE (476)***   **98**

        Activities   101

        Review 7: Lessons 19–21   103

WORKSHEET 1: Lessons 1–21   **105**

*All lesson titles in bold caps and dates in bold are key events and dates to memorize. There are 12 key items in this volume.

WEEK 8 / Pretest **117**

    Lesson 22: **Daily Life in the Dark Ages** (c. 500–1000)   **118**

        Activities   122

    Lesson 23: **King Arthur and the Knights of the Round Table** (503)   **123**

        Activities   127

    Lesson 24: **Justinian I and Theodora,**

               Rulers of the Byzantine Empire (527–565)   **128**

        Activities   131

        Review 8: Lessons 22–24   132

        Week 8: Exercise   133

WEEK 9 / Pretest **135**

    Lesson 25: **Columba, Missionary to Scotland** (563)   **136**

        Activities   137

    Lesson 26: **Early Japan and Prince Shotoku** (573)   **139**

        Activities   141

    Lesson 27: **Gregory the Great** (590)   **143**

        Activities   146

        Review 9: Lessons 25–27   148

        Week 9: Quiz   152

WEEK 10 / Pretest **154**

    Lesson 28: **The Sui and Tang Dynasties of China** (589, 618)   **155**

        Activities   158

    Lesson 29: **Mohammed and the BIRTH OF ISLAM (622)***   **160**

        Activities   165

    Lesson 30: **The Spread of Islam** (632)   **166**

        Activities   170

        Review 10: Lessons 28–30   172

        Week 10: Exercise   174

WEEK 11 / Pretest **175**

    Lesson 31: **Wu Zetian, the Empress of China** (690)   **176**

        Activities   178

    Lesson 32: **The Epic of *Beowulf*** (Early 700s)   **179**

        Activities   181

    Lesson 33: **Al-Andalus: "The Ornament of the World"**

               in Medieval Spain (711)   **182**

        Activities   187

        Review 11: Lessons 31–33   189

        Week 11: Quiz   191

All lesson titles in bold caps and dates in bold are key events and dates to memorize. There are 12 key items in this volume.

WEEK 12 / Pretest **193**

    Lesson 34: **St. Boniface, Apostle to Germany** (718)   **194**

        Activities   196

    Lesson 35: **The Iconoclast Controversy** (726)   **197**

        Activities   200

    Lesson 36: **Charles "Martel" and the BATTLE OF TOURS (732)***   **201**

        Activities   202

        Review 12: Lessons 34–36   204

        Week 12: Exercise   205

WEEK 13 / Pretest **206**

    Lesson 37: **Charlemagne** (768)   **207**

        Activities   210

    Lesson 38: *The Thousand and One Nights:* **Tales from Arabia** (786)   **211**

        Activities   213

    Lesson 39: **INVASION OF THE VIKINGS (793)***   **214**

        Activities   217

        Review 13: Lessons 37–39   218

        Week 13: Quiz   220

WEEK 14 / Pretest **221**

    Lesson 40: **The Vikings: Their Families, Their Homes,**
           and Their Faith (c. 800–1100)   **222**

        Activities   225

    Lesson 41: **Methodius and Cyril, Missionaries to the Slavs** (863)   **226**

        Activities   227

    Lesson 42: **Alfred the Great, King of England** (871)   **228**

        Activities   231

        Review 14: Lessons 40–42   234

WORKSHEET 2: Lessons 22–42   **235**

SEMESTER I TEST: Lessons 1–42   **242**

SEMESTER II
THE MIDDLE AGES ◆ 247

QUARTER 3 — The Fire Grows: 874 to 1192   **249**

Around the World ◆ 249

WEEK 15 / Pretest **253**

    Lesson 43: **Lydveldid Island (Iceland)** (874)   **254**

        Activities   256

All lesson titles in bold caps and dates in bold are key events and dates to memorize. There are 12 key items in this volume.

Lesson 44: **The Maori of New Zealand** (c. 900)   **257**

    Activities   261

Lesson 45: **The Great Zimbabwe of Africa** (c. 900)   **262**

    Activities   265

    Review 15: Lessons 43–45   266

    Week 15: Exercise   268

WEEK 16 / Pretest **269**

Lesson 46: **"Good King Wenceslas"** (929)   **270**

    Activities   272

Lesson 47: **Otto I and the Holy Roman Empire** (936)   **273**

    Activities   275

Lesson 48: **Vladimir I of Russia** (c. 956)   **275**

    Activities   277

    Review 16: Lessons 46–48   279

    Week 16: Quiz   280

WEEK 17 / Pretest **281**

Lesson 49: **The Song Dynasty of China** (960)   **282**

    Activities   285

Lesson 50: **St. Simon and the Coptic Orthodox Church** (979)   **286**

    Activities   289

Lesson 51: **Eric the Red and the Settlement of Greenland** (985)   **290**

    Activities   293

    Review 17: Lessons 49–51   295

    Week 17: Exercise   297

WEEK 18 / Pretest **299**

Lesson 52: **LEIF ERICSSON DISCOVERS AMERICA (c. 1003)***   **300**

    Activities   302

Lesson 53: **Macbeth, King of Scotland** (1040)   **303**

    Activities   305

Lesson 54: **El Cid, a Spanish Hero** (1040)   **305**

    Activities   307

    Review 18: Lessons 52–54   309

    Week 18: Quiz   311

WEEK 19 / Pretest **313**

Lesson 55: **William the Conqueror and the BATTLE OF HASTINGS (1066)***   **314**

    Activities   317

Lesson 56: **Pope Gregory VII, Henry IV, and the Investiture Controversy** (1076)   **318**

    Activities   322

*All lesson titles in bold caps and dates in bold are key events and dates to memorize. There are 12 key items in this volume.

Lesson 57: **THE EARLY CRUSADES (1096)***   **323**

     Activities   325

     Review 19: Lessons 55–57   327

     Week 19: Exercise   329

WEEK 20 / Pretest **332**

     Lesson 58: **The Petrobrusians and the Waldensians** (1100s)   **333**

     Activities   335

     Lesson 59: **Eleanor of Aquitaine, the Queen of Two Nations** (1154)   **335**

     Activities   339

     Lesson 60: **The Jews of the Middle Ages** (c. 12th Century)   **340**

     Activities   344

     Review 20: Lessons 58–60   346

     Week 20: Quiz   347

WEEK 21 / Pretest **349**

     Lesson 61: **Richard the Lionhearted, Saladin, and
the Third Crusade** (1192)   **350**

     Activities   352

     Lesson 62: **The Classic Tale of Robin Hood** (Unknown)   **353**

     Activities   356

     Lesson 63: **The Shoguns and Samurai of Japan** (1192)   **356**

     Activities   359

     Review 21: Lessons 61–63   361

WORKSHEET 3: Lessons 43–63   **362**

QUARTER 4 — The Fire Shines: 1210 to 1456   369

Around the World ◆ 369

WEEK 22 / Pretest **373**

     Lesson 64: **St. Francis of Assisi, St. Clara, and
St. Dominic** (1210, 1212, 1216)   **374**

     Activities   379

     Lesson 65: **The Children's Crusade** (1212)   **380**

     Activities   382

     Lesson 66: **King John and the Magna Carta** (1215)   **383**

     Activities   385

     Review 22: Lessons 64–66   386

     Week 22: Exercise   387

WEEK 23 / Pretest **390**

     Lesson 67: **Frederick II, "The Amazement of the World"** (1229)   **391**

     Activities   394

All lesson titles in bold caps and dates in bold are key events and dates to memorize. There are 12 key items in this volume.

Lesson 68: **St. Thomas Aquinas, Philosopher of the Middle Ages** (1252)   **395**
     Activities   398
Lesson 69: **Roger Bacon, Scientist of the Middle Ages** (1253)   **399**
     Activities   401
     Review 23: Lessons 67–69   403
     Week 23: Quiz   405

WEEK 24/ Pretest **408**
Lesson 70: **The Great Khans and the Mongol Invasion of China** (1260)   **409**
     Activities   411
Lesson 71: **MARCO POLO TRAVELS EAST (1271)***   **412**
     Activities   415
Lesson 72: **Sir William Wallace and Robert Bruce,**
       "Bravehearts" of Scotland (1298, 1314)   **416**
     Activities   418
     Review 24: Lessons 70–72   419
     Week 24: Exercise   420

WEEK 25/ Pretest **425**
Lesson 73: **Dante Alighieri, Poet of the Middle Ages** (1318)   **426**
     Activities   428
Lesson 74: **The Aztecs (The Mexica)** (1325)   **429**
     Activities   433
Lesson 75: **The Hundred Years' War** (1337–1453)   **434**
     Activities   436
     Review 25: Lessons 73–75   437
     Week 25: Quiz   438

WEEK 26/ Pretest **441**
Lesson 76: **The Black Death of Europe** (1348)   **442**
     Activities   444
Lesson 77: **The Ming Dynasty of China and the Forbidden City**
       (1368–1644)   **445**
     Activities   448
Lesson 78: **JOHN WYCLIFFE, "MORNING STAR OF THE**
       REFORMATION" (1377)*   **449**
     Activities   452
     Review 26: Lessons 76–78   454
     Week 26: Exercise   455

WEEK 27/ Pretest **456**
Lesson 79: **Geoffrey Chaucer and *The Canterbury Tales*** (1387)   **457**
     Activities   460
Lesson 80: **John Huss** (1415)   **462**
     Activities   466

*All lesson titles in bold caps and dates in bold are key events and dates to memorize. There are 12 key items in this volume.

Lesson 81: **The Life and DEATH OF JOAN OF ARC (1431)***   466
    Activities   470
    Review 27: Lessons 79–81   472
    Week 27: Quiz   474

WEEK 28/ Pretest   476
    Lesson 82: **The Inkas of South America** (1438)   477
        Activities   481
    Lesson 83: **The Ottoman Turks Take Constantinople** (1453)   482
        Activities   485
    Lesson 84: **Johannes Gutenberg Invents the Printing Press** (1456)   486
        Activities   488
        Review 28: Lessons 82–84   490

WORKSHEET 4: Lessons 64–84   491

SEMESTER II TEST: Lesson 43–84   497

Outline Maps   503

Appendix   561
   Section A: Would You Like to Belong to God's Family?   563
   Section B: Activity Supplement   565
   Section C: Supplemental Books and Resources   624
   Section D: Materials Lists   643
   Section E: Bibliography   667
   Section F: Pretest Answer Key   671
   Section G: Answer Key   680

Index   703

All lesson titles in bold caps and dates in bold are key events and dates to memorize. There are 12 key items in this volume.

PREFACE

This is the place in this book where I am allowed to say, "please excuse this or that." Bear with me through these important disclaimers.

First, I apologize for the great length of time it took me to complete this volume. I never dreamed it would take me three times as long as it did to write Volume I. But, for the integrity of the material, I believe it was necessary. A good deal of my time was spent on research. Based on input from Volume I, I sought to improve and lengthen the weekly lessons. One positive result of the long wait for Volume II is that a healthy demand was created for this book, for which I'm grateful.

Second, for the sake of easier reading, I frequently use the terms *man* or *mankind* (and sometimes *his* or *him*) to refer to male and female alike. This in no way diminishes the beautiful, unique, God-given design for the genders.

Third, all Scripture used in this text is quoted from the New King James Version of the Bible.

Fourth, it is my suggestion that families and individuals consider for themselves the appropriateness of each book or film listed on the Supplemental Resource List. Though I have entrusted the compilation of this list to a knowledgeable, conservative book enthusiast, opinions may vary on the suitability of the materials. Please use your own discretion in your selections and view the reading list as a guide to expanding your knowledge base of history.

Fifth, it would be negligent of me not to mention that though I've tried to make this a true history of the world there is inevitably some bias toward the history of Western Civilization. The history of the Western world has had more impact on my own heritage and more than likely the heritage of most of my readers. This is in no way meant to reflect an opinion of superiority of my heritage, my race, or my culture.

Sixth, without apology, this book is written from a Christian worldview due to my personal faith in Jesus Christ. I entered into a personal relationship with Him at 17 and remain one of His followers. I have tried to carefully handle the discussion of other faiths with dignity and respect without compromising my own beliefs.

Finally, it is likely that as time moves forward, mistakes in this book will be found. I apologize ahead of time for them. What I present here is, to the best of my knowledge, historically accurate and biblically based information. Invariably, archaeologists will unearth keys to the past and force us to retell the stories of old. I ask for your patience with the publishing process as we update, improve, correct, and append future printings of this curriculum.

Linda Lacour Hobar

LETTERS TO THE STUDENTS

Younger Students

Hi! My name is Mrs. Hobar. Some of you might already feel like you know me because you read Volume I of *The Mystery of History*. Some of you might be new to this series. Either way, I'm glad you are reading this. It means that you are about to start the second volume of *The Mystery of History*.

I think you are going to like it! You know why? Because there are stories of big volcanoes in this book — massive ones that swallowed up entire towns! And there are stories of kings and queens and knights who lived in great castles and fought dragons and stuff like that. And there are stories about samurai soldiers who lived in Japan and carried long, sharp swords and wore big clothes to make them look tough!

You know, that's what history is. It's a book about people and the exciting, happy, sad, or *unusual* lives they led. Some of these people were nice and kind. Some were purely wicked and selfish. Some were sort of in between. Though many of our customs have changed since the Middle Ages, men and women and boys and girls are still very much the same. Some people are still nice, some are still mean, and some are kind of both. And just like the people of the Middle Ages, most of us are people who work and play, who laugh and cry, and usually go to school. We are also people who are trying to understand what life is all about.

Some of the people we will study had a good understanding of what life is all about. They understood it because they knew God, the One who gave them life in the first place, personally. I hope you are one of those people too. I hope that you know God personally. If you are not sure about that relationship, I encourage you to read "Would You Like to Belong to God's Family" in the Appendix of this book. It explains how we *can* know God through Jesus Christ. You might want to discuss this matter with your teachers or parents.

As for history, I hope this book is exciting to you. But remember, I wrote this book for people of *all* ages, so I don't expect you to be able to understand all of it. You might not be able to do all the quizzes or maps or older student stuff. But that's okay. I have kept you in mind when I wrote and have given you plenty of things to do that I think you can handle — like making treasure maps and building castles. So have fun, and enjoy learning! You are in my prayers.

For the sake of the Mystery,
Mrs. Hobar
2004

Middle Students

Hi! My name is Linda Hobar. I wish so much that I could meet you personally. I think about you all the time. I like your age group. You are still young enough to have fun in school, but you are old enough to really learn.

I have kids too. They are presently 19, 15, and 11. That means that my youngest kid is about your age. She has helped me a lot with this book. You will see pictures of her completing some of the cool activities that you'll be doing.

And though I really want you to have fun with history projects, I will expect more from you at your age. I expect you to try to understand what history is all about. If you think about it, history is really a long story. It's the story of one life after the other. Over time, they connect the past with the present.

You know, some of the people from the Middle Ages were tremendous. There were many saints and missionaries and godly kings and knights. They were dedicated to knowing God and to making Him known. Others, you will learn, fell short of bringing glory to God. They led desperate lives that caused ruin and despair. Like others from the past, some people today know God and some don't. I wonder, what kind of relationship do you have with God? Do you know Him?

If you are not sure about that, I encourage you to read "Would You Like to Belong to God's Family" in the Appendix of this book. It will explain how a person can know God personally through faith in Jesus Christ. I became one of Christ's followers when I was 17 years old. I haven't been the same since.

I hope that by encountering God and growing in your relationship with Him, that you are not the same either. I hope that as the stories of history unfold you are amazed and in awe at the world that we live in. It is an amazing world because it was created by an amazing God.

So, as you read about the heroes, the saints, the martyrs, and the emperors of the past, think about God seeking to reveal Himself over the ages. It is the greatest epic ever told. And have some fun while you do it through the activities suggested here and by exploring, researching, and reading beyond what is presented here. I couldn't begin to include everything in this book that there is to know about the Early Church and the Middle Ages. I'm counting on you to dig deeper into the stuff that you really find interesting. Remember, I do pray for your growth.

For the sake of the Mystery,
Linda Hobar
2004

Older Students

Hi! Allow me to tell you something about myself. My name is Linda Hobar, and I am the mother of three children, ages 19, 15, and 11. That means that I have two teenagers. So I am in the midst of parenting kids about your age.

To some that is a frightening thought, but I love it. I'm very close to my kids though we're many years apart. I think one reason we are so close is because we talk about a lot of things. I am open with my struggles and they are open with theirs. We are not a perfect family, but we serve a perfect God. By His grace, we are still in process — together.

I share all of this because I have the privilege of sharing information with you through this history course that will keep you in process as well. Though there are many facts, legends, and biographies to learn here, this course is more than that. This course is designed to tell a great story — one that is still going on. That is the story of God revealing Himself to man over the ages. He did it best through the life of Jesus Christ.

If you don't have a personal relationship with God, or you are unsure of it, I encourage you to read "Would You Like to Belong to God's Family" in the Appendix of this book. It tells how you can know God personally. I came to know Christ when I was 17. My life has never been the same.

As for history, it can be fascinating. At least *I* think so. I love the tragedies, the romance, the miracles, and the drama. It's as if we are all part of a big story — an epic that started at Creation and hasn't ended yet.

I don't know where you are in this story, but I hope you are growing. I hope that this book serves as a guide to take you further along your journey. Because I wrote this book for all ages, you will need to do more research, more reading, and more exploring than what is given in each lesson. You will need to read some of the recommended supplemental books and take the activity suggestions seriously to get the most out of this course. But I think you can do that easily if you follow your interests. Not every topic will inspire you, but sooner or later, some will. Find out what grips you, what moves you, and what intrigues you, then go for it! The world is waiting for people like you who will take the time to grasp the meaning and purpose of history and apply it to today. In fact, the world is desperate for it.

I wish I had more personal time with you as a teacher or as a friend. There's a lot we could talk about. Please know I do pray for you!

For the sake of the Mystery,
Linda Hobar
2004

LETTER TO THE TEACHER

My dear friends,

Welcome to the *The Mystery of History, Volume II*. For many of you, this will be a familiar journey. I'm referring to those of you who have already been through Volume I. For you, I hope this is an anticipated *return* to a story—a story that began with Creation and followed with the miraculous coming of Jesus Christ. Volume II essentially continues where Volume I left off. The theme of the book is the same, but the time period is different. In fact, many aspects of Volume II are exactly the same as Volume I. But you will want to read through the rest of this letter to learn of a few changes and improvements.

If you are new to *The Mystery of History*, then first I welcome you. I am delighted you will join us in the study of the Early Church and the Middle Ages as found in Volume II. You will want to finish reading through this letter to understand why I wrote this curriculum and why things are laid out as they are. Overall, I think you will find this curriculum to be user-friendly, informative, inspiring, and even a little fun. At least that is my intent.

But more than that, my prayer for all is that in studying *The Mystery of History*, each will come to more deeply appreciate the role of God throughout the ages. I hope that each of us, in our own way, would marvel at His Creation, be humbled by His plan of redemption, and be inspired by His faithful followers. I believe God seeks to reveal Himself to us and to invite us into His very presence so that He might not be a mystery at all.

I. Why I Wrote This Curriculum

There are many reasons why I wrote *The Mystery of History*—the main reason being that I felt the Lord call me to do it when He seemed to whisper the title of the book in my ear. That was over three years ago. But let me give you this background to the story.

After homeschooling my children for many years, I made the observation that there seemed to exist two kinds of learning—short term and long term. It appeared to me that my children could easily accumulate volumes of long-term information in certain subjects like math and language. They seemed to retain this information because of repetition and review. On top of that, they would build on what they had already learned to expand their knowledge even further.

As for the short term, it appeared to me that my children and I could learn just about any general piece of information in science, social studies, or history given the right materials to work from. For example, in one or two afternoons we could learn the parts of a flower, cloud formations, or the story of Cleopatra. We could read about inventions, the human cell, or the American Revolution. But I couldn't say that we always *remembered* these kinds of things. Our base of knowledge in these kinds of broad subjects was often disjointed and spread out. I often found myself discouraged over this situation at the end of a week or the close of a unit. It led me to question the benefit of spending so many of our hours "learning" things that seemed to sit only for a little while in our short-term memory banks.

In my questioning of our method of education, I found myself really asking something far bigger—and that was the question, "Why?" Why are we doing this? (Of course, we all might ask that on a bad day!) But I wondered even more, why learn anything at all? Why do we even exist? Now, maybe you haven't felt the need to answer these particular questions when it comes to homeschooling. But for me it was necessary to find more meaning and purpose behind it all. Though I enjoyed learning and teaching, and believed it could glorify God, I needed a bigger picture than that.

After much pondering, an answer came for me in this thought—I concluded that one of the only reasons why we are here on earth is ***to know God and to make Him known***. We are designed for relationship. With that being the case, then the *story* of God and man was really worth my extra attention! And I wanted this incredible story to be far more than the short-term accumulation of scattered dates and events. I wanted the living story of God and man to be one of our "long-term" core subjects.

That leads me to the study of world history and the Bible. I think one of the easier ways to "know God better and to make Him known" is to first *know* the stories of Him found in history and the Bible from the beginning to the end! That to me *is* history. I believe history is the story of God revealing Himself to mankind and that He did it most perfectly through the person of Jesus Christ. For that reason, I call this course *The Mystery of History*, believing that the "mystery" is the gospel of Jesus Christ. That is what I hope your children and mine will remember for a lifetime. That is why I write!

As an additional note, you will find that I have at times chosen difficult topics to write about in Volume II. That is in part because there are so many difficult things that happened in the Middle Ages! There were persecutions, revolts, natural disasters, and the Crusades. There were murders, rebellions, wars, and plagues. Though morbid, these stories are part of history. They are the result of relationship— both good and bad—between God, man, and nature. My hope is that the emotion provoked by reading them will pierce the soul and make history more real. If the sad stories don't move your students, then perhaps the inspiring ones will. There are plenty of impressive stories of heroes, saints, and great leaders in this volume, too.

II. The Curriculum Layout

With all these thoughts in mind, please consider now the layout of the curriculum. Remember that there is a reason behind every aspect of it. It is designed to make history more than a short-term project of memorizing dates and events. Though memorization may be part of this curriculum, it is not the core of it. This is an *experiential* curriculum designed to tap into the five senses through activities, research, and cumulative review. It is written to be remembered for a lifetime—not every detail of the book, but the central theme. Though there is purpose behind the design, I hope you experience the freedom to adapt these materials to meet the needs of your own family or classroom.

Step #1—Quarter Summaries ("Around the World")

There are four quarters to this book. At the beginning of each quarter you will find a page titled "Around the World." This is an introduction to the time period and an overview of lessons to come. There are no quiz or test questions taken from this bonus material. These summaries are designed to simply give a big picture to the fascinating world we live in.

Step #2—Pretests ("What Do You Know?")

Students (and teachers alike if they wish) will begin each week by taking a Pretest titled "What Do You Know?" This eight-question pretest introduces students and teachers to people, places, and events that they may or may not have ever heard of before. Though some questions can be answered with pure logic, I would not expect most students or teachers to actually *know* the answers since this volume covers a vast spectrum of world history. My intent is not to discourage students with what they don't know, but rather to stir their curiosity for what they will know! The answers to the questions will be revealed to them throughout the week as they delve into the material. Though I do suggest that the pretests be graded, I do not recommend keeping scores that would count toward a grade in the course. (It would be unfair in my mind to be tested over material not yet learned!) Most of the pretests are simple enough to answer out loud, which is good for the pencil-weary student.

Step #3—Lessons

Most of the lessons in *The Mystery of History* are real-life biographies. I feel that history is far more interesting when seen as the story of men and women who have helped shape the world through both their good and their bad character. The story of God revealing Himself to mankind is woven throughout. Though you will find in Volume II that much emphasis is placed on the nations of Europe through the Middle Ages, I have tried to make it a true world history course and include cultures from all over the world at significant stages of their development. You will also find that there are fewer lessons in this book (only 84) than there were in Volume I (108). But these lessons are **longer!** I made Volume II lessons longer at the request of many families who felt they would rather have "more" than "less" material to draw from. For the sake of those students who might find them a bit too long, I have provided natural breaks in the lessons with the inclusion of **subtitles**. These subtitles will also be helpful when skimming a lesson for information.

Another change in the lessons is the appearance of **key words in bold print.** I felt it might benefit students searching for major names, places, or items in a lesson if these key terms were in bold. Some may choose to make a separate vocabulary list from these words, though I do not give a particular instruction to do so.

Step #4—Activities

After every lesson you will find a section of optional activities. You will see that they are broken into three age levels to accommodate the abilities of all the children in your family or classroom. I have tried to remain consistent with the level of difficulty for each group, but there is room to improvise here.

"Younger Student" activities generally use the five senses to help them "experience" history and better retain it. "Middle Student" activities are a mixture of hands-on work and research, as I would hope to stretch their minds beyond their senses. "Older Student" activities are primarily research oriented. It is for the sake of higher learning that I would expect them to be digging deeper through application, analysis, and synthesis.

With all of that, I have two very important things to add here: First, there are many activities to choose from—more than in Volume I. I would never expect a student or family to do them all! My own family did not. But I am offering *more* choices in this volume so that families or classrooms can make *better* choices based on the resources available to them. On some days, the *wisest* choice may be to not attempt an activity at all in light of other demands or priorities!

Second, there will be many times that Middle or Older Students may prefer Younger Student activities because they better match their learning style or they just appear to be more fun. And there may be Younger Students very open to Older Student topics because they sound interesting. I say this hoping that you will feel the freedom to choose the activities that genuinely interest your students, no matter the age level. Also, for the sake of streamlining *your* energy, it would be very appropriate for an entire family or class to choose only *one* activity, regardless of age level. The best advice I could give here is to choose only those activities that will help maintain the precious joy for learning.

Step #5—Memory Cards

In the last Activity section for each week, I remind students to make their Memory Cards. These are fact cards made by the students on 3-by-5-inch ruled index cards. I recommend that the student or teacher create one card per lesson. Write the lesson title on the blank side of the card. On the ruled side, summarize the main points of the lesson in a few sentences or phrases. Include the timeline date of the lesson underneath the summary.

Younger Students may not have the writing skills to make these cards yet, but they could be involved in the process by narrating to the teacher. Middle Students could participate in writing the cards themselves through dictation, copying, or formulating their own thoughts. Older Students should utilize this valuable tool for the practice of summarizing important facts.

Though some families may choose to have every student make a set of Memory Cards, it is only necessary that there be one complete set per family to use as flashcards. There is more information on these cards and how to make them in the section titled "Memory Cards."

Step #6—Reviews ("Take Another Look!")

At the end of each week, or however long it takes to complete the three lessons for the week, there is a Review section titled "Take Another Look!" This section offers guidelines for timeline and mapping work that corresponds to the material from that week. Though some families may prefer to do a little timeline and mapping work with *each* lesson, it might be easiest to pull out the necessary items for timeline and mapping work only once a week, on review day. Furthermore, delaying timeline and mapping work until a later day in the week naturally brings back information previously learned, making it a true "review."

"Wall of Fame." As in Volume I, the Review section contains instructions each week for creating your own paper timeline figures using simple household items to bring them to life. I recommend placing the figures on a wall, on a pattern-cutting board (sewing board), or in a notebook. There are many great variations to building a meaningful and attractive timeline. Generally speaking, I think the younger the student, the larger the timeline should be to give a visual of when things happened in history.

For those needing something a little easier, I have added a **new feature** to Volume II. In every Wall of Fame section, I make reference to beautifully illustrated timeline figures that are *already* drawn for you. These figures are part of a timeline packet called *History Through the Ages—Resurrection to Revolution* (copyright 2003). Created by Amy Pak of Home School in the Woods, this packet contains hundreds of lovely hand-sketched figures that can be cut, colored, or photocopied to add to any timeline. (Note: The original, copyright 2002 version of *History Through the Ages* is not complete for use with *The Mystery of History, Volume II*.) There is more information and photos on how to make a foldable, portable, and attractive timeline in the section titled "Wall of Fame Timeline Suggestions."

"SomeWHERE in Time." Also as in Volume I, the Review section contains mapping projects for each week to correspond to the lessons. Generally speaking, the mapping projects are listed on each review from simplest to hardest. As with the activities, choose only the appropriate mapping projects for your students, considering their skill and interest levels. It will be helpful to have available a globe, a historical atlas, and a modern atlas. The publisher has made every effort to make sure that the assignments can be completed using Internet research or commonly found atlases such as the following:

Rand McNally *Student World Atlas* (ISBN: 978-0-528-01344-7)

Rand McNally *Historical Atlas of the World* (ISBN: 528-83969-1)

The Student Bible Atlas by Tim Dowley (ISBN: 0-8066-2038-2)

These atlases, WonderMaps, and the timeline figures, are available through Bright Ideas Press.

For your convenience, the specially designed outline maps are located toward the back of the book, just before the Appendix. Many of the maps will be used several times, so you will want to photocopy them in the quantities recommended on the opening page of the Outline Maps section at the back of the book. A **mapping answer key** is available at:

https://www.brightideaspress.com/shop/mystery-of-history-vol2/

Step #7—Exercises ("What Did You Miss?")

At the end of each week you will find either an exercise or a quiz. (I explain the quizzes in the next section.) The exercises are titled "What Did You Miss?" Using simple, fun formats and some occasional games, the exercises prompt students to recall material already learned or to think about it more deeply.

Students are encouraged to use their textbooks, Memory Cards, and timelines to help them complete the exercises.

The exercises are cumulative in nature, meaning that they ask questions about content from the very beginning of the book! Almost every question is presented in chronological order so that students see the events in history in the same order in which they happened. I hope you can appreciate this unique feature of *The Mystery of History*. Very few history programs provide cumulative review, which in my opinion helps move the material from short-term to long-term storage. I suggest that grades be kept on the exercises to encourage students to take them seriously.

Step #8—Quizzes ("What Did You Learn?")

Every other week in the book concludes with a quiz titled "What Did You Learn?" Like the exercises, the quizzes are cumulative in nature. That means they ask questions from the entire book. And like the exercises, these questions are most often presented in chronological order so the student consistently sees history in the order in which it happened. I don't believe in giving tests for the sake of "busy work," nor do I believe that tests or quizzes can always reflect true learning. However, I do think these simple cumulative quizzes will help students remember the important things they've learned.

Unlike the exercises, I would not recommend that Middle and Older Students be allowed to use their textbooks, Memory Cards, or timelines to answer the quiz questions. Though the quizzes are not overly difficult, they will require study and preparation—and that's a good time to pull out the Memory Cards!

As for Younger Students, or those with learning disabilities, I suggest that you determine the age at which they are ready for the challenge of a quiz. Teacher assistance, oral test-taking, or group work might be a suitable way for these students to get the review of the quiz without the stress of it.

You will notice that both the exercises and the quizzes grow in length throughout the book, but they are not particularly any more difficult. The extra length is necessary to accommodate the growing amount of information covered.

Step #9—Quarterly Worksheets ("Put It All Together")

By the end of each quarter, the students will have learned a lot! To help them "Put It All Together," students are asked to complete a worksheet at the end of each seven-week quarter. As with the exercises, students are encouraged to use their textbooks, Memory Cards, and timelines to help them answer the questions. The worksheets are similar to the exercises and quizzes in format but are longer and cover only the content of one quarter.

Step #10—Semester Tests

At the end of each semester, the students are given a long test. The test covers only the material from that semester (which is two quarters). As with the quizzes, Middle and Older Students should not be allowed the use of their textbooks, Memory Cards, or timelines. Younger Students, or those with special needs, will require assistance but can still benefit from the review experience.

Step #11—Student Notebooks

Though families or classrooms might share *The Mystery of History* textbook, I recommend that each student compile his or her own Student Notebook. This notebook should contain eight dividers—one for each of the seven continents and one for a Miscellaneous/Exercise/Quiz section. This notebook will grow over time or can be continued from the first volume. As students complete an activity or map, they can file their work behind the proper continent divider.

Subsequent dividers for the names of individual countries can be made out of simple notebook paper as the countries arise in their study. For example, in an activity from a lesson on China, I may instruct students to file their work under "Asia: China." The continent name is always written first, followed by the name of the country.

Step #12—"Supplemental Books and Resources"

For families who desire more, there is Section C in the Appendix, "Supplemental Books and Resources." Please bear in mind that these are merely suggested books, movies, and other resources that could *enhance* your study of the Early Church and the Middle Ages through spice and variety—but they are not necessary to complete this course. Many will choose additional resources because of a particular fascination with a topic or merely to overlap general reading with history. Besides that, there can be great joy in reading "living books" through good historical fiction.

Though there are almost endless books, movies, and other resources available, the ones in the list were chosen based on their excellence as well as availability. Many of the books and movies are common in homeschool circles, which will ease your hunt in finding them at your local homeschool conventions or through catalogs or the Internet.

I strongly suggest that you as the parent or teacher have the final word on the suitability of *any* additional resource suggested. Though all books and movies have been carefully selected from a conservative angle, families inevitably vary in their standards, and each should be responsible for making their own final choices. When caution is due on a resource that I am familiar with, a note has been made of that for you. Forgive me ahead of time if any that you find offensive have slipped by me. Feel free to let me know of them for future editions.

III. Suggested Schedules and Adaptations

Younger Students

For those whose oldest students are still in the kindergarten to 2nd grade stage, I would consider choosing two to three lessons a week to read and doing one to three corresponding activities. (The curriculum would last more than one year at this pace.) Some children with shorter attention spans may prefer one small bit of work a day. That could mean reading the lesson one day and doing the corresponding activity the next day. I would not necessarily suggest that younger students take pretests or complete all the exercises or the quizzes unless they are particularly inclined to sit-down work. The questions of the pretests, exercises, or quizzes could be skipped altogether or presented orally instead and kept "fun." Memory Cards could be made by the teacher and pulled out for games or drills.

Timeline figures could be made for favorite figures in history but not for all. Maps could be done on an "as-interested" basis. Many of the geography skills involve only "finger mapping," where a student finds a spot on a globe or map with his finger but is not required to transfer this information to paper. These exercises would be very appropriate for children to learn about the basic makeup of their world without stressing them out over more paperwork.

To summarize, here might be a typical week for a family with the oldest child being the age of kindergarten up to 2nd grade.

Mon	Tues	Wed	Thur	Fri
Oral Pretest; Lesson 1	Activity 1	Lesson 2	Activity 2	Timeline

A variation to this format could be:

Mon	Tues	Wed	Thur	Fri
Lesson 1; Activity 1	No history	Lesson 2; Activity 2	No history	Mapping

Or:

Read Lesson 1	Read Lesson 2	Read Lesson 3	Do one activity from Lesson 1, 2, *or* 3	Oral quiz

Middle and Older Students

For the family who has the oldest child in 3rd–8th grades, a schedule might be as follows:

Mon	Tues	Wed	Thurs	Fri
Pretest; Read Lesson 1; Activity 1	Read Lesson 2; Activity 2	Read Lesson 3; Memory Cards	Review; Exercise or Quiz	OFF

The activities may be skipped sometimes as in the example above on Wednesday. The other activities are chosen based on what is best for the 3rd–8th grader as well as any younger siblings. If the activities are simple, a family may have two children doing a fun, hands-on project and two working on more challenging research—whatever accommodates the family as a whole.

Another sample week (that fits what we most often preferred) would look like the one below. My children are older and have longer attention spans. Therefore, it is a better use of our time to do a lot of history on one day rather than a little every day. Besides, my kids love science and don't want to share those days with history!

Mon	Tues	Wed	Thurs	Fri
Pretest; Read Lesson 1–2 Activity 1 *or* 2	Science day, no history	Read Lesson 3; Activity 3; Make Memory Cards	Science day, no history	Review; Exercise or Quiz

For those who may have **high schoolers**, this material could serve as a **framework** for further research and study on their part. Some of the "Older Student" activities are perfectly suitable for the high schooler.

Keep in mind that high school students traditionally receive one year of world history and one year of American history. This is what colleges would expect to see on a high school transcript. Economics and government are generally taught together to comprise the senior year of high school. That would total three years of history in high school.

I opt instead for teaching history in four years. I would teach what I call "World History and Geography" in two years (9th and 10th grades) and what I call "American and Modern History" in 11th. The senior year can still be reserved for economics and government. My reasoning for two years of world history rather than one is simply that I believe it is too vast a subject to teach adequately in one year! And I have not found any colleges that are unhappy to find more world history on a transcript.

Depending on what a high school student has studied in junior high, a possible scope and sequence could look like this for a high schooler:

Volume I or II	9th or 10th grade
Volume III or IV	11th or 12th grade

IV. Final Thoughts

As a summary to the features you just read about, let me point this out: Ideally, if students *were* able to go through the steps in this curriculum as laid out, it would give them approximately 13 "experiences" with each new lesson in history. That should be plenty to help students grasp the importance of a new person, place, or event. They won't necessarily retain every detail of the story in long-term memory, but they should have a good handle on the significance of it.

In reality, there will be some busy weeks where many of these features might have to be skipped. Nonetheless, even incorporating a *few* of these features, will give students far more experience with history than the three-step approach found in traditional textbooks (which generally include a reading assignment, a review, and a test.).

As an example of the students' learning experience in this curriculum, consider with me the life of Augustine. He was a rather important figure in church history, but his is not exactly a household name. Follow along with me to get a feel for what learning about Augustine looks like in *The Mystery of History*.

- **First**, students read of him in an *Around the World* page. It is a very general introduction, but it is a chance to hear his name for perhaps the first time.

- **Second**, students learn three facts about Augustine through the taking and grading of a pretest. These facts include the name of his autobiography (*Confessions*); the location of his home (Hippo, Africa); and the meaning of the word "rhetoric," which was his area of giftedness.

- **Third**, students read (or have read to them) an entire lesson about the life and ministry of Augustine, learning of his doubts about Christianity, his conversion, and his great ministry and legacy as a church father.

- **Fourth**, students have an opportunity to do an experiential activity related to the lesson. The Younger Student records a praise song because Augustine was influenced by the singing of children when he came to Christ. The Middle Student researches a man who was representative of an erroneous view of pleasing God that was common during Augustine's era—representative because he spent 37 years on top of a stone pillar to prove his piety. The Older Student discusses "mentoring" because Augustine had a mentor in his life and/or reads some of the original works of Augustine.

- **Fifth**, students make a Memory Card on Augustine, recording important facts about his life.

- **Sixth**, in the Review section, students make or cut out a timeline figure of Augustine and place it on a wall or in a notebook alongside his contemporaries, who were the Maya of Mexico, Jerome, and the legendary St. Patrick.

- **Seventh**, students do some mapping work in the Review section to become acquainted with Northern Africa, Augustine's home when it was part of the Roman Empire.

- **Eighth**, students see Augustine again on a cumulative quiz at the end of the week, which asks one simple question about him. They continue to see his name on other quizzes throughout the year.

- **Ninth**, students see Augustine periodically on alternating exercises in weeks when there is no quiz.

- **Tenth**, Augustine appears on a lengthy worksheet.

- **Eleventh**, he is on a semester test.

- **Twelfth**, each student files his activity and/or mapping exercise on Augustine in his Student Notebook, which hopefully will be proudly displayed as a scrapbook of accomplishments.

- **Thirteenth**, as a final option, students can explore any of the supplemental books or resources suggested in the back of the text that pertain to the extraordinary life of St. Augustine.

If experiential learning is what you are looking for, you have found it in *The Mystery of History*! May the Lord bless you in your efforts to teach and in the adventure of learning.

A CLASSICAL APPROACH TO EDUCATION

I want to expand on the design of this curriculum in regard to the classical approach to education. For those of you not familiar with that philosophy, let me explain.

A classical education is one that is language-centered, which means that students will do great volumes of reading, listening, and writing to learn. Furthermore, a classical education observes three stages of training the mind. The three-stage process is called the *trivium* of learning. I will briefly describe each.

Stage one is referred to as the **grammar** stage. It would primarily describe children in the grades of kindergarten through third or fourth grade. The authors of the book *The Well-Trained Mind* consider these ages as those that are most ***absorbent***. They believe it is not so much a time of self-discovery as it is the accumulation of new ideas, new words, new stories, and new facts. This can be a fun stage for a teacher. At the same time, the immaturity of this age range can create a battle for *how* this information is obtained!

Stage two is referred to as the **logic** stage because children of this age group are beginning to process information they've obtained and to ***question*** it. This group would include fourth and fifth graders through about eighth grade. The reason that students begin to ask more *why* questions at this stage is because their ability to think abstractly has been further developed. They should begin to process things more logically. Unfortunately, some children question authority at this stage as well!

The third stage of the trivium of learning is referred to as the **rhetoric** stage. These are students from ninth grade and up. By this stage, students should be *applying* information that has been learned. The challenge I have found at this last stage is in the interest level of the student. Ability does not always equate with desire!

Basically, the grammar student absorbs information, the logic student questions information, and the rhetoric student should be able to analyze or defend information. Of course, these stages are only generalities. Learning styles, personalities, and maturity can certainly affect the way any student learns.

I have considered the trivium of learning in the construction of this curriculum and have endeavored to incorporate it throughout. Here is how.

The **grammar stage:** I believe the *reading* of the lessons *is* the primary source of absorbing new information for these students. The activity is then designed to be fun and to reinforce what they have learned. This student may be interested in the activity for either the Younger Student or the Middle Student. The Memory Cards will be especially helpful in capturing the new information the student has learned.

The **logic stage:** Again, the reading of the lesson is the primary source of absorbing new information. However, these students will find that the Middle Student and Older Student activities force them to a more in-depth handling and processing of the information. Some activities are merely fun, whereas others are designed to be thought-provoking. The biweekly exercises and quizzes complement the handling of the material when the student is required to make lists, compare dates, and so forth. Memory Cards will be essential in summarizing and organizing what the student has learned.

The **rhetoric stage:** This begins for most students in high school, but I know there are some mature sixth through eighth graders who are ready to touch on this level of interpreting and applying information. Therefore, some of the Older Student activities were written with them in mind. Many of these activities are research-oriented or at least require further reading and writing. I wrote many of the activities for older students with the hope of developing a strong Christian worldview in a student. I especially want the older students to become masters at expressing thoughts.

One last aspect of classical education is the process of repeating the presentation of some material at each level of the trivium. In other words, a good classical education would provide information to a student in the younger years, repeat it on a higher level in the middle years, and repeat it again at an even higher level of learning in the older years.

Not all curricula will fit that mold. My hope is that *The Mystery of History* will, in one way or another. I hope you will repeat the volumes of *The Mystery of History* as your students grow, bumping them up to higher levels of activities each time through.

While we're on the subject, I wish I could provide for you a perfect scope and sequence that would line up your students for two or three cycles of all four volumes of *The Mystery of History*! But in reality, "one size does *not* fit all." The age of your children, and their spacing, will create endless combinations for when you might teach each volume. I can, however, provide you with these ideas to consider in your planning:

1. Each volume of *The Mystery of History* gets more difficult in content and the lessons grow longer.

2. In fact, because of the more difficult and serious themes of Volume IV (i.e., Darwinism, communism, fascism, terrorism), some lessons will not be suitable for Younger or Middle students at all. Teachers will want to be sensitive to which lessons are appropriate for younger ones who may be "tagging along" and listening. (As in all volumes, there are age-appropriate activities provided for all ages that might be "joining in.")

3. The addition of American history is best placed after *The Mystery of History*, Volume III.

4. Most American high schools require one year of world history, one year of American history, one half year of economics, and one half year of government.

5. While not "necessary," I recommend two years of world history in high school. It's not for everybody, but I think one year is not enough for students interested in the subject.

6. Any volume of *The Mystery of History* can be made a high school credit.

7. Volumes III and IV, because they are more difficult, are easier to use "as is" in high school.

I want to close this section with these words of encouragement. While academics *are* important, our highest calling as teachers is to mold, shape, and disciple our children and students in the ways of our Savior. So, above all else, I exhort you to follow the Lord's model of education! Deuteronomy 6:7–9 gives us these beautiful guidelines for teaching His words, which I hope will inspire you in teaching all subjects:

"You shall teach them diligently to your children, and shall talk of them when you sit in your house, when you walk by the way, when you lie down, and when you rise up. You shall bind them as a sign on your hand, and they shall be as frontlets between your eyes. You shall write them on the doorposts of your house and on your gates."

MEMORY CARDS

I. Making the Cards

Ideally, students will make Memory Cards as a tool for reinforcing the material they have learned. The cards serve as a set of flashcards made personally by the student. The process of making the Memory Cards is in and of itself an exercise in summarizing the main points of a lesson. (Younger students whose hands tire of written work may be the exception.) By making your own cards, the cost for this course is kept down and students are given the challenge of organizing thoughts. In preparing for quizzes and tests, the cards can be used as quick study guides.

For this volume, you will need 84 3-by-5-inch ruled cards. White cards will be sufficient. For future reference, there will be eight time periods to study in the four volumes of *The Mystery of History*, so you will need eight colored markers to distinguish these eras from one another. These are the colors I will be using on my cards. Follow if possible because I may refer to the colors in future memory games.

• Volume I-A	Creation and Early Civilizations	dark green
• Volume I-B	The Classical World	red
• Volume II-A	The Early Church	light purple
• Volume II-B	The Middle Ages	gray
• Volume III-A	The Reformation and Renaissance	light green
• Volume III-B	The Growth of Nations	dark blue
• Volume IV-A	The Struggle of Mankind	dark pink
• Volume IV-B	Mankind's Hope in Christ	black

Using a light purple marker, set up the cards for Volume II-A to look similar to these samples.

This is what my Younger Student wrote for Lesson 24. (To be realistic, I left in the typos.)

(Front, blank side)   (Back, lined side)

Justinian I and Theodora Rulers of the Byzantine	**Vol. II A 24** *They were both pore and grew up to be king and Queen. (They were lucky.) Theodora was brave smart so she helped Justinian Rule the empire. Justinian wrote a code of laws. he was religious and fasted a lot.* **527-565**

This is what my "Middle/Older Student" wrote for Lesson 26. (I left his typo in also.)

Early Japan and Prince Shotoku	**Vol. II A** **26** *Japan is an archipelago off the coast of China. The archipelago is actually made up of 4,223 islands, only 600 of these are lived on by humans. Prince Shotoku brought a new form of government. He also brought budism to Japan. Basically he brought together Japan.* **573**

The front of the card is simply the name of the lesson as listed in the Table of Contents. For neatness, efficiency, and consistency, I chose to write the lesson titles on the cards well before they were needed. You may choose to do the same, especially if younger students are involved. The back of the card should contain the following four items:

1. The upper left corner should state the volume number and either an *A* or a *B*. An *A* refers to the first semester of study. A *B* refers to the second semester of study. Each volume will cover two time periods, or semesters, of study. This too might be done ahead of time by the teacher.

2. The upper right corner should state the number of the lesson as listed in the Table of Contents and on the lesson page itself. Teachers may opt to do this ahead of time as well.

3. The middle of the card allows ample space for a simple summary of the lesson. (I suggest pencil for this to allow for remedy of mistakes and because the marker will be too broad.) Younger children may choose to narrate their sentences to the teacher, copy sentences from the lesson, or create their own. Middle and older students should be able to put their own thought into the summary — perhaps with some prompting by the teacher. I encourage the use of the book as a reference.

4. The very bottom of the card should give the date from history of the lesson or its approximate time span. It's probably a good idea to allow the student to copy this from the book for reinforcement.

II. Using the Cards

I recommend that a student (or siblings who share the job) make the cards at one time about every three lessons. I remind students about these cards on the activity page of every third lesson.

Families and groups should incorporate review of the cards in some systematic fashion. The cards could be pulled out, shuffled, and refiled. They could be brought out before quizzes to see what topics need to be studied. They might be used in games of trivia. Co-op classes could open with a quick review of random Memory Cards. Use your own imagination.

I do not necessarily expect every date and lesson to be memorized. Maybe some of you will choose to be that industrious. I prefer instead that a student be able to place a lesson in the proper time period. That is the reason for the emphasis on the specific marker color on the card. The colors will help the mind to visualize where a piece of information fits into history.

However, as in Volume I, there are 12 significant dates in Volume II that I recommend students memorize. I will make reference to them throughout the text.

III. Storing the Cards

I recommend a short-term and long-term approach to storing your Memory Cards. First, for the short term, there are numerous selections at office supply stores for small, two-ring binders. Most will hold about 50 index cards. Consider the purchase of two to last you one school year. (You are going to have approximately 84 cards by the end of the year.) Another option is to punch a single hole in the corner of each card, and slip all the cards on a ring that clamps shut. If all else fails, rubber bands work just fine! A thick ribbon wrapped around the cards will add a little charm.

Second, for the long term, if you envision yourself studying all four volumes of *The Mystery of History*, then you are going to end up with approximately 360 cards. For storing these cards at the end of a school year (until you repeat the course), I would consider the purchase of a decorative photo file box, a large 3-by-5-inch card file, or a small shoebox—to be decorated by your students, of course. Younger and Middle Students might enjoy creating a "treasure box" for these cards to pull out over and over again. It's rewarding to see these cards "mature" as the students grow in years.

WALL OF FAME TIMELINE SUGGESTIONS

Part of the review for each week consists of adding timeline figures to the Wall of Fame. Because I receive so many questions about timelines, I want to elaborate rather extensively on some suggestions for putting one together.

Understand first that there are many different methods for assembling attractive and functional timelines. I've seen them in notebooks, on walls, on butcher paper, wrapped around stairwells, and placed on pattern cutting boards (my personal favorite). I've even seen a timeline adorning a bathroom wall for friends and family to study while using the facilities! The important thing is to make a timeline for your family or classroom that will work for you *this* year with *this* volume based on your students' interests and the space you have available. Inevitably, students learning styles, interests, and abilities will change over the years as they mature (along with how much wall space you have!). It is reasonable to imagine that a large timeline on a wall or pattern cutting board might appeal to a visual learner or younger student now. But, this same student, or one who has a bent toward detail work, might prefer a notebook style timeline in the future when they are older. I suggest you adapt your methods of keeping a timeline *as you go* rather than stress out over choosing one that will work for the next 5 – 10 years.

I bring this up because I know from experience that some of you will stress out (as I have) over starting a timeline. I have the emails to prove it! I too have been trying to create a perfect system that will work for years to come. It is a worthy goal, but I'm not yet sure if it is attainable. I have 13 years of homeschool experience to draw from, but I don't have all the volumes written yet for *The Mystery of History*. So, bear with me, please, volume by volume, as I tweak, adapt, and modify suggestions for making a timeline. My favorite method for keeping a timeline on a pattern cutting board (sometimes referred to as a sewing board), may very well suit every volume of *The Mystery of History*, but I'm not guaranteeing it.

All of that aside, let's move on to two suggestions for making a foldable, portable, and attractive timeline for Volume II. Both of the plans presented here are on a pattern cutting board (though either plan could work as well on a wall.) When held vertically, it is the inside of the board that serves as the

backdrop for the placement of time strips and figures. One plan, which I will call *Plan A*, follows my ideas for making your own decorative figures as described on each Take Another Look review page in this book. This plan might appeal to students who are artistically inclined, or who really favor hands-on work. There is a little bit of built-in fun as some figures require wrinkling, burning, tearing, and so forth.

The other plan, which I will refer to as *Plan B*, uses the beautifully illustrated figures by Amy Pak from *History Through the Ages*. For your convenience, I reference these figures as well on each Take Another Look review page in this book. This plan might appeal to children who like to color, families with older students, or those who just feel too busy to make their own. Regardless of whether you use Plan A or Plan B, I suggest you set up a pattern cutting board as follows. (I recommend families only attempt to make one timeline of this magnitude, though some students may be more industrious than others and choose to each make their own.)

I. Set up of the timeline

In Volume I, I gave elaborate directions for setting up a pattern cutting board which included *dated* strips. Timeline figures were added to the strips throughout the course. Since then, I have learned some things. Predating the strips requires a lot of preliminary work. And I found that my strips were blank in some places and quite jumbled up in others since we have no control over who lived when. To remedy the situation, I experimented with making a timeline with strips that are *not* dated at all. Rather, each *figure* added to the timeline is dated. It was a simple adjustment, but one that proved to make a very neatly organized timeline. I also found ways to make a cardboard sewing board more attractive by covering it with decorative adhesive paper. I also found it easy to use packing tape or duct tape for the time strips rather than laminated poster board. Here are steps and materials to make these improvements should you so desire:

A. Materials needed:

- One foldable pattern cutting board

    To my knowledge, two brands of these boards exist. The *Wright's* brand, available at most Hobby Lobby stores, is the smaller of the two at 36″ x 60″. The Dritz brand board, found at most Wal-Mart stores, is larger at 40″ x 72″. My directions will work for either, except the larger board will give you much more space to work with and will require more than one roll of adhesive paper for covering.

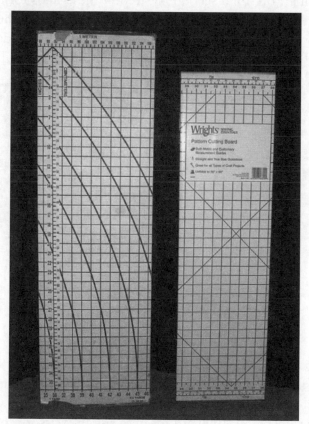

- One or two rolls of self-adhesive decorative covering, more commonly referred to as *Con-Tact* paper

    Purchase one or two rolls, depending on which cutting board you are using. Choose a color or motif of your liking. (For Volume II, I chose a green marbled look of Con-Tact adhesive paper called Pompeii Green, which is product # 997800).

- One roll of colored packing tape or duct tape (1.88″ x 20 yards)

I chose green duct tape for this volume to match the green marbled adhesive paper.

- One yard of piping or trimming cord or ribbon to make a closure for the board
  I chose a white rope cord to match the white of the marbled adhesive paper.

- One foot of clear adhesive tape
  I use this to secure the closure of the board.

- A yardstick

- Scissors

- A helper

B. **Covering the board** (It will take approximately 45 minutes to complete this preliminary task):

1. You will not want to begin this project without the extra hands of an older child or another adult to help you lay the adhesive paper. Otherwise, it will take you much longer to lay the adhesive paper without it crinkling. (I tried!)

2. Lay the pattern cutting board open on the floor. Unroll the adhesive paper, and measure a strip the width of your board (the short direction, not the long direction). Cut the strip, peel the backing off, and use your helper to lay the adhesive paper down. If it is crooked, or has folds, it will lift off for a second try. Repeat these steps for both the front and the back of the cutting board, overlapping each strip a few inches over the last. When you reach the ends of the board, it is easiest to stop the adhesive paper at the edge, rather than attempt to wrap it around the edges. The exposed edges of raw cardboard will not present a problem.

3. With both sides of the board covered, you will notice that the board is tight and hard to fold up. To correct this problem, use a sharp pair of scissors to score the outside of the cutting board in several places. By that I mean to run the scissors down a few outside creases to cut a slight gap in the adhesive paper. It will cause a small part of the board to be exposed, which is why I suggest doing this on the outside rather than the inside. It is the inside of the cutting board that will serve as the place for placing all the timeline figures.

4. Open the cutting board so that the inside is facing up. It is now time to mark the places for the tape strips.

a. For the Wright's cutting board: use a yardstick and pencil to mark 2 inches, 4 inches, 6 inches, and 8 inches from the top of *each* panel on the edge of the cutting board. Make the marks evenly on both edges of the board. Unwind a length of duct tape or packing tape that will go across the width of the cutting board with a little length to spare. Carefully lay the tape strip down horizontally between the 2-inch mark and the 4-inch mark. The tape is fairly forgiving should you need to lift and reapply. Trim the excess. Repeat this step, laying down tape between the 6-inch mark and the 8-inch mark. You are laying two parallel strips on each panel. There will be 12 tape strips in all.

b. For the Dritz cutting board: use a yardstick and pencil to mark 2 1/2 inches, 4 1/2 inches, 7 inches, and 9 inches from the top of each panel on the edge of the cutting board. (Remember, this board is larger and requires the strips to be spaced further apart.) Make these marks evenly on both edges of the board.

Unwind a length of duct tape or packing tape that will go across the cutting board with a little length to spare. Carefully lay the tape strip down between the 2 1/2 inch mark and the 4 1/2 inch mark. The tape is fairly forgiving should you need to lift and reapply. Trim the excess. Repeat this step laying down tape between the 7-inch mark and the 9-inch mark. You are laying two parallel strips on each panel. There will be 12 in all.

5. To make a cool closure for the board, fold it all the way shut and mark the center point of the back of the board. Find the middle of the length of one yard of cord. Use clear packing tape to adhere cord at its middle to the center point of the back of the board. This cord can be tied and untied by students when they get the board out to work on it.

6. Finally, I suggest that a title cover be attached to the outside of the board to identify its time period. It might read, "The Mystery of History, Volume II — The Early Church and the Middle Ages."

II. Preparing the figures

Now that your board is assembled, remember that you have two plans to choose from for adding figures to your timeline. You can make your own figures following my suggestions (Plan A) or use pre-drawn figures from *History Through the Ages* (Plan B). I have a few tips for each.

A. Plan A figures (making your own)

I find it easiest to make my own figures on white card stock paper using colorful markers to outline and decorate with. Blank 3-by-5-inch index cards will work for some figures, but are not large enough for all. In Volume I, I suggested the use of colored index cards to code various people groups such as the Egyptians, the Greeks, and so forth. But for Volume II, this will not be practical as the number of people groups being covered has expanded. On Take Another Look review pages, I give ideas for making and decorating your figures. Feel free to elaborate! Your children's interest level may dictate how many details you add. I have certainly helped my own children make several figures over the years to assist them in moving along in the process.

For the times that I request they make a person, I have provided a stencil of a man or a woman. I recommend that you photocopy these to make a pattern. It would be wise to trace the pattern ahead of time for students putting several on a page with ample space around each character. However, I would not cut the patterns out ahead of time because I often ask the students to add something to their character (like a harp, a book, or a crown). In those instances, it is far easier for students to draw these items around the pattern and *then* cut them out. Of course, not all the figures will be people. I also ask students to make boats, mountains, documents, maps, and so forth.

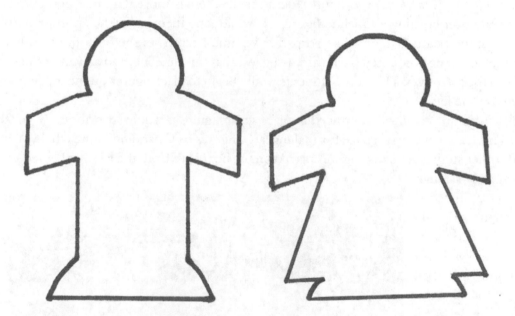

B. Plan B figures (using pre-drawn figures)

Rather than make your own figures, you may choose to use the ones pre-drawn from *History Through the Ages*. These figures, which are a separate purchase, can be photocopied onto colored paper to match the theme of the time period or used as is. Students can color and cut the figures prior to hanging them on the timeline. I copied the figures onto light green colored paper to match the green marbled adhesive paper. You can make this option as simple or as complicated as you want. Some students may want to even incorporate some of the creative ideas from Plan A into Plan B by decorating the pre-drawn figures with a few extras.

III. Attaching the figures

I found it most convenient to work on our timeline only once a week. Though some families prefer to make the timeline figures on the day that they study the corresponding lesson, I like to do the exercise later in the week as a means of reviewing and bringing characters back to mind from days earlier.

On review day we usually needed to create only three figures, one from each lesson of the week. If using *History Through the Ages* figures, occasionally there is more than one figure for each lesson. Either way, after creating a timeline figure, we would tape them on at the appropriate place on the pattern cutting board. The timeline strips for Volume I ran from the bottom up to help a student grasp that B.C. time is counted backward. I suggest that this timeline, and all future ones in A.D. time, run from the top down. Therefore, students would begin to place figures on the top line of the board, starting on the left.

If using Plan A, you will only need to place seven figures per time strip about two or three inches apart. This leaves plenty of space for making large figures or for adding figures that you come across in your other studies. The first figures placed on the board are from the lessons Pentecost, Saul/Paul, and Paul's Missionary Journeys as listed in bold print on Take Another Look in Week 1, Review 1. You may want to turn there now to follow along with me. Students will make figures of a flame, a man, and a boat. From Review 2, students would add figures to represent Nero, Martyrs of the

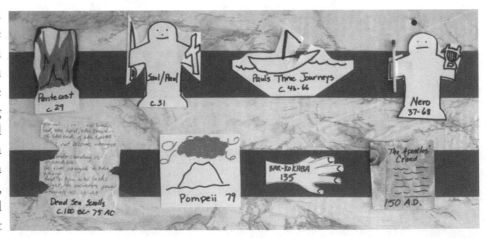

Early Church, and Josephus. To complete the first strip, students would later add a figure for Masada and then drop to the next line to add something for The Dead Sea Scrolls and The Buried City of Pompeii.

If using Plan B's pre-drawn figures from *History Through the Ages*, students will need to add about 10 figures per time strip placing them about two inches apart. The first figures on the board would be those titled *Day of Pentecost, Stephen,* and *Paul and Peter.* From Review 2, students would add the figures titled *Nero, Domitian, Trajan, Ignatius, Polycarp,* and *Marcul Aurelius.* Dropping to the next time strip, students would continue to add figures titled *Tertullian, Josephus,* and *Titus.* From Review 3, students will add the figures titled *Masada, Dead Sea Scrolls, Pompeii,* and so forth.

Upon filling up one row, I suggest the next row of figures start from the left to right as well working your way all the way down to the bottom of the board. It is a great visual for students to chart their progress through the course of history by the growing number of figures on their timeline. As a final note, on the top center point of my timeline, I used a hole-punch to create a hole just large enough so that I can hang my timeline on a nail in the wall while we are using it. I highly recommend this if space allows. When not in use, you can fold your timeline, tie it off with the closure cord wrapped around it, and tuck it away behind a cabinet or under a sofa.

From time to time we made a game of searching for a character on the board or pointing blindly to a random character and asking the student to supply some information about him or her or it. Remember, your timeline may not turn out perfectly, but it is just one of many ways to observe and appreciate God's marvelous hand in history. I hope you enjoy it!

THE X FILE:
TIPS ON GRADING

To aid you in the philosophy of grading and record keeping, I have created a diagram that I hope you'll find helpful. As you can see from the diagram, at the younger grade levels I believe that grading and daily lesson plans should be loosely kept. The main reason is that teacher involvement is naturally high. The teacher will know how well lessons are being grasped because of one-on-one interaction. Younger students need most things read and explained to them. Enjoy this time; it's rewarding to be directly interacting with their young minds. Their questions and perspectives are amazing.

On the other end of the spectrum, the older student should be well into studying independently. Therefore, grades and lesson plans are absolutely essential in giving them guidance and in knowing whether or not they are learning the material. Teacher involvement will be lower usually because there are younger children to be taught and most homeschool teachers are mothers. We are not biology teachers, algebra teachers, or Latin teachers. Teachers can give guidance and help, but I have observed that successful older homeschool students are those who find that THEY must take the responsibility to learn. They become self-teachers, which is a great achievement in and of itself.

I believe the middle years are the more trying ones, as teacher involvement naturally goes down and the need for grades and efficient record keeping goes up. Middle students need to be weaned from too much teacher involvement (assuming the student can read and follow directions), while at the same time they still need to be well taught! Too much help from a teacher can lead to students becoming lazy with their work and leaning on the teacher to get it done. Not enough help can lead to student frustration and poor understanding. It's a delicate balance, requiring frequent adjustments with a varying need for teacher involvement.

To summarize, I don't feel it is necessary for younger students to have grades per se, and my lesson plans are loosely kept to allow for creative bursts. For the middle student, however, I record grades in essential courses and maintain basic lesson plans. For the older students, I feel it is absolutely necessary to record grades and map out the work to be completed with detailed lesson plans. Thus a shift takes place from teacher to student as the diagram represents.

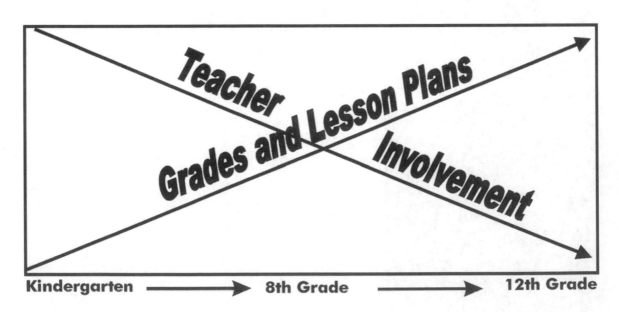

With that philosophy lesson behind us, let me give you a systematic plan for keeping the grades that you decide to keep. I don't mean to insult you, but I will be very specific. For some of you, this is new territory.

Beginning with the pretests, I would grade one just after it was taken, but I would not necessarily *record* the grade. I would simply let the student take the pretest and grade it with a 100 percent if they are all correct. Or, give them a fraction on the top of the page made up of the number of questions answered correctly over the total number of questions on the pretest. For example, 6/8 means the student missed two questions. The purpose of the pretest is not to measure what they know. It is to spark interest.

For the quizzes and exercises, however, I would begin to record these grades and accumulate them. The quizzes ARE designed to measure what they have learned. First you have to grade them with a fraction to represent the number of questions answered correctly over the total number of questions on the quiz. For example, 14/18 means that the student missed four questions. If you punched those numbers into a calculator, you would do 14 divided by 18 equals 78. On a scale of 1 - 100, a 78 means something to a student. You may decide on your own grading scale as to what you believe is a fair letter grade. I keep it simple with 90 - 100 being an A, 80 - 90 a B, and so on.

As I go through the year, I choose to record the fractions, not the final letter grade. This is why. The fractions will automatically "weigh" the quizzes, tests, and worksheets fairly. You see, the worksheets and tests are longer, giving the fractions greater denominators. A test grade may look like 28/36. They missed far more than the earlier quiz I described. They missed eight questions instead of four. But, if you put 28/36 on a calculator, it also equals 78 percent. The student answered more questions correctly because there were more questions! Hope you follow that.

Throughout the year I keep track of their fractions, so that at any given time I can stop and calculate their present grade. I simply add ALL the denominators of the fractions and write this number down. Then I add ALL the numerators of the fractions and write this down. Next, I divide the numerator sum by the denominator sum, and voila, I have a numerical grade that I can now assign a letter grade to based on my grading scale.

If you think that your student does not perform well on quizzes or tests, consider stacking up his or her grade average with credit for lessons and/or activities. If he reads his lesson, he could get a 10/10 to average in. If he completes an activity, give it a 10/10. If he gets sloppy on activities, give him less credit, like a 7/10. That will bring down his average, as maybe it should. Use the grades as you need them to motivate, reward, or discipline.

I like to use grades to reward hard work done, like reading, being creative, or having studied hard for a test. You can determine what to grade and when to grade and throw them all in the same pot for an average each quarter. At the end of this section, I have provided a grid on which to record grades that pertain to *The Mystery of History* based on seven weeks per quarter. Some days may remain blank. If you have two graded pieces fall on the same day, just record them together. Add the numerators and the denominators separately. They will average out the same.

In regard to special activities or larger projects, I recommend establishing a point system. For example, if your student is going to do a particularly hard project, make it worth 50, 75, or 100 points. Then break it down such as neatness = 10 points, creativity = 10 points, content = 15 points, research = 10 points, and so forth. Then your student might achieve 43/50 points on a special project, and that fraction can be averaged into his grade.

I do present my children with a report card every quarter of the school year so they know where they stand. This gives ample time for pulling up grades if need be. It is also a healthy tool for keeping family members informed as to how the students are performing.

I find this form of record keeping the least painful way to track the work my middle and older students are doing. For a student below fourth grade, I don't bother at all with the grade average. For middle or older students, I use this same method in all the courses that I keep grades for: spelling, math, and so forth. I can quickly look at the grade record to see what the student has completed and what I have graded. I may only actually grade their work every week or so and at that time fill in a week of grades. But with one glance at the grade record, I can pick up where I left off and stay on track.

Grade Record

Student _____ **Grade** _____

Subject _____ **Year** _____

QUARTER 1 (SEMESTER I) – THE FIRE IGNITES

	WEEK 1 (1)	WEEK 2 (2)	WEEK 3 (3)	WEEK 4 (4)	WEEK 5 (5)	WEEK 6 (6)	WEEK 7 (7)
MONDAY							
TUESDAY							
WEDNESDAY							
THURSDAY							
FRIDAY							

QUARTER 2 – THE FIRE SPREADS

	WEEK 1 (8)	WEEK 2 (9)	WEEK 3 (10)	WEEK 4 (11)	WEEK 5 (12)	WEEK 6 (13)	WEEK 7 (14)
MONDAY							
TUESDAY							
WEDNESDAY							
THURSDAY							
FRIDAY							

QUARTER 3 (SEMESTER II) – THE FIRE GROWS

	WEEK 1 (15)	WEEK 2 (16)	WEEK 3 (17)	WEEK 4 (18)	WEEK 5 (19)	WEEK 6 (20)	WEEK 7 (21)
MONDAY							
TUESDAY							
WEDNESDAY							
THURSDAY							
FRIDAY							

QUARTER 4 – THE FIRE SHINES

	WEEK 1 (22)	WEEK 2 (23)	WEEK 3 (24)	WEEK 4 (25)	WEEK 5 (26)	WEEK 6 (27)	WEEK 7 (28)
MONDAY							
TUESDAY							
WEDNESDAY							
THURSDAY							
FRIDAY							

Semester 1

The Early Church

CONTENTS

QUARTER 1   The Fire Ignites: c. A.D. 33 to 476

Pages

Around the World 3–5

Weeks 1–7 7–104

Put It All Together (Worksheet 1) 105–111

QUARTER 2   The Fire Spreads: c. 500 to 871

Around the World 113–115

Weeks 8–14 117–234

Put It All Together (Worksheet 2) 235–241

SEMESTER 1 TEST 242–245

QUARTER 1

THE FIRE IGNITES:
C. A.D. 33 TO 476

Are you ready to go around the world? In a way, that's just what we're going to do. At the beginning of each quarter, I'm going to summarize what was going on around the world during that time period. Of course, it's impossible to cover everything. Only the Creator of mankind knows every person's story that makes up the history of the world. But fortunately, we have a record of quite a few people—both good and bad—who have shaped history. That's what this book is about.

But this book is also about God. I believe He seeks to reveal Himself to mankind that we might know Him personally. How does He do that? He ultimately came to earth Himself in the form of a man. That is, in the person of Jesus. In doing so, He came to give His life for our sins—dying on a cross that we might spend eternity with Him, forgiven and redeemed! But what about after the resurrection of Christ? How does God reveal Himself to man then?

We're going to get to that throughout this book. We will first look at a time called *Pentecost* when the Holy Spirit was poured out on the first followers of Jesus. They were empowered with supernatural abilities to help spread the message of the Gospel. The Bible says in the story of Pentecost, *"Then there appeared to them divided tongues, as of fire, and one sat upon each of them. And they were all filled with the Holy Spirit . . . "* (Acts 2:3–4) For that reason I'm titling this quarter, "The Fire Ignites." To me it describes the beginning of supernatural power that was coming through the Holy Spirit so that God would be made known.

But as the Gospel spread across Europe, there were, unfortunately, enemies who tried to stop it. *Saul of Tarsus* was one such enemy, as were *Nero* and many other Roman emperors. These men sought to hurt and destroy Christians. We call that *persecution*. You will find many grueling stories of persecution in this book, particularly in the first quarter. They are not very pleasant to learn about. But don't let it spoil the rest of the book for you. Not all the quarters will be as sad as this one. Remember, too, that at least in studying persecution, we can be inspired by the great faith of thousands of men and women who have helped keep the Christian faith alive through their own deaths.

3

We will also look at the *Jews* of this time period just after the life and death of Jesus. What became of those who did not believe Jesus was the Messiah? Many of them died a brave death at a place called *Masada*. Masada was a great fortress where almost a thousand Jews tried to hide from the Romans after Jerusalem was destroyed. When that failed, there were many who tried to revolt against Roman rule. They followed a man who claimed to be their long-awaited messiah. His name was *Bar-Kokhba*. He failed them, too.

Since I've mentioned Rome here, you may want to know ahead of time that there is a lot of *Roman* history in the beginning of this book. Why? It's simple. At the time of the Early Church, Rome was the biggest empire in Europe. The Romans were strong, powerful, and inventive people. The great *Colosseum* of Rome was built and dedicated around A.D. 80. And Roman leaders had a great effect on the world—especially an emperor by the name of *Constantine*. In 313

The great Colosseum in Rome stands about 600 feet long, 500 feet wide, and over 150 feet high.

he declared it illegal to persecute Christians. It was a great relief to the Early Church.

Now, back to God revealing Himself to mankind. He has always done so through His written word. You will learn about how the Scriptures were preserved in the *Dead Sea Scrolls* and how they were translated for the common man. Both of these are truly significant events that still influence us today.

You will also learn of many great men who were messengers of the Gospel. First, we will study a few of the *apostles*, such as *Peter, John, and Paul*. An "apostle" is someone who has a special calling. In the New Testament, the word *apostle* generally refers to the 12 disciples of Christ *after* the resurrection of Jesus. (Paul, who was not one of Christ's 12 disciples, was added to this list after his conversion.) We will also look at a few men who have been given the title of *saint*, such as *St. Valentine, St. Patrick, St. Augustine, and St. Jerome*. Though in reality all believers in Jesus Christ are considered "saints" (Rom. 1:7, 1 Cor. 1:2), there are some special men and women who have been given that title in history for the outstanding lives they lived. Some "saints" have their own holidays to remember them by.

Though most of this quarter will cover the history of Europe, we are going to peek at the rise of two amazing cultures in other parts of the world. First, on the continent of Asia, we will look at *India*. During the time of the Early Church, it was one of the most prosperous countries of the world! The Indians (as the people of India are called) understood certain kinds of math long before anyone else did. And strangely, on the other side of the world at the very same time, the *Maya* of *Mexico* and *Central America* were figuring out advanced mathematics, too. As far as we know, both the Indians and the Maya invented the use of zero. (We can't imagine life without it!)

We will end this quarter with the fall of the Western Roman Empire. You might already have heard of it. It was a very important event in history. You will learn that after the great empire of Rome fell, a dark time in history covered most of Europe. We call it the *Dark Ages*. It ushered in the *Middle Ages*. But I'm getting way ahead of myself here. I'll tell you much more about the Middle Ages when we get to it.

In closing, I want to mention some things about how we count time. The term B.C. means *Before Christ*. It refers to the time period *before* the life of Jesus. We count it backward. For example, if something happened 50 years before Jesus was born, we call it 50 B.C. If something happened 1,000 years before Christ was born, we would call that 1000 B.C. So, the bigger the numeral before the letters B.C., the longer ago it happened; that is, the more ancient it was in time. Take the first Olympics, for example. They took place in 776 B.C. That means that seven hundred and seventy-six years before Jesus lived, the Greeks were playing the first Olympic games. That was a long time ago.

On the other hand, the term A.D. stands for *Anno Domini*. It is Latin for *"in the year of the Lord."* It refers to time *after* the birth of Jesus Christ. These numbers are not counted backward, but forward. So, something that happened 50 years *after* Jesus was born is called A.D. 50. Something that happened 1,000 years after Jesus was born is called A.D. 1000. The bigger the numeral after the letters A.D., the more recent the event was. Take the year A.D. 2000 for example. It refers to time just a few years ago that was 2,000 years after Jesus was born.

Now here is the confusing part I want to clear up. Somewhere along the way historians found the calendar to be off by a few years. It has been determined that Jesus was actually born around 4 B.C. Since He lived for about 36 years, that puts His death around A.D. 33. And that is where this book will begin, at A.D. 33.

Volume I of *The Mystery of History* covered Creation to the Resurrection of Jesus (c. 4004 B.C. to A.D. 33). I hope you were able to read that first. But if not, you can pick up and join us where Volume II begins—on the Day of Pentecost. According to the Book of Acts, Pentecost occurred just after the ascension of Christ, which is where Volume I concluded.

You may notice, too, that I quit writing A.D. by the time my stories reach the 300s. It just seems too tedious to read and write. And after we get to the 300s, you should remember that everything in this volume is from the A.D. time period. Now, with all of that, let's begin Volume II of *The Mystery of History*.

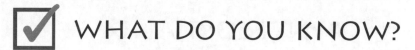

✓ WHAT DO YOU KNOW?

PRETEST 1

Pretests are just what they sound like. They are a "pre" test, not a real test. They are designed to introduce new people and places, stir your curiosity, and find out what you might *already* know about the lessons to come. Keep it fun! I suggest you check your answers but not record your grade. Chances are you will miss a lot of questions! But that's OK. If you knew all the answers, you wouldn't need to take this course! Hopefully this pretest will give you a glimpse of what you WILL be learning for the week.

Who/What Am I? Choose the best answer from the list below.

1. Before I left the earth and ascended into heaven, I told my followers, "But you shall receive power when the Holy Spirit has come upon you . . ." (Acts 1:8) Who am I?

2. As Jesus said would happen, I came upon the apostles at Pentecost. Who am I?

3. I was stoned to death and became the first Christian martyr. Who am I?

4. Jesus spoke to me on the road to Damascus and I was blinded. Who am I?

5. I am the city from which the first Christians were sent out as missionaries. What am I?

6. I traveled with Paul on his first missionary journey to nine cities. Who am I?

7. I am the place in Athens, Greece, where Paul preached a powerful sermon. What am I?

8. I am an island in the Mediterranean where Paul was shipwrecked for three months. What am I?

WORD BANK

Mars Hill	Antioch	Jesus	Stephen
Barnabas	Holy Spirit	Malta	Saul (or Paul)

PENTECOST AND
THE FIRST FOLLOWERS OF JESUS
LESSON 1

Imagine the first men and women who were followers of Christ. Most of them heard Jesus teach with their own ears. Some had seen Him die with their own eyes. Many saw Him face to face after He rose from the dead. The first believers experienced things that were more than amazing. But what happened next to these men and women was enough to forever shape history!

You see, just before Jesus left this earth and ascended into heaven, He told His followers that they would receive the **Holy Spirit** as promised by the Father. *"But you shall receive power when the Holy Spirit has come upon you; and you shall be witnesses to Me in Jerusalem, and in all Judea and Samaria, and to the end of the earth."* (Acts 1:8) Notice the two things Jesus stressed here: that people would receive *power from the Holy Spirit* and that they would be His *witnesses.*

This one promise in the Bible is incredible! Do you think it came true? According to the Book of Acts, it did. And better yet, the Bible says it is *still* coming true! (John 14–16; Rom. 8:16; 10:13–17) In Acts, Chapter 2, we learn that as the apostles were gathered:

*"suddenly there came a sound from heaven, as of a rushing mighty wind, and it filled the whole house where they were sitting. Then there appeared to them divided tongues, as of fire, and one sat upon each of them. And they were all **filled with the Holy Spirit** and began to speak with other tongues, as the Spirit gave them utterance."* (Acts 2:2–4) (Bolded letters are mine for emphasis.)

As a result of this incident, the Bible says that the multitudes were *"confused, because everyone heard them speak in his own language. Then they were all amazed and marveled, . . . "* (Acts 2:6–7) Because different languages were all being spoken, some people thought that the disciples were drunk with wine in the middle of the day. How wrong they were.

Acts 2:14 tells the rest of the story. After the Holy Spirit had come upon those who were gathered, **Peter** began to preach and explain what was happening. As a result, the Bible says that 3,000 people were saved that day! Not bad results for a first sermon. And, what makes the story even more special is to know that Peter was the disciple who *denied* he knew Jesus three times just before Jesus was crucified. What a turnaround of courage for Peter.

The event of the coming of the Holy Spirit happened on what is called the **Day of Pentecost, c. A.D. 33.** Pentecost means "fifty" in Greek.

"And they were all filled with the Holy Spirit . . ." (Acts 2:4)

What does fifty have to do with it? Well, the coming of the Holy Spirit happened *fifty* days after the Passover. What makes this particularly meaningful is that in the Old Testament, the Jews were given the Law of Moses *fifty* days after the Exodus. (Recall that the Exodus was the time when the Jews left Egypt and were freed from slavery.)

This is an amazing spiritual parallel from the Old Testament to the New Testament. For just as the Jews received *freedom from physical bondage* and were given the *LAW* to live by, the early Christians received *freedom from spiritual bondage* and were given *POWER* to live by—the power of the Holy Spirit! It's also interesting that in the Old Testament there is a story of 3,000 people dying from disobeying the Law after it was given. (Exod. 32:28) But in the New Testament, we see 3,000 people being saved after Peter's first message was given. What a contrast!

After Pentecost

After the Day of Pentecost, we continue to see the Holy Spirit working supernaturally through the apostles and these first believers in order that *others* might believe that Jesus was God. A great example of this is in the Book of Acts when Peter and **John** healed a lame man at the **Beautiful Gate** of the Temple. (Acts 3:1–10) Picture a crippled man sitting and begging in the Temple at the same place day after day, year after year, completely depending on others to survive. Peter and John not only noticed the lame man, but they healed him in the name of Jesus! This healing act was so powerful that it led a great crowd to be filled with *"wonder and amazement"* and once again Peter was given an opportunity to preach.

Furthermore, the Bible says:

Some city streets in Jerusalem haven't changed much from the days when Peter passed through them.

*"through the hands of the apostles many signs and wonders were done among the people . . . And believers were increasingly added to the Lord, . . . so that they brought the sick out into the streets and laid them on beds and couches, that **at least the shadow of Peter passing by might fall on some of them.** Also a multitude gathered from the surrounding cities to Jerusalem, bringing sick people and those who were tormented by unclean spirits, and they were **all** healed."* (Acts 5:12–16) (Bolded letters are mine for emphasis.)

Think about how incredible it would have been to witness these kinds of miracles with your own eyes! It caused many to believe.

One more story of great significance in Acts was when the Holy Spirit fell upon the **Gentiles.** You see, a Gentile is a person who is not of the Jewish race. Many Jewish Christians believed that they alone would be saved and thus receive the Holy Spirit—because they thought that only the Jews were the chosen people of God. But what we find in Acts 10:44–48 is God revealing Himself through the Holy Spirit to people who were *not* Jewish. It says, *"And those of the circumcision* [meaning the Jewish believers] *who believed were astonished, as many as came with Peter, because the gift of the Holy Spirit had been poured out on the Gentiles also."* (Acts 10:45) (Brackets are mine.)

This outpouring of the Spirit is profound! Why? Because it means that redemption is available to everyone. And it shows, too, that God kept his promise to Abraham in the Old Testament when He said, *"And in you* [Abraham] ***all*** *the families of the earth shall be blessed."* (Gen. 12:3) (Brackets and bold letters are mine.) That is good news for our world!

Unfortunately, this good news and the great miracles described above were perceived as a threat to the Jewish leaders. Peter and John were thrown in prison on more than one occasion for preaching about Jesus. **Stephen** was stoned to death after giving a great sermon and became the first Christian **martyr.** (A martyr is a person who dies for his or her beliefs.)

As awful as that sounds, I believe we can still see where God was at work. While Peter and John were imprisoned, not even chains were able to stop the power of the Holy Spirit that Jesus had promised them. Acts 5:19 tells us that *"at night an angel of the Lord opened the prison doors and brought them out, and said, 'Go, stand in the temple and speak to the people all the words of this life.' "* They did this with great boldness. And when Stephen was being stoned, he said, *"Look! I see the heavens opened and the Son of Man standing at the right hand of God!"* (Acts 7:56) That means that even in his tragic death, Stephen proclaimed the Gospel!

It is sad but true that as long as men have been preaching the truth of the Gospel, there has been an enemy trying to stop it. (John 15:18–27). Over the centuries, men and women have been arrested, tortured, and even killed because of their love and devotion to Jesus and their desire to be His witnesses. But, has the enemy stopped the spread of the Gospel yet? Not hardly! Jesus Himself promised the power of the Holy Spirit so that we might be His witnesses in all the earth. (Acts 1:8) As **Gamaliel,** a Pharisee and teacher of the Law, said in Acts 5:38–39, *"let them* [the apostles] *alone; for if this plan or this work is of men, it will come to nothing; but if it is of God, you cannot overthrow it."* (Brackets are mine.) Evidently the plan to spread the Gospel *has* been of God because more than 2,000 years later, it is still happening!

ACTIVITIES FOR LESSON 1

ALL STUDENTS

I recommend that students memorize 12 specific dates in this volume. The first date to memorize is Pentecost (c. A.D. 33). On your Memory Card, highlight this name and date in yellow so that it stands out from the other cards.

1A—Younger Students

Re-enact the healing of the lame beggar at the Beautiful Gate. Read Acts 3:1–10. It might remind you of a popular children's praise song based on this story and titled "Silver and Gold Have I None." For the words and music to this song, visit www.jlfoundation.net/payoff.html. Sing it as part of your re-enactment.

1B—Middle Students

1. Do you think men or women have ever been guilty of wanting power for the wrong reasons? Read Acts 8:14–25 to learn the sin of Simon, the sorcerer, who hoped to "buy" the power of the Holy Spirit. Discuss with your teacher the way our society perceives power (money, position, and strength) versus the genuine power of God. Pray and thank God that He ultimately is the greatest power!

2. Read more stories in the Book of Acts revealing the power of the Holy Spirit. I recommend the

story of Philip who preached to the Ethiopian and was miraculously transported somewhere else. (Acts 8:26–40) There is also in Acts (10:1–43) the amazing conversion of a Roman centurion named Cornelius. (A centurion was a leader in the army.)

3. Do you know when or where the followers of Christ were first called Christians? Look up Acts 11:26 to find out.

1C—Older Students

1. Have you ever preached a sermon? On a tape recorder or through a video camera, practice preaching Stephen's sermon, as given in Acts 7. Notice how often he used Scripture to defend his statements.

2. Have you ever witnessed a miraculous answer to prayer? Thank the Lord now for the privilege of this experience to build your faith. Write it down and file it in your Student Notebook under the country in which it happened.

3. Have you ever witnessed to someone about the Christian faith? If not, become acquainted with materials that will help you to prepare. Begin to pray that you would be like the early disciples who changed the world through their bold witnessing.

"SAUL, WHO ALSO IS CALLED PAUL"
LESSON 2

You may have heard of a man named **Paul.** He is mentioned many times in the New Testament because he *wrote* most of the New Testament. He wrote it in the form of letters. The Book of Acts tells the amazing life story of Paul, from his zealous younger years to his older wiser years. It was in his younger years that he was most often called **Saul of Tarsus.** (Tarsus was a city in Turkey.) Today we'll look at what made this man such an incredible witness for Jesus Christ.

Let's consider first who Saul was *before* he knew Christ. (The Bible most often calls Paul "Saul" until he began his ministry. For consistency, I will do the same.) Believe it or not, Saul was a great enemy to the early Christians. Yes, an enemy! Saul was actually one of the very men who persecuted the first believers! In fact, according to Acts 7:58, Saul was at the scene and possibly led the stoning of **Stephen,** the first Christian martyr. Acts 7:58 says, *"And the witnesses laid down their clothes at the feet of a young man named Saul."* Further in the Book of Acts (8:3), it states, *"As for Saul, he made havoc of the church, entering every house, and dragging off men and women, committing them to prison."*

From what you might already know about Paul, that he was a "good guy," you may be wondering what possessed him to be so hard on the early believers. Well, it had everything to do with his religious background. Saul of Tarsus was a very devout Jew and the son of a **Pharisee.** Pharisees were considered the most faithful Jews of their day. They were particularly dedicated to the **Law** (the commandments given to Moses). Saul was, in fact, so devout in his Jewish customs that he said this of himself:

"If anyone else thinks he may have confidence in the flesh, I more so: circumcised the eighth day, of the stock of Israel, of the tribe of Benjamin, a Hebrew of the Hebrews; concerning the law, a Pharisee; . . . concerning the righteousness which is in the law, blameless." (Phil. 3:4–6)

As is clear from this statement, it was Saul's strict **Judaism** (or Jewish heritage) that most led him to persecute the Early Church. As a dedicated follower of the Law, Saul was extremely upset when he heard Jesus' claims to *be* God. He thought it was **blasphemy** and he was willing to do anything to stop it. (Blasphemy means to insult God or fail to show Him respect and reverence. It was a serious crime to the Jews.)

Now you may be wondering exactly how Saul of Tarsus went from killing Christians to *being* a Christian. Well, God works in amazing ways. Acts, Chapter 9, tells the story of his incredible conversion that occurred **about A.D. 35.**

"As he [Saul] journeyed he came near Damascus, and suddenly a light shone around him from heaven. Then he fell to the ground, and heard a voice saying to him, 'Saul, Saul, why are you persecuting Me?' And he said, 'Who are You, Lord?' Then the Lord said, 'I am Jesus, whom you are persecuting. It is hard for you to kick against the goads.' So he, trembling and astonished, said, 'Lord, what do You want me to do?' Then the Lord said to him, 'Arise and go into the city, and you will be told what you must do.' And the men who journeyed with him stood speechless, hearing a voice but seeing no one. Then Saul arose from the ground, and when his eyes were opened he saw no one. But they led him by the hand and brought him into Damascus. And he was three days without sight, and neither ate nor drank." (Acts 9:3–9) (Word in brackets is mine for clarity.)

I suppose it would have been hard for anyone to eat or drink after an experience like that! The Lord Jesus made a bold believer out of Saul by calling to him as dramatically as He did. And He did so for good reasons. Saul was going to live through many challenges and dangers for the sake of Christ before his life was over.

For starters, the early Christian believers were terribly frightened of Saul. They knew him as the one who murdered their Christian brothers and sisters! On the other hand, the devout Jews and Pharisees were shocked at Saul for becoming a Christian. They in fact hated him for it! This young man had completely changed sides, from being the one to persecute, to being the one who was persecuted!

Imagine the best player on a soccer team changing sides in the middle of a game. Would *either* side trust him at first? I don't think so! With so many people in an uproar over Saul's conversion, he had to escape from his home in

"And the witnesses laid down their clothes at the feet of a young man named Saul. And they stoned Stephen as he was calling on God . . ." (Acts 7:58–59)

Damascus in the middle of the night. He pulled this off by having friends secretly lower him in a basket over the huge city wall. For good reasons, Saul was afraid for his life and returned to his original home in Tarsus. He stayed there for nearly 10 years, preaching and teaching Christ.

But the Lord had much bigger plans for Saul of Tarsus. He sent a godly man by the name of Barnabas looking for him. The Bible says:

"Then Barnabas departed for Tarsus to seek Saul. And when he had found him, he brought him to Antioch. So it was that for a whole year they assembled with the church and taught a great many people. And the disciples were first called Christian in Antioch." (Acts 11:25–26)

It must have been a glorious assembly there in Antioch. Imagine the teaching and the strong testimonies of those in the congregation. I think it is beautiful that the disciples were first called Christians there. That means they were willing to bear the name of the Lord Jesus Christ. Saul was there too, proving once and for all that he was a true believer to any who might have doubted. I wonder how many times he stood up to retell his dramatic encounter with the Lord on the road to Damascus.

It was from the growing church at Antioch that Barnabas and Saul were first sent on a short mission. Their job was to bring relief to their suffering brethren in Judea. But the Lord had even more planned for Saul! It says in Acts 13:2, *"As they ministered to the Lord and fasted, the Holy Spirit said, 'Now separate to Me Barnabas and Saul for the work to which I have called them.' "*

Coincidentally, it is just after this special calling that the writers of the New Testament begin to refer to Saul as Paul. Acts 13:9 says, *"Then Saul, who also is called Paul, filled with the Holy Spirit . . . "* Mistakenly, many people think that Saul *changed* his name to Paul. But the Bible doesn't really say this. Some scholars believe the name Paul was used to signify the great transformation in his life. Others believe Saul took the name of one of his first converts, **Sergius Paulus.** Or it may just be that Saul was his Jewish name (named after King Saul, the first king of Israel) and Paul was his Roman name. As he ministered to many non-Jewish people, he may have preferred to use his Roman name. Regardless of what name he went by, Paul was truly a remarkable man!

The work Paul was called to was nothing less than miraculous. The rest of his life is best described through his missionary journeys. There is so much to tell about these that I'll save it for the next lesson. Let's just say that if you like adventure, you'll like the journeys of Paul. He was kicked out of town, stoned, imprisoned, shipwrecked, and chained to a Roman soldier—all for the cause of Christ!

ACTIVITIES FOR LESSON 2

2A—Younger Students

When the Lord spoke to Saul on the road to Damascus, he struck him with blindness for three whole days. He had to be led around by the hand. Have your teacher blindfold you and lead you around your home or classroom. Total blindness can be frightening when you're not used to it. Why do you think the Lord wanted Saul to experience this? Discuss possible reasons with your teacher—for example, to teach Saul that he was spiritually blind without Christ (John 9:39–41), to emphasize Paul's dependence on the Lord, to teach humility, and other possible reasons.

2B—Middle Students

Saul had a very dramatic conversion experience when he became a believer in the Lord Jesus. Not all Christians do. Do you believe God has saved you by making you a believer in Christ? If so, write a brief explanation of how you know this. I recommend this simple guideline:

1. Explain what you need to be saved from (your sinfulness and rebellion against God);

2. Explain what God has done in Christ to provide you with salvation (His death being a payment for your sin; His life giving you righteousness);

3. Explain when, where, and to whom you first professed your belief in Christ (recognized and turned from your sinfulness; expressed faith in Christ's ability to save you); and

4. Explain how you now live as a Christian (expressing faith through obedience; expressing repentance when sinning).

For each point, write no more than two or three sentences. If you're not sure yet that you've experienced salvation through Christ, discuss this with your parent, teacher, or pastor.

2C—Older Students

In the story of Saul, we are shown that even "enemies" of the Lord can become believers. Go through a local newspaper today and choose the name of one person who appears to be opposed to the things of God. Cut out the article and post it in a place where you will be reminded to pray for that person. Pray that he or she, like Paul, will become a great witness for Jesus Christ rather than a persecutor of the Christian faith.

PAUL'S MISSIONARY JOURNEYS
LESSON 3

In the last lesson we learned that **Saul** (who also was called Paul) was dramatically converted from being an *enemy* of Christ to being a true *believer* in Him. It's an incredible story. From Paul's New Testament letters we know even more amazing things about him. He traveled to cities all over Europe and Asia teaching and preaching the gospel of Christ. We group his travels into three major journeys, extending from **about A.D. 46–66.** Each was full of tough challenges and wonderful miracles.

A church in **Antioch** commissioned Paul and his friend **Barnabas** as the very first **missionaries** of the gospel of Christ. (Acts 13:2–3) Their mission was to teach others the very things that Jesus taught about who He was and what He had done to provide redemption for people. And when others believed, Paul and Barnabas sought to teach them how to live as Christians in spiritual families of God called **churches.**[1] This was what Jesus had instructed them to do in what is called the Great Commission. (Matt. 28:19–20; Mark 16:15)

Paul's First Journey

On the FIRST missionary journey, Paul and Barnabas traveled to nine different cities. Because Paul was a Jew by birth and a respected Pharisee, he was allowed to teach in the different **synagogues** that were scattered across Europe and Asia. (A synagogue is a Jewish place of worship and teaching.) Most of the time, Paul and Barnabas saw incredible results from their work. Paul performed miracles that proved

---

1. Middle and Older Students: The name of the "church" will vary throughout this course because historians typically use various terms to label the church at different time periods. The general breakdown is as follows:

The New Testament Church—the earliest church as established by the apostles.

The Apostolic Church—the church from c. A.D. 70–120.

The Early Church—the church from c. A.D. 150–500 (sometimes up to 1070).

The Western Church, Latin Church, or Medieval Church—the church in Europe that remained after the fall of the Western Roman Empire. In this volume I will most often use the term *Medieval Church*.

The Eastern Church or Byzantine Church—the church of the Byzantine Empire. I will call it the *Eastern Church* in this volume.

The Roman Catholic Church—this term was not used until 1560 when Roman Catholics distinguished themselves from Protestants during the Reformation. You'll read more about that in Volume III.

their teachings were of God. Many Jews listened and believed, but there were also many who did not! Those who didn't believe were angry enough to kill. In one city, a vicious mob threw stones at Paul until they believed him to be dead! Miraculously, Paul survived. This was just the beginning of many trials and victories for him.

Paul's Second Journey

On Paul's SECOND missionary journey, he visited 12 cities. This time, though, he traveled with a disciple named **Silas** and later with **Timothy.** (Paul and Barnabas went on separate missionary journeys this time because they disagreed over whom to bring along.)

Paul continued to teach in the synagogues and perform life-changing miracles. He once healed a slave girl from demon possession! This was a good thing. But the girl's owners were upset over it. It seems they tried to use her demonic fortune-telling powers to make money. The slave owners dragged Paul and Silas to the city judges and accused them of causing problems. (Acts 16:17–23) Paul was severely beaten for healing the slave girl and thrown in prison.

Paul, along with Peter, was one of the most influential apostles of Jesus Christ.

Even in prison, Paul was used to demonstrate God's supernatural power. Acts 16:25–26 tells us:

"But at midnight Paul and Silas were praying and singing hymns [praises] to God, and the prisoners were listening to them. Suddenly there was a great earthquake, so that the foundations of the prison were shaken; and immediately all the doors were opened and everyone's chains were loosed." (Brackets indicate translation in the King James Version.)

God used this miracle to convict the jailer of his sin of unbelief. He chose to become a follow of Jesus Christ that very night!

Worse things might have happened to Paul after his beating and imprisonment, but the authorities discovered that he was a **Roman citizen.** Back then, a Roman citizen had certain privileges. One of those was that a Roman citizen couldn't be punished for a crime without having a trial. Those who had beaten Paul had *not* given him a trial like they should have. So that they wouldn't get in trouble, the authorities just asked Paul to leave the city. Though the Roman government was sometimes evil, in that instance God used the Roman law to protect Paul.

Toward the end of his second journey, Paul ended up in **Athens.** Think with me about what you might already know about Athens. It was the largest city in Greece and was immersed in mythology and idolatry. Imagine Paul's feelings when he walked the streets of this ancient city. Athens would have been decorated from end to end with statues to pagan gods and goddesses. To some it might have seemed impossible to reach the Greeks because of all their mythology.

But Paul, in his wisdom and zeal, delivered a sermon to the Athenians that is still talked about today. It's referred to as the sermon at **Mars Hill.** (Acts 17:16–34) Rather than put down the Athenians for their beliefs, Paul encouraged them to think about the possibility that there was just *one* God over everything.

He appealed to the deep thinking that the Greeks were known for through their famous philosophers. I'm happy to say that Paul's approach was effective, and God used it to bring many Greeks to belief in Christ.

At the close of his second journey, Paul stayed for awhile in the city of **Corinth.** (The church at Corinth is one that Paul later wrote letters to. We know them now as the books of 1 and 2 Corinthians in the New Testament.) Paul spent almost a year there with the believers of Corinth. His extended stay may explain why his letters to them were so long and detailed. They were his good friends, especially a couple named **Aquila and Priscilla.** They made and sold tents with Paul in Corinth to help him support his ministry.

You can still see the ruins of the theater in Ephesus where Demetrius led a riot against the teachings of Paul.

Paul's Third Journey

Paul's THIRD missionary journey around Europe and some parts of Asia proved to be one of the most interesting. The Bible says, *"Now God worked unusual miracles by the hands of Paul, so that even handkerchiefs or aprons were brought from his body to the sick, and the diseases left them and the evil spirits went out of them."* (Acts 19:11–12). Paul even raised from the dead a man who had fallen out of a window during a late-night sermon! (Acts 20:7–12) I would call that some amazing power!

Through such miracles, many people came to believe in Christ. **Sorcerers** were known to burn their books of magic to completely turn from evil and follow Jesus. Paul's teachings had such an impact in Ephesus that a silversmith named **Demetrius** led a riot against the apostles. Demetrius gathered a large crowd at the theater in Ephesus to protest because he and other craftsmen were losing money making idols! (Acts 19:21–41)

As had been the case before, many of the Jewish leaders were threatened by Paul's miracles and teachings, and he was thrown in prison again. While Paul was in **Jerusalem,** at least 40 Jews conspired together that they would not eat or drink until they killed Paul. By God's providence this plot was discovered by Paul's young **nephew.** We don't know this boy's name but he was very brave in helping Paul. The boy reported the murder plan to a **Roman centurion** (a soldier in charge of at least 100 men). The centurion in turn decided to sneak Paul out of Jerusalem at night—protecting him with 200 soldiers, 70 horsemen, and 200 spearmen and delivering him to the Roman governor in **Caesarea.** It was an incredible escape! (Acts 23:11–35)

For about two years Paul remained a prisoner in Caesarea under the protection of the Romans while waiting for a trial. (Acts 24–26) Eventually Paul was made to stand trial before three Roman rulers named **Felix, Festus,** and **Herod Agrippa.** On each occasion, Paul was able to share the Gospel of Christ with these men and with all who attended his trial. Believe it or not, each of these three Roman rulers found Paul to be innocent of any crime against Rome!

But the Jews persisted in trying to stop Paul from preaching by accusing him of breaking Roman law. By A.D. 60, Paul requested that the **emperor** of Rome himself hear his case. But since obviously the emperor of Rome lived in the city of Rome, Paul had to travel by ship to get there. This is when his story gets even more interesting. It was on that long voyage across the stormy **Mediterranean Sea** that Paul was shipwrecked! (Acts 27) After all he had been through, he was nearly lost forever at sea.

But, for several reasons, Paul knew that he was going to survive the incident. Acts 23:11 tells us that earlier, when Paul was still a prisoner in Jerusalem, the Lord stood by him and said, *"Be of good cheer, Paul; for as you have testified for Me in Jerusalem, so you must also bear witness in Rome."* And God had also spoken to Paul through an angel the very night of the shipwreck, telling him they would survive. (Acts 27:21–24) Thus, Paul was able to confidently inform his companions, all 276 of them on board the ship, that not one of them would perish that night. And not one of them did!

For three months Paul and the other survivors lived on the island of **Malta** until other arrangements could be made to get them to Rome. Isn't it like God to sometimes throw "detours" in our lives and make something good of it? The months at Malta were certainly unplanned by Paul and his shipmates.

The ruins of an ancient library still stand in Ephesus.

But it turned into an opportunity for ministry. Paul miraculously survived a poisonous snakebite, and he healed a man of severe fever. (Acts 28:1–10) As a result, many on the island of Malta came to believe in Christ and were healed.

The Book of Acts closes with the story of Paul *finally* making it to Rome. There, in one of the greatest cities of the ancient world, Paul had the opportunity to really preach. He was also granted partial freedom. He was under what is called "house arrest." It means that he lived in a house rather than a prison, although he was probably chained to a Roman soldier at all times! Acts 28:30–31 says, *"Then Paul dwelt two whole years in his own rented house, and received all who came to him, preaching the kingdom of God and teaching the things which concern the Lord Jesus Christ with all confidence, no one forbidding him."*

I'm glad Paul had those last two years of fruitful ministry in Rome because from other New Testament books, we learn that Paul was later imprisoned again! As an older man, after all his years of teaching, miracles, healings, beatings, trials, and imprisonment, Paul was put behind bars one last time. It is believed that he died a short time later as a martyr under the rule of a terrible man named **Nero.** We will learn in the next lesson just how awful Nero was toward many thousands of Christians. Though it's a horrifying story, it can't begin to negate the devoted and powerful life that Paul led.

ACTIVITIES FOR LESSON 3

ALL STUDENTS

It's time to make your 3-by-5-inch Memory Cards for Lessons 1–3. Follow the directions for making these cards given in the section "Memory Cards" in the front of this book. I think it will be easiest for you to make three cards at a time, so I will remind you every three lessons to make your cards. You may prefer to make one card every time you read a lesson. You decide what works best for you! The cards are designed to help you remember the lessons and to be used in games; they are not intended to be a burden. Your teacher may opt to write the cards for younger students. Try to use LIGHT PURPLE markers on the front side of the cards for the first semester ("The Early Church"). We will use GRAY later to distinguish "The Middle Ages," the title of the second semester.

Memorize the date of Pentecost (c. A.D. 33) and highlight the Memory Card if you did not already do so.

3A—Younger Students

1. Become a pen pal to a missionary. Do you know anyone who is a missionary? A Christian missionary is someone who feels a special calling to share the Gospel of Jesus with others. Many times, missionaries live in other countries. Some of them live right where you do. Through your church or family, find the name and address of a missionary family. "Adopt" them as a family by sending letters or e-mail and praying for them. They may have special financial needs you can contribute money toward. Create an information page about the family you choose and place it in your Student Notebook under the country where they live.

2. For educational purposes, visit a synagogue in your community with your family. Imagine Paul preaching about Christ in synagogues across Europe and Asia. He was very brave to speak of his faith.

3B—Middle Students

1. Pretend you were shipwrecked with Paul. Try writing a letter to your family from the island of Malta to explain your three-month delay! Use the text from Acts 27–28 to add real facts to the story. File your story in your Student Notebook under "Asia: Malta."

2. Are you familiar with the New Testament books that Paul wrote? Using a Bible, create a list of each of Paul's letters. On a Bible map, find the corresponding cities to which he wrote. File your list in your Student Notebook under "Miscellaneous."

3. Memorize the Great Commission passage found in Matthew 28:19–20.

3C—Older Students

1. In Acts 17:16–34, we see that while in Greece Paul was challenged by both *Stoic* and *Epicurean* philosophers. Using a Bible dictionary, find and write a definition for the philosophies of the Stoics and Epicureans. You will learn that one group favored living for pleasure while the other group believed in controlling one's desires. Discuss the barriers that each of these philosophies would present in understanding the Gospel. Toward which philosophy does our present age lean? File your definitions of these philosophies in your Student Notebook under "Europe: Greece."

2. Research the validity of a story that archaeologists may have recently discovered three anchors at the bottom of the Mediterranean Sea that they believe are from Paul's shipwreck. This may require some digging of your own!

Wall of Fame

This is the place in our study where you will create miniature historical figures and attach them to a timeline. As your timeline grows you can chart your progress through the book. Your timeline may be in the form of a notebook, a poster, or a large sewing board. (Details for how to make a timeline out of a foldable sewing board are in the "Wall of Fame Timeline Suggestions" section in the front of this book.)

As an option to making your own figures, you may purchase beautifully drawn figures by Amy Pak in her series *History Through the Ages—Resurrection to Revolution*. Amy Pak of Homeschool in the Woods has shared her artistic talent and created sketches to correspond to the lessons in *The Mystery of History*.

Below are directions for making your own figures. In brackets underneath each entry I have designated the corresponding figures from *History Through the Ages*.

1. **PENTECOST (c. A.D. 33)**—Draw a flame of fire with the word "Pentecost" on it. **With parental supervision,** slightly burn the outside edges of your paper to remember Acts 2:3, *"Then there appeared to them divided tongues, as of fire, and one sat upon each of them."* **Remember, this is a date to memorize.** [From *History Through the Ages,* use *Day of Pentecost.*]

2. *Saul/"Paul" (c. A.D. 35)*—Draw a line down the middle of your figure to depict Saul before and after his conversion to Christ. In one hand, place a sword. In the other, place a cross. [Use *Stephen.*]

3. *Paul's Missionary Journeys (c. A.D. 46–66)*—Draw a picture of a boat. In big letters, write "Paul's Three Journeys." Tear the boat just slightly to depict the shipwreck! [Use *Paul and Peter.*]

SomeWHERE in Time

In this section, I will be asking you to find and/or color places on maps and globes that directly correspond to the people or events that we've been studying. Each list of mapping exercises begins with easy map work and ends with more difficult map work. Please choose carefully to be sure the mapping exercises used are on a level appropriate for each child. I would not expect a student to do all the exercises given!

As described earlier in this book, I want you to keep a separate Student Notebook with dividers for each of the seven continents. Hopefully you can file all kinds of information in your notebook that, along with your map work, will help you learn and remember the places in the world where great history has taken place.

1. Using a globe, I want you to familiarize yourself with the Earth. With your finger, find where you live. Then find where your grandparents live. Find and name the seven continents. They are *North America, South America, Europe, Africa, Asia, Australia,* and *Antarctica.* Find and name the major oceans. They are the *North Atlantic Ocean, the South Atlantic Ocean, the Indian Ocean, the North Pacific Ocean,* and *the South Pacific Ocean.* Which is the closest ocean to you?

2. Using a map or globe, find the small country of *Israel.* This is where Jesus lived and died. If you look very closely you will even find Jerusalem. This is the city where the apostles were filled with the Holy Spirit after Jesus ascended into heaven. From that tiny place, the rest of the world has been influenced as men and women left there to be witnesses of all that Jesus had done.

3. There were many ancient cities named Antioch. Using a Bible atlas, find the city of Antioch in Syria and the city of Antioch in Turkey. The city in Syria is now called Antakiyeh. It was from this city of Antioch that Paul and Barnabas were sent out as the first missionaries. Using a modern atlas, locate the city of Antakya, Turkey. In biblical times, this city, too, was called Antioch. Paul visited this city of Antioch in all three of his missionary journeys. It is easy to confuse these two cities with the same ancient name!

4. The names of nine New Testament books (Romans, 1 and 2 Corinthians, Galatians, Ephesians, Philippians, Colossians, 1 and 2 Thessalonians) are derivatives of the names of seven cities that Paul journeyed to. In a Bible atlas, find the following locations: *Rome, Corinth, Galatia, Ephesus, Philippi, Colossae,* and *Thessalonica.* Record these cities on Outline Map 1, "Mediterranean," and file it in your Student Notebook under "Asia: Syria" (because Paul was commissioned from the church in Antioch, Syria).

5. Using a Bible atlas as a resource and Outline Map 2, "Eastern Mediterranean," create your own map of Paul's missionary journeys. Denote the line of his first trip with blue; the second, green; and the third, red. (Some Bible maps may denote Paul's final trip to Rome as a fourth, or separate, journey from the third. To simplify, you may keep this in red as well since the trip was an extension of his third missionary journey. Notice the great number of cities Paul visited. It is no wonder that he was greatly responsible for the spread of the Gospel of Jesus Christ to Europe and Asia Minor. (Asia Minor is the name of the westernmost part of Asia, which now forms the greater part of modern-day Turkey.)

WHAT DID YOU MISS?

At the end of each week, you will find either an exercise or a quiz. The unique thing about these is that they will not only test your knowledge about what you just learned, but they will also test your knowledge about things from the beginning of the book and beyond. It's a built-in review system reminding you of who was who and what was what. These are not meant to be difficult but rather to help you remember the lessons. I have made the exercises a bit more challenging, however, because you are allowed to use your books for these. As for quizzes, I suggest you study for them because you should *not* use your book to answer the questions!

Scripture Search.   For your first exercise, use a Bible and/or your textbook to match the important Scriptures below with their Bible reference. (A Bible reference is like an address for a verse in the Bible. It tells you the name of the book of the Bible, the chapter, and the numbered location within that chapter where the verse is found.) Place the proper reference in the blank after each Scripture.

Acts 1:8	Acts 2:2–4	Acts 5:38–39	Acts 9:3–4
Acts 10:45	Acts 16:25–26	Acts 17:16–34	Acts 19:11–12

1. "And those of the circumcision who believed were astonished, as many as came with Peter, because the gift of the Holy Spirit had been poured out on the Gentiles also." _____

2. "As he journeyed he came near Damascus, and suddenly a light shone around him from heaven. Then he fell to the ground, and heard a voice saying to him, 'Saul, Saul, why are you persecuting Me?' "

   _____

3. "And suddenly there came a sound from heaven, as of a rushing mighty wind, and it filled the whole house where they were sitting. Then there appeared to them divided tongues, as of fire, and one sat upon each of them. And they were all filled with the Holy Spirit and began to speak with other tongues, as the Spirit gave them utterance." _____

4. "But you shall receive power when the Holy Spirit has come upon you; and you shall be witnesses to Me in Jerusalem, and in all Judea and Samaria, and to the end of the earth." _____

5. The sermon at Mars Hill. _____

6. "Now God worked unusual miracles by the hands of Paul, so that even handkerchiefs or aprons were brought from his body to the sick, and the diseases left them and the evil spirits went out of them."

   _____

7. ". . . let them alone; for if this plan or this work is of men, it will come to nothing; but if it is of God, you cannot overthrow it." _____

8. "But at midnight Paul and Silas were praying and singing hymns to God, and the prisoners were listening to them. Suddenly there was a great earthquake, so that the foundations of the prison were shaken; and immediately all the doors were opened and everyone's chains were loosed."

   _____

✓ WHAT DO YOU KNOW?
PRETEST 2

Scramble! Unscramble the words to fill in the blanks. Use the word bank below only if you need to!

1. Nero was one of the most evil (Ranom) _____ emperors that ever lived.

2. When the city of Rome burned, Nero played the (ryle) _____ at his window.

3. The Roman emperor Trajan made it a capital (remic) _____ to be a Christian.

4. Ignatius was thrown to the (soiln) _____ in the Colosseum of Rome.

5. Tertullian wrote, "The (doobl) _____ of the martyrs is the seed of the church."

6. Like Paul, Josephus was a strict (eesirahP) _____.

7. Josephus was impressed with Rome but still fought in the First Jewish (lotveR) _____.

8. Josephus became a great Jewish (sotiryh) _____ writer.

WORD BANK

lions	Revolt	Roman	lyre	blood
history	crime		Pharisee	

The Mystery of History–Volume II

NERO

LESSON 4

Throughout this course, you are going to learn about some great people who helped shape the course of history for the better. But on the other hand, you are also going to learn about some terrible men and women who left the pages of history with ugly scars. Today's lesson is about one of those terrible men. His name is **Nero.** Born in A.D. 37, he was quite possibly one of the most evil Roman emperors that ever lived, and he definitely left a trail of scars behind him.

Nero was one of the most despised of all Roman emperors for his self-indulgence and persecution.

Before I tell you about this wicked man, let me back up a little bit and review the history of Rome with you. Before Jesus lived, **Julius Caesar** tried to conquer Rome as a single emperor. He was a brilliant man, but the Roman Senate assassinated him for trying to be a dictator and rule the world with **Cleopatra** of Egypt. After his death, the name "Caesar" was used in his memory as a title for other emperors of Rome. (That's why it's easy to mix them up!)

After Julius Caesar was murdered, his nephew **Octavian** managed to win the favor of the Senate and become the first true emperor of Rome. Octavian was later called **Augustus Caesar.** You can find his name in the New Testament story of the birth of Christ. *"And it came to pass in those days that a decree went out from Caesar Augustus that all the world should be registered."* (Luke 2:1) I find it incredible that God had his hand on these rulers in order that the prophecy would come true about where Jesus would be born! (The prophecy said Jesus would be born in Bethlehem, and He was—because Mary and Joseph were traveling for the census that Augustus declared.)

Augustus Caesar did a pretty good job of ruling over the massive Roman Empire. Rome was said to be in its **Pax Romana**, or a time of "Roman peace" under his leadership. But after him, things really went downhill. There were a couple of Caesars who were so unpopular they were assassinated. Being the emperor of Rome wasn't easy.

The fifth man to attempt the job was hardly a man at all. At just 17 years of age, Nero became the emperor of Rome with the help and manipulation of his mother. The rest of this lesson is the story of how he ruled Rome and what he did that earned him such a terrible reputation.

In the beginning, Nero showed some genuine humility as the young leader of Rome. When told that a silver and gold statue would be built in his honor, Nero shyly asked that it not be done. And when it was requested that he sign his first death sentence for a criminal, Nero said with great reservation, "Would that I had never learned to write."[1] That means it bothered him to think of ending someone's life with merely his signature. Young Nero was also bothered by the Roman gladiator system in which

---

1. Will Durant, *Caesar and Christ*. Vol. III of *The Story of Civilization*. New York: Simon and Schuster, 1944; p. 275.

men were forced to fight to the death. He felt it was barbaric! (Which of course, it was.) Unfortunately, both his humility and compassion were soon to wear off.

In time Nero became a man of great indulgence, with the power and wealth of Rome completely available to him. He lived for the "pleasure" of things above all else. It's been written that he slept most of his days away and partied and carried out business through the night. In living for so much pleasure, Nero developed a selfish, cruel, and paranoid disposition. (Paranoia is great, unfounded fear.) At one point, he went so far as to have his own mother killed for fear she was trying to take over his kingdom! Nero's mistress, **Poppaea,** convinced him it was true. Maybe it was, although Nero's mother was the very person who helped put him on the throne to begin with.

Nero's mother was just one of many people Nero had killed. Much like **Herod the Great** who lived earlier, Nero went on a killing spree to rid his empire of anyone who appeared to threaten him. This included a wife

The ancient city of Rome was crowded, leaving little room—if any—for Nero to build new palaces.

named **Octavia;** a half brother; and **Seneca,** one of his chief officers. Nero's behavior became even more lewd and vulgar after his wife's death.

Strangely enough, in some ways Nero acted like he didn't want to be a Roman emperor at all. On one occasion he dressed up like a commoner and roamed the streets of the city, getting into all kinds of mischief. He hung out with gangs and street ruffians and beat up innocent people! Not exactly fitting behavior for an emperor. Furthermore, Nero appeared to spend more time in Greece than he did in Rome. He did this because of his love for art, music, and theater, which were far more popular in Greece than in Rome. Unlike any of the other Roman emperors, Nero regularly performed in Greek theater. At every opportunity he could create, he sang, played the harp, read poetry, or acted. He was so serious about his career in the arts that he made it against the law to leave a theater where he was acting or to fall asleep during one of his performances!

The Romans were appalled at Nero's behavior. They didn't like the idea of their emperor "mingling" with the artists and musicians of Greece. What did it say about the Romans? Nero ignored their ridicule and went on to compete in Greek sporting events. His favorite was **chariot racing.** Nero received 1,808 winning crowns for all the *Greek* competitions he was involved in! This *really* bothered the prideful Romans. Nero was told he ought to just kill himself rather than bring such shame to Rome, but his behavior remained unchanged.

To make himself even more unpopular with the Romans, Nero publicly whined about the layout of the crowded city of Rome. He didn't like where all the buildings were situated. It was true that Rome had grown rapidly and was very congested. Streets had not been well laid out, leaving Nero little room—if any—to build new palaces. Knowing that that is how Nero felt, it only makes you wonder if he was indeed the one behind the great burning of Rome.

You see, for almost a full week in A.D. 64 the city of Rome went up in flames. The great fire raged out of control. About two-thirds of Rome was destroyed, and many people lost their lives. During the fire Nero is said to have nonchalantly played the **lyre** (a stringed instrument) while gazing out his window at the smoke and debris.

Persecution Begins

To most Romans, Nero appeared quite guilty of starting this catastrophic fire. To keep himself from looking so suspicious, Nero set up relief stations for the homeless. But he also looked for someone to blame for the fire. Do you want to guess whom he found? Nero discovered that a new religious sect was growing in Rome and stirring up trouble among the Jews. These people were the early **Christians**!

Nero intentionally blamed the burning of Rome on these innocent believers and had thousands of them killed. According to Nero, they deserved death because they were "cannibals" who drank blood and ate human flesh. This rumor was started because of the sacrament of **communion** (where Christians break bread and sip wine to remember Christ's body and shed blood on the cross). Christians became what we would call **scapegoats**—people who take the blame for something they didn't do. Ironically, the expression comes from Jewish tradition when they would sacrifice a goat for their sins. (Lev. 16) Of course, Christians believe that Jesus Christ was the ultimate sacrifice for sin. That's what makes the story so ironic.

It is probably not necessary for me to share gory details of just how some of the early Christians died under Nero's persecution. But I feel it is important to appreciate what these believers endured because of their great faith in Jesus Christ. One historian wrote that some people were torn apart by wild beasts in the numerous sporting arenas. Others were covered with pitch, raised on poles, and left to burn as torches in Nero's personal gardens. **Peter** and **Paul** are believed to have died under Nero. Paul was beheaded, and Peter was crucified upside down. Peter chose to be crucified that way because he didn't feel worthy to die in the same manner that Jesus did.

Because of these horrible conditions, some Christians gathered to hide in what are called the **catacombs.** The catacombs were underground chambers used as burial grounds beneath the city streets of Rome. These chambers were only about 10 feet wide and 6 feet high but they extended for miles and miles under the ground. The catacombs made a perfect secret location for early Christians to meet for worship and prayer. And it is estimated that between 2 and 7 million Christians who died sometime in the first century are also buried there.

It is very sad to think about these tragedies. But it is also encouraging to remember how brave the Christians were. Had they only renounced (or denied) their faith in Jesus, their lives would have been spared. But they wouldn't deny who they believed Jesus to be, and that was God.

As for Nero, he didn't live a very long life either. By the time he was 30 years old, the Roman Senate was completely fed up with him. Soldiers went on a massive manhunt for Nero with every intention of torturing and killing him. Nero became aware of it and went into hiding. But he couldn't escape for long. Rather than face a slow and agonizing death by torture, Nero tried to kill himself with a sword in A.D. **68.** According to Will Durant in *Caesar and Christ,* Nero's assistant actually finished driving the sword through Nero that caused his death because the emperor himself found it too painful to do.[2]

Despite the cruelties, the quirks, and the unusual behavior of Nero, when news spread in Rome of his death, there were mixed reactions from the masses. Will Durant wrote, "Many of the populace

---

2. Ibid., p. 284.

rejoiced at his death and ran about Rome with liberty caps on their heads. But many more mourned him, for he had been as generous to the poor as he had been recklessly cruel to the great."[3]

It is an odd summary, isn't it? But then Nero was an odd man who appeared to live more for himself than for anyone else.

I warned you in the beginning of this lesson that some people we'll be studying were pretty awful. I think that by now you can clearly see the depraved life that Nero led. It is very sad that so many people suffered and died under his rule.

ACTIVITIES FOR LESSON 4

4A—Younger Students

Make a pretend lyre. Directions are in the Activity Supplement in the Appendix. Or, locate the sounds of a lyre using a computerized encyclopedia with CD-ROM capabilities. Listen to it with your teacher. What type of instrument that we use today does it resemble?

4B—Middle and Older Students

The Colosseum of Rome is one of the most spectacular Roman ruins still standing today. Research this magnificent structure. (It was not dedicated until A.D. 80, about 12 years after Nero died. Though many Christians died there through persecution, it would not have been under Nero.)

Find out the Colosseum's size, the meaning of its name, and how it was used. Write three to five paragraphs on your findings. Photocopy the ruins of the Colosseum from a reference book or print it from the Internet and include it in your mini-report. File it under "Europe: Rome" in your Student Notebook.

4C—Middle and Older Students

1. Research the catacombs of Rome and/or other cities. One suggested Internet link is:

   www.scrollpublishing.com/store/catacomb-pictures.html

   Investigate the artwork that has been discovered in some catacombs. Christians were known to leave secret signs like a fish or *Chi-Rho* (the first two letters of "Christ" in Greek) to communicate that they were believers. These symbols are found in the catacombs. Photocopy or print examples. Write a few paragraphs on the catacombs. Combine these and file them in your Student Notebook under "Europe: Rome."

2. If you are part of a co-op or school group, create symbols to lead believers to a meeting place. Gather "secretly" in a dark room of your school or home to quietly sing praise songs and read Scripture. Consider that many Christians today meet in such conditions to avoid persecution!

3. ***Adult Supervision Needed.*** A record has been kept of a letter written by Nero's mother to him. Her name was Agrippina. In this emotion-filled letter, she pleads for her life. Read this for yourself in the Activity Supplement. Draft your own letter as an in-law of Nero, a Roman official, or a Christian leader pleading that he not kill Christians. Burn the edges to make it look more authentic. File it under "Europe: Rome" in your Student Notebook.

---

3. Ibid.

MARTYRS OF THE EARLY CHURCH

LESSON 5

(NOTE TO TEACHER: Preview this lesson for graphic details that may be unsuitable for some children. Paraphrase as needed.)

For many people, the thought of dying is a scary one. It is not something most of us look forward to. But for Christians it is less frightening because there is hope for eternal life! It is this indescribable hope and yearning for heaven that I imagine has calmed the countless number of men and women who have died because of their belief in Christ. We call them **martyrs.**

The first people to persecute the Christians were the Jews themselves, like **Saul of Tarsus** for example. (It is ironic that the very race that Christ was born into was first in trying to erase Him from history.) But eventually the Jews lost power over Israel and were no longer able to persecute Christians. What we find is that the Romans picked up where the Jews left off in trying to stop the spread of Christianity.

The FIRST wave of Christian persecution in the Roman Empire was that which occurred under the depraved leadership of Nero. Both **Paul** and **Peter** of the New Testament were victims of Nero's deadly reign. If you recall, Nero blamed the newly formed sect of Christianity for the great fire of Rome in **A.D. 64.** Unfortunately, persecution of the New Testament Church didn't end with Nero's death.

Roman Emperor Domitian exiled the apostle John to the Isle of Patmos for refusing to worship him.

The SECOND onslaught on believers occurred under the Roman emperor **Domitian** between A.D. 81 and 96. Domitian, like many of the other Roman emperors, claimed to have divine power and expected to be worshiped. Though many of his demands were just a formality, Domitian really wanted people to burn incense and chant their loyalty to him as emperor! Those who wouldn't bow down paid for it with their lives or were exiled from Rome. In fact, the apostle **John** who wrote the Book of Revelation was exiled to the **Isle of Patmos** for refusing to worship Domitian.

Roman Emperor Trajan made it a crime punishable by death to be a Christian.

The THIRD wave of persecution came under the leadership of **Trajan.** He made it a capital crime to be a Christian. A capital crime is one punishable by death. One of the dear saints who lost his life under Trajan was a man named **Ignatius.** He was a bishop. Tradition says that Ignatius may have been one of the small children that Jesus Himself held in his arms and blessed as an object lesson to the disciples who were trying to shoo them away. If it is true, it may have been this very encounter with Jesus that helped inspire the great faith of Ignatius. When being thrown to the lions in the great **Colosseum** in Rome, Ignatius responded with a prayer like this: "I am God's grain, to be ground between the teeth of wild beasts, so that I may become a holy loaf for the Lord."[4]

---

4. George T. Thompson and Laurel Elizabeth Hicks, *World History and Cultures in Christian Perspective*, Pensacola, FL: A Beka Book, 1985; p. 118.

Ignatius was thrown to the lions in the Colosseum under the rule of Trajan.

Also under Trajan, a widow named **Symphorosa** and her seven sons perished. They were commanded to sacrifice to the false gods but refused. As punishment, Symphorosa was hung by her hair and then drowned. Her sons were each stabbed to death.

About this time there were also two brothers who died for their beliefs. They were named **Faustines** and **Jovita.** It has been recorded that they so patiently endured their tortures that a heathen man came to believe in their God just by watching them die! He cried out at their execution, "Great is the God of the Christians."[5] The crowd then killed him, too.

In A.D. 155 an aged bishop from **Smyrna** named **Polycarp** was martyred for his faith. Under the emperor **Hadrian,** Polycarp was asked to renounce his belief in Jesus Christ. Here is how he responded: "Eighty and six years have I served Christ, and He has done me no wrong; how then can I blaspheme my King who has saved me?"

As Polycarp was bound at the stake to burn alive, he prayed out loud, "Lord God, Father of our blessed Savior, I thank Thee that I have been deemed worthy to receive the crown of martyrdom, and that I may die for Thee and Thy cause."[6]

Isn't it touching that he felt *honored* to serve the Lord in the manner of his death? It is no wonder then that Polycarp's death was so dramatic. It seems his persecutors had a difficult time killing him. The fire they started kept going out! An eyewitness wrote, "He was in the middle, not as burning flesh, but as bread baking or as gold and silver refined in a furnace. And we smelled such a sweet aroma as the breath of incense or some other precious spice."[7] Polycarp's body wasn't truly burned until he was already dead from stab wounds. Because of this miracle, many around him believed in the God of the Christians.

The inside of the Roman Colosseum had four tiers of marble seats that could hold 50,000–80,000 spectators.

Persecution Slows, Then Grows

Fortunately for the believers, the persecutions slowed down for a time. A few years before Hadrian died, he made it illegal to kill Christians.

After Hadrian, the emperor **Antonius Pius** maintained this law of mercy. In taking the throne, he issued this edict, "If any hereafter shall vex or trouble the Christians, having no other cause but that they are such, let the Christians be released, and their accusers punished."[8]

---

5. *Foxe's Christian Martyrs of the World.* The Christian Library series. Westwood, NJ: Barbour and Co., Inc., 1985; p. 53.

6. George T. Thompson and Laurel Elizabeth Hicks, *World History and Cultures in Christian Perspective,* Pensacola, FL: A Beka Book, 1985, p. 118.

7. A. Kenneth Curtis, J. Stephen Lang, and Randy Petersen, *The 100 Most Important Events in Christian History.* Grand Rapids, MI: Fleming H. Revell, 1991; p. 21.

8. *Foxe's Christian Martyrs of the World.* The Christian Library series. Westwood, NJ: Barbour and Co., Inc., 1985; p. 54.

However, the next Roman emperor was oblivious to the sufferings of the Christians. So began the FOURTH persecution of the Early Church under **Marcus Aurelius,** emperor of Rome from A.D. 161–180. By this point in time, the common people of Rome had grown callous to the killing of Christians. "The Christians to the lions!"[9] they would chant. For just about any calamity or disaster that struck, Christians were blamed and killed.

Justin Martyr, from whose name the term *martyr* originated, died under Marcus Aurelius. Justin was a great philosopher. He spent his life teaching both Jews and Gentiles about the Christian faith. He wrote many things that explained exactly what Christians believe. We call these types of writings "apologies," or **apologetics,** of the faith. It was Justin's apologetics that got him into trouble. He was challenged by other philosophers to debate his beliefs. This eventually landed him in a trial where he was asked to deny his faith and sacrifice to idols. Refusing to do either, he was scourged and beheaded. He wrote, "You can kill us, but cannot do us any real harm."[10]

Polycarp prayed, "I thank Thee that I have been deemed worthy to receive the crown of martyrdom, and that I may die for Thee and Thy cause."

We also have record of several young women who suffered and died for their faith. One was a young slave girl named **Blandina.** Though tortured for her beliefs, she is remembered as saying, "I am a Christian; among us no evil is done."[11] Almost 30 years later, under the FIFTH persecutor, a noblewoman named **Perpetua** and her slave **Felicitas** died. They were trampled to death by wild animals though each had a young baby to care for. No mercy was shown to these mothers.

I know that all these persecutions sound terrible. But they got even worse. In the SIXTH and SEVENTH persecutions, Christians were not only killed but also brutally tortured if they failed to sacrifice to the Roman gods. I can't even write about the atrocities that some of the saints had to endure! And by the EIGHTH persecution, in **A.D. 257,** Christians were stripped of property, exiled, or forbidden to gather for worship. **Cyprian of Carthage** is one of those who was beheaded for not sacrificing to the Roman emperor **Valerian.** He was so loved by his students that handkerchiefs stained with his blood were kept as mementos of his greatness.

Roman Emperor Marcus Aurelius led the fourth wave of persecution of the Early Church.

There are even more persecutions to write about, but I'm going to stop here for now. I hope that as we read and write these names, we feel in our hearts for our Christian brothers and sisters, both then and now, who die for their faith. Jesus Himself suffered the cross for all our sins. He promised in the Beatitudes:

"Blessed are those who are persecuted for righteousness' sake, for theirs is the kingdom of heaven. Blessed are you when they revile and persecute you, and say all kinds of evil against you falsely for My sake. Rejoice and be exceedingly glad, for great is your reward in heaven, for so they persecuted the prophets who were before you." (Matt. 5:10–12)

---

9. George T. Thompson and Laurel Elizabeth Hicks, *World History and Cultures in Christian Perspective*, Pensacola, FL: A Beka Book, 1985, p. 118.

10. A. Kenneth Curtis, J. Stephen Lang, and Randy Petersen, *The 100 Most Important Events in Christian History.* Grand Rapids, MI: Fleming H. Revell, 1991; p. 19.

11. George T. Thompson and Laurel Elizabeth Hicks, *World History and Cultures in Christian Perspective*, Pensacola, FL: A Beka Book, 1985, p. 118.

Be encouraged that despite persecutions for more than 2,000 years, Christianity *has* grown and continues to grow. **Tertullian,** one of the founding fathers of the Early Church, said it this way; "The blood of the martyrs is the seed of the church."[12]

ACTIVITIES FOR LESSON 5

5A—Younger Students

1. ***Adult Supervision Needed.*** Polycarp was said to have a sweet aroma about him "as the breath of incense or some other precious spice." It reminds me of the beautiful passage found in 2 Corinthians 2:15–16, which says:

   "For we are to God the fragrance of Christ among those who are being saved and among those who are perishing. To the one we are the aroma of death leading to death, and to the other the aroma of life leading to life."

   Tertullian, the theologian, said, "The blood of the martyrs is the seed of the church."

   In honor of Polycarp, burn a spice-scented candle in your home or classroom today. Discuss how a pleasant fragrance makes you feel and how as Christians we ought to be an aroma of "life."

2. Today would be a good day to pray for someone who is suffering for being a Christian. There are many places in the world today where it is forbidden to worship Jesus Christ. Pray that Christians will be protected from evil and that the gospel of Jesus Christ will continue to spread until He returns.

5B—Middle Students

Familiarize yourself with *Foxe's Christian Martyrs of the World*. (It is sometimes called *Foxe's Book of Martyrs*.) It is a collection of stories of those who have died for Christ. Chapters three through eight give particular detail to the 10 Roman persecutions beginning with Nero.

5C—Older Students

1. Choose one of the bishops in today's lesson and seek original works written by him. It is particularly rich to be able to read the sentiments of the men and women who lived so near the time that Christ lived. We can draw much strength and wisdom from their firsthand experiences of the Early Church. Write a short paper on the saint you choose and file it under "Europe: Ancient Rome" in your Student Notebook.

2. With parental discretion, view the 1960s film *Quo Vadis* (starring Peter Ustinov). (Because it is an accurate portrayal of this era of persecution, it does have some disturbing content.)

12. A. Kenneth Curtis, J. Stephen Lang, and Randy Petersen, *The 100 Most Important Events in Christian History*. Grand Rapids, MI: Fleming H. Revell, 1991; p. 15.

JOSEPHUS

LESSON 6

Why do people write history books? I ask myself that question a lot since I *am* writing a history book. About two thousand years ago, a man named **Josephus** (Joe SEE fuss) asked the very same question. Today I'm going to share with you what his answer was to this question and what he did with his life. But we'll start with some background on him.

Josephus was born of a royal Jewish family about eight years after Jesus was crucified. In fact he was born about the same year as **Nero.** Josephus and Nero would be what we call "contemporaries" of one another; that is, they were of the same age or of the same generation. While Nero was being groomed as a young teen to serve as the next emperor of Rome, Josephus was doing his "homework." Literally. He was a very serious student.

Josephus wrote this about himself:

"when I was a child, and about fourteen years of age, I was commended by all for the love I had to learning; on which account the high priests and principal men of the city came then frequently to me together, in order to know my opinion about the accurate understanding of points of the law." [13]

Josephus is one of the greatest Jewish historians that ever lived.

Though Josephus may have been bragging about himself a bit here, it is probable that he was quite an intellectual for his age.

When Josephus was 16 years old, he decided that he would study the three different sects of Judaism that were around him in order to decide where he belonged. He studied the **Pharisees,** the **Sadducees,** and the **Essenes** (es SEENZ). After three long, hard years he decided that he most agreed with the teachings of the Pharisees. At 19 years of age, Josephus joined them.

Do you remember who had been a strict Pharisee? It was **Paul.** He and Josephus would have had a lot in common. But unlike Paul, Josephus never claimed to have encountered Jesus personally. He remained a faithful and devout Jew all his life.

By the time he was 26 years old, Josephus had become an important figure. He traveled to Rome to stand before Nero and plead for the release of some Jewish priests. He won his case before Nero, and the priests were freed.

But more than that happened on his trip to Rome. For Josephus it was an eye-opening experience that altered how he felt about the **Romans.** You see, most Jews back then despised the Romans for being evil oppressors. They opposed them so much that they were preparing for war. But not Josephus. When he visited Rome, he was impressed with its wealth and splendor. He was also amazed at the strength of

---

13. Flavius Josephus, *The Works of Josephus,* translated by William Whiston, A.M. Peabody, MA: Hendrickson Publishers, 1988, p. 1.

Rome's army. Josephus concluded that the Jews didn't stand a chance in fighting against them. He tried desperately to convince them *not* to go to war against Rome.

Unfortunately, it's hard to turn rebellion around. Despite the warnings by Josephus, the Jews rebelled against the Romans in A.D. 66. It was the beginning of a war that lasted for four years. Rather than just sit back and watch, Josephus joined the war as a commander of the **Galileans.** He was absolutely right, though, about the Romans. They were too tough to beat. Josephus, along with many others, was forced to surrender his small command and was imprisoned for being part of the revolt.

This is a model of the Temple of Solomon, which was destroyed in ancient times. It was rebuilt by Zerubbabel, lavishly remodeled by Herod the Great, and then destroyed by the Romans.

But even in prison, Josephus remained an influential man. So much so that Josephus gained great favor with a Roman commander named **Vespasian** (veh SPAY zhuhn). It just so happened that after Nero died, Vespasian became the next significant emperor of Rome. How convenient for Josephus to have become close friends with the next emperor! By A.D. 69, Vespasian set Josephus free because of their friendship.

Titus Flavius was the Roman emperor who employed Josephus and extended him his family name.

Upon receiving his freedom, Josephus went home to **Jerusalem.** This time he was employed by Vespasian's son **Titus** as an interpreter and mediator. But the same problems existed as before between the Jews and the Romans. The Jews planned another revolt against Rome—but this time an even bigger one. What was Josephus to do? He loved his Jewish homeland but had close connections to the Roman world. The war was painful for him because he was torn between these two worlds. He tried again to persuade the Jews from war, believing that they would be demolished. And he was right.

The Destruction of Jerusalem

In A.D. 70, Jerusalem was hit so hard by the Romans that it didn't recover as a Jewish land for more than a thousand years. Historians call this the end of the **First Jewish Revolt.** (In Luke 19:41–44 and 21:20–21, Jesus Himself prophesied that this would happen.) The Temple was completely destroyed. I don't mean that it was just toppled over, I mean it was obliterated! The Romans stole every imaginable treasure out of it and tore it down stone by stone to the very foundation. The large front brass doors were melted into a mere puddle. In prideful victory, the Romans paraded down the streets, waving the priceless sacred treasures from the Temple and dragging Jewish prisoners behind them.

To the Jews, the loss of the Temple was an unbearable catastrophe. It was, by the way, the Temple that Herod the Great had begun to remodel just before Christ came. It had been completed only a few years before this massive destruction! Without this place of worship and with their homeland in ruins, the Jews were more than defeated. Those who survived the attack on Jerusalem were forced from Israel to settle anywhere they could find work. This dispersion of the Jewish people to other countries is called the **diaspora.**[14]

But what about Josephus? What did he do after this heartbreaking loss? Well, despite his mixed loyalties, he kept his job working for Titus—a Roman. He even adopted Titus's family name, which was **Flavius.** Was he being disloyal to the Jews by working for the Romans? I don't know. But I think it was the love he had for his Jewish heritage that drove him to his life's work. He decided to write the **history** of the Jews from beginning to end as he was taught it, lived it, and understood it. Perhaps he hoped that the history of the Jews in written form would help the Romans better understand his people.

Some would say that Josephus is the best Jewish historian that ever lived. You can still read what are called ***The Works of Josephus.*** They are kind of long, hard reading but they're very interesting. Besides the fabulous stories of Creation and the Old Testament, Josephus includes his own adventures as a commander, the shipwrecks he survived, and the rescues he performed. His history records give us a great glimpse into the time period in which he lived as well as an account of Old Testament events.

I like what Josephus had to say about why he wrote the history of the Jews. He observed that people write history for three reasons: (1) to show that they have a skill at writing, (2) for the sake of others, or (3) because they are "driven to write history, . . . and so cannot excuse themselves from . . . writing."[15] Josephus claims he wrote for the last two reasons—he was *driven* to write, but it was for the benefit of others. His reasons sound good to me!

ACTIVITIES FOR LESSON 6

ALL STUDENTS

Make your Memory Cards for Lessons 4–6.

6A—Younger Students

Do you have any family stories that show how God has worked in your life? For example, have you ever prayed for a really big thing and then seen God answer that prayer? Dictate to your teacher a special family story. Illustrate it, too. Consider that you are being a "historian" by writing these things down. File your story and drawing in your Student Notebook under the continent and country where the story took place.

6B—Middle and Older Students

1. Using a Bible encyclopedia or other resource, look up and define the three sects of Judaism that Josephus studied. They were the *Pharisees,* the *Sadducees,* and the *Essenes.* It is particularly helpful to be familiar with the first two as they are frequently mentioned in the New Testament. The third group, the Essenes, was probably responsible for writing the Dead Sea Scrolls. (But that's another lesson.) Write down these definitions and file the information in your Student Notebook under "Asia: Israel."

2. From time to time, I run out of space to include all the stories I would like to in this book. I challenge you to fill in the gaps! Research a woman of this time period named *Boudicca.* She was from England. Learn of her heroic efforts to fight off the Romans. Discover how she died. File a short paper on her life under "Europe: England" in your Student Notebook.

---

14. The term *diaspora* refers also to other times in history when the Jewish people were driven from their homeland (i.e., the deportation to Assyria and the Babylonian Captivity). The incident in A.D. 70 was just the beginning of a wave of dispersions that was completed in A.D. 135.

15. Flavius Josephus, *The Works of Josephus,* translated by William Whiston, A.M. Peabody, MA: Hendrickson Publishers, 1988; p. 27.

6C—Older Students

1. Through a library or the Internet, obtain the original works of Josephus. Read for yourself his testimony on Creation. Then compare it to the biblical record of Creation. How important is it that Josephus was a good historian? Of what significance are his stories in defending the validity of the Bible? Discuss these matters with your teacher.

2. Research the history of the Temple of Jerusalem beginning with Solomon. Write a brief synopsis of who held it when. Include sketches of the Temple. Discover what is found at the Temple site now. It is very fascinating. File your research under "Asia: Israel" in your Student Notebook.

TAKE ANOTHER LOOK!

REVIEW 2: LESSONS 4–6

Wall of Fame

1. *Nero* (A.D. *37–68*)—Place a small lyre (a violin-looking instrument) in one of his hands and **(with adult supervision)** a burned match in the other. [From *History Through the Ages*, use *Nero*.]

2. *Martyrs of the Early Church* (c. A.D. *64–280*)—Draw a thick cross and on it write the names of some of the martyrs from this lesson. [Use *Domitian, Trajan, Ignatius, Polycarp, Marcus Aurelius,* and *Tertullian*.]

3. *Josephus* (A.D. *66*)—Draw two hearts on him. In one heart, write "Israel." In the other heart, write "Rome." [Use *Josephus and Titus*.]

SomeWHERE in Time

1. Find the modern city of Rome on a map. This is where Nero lived. What country is it in? In a historical atlas, find a map of the Roman Empire at its height. Compare the size of the city of Rome today with the size of the Roman Empire. It is sometimes confusing that "Rome" refers to both a once-large empire and a modern city.

2. The tiny island of Patmos (which now belongs to Greece but lies just off the coast of Turkey) is located northwest of the island of Rhodes. Patmos will be very difficult to find in most atlases, but you might enjoy looking for it on the Internet. A search at www.Google.com revealed several nice sites when I keyed in "Patmos Island."

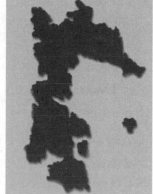

Island of Patmos

Patmos is where John was exiled for not worshiping Domitian. It was from here that he wrote the Book of Revelation. This tiny volcanic island is only 10 miles long and 6 miles wide. With an irregular coastline that makes the island resemble a horse's head, Patmos is only 13 square miles in area.

Today I want you to recreate the dimensions of this diminutive island on paper. Using a ruler, draw a rectangle that is 10 inches long and 6 inches wide. Cut it out. Now, using scissors, cut jagged chunks out of the edges of the rectangle to reduce the area of it. Use the little map shown here as a guide.

You see, as a smooth rectangle, the area of the island should have been 60 square miles. But because of the sharp inlets jutting in and out of the coast, the island is really only 13 square miles in area. Glue your little island onto a piece of notebook paper and write "Patmos" on it. File it under "Asia: Turkey" in your Student Notebook.

3. In a Bible atlas, find the province of Galilee. Josephus was a commander of the Galileans in the battle against the Romans in A.D. 66. Jesus once spent a lot of time in Galilee. It was at the Sea of Galilee that Jesus calmed a storm and walked on the water. In your atlas, find the city of Jerusalem and the city of Rome. We know that Josephus lived in all three areas. On Outline Map 1, "Mediterranean," record the province of Galilee and the cities of Jerusalem and Rome. Label your map "The Homes of Josephus" and file it under "Asia: Israel" in your Student Notebook.

Name _____ Date _____

 # WHAT DID YOU LEARN?

WEEK 2: QUIZ

Multiple Choice. Circle the correct answer for each question.

1. In the Book of _____, Jesus told His followers that they would receive the Holy Spirit.

    a. Ruth

    b. Acts

    c. Romans

    d. Revelation

2. On the road to _____, Jesus spoke to Saul and he was blinded for three days.

    a. Antioch

    b. Jerusalem

    c. Damascus

    d. Eden

3. After a shipwreck, Paul spent three months on the island of _____.

    a. Crete

    b. Malta

    c. Cyprus

    d. Sicily

4. Nero was one of the most evil _____ emperors ever to live.

    a. Roman

    b. German

    c. Persian

    d. Jewish

5. Under Saul of Tarsus and others, the very first people to persecute the early Christians were the _____.

    a. Jews

    b. Persians

    c. Babylonians

    d. Romans

6. Bishop Ignatius was thrown to the lions in the _____ of Rome.

    a. Parthenon

    b. circus

c. Colosseum

d. catacombs

7. Josephus was one of the best Jewish _____ who ever lived.

   a. dancers

   b. architects

   c. generals

   d. historians

8. Though he was impressed with the Romans, Josephus fought against them in the First Jewish _____.

   a. Council

   b. Revolt

   c. Feast

   d. Retreat

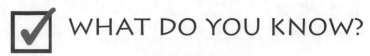

WHAT DO YOU KNOW?

PRETEST 3

True or False? Circle your answers.

1. Masada is the name of a great fortress in China.   T   F

2. Rather than be captured by the Romans, nearly 1,000 Jews killed
   themselves at Masada.   T   F

3. The Dead Sea Scrolls were discovered by a troop of Girl Scouts.   T   F

4. The Dead Sea is the lowest place on earth.   T   F

5. Nearly 800 Scrolls hidden by the Essenes have been found in caves
   near the Dead Sea.   T   F

6. Mt. Vesuvius is a volcanic mountain in Italy.   T   F

7. The city of Pompeii has never been seen again since being buried by
   volcanic ash 1,500 years ago.   T   F

8. Mt. Vesuvius blew so hard in A.D. 79 that it shot hot magma 12 miles high
   for 11 hours.   T   F

MASADA
LESSON 7

(Note to Teacher: I recommend previewing this lesson to determine which parts are suitable for your children. The more graphic paragraphs are marked and may be skipped without losing the content of the story.)

Have you ever seen a movie or read a book that made you cry? I have. I just can't get through some stories without at least a lump rising in my throat. Well, today's lesson is one of those kinds of stories. It made me cry when I first read about it. Unfortunately, some things in history are just that sad.

Masada is not the name of a person or a city, but it is the name of a place. It is a massive **fortress** that still stands today on a steep plateau in **Israel.** The fortress itself isn't the sad part of the story, but what happened there was absolutely tragic.

In review, do you remember the war that **Josephus** was involved in? He was caught up in the First Jewish Revolt against the Romans in A.D. 66–70. Josephus warned the Jews not to even *try* to fight the powerful Romans. But they wouldn't listen, and many were killed. The beloved **Temple** of the Jews was completely destroyed. To add insult to injury, the Romans robbed the Temple of some of its sacred treasures and paraded them through the streets. Worse than that, Jewish prisoners were dragged past the sneers and shouts of their enemies! Some were dragged to their death.

Well, sometime around A.D. 66, at the beginning of the war between the Jews and Romans, there were some Jews who agreed with Josephus that they ought *not* to fight the Romans. They had no confidence they would survive. So rather than fight, they fled. They thought their

This is a model of the massive but beautiful fortress of Masada. It was once a palace retreat for Herod the Great.

best option might be to hide from the Romans and then defend themselves if necessary. I will refer to the Jews who fled as the **Zealots,** as most history books would call them. They are also named the **Sicarii** for the method in which they fought, which was with daggers. In Latin, *sica* means "dagger," so the Zealots were sometimes called the "Sicarii," or **daggermen.**

After some years on the run, the Zealots grew weary of not having a home. They needed a place to live that would give them protection. What they discovered was Masada. The Masada fortress had been built many years earlier. **Herod the Great** (the Herod in the Bible who sent out the wise men to find Jesus) lived at Masada when he was just a young boy. It was used as a fortress in wars against the **Parthians.** Later in Herod's life, he returned to Masada to make it an even better, stronger fortress. Herod was so fearful that someone was out to kill him, that he needed a solid place like Masada for protection. (He was probably right, too, that someone somewhere wanted to kill him. He had a lot of enemies!)

So Herod the Great remodeled Masada into an unbelievable stronghold. He cut out great caverns and cisterns that would hold many years' worth of rainwater. He built storehouses that would keep years of preserved food. He added two ornate palaces to help him fight boredom should he get stranded there. The place was an ideal refuge.

The Romans spent seven months erecting a huge ramp of earth to help them overtake Masada.

In its natural state, Masada was difficult to get to. That alone made it a great fortress. It was located on the western shore of the **Dead Sea,** about 30 miles southeast of **Jerusalem.** The fortress was on top of a plateau that jutted up 400 meters above the Dead Sea. Steep limestone cliffs surrounded it. Only two paths existed to climb the great plateau: one short, steep path on the west side and a long torturous snake path up the east side.

But back to the Zealots . . . in the midst of the war with Rome, they poured out of Jerusalem and other villages by the hundreds and headed to the refuge of Masada under the leadership of **Eleazar Ben Yair.** A few Roman soldiers were occupying Masada at the time, but they were easily overtaken. Masada then belonged to the Jews! At least for awhile.

Life for the Jewish Zealots at Masada was a relief at first. Considering that they had been living in fear for years in their villages, the rugged surroundings of Masada were bearable. For many of them it was the first time in their lives that they were free of Roman rule. They were free to worship as they liked. Free to pray as they liked. Free to be the people they wanted to be.

The Romans Attack

In time, however, word got back to the **Roman emperor** that nearly a thousand Jews were in hiding at Masada. He would not tolerate their rebellion and escape! The emperor sent a myriad of legions to try to stomp out these devout Jews who would *not* submit to the Roman government. According to Josephus, who wrote about the incident at Masada, as many as 20,000 Roman soldiers marched on the great fortress.

Since I already told you this was a sad story, you may think you know what happens next. You would think that 20,000 Roman soldiers could have just scaled up the cliffs and easily overtaken 1,000 Jewish civilians. But, according to Josephus, that's not at all what happened.

The Romans quickly learned that Masada was impenetrable. That means it was impossible to break into. When they tried to scale the cliffs, the Jews showered them with rocks and weapons from above. In every instance, the Jews had the advantage from being up so high on the plateau. And with all the food and water stored at Masada, the Romans couldn't even starve out the Jews.

But someone in the Roman camp came up with a scheme to get to the top of the towering plateau. They would build a **dirt ramp.** That is, a really *big* dirt ramp. Using Jewish prisoners as part of the workforce, the Roman soldiers erected a massive ramp of earth and wood that took them seven months to build.

Imagine for seven months watching the slow progression of the enemy as they inched their way higher and higher to the top of the fort. I can picture the faces of terrified children peeking over the great walls. I can hear them asking their moms what would happen next. I'm glad that they couldn't have known.

When the Romans completed their building, in A.D. 73, they pushed and pulled huge weapons of war up the long earthen ramp. One weapon was called a **battering ram** because it repeatedly rammed a huge boulder through anything in its path. It successfully knocked down outer walls of the fortress, and the Romans set fire to the wooden gates. However, they underestimated the great weight of their weapons. Part of the ramp collapsed and caught on fire. Humiliated at this setback, the Romans yelled, "We'll get you tomorrow!" and they departed for the night to their tents below.

Josephus claims that early the next morning, thousands of Roman soldiers marched back up the ramp with every intent of taking Masada for good. But rather than encounter mobs of fighting Jews, as would be expected, they were greeted by complete silence! Not one person was stirring! Where were the Jews that the Romans had spent seven months preparing to capture? Well, this is the sad part of the story. They were all dead. Through the night, 960 men, women, and children killed themselves. Rather than face Roman rule and imprisonment, they died by their own hands!

(Teacher: The next two paragraphs may be disturbing for some children. Use your discretion in reading them.)

Josephus tells us, however, that two older women and five children survived the mass suicide to explain exactly what transpired that tragic night. According to the witnesses, Eleazar Ben Yair gathered the people around him one last time. He shared with them that they had but two choices. They could be tormented as prisoners of Rome or they could take their own lives and die as free people. After all they had been through, including seven months of anticipating their fate, the idea of taking their own lives was apparently less painful to consider.

To carry out the horrible task, Eleazar instructed families to first burn all their personal belongings. They didn't want the Romans to walk away with even one of their meager possessions or a cent of their wealth. Then, most tragic of all, each man was to slay his own wife and children. Names were then drawn between the men to kill each other.

(Resume reading here.)

There are hardly words I can write that express how this story makes me feel. Thousands of people travel every year to the site of Masada and experience the same problem. They are left in complete awe over the tragedy that occurred there nearly 2,000 years ago. Of course thousands of people have died in multitudes of other wars, but few have died as tragically as these did by the hands of their own loved ones.

Today, the Jewish army uses the ruins at Masada as the place where soldiers swear their allegiance to Israel. It is no wonder that in Israel, postage stamps and medallions display the words, "Masada shall not fall again!" Hopefully there never *will* be an incident like Masada again. Hopefully we've learned from history other ways to achieve freedom than through such tragedy.

ACTIVITIES FOR LESSON 7

7A—Younger Students

1. Create a medallion with the words "Masada shall not fall again!" inscribed on it. Use cardboard, ribbon, and markers.

2. Masada was well equipped for storing preserved foods. For lunch today, try eating dehydrated foods such as raisins, beef jerky, prunes, dried apples, and soup in a paper cup that you add hot water to, etc. If you have a dehydrator, make some of your own dry foods and store them. It would be hard to live on these kinds of foods for months and months at a time. Discuss with your teacher the pleasure of eating freshly prepared foods and be thankful to have these available.

7B—Middle Students

1. Using outside sources, research ancient weapons like the battering ram and the assault tower. Try to find a picture of both to help you grasp why the earthen ramp at Masada collapsed under their weight. Photocopy and color your findings and file them in your Student Notebook under "Asia: Israel."

2. Create a small system of cisterns. A cistern is a method of collecting rainwater. I suggest you do something like this: Cover several large plastic bowls with pieces of mesh cloth. Secure the cloths with rubber bands or string. Place clean rocks or weights on the cloths to direct water to seep down into the containers. (The cloths will slow down the amount of water that seeps in, but they will serve as screens to keep bugs out!) Set the containers outdoors for two weeks or more, depending on the season. Monitor the weather and check your cisterns for rainwater collection. Rainwater is supposed to be excellent for washing hair because it lacks the hard minerals found in tap water. If you can collect enough rainwater, try it out—even if you have just enough for a final rinse after you've shampooed.

7C—Older Students

1. Obtain the original works by Josephus that explain the entire Masada incident. He wrote of it in his book *The Jewish War.* For centuries historians thought this story was fiction. However the great fortress was discovered and excavated in the 1800s to prove that the story was unfortunately quite real. Debate still exists, however, as to whether the mass suicide was as extensive as Josephus made it out to be. Research the debate yourself and draw your own conclusions. Did Josephus exaggerate the mass suicide or did it happen exactly as he wrote it? The findings of archaeologists are some of our only keys to the past! Record your findings in your Student Notebook under "Asia: Israel." (Or send them to me if you'd like! I'd love to know what you discover!)

2. Discuss the ethics of suicide with your teacher or classroom. What are the statistics of suicide in your nation? What does God's word have to say about it? Consider the present-day debate over Dr. Jack Kevorkian's suicide machine.

C. 100 B.C.– C. A.D. 75

THE DEAD SEA SCROLLS
LESSON 8

Over the centuries, archaeologists have found lots of things that help support the stories of the Bible. But none could be more significant than the **Dead Sea Scrolls.** That is the name given to some well-preserved biblical documents that were written thousands of years ago but were only found in the last century by a young boy.

As the story goes, in 1947 a **Bedouin** (BED oo in) shepherd boy was exploring some caves near the **Dead Sea** when he discovered hundreds of parchments. These were no ordinary documents. What the boy found were fragments of the entire **Old Testament,** except for the Book of Esther.

It turned out that archaeologists and other Bedouins found 10 more caves in the nearby area. Hundreds more parchments were found. These included parts of the **Apocrypha** and records of customs of the people who wrote these documents. (The Apocrypha is a book of religious writings that complement the Bible but were not included in it.)

Who wrote the Dead Sea Scrolls? Most scholars agree that the Jewish sect called the **Essenes** (es SEENZ) wrote the Scrolls. Do they sound a little familiar to you? I introduced you to them in the lesson on **Josephus.** Josephus had studied the lives of the Essenes as well as the **Pharisees** and **Sadducees** before deciding to join the Pharisees.

For centuries the Dead Sea Scrolls were well preserved by the dry air of the region.

The Essenes were a strict group of Jews that may have sprung from the former **Maccabees.** (See Volume I of *The Mystery of History* for the story of Judas Maccabee and the first Hanukkah.) As devout Jews, the Essenes felt they should live "separate" from the corrupt world around them. So, they usually lived far away from big cities.

That may be one reason why their "library" of sacred writings was discovered near the Dead Sea. This location, which is also called **Qumran,** was not exactly a popular spot. Qumran is situated near limestone cliffs and the low-lying fossil bed of the Dead Sea. The Dead Sea lies farther below sea level than any other place on earth! It is so hot there, that as fresh water pours into the Dead Sea from nearby rivers, it quickly evaporates. This process leaves behind so much salt and mineral sediment that fish can't survive in the sea. In fact, the salt and mineral content is so high in the Dead Sea that a person will float in the water without even trying!

Well, all in all, a total of 800 writings have been retrieved from the desert spot in Qumran. Most were written in **Hebrew,** some were in **Aramaic,** and a few were in **Greek.** To this day, scientists are still piecing together some of the writings like a giant jigsaw puzzle.

Nobody knows for sure why the Dead Sea Scrolls were systematically stored as they were. It may have been a response to the difficult times the Jews were having against the Roman government. It may simply have been an act of preserving sacred Jewish history.

Unlike most documents of that era, these Scrolls were really well preserved. They probably lasted so long because of the extremely dry air in the region and the materials used to write them on. Some writings were found on **calfskin** and **sheepskin.** Most were on **parchment** and **papyrus.**

What do we know about the lives of the Essenes? For about two centuries, from **c. 100 B.C. to c. A.D. 75,** they lived "separate" from the world. From excavating the area, scientists know that the Essenes lived in communes and shared their wealth with one another. Their writings state that "they shall eat in common and bless in common and deliberate in common."[1] From this we conclude that besides living together as neighbors, they ate together in one large group. And it *was* a rather large group. Anywhere from 200 to 400 people made up the commune at Qumran.

The Essenes were self-sufficient, as was necessary for living out in the wilderness. They raised sheep and cattle, farmed, and made date honey. Evidence of a potter's workshop has been found as well

1. *Dead Sea Scrolls.* New South Wales: Art Gallery of New South Wales, 2000; p. 22.

as a tannery. (A tannery is a place where leather is made.) But the main occupation of the Essenes was the preservation of the Scriptures.

Eventually the Essenes disappeared from history. **Earthquakes** violently shook the region, forcing many of them to leave. Wars with Rome may have forced them out too. Though we don't know much more about the Essenes, we can be grateful for their dedication to the preservation of the Scriptures. The copies they left behind are priceless to Jews and Christians alike because they provide additional historical evidence of the accuracy of the Bible.

ACTIVITIES FOR LESSON 8

8A—Younger Students

Create an ancient document. (This activity will take two days to complete.)

Materials: Paper, pencils, four black tea bags, water, pot for boiling, tongs, shoes, matches, three-hole plastic sleeve for notebook

Adult Supervision Needed

1. Have your teacher place a few cups of water to boil on a stove.

2. When the water boils, add four black tea bags and remove from heat.

3. Set tea water aside to steep and cool.

4. On a piece of paper, write in dark pen several of your favorite Old Testament Bible verses in your best handwriting.

5. Crumple the paper into a tight ball. Straighten it out.

6. Using tongs, slowly lower the paper into the tea water. Leave for several minutes.

7. Use tongs to carefully remove the paper; allow it to drip-dry overnight.

8. Assuming your paper is now dry, have your teacher locate a safe place outdoors where you can burn the edges of the paper. This will give your document an aged appearance. For safety, I recommend shoes on all participants as well as an extra shoe in hand to stomp out the smoldering edges!

9. When the document has completely cooled, I suggest you store it in a three-hole plastic sleeve that can easily go into your Student Notebook under "Asia: Israel."

8B—Younger and Middle Students

Grow salt crystals!

Background Information: The Dead Sea is sometimes referred to as the Salt Sea in the Bible because of its high content of salt. Along the southeast end of the Dead Sea, there lies a ridge of earth 300 feet high and 5 miles long that appears to be covered with *salt crystals*.

Materials: 2 tablespoons of Epsom salt, black construction paper, scissors, foil pie pan or shallow saucer, ½ cup of water, small plastic container with a lid

1. In a small plastic container, add ½ cup of water and 2 tablespoons of Epsom salt.

2. Close the container with a lid and shake hard for about a minute.

3. Cut a black piece of construction paper to fit the bottom of your pie pan or shallow saucer.

4. Pour the saltwater solution gently over the paper in your pan or saucer.

5. Set the pan near a sunny place where it won't be bumped for a few days.

6. Observe the growth of long, beautiful salt crystals as the water evaporates.

7. Take a photo of your salt crystals and file it under "Asia: Israel" in your Student Notebook. Title the page "The Dead Sea Is Salty."

8C—Older Students

1. Examine actual photos of the Dead Sea Scrolls on the Internet. If these sites are not working, do a search for current sites.

   www.loc.gov/exhibits/scrolls/toc.html   (sponsored by the Library of Congress)
   www.usc.edu/dept/LAS/wsrp/educational_site/dead_sea_scrolls/

2. Using a Bible dictionary, research the *location* of the ancient cities of Sodom and Gomorrah. Genesis 19:24–26 explains how these cities were destroyed by God and the fate of Lot's wife, who was turned into a pillar of salt. What scientific facts about the Dead Sea could support this biblical account in Genesis? Write three paragraphs on the topic and file your research under "Asia: Israel" in your Student Notebook.

A.D. 79

THE BURIED CITY OF POMPEII
LESSON 9

On the morning of August 24, A.D. 79, the Roman city of **Pompeii** was bustling about like normal. Fathers were going to work in their shops, mothers were cooking and cleaning, and children were finishing chores so they could go outside to play. But under the ground, something was churning and burning that would forever change this city. A nearby volcano called **Mt. Vesuvius** was about to bury Pompeii in ashes and leave it covered in eerie silence for nearly 1,500 years!

As hard as it is for us to imagine, the ancient city of Pompeii was very modern and much like one of ours. Streets were systematically laid out; homes were lavishly decorated with paintings, mosaics, and marble floors; and the city was undergoing **elections.** Just like our neighborhoods around election time, people staked signs in their yards telling whom they would vote for. Some people even made sport of it and created sarcastic signs to heckle the politicians. For example, some signs read "The Town Drunks Vote for Maximus" and "Thieves Are Voting for Scipio."

Pompeii was a significant port city because it was strategically located near the sea on the western banks of **Italy.** The people of Pompeii traded with faraway **Egypt** and **Spain** as well as with other local Roman cities. With a population of 10,000 to 20,000 people, things were busy. Farmers and shepherds raised olives, grapes, grain, sheep, and flowers. With these products, the bakers and craftsmen made olive oil, wine, bread, wool, perfumes, and flowering garlands.

Pompeii sounds like a neat place, doesn't it? It was in many ways. But in one long and terrifying day, it was obliterated! Had the people of Pompeii better understood the warning signs of a volcano, they might have been spared. But people that long ago had far less knowledge and capability to predict natural events than we have today. For example, in the year A.D. 62, a few years before Vesuvius showered Pompeii, a massive **earthquake** had rocked the entire town. The earth shifted so suddenly that a huge portion of Pompeii was damaged. Even by the year A.D. 79, some buildings and statues in Pompeii were still in shambles from never having been rebuilt.

Despite that incident, nobody in the year A.D. 79 knew what was brewing in the peaceful-looking mountaintop of Vesuvius. The lurking volcano appeared harmless, with layers of lush, green landscape draping across it. The mountain provided enough vegetation for animals to graze there unaware of their fate. Life was seemingly normal.

When Mt. Vesuvius erupted in A.D. 79, it buried the city of Pompeii in 12 feet of ash.

To better understand what happened at Pompeii, let me explain a little bit about how volcanoes work. Miles underneath the ground, it's hot—extremely hot! Sometimes it becomes so hot that rocks melt and gases are created. This hot melted rock is called **magma.** We call the same stuff **lava** when it spews out of a volcano. In a normal volcano, gases build up like a massive teakettle and blow the top right off a mountain. Hot lava then oozes out and burns up everything in its path. But at Vesuvius, something strangely different happened.

Vesuvius Erupts

The pressure under Vesuvius was so great that it blew the contents of the mountain 12 miles straight up into the sky where it hung suspended for hours above the spewing gases! Though some of the debris solidified into porous rock called **pumice** and plummeted back to the earth, most stayed up in the sky. It would have been a frightening sight. The strength of Vesuvius was more like that of a nuclear bomb! It is thought to have been 10 times stronger than the eruption of **Mt. Saint Helens** in the United States on May 18, 1980.

I share all of this with you that you might grasp just what happened to the ancient city of Pompeii and its people that hot August day. Just before one o'clock in the afternoon, so much heat was building up under Vesuvius that the streams and creeks evaporated, animals grew restless, and the nearby sea heaved. Then the top blew! Red-hot stones and pumice shot thousands of feet into the sky. Smoke blocked out the sun, and the whole region shook.

The people indoors probably thought it was another earthquake and braced themselves under shelter. But one look outdoors would have given away the truth. A red cloud hovered and glowed above Vesuvius like a giant **mushroom,** and debris showered the streets. Of the thousands of people who lived there, most had time to escape if falling rocks didn't hit them. Remember there was no hot lava to stop them because the majority of magma from Vesuvius was suspended overhead! People fled by boat, on foot, or on horseback. However at least 2,000 residents were not so fortunate. Ash fell from the sky at the rate of 6 inches per hour! That alone suffocated hundreds who were left in Pompeii.

But what really destroyed the remaining city was an avalanche of **hot air** and **gases.** You see, after about 11 hours, the pressure of the volcano weakened. As it cooled, the great column of ash and rock that hung in the air collapsed. Six different times the column surged downward from the sky before it completely ripped through Pompeii like a hurricane! Anyone who might have lived up to this point would have instantly been killed by the scorching heat and vapors. Twelve feet of ash buried the entire town. The harbor became impassable to boats as ash turned the water to mush.

The fate of Pompeii is like none other. Because of the amount of ash that fell and the absence of hot lava, people were frozen in time like statues in a museum. In the 1700s, local diggers discovered the town almost completely undisturbed. Like giant fossils, shop owners, slaves, children, gladiators, food, animals, and homes were found by archaeologists in the exact positions in which they perished! Some people were found clutching their loved ones, others were found holding bags of jewelry and money. Most died with expressions of terror on their faces at the realization that they weren't getting out.

It is hard to believe that a city could remain covered for nearly 1,500 years! I suppose some of those who fled returned to try to find what had been lost there. But it would have been of no use. Deadly pockets of gas would have still overcome anyone brave enough to begin to dig out Pompeii. Eventually the city was completely abandoned and forgotten. Local people referred to it as **civitas,** meaning "ancient city" in Latin.

If you were to visit Pompeii today, you would learn a great deal about the way of life in ancient Rome. Because the gases have now subsided, nearly the whole city has been unburied to reveal a past life suspended in time. Archaeologists discovered ways to preserve the hollow, ash-covered bodies. They poured plaster into the cavities where the bodies had deteriorated. What remained were three-dimensional representations of real people. It is a fascinating accomplishment. Even the names of families have been traced through the election signs posted in yards.

Why should we care so much about the study of the Romans? Weren't they the bad guys who oppressed the Jews and persecuted the early Christians? Well, many Romans were guilty of such crimes, but not all of them of course. And good or bad, our government and many Western philosophies have been patterned after the Roman way of thinking. So a day in the life of Pompeii is very interesting to historians. Besides that, the story is a sobering reminder of the uncertainty that life holds. Vesuvius remains an active volcano that is regularly monitored in hopes that it will *never* do again what it did in A.D. 79!

ACTIVITIES FOR LESSON 9

ALL STUDENTS

Make your Memory Cards for Lessons 7–9.

9A—Younger and Middle Students

Make your own volcano.

Materials: Short plastic bottle (like an 8-ounce water bottle), vinegar, funnel, baking soda, red food coloring, liquid dish soap, dirt, water, box

Fill an old box with dirt and add water to make it moist enough to sculpt. Nestle a bottle into the dirt and continue to build up the sides to resemble a mountain. Using a spoon or funnel, add 2–3 tablespoons of baking soda to the bottle. Add a few drops of red food coloring and dish soap for effect. Then carefully and slowly pour about ½ cup of vinegar into the hole of your "volcano." It should react with the baking soda and begin to ooze out of the top of your bottle. Add more ingredients if needed. Take a picture of your creation. File it under "Europe: Italy" in your Student Notebook.

9B—Younger and Middle Students

Some of the everyday discoveries at Pompeii help us to see the ancient residents as real people. One of the many things found there was a sign in Latin that read *Cave Canem*. It means "Beware of the Dog." The Romans also left behind a lot of graffiti. "Graffiti" is what we call words spontaneously, and sometimes illegally, scribbled in unusual places for others to read. (Like in a public bathroom stall!)

Nearly 2,000 years ago, someone in Pompeii scribbled the statement "May you sneeze sweetly." It was a gesture of wishing someone good luck. A school student engraved the words, "I was whipped for the 3rd time," referring to his consequence for misconduct.

If someone were to discover your city or home in 1,500 years, what kind of words would they find there? Make up a page of popular slogans or advertisements of our day. File it in your Student Notebook under "Europe: Italy."

9C—Older Students

1. The type of eruption at Vesuvius has been termed a "Plinian" eruption after a historian named Pliny the Younger. Turn to the Activity Supplement in the Appendix to read his account of what happened in the year A.D. 79.

2. Vesuvius was not completely without lava although it wasn't lava that destroyed Pompeii. Research a nearby city in Rome called Herculaneum. It also was destroyed by the volcano of A.D. 79 but in a different manner. Investigate the hundreds of skeletons that were discovered in 1982 along the beach of the city. It is very interesting. Suggested resource is a library book titled *Pompeii: Nightmare at Midday* by Kathryn Long Humphrey, published by Franklin Watts, 1990. See Chapter 8 in Humphrey's book for more about the skeletons.

3. Over the years, Vesuvius has erupted many times. One of the more recent eruptions was in 1944. Research this eruption on the Internet or in an encyclopedia (I recommend *World Book*) to find pictures of Vesuvius during a blast.

TAKE ANOTHER LOOK!

REVIEW 3: LESSONS 7–9

Wall of Fame

1. *Masada* (A.D. *66–73*)—Create a small banner or medallion that says, "Masada shall not fall again!" [From *History Through the Ages,* use *Masada.*]

2. *Dead Sea Scrolls (c.100* B.C.–C. A.D. *75)*—In tiny writing, use a light-colored pencil to copy a verse from Isaiah on a small piece of paper. Then crumple it up to make it appear aged and wrinkled. In larger letters, write in ink "Dead Sea Scrolls" over the top of your paper. [Use *Dead Sea Scrolls.*]

3. *The Buried City of Pompeii* (A.D. *79)*—Draw a small mountain with a large red cloud hovering over it. Write the name "Vesuvius" on it. [*Use Pompeii.*]

SomeWHERE in Time

1. How well do you know the directions east, west, north, and south? In a Bible atlas, find the city of Jerusalem with your finger. Move your finger just a little in the direction of south. Now move it just a little east. You should be right on the western shore of the Dead Sea. This is where the fortress of Masada stands.

2. "There are over 500 active volcanoes in the world, some of which are under the sea. Two major areas of volcanoes exist. (Earthquakes are common in these areas, too.) The first is called the 'Pacific Ring of Fire.' This area circles around the edge of the Pacific Ocean and has many active volcanoes. It includes the western coast of North and South America (including Mt. Saint Helens in Washington state). It also includes Mt. Fuji in Japan, from Guam to Samoa, to New Zealand, then down and across to the southern coast of South America. The second chain forms a line along the Azores, Canary Islands, and east to Europe and Asia."[2]

On Outline Map 3, "World," label the following volcanoes using an atlas and/or other reference materials. Which are located in the Pacific Ring of Fire? A helpful website is:

www.mapsofworld.com/major-volcanoes.htm

Volcano	Country
Mt. Aconcagua	Argentina
Mt. Fuji	Japan
Mt. Saint Helens	Washington state
Lassen Peak	California
Mt. Etna	Sicily

---

2. From *The Ultimate Geography and Timeline Guide,* by Maggie S. Hogan and Cindy Wiggers. Published by GeoCreations, Ltd., 1998; p. 116.

Match and Mark. This is a matching exercise with an artistic variation. You will need colored pencils to complete it. Not only do I want you to match the items in the two columns by placing the correct letter next to the number, but I also want you to follow the directions to artistically "mark" the items as described.

Remember, these exercises and quizzes are designed to take you back to some of the first lessons we learned. On an exercise, you can use your book as a reference if you need to. The lesson numbers are provided for you in parentheses.

_____1. Using a pink pencil, write the number "50" over the Greek word with that meaning. (1)

a. Josephus

_____2. Using a black pencil, draw "x's" on a smiley face next to the name of the man who met Jesus on his way to Damascus. (2)

b. Tertullian

_____3. In green pencil, draw a tent over the name of the couple who made and sold tents with Paul. (3)

c. Pentecost

_____4. In yellow and orange pencil, draw flames around the name of the emperor who blamed the Christians for the burning of Rome. (4)

d. Vesuvius

_____5. In red pencil, draw a drop of blood next to the name of the philosopher who said, "The blood of the martyrs is the seed of the church." (5)

e. Saul

_____6. In gray pencil, draw jail bars over the name of
the historian who was forced to surrender to
the Romans. (6)   f. Dead

_____7. In purple, draw a sword under the name of the
leader of the Zealots at Masada. (7)   g. Pompeii

_____8. In blue pencil, draw waves around the name
of the sea where hundreds of parchments of
Scripture were found in 1947. (8)   h. Eleazar

_____9. In brown pencil, draw the shape of a mountain
around the name of the volcano that erupted
in A.D. 79. (9)   i. Nero

_____10. Using brown, black, and gray pencils, draw a
shower of ash falling on the name of the city
that was buried for 1,500 years. (9)   j. Priscilla
                                                                        and Aquila

WHAT DO YOU KNOW?
PRETEST 4

Circle Sense. In the sentences below, *circle* the word that makes the most *sense*.

1. In the First Jewish Revolt, the (Temple, Eiffel Tower) was destroyed by the Romans.

2. To be a member of Bar-Kokhba's army, a man was required to cut off part of his (nose, finger).

3. Yigael Yadin, a famous (archaeologist, mathematician), uncovered evidence that proved Bar-Kokhba was more than a legend.

4. A creed is a statement of (birthdays, beliefs).

5. The apostles wrote a church creed just (100, 1,000) years after Jesus walked the earth.

6. St. Valentine is remembered in the month of (January, February).

7. Lupercalia was a Roman festival of (frog hunting, love).

8. According to Roman mythology, one shot from Cupid's (arrow, rubber band) made a person "fall in love."

BAR-KOKHBA
LESSON 10

Do you think that history ever changes? Your first thought may be "No, you can't change the past." Well, that may be true. But because of the intricate work of archaeologists, the things we *know* about history are always changing! Such is the case with **Bar-Kokhba** (bar KOCK bah). The existence of a man named Bar-Kokhba had been considered only a legend for centuries. That is, until some rather daring archaeologists went digging around the **Dead Sea.** Let me explain the whole story.

Like the name "Hercules" or "Robin Hood," the name "Bar-Kokhba" was familiar folklore to the Jews of long ago. Some would have considered him only a myth. Others believed he was a hero in the **Second Jewish Revolt** against the Romans. But before I explain the Second Jewish Revolt, let's review the first one so we don't get the two confused.

The **First Jewish Revolt** ended in A.D. 70. That was when the Jews rose up in rebellion against the Romans for ruling Israel. It's the same revolt that Josephus tried desperately to persuade the Jews *not* to get involved in. Do you remember that story? Josephus feared the Jews didn't stand a chance against the Romans, and he was right. The Romans utterly destroyed Jerusalem as well as the Temple—the most important place of worship for the Jews. The Jews who survived the massacre fled. We call that the diaspora, or dispersion of the Jews. Some Jews, as you'll remember, fled to Masada where unfortunately they perished. (See Lesson 6.)

Well, the Jewish Revolt in A.D. 70 was not the last time the Jews rebelled. Though the Jews had been defeated and scattered, they continued to regroup, grow in numbers, and try again to break free of Roman rule and occupy Jerusalem. More than anything, they wanted access to the site of the Temple. As early as A.D. 115, groups of restless Jews started uproars in places such as Egypt, Mesopotamia, and Cyprus. An unknown number of Roman legions were slain in these rebellions. But about 17 years later, a much more serious revolt erupted. This one was led by Bar-Kokhba; thus we have what historians call the *Second Jewish Revolt* in A.D. 132.

Ruins are still present today in Jerusalem as testimony to the destruction of the city.

More than likely, the cause of the Second Revolt had to do with what happened to Jerusalem. After Jerusalem was destroyed in A.D. 70, the Roman emperor **Hadrian** had another city built right on top of it. In complete arrogance he renamed it **Aelia Capitolina** after himself. (Hadrian's middle name was Aelius.) To make matters worse, Hadrian built a temple to the Roman god **Jupiter** on the very spot where the Jewish Temple had been! You may recall from Volume I of *The Mystery of History* just how special the

Temple was to the Jews. It was considered the very dwelling place of God! The temple to Jupiter that now stood in its place was an outrage and an insult to the Jews who were scattered around the region.

So what about Bar-Kokhba? Who was this legendary hero? We don't know a whole lot about him personally. For a long time even the spelling of Bar-Kokhba's name remained a mystery as well as when his rebellion started and where it was fought. Josephus, the great historian, had died by the time Bar-Kokhba led the Second Revolt. So we don't have good records of exactly what happened. What we do know is that Bar-Kokhba had a strong, charismatic personality. He was a powerful military leader, and he called himself the **prince of Israel.** He couldn't claim to be a priest or a king because he was not from the proper family to have those titles.

By A.D. 132, Bar-Kokhba raised an army estimated at 400,000 men. Though we would consider it barbaric, there was one unique qualification for being in his army. Bar-Kokhba required his men to have part of their fingers cut off to prove their loyalty to him and to Israel! This is just one example of Bar-Kokhba's strong influence over people. As for physical strength, legend claims Bar-Kokhba stopped a cannonball with his leg and kicked it back on the enemy! In letters he wrote to his generals, we learn he was very strict. He threatened to punish his men if they didn't do *exactly* what he said. He supposedly kicked to death one of his priests for suspecting him of giving in to the enemy. Bar-Kokhba was known, too, for persecuting Christians because they opposed his plan to restore Israel.

All these aspects of Bar-Kokhba's personality and behavior helped to give him a fearsome reputation. But probably the main reason Bar-Kokhba became a "hero" of sorts is because he claimed to be the **Messiah**—the one the Jews were waiting for! A leading Jewish priest of that time period believed it to be true and convinced many to follow Bar-Kokhba for that reason. You see, the Jews believed that the true Messiah would be the one who could lead them to freedom from the Romans. They believed that the Messiah would be a *military* conqueror and deliver them from their evil oppressors.

As you probably already know, **Jesus Christ** of Nazareth claimed to be the real Messiah about 130 years before this event. Though He did many supernatural things, Jesus never attempted to conquer Rome. He was not on earth to save the Jews from the Romans, but to save people from their sins! Instead of overthrowing the Romans, Jesus suggested the Jews obey them and pay their taxes. For that reason, as well as many others, there were thousands of Jews who never believed that Jesus was the Messiah. And they still don't.

So, when someone like Bar-Kokhba came along, with promises of conquering the Romans, many Jews believed that he was perhaps the long-awaited Messiah—the Deliverer! They wanted nothing more than for Bar-Kokhba to return them to Jerusalem and rebuild the Holy Temple.

The Second Jewish Revolt

The Second Revolt, under this "prince of Israel," lasted for three years. And in many ways, Bar-Kokhba was successful. Thousands of Romans were killed. For a time, a Jewish state, or government, was established, and the Jews actually regained Jerusalem. New **coins** were shaped on top of the old Roman ones, with the words inscribed, "Year One of the Redemption of Israel" and "Year Two of the Freedom of Israel." Other coins were stamped with pictures of holy relics of the Temple. It seemed that Israel was going to recover as a nation.

But as you may have already guessed, this surge of hope didn't last very long. In A.D. **135** endless Roman armies stormed the Jews again. This time they attacked a city named **Bethar,** a Jewish stronghold not far from Jerusalem. As bad as the First Revolt ended for the Jews, the conclusion of the Second Revolt was even worse. Anywhere from 80,000 to 580,000 Jews are thought to have been killed! People and holy books were crushed and burned. Hundreds of phylacteries were stripped from the Jewish men and tossed aside in baskets (Phylacteries are tiny containers of Scripture worn on the hand or head). No decent burials were allowed.[1] And worst of all, Bar-Kokhba, the "prince of Israel," was killed in battle!

So what now of the so-called Messiah? Bar-Kokhba was dead, and the Jews were *not* delivered! The hope of Israel was shattered. The "messiah" was gone without saving Israel, without performing miracles, without fulfilling prophecy, and without rising from the dead. Bar-Kokhba appeared to most to have been a "misguided" messiah or in some cases, an outright fraud. Hecklers changed a letter in his name to give it the meaning of "liar" instead of "star." ("Star" was the original meaning of Bar-Kokhba's name.) Many Jews felt betrayed by this man who was so full of promises, but was now cold and dead.

The Jews who survived the massacre were scattered. Some escaped to caves in the canyons near the Dead Sea, which had served as a hideout for years. But without enough food or means of starting a new life, an unknown number of men, women, and children died from starvation in the cave dwellings. No one knows for sure what their final fate was. No one knows for sure how long these people hid from the Romans who camped nearby. No one knows for sure how many even tried to survive the nightmare.

Despite the number who perished and the hopes that were dashed, legends of heroes have a way of sticking around. Though Bar-Kokhba failed to save Israel, he was remembered for trying. Though some men cursed him, others honored him. In the same way that American boys and girls used to play cowboys and Indians, so European Jewish children played "Bar-Kokhba and the Romans." It was the spirit of Bar-Kokhba that lived on. Over centuries of time, historians wondered if Bar-Kokhba was a real hero or just perhaps a legend because so little had been documented of his life.

Well, this is the part of the story where **archaeologists** come in. You see, after the Dead Sea scrolls were discovered in the 1940s, many archaeologists visited the area with hopes of finding more. Not that that was easy. Excavating caves around the Dead Sea is dangerous work! The entrance to some caves is nearly impossible to reach without scaling rocky cliffs and dangling from ropes over deep canyons! To add to the danger, imagine doing that with tools, lights, ladders, and cameras! That's exactly what a group of daring archaeologists did.

Under Bar-Kokhba, new coins were made declaring the freedom of Israel.

In 1960 and 1961, a Jewish man named **Yigael Yadin** and his crew took on the challenge of excavating certain caves around the Dead Sea without any idea of what they were going to discover. They specifically targeted a canyon named **Nahal Hever.** (*Nahal* means a dry river or canyon.) Much like the Dead Sea Scrolls, the things they found were in remarkable condition because of the dry air of the region. First they found ordinary things such as coins, pots, clothes, tools, deeds, documents, and the like. Even these ordinary things were amazing because they gave evidence to the fact that people had actually lived in the caves for a time after the Second Revolt. Second, and the saddest though, was the discovery of numbers of skeletons. These gave evidence to the fact that families hid in the caves until most likely they died of starvation.

---

1. Yigael Yadin, *Bar Kokhba: The Rediscovery of the Legendary Hero of the Last Jewish Revolt Against Imperial Rome*. London: Weidenfeld and Nicolson, 1971; p. 26.

But the most significant discoveries of all were letters written by Bar-Kokhba to his generals. These letters referred to Bar-Kokhba with the title **"President of Israel."** Do you know what that discovery meant to the Jews in 1961? It meant that Bar-Kokhba *was* a real hero at one time in history. He was more than a myth. With this new information, the Jews now consider Bar-Kokhba the last real president of Israel before it lay a dead nation for 1,500 years! You see, Israel was not made a nation again until after World War II! (On May 15, 1948, to be exact.) The Israelites were without a nation and a president that whole time.

It may be hard for *us* to grasp the significance of Bar-Kokhba. But I want us to learn this lesson from his story: we need to be careful whom we follow! Well-intentioned Jews followed Bar-Kokhba as their Messiah because he showed unusual military strength. Their misunderstanding led to great tragedy. I hope you remember also that ancient history can still be changed. At least our perspective of it can. We've no idea what archaeologists may dig up next that will give us new stories about the past.

ACTIVITIES FOR LESSON 10

10A—Younger Students

Excavate an archaeological dig! (This activity requires teacher preparation.)

Materials: To make dig site: About 3 pounds of mulch, sand, potting soil, or leaves and pine needles; also, medium-sized box (any shape, somewhat larger than a shoebox), hand/garden shovel, large slotted spoon, tongs and/or tweezers, small paint brush, colander and/or strainer, newspaper, several sandwich-sized plastic bags, permanent marker

To create relics, choose a few of the following to fit into your box: An assortment of coins (foreign and/or local), a sandal, small mirror, small tool, coffee mug, ball of yarn, scrap pieces of fabric, blank stationery rolled like a scroll and wrapped with raffia ribbon, wrinkled documents with the name "Bar-Kokhba" included

TEACHER: Create "relics" from the list above. These items represent some of the things found by Yadin near the Dead Sea. (The blank stationery represents rolls of unused parchment that were discovered.) Partially fill a medium-sized box with either mulch, sand, potting soil, leaves and pine needles—or a mixture of all of these. Creatively hide the relics in the box and add more dirt material to cover.

STUDENT: Working outdoors, in a garage or on a hard floor, spread newspaper out in a wide area. Have your teacher hand you your prepared box to excavate. Begin to slowly dig through the dirt and/or sand using tools such as a small shovel and large slotted spoon. When you come across an item, use tongs or tweezers to carefully raise it out of the dirt. Coins may need to be washed in a strainer or colander. With a paintbrush, dust dirt off the item and place the relic in a plastic bag. Label your bags with what you found and number them in the order you found them. This is what real archaeologists do! Take a picture of your relics and place it in your Student Notebook under "Asia: Israel."

10B—Younger and Middle Students

In remembrance of Jewish tradition, make a phylactery. (Teacher: See the "Note to Teacher" at the end of this activity.) A phylactery was a small box used to hold selected Scripture from the first five books of the Old Testament. The container was tied either to a Jewish male's forehead or left hand during times of worship. A boy had to be 13 before he could wear one. The tradition can be traced back to Deuteronomy 6:8, which reads, *"You shall bind them* [God's words] *as a sign on your hand, and they shall be as frontlets between your eyes."* (Words in brackets are mine.)

Materials: Old lipstick or lip balm tube (or inexpensive new one), black spray paint (optional), Bible, small strips of paper, writing pen, hot-glue gun, narrow strip of cloth (about ½ inch wide and long enough to tie around student's head or wrist)

Empty and wash out an old lipstick or lip balm tube. If desired, spray-paint it black. Using a Bible, select one to three verses from any of the first five books of the Old Testament. On tiny strips of paper, write out your verses in the smallest print you can create (or choose a small font off the computer). Roll up your paper as tiny as possible and slip it into the lipstick tube. Lay the tube lengthwise to the cloth and carefully glue it to the strip.

Attach the phylactery to either your head or wrist. Take a photo and file it under "Asia: Israel" in your Student Notebook.

Note to Teacher: Please discuss with your student the following theological point. The original intent of the phylactery was to honor God's Word. Over time, however, many Jews replaced true holiness with the practice of keeping traditions like the wearing of the phylactery. It was an outward symbol that didn't necessarily deal with the heart. Discuss with students the fact that legal practices don't create holiness or grant us our salvation. (Mark 7:1–23) Discuss how we do achieve salvation (through Jesus Christ) and how we can strive for holiness (through the power of the Holy Spirit.) Discuss also the potential legalistic traps that Christians might fall into today.

10C—Older Students

Try to name at least 10 things that qualified Jesus Christ as the Messiah. Use Scripture from both the Old Testament and the New Testament to support your claims. File this under "Asia: Israel" in your Student Notebook.

A.D. 2ND –7TH CENTURIES

THE APOSTLES' CREED

LESSON 11

History is most fascinating to me when it directly connects the present with the past. Today's lesson does just that. The **Apostles' Creed** is presently recited by millions of Christians at church on Sundays although it comes straight from the Early Church!

A **creed** is simply a statement of beliefs. It comes from the Latin word *credo*, which means "I believe." The Apostles' Creed exists in two forms, a short one and a long one. The short one, which is also called the **Old Roman Creed**, dates back to the middle of the **second century**.[2] (That's a long time ago!) Legend says the apostles recited the Old Roman Creed on the day of Pentecost, with each apostle contributing a line or two. This story can't be confirmed, but fourth-century copies of the Old Roman Creed exist in both Greek and Latin.[3]

The longer form of the Apostles' Creed is very similar to the Old Roman Creed, but a few words were added as late as the **seventh century**. This is the creed that most Christians are familiar with and that you may recite out loud at your church.

The Apostles' Creed was written by early Christians for several reasons. It was used at the **baptism** of new Christians to confirm what they believe. It was probably used to teach others about Christianity, and it certainly helped bring churches together. The Apostles' Creed was undoubtedly memorized in the Early Church and then taught on deeper levels. It would have been like a curriculum for a new believers' class. And of great importance, the Apostles' Creed served as an anchor for early Christians who were persecuted. In other words, the creed may have helped Christians understand what they were dying for if indeed they were put to death for their faith.

One version of the Apostles' Creed as used in modern-day Protestant churches goes like this:

I believe in God the Father Almighty, Maker of
heaven and earth;
And in Jesus Christ his only Son, our Lord;
Who was conceived by the Holy Ghost,
Born of the Virgin Mary,
Suffered under Pontius Pilate,
Was crucified, dead, and buried:
He descended into hell;
The third day He rose again from the dead;
He ascended into heaven,
And sitteth on the right hand of God the Father
Almighty;
From thence He shall come to judge the quick
and the dead.
I believe in the Holy Ghost;
The holy catholic[4] *Church;*
The communion of saints;
The forgiveness of sins;
The resurrection of the body;
And the life everlasting.
Amen.

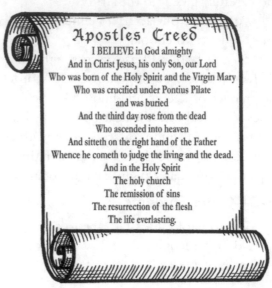

Though written nearly 2,000 years ago, the Apostles' Creed is still recited in many churches today.

This simple but profound creed became one of the cornerstones of the Early Church. How important is the Apostles' Creed? You will learn as we study through centuries of history that it is very important. Over time, people have intentionally and unintentionally reinterpreted Scripture to say things completely different than what Jesus said. Out of error, many **cults** have arisen from these interpretations and led people away from the Christian faith. A solid statement like the Apostles' Creed could help a person *not* be led astray by false doctrine.

Remember, too, that the earliest version of the Apostles' Creed, the old Roman Creed, was written only 100 or more years after Jesus Himself directly taught these things to His followers. That makes the creed very close in time to eyewitnesses of Christ's life and teaching. That gives it great **credibility** (meaning it's reliable).

Isn't it wonderful that Christians still use the Apostles' Creed nearly 2,000 years after it was written? Maybe you've recited it at your own church. I think it's a great example of history coming to life.

---

2. Elliot Ritzema, "The Apostles' Creed: Its History and Origins." April 11, 2015. Accessed on the Faithlife/Logos Bible Software blog: https://blog.faithlife.com/blog/2015/04/the-apostles-creed-its-history-and-origins.

3. The Old Roman Creed was recorded in Greek by Marcellus of Ancyra in A.D. 341. It was preserved in Latin by Rufinus in A.D. 390.
4. The term *catholic* as used in this creed means "the universal church"; not to be confused with the *Roman Catholic Church*, which was named as such later in history. In general, when *catholic* is not capitalized, it means *universal*; when *Catholic* is capitalized, it refers to the *Roman Catholic Church* or members of it.

ACTIVITIES FOR LESSON 11

11A—Younger Students

Go over the Apostles' Creed with your teacher. Discuss the meaning of some of the words, such as "quick," "catholic," and "communion." Look up these words together if you are unsure of their meaning.

11B—Younger and Middle Students

Make the creed into an ancient manuscript. This is similar to the activity for the Dead Sea Scrolls and may take more than one day to complete.

Materials: One photocopy per student of the Apostles' Creed from the Activity Supplement in the Appendix, four black tea bags, water, pot for boiling, tongs, shoes, matches, three-hole plastic sleeve for notebook

Adult Supervision Needed

1. Have your teacher place a few cups of water to boil on a stove.

2. When the water boils, add four black tea bags and remove from heat.

3. Set tea water aside to steep and cool.

4. Crumple the photocopy of the Apostles' Creed into a tight ball. Straighten it out.

5. Using tongs, slowly lower the paper into the tea water. Leave for several minutes.

6. Use tongs to carefully remove the paper; allow it to drip-dry overnight.

7. Assuming your paper is now dry, have your teacher locate a safe place outdoors where you can burn the edges of the paper. This will give your document an aged appearance. For safety, I recommend shoes on all participants as well as an extra shoe in hand to stomp out the smoldering edges!

8. When the document has completely cooled, I suggest you store it in a three-hole plastic sleeve that can easily go into your Student Notebook under "Europe: Ancient Rome."

11C—Middle and Older Students

1. If you have not already done so, memorize the *Apostles' Creed.*

2. As in the activity on Josephus, I have the story of another woman who was brave enough to fight against the Romans for you to res earch. Her name was Queen Zenobia. Different from Boudicca, there is a twist to the story of Queen Zenobia's fate. Write a short paper on this character and file it under "Europe: Rome" in your Student Notebook.

A.D. 269

ST. VALENTINE

LESSON 12

Every year on February 14, people exchange "valentines." It's a beautiful way to express love with cards, flowers, and candy. But do you know how the tradition was really started? It might surprise you.

There were two Christian men, each by the name of **Valentine,** who lived in and around Rome in the third century. Unfortunately, like so many other Christians, they were martyred for their faith. The date? February 14, A.D. **269.** Are you beginning to see the connection?

One of the men named Valentine was supposedly beheaded in **Rome.** The other Valentine is thought to have died in **Interamna,** a town 60 miles from Rome. The Valentine of Rome was a priest. In 350, a church was built in his honor, and Valentine's bones are buried there.

We're a little unsure of who the other Valentine was. Some scholars speculate that there was really only one Valentine and that church records were mixed up as to where he died—making it appear there were two! Nobody knows for sure.

Now you may still be wondering what martyrdom has to do with the tradition of pink hearts, lace, and chocolate. Nothing really. But February *fifteenth* happened to be the date of a Roman festival of love. On this feast day, which was called **Lupercalia,** the Romans honored **Juno,** the supposed goddess of women and marriage. They also honored **Pan**—believed to be the god of nature.

During the festival of Lupercalia, young men and women would draw names out of a box for a partner. The couple would spend time together and exchange gifts. Some of these couples would marry as a result of the courtship. Somehow **Cupid** was believed to be involved. According to Roman mythology, Cupid was the "god of love" and the son of **Venus,** the supposed "goddess of love." It was thought that a shot from one of Cupid's **arrows** made a person fall in love! To this day he is depicted as a chubby little boy with golden wings, usually holding a bow and arrow.

As you can imagine, it was difficult for the Christians living in Rome to deal with all the pagan festivals that surrounded them. Christians didn't believe in the fanciful Roman gods and goddesses. They certainly didn't believe that true love came from Cupid's little arrows! So in 495, **Pope Gelasius** decided to declare February 14 as **Saint Valentine's Day** to replace the pagan festival of Lupercalia on February 15. It was a gesture to Christianize a pagan tradition. (Early Christians did the same with Halloween. See Activity 12C at the end of this lesson.)

Was Pope Gelasius very successful? Did he change the Roman tradition? For a time his plan may have worked. I imagine that for centuries Christians spent time on February 14 remembering the saints and praying for the persecuted. But almost 2,000 years later, one trip to a drugstore in early February will tell

Valentine died a Christian martyr on February 14, A.D. 269.

you differently. Instead of remembering the saints, we are bombarded with pink trinkets, red candy, and greeting cards of all shapes, sizes, and scents. Cupid is just about everywhere!

It's not that it's bad to express love and friendship on February 14. I kind of like it! It's just a shame that St. Valentine, as a martyr, isn't better remembered for what he and hundreds of other saints endured. I believe it's important to reflect on the hardship and sacrifice they made. Maybe next Valentine's Day, besides sending sweet notes to loved ones, you'll remember what **Jesus** said about love. *"Greater love has no one than this, than to lay down one's life for his friends. You are My friends if you do what I command you."* (John 15:13–14)

The Mystery of History-Volume II

ACTIVITIES FOR LESSON 12

ALL STUDENTS

Make your Memory Cards for Lessons 10–12.

12A—Younger Students

1. Take time today to make a special card and give it to someone who really needs a boost. Maybe it's your own mom or dad. Or perhaps you know an elderly person who could use some encouragement. Just show somebody that you really care for him or her!

2. Bake heart-shaped sugar cookies to share with your family or classroom.

12B—Middle and Older Students

Investigate how chocolate is made. What are the main ingredients? Visit a chocolate factory if there is one in your area or make something from chocolate. (For research purposes, of course! ☺)

12C—Older Students

Valentine's Day is not the only pagan holiday that early believers tried to Christianize. Many of our Christmas traditions blend pagan rituals with Christian symbolism. Research the history of St. Nicholas who evolved into present-day Santa Claus. St. Nicholas lived in the 300s and was the Bishop of Myra in Lycia on the coast of Asia Minor. I'll leave the rest of the research up to you! File your report on St. Nicholas under "Asia: Turkey" in your Student Notebook.

TAKE ANOTHER LOOK!

REVIEW 4: LESSONS 10–12

Wall of Fame

1. **Bar-Kokhba (A.D. 135)**—Draw a hand. Cut off one of the fingers to depict the unusual ritual of losing a finger to join Bar-Kokhba's army! Write "Bar-Kokhba" on the hand. [From *History Through the Ages,* use *Bar-Kokhba.*]

2. **The Apostles' Creed (A.D. 2nd–7th Centuries)**—Create a tiny document, wrinkle it. Write on it "The Apostles' Creed." [Use *The Apostles' Creed.*]

3. **St. Valentine (A.D. 269)**—Make two rectangles side by side. On the top of the left rectangle, write "Feb. 14." Underneath it, draw a cross and the name of Valentine to depict his death. On the top of the right rectangle, write "Feb. 15." Under it, color a pink heart and write "Lupercalia" over it. The two rectangles, side by side, should help you remember how the holidays blended together over time. [Use *St. Valentine.*]

SomeWHERE in Time

1. Using a globe, find the city of Rome where Valentine was martyred. To familiarize yourself with "scales" of maps, I want you to try to determine how far the city of Rome is from where you live. On a legend on your globe, there should be a scale to depict how many miles are represented by one inch or one centimeter on your globe. For example, the legend on my globe indicates that every inch is about 500 miles. Using a soft tape measure, connect your home to the city of Rome. Determine about how many inches or centimeters that distance is. Multiply to determine how many miles it is to Rome.

2. There are so many significant things that happened around the Dead Sea. I want you to make a salt map of the region with markings of some special places. (The salt will also help you remember the saltiness of the Dead Sea!)

   Materials: Outline Map 4, "Israel"; Outline Map 5, "Review 4 Answer Key"; Bible atlas with a topographical or relief map of Israel or ancient Palestine; piece of cardboard about 10 by 13 inches; salt dough (1 cup salt, 1 cup white flour, and enough water to thicken like mud); food coloring; toothpicks; paper for small flags; tape

   a. Glue the outline map of Israel to the center of the cardboard. Set aside to dry.

   b. Using food coloring, dye half of the dough blue and the other half brown.

   c. Following the terrain of your topographical map, sculpt the land around the Dead Sea using your brown dough.

   d. Sculpt the Dead Sea, the Sea of Galilee, and the Mediterranean Sea using the blue dough.

   e. With paper, tape, and toothpicks, create flags for: (1) Jerusalem; (2) Nahal Hever, a canyon region where many artifacts were found to attest to Bar-Kokhba's existence; (3) Masada; and (4) Qumran (or Khirbat Qumran), location of the Dead Sea Scrolls. Place these flags in the right locations following the guide provided in the Answer Key Map.

   f. Take a photo of your map and place it under "Asia: Israel" in your Student Notebook.

WHAT DID YOU LEARN?

WEEK 4: QUIZ

Who/What Am I? Choose the best answer from the word bank below.

1. According to the Book of Acts, I fell upon believers at the Day of Pentecost. Who am I?

2. I was a devout Jew, a Pharisee, and a persecutor of early Christians. Who am I?

3. At Antioch I was commissioned with Paul as one of the first missionaries. Who am I?

4. My mother helped me become emperor of Rome, but I mistrusted her and had her killed. Who am I?

5. As an emperor of Rome, I made it a capital crime to be a Christian. Who am I?

6. I observed and recorded the destruction of the Temple in the First Jewish Revolt. Who am I?

7. Herod the Great remodeled me to be a self-sustaining fortress. What am I?

8. We copied hundreds of parchments and hid them in caves around the Dead Sea. Who are we?

9. Once covered with ash from a volcano, I sit on the western banks of Italy. What am I?

10. Some considered me a hero of the Second Jewish Revolt; others thought I was just a legend. Who am I?

11. I am a statement of beliefs written for early Christians. What am I?

12. I was martyred on February 14, 269. Who am I?

WORD BANK

Apostles' Creed	Masada	Saul	Essenes
Bar-Kokhba	Nero	St. Valentine	Pompeii
Holy Spirit	Barnabas	Josephus	Trajan

WHAT DO YOU KNOW?

PRETEST 5

Match Me! Connect the words on the left to the definitions on the right. (Using different-colored pencils may make it more fun to work and easier to grade.)

1. Diocletian

a. Latin for "Our Lord"

2. *Dominus* Noster

b. A country in Asia

3. Jupiter

c. A law for religious freedom

4. Constantine

d. Sacred poem of India

5. Edict of Milan

e. Hindu belief of coming back to life

6. India

f. Founded Constantinople

7. *Ramayana*

g. Shared the Roman Empire

8. Reincarnation

h. Father of the mythological Roman gods

DIOCLETIAN DIVIDES THE ROMAN EMPIRE
LESSON 13

Do you find it easy to share? Most of us don't, but we learn that it's usually the right thing to do. There was a Roman emperor who learned to share on a rather large scale. His name was **Diocletian.** He decided to share half of his country with another ruler because it was the best thing to do for the Roman Empire.

If you remember, one of the last Roman emperors we studied was **Marcus Aurelius.** He was the fourth emperor to persecute Christians. Well, in a hundred-year period between Aurelius and Diocletian there were at least 28 men who tried to be emperor. None of them lasted very long. All but four of them were assassinated! This left the Roman government shaky and the people very unhappy.

But Diocletian was working his way up into the ranks. Though he was born into poverty, Diocletian's abilities as a soldier made him popular. The army voted him to be emperor in **A.D. 284**. Though this was a great honor, Diocletian was smart enough to know that in those days emperors didn't live very long in Rome. Most were assassinated. If he wanted to stick around awhile, he was going to have to change the way things were done.

Diocletian's first conclusion was that the Roman Empire was just too big for one person to look after. After all, it included England, almost all of Europe, part of Asia Minor, and the northern coast of Africa! To make it more manageable, Diocletian selected a man by the name of **Maximian** to rule the western half of Rome. Diocletian kept the eastern half. They called themselves the **Augusti** rulers. The men serving under them were **Caesars.** Now, if you know anything about the history of Rome, it is ironic (which means "almost funny") that *two* men were ruling Rome again. For that is the very way the Roman Republic started hundreds of years before. Rome was founded on the basis that *two* rulers were better than one!

Anyway, there was great potential in Diocletian's plan. He subdivided each man's region into even smaller parts. He created **prefectures** ruled by **prefects, dioceses** ruled by **vicars,** and **provinces** ruled by **governors.** Rome was neatly divided into 120 provinces overall.

Diocletian divided the Roman Empire into 120 provinces.

Now before I make Diocletian sound too good for sharing, you should know he was also the *cause* of some problems in the Roman Empire. To boost the economy, Diocletian tried making more gold and silver coins. But instead of making people feel like they had more money, it caused **inflation.** (Inflation is when the prices of goods go higher.) Diocletian then tried to put limitations on how much money a person could make. Anyone caught violating his plan was sentenced to death. I'm sure that didn't make him very popular!

As you can imagine, Diocletian's harsh economic plan didn't work very well. It led to an economic depression. Food was scarce and rioting broke out. The population of Rome went down and taxes went up. All in all, because money is so important to the health of a nation, Rome was in bad shape under Diocletian.

But the worst part of Diocletian's reign was his attitude toward **Christians.** More than *any* of the Roman emperors before him, Diocletian was determined to obliterate the Christian faith for good! His wave of persecution was the last of 10 that existed from the time of Nero until about 311.

One of the problems between Diocletian and the Christians was in the title that Diocletian gave himself and Maximian. The men went by **Dominus Noster,** which is Latin for "Our Lord." Faithful Christians were not at all comfortable calling an emperor their "lord." But worse than expecting to be called lord, Diocletian demanded he be *worshiped* as **Jupiter,** the father of the Roman mythological gods!

One of the men who refused to worship Diocletian was named George. He was one of the emperor's high-ranking soldiers. George was tortured and put to death on April 23, 303. This date has been remembered ever since as the feast day of St. George. But most people today remember St. George for the legend that he slew a dragon that was going to eat the king's daughter! (Just an interesting side note to the story.)

As revenge on the Christians who wouldn't bow down to Diocletian (and many like St. George wouldn't), Diocletian destroyed all copies of Scripture he could find. Bibles and manuscripts were brought by the cartloads to the city square and burned like rubbish. Diocletian completely forbid Christians to meet and assemble. Churches were recklessly destroyed by Roman soldiers.

It is recorded that in **Phrygia,** an entire Christian village and its inhabitants were burned. Not one man, woman, or child spoke against Christ to save their life, but each painfully endured the fire. And supposedly, under Diocletian, there were so many Christians thrown to the wild animals in the sporting arenas that the animals became full and quit eating! It was a horrific time to be a Christian in Rome.

By the grace of God, there did come an end to these tortuous times. Three hundred grueling years of Roman persecution ended after Diocletian's reign. When you think about it, it is amazing that the Early Church survived at all. But then, I believe we serve an amazing God, Who has through time continued to reveal Himself and keep the church alive!

ACTIVITIES FOR LESSON 13

13A—Younger Students

Create a puzzle of the United States.

Materials: Two photocopies of Outline Map 6, "United States"; fine-point pen; lightweight cardboard or poster board; glue; crayons or colored pencils; scissors; a plastic bag that zips closed

Whether you live in the United States or not, consider how it is divided into 50 states to make it more manageable. If you don't already know the states, this would be a good time to try to name them all. Photocopy two maps of the United States. On the first map, have your teacher write in the name of each state using a fine-point pen. Glue this map onto a light piece of cardboard or poster board. While the teacher is writing in the names of the states, color the states on the other map using colored pencils or crayons. When you have done that, allow your teacher to help you cut out each state. Some states are shaped like rectangles and are very easy to cut out. Others are very hard because the borders follow uneven rivers or mountain ranges. (I suggest that you keep the smaller states in the Northeast together as one piece.) When you have done all of this, practice laying the states down like a puzzle on your good map. Do this often until you can match the states quickly. Make a game of guessing the name of a state before you pick it up and read it underneath.

13B—Middle Students

1. Similar to the governor of a province in ancient Rome, the term *governor* is used in the United States today to describe the chief executive of a state. If you live in the United States, find out the name of your state governor. Research the duties of a governor in an encyclopedia. List them on paper and file it in your Student Notebook under "North America: United States."

2. If you are a United States resident, work on knowing your states and capitals. Make your own flashcards out of 3-by-5-inch index cards. Write the name of each state on the front of the card and the name of its capital on the other side of the card. Drill yourself by guessing the capital city of each state, and then guess the state that goes with each capital city. For fun, drill your parents!

13C—Older Students

1. Using an encyclopedia, research the myth of Jupiter. He was called Zeus by the ancient Greeks. One of my observations about mythology is that, like mankind, the gods and goddesses of Rome and Greece were fallible. Think about this and what little hope mythology gave to the ancient world. What hope was there for mankind if even the gods couldn't get along? Contrast this to Christianity. What Scripture can you find to support the truth that God is infallible, holy, blameless, and perfect? What hope does that offer mankind? Write down your conclusions and file them in your Student Notebook under "Miscellaneous."

2. Who was the real St. George? Visit the Web sites below to answer the following questions: Where was George born? Where did he die for his faith? In what country did he allegedly slay a dragon? What 11 countries name George as their patron saint? When is St. George's Day in England? What does the St. George flag look like and why? File your questions/answers and a copy or drawing of the St. George flag under "Europe: England" or "Miscellaneous."

www.projectbritain.com/stgeorge2.html (*and*
www.projectbritain.com/stgeorge3.html*)*

313

CONSTANTINE I
AND THE EDICT OF MILAN
LESSON 14

For three long centuries after the resurrection of Christ, Christians were persecuted. They were imprisoned, tortured, burned, crucified, and mauled by wild animals. Thousands of people died for the cause of Christ. Finally, though, there came a time when the persecutions stopped. It was **Constantine I** who officially brought the bloodshed to an end. For this important reason and many others, he is sometimes called **Constantine the Great.**

As a young man, Constantine was an able soldier. His father was an emperor of the **Western Roman Empire.** When his father died in 306, Constantine naturally claimed the throne. But it wasn't easy to become emperor. In 312 Constantine had to beat out his greatest rival, **Maxentius,** in the **Battle of Milvian Bridge.** The beautiful **Arch of Constantine** in Rome was built to commemorate the great victory.

Constantine used the cross and the Greek letters chi and rho as his battle symbol.

According to legend, Constantine had a spiritual experience during the Battle of Milvian Bridge that forever shaped his outlook on Christianity. Supposedly he saw a cross in the sky with these Latin words inscribed on it, ***In hoc signo vinces,*** meaning *"In this sign you shall conquer."* Later, Constantine supposedly had a vision of Christ and in a dream saw the Greek letters *chi* and *rho,* the first two letters of *Christos.* From that time on, Constantine viewed Christianity with great respect. He used the cross and the Greek letters as his battle symbol.

As a result of his experience, Constantine did something very incredible for the Early Church. In **313** he signed the **Edict of Milan.** The edict was a document that ensured freedom from persecution for *all* Christians in the Roman Empire, both East and West. It said, "Our purpose is to grant both to the Christians and to all others full authority to follow whatever worship each man has desired."[1] What celebrating there must have been! What tears of joy must have fallen! Finally, Christians were free to worship without fear for their lives. No more hiding, no more jail, no more martyrdom in the Roman Empire! The edict was a tremendous gesture of mercy by Constantine.

Was Constantine then a believer? We don't know for sure. Though he respected Christians and freed them of persecution, he didn't profess to become a Christian until near his death. It was then that he was baptized. His mother, however, had a genuine conversion experience to Christianity. She traveled to the Holy Lands to better understand her newfound faith. Whether or not she influenced her son, we don't know for sure. But if she did, it is a beautiful illustration of the answer to a mother's prayer and the fulfillment of God's promise to bless one's children with salvation. (Acts 2:38–39)

As an emperor, Constantine was very capable. Though the Roman Empire had been divided under Diocletian, Constantine decided he wanted to rule the *entire* empire. And he did that by defeating the emperor of the East in 324. It was then that Constantine made a significant decision. He moved the capital of the Roman Empire to the ancient city of **Byzantium.**

Byzantium (which is modern-day **Istanbul,** Turkey) is a great location for a capital city. It sits at the entrance to the **Black Sea** between Europe and Asia, making it a perfect place for traders of the East to meet with traders of the West.

The Basilica Nova was one of the last great building projects of the Roman Empire. It was started by Maxentius but completed by Constantine.

---

1. A. Kenneth Curtis, J. Stephen Lang, and Randy Petersen, *The 100 Most Important Events in Christian History.* Grand Rapids, MI: Fleming H. Revell, 1991; p. 33.

Constantine renamed the city New Rome. But it quickly became known as **Constantinople,** meaning the *city of Constantine.*

Besides establishing a new capital, Constantine did his best to help the Early Church become better established. A great example of this was his calling together leaders of the church to settle their disputes. You see, some Christians were convinced that Jesus was the same as God, but some believers thought He was not. There was also the problem within the church as to when the Resurrection ought to be celebrated. At what has been named the **Council of Nicaea,** in 325, Constantine invited 300 bishops, or church leaders, to discuss these serious differences.

On the Arch of Constantine, these words are inscribed, "Constantine overcame his enemies by divine inspiration."

As a result of the council, the **Nicene Creed** was written. It was a document very similar to the Apostles' Creed, which states exactly what Christians believe to be the truth about Jesus Christ. In summary, the Nicene Creed states that Jesus is the *same* as God; that is—He *is God,* not just similar to God. This creed is of great significance to Christians even now.

I hope you are beginning to appreciate Constantine for all he did. He allowed the Christians to worship freely; he brought Rome back together as one empire; and he helped settle disputes in the church. However, there was one downside to this. In an effort to bring unity to Rome, Constantine was beginning to blend the authority of the government *with* the authority of the church.

One example of this was a change in the court system. You see, by the time of Constantine, almost half of the Roman Empire had converted to Christianity. These converts were very unhappy with the Roman court system. It seemed to them pagan and unfair. So they set up their own courts. When Christianity became legal under the Edict of Milan, these Christian courts grew to be even more popular. Even the pagan people preferred them. Of course, the men who served in these Christian courts were also church leaders. Under Constantine these church leaders were required to wear long robes or gowns like the Roman court officials did. That is why today some church leaders *still* wear long robes or gowns in their churches. This tradition goes all the way back to the early Middle Ages!

Although it was beneficial for Christians to establish a court system, it created problems, too. It eventually led to the idea that the emperor could use the courts to mandate what people ought to believe and what religion they had to practice! Christianity was never meant to be forced on people like that. You'll learn later that at times during the Middle Ages, it was.

ACTIVITIES FOR LESSON 14

ALL STUDENTS

Memorize the date when the Edict of Milan was signed (313).

14A—Younger and Middle Students

1. Make a battle shield with the symbol of a cross and Greek letters.

Materials: Large white piece of cardboard, pencil, sheet of carbon paper, stapler, tape, black marker, red marker or crayon, photocopy of cross from the Activity Supplement in the Appendix, two pieces of elastic, stapler

a. Cut a white piece of cardboard in the shape of a shield, as shown.

b. Place the sheet of carbon paper underneath the photocopy of the cross. Staple them together.

c. Center the papers over the middle of your shield and secure them lightly with tape.

d. Use a pencil to trace the outline of the cross onto the shield Trace the Greek letters, too.

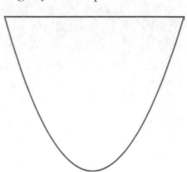

e. Carefully remove the photocopy and carbon paper.

f. Use a black marker to darken the edges of the cross and letters.

g. Fill in the cross with red crayons or marker.

h. With a stapler, attach the elastic bands to form an "X" on the back of the shield.

i. Take a photo with your shield and file it under "Europe: Rome" in your Student Notebook.

2. Create a cloth document of the Edict of Milan.

Materials: A 20-inch length of muslin-type cloth, a yardstick, a pencil, ½ yard of gold ribbon or cord, scissors, two empty paper-towel holders, glue, permanent marker

a. Cut the cloth 10 inches wide to create a rectangle that is 10 inches by 20 inches.

b. Lay the cloth vertically on your workspace. Drop down 6 inches from the top of your cloth and draw a horizontal line with a light pencil. You will need this border later to mount the edict. Repeat this step, marking off 6 inches from the bottom of the cloth.

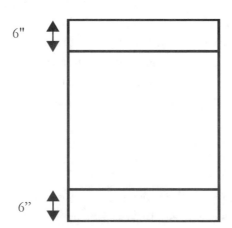

c. Again, lay your cloth vertically on your workspace. On the 8 inches in the middle of your cloth, write out (or have your teacher write out) the words to the edict as given in the lesson. You might want to write the letters lightly in pencil first and then apply the permanent marker. Title it "The Edict of Milan" and add the name of Constantine on the bottom.

d. Wrap the top of the cloth around an empty paper-towel holder and glue it in place. Repeat this step for the bottom.

e. Drop gold ribbon or cord through the paper-towel holder at the top of your cloth. Tie it together as a holder. Hang your document in a prominent place as a reminder of religious freedom.

f. Take a photo of your edict and place it in your Student Notebook under "Asia: Turkey." (Turkey because Constantine's capital city of Constantinople is now the city of Istanbul in Turkey.)

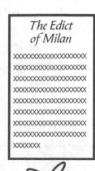

14B—Middle and Older Students

Read the Nicene Creed in the Activity Supplement of this book. Discuss the meaning and content with your teacher.

14C—Middle and Older Students

Research the modern city of Istanbul (formerly Constantinople). Who lives there now? What religions are practiced in this city? Is there freedom to worship or does persecution exist? Pray for the unsaved living in Istanbul. Write a few paragraphs on Istanbul and file the information in your Student Notebook under "Asia: Turkey."

C. 320–500

THE GOLDEN AGE OF INDIA
LESSON 15

Like ancient Greece and ancient Rome, the country of India experienced a time in its history that was rich and luxurious. It was a time when the people of India had the wealth and freedom to flourish in the sciences, the arts, and religion. Today we'll look at this prime time in India. It's referred to as the **Golden Age.**

What started this prosperous time in India? It had a lot to do with the kings of that era. The ruling family of the Golden Age was the **Gupta** (GOOP ta) **dynasty.** It united northern India from **about 320–500.** The most famous of the Gupta leaders was **Samudragupta** (sa mood ra GOOP ta). He reigned as king of India for 50 years. Many good things happened under his rule.

Besides moving the capital and expanding his empire, Samudragupta accumulated a great amount of wealth for his country. Instead of just spending money on himself, he invested money in the people of India. Samudragupta generously sponsored the work of **scientists, artists, architects,** and others. Samudragupta himself earned the reputation of being a great poet and musician. No wonder he advanced the work of artists. He was one!

In the field of science, it was early in the history of India that **astronomers** explained things like eclipses, the revolution of the earth, and the arrangement of the stars. Amazingly, the Indians accurately calculated the diameter of the moon, the position of the earth's poles, and a 12-month calendar! Not bad considering their lack of modern tools.

Advanced science also contributed to superb **ironmaking.** For example, there was an iron pillar erected in the city of Delhi over 1,900 years ago and it *still* stands untarnished! It was made of such fine iron that scholars are perplexed even today at how it was done. **Chemistry** also proved itself to be unsurpassed during the Gupta dynasty, as even the brilliant Romans looked to India for the creation of new dyes, soaps, glass, and cement.

Mathematicians from India were the first to create **Arabic numbers.** Arabic numbers are the kind used around most of the world today. They were found in India as early as 256 B.C.! As part of that number system, the Indians invented the amazing concept of "zero." Now the use of zero may sound like a little thing, but it was a big thing. We can't even imagine counting without it. Furthermore, the mathematicians of India were almost a thousand years ahead of the rest of the world in understanding **decimals** and **algebra.** That's a big thing, too.

A description of ancient India would not be complete without mentioning their ability to create beautiful and comfortable **cloth.** The making of cloth became an art form in and of itself. It was the Indians who first used **cotton.** The Arab word *quttan* is where we get our word "cotton." The terms **muslin** and **calico** come, too, from the influence of India. Calico gets its name from the Indian city of Calicut. So fine was the craftsmanship and embroidery of Indian cloth that it was traded all over the Mediterranean world.

As for charities, every five years a great festival was held to benefit the needy. All religious workers and the poor were invited to receive what they needed from the government. At this special festival, mounds of silver, gold, jewelry, and fine fabrics were piled in the city square. After three days of religious services, distribution of these items began. Ten thousand monks were fed and each received pearls, clothes, perfumes, flowers, and gold. It took as long as three to four months just to hand everything out! As a final act of charity, the king of India himself would remove his heavily decorated robe and all his fine jewelry to give to the needy.

As for the appearance and cleanliness of the Indians, an observer once wrote:

> "The people had a refined appearance, and dressed in glossy silk attire . . . Before every meal they must have a wash; the food utensils are not passed on; those which are of pottery or of wood must be thrown away after use, and those which are of gold, silver, copper or iron get another polishing. As soon as a meal is over they chew the tooth-stick and make themselves clean." [2]

Long, beautiful, and flowing, the clothes of India are still a fine form of art.

Sacred Literature and Religion

I've shared with you now many things about India and its people, but to really understand this culture, it's important to know something about its sacred literature. The two most famous works are the ***Mahabharata*** (ma ha BA ra ta) and the ***Ramayana*** (ra MA ya na). Both are beautiful poetic tales of legendary kings, queens, and princes and the wars they fought for life and love. These stories are considered more than great literature to the people of India. The good characters in these stories are regarded as virtuous role models to live by.

The *Mahabharata* is considered by far to be the greatest literary work of Asia and is seven times the length of the famous *Iliad* and *Odyssey* of Greece. Though composed during the Gupta dynasty, hundreds of years before the Greek works, the *Mahabharata* was lengthened to include the religion of the Hindu priests. It states:

---

2. Will Durant, *Our Oriental Heritage.* Vol. I of *The Story of Civilization.* New York: Simon and Schuster, 1954; pp. 481, 497.

"If a man reads the Mahabharata and has faith in its doctrines, he becomes free from all sin, and ascends to heaven . . . as butter is to all other food, as Brahmans [priests] are to all other men, . . . as the ocean is to a pool of water, . . . so is the Mahabharata to all other histories . . . He who attentively listens . . . and has faith in them, enjoys life and solid reputation in this world and an eternal abode in the heavens in the next." [3] (Word in brackets is mine.)

Despite the incredible significance given to the *Mahabharata*, the *Ramayana* is probably the better loved of the two works and easier to read. It contains stories of love and devotion that are still quoted in weddings of Indian couples today. Indians love reciting and acting out these sacred stories as well as dozens of other fables.

Of course the Bible doesn't teach that salvation can be earned by reading the *Mahabharata* and following its doctrine. Neither does the Bible tell us to follow the examples of the characters of the *Ramayana* to earn God's favor. Instead, the Bible tells us to believe that salvation comes from faith in Christ and His work on the cross. But I want you to be familiar with the literature from which the people of India derive their moral teachings.

It's important, too, to understand India's main religion, **Hinduism.** In fact, the Golden Age of India is sometimes called the **classical Hindu** period because Hinduism was thriving just as strongly as the culture was. Hinduism is one of the oldest religions of the world. Unlike Judaism or Christianity, the Hindu faith is not based on a belief in a personal god. The Hindus hold to traditions that have been passed down for thousands of years in the form of hymns and writings called ***Vedas,*** which stress that there are hundreds of gods, all leading to one. Because there are seemingly Hindu "gods" for everything, India appears to be one of the most religious countries in the world.

Unlike other religions, Hindus don't believe in salvation from sin. They believe instead that people are given chance after chance to live life perfectly. This process of reliving life is called **reincarnation.** From this belief system, Hindus think that a person can even come back to life as an animal! They therefore choose not to eat the flesh of animals or to use their skins (leather for instance). (See Volume I of *The Mystery of History* for more details on Hinduism.)

Though life was rich and religion was flourishing during the Golden Age of India, there came a time when these things grew dim. Despite the strength of their sciences, arts, and religion, the Indians were not strong militarily. Among other problems, roadways and means of communication were weak. Over time, greedy outsiders sought to rob India of its rich resources. Unfortunately for the Indians, this happened all too easily. So, because of years of invasions and for many other complicated reasons, India is known today for having some of the worst poverty and hardship in the world. This reminds us that, unfortunately, golden ages don't last forever!

During the Golden Age of India, classical Hinduism thrived and grew.

3. *Ibid., p. 571.*

ACTIVITIES FOR LESSON 15

ALL STUDENTS

Make your Memory Cards for Lessons 13–15. The Edict of Milan (313) is a date to memorize. Highlight the card accordingly.

15A—Younger Students

1. Consider the comments made by an observer that the Indians wore "glossy silk attire" and cleaned their teeth with a "tooth-stick" at the end of each meal. Just for fun, wear silky clothes at your next meal and use a toothpick after you eat. Discuss with your teacher how historians might describe the mealtime habits of families in your culture.

2. The charity of the Indians is a reminder of the importance of giving. With your teacher, discuss what unused items in your home you could give away to those in need. List the items you come up with on paper or take a photo of them. File this list or photo in your Student Notebook under "Asia: India." Before the week is over, collect your items and take them to a place where they can be used.

3. The people of India were known for making fine cloth. Search your home or classroom for samples of cotton, muslin, and calico. (Calico is actually a plain weave of cotton made into a coarse fabric.) The next time you visit a store that sells fabric, ask for a sample of each and glue it onto a piece of paper. File it in your Student Notebook under "Asia: India."

15B—Middle Students

1. Have you ever witnessed a lunar or solar eclipse? Research this amazing phenomenon. Gather enough information so that you can construct a model of an eclipse using a large ball for the sun, a medium ball for the earth, and a small ball for the moon. Use a flashlight for your demonstration as your source of light for the sun. Take a picture and file it under "Asia: India" in your Student Notebook.

2. Do you know the diameter of the moon? From an encyclopedia or reference book, record this information and file it in your Student Notebook under "Asia: India." How difficult might it have been for the mathematicians of India to figure this out?

3. Glassmaking was a valued skill during the Middle Ages. Research the technique of making glass. What is it made from? Write a paragraph about it and file it in your Student Notebook under "Asia: India."

15C—Older Students

1. Have you ever tried to solve Hindu algebra? Here's your chance. The following are two actual word problems from a Hindu algebra text.[4] Notice that they're written very poetically, as was most of their literature.

   a. "Out of a swarm of bees one-fifth part settled on a Kadamba blossom; one-third on a Silindhra flower; three times the difference of those numbers flew to the bloom of a Kutaja. One bee, which remained, hovered about in the air. Tell me, charming woman, the number of bees."

   b. "Eight rubies, ten emeralds, and a hundred pearls, which are in thy earring, my beloved, were purchased by me for thee at an equal amount; and the sum of the prices of the three sorts of gems was three less than half a hundred; tell me the price of each, auspicious woman."

---

4. As cited in Will Durant, *Our Oriental Heritage*. Vol. I of *The Story of Civilization*. New York: Simon and Schuster, 1954; p. 528.

(Note to Teacher: My resource for these problems did not provide the answers. However, with the help of one of our families and a friend who is a math whiz, we have come up with what we think are the solutions and answers. They can be found in the Pretest Answer Key in the Appendix.)

2. With parental approval, search the Internet or your local library for copies or a summary of the *Bhagavad Gita,* or "Lord's Song." This poetic portion of the *Mahabharata* is considered one of the world's finest pieces of literature. With great emotion it depicts the struggle of a prince named Krishna in fighting his own relatives in war. Be conscious of a worldview far different from that of Christianity.

3. Research the poverty of present-day India. From your findings, what factors do you believe contribute to the situation? Make a list of at least five things. File it under "Asia: India" in your Student Notebook.

TAKE ANOTHER LOOK!

Wall of Fame

1. **Diocletian (A.D. 284–305)**—Draw an oblong shape and write the words "Roman Empire" on it. Tear it in half. On the right half, write "Diocletian" (to depict the Eastern Roman Empire). On the left half, write "Maximian" (to depict the Western Roman Empire.) Attach these to your timeline, side by side. [From *History Through the Ages,* use *Diocletian.*]

2. **Constantine I and the EDICT OF MILAN (313)**—Create the figure of a man with a smile holding the Edict of Milan. **Remember, the Edict of Milan (313) is a date to memorize.** [Use *Constantine and the Council of Nicaea.*]

3. **The Golden Age of India (c. 320–500)**—On a little square of cotton fabric, draw a crescent moon (to depict an eclipse), a decimal number, a zero, and a star to remember just some of the great achievements of the people of India. [Use *The Golden Age of India.*]

SomeWHERE in Time

1. To remember the city with three names (Byzantium, Constantinople, and Istanbul), create a trifold map for your Student Notebook.

   Materials: Sheet of colored paper (8½ by 11 inches), markers or colored pencils, ruler, scissors, glue, sheet of notebook paper.

   On a globe or in an atlas, find the modern cities of Rome and Istanbul. Though Diocletian had systematically divided the Roman Empire into the East and the West, Constantine put it back together. It was then that he moved the capital of the Roman Empire from Rome to Byzantium. People began to call it Constantinople after Constantine. You will learn in the last week of this book, that the city was renamed Istanbul in 1453. It bears that name today.

   a. Fold the colored paper in half lengthwise. Cut on the fold and discard one half.

   b. With a light pencil mark, make a line at 3½ inches from the top and 3½ inches from the bottom. Fold at the lines. I will refer to the three segments you created as "A," "B," and "C," as shown in the diagram.

3 ½" {   A

B

3 ½" {   C

c. Glue the bottom of segment B vertically onto the middle of your piece of notebook paper.

d. Fold flap A down at the crease. On the outside of the flap, write in large letters, "Byzantium (500 B.C.–A.D. 300)."

e. Fold flap C up at the crease. On the outside of the flap, write in large letters, "Constantinople (A.D. 324–1453)."

f. Open both flaps to view segment B. It should be blank. On it, write in large letters, "Istanbul (1453–Present)."

g. Open and close the flaps a few times in the order which the city changed its names.

h. At the top of your notebook paper, write the title, "The City of Three Names." File it in your Student Notebook under "Asia:Turkey."

2. This is a three-part mapping activity. The parts progress from easy to more difficult. It should be completed as is suitable for each student. All will use Outline Map 7, "East Asia."

a. Using a globe or world map as a resource, write the names of these countries on the map of East Asia: India, Pakistan, Afghanistan, Nepal, Bangladesh, and China.

b. Add the capital city to each of the countries above. I will provide the city names, but you will need to find where each belongs. The city names are Kabul, Dhaka (or Dacca), New Delhi, Beijing, Kathmandu (or Katmandu), and Islamabad.

c. Add these major cities and rivers to your map using an atlas as a resource. (1) Cities: Delhi, Calcutta (Kolkata), Bombay (Mumbai), and Madras (Chennai). (I am including both traditional names and current names.) Hyderabad is the name of cities in both Pakistan and India. Label them both. (2) Rivers: Indus (though located in Pakistan, this river gives India its name), Ganges, Godavari, and Krishna (formerly Kistna).

Famous Phrases. For this exercise, you need at least two participants. Photocopy this page or hand copy each of these names on a small piece of paper. Fold them in half and drop them in a hat. Pass the hat around, allowing each participant to draw one name at a time until all have been drawn. Take turns acting out the character you drew, using a "famous phrase" your character might have said. Use your imagination! Because this is an exercise, you may refer to your book for ideas on what to say or for help in guessing the characters.

Stephen

Paul

Nero

Domitian

Josephus

Eleazar Ben Yair

Bedouin boy

Bar-Kokhba

An apostle writing the Apostles' Creed

Cupid

Diocletian

Constantine

Samudragupta

WHAT DO YOU KNOW?

PRETEST 6

Jeopardy. Just as they do on the *Jeopardy* television game show, I have provided the answers. You find the right question for each answer from the bottom of the page.

1. A people group that practically vanished from Mexico and Central America.

2. A small body of water between Asia and North America.

3. A picture or sound that makes a word.

4. The art of speaking and writing.

5. A city in North Africa.

6. The autobiography of St. Augustine of Hippo.

7. Hebrew, Aramaic, and Greek.

8. The Bible written in Latin.

> What is a hieroglyph?
> What is *Confessions*?
> What is Hippo?
> Who are the Maya?
> What is the Bering Strait?
> What is the Vulgate?
> What are the original languages of the Bible?
> What is rhetoric?

THE MAYA

· LESSON 16

Can you imagine the United States disappearing from history? It's hard for us to believe that an advanced civilization could be "lost." However, it *has* happened! For thousands of years there were people living in **Mexico** and in the rain forests of **Central America** who later seemed to practically vanish! Who were these mysterious people? They were the **Maya** (MY yuh). (The plural is sometimes written as *Mayas*, but I am using *Maya* for both singular and plural.)

Early Mayan history dates back thousands of years before Christ. The exact date of their beginnings is unknown. However, historians suspect that the Maya migrated to North America from Asia way back when there existed a land bridge between the two continents. If you looked at a globe or atlas now, you would see that the **Bering Strait,** a small body of water, is presently between Asia and North America. Well, at some point in history there was exposed land in this area, making it easy to cross on foot from one continent to the other (without getting wet!). It appears that's how the Maya originally arrived in Mexico and Central America.

For centuries the Maya lived as hunters and gatherers in the **rain forests** of the region. But sometime around 350, the Mayan culture really took off. From **about 350–900,** the Maya experienced what we could call their **classical period.** It was a time when they were most prosperous.

What made the Maya flourish? Lots of things. For one, like the mathematicians in India, they too developed the concept of "zero." This was done miles and miles apart from other civilizations that were just beginning to use zero. The Maya were also masters at astronomy. They accurately estimated the number of days in a year and, like the Indians, calculated when to expect eclipses. They also figured out the orbit pattern of Venus. Neither the Romans nor the mathematicians of India had accomplished that!

The Mayan Temple of Five Stories (at Edzna, Mexico) faces west so that on May 1 and August 13 when the sun reaches its highest point, it shines directly into the temple's rooms.

When it came to education, most Mayan children were homeschooled by their parents! I doubt that **homeschooling** back then was as extensive as it is today. But nonetheless, parents took responsibility to teach their children as best as they could with what they knew. Formal schooling was reserved for children of the nobility. All children had to memorize chants that explained the legends and history of their people.

Unlike other native Americans, the Maya had a **written language.** Their writing was a form of hieroglyphics combining pictures and sounds to make words. The understanding of the Mayan language has taken more than a hundred years to figure out! But once these hieroglyphics were decoded, Mayan history has been better understood. The Maya wrote on just about everything to tell us who they were. They wrote in books, on pots, up stone pillars, and throughout their ornate murals. What is most amazing about their carved writings is that they were made with stone tools. There were no metals used in classic Mayan times.

As for **art,** the Mayan people used extremely bright colors to express themselves. Their distinctive art form depicted daily life and their religious beliefs. Their architecture (or buildings) also reflected their religious beliefs. Tall, towering, step pyramids were typically built for the priests so that they might be closer to the gods. Low-lying palaces served to meet the daily needs of the priests and other royalty.

What were the **religious beliefs** of the Maya? It seems that they worshiped gods representing nature, such as the rain, sun, corn, and soil of the earth. They thought that everything descended from the moon or the sun, calling these "our mother" and "our father." Unfortunately, the Maya appear to have practiced some *human* sacrifice to their gods! They later adopted the worship of **Kukulcan,** from the people of Mexico. Kukulcan was a feathered serpent-god.

To make a living, most of the Maya worked as **farmers.** They were scattered in small villages throughout present-day Mexico, Guatemala, and Honduras. The cities were reserved for priests and the nobility. On religious occasions, farming families would travel to the cities where the roads were paved and the trading was good. These were important social occasions, too.

One of the more exciting events found in the cities was a crude form of **basketball.** The Mayan men had to bounce a ball up and down a court and try to pass it through a raised hoop. However, the ball couldn't touch the ground! It had to be bounced off the player's thighs, hips, and elbows instead. It was apparently so difficult to achieve this that as soon as one team scored, the game was over! The losers not only lost their dignity, but also their clothes and jewelry to the winners!

The Maya dressed lavishly with much ornamentation, color, and jewelry.

Do you wonder what the Maya looked like? From their artwork we have a pretty good idea that most of them were short and stocky, with particularly round heads and dark hair. It seems, too, that the culture so valued a *sloping forehead* that mothers would wrap their babies' heads to make them grow that way! Mothers were also inclined to dangle beads in front of the eyes of their babies, believing it would help them become cross-eyed, which they considered beautiful.

Like their artwork, the **clothes** of the Maya were colorful and showy. Garments were painted, embroidered, and decorated in bright colors with feathery fringes. Men and women alike wore jewelry, which included earrings and necklaces of seeds, shells, jade, and even the wings of beetles. Mayan attire was loud and festive compared to their European contemporaries in Rome.

The Mayan Platform of the Knives in Edzna, Mexico, was so named because some flint ritual knives were discovered buried beneath it.

So, with all this great achievement, how and why did the Maya nearly disappear? Nobody knows for sure. Apparently sometime around 800 or 900, the Maya completely abandoned their elaborate cities. They left the temples, the palaces, and the ball courts. Eventually they left their farms, too. It may have been a combination of economic problems, disease, and crop failure that drove the Maya away.

How do we know so much about these people if they were "lost" in history? Well, it goes back to solid archaeological work. In the late nineteenth century, dedicated people began to unearth the palaces, the temples, and the plazas of the Maya. For almost a thousand years these sites had been completely hidden behind and under dense forests and high mountains in that region. Except for the patience of the diggers, these landmarks might never have been found!

Besides these ruins that attest to the once great Maya, there are millions of people now living in Mexico, **Guatemala,** and **Belize** who claim to be "modern" Maya. They are actually a blend of many native peoples from Mexico and Central America, including descendants of the ancient Maya. With pride in their heritage, the modern Maya help to keep alive the mysteries of the past.

ACTIVITIES FOR LESSON 16

16A—Younger Students

1. If you had been raised in a rain forest, what kind of animals might you have seen? In an encyclopedia or library book, find out about some of the unique animals that live only in rain forests. Photocopy pictures of them and place them in your Student Notebook under "North America: Mexico."

2. Make a necklace using things like beads, seeds (pumpkin, sunflower), and insect wings. Locust wings may work or have your teacher help you "create" insect wings out of waxed paper or tissue paper.

3. In black and white, photocopy images of the Maya from a reference book. Color these with your own bright colors. Place your pictures in your notebook under "North America: Mexico."

16B—Middle Students

1. Research the life of David Stuart. At age 8 he began to sketch hieroglyphics from Mayan carvings. By age 12 he was a world-known cryptographer! Discover what you can about him. Record your findings and file them under "North America: Mexico."

2. For a fun hieroglyph test, visit this site on the Internet:

   www.pbs.org/wgbh/nova/maya/glyp_wave.html

16C—Older Students

What is the modern-day debate over rain forests all about? How much of the earth is made up of rain forests, and how quickly are they being destroyed? How far should man go to protect his environment? Discuss these matters with your class or teacher.

ST. AUGUSTINE OF HIPPO
LESSON 17

Think of someone you know who is really, really smart. I mean a person so smart that they "make you think" when they speak. Well, over a thousand years ago, there lived a man with this kind of intelligence. Through his profound speaking and writing, he made lots of people think. In fact, his written works are *still* challenging people today. This man's name was Aurelius Augustine, later named **Saint Augustine.**

Augustine was born in **North Africa** in **354.** His mother, **Monica,** was a devout Christian. His father, **Patricius,** was a Roman official and a pagan. (A pagan is someone who doesn't believe in God.) Though this couple's religious beliefs were different, Augustine's parents agreed on one thing. They knew their son was brilliant! Because of his giftedness, they sent him to the finest schools in Carthage, a city in North Africa.

Augustine studied hard in Carthage. He was well educated in grammar, math, music, and rhetoric. **Rhetoric** is the art of speaking and writing. Augustine became a master in this field and accepted a position teaching others the skills of rhetoric.

Though Augustine had proven himself to be intelligent, he was not always wise. Unlike his prayerful mother, young Augustine was not a Christian. He believed Christianity to be for the "simple-minded." At age 18 he fathered a child, even though he wasn't married. He lived to later regret his immoral actions and wrote, "I came to Carthage, where a cauldron of unholy loves was sizzling and crackling around me."[1]

Despite the temptations he fell to, Augustine was a genuine seeker for truth. He immersed himself in studying all kinds of philosophies, one after the other, looking for answers to life. In his searching, Augustine moved to the city of **Milan** in 384. It was there that his mother introduced him to someone nearly as brilliant as himself. The man's name was **Ambrose.** He was the **Bishop of Milan,** which means he was a high leader of the Early Church.

Augustine was deeply struck by the fact that this intelligent man professed a strong faith in Jesus Christ and yet wasn't "simple-minded" at all! On the contrary, Augustine found Bishop Ambrose to be a great scholar. Augustine, now 29, was greatly challenged. His friendship with the bishop forced him to examine his own life and beliefs. In his struggle to understand obedience to God, he humorously wrote, "Lord, make me chaste [or pure], but not yet."[2] (Words in brackets are mine.) It sounds to me like Augustine was at least beginning to want to please God with his life. He just wasn't sure how to let go of the things of the world.

Augustine used his gift of rhetoric to explain his deep faith in God.

1. A. Kenneth Curtis, J. Stephen Lang, and Randy Petersen, *The 100 Most Important Events in Christian History.* Grand Rapids, MI: Fleming H. Revell, 1991; p. 41.
2. Ibid.

However, according to Augustine himself, there came a day in 387 when he could no longer put off the call of God in his life. He was meditating in a garden when he heard something like children singing, "Take it and read; take it and read." So he did. Augustine reached over to a copy of the scripture and read from Paul's letter to the Romans. The passage says:

"Let us walk properly, as in the day, not in revelry and drunkenness, not in licentiousness and lewdness, not in strife and envy. But put on the Lord Jesus Christ, and make no provision for the flesh, to fulfill its lusts." (see Romans 13:13-14)

From that moment on, Augustine claims he became a true believer in Christ. He said, "It was as though the light of faith flooded into my heart and all the darkness of doubt was dispelled."[3] He and his son were soon baptized together on the night before Easter. His conversion, like Constantine's (Lesson 14), is another beautiful example of God answering the prayers of a devout mother. Just four years later, in 391, Augustine was ordained a priest, and by 395 he became the **Bishop of Hippo,** a city in North Africa (now Annaba, Algeria). Because of his quick learning as a Christian and his great leadership skills, one historian said of Augustine, "from this foot of earth he moved the world."[4]

These majestic Roman ruins stand in Tunisia, Northern Africa, as a reminder that for centuries, including during Augustine's lifetime, Tunisia was part of the vast Roman Empire.

One way that Augustine "moved the world" was through his many writings. If you remember, he was a master of rhetoric, and he used this gift to glorify God. He wrote about his conversion to Christianity in a book titled ***Confessions.*** In this autobiography that was written "to God," Augustine openly shared his life and sins *before* knowing Christ personally. (It was shocking to the Early Church!) The book opens with the saying, "Our hearts are restless until they rest in You."[5] Augustine also authored a book titled **On the Trinity,** which helped to explain complex ideas about the godhead. It took him 15 years to complete this difficult work.

Coincidentally, around this time the Roman Empire was beginning to crumble. Some Romans blamed the Christians for this, believing that they had upset the mythological Roman gods with their beliefs in Christ. To help the Romans better understand God and the Bible, Augustine wrote a masterpiece called **The City of God.** In it he described that, since the earliest of time, there have always been cities built by

3. Ibid., p. 42.
4. Will Durant, *The Age of Faith*. Vol. IV of *The Story of Civilization*. New York: Simon and Schuster, 1950; p. 67.
5. A. Kenneth Curtis, J. Stephen Lang, and Randy Petersen, *The 100 Most Important Events in Christian History*, Grand Rapids, MI: Fleming H. Revell, 1991; p. 42.

men and cities built by God. He claimed that cities whose foundations were laid by God would last, and those that weren't would fall. As Rome was falling to the attack of outsiders, he was pleading with the Romans to place their faith in the One true God. He influenced many people through this profound book.

Unfortunately, the city that Augustine physically lived in was crumbling under a siege. In a war there in **430,** Augustine was killed in an attack! Many grieved the loss of this brilliant scholar. Though Augustine no longer lived, his influence lasted for centuries to come through the Middle Ages and the Reformation. Great men like **Martin Luther** and **John Calvin** used his writings as a basis for some of their ideas. The church gave Augustine the title of **saint.** And in his honor, a group of **monks** used Augustine's name to identify themselves.

Personally, I hope that Augustine's testimony of great intelligence *and* faith will still challenge people today. His conversion should help others see that Christianity is certainly not just for the "simple-minded."

ACTIVITIES FOR LESSON 17

17A—Younger Students

Did you notice in the story of Augustine that something "like the singing of children" influenced him? Can you think of any praise songs you know that tell others about the love of God? Practice singing them together with your teacher today and make a cassette recording of it. Send your tape to a friend or relative who might benefit from listening. Remember that God can use the praises of children to make Himself known.

17B—Middle Students

Near this time, there were some Christians who believed that they had to punish or torture themselves to earn God's love. One of these men was Simeon Stylites (390–459) who lived on top of a 50-foot stone pillar for 37 years! Research the details of his unusual life and the impact he had. What do you think was inaccurate about his theology? Discuss this with your teacher or class.

17C—Older Students

1. Bishop Ambrose had a great influence on Augustine. Is there someone in your life who influences you or who needs your influence? Pray about being mentored by an older person whom you admire or your mentoring a younger person in your life. The life of Ambrose is a reminder of the difference one person can make.

2. Seek the original works of St. Augustine. I've included a beautiful short excerpt from *Confessions* in the Activity Supplement in the Appendix. A modern translation of *The Confessions of St. Augustine* is available at many bookstores. Consider his gift of rhetoric. What might be your spiritual gift? How can you use it bring glory to God?

THE HOLY BIBLE
AND THE VULGATE BY JEROME
LESSON 18

Have you ever wondered where the **Bible** came from? To some degree the answer is simple—God wrote it! But when you consider all the special details of this book, it's really more complicated than that. Today we'll look at how the Holy Bible was put together. We'll also learn about a man named **Jerome** who translated the entire Bible into Latin. To say the least, he was quite dedicated to preserving the word of God.

As for the Bible, did you know that it says it was inspired by God? In 2 Timothy 3:16, it says, "*All Scripture is given by inspiration of God . . .*" This means that God gave the words to men to write. Peter affirms this when he wrote, "*for prophecy never came by the will of man, but holy men of God spoke as they were moved by the Holy Spirit.*" (2 Pet. 1:21) In simpler terms, this means that God, through the Holy Spirit, used men like Moses, David, Matthew, Paul, and others to write the things He wanted. These sacred writings have become what we call the Bible.

As you may already know, the Bible is divided into two main parts, the **Old Testament** and the **New Testament.** The Old Testament contains 39 books, which were written in two different languages—Hebrew and some Aramaic. These writings are divided into the **Pentateuch,** which comprises the first five books of the Old Testament, or the "Law"; the **Writings**, which are 17 books of history, poetry, and wisdom; and the **Prophets,** which are 17 books of prophecy. These books were written over about a 1,000-year time span by kings, prophets, and special men of God. Jewish leaders of long ago compiled the Old Testament by determining which books they believed were inspired and in what order they should appear.

It took Jerome 23 years to translate the Bible into the Latin Vulgate.

The New Testament was originally written in the Greek language. It contains 27 books that can be described in four groups. Those groups are the **Gospels** (4), the **Book of Acts** (1)**,** the **letters of the apostles** (21), and the **Book of Revelation** (1)**.** Most of these books were written within 50 to 100 years after the resurrection of Christ by actual eyewitnesses to the life of Christ! This fact gives the books much credibility from a historical perspective.

If you remember the lesson on **Diocletian,** you may recall that he severely persecuted Christians and tried to destroy their sacred writings at the beginning of the fourth century A.D. At that time the Scriptures had not yet been compiled into what we now know as the Bible. Writings of the apostles had been circulated for centuries and were considered divinely inspired. Because of the persecutions going on, it was important for believers to completely agree on which writings were worth dying for! So, in 393, church leaders officially standardized the books of the New Testament at a meeting in **Hippo.**

Though many things were considered at this meeting, there were at least five criteria that church leaders agreed upon when deciding which letters of the apostles were God's revelations. According to Josh McDowell,[6] the criteria were:

1. Was the book written by one of God's prophets?

2. Did the book contain miracles to affirm God's acts?

3. Did the book tell the truth about God?

4. Was the book powerful enough to be life changing?

5. Did the early Christians accept the book?

Despite these criteria, some would put it this way: It was not a matter of man *deciding* what books went into the Bible, but it was up to man to *discover* the books that God had inspired! I think that's a valuable way to consider how the Bible was put together.

Do any of the original documents of the Bible exist? No they don't; but fortunately, Jewish scribes have kept meticulous copies of the Old Testament for centuries. And the New Testament was copied over and over by early Christians. In fact, today there exist some New Testament letters that were copied only 30 to 50 years after the apostle Paul wrote them! As stated in the book, *A Survey of Bible Doctrine,* "More than 5,000 manuscripts of the New Testament exist today, which makes the New Testament the best-attested document in all ancient writings.[7]

Jerome Translates the Bible Into Latin

If you have already studied Volume I of *The Mystery of History,* you may remember learning about the **Septuagint.** It was the very first Old Testament to be translated from one language to another. Writers of the Septuagint translated Hebrew and Aramaic Scriptures into Greek. This was done so that the Jews who spoke only Greek could study the Scriptures themselves.

For years the Greek Septuagint served the early Christians as the *only* version of the Old Testament. But not everyone in Europe could read or write Greek. There was a great need for the Bible to be translated into a language for the common man. And that common language would be Latin, the language of the Roman Empire that had spread over most of Europe.

That brings us to the Latin Bible translated by Jerome. It is also called the **Vulgate.** The word *Vulgate* simply means "common." The *Vulgate* was written in Latin so that the common man could read it.

The details of translating the Vulgate are not particularly exciting. But Jerome, the man who did the translating, was an interesting and unusual character. Jerome was such a devout Christian that he was strangely impatient with himself for having any human weaknesses at all. He so wanted to be like Christ that, unfortunately, he was said to be critical of sin in himself *and* in others. This critical trait didn't make him very popular! He found it suited him best to follow the simple solitary life of the monks, remaining poor and unmarried his whole life.

However, Jerome wasn't that simple of a man. Like Augustine of Hippo, Jerome was brilliant. He became a priest and a secretary to the bishop. It was **Bishop Damasus** who challenged Jerome to take scattered versions of the Bible that had already been written in Latin and translate them more properly. This challenge turned into a 23-year project! It lasted from **382 to 405.**

---

6. Josh McDowell, *The New Evidence That Demands a Verdict.* Nashville: Thomas Nelson Publishers, 1999; pp. 21–22.
7. Charles C. Ryrie, *A Survey of Bible Doctrine.* Chicago: Moody Press, 1972; p. 46.

For most of those 23 years Jerome lived in a cell-like cave with little more than heaps of books and papers. Daily he poured over the details of the Bible, remaining focused and committed to his task. Much was on his shoulders to accurately translate the Word of God. It helped greatly that he already knew Hebrew from having lived in Bethlehem. He did an incredible work considering the crude times in which he lived.

Note the beautiful hand-drawn artwork and lettering of this early Bible.

Jerome liked to call the Bible a "divine library." His work of putting the divine library into Latin was one of the greatest literary gifts of the fourth century! For years and years the Vulgate was used by ordinary people, as well as scholars, to understand the word of God. For as long as Latin was used in everyday life in Europe, the word of God was available.

As a side note to older students, it was Jerome who first named the group of literature that is called the ***Apocrypha***. The word *apocrypha* means "hidden things." It refers to ancient writings (14 books) that, though included in the Septuagint and the Vulgate, were historically not recognized by the church as inspired. Jerome defined them as books that were outside the Hebrew canon. According to Unger's Bible Dictionary, "The Old Testament apocrypha have an unquestioned historical and literary value but have been rejected as inspired."[8]

In closing, there are many fascinating things to know about the Word of God, but I will end with these beautiful passages to reflect on. The last is one of my favorites.

> *"So shall My word be that goes forth from My mouth; it shall not return to Me void, but it shall accomplish what I please, and it shall prosper in the thing for which I sent it."* (Isa. 55:11)

> *"Most assuredly, I say to you, he who hears My word and believes in Him who sent me has everlasting life . . . "* (John 5:24)

> *"The words that I [Jesus] speak to you are spirit, and they are life."* (John 6:63) (Word in brackets is mine.)

> *"For the word of God is living and powerful, and sharper than any two-edged sword, . . . "* (Heb. 4:12)

> *"And the Word became flesh and dwelt among us, . . . "* (John 1:14)

ACTIVITIES FOR LESSON 18

ALL STUDENTS

Make your Memory Cards for Lessons 16–18.

18A—Younger Students

1. Do you know the books of the Bible by heart? If not, this might be a good time to memorize them. Perhaps you may earn as a reward a new Bible or Bible cover.
2. Sing "The B-I-B-L-E."

---

8. Merrill F. Unger, *Unger's Bible Dictionary*. Chicago: Moody Press, 1979; p. 70.

The B-I-B-L-E
Yes, that's the book for me;
I stand alone on the Word of God,
The B-I-B-L-E.

The words to this and many other hymns can be found on the Web site: www.cyberhymnal.org.

3. Copy by hand a verse of the Bible in Latin. (See the one written out for you below.) For fun, write the verse in a "cave" like Jerome did! A "cave" might easily be formed by throwing large sheets or blankets over a kitchen table.

"Quia natus est vobis hodie Salvator, qui est Christus Dominus, in civitate David." (Luke 2:11)

Look in your Bible for the translation in English. You can probably guess what some of the words mean without looking! File this verse in your Student Notebook under "Europe: Rome."

18B—Middle Students

1. Memorize the verses about God's word included at the conclusion of this lesson.

2. Research the number of Bibles that have been printed. How many are in your own home? Do you have any extras that can be donated to a mission group?

3. Bible translation is an ongoing work by missionaries. Research the number of languages that *still* need a translation of the Bible. Consider Wycliffe Bible Translators as a resource.

18C—Older Students

1. Bible translation is no small matter. Men have died over the centuries for their dedication to preserving the Bible. Familiarize yourself with these ancient manuscripts found in later centuries. They are the Codex Sinaticus from 330, the Codex Vaticanus from 340, and the Codex Alexandrinus from 425. These, along with the Dead Sea Scrolls found in 1947, have spurred the writing of many new translations of the Bible since 1952.

2. Research the dangers of smuggling Bibles into closed countries.

3. Familiarize yourself with the books of the Apocrypha. Discuss the historical validity of the books versus the theological perspective of them. (Churches vary on their viewpoint toward the Apocrypha.)

TAKE ANOTHER LOOK!

REVIEW 6: LESSONS 16–18

Wall of Fame

1. **The Maya (350–900)**—With a pencil, draw some stick figures of people. Now erase them. Label it "The Maya Disappear." [From *History Through the Ages*, use *The Maya*.]

2. **St. Augustine of Hippo (354–430)**—Draw a small lightbulb over the figure of a man. Draw a cross in the lightbulb. Write Augustine's name across his chest. [Use *Augustine*.]

3. **Jerome (382–405)**—Depict a man with a pen and a book. [Use *Jerome*.]

SomeWHERE in Time

1. Make the Maya "disappear" with a map overlay.

   Materials: Outline Map 8, "Mexico and Central America"; historical atlas with map of Mayan World; modern-day atlas; a clear transparency; transparency marker*; colored pencils; scissors; stapler; three-hole punch. *(A water-based marker will smudge, but it is erasable for errors; permanent is, well, permanent. It doesn't smudge after it dries, but it doesn't allow much room for errors. Your choice!)

   a. Lay the clear transparency over the unused outline map. Use a marker to trace the outline map onto the transparency and then label the region on the transparency according to the Mayan World map in your historical atlas.

   b. Now use the pencils to color each of the modern-day countries a different color on the paper outline map.

   c. Lay the transparency over the paper outline map. Line up the maps.

   d. Staple the top edges together.

   e. Open and close the overlay to make the Maya appear and disappear.

   f. Punch three holes in them and place in your Student Notebook under "North America: Mexico/ Central America."

2. Northern Africa has changed since St. Augustine lived there. The city of Hippo is no longer on the map. It once stood, however, on the coast of the Mediterranean Sea near what is today the city of Annaba, Algeria. (Annaba is not far from Tunis, Tunisia.) Today I want you to become more familiar with present-day northern Africa. This is a multistep mapping activity. The parts progress from easy to more difficult. Complete as is suitable for each student. All will use Outline Map 9, "Northern Africa."

   a. Using a globe or an atlas as your resource, write the names of the following countries on a blank map of Northern Africa: *Morocco, Algeria, Tunisia, Libya,* and *Egypt.* These five nations are called *Saharan Africa* because of their closeness to the Sahara. Color each country a different color.

   b. Add these following bodies of water to your map: *Atlantic Ocean, Mediterranean Sea, Red Sea,* and the *Nile River.* Color them various shades of blue.

   c. Using a globe or atlas, match the following capital cities to their countries: *Tunis, Cairo, Rabat, Tripoli,* and *Algiers.*

d.   Add the *Sahara, Atlas Mountains,* and *Libyan Desert*.

e.   Add the five countries and their capitals just south of the Saharan nations. They are *Mauritania, Mali, Niger, Chad,* and *Sudan*. These are considered the countries of the *Sahel* or *Sudan*.

f.   File your map under "Africa: Algeria" in your Student Notebook.

WHAT DID YOU LEARN?

WEEK 6: QUIZ

True or False? Circle your answers.

1. Nero blamed the burning of Rome on Christians.   T   F

2. Trajan, a Roman emperor, allowed freedom of religion.   T   F

3. Josephus despised the Romans and spent his entire life in prison
    for it.   T   F

4. Masada was destroyed and buried by a terrible earthquake.   T   F

5. The Essenes wrote the Dead Sea Scrolls and then vanished from history.   T   F

6. Hot lava flooded the streets of Pompeii when Vesuvius blew
    in A.D. 79.   T   F

7. Bar-Kokhba's existence has never been proven.   T   F

8. The Apostles' Creed was written about 100 years after Christ lived.   T   F

9. Lupercalia, the Roman festival of love, falls on Easter every year.   T   F

10. Diocletian divided the Roman Empire to make it more manageable.   T   F

11. Constantine threw Christians to the lions in the Roman Colosseum.   T   F

12. Hinduism grew during the Golden Age of India under the
    Gupta dynasty.   T   F

13. The Maya of Mexico and Central America had no written language.   T   F

14. St. Augustine was gifted in rhetoric, the art of speaking and writing.   T   F

15. It took Jerome only 23 months to translate the Bible into the
    Latin Vulgate.   T   F

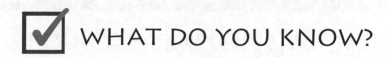

WHAT DO YOU KNOW?

PRETEST 7

Fill in the Blanks. Using a word from the bottom of the page, fill in the blanks.

1. At 16, Patrick was _____ by Irish pirates.

2. St. Patrick used the symbol of the three-leaf _____ to explain the Trinity to the Irish.

3. As nomadic people, the Huns relied heavily on _____ for food, milk, and transportation.

4. Attila the Hun was nicknamed the "_____ of God" by those who feared him.

5. Like a bribe to a bully, Theodosius II paid _____ to Attila the Hun to leave the Eastern Roman Empire alone.

6. The name "_____" was given by the Romans to anyone from a tribe outside of Rome.

7. The Vandals _____ much of the city of Rome to the ground.

8. The fall of the Western Roman Empire led to a period in time that is called the _____
_____.

WORD BANK

burned	scourge	shamrock	kidnapped
tribute	Dark Ages	horses	barbarians

ST. PATRICK, MISSIONARY TO IRELAND
LESSON 19

Have you ever worn green for **St. Patrick's Day**—or been "pinched" for forgetting? The "wearing of the green" is a common custom in the United States. But do you know anything about Patrick? Do you know why was he called a saint? Most of us don't, but if you like adventure stories, you'll like this lesson about **St. Patrick.**

Patrick was born about **389** in a region of Great Britain that at the time was under Roman rule. (He was not Irish as most people think but was probably of Celtic descent from Wales or Scotland.) His parents were strong Christians. His father was a deacon in a church, and his grandfather was a pastor. But Patrick didn't share the faith of his family. He was the type of kid who would rather play on the beach than go to church with his family.

One tragic day, Patrick's youthful rebellion cost him his freedom. While playing on the rocky shores of the British coast at the age of 16, Patrick was kidnapped by Irish pirates! Imagine one minute hanging out on the beach with your friends and the next minute being thrown on a pirate ship in chains! Patrick didn't know if he would see his home or his family again.

The pirates sold Patrick to other Irishmen who kept him in slavery for six years! Like the parable of the Prodigal Son, Patrick's job was taking care of pigs. In the first year of Patrick's imprisonment, he thought long and hard about the things his parents had taught him. He especially thought about the faith he had rejected. In his words, this is what happened:

Patrick dreamed that Irish children were calling him back to Ireland, where he had been a slave.

> "I was sixteen years old and knew not the true God; but in that strange land the Lord opened my unbelieving eyes, and, altogether late, I called my sins to mind, and was converted with my whole heart to the Lord my God, who regarded my low estate, had pity on my youth and ignorance, and consoled me as a father consoles his children."[1]

From this testimony, we gather that Patrick became a genuine Christian. For the next several years he learned how to pray, as he never had before. His main prayer, of course, was for his **freedom.** The Lord heard young Patrick's prayers and had mercy on him. Though some never escape slavery, Patrick did! Thinking his only hope of escape would be by ship, Patrick raced toward the sea nearly 200 miles away. As another answer to prayer, Patrick found a ship with a captain willing to take him aboard as a dog keeper. Without hesitation, Patrick took the job—hoping it would eventually lead him home.

---

1. George T. Thompson and Laurel Elizabeth Hicks, *World History and Cultures in Christian Perspective.* Pensacola, FL: A Beka Book, 1985; p. 133.

After a stopover in France, Patrick's wishes came true, and the day came when he finally made it back to Great Britain. Can you imagine his parents' reaction to seeing him again? I doubt they had known if he was dead or alive. And to make the reunion even more special, Patrick's parents learned of their son's conversion. I suspect his return home, as well as his new faith, brought unexplainable joy and was another example of God answering the prayers of parents for their children.

As great as it was to be home, Patrick found himself having strange **dreams** at night. He dreamed that Irish children were calling him *back* to the pagan country of Ireland! In his dreams, he was teaching them about God. You would think that after spending six grueling years in Ireland as a slave, Patrick would have absolutely no desire to return. But, you know what? He did. That's perhaps one reason why he's considered a saint!

Patrick Returns to Ireland

In 432, after receiving training as a minister in **France,** Patrick returned to Ireland. He returned to minister to the people who had once held him captive. He returned with a heart full of love and forgiveness. It was a remarkable step of faith.

For nearly 30 years, Patrick ministered and preached the Gospel in Ireland. To help you appreciate this difficult task, let me explain the condition of this pagan country. For hundreds of years, Ireland was ruled by **tribal chiefs.** And none of these chiefs got along very well. War after war was fought between the different tribes of people. In fact, war was so common to the Irish that soldiers were buried standing up and facing their enemies. Why? So that even in death they were ready for battle!

As for the **spirituality** of the Irish, few people were more superstitious than they were. The Irish believed in all kinds of magic, from which come the fanciful stories of fairies, elves, and leprechauns. One Celtic (KELT-ick) religion was that of the **druids.** (The **Celts** [Keltz] were early Indo-European peoples that had scattered throughout Europe.) White-robed druid priests worshiped the sun, the moon, and the stars and performed all kinds of magic rituals. In fact, many of today's **Halloween** symbols come from the druids.

Other British missionaries had tried to share the Gospel of Christ in Ireland but without much success. The British had difficulty relating to Irish customs. But Patrick, because of his years of imprisonment there, found it easy to communicate with the warring, superstitious Irish. He was most well known for using the three-leaf **shamrock** (or clover) as a symbol of the Trinity, or the three persons of the Godhead. As a result of his teachings, the common masses of people loved Patrick. They knew he had returned to them out of compassion, and they eagerly embraced his message. But not all the people loved Patrick so easily. His greatest opposition was from the druid priests and tribal chiefs. He wrote in his autobiography that at least 12 times his life was in danger; that he was seized on numerous occasions; and that he was held captive! I wonder if he had flashbacks to his former days of slavery. Despite those troubles, Patrick persevered in his mission. It has been said of him that he "found Ireland all heathen and left it all Christian."[2]

In fact, Patrick started at least 300 churches and baptized 120,000 people! His ministry was amazing. Much like the early apostles, Patrick performed **miracles** that led many to believe. He supposedly gave sight to the blind and hearing to the deaf, cleansed lepers, cast out demons, and raised nine people from the dead! His ministry was so incredible that many legends and stories of Patrick grew that may or may not have been true. One tale suggests that he led snakes to the sea to drown. He was also said to have dug a hole to the underworld and sent monks down into it to give a report on Hades! It seems that the love of fanciful stories never completely left the Irish people although they grew to be a strong Christian nation.

---

2. *World Book Encyclopedia*, 50th Anniversary ed., s.v. "Patrick, Saint." Chicago: Field Enterprises Educational Corp., 1966.

Unlike most of the early apostles, Patrick fortunately never had to face a martyr's death. He died of natural causes in **461.** After 30 years of ministry, he left the church in Ireland strong and growing. Irish abbots were dedicated to the pure teaching and preaching of Christ, copying the Scriptures by hand, and ministering to the poor.

It is no wonder that Patrick has been so well remembered. I hope that on March 17, which has been dedicated in his honor, you do more than wear green for "good luck." I hope you remember the great dedication of St. Patrick to ministering to his one-time captors and preaching the Gospel of Christ.

ACTIVITIES FOR LESSON 19

19A—Younger Students

1. Have your teacher help you sketch a large three-leaf clover on a piece of notebook paper. On each leaf, write the name of one of the three parts of the Trinity. They are the Father, the Son, and the Holy Spirit. Color your clover green and file it in your Student Notebook under "Europe: Ireland."

2. With your teacher's help, make a list of the symbols and traditions we see on St. Patrick's Day. Talk about the meaning of "traditions" with your teacher.

19B—Younger and Middle Students

In a hymnal, look for the songs written by St. Patrick titled "I Bind unto Myself Today" and "Christ Be Beside Me." Read or sing these. Isn't it beautiful that we have some of his songs in our modern hymnals?

19C—Older Students

Research the ancient druids and their customs that are held to today through the celebration of Halloween. Suggested resource is *Handbook of Today's Religions* by Josh McDowell and Don Stewart. See "Witchcraft."

434–453

ATTILA THE HUN

LESSON 20

Attila the Hun. What a name! The very sound of it is intimidating. In the fifth century, it was more than the name of Attila that scared people. It was the man. **Attila the Hun** was an incredible warrior king who did serious damage to the Roman Empire.

So who were the "Huns" anyway? They were a nomadic people who began to invade Europe from somewhere in central Asia. Strangely, no one knows exactly where they came from. But they literally swept from the East to the West, attempting to take everything in their path.

The stature and customs of the Huns are part of what made their reputation a fierce one. The Huns were short, thick people with flat noses and small "pig-like" eyes.[3] Parents are said to have scarred their children's faces to teach them to tolerate suffering and pain. Of course it made them look scary, too!

---

3. T. Walter Wallbank and Alastair M. Taylor, *Civilization Past and Present*. Chicago: Scott Foresman and Company, 1949; p. 230.

Attila the Hun used his evil reputation to help him win battles against the Romans.

The Huns are further described as rather bow-legged people. It was probably because of how much time they spent on horses. You see the Huns didn't migrate to Europe on foot; they stormed through on horses! It is said that they so relied on horses for their livelihood that they drank horse milk, ate horsemeat, and "cooked" food situated under their saddles as they rode! (The friction of the rider against the horse supposedly did the cooking, but I wouldn't want to try it myself.)

Now that you have a picture of these barbaric people, imagine the man who was their king from **434–453.** He was Attila the Hun. The Romans and Germans who feared him nicknamed him the "scourge of God." What did they fear? For one, Attila had an army of half a million men. That's a big army for a king without a country. I suppose that's why he went out to conquer new land. The empire he went after was the biggest one around—he went after Rome!

In 447 Attila the Hun began his blitz of terror by invading the **Eastern Roman Empire.** In order to make peace, **Theodosius II** (the Roman emperor of the East) agreed to pay Attila a **tribute.** A tribute is a large sum of money. Paying a tribute to another king is like bribing a bully. The Romans in the East basically *paid* Attila to not hurt them anymore! To Attila, it was a victory. To the Romans, it was humiliating.

With renewed confidence, Attila decided to see what he could gain from the Western Roman Empire. In 451 Attila managed to not only receive tribute money from the emperor of the West, but he also received a gift of land south of the **Danube.** This spurred him on to blast through the country of **Gaul** (later known as France), ransacking towns and cities by killing men and capturing women.

Now I know I've made this guy sound pretty terrifying. But according to some historians, Attila was no more ruthless than Julius Caesar, whom many hold to be one of the greatest generals that ever lived. Some say Attila was in fact *merciful* to those he captured and treated them fairly. Supposedly, he was good to his own people and ruled them very well.

As for lifestyle, Attila's was unusually simple. Although he was a king, Attila dressed in plain clothes; he ate and drank like common people; and he put luxuries aside for others to enjoy. For example, Attila's palace was formed out of nicely carved wood but only draped with ordinary animal skins to keep out the cold. You could say he was far more practical than he was extravagant.

It seems to me, then, that to develop such a fearsome image, Attila was probably more clever than he was savage. Though unable to read or write, he was obviously smart when it came to being a conqueror. Attila allowed the evil reputation of the Huns to win some of his battles before he even fought them.

Well, whether it was brains or terror that made Attila the most powerful man in Europe, it didn't last. In June of 451, one of the bloodiest battles ever fought brought the fearless Attila to a stop. Both the Romans and the **Visigoths** (a Germanic tribe) had had enough of Attila. They joined forces together at what is called the **Battle of Chalons-sur-Marne.**

In the massive fight, 162,000 men died on the battlefield! This death toll included the king of the Visigoths, who was helping the Romans fight off the Huns. Attila survived the battle and within a year moved southward to conquer Italy. It could have been a disaster. But somehow, a church leader managed to talk Attila out of conquering the city of Rome. For reasons no one knows, Attila headed back through the Alps to where he came from. Perhaps he was retreating to make a new plan of attack. Or perhaps he was giving up.

What Attila didn't know was that his life was about to come to an abrupt end—not from battle however. In 453 Attila died in his bed from a ruptured blood vessel. It may be that he overindulged in food and drink during his own wedding festivities. His death occurred on one of his many wedding nights. The Huns never fully recovered from the loss of their king. The Romans and the Germans, however, were relieved at the news that the "scourge of God" no longer lived to terrorize them.

What we learn from the life of Attila the Hun is that warrior-type power isn't lasting. After Attila's sudden death, his two sons divided his kingdom. Neither one was a capable ruler, however, and the agonizing reign of the Huns ended as quickly as it started. The name of this legendary warrior king remains in our history books, but little else exists to testify to the terror of the Huns.

ACTIVITIES FOR LESSON 20

20A—Younger Students

Ride a broom horse!

In the lesson, I stated that the Huns "swept from the East to the West, attempting to take everything in their path." Do you know which way is east and which way is west in your home or school? Use the direction of the sun, which rises in the East, as a guide.

Now, just for fun and to remember the Huns sweeping "from the East to the West," ride a *broom horse* from east to west across your home or classroom.

20B—Middle Students

Though it may be appalling to imagine drinking horse milk or eating horsemeat, list different products we do use that come directly from animals such as cows or pigs. Don't forget all the dairy products made from milk. Much like the Huns, our culture relies heavily on the use of animal products.

20C—Middle and Older Students

As you learned in the lesson, Attila had a terrifying reputation. From the Activity Supplement in the Appendix, read the descriptive paragraph of Attila as written by a Gothic historian. With that narrative in mind, write your own descriptive paragraph of a modern-day leader. Describe the walk, the talk, the gestures, and the reputation of the leader you chose. Without telling who it is, see if family members or your class can identify the leader you wrote about.

476

FALL OF THE WESTERN ROMAN EMPIRE
LESSON 21

Thousands of years ago, Rome was just a tiny village. But that village grew into a bustling city; that city became a major republic; and that republic expanded to become the largest and most powerful empire that had ever been! But, as many nations rise and fall over time, so even the Roman Empire fell. Today we'll look at how such an enormous empire could collapse—that is, at least how *half* of it collapsed in **476.** It certainly wasn't easy!

The last time we took an in-depth look at the Roman Empire, it was under the rule of **Constantine the Great.** He's the one who made it against the law to persecute Christians in 313. After Constantine, the leadership of Rome passed through many different emperors over the course of a hundred years.

Some were good and some were bad. At the height of the empire, Rome ruled almost all of Europe, parts of the Middle East, and the northern coast of Africa. That's part of three different continents! The proud Romans even claimed the Mediterranean Sea as their own and called it **Mare Nostrum** (MAY ree NAHS truhm). That's Latin for "our sea."

It may be in part the huge size of Rome that had something to do with its downfall. As Rome swallowed up more nations, it was harder and harder to find enough soldiers to defend these newly conquered territories. So the Roman Empire began to hire foreigners and outsiders as soldiers. This worked to give the Romans *more* soldiers, but then the Roman army wasn't purely Roman anymore! It was made up partly of rebellious **"barbarians"**! (The Romans used the term *barbarian* to describe anyone from a tribe outside of Rome. It meant "ignorant one.")

To complicate matters, it cost a lot of money for the Romans to hire outsiders for their army. To pay for more soldiers, the government did two things: they raised taxes and they devalued money. The result of these actions was that prices rose sharply on things people bought, such as food, clothing, and houses. We call that **inflation.** With inflation and rising taxes, many people left the busy cities and headed to the country. This caused business and trade between the cities of the empire to suffer.

If these problems weren't enough to shake the Roman Empire, it so happened that tribes outside of Rome were looking for places to live. Remember the **Huns**? They are just one example of a nomadic group of people looking for land in Rome. Unfortunately for the Romans, there were many other groups doing the same thing.

The widest extent of the Roman Empire, c. 98 AD

By the year 98, the Roman Empire covered parts of three continents—Europe, Africa, and Asia.

To keep these different people groups straight, we'll look at them in alphabetical order in the following paragraphs. First there were the **Angles.** These "barbarians," as the Romans would have called them, began to move into the Roman region we now call England. In fact, the name England comes from the Old English words *Engla* and *land,* which together meant "land of the Angles." They were joined by

Pillars of ancient Roman buildings still rise over the city of Rome today or lie toppled on the ground in silence.

the **Jute** and **Saxon** tribes. You've probably heard of the *Anglo-Saxons*. The term comes from the blend of the Angles and Saxons who settled in England at the fall of the Roman Empire. (Most of our English language comes from these people!)

Another invading group was the **Franks.** The Franks were of German descent. Under the leadership of a king named **Clovis,** the Franks took northern Gaul from the Romans in 486. The area became so well populated by the Franks that it was named **France** after them. Interestingly, Clovis converted to Christianity at some time during his reign. His beliefs helped shape the future of France.

The **Goths** were another Germanic tribe that invaded the Roman Empire. The Goths split into two groups—one called the **Visigoths** (Western Goths) and the other, the **Ostrogoths** (Eastern Goths). The names are easy to confuse. If you remember, the Visigoths are the ones who helped Rome fight off Attila the Hun. Because they helped, the Visigoths were offered a small part of the Roman Empire. They were supposed to remain there in peace, but they didn't. In 409 the Visigoths rallied together and stormed Italy. By 410 they did the unthinkable and sacked the city of Rome itself! This capital city hadn't been invaded for nearly 800 years. It was a tough blow to the entire empire.

Vandals Attack the City of Rome

But the hardest blow to Rome was yet to come. In 455 there was yet another Germanic tribe seeking to conquer Rome. They were the **Vandals.** To this day the term *vandal* refers to someone who sets out to destroy or plunder someone's property. The term accurately fits that which happened in 455. The Vandals hit the city of Rome like a hurricane, and for two straight weeks they ripped it apart through looting and violence!

The attack by the Vandals came somewhat as a surprise because of the way they traveled to get to Rome. Instead of coming from the North as might have been expected, the *Vandals* attacked Rome from the South. They did this by crossing into Africa from Spain and then sailing across the Mediterranean. Once on the coast of Italy, the Vandals traveled up the Tiber River and burned much of Rome to the ground.

If burning the city wasn't harsh enough, thousands of Romans were taken as slaves. Men were taken from their families, and children were ripped away from their parents. Thousands of farms were ruined; fields and businesses were abandoned; and the population dropped from 1,500,000 to 300,000 in just 10 years. To protect themselves from complete destruction, village residents used debris from the cities to build walls around their towns. Italy was in terrible chaos.

You won't believe what was included in some of the looting by the Vandals. It seems they stole from the Romans what the Romans once stole from the Jews! I'm referring to the sacred items from the Temple. You see the Romans had kept some of the treasures from the Temple in Jerusalem when the emperor **Titus** attacked it in A.D. 70. Masses of golden candle-stands, special goblets, precious metals, and remnants of furniture were stored by the Romans for over 300 years until the Vandals swiped it all right out from under them. Kind of interesting, don't you think?

For centuries, the Romans had bullied and brutalized most of Europe into submission and murdered many a saint. **Daniel** of the Old Testament said in his prophecy that the fourth beast, referring to Rome, would be *"exceedingly dreadful"* and *"devour the whole earth, trample it and break it in pieces."* (Dan. 7:19, 23)

Daniel was accurate in his prophecy, but the long reign of Roman terror did end. The very last western Roman leader, a youth named **Romulus Augustus,** was ousted from the throne by **Odoacer,** a German war chief. This happened in 476. It's been called the fall of the Western Roman Empire ever since. And although much of the fall was due to invasion by barbarians, the moral decline of Rome had much to do with it, too. From so many years of bloodshed, the Romans had lost the value of human life. Marriage was no longer sacred and materialism (too much wealth) had spoiled the masses.

Knowing all of this, you may now better understand why the *early* Middle Ages are sometimes called the **Dark Ages.** You see, the fall of the Western Roman Empire ushered in a dark time in the history of Europe. It was dark from the moral decay of Rome and for the lack of progress. The arts completely dwindled as prosperity collapsed. Scholars fled to what remained of the *Eastern* Roman Empire. (It was later called the Byzantine Empire.) People lost interest in education as they fought just to survive. Barbarian raiders destroyed books and schools so that over time, many lost the skill of reading or writing. That included the loss of reading God's Word!

Despite the numerous flaws of the Roman Empire, the Romans contributed many important things to the rest of the world. The Latin language that came from the Romans is the basis of five modern languages and has heavily influenced many others (including English). Engineering and architecture reached new heights under the Romans. This is made clear by the fact that some Roman roads, aqueducts, and bridges are *still* in use. Most importantly, Roman law and government provided a foundation for many governments today, including my own.

In closing, the fall of the Western Roman Empire is important history to know. With moral decay and materialism invading modern nations today, we could make the same mistakes as the Romans! Pray that we learn from history and not neglect its great lessons.

Ancient Roman pillars and frescoes lie abandoned, but not forgotten, in the city of Rome.

ACTIVITIES FOR LESSON 21

ALL STUDENTS

Make your Memory Cards for Lessons 19–21. The fall of the Western Roman Empire (476) is a date to memorize. Mark the card accordingly.

21A—Younger and Middle Students

Play a shopping game to understand "inflation."

Materials: One fresh vegetable, one piece of fruit, a loaf of bread, a pair of blue jeans, one blanket, one bar of soap, a roll of toilet paper, one package of gum or candy, one small toy, one piece of jewelry, 10 dimes (exact change is necessary!)

1. With your teacher, set up a pretend store with the first 10 items listed above. (You may substitute with similar items.)

2. Your teacher will then give you the 10 dimes so you have a dollar's worth of spending money.

3. Pretend to "shop" and buy each item for one dime. Use your full dollar and buy *everything* your first time through.

4. Return your items to the store and the money to your pocket. Shop again, but this time each item you want to buy costs two dimes! You will quickly see that you won't have enough money to buy everything. You'll only be able to afford five things! Decide what you would buy if this were the only money you had for a month.

5. Play "store" again, but this time each item costs you three dimes! Now you can only afford to buy three of the items (with one dime left over). You may only be able to afford food!

6. Play one more time, with each item costing you a dollar! This time you can only afford *one* thing in your store. What would you buy if that were your only money for one month?

The game you just played depicts what happened in Rome when prices were "inflated." When prices for things go up, people cannot afford to buy as much. Discuss with your teacher how a bad economy contributed to the fall of the Roman Empire.

21B—Middle Students

Research the way of life in monasteries during the early Middle Ages. Investigate **St. Benedict of Nursia,** the founder of Benedictine monasticism. St. Benedict lived around 543. He taught that "idleness is the enemy of the soul." Write a short report and file it under "Europe: Italy" in your Student Notebook.

21C—Older Students

1. The fall of the Western Roman Empire occurred when Jerome (the saint who translated the Latin Vulgate) was about 70 years old. He was living in Bethlehem when he heard the news. In the Activity Supplement, read portions of a letter he wrote to a friend in response to the event. How would you expect an older, godly man to respond to the fall of Rome? Would he rejoice or would he weep?

2. Research a man by the name of **Stilicho.** By bloodline, he was half-Roman and half-Vandal. Who do you think he became a general for—the Romans or the Vandals? Write a short report on this fascinating story. File it in your Student Notebook under "Europe: Rome."

TAKE ANOTHER LOOK!

Wall of Fame

1. *St. Patrick of Ireland (c. 389–461)*—On a three-leaf clover, write the three parts of the Trinity: the Father, the Son, and the Holy Spirit. Write Patrick's name beneath. [From *History Through the Ages*, use *Patrick*.]

2. *Attila the Hun (434–453)*—Give him a face with scars. [Use *Attila the Hun*.]

3. *FALL OF THE WESTERN ROMAN EMPIRE (476)* Draw a stick figure of a throne. Write the name of the Western Roman Empire on it. Attach the throne toppled on its side to depict that it "fell." **Remember, this is a date to memorize.** [Use *The Fall of the Western Roman Empire*.]

SomeWHERE in Time

1. Make a puzzle of Great Britain and Ireland. But first, let's start with some definitions.

   • The term "British Isles" is a geographic reference, specifically referring to the United Kingdom, Ireland, and adjacent islands.

   • The island of Ireland is divided between the Republic of Ireland and Northern Ireland (which forms part of the United Kingdom).

   • Great Britain consists of England, Scotland, and Wales.

   • Great Britain PLUS Northern Ireland equals "The United Kingdom of Great Britain and Northern Ireland," often called the United Kingdom or "UK" for short.

   Now, let's get back to that puzzle of Great Britain and Ireland:

   Materials: Outline Map 10, "British Isles"; colored pencils; poster board or light cardboard; glue; scissors; two plastic sandwich bags; permanent marker

   a. Color the map of Great Britain and Ireland these colors:

   England – brown

   Scotland – orange

   Wales – yellow

   Northern Ireland – green

   Republic of Ireland – purple

   b. Glue this colored map onto a piece of poster board or light cardboard.

   c. Cut out each of the above pieces.

   d. Place in one bag the countries of England, Wales, Scotland, and Northern Ireland. Label this bag "United Kingdom."

   e. In the other bag, place the Republic of Ireland. Label it "Ireland."

   f. The two bags will help you remember that Ireland has two parts—one is part of the United Kingdom, the other is an independent republic. Practice putting the pieces together.

2. To see how the Roman Empire of the first century (c. A.D. 98) compares in size to three modern countries, try this simple activity. Using Outline Map 3, "World," the map of the Roman Empire on page 99, and a modern atlas, complete the following steps:

a. On the map of the world, find and sketch the widest boundaries of the Roman Empire in pencil using the map on page 99 as your guide. Label it and color the area purple.

b. Using the atlas, find and sketch the modern boundaries of China. Label the country and color the area red.

c. Label Australia and color it gold.

d. Label the United States and color it blue.

e. At the bottom of the map, make a key ranking each of these places from largest to smallest—but don't trust your eyes! Do a little research to determine the approximate size of each. Answers are provided in the Answer Key.

PUT IT ALL TOGETHER

You have had 21 lessons in the first quarter of this history course. It's time now to "Put It All Together." Using your textbook, Memory Cards, maps, and timeline, go through this worksheet and answer the questions. This is not a test. This is an exercise in reviewing what you've learned. Just like the muscles have to be worked to stay in shape, so our minds have to work to stay in shape too! Allow yourself plenty of time to complete this worksheet.

I—Dates to Memorize

I don't expect you to memorize the date of every lesson we learned, but I do want you to remember 12 dates from this volume. (*Note to Teacher*: This number can be modified for younger students.) Three of those dates are from the first quarter.

For practice, write out the names and dates that I have asked you to memorize four times each on the lines below.

Pentecost   c. A.D. **33**

1. _____

2. _____

3. _____

4. _____

Edict of Milan   **313**

1. _____

2. _____

3. _____

4. _____

1. _____

2. _____

3. _____

4. _____

II—Order of Events. Put the following events from Paul's life in order by placing a number from 1 to 8 to the left of each sentence below.

_____a. Paul is shipwrecked off the coast of Malta.

_____b. Saul meets Jesus on the road to Damascus.

_____c. Paul travels to nine cities with Barnabas.

_____d. Paul is under house arrest in Rome awaiting his trial.

_____e. Saul persecutes members of the Early Church.

_____f. Paul travels to 12 cities with Silas and later Timothy.

_____g. From Antioch, Paul and Barnabas are sent out as missionaries.

_____h. Paul lives a year in Corinth, making and selling tents with Priscilla and Aquila.

III—Matching Romans. Match the following Roman emperors by placing the correct letter next to the number. The lesson number where the answer can be found is in parentheses.

_____1. Nero (4)   a. Persecuted Justin Martyr in the fourth wave of persecution

_____2. Domitian (5)   b. Put Polycarp to death, then made it illegal to persecute Christians

_____3. Trajan (5)   c. Issued the Edict of Milan to end persecution

_____4. Hadrian (5)   d. Spent more time in Greece than in Rome

_____5. Antonius Pius (5)   e. Last Western Roman emperor

_____6. Marcus Aurelius (5)   f. Claimed divine power; exiled John to Patmos

_____7. Valerian (5)   g. Maintained Hadrian's law of mercy

_____8. Diocletian (13)   h. Divided Rome; led last wave of persecution

_____9. Constantine (14)   i. Persecuted Ignatius, Symphorosa, Faustines, and Jovita

_____10.Romulus Augustus (21)   j. Persecuted Cyprian of Carthage in eighth wave

IV—Which Amazing Number? Circle the right number in each sentence to make it correct. Refer back to Lessons 7 to 9 in Week 3 if you need assistance.

1. The fortress of Masada stands (40 or 400) meters above the Dead Sea.

2. Masada was attacked by (200 or 20,000) Roman soldiers.

3. Through the night, (96 or 960) Jews committed suicide at Masada to avoid capture by the Romans.

4. A Bedouin boy discovered the Dead Sea Scrolls in (1947 or 1987).

5. A total of (80 or 800) compositions have been retrieved from the desert spot of Qumran.

6. Anywhere from (200–400 or 2,000–4,000) Essenes made up the commune at Qumran.

7. The city of Pompeii was buried for nearly (500 or 1,500) years.

8. At least (2,000 or 20,000) people died from the eruption of Mt. Vesuvius in A.D.79.

9. The blast of Vesuvius was so strong that a cloud of hot air and gases hung over Pompeii for almost (1 or 11) hours before collapsing through six surges.

V—First or Second? I have listed several facts from the First and Second Jewish Revolts. Circle appropriately, depending on whether the fact is true of the First or the Second Revolt. Answers can be found in Lessons 6 and 10.

1. The Temple was destroyed.

          First   Second

2. A Jewish state was established.

          First   Second

3. Eighty thousand to 580,000 Jews were killed.

          First   Second

4. Temple treasures were stolen and paraded by the Romans.

          First   Second

5. Though doubtful of victory, Josephus was involved in this revolt.

          First   Second

6. Jewish coins were made and stamped on top of Roman ones.

          First   Second

7. The city of Bethar was attacked by the Romans.

          First   Second

8. Bar-Kokhba, the "prince of Israel," was killed.

          First   Second

9. After this revolt, some Jews fled to Masada for refuge.

    First   Second

10. After this revolt, some Jews fled to caves near the Dead Sea.

    First   Second

VI—Scientists and the Stars. Though continents apart, the brilliant scientists of India and of the Mayan culture made two similar breakthroughs, one in math and one in astronomy. Use Lessons 15 and 16 to find and list these two breakthroughs in the overlapping oval labeled "Both" on the next page. Other than that, each group of scientists made its own significant discoveries. Give credit where credit is due by listing them in the proper ovals on the next page. As it will be hard to squeeze in the full phrases, you may abbreviate your list using the words in bold.

▸▸ Diameter of the **moon**

▸▸ Orbit of **Venus**

▸▸ **Revolution** of the Earth

▸▸ Concept of **zero**

▸▸ 12-month **calendar**

▸▸ Use of decimals and **algebra**

▸▸ Days in a **year**

▸▸ **Eclipses**

▸▸ Position of the Earth's **poles**

▸▸ Arrangement of the **stars**

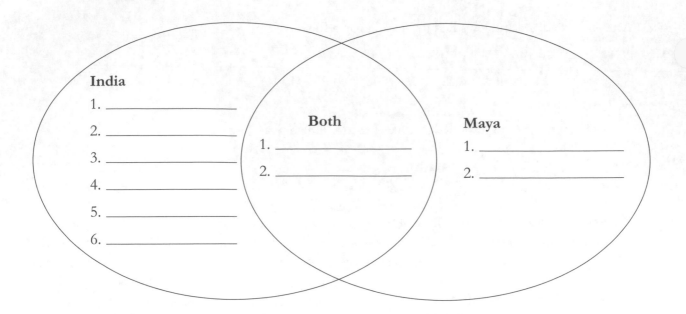

India
1. _____
2. _____
3. _____
4. _____
5. _____
6. _____

Both
1. _____
2. _____

Maya
1. _____
2. _____

VII—Great Writings. Many great writings emerged from this time period. Using colored pencils, connect the following authors to their famous works.

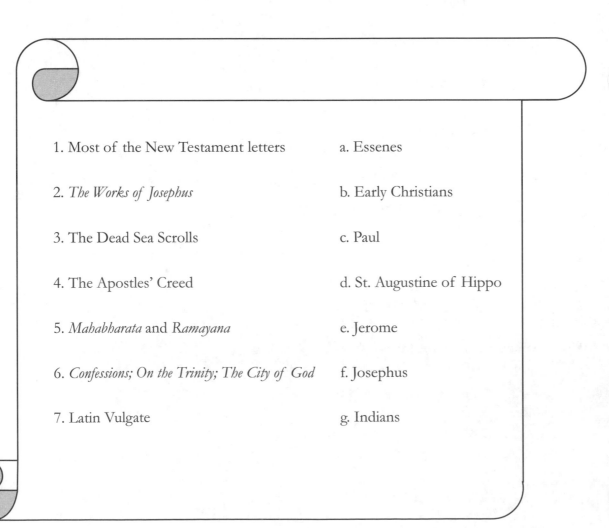

1. Most of the New Testament letters

a. Essenes

2. *The Works of Josephus*

b. Early Christians

3. The Dead Sea Scrolls

c. Paul

4. The Apostles' Creed

d. St. Augustine of Hippo

5. *Mahabharata* and *Ramayana*

e. Jerome

6. *Confessions; On the Trinity; The City of God*

f. Josephus

7. Latin Vulgate

g. Indians

VIII—What a Saint! Use each symbol twice to identify the following statements about the saints.

• St. Patrick – a clover

• St. Valentine – a heart

• St. Augustine – a lightbulb (for being smart)

• St. Jerome – a feather pen

_____1. I lived in Rome and was martyred for my faith.

_____2. As a young teen, I was captured by pirates.

_____3. I lived in a small cell-like cave for 23 years to translate the Bible.

_____4. Though I was not born in Ireland, I started at least 300 churches there.

_____5. I was inspired to read the Bible through the singing of children.

_____6. I died on February 14, and Pope Gelasius made it a holiday.

_____7. I was a poor monk, a priest, and a secretary to a bishop.

_____8. My mother, Monica, was a devout Christian and prayed for my salvation.

IX—Bonus: Why the Fall? Using Lesson 21 as a reference, earn extra points in this bonus section by naming factors that contributed to the fall of the Western Roman Empire. (Inflation is one example.) Receive half a point for every good answer. Write in complete sentences and use a separate sheet of paper if necessary.

THE FIRE SPREADS: C. 500 TO 871

I briefly mentioned in our last "Around the World" summary that the fall of the Western Roman Empire ushered in the *Dark Ages*. That's exactly where this quarter will start—at the beginning of the Dark Ages. So let me first explain that term a little better.

The Dark Ages generally refers to the time period in Europe when life was particularly dark and difficult, from the late 400s to the 1000s. Why was life difficult? Well, the Roman government that *had* been in control there for centuries was now gone. Without a government in place, things were chaotic. Think about it for a minute. What if there were no police, sheriffs, or officials in your town? What if the banks were closed, the markets were shut down, and transportation stopped? What would people do?

Some people would take advantage of the mess. Without laws and governors, some people would steal, kill, and plunder. Others would suffer from the hardships. Without a stable economy (economy is another name for a money system), many people would be poor. When people are poor and struggling to survive, their priorities often change. Even to read and learn would be considered a luxury compared to eating and having shelter. And that's what happened in Europe. People abandoned the arts and higher learning just to survive. It's been called the Dark Ages ever since.

Though inviting from the outside, castles of the Early Middle Ages were usually dark and dreary on the inside.

Some historians would instead call this time period the *Early Middle Ages*. You've probably heard of that before. The term *Middle Ages* makes sense from our perspective as we look at the era as dividing *ancient history* from *modern times*. It's the time in the *middle*, the *Middle* Ages. But remember, to the people living then, it was the present time! So *they* would never have said that they were living in the Middle Ages.

When you and I hear of the Middle Ages, we most often have visions of kings with beautiful queens, knights in shining armor, and adventure in glittering castles. Although that's not the whole picture of the Middle Ages, we are still right to do so. With the collapse of the Roman government, power shifted from the emperors to small kings and their kingdoms. Many of these kingdoms really *were* protected by knights in full body armor as tales and stories would suggest. The word *romance*, which we might picture in this setting of ladies and knights, means a story from the lands once settled by the Romans.

You may also hear this era referred to as the *medieval period*. This term comes from the Latin words *medium aevum*, or "middle era." It is properly pronounced *meed ee EE vuhl* although most people shorten it to *mid EE vil*. No matter what you call it, the entire Middle Ages lasted about 1,000 years, starting with the fall of Rome. As Roman rule faded, the individual countries of Europe began to take shape and small kingdoms emerged.

In Old English, the term knight *means "household retainer," referring to one who protected or retained the home.*

Though built in the 1800s, the Neuschwanstein Castle in Germany was designed to mimic the majestic style of medieval times.

But this book isn't just about Europe. And certainly not all of life was *dark* and difficult during the Dark Ages. In fact, in some parts of the world, the opposite was true! Take the *Byzantine Empire*, for example. The Byzantine is another name for the *Eastern* Roman Empire. Unlike the West, the Byzantine was booming. Many of the great scholars of the West found great wealth and opportunity there. Naturally they moved, making the Byzantine even stronger.

And then there was *Japan*. This small chain of islands became much stronger in the Early Middle Ages under the leadership of *Prince Shotoku*. He is considered the "founder of Japanese civilization." Next door to Japan, *China* was growing even stronger. In fact, it was during the Dark Ages of Europe that China was in its golden age! Unlike the Europeans who were struggling to survive, a great number of Chinese were enjoying all kinds of luxuries and spectacular celebrations through the invention of fireworks.

And though they didn't have fireworks, the people in southern Spain were enjoying a great deal of luxury and celebration, too. Under the leadership of the Umayyad family (an Arabic people), southern Spain was nicknamed "the ornament of the world." It was so called for its unbelievable splendor, wealth, and high society. Unlike Europe in the Dark Ages, southern Spain had palaces made of gold, enormous libraries, exotic zoos, and well-paved streets. This magnificent center of culture was named *al-Andalus* by the Arabs. It was named *Sefarad* by the Jews. The Christians called it the home of the *Moors*. The amazing thing about the region, whatever it was called, was that Christians, Jews, and Arab *Muslims* lived there together, worked there together, and learned there together—in some form of harmony.

Who are the *Muslims*? That is a topic we will discuss in great length in this quarter as we learn of the life of *Mohammed*. He was an Arabian. Through what *he* believed were divine revelations, he started an entirely new religion called Islam. Followers of this religion are known as Muslims. I feel it will be of great value for us to try to understand the roots of this religion because Islam remains an active faith today. And unfortunately, it is a faith in great conflict with both Jewish and Christian doctrine. This conflict has been the source of numerous crusades, wars, and acts of terrorism.

On the positive side, I've named this quarter "The Fire Spreads" because it was also during this time that the Gospel of Christ was spreading through the power of the

This stained-glass window of a mosque reflects the geometric design found in most Islamic art.

Holy Spirit. Through missionaries like *Columba*, *Boniface*, *Methodius*, and *Cyril*, more people were hearing of Christ in Europe. In fact, by the year 500, about one-quarter of the world had become Christian and more than 40 percent had heard the Gospel.[1] It was a good thing, too, because some parts of Europe were being ravaged by the *Vikings*. You have probably heard of them. Though fascinating, the Vikings of Scandinavia were so ruthless and so cruel that many Europeans felt the need to turn to God for protection and comfort.

Keep in mind, however, that Christianity was not the only religion to spread in the Early Middle Ages. In 550, *Buddhism* spread from China to Japan, Burma, Thailand, Cambodia, and Korea. In 624 Buddhism was declared the official religion of China. And after Mohammed died, Islam spread to all corners of the Arabic world.

Large images of Buddha are popular in many parts of the world where Buddhism is still practiced today.

I believe the spread of religion is a reminder to us that people are hungry for the knowledge of God. How much more exciting is it to know that one *can* have knowledge of God through Jesus Christ. I hope it motivates you to keep learning and to share Jesus, the Mystery of History!

1. Mark A. Beliles and Stephen K. McDowell, *America's Providential History*. Charlottesville, VA: The Providence Foundation, 1989; p. 37.

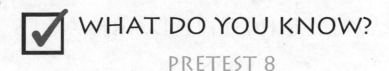

☑ WHAT DO YOU KNOW?

PRETEST 8

Who/What Am I? Choose the best answer from the list below.

1. I was the lowest rank of the peasants in the Dark Ages of Europe. Who am I?

2. During the Dark Ages, I was the man in town responsible for "bloodletting." Who am I?

3. According to legend, Arthur became king when he drew me out of a stone. What am I?

4. According to Joseph of Arimathea, I was used to collect some of the blood of Christ. What am I?

5. I was the unfaithful queen of King Arthur. Who am I?

6. Though I grew up a peasant, I became the king of the Byzantine Empire. Who am I?

7. I grew up in the circus and became a queen. Who am I?

8. I was built to be more magnificent than the Temple of Solomon. What am I?

WORD BANK			
Theodora	Holy Grail	barber	Guinevere
Justinian	a sword	serf	cathedral of Saint Sophia

DAILY LIFE IN THE DARK AGES
LESSON 22

As you may have noticed by now, I like to teach history through the lives of famous people. But sometimes it's interesting to take a look at *ordinary* people and *ordinary* lives. Though their names may never be written down in a history book, these people are part of history, too. Today we will focus on what common life was like in the **Dark Ages** of Europe—sometimes called the **Early Middle Ages** and encompassing approximately the years **500–1000.** Whatever you call the time period, it certainly wasn't an easy time to live.

Homes

Ordinary homes were nothing like the lofty, beautiful castles that we associate with the Middle Ages. Nor were they very comfortable. Ordinary homes were dark, damp, drafty, and made of wood. House fires broke out easily from these conditions because a fire was almost always lit for cooking, heating, and keeping flies away. Furniture was made of hard wood, mattresses were of prickly straw, and blankets were made of scratchy wool. And to make matters worse, most homes were used for stables, too, or had stables attached nearby. That means the smell was awful! Cows, sheep, chickens, and even rats—everyone shared the same roof if you didn't have much money!

Toilets were practically unheard of in poorer homes. People used buckets to collect their waste or just relieved themselves outdoors. Some nicer homes had restrooms in which the toilet was a seat built over a hole that allowed waste to fall below into another room. Though using a restroom like that was a little more convenient than going outdoors, the lower room had to be shoveled out regularly—a most unpleasant chore!

Food

The diet of an average person in the Dark Ages was rather bland and boring. A family would eat the same kinds of foods over and over. Bread was the main staple served morning, noon, and night. Bread was so important that if a baker sold moldy bread or if it weighed less than advertised, the baker was dragged through the city streets as punishment for his crime. Villagers would shout and throw things at him!

Dinner might have been a soupy stew made with beans, vegetables, and bones. It was seasoned with garlic, peppers, and herbs. Wealthier people had meat, cheese, and eggs from time to time, but these were scarce for the common man. For drinking, milk and cold water were not very safe. It was better for people to drink a weak type of ale or beer. The ale contained alcohol that prevented the growth of germs.

For special occasions, pies were very popular. The most creative kind was cleverly baked with live birds in it. When served,

As in the Dark Ages, fresh bread from a bakery is very important to Europeans.

the birds would fly away unharmed. It is probably from this unusual custom that we have the nursery song "four-and-twenty blackbirds baked in a pie . . ."

Schools

The opportunity to receive an education in Europe depended greatly on what kind of family you were born into and whether you were a girl or a boy. Girls from poor families would learn the skills of farming, cooking, storing food, and cleaning. They would learn most of this at home from their parents, especially from their mothers.

Girls from wealthy homes would learn skills for taking care of a large household. This might include having a tutor to teach them math calculations and reading so they could help buy things for a large estate. They would also be trained in entertaining, dancing, singing, and sewing. Some wealthy girls were fortunate enough to learn to ride horses just for fun.

Peasant boys learned how to farm, as well as how to fight, from their dads, uncles, or brothers. For the poor, formal school in a classroom was rare. Merchants' sons, however, might attend school in a village to learn reading and math for running a small business. Noblemen's sons would probably receive better schooling through private tutors at home. (It was probably a form of "homeschooling"!)

Work

About 80 percent of the population in Europe during the Dark Ages consisted of poor peasant farmers. The **serfs** were the lowest of these peasants. They were practically slaves in that they worked long, hard hours for a lord, a duke, or a count without receiving any pay at all! However, they did receive food, clothing, a house, and protection in exchange for their labor. If they were able to escape from their lord for a year and one day, they were considered free! Of course, escape was not an easy thing to do in a small community. Practically everyone knew everyone else, making it difficult to get away.

Just above the serfs were the **villeins.** They were freer than the serfs and controlled a small plot of land to farm. But they didn't own it. Villeins were expected to pay their landowners with food they grew themselves or animals they raised. It was terribly difficult to ever rise out of being a poor farmer. In fact, today's term *villain*, which means a scoundrel or person of poor manners, stems from this unfortunate class of people who were not widely respected.

Some commoners who populated the towns were a bit more fortunate. Rather than toiling endless hours in the fields, they became **merchants** or **craftsmen.** It was common in the towns for a merchant to rent a two-story dwelling from the nearest lord. The merchant and his family could live upstairs and work downstairs. (These cozy shops and homes are still a common sight in Europe today.) Since most people couldn't read or write, the merchant would hang a picture sign over the door of his shop to lure customers in. Walking through the town one might see a picture sign of bread for the baker, shoes for the cobbler, a coat for the tailor, and more.

As towns grew, so did the number of merchants and craftsmen. To protect themselves from being taken advantage of, these townspeople created **guilds.** A guild was a group of people who practiced the same trade—like that of being a silversmith, for example. But to become a part of a guild was a long ordeal. At about 7 years of age, a boy was trained as an **apprentice** to a **master** merchant or craftsman. An apprentice wasn't paid for his work but was given food and lodging. If the apprentice was good and learned his skill well, he could be promoted to a **journeyman.** Fortunately, a journeyman was paid for his work! If approved by the guild, a journeyman could eventually open his own shop to sell his goods. If he was especially successful, he could then become a master of his trade. And the cycle went on and on. Though conditions were often difficult, this system provided incentive for people to work hard and take pride in their goods and crafts.

Healthcare was definitely questionable during the Dark Ages in Europe. Doctors had some unusual ideas for making people well. It was believed at one time that a doctor could drill holes into someone's head to help relieve the symptoms of mental illness! And procedures like that were often done without any anesthetics (the special chemicals that keep us from feeling pain during surgery). How awful!

It was also believed that if a doctor could remove "bad" blood from a patient, he could heal them of disease. Doctors would use leeches, a blood-sucking worm, to literally suck blood from patients. Or, the doctor would make cuts on the patient (called "bloodletting") to drain them of "bad" blood.

Modern barbershops still bear the red, white, and sometimes blue striped emblem of the barber pole that originated in the Middle Ages.

It may be of interest to know that barbers, men who cut hair, were also used in the business of bloodletting—probably because they owned instruments sharp enough for cutting. In fact, the traditional barber pole, a white pole with red stripes around it (and sometimes blue), was designed as a symbol of bloodletting. The white stripe was symbolic of bandages and the red stripe, of blood.

As you can tell, some medical practices of the Early Middle Age were brutal. But, on the positive side, there was also a wide use of herbs and other natural remedies to help the sick.

Church

Last, I think you should know just how important the church became to the everyday life of those living in the Dark Ages. The Medieval Church became the foundation of civilization in mainland Europe![1] The lives of both the rich and the poor were touched by it. The church was responsible for teaching faith, baptizing children, performing weddings, and burying the dead.

As we learned in the last quarter, the church had once been *persecuted* in Europe under the Roman Empire. Under persecution, Christians met secretly in homes to worship. But after Constantine I granted Christians the freedom to worship in public, they began to build churches as places to worship. By the fifth century, one could find a small **parish church** in nearly every medieval village in Europe. Most started as extensions of private homes and then grew. The first church buildings were patterned after a Roman structure called a **basilica.** These long rectangular buildings with high-domed ceilings were once used as Roman courtrooms or meeting halls. They were perfect for the gathering and worship of small congregations.

The **parish priest** lived near the church in a home only a little better than the cottage of a serf. As the only priest in the village, he was expected to do far more than preach on Sundays. The parish priest kept an eye on everyone's moral behavior, took care of the sick, and even arranged town

Small stone churches like this one adorn the countryside of Germany.

---

1. *Mainland Europe* refers here to regions of Europe not including England. At this time in history, the churches in England were operating individually under the Celts. They were not centralized like the churches of Europe until the late 500s.

games. Though some priests slipped into bad behavior themselves, most were well loved and respected by their townspeople for their devoted service.

Above the parish priest was the **bishop.** A bishop usually lived in a larger town and managed a **diocese,** which consisted of several small nearby parishes. As a landowner under the nearest lord or duke, a bishop had a lot of authority in his community. He took on what used to be the role of a Roman governor. So, besides overseeing the business of his church and surrounding parishes, the bishop was busy with civil matters. He helped settle court cases between neighbors and bickering husbands and wives, as well as give direction in military affairs. Unlike the parish priests, the bishop lived in nice quarters. And his church building was more like a small cathedral.

On the next level of the church, the **archbishop** ruled over a group of bishops in what was called a **province.** The archbishop lived in the big city, so to speak, and carried a great amount of authority—both in the church and in the community. And with his high position came even more spectacular cathedrals to oversee. In time, these cathedrals grew to be great works of **Gothic architecture,** like Notre Dame in France for example. These massive Gothic cathedrals are an incredible testimony to the genius of mankind.

In the fifth century, **Emperor Valentinian III** decided that all the archbishops should be in obedience to one head bishop. And since Rome was still the largest city in Europe, the bishop of Rome naturally became the one to take that position. (Besides that, Peter, who *some* would consider the first bishop,

The famous Cathedral of Notre Dame in Paris, France, was started in 1163. It is one of the greatest examples of early Gothic architecture ever built.

was martyred in Rome after serving in Jerusalem and Antioch.) From that point on, the bishop of Rome was called the **pope.** It means "papa." The pope obtained a great amount of authority in the Middle Ages and grew to have the most extravagant cathedral in Europe. We will talk more about the pope in lessons to come. You will learn that, over time, there was disagreement about this structure of the church. Many Christians disagreed about the role of the pope as well as about many other things.

In closing, I remind you that far more important than the *structure* of the church in the Dark Ages was the *purpose* of it. According to the Bible, it is the Lord's plan that "*the manifold wisdom of God might be made known by the church.*" (Eph. 3:10) So, though daily life in the Dark Ages was dark and sometimes difficult, there was light and hope for those who followed the wisdom of God.

St. Peter's Church, located in Vatican City within Rome, is the largest church in the world and the home church of the pope today.

ACTIVITIES FOR LESSON 22

ALL STUDENTS

1. Experience a bland peasant diet. For dinner, eat only vegetable stew and bread for three nights in a row! How did it make you feel? Consider the luxury you have today of experiencing a variety of foods in your diet.

2. If you are part of a co-op or larger class, consider hosting a Merchant/Craftsman Trade and Barter Day. Suggestions for such an event are located in the Activity Supplement in the Appendix. It will require extensive preparation but can be a lot of fun as well as educational.

22A—Younger Students

Make a barber pole.

Materials: An empty paper-towel roll, a plain sheet of paper, red marker or wide red tape, clear tape

Tape a blank piece of white paper onto an empty paper-towel roll. Try to keep it smooth. Using a red marker, draw a wide line all the way down and around the tube like a candy cane. (It might be easiest if the teacher sketches the place to color with a pencil first.) Or, adhere a piece of wide red tape down and around the pole instead. When the tube is complete, tape it vertically to a wall the way a barber's pole would hang. Use it when you play doctor!

22B—Middle Students

A variety of things were used in medieval days for keeping time. For example, sundials, hourglasses, bell towers, and candles were all used to track time. Following the directions given below, make your own "hour" candle.

Materials: Tape measure or ruler, a slender 8- or 9-inch candle (approximately ½ inch in diameter), candleholder, matches, timer, pencil

Adult Supervision Needed

1. Using a tape measure or ruler, measure the exact length of your candle. Write down this measurement (Measurement A).

2. Place the candle in a sturdy candleholder.

3. Light the candle (**with an adult**) and write down the time on the clock. Set a timer for exactly one hour.

4. When one hour has passed, blow out the candle. When the wick has cooled, again measure the length of your candle. Write down this figure (Measurement B).

5. Subtract the second measurement from the first measurement (A minus B). This will tell you how much your candle burned down in exactly one hour. We'll call the difference "Measurement C."

6. With this completed, now take the figure that you calculated (C) and use it to mark off your candle in hours. For example, if you calculated that your candle burned down 1 inch in an hour, then you are going to take your candle, lay it next to a ruler, and make a mark with a pencil for every inch left on your candle. You now have an "hour" candle that will tell the time for you as it burns. **As always when working with candles, do it with adult supervision.**

7. How many hours will your candle burn? Can you think of pros and cons to counting hours this way?

Take a picture of your hour candle and file it in your Student Notebook under "Miscellaneous."

22C—Older Students

1. BOYS: Young merchants in the Middle Ages were expected to learn business skills at home or school. Do you know how to balance a checkbook or savings account? Practice this important skill.

2. GIRLS: Young girls of the nobility were expected to know how to entertain guests. Obtain an etiquette book and look up the section on proper table settings. Practice on your own family for dinner one night this week. Take a photo of your place setting and file it in your Student Notebook under "Miscellaneous."

3. Using a Bible concordance, look up the term *church*. Evaluate its many meanings: It can refer to God's redeemed people as a whole as well as to a particular group of believers in a specific location. Find examples in your Bible.

503

KING ARTHUR AND THE KNIGHTS OF THE ROUND TABLE
LESSON 23

Have you ever wished you could go back in time? I have. And if I did, I'd want to go back to the enchanting castle of **Camelot,** the legendary home of **King Arthur and the Knights of the Round Table.** Adventure, romance, drama, and mystery! It's all there in the tales of King Arthur. However, historians are perplexed about King Arthur. Some say he was only a magical myth—a figment of literary imagination. Others say he had to be real because so much legend exists around his name and the adventures of his knights. Real or not, the stories of King Arthur and the Knights of the Round Table give us a great glimpse of life in the Early Middle Ages.

In order to understand who King Arthur might have been, I need to take you back to early **England.** A long, long time ago, about 600 years before Christ, there was a group of people called the **Celts** (keltz). They lived in Europe and were known for being artistic, brave, and good ironmakers. As they scattered across Europe, some crossed the sea to settle the rock-edged island of England. The Celts never had their own written language, so not much is known of their early history.

About 550 years later, just 50 years before Christ was born, the Romans invaded England under **Julius Caesar.** When the Romans met the Celts in England, they called them "Brythons," meaning, "tattooed men." Apparently the Celts were fond of tattoos. It is from this Roman term that **Britain** later got its name.

Arthur became a legendary hero in England for his fight against the Saxons and the magical tales that surrounded his court.

The **Romans** remained a major ruling power over England for about 300 years. That's a long time! In this time the Romans lived mostly in peace among the Celts and contributed a lot to their way of life. The Romans built great roads, bathhouses, and homes with central heating and glass windows. In the second century, one Roman emperor by the name of **Hadrian** went so far as to build a great wall in northern England to protect it from the Scottish. In a way, the Romans seemed to "guard" the native Celts and actually help them to flourish.

Roman Emperor Hadrian built "Hadrian's Wall" across Britain to protect it from Scottish tribes in the north.

But as you know from our last lesson, the Western Roman Empire began to collapse in the late 400s. When this happened, it caused real problems for the Celts. As Romans fled the country, other tribes invaded and the Celts had no way of protecting themselves. In particular, it was the **Angles,** the **Saxons,** and the **Jutes** that invaded England from other parts of Europe. I mentioned these groups to you in a past lesson about the fall of the Roman Empire. The Saxons were particularly brutal in their takeover of the island. They once killed 1,200 Celtic pastors who were meeting for prayer!

Arthur, the Celtic King

This finally brings us to **King Arthur.** Most historians believe he was a **Celtic king** or war chief who lived in England just about the time that the Romans left and the Saxons invaded. Now think about that for a minute. With the great power of Rome leaving and the ruthless Saxons invading, this could have been a difficult time to be a king. But not so for Arthur! Like a storybook coming to life, he rose to defend his beloved homeland. At least, that's what many believe. In doing so, he became a legend. It is no wonder that many fabulous tales exist about him in English literature.

So what exactly are the great tales surrounding King Arthur? I will try to summarize them in case you've never read them (but I hope someday you do). First, according to legend, Arthur is said to have become a king in a most unusual way. A story circulated that no one could remove a certain "sword in the stone" except the man who would be the next king of England. Many men of great strength had tried and failed.

As the legend goes, one day Arthur—who was just a teen at the time—passed by the sword in the stone. As a young squire, he was supposed to be going home to fetch a sword for a knight. But rather than run all the way home, he decided to save himself the trip and grab the one he saw. With just a tug or two, the sword gave way and glistened in his hands! He hardly knew what to think. Arthur was immediately surrounded by the townspeople and declared the king. "Long live the king!" the crowd chanted. And so Arthur became the greatest, most courageous, most noble king that England ever had! (According to legend, of course. An image of a sword in a stone had been a long-time icon for the Roman cavalry, which probably had something to do with the story!)

In becoming king, Arthur had much to learn. Most of his wisdom he attributed to a magician named **Merlin,** who was his childhood teacher. In story form, Merlin was said to be a magical wizard who could change people into animals. Though that part of the

This unusual medieval castle in Italy is "round" like King Arthur's table!

story is pure fiction, it stirs the imagination. Like a wise teacher or a mentor, Merlin supposedly guided Arthur through all his years as king.

According to numerous tales, one of the wisest things Merlin ever did was to help Arthur make what is called the **Round Table.** It was exactly what its name implied—a huge table that was completely round. Why? Because it gave the knights of the castle a place to sit without arguing over who would be seated next to the king! It was this type of diplomacy or fairness that made Arthur so famous. In all the stories that surround him, he was just, brave, wise, and extremely loyal to his knights.

So what do kings and knights do to keep a kingdom? Mainly, they fight to protect it. Some of the fights were against "dragons," according to countless tales of Arthur. I speculate that some of these tales may be true if smaller species of dinosaurs were still troubling the region! Others would suggest that "dragons" were symbolic of people who were enemies. Either way, most of the fighting would certainly have been against the invading Saxons. Arthur supposedly fought 12 battles against the Saxons, the last one being the **Battle of Mount Badon** in **503.** He was almost always victorious. It is from these victories that there exists some evidence of a true war hero named Arthur, the **Dux Bellorum,** which means "Lord of the Battles." Many believe that this Arthur, though never a king, was the sole inspiration for all the folklore that followed.

One writer claims that Arthur single-handedly fought 900 of his enemies at one time. He was known for wearing a gold-crested helmet shaped like a dragon and leading his army on a white horse. Arthur's inspiration was said to be from an image of the Virgin Mary etched on his armor. Religious zeal was common among the knights. Though not all were genuine believers, they swore an oath to uphold Christ and keep down the heathen.

Though we think of all knights as wearing full armor, it was not until the late 1400s that plate armor completely covered a knight's body for protection.

The Holy Grail

Because of their zeal, one of the more interesting pursuits of the knights was their "quest to find the **Holy Grail.**" Let me explain. In Matthew 27:58–60, the Bible says that **Joseph of Arimathea** asked Pilate for Jesus' body and that he placed it in his own tomb for burial. According to the Bible, this is a fact. But tradition adds that Joseph of Arimathea somehow acquired the cup that **Jesus** used at the Last Supper with his disciples. With that cup, Joseph is said to have collected some of Jesus' blood while He hung on the cross. No one knows for sure if there is any truth in this tradition. It is true, however, that Joseph later traveled to England. And if he had the holy cup, he probably took it with him. It was believed that the cup of Jesus' blood had healing powers. Thus it was called the "Holy" Grail. (Grail is an old English term for cup.)

As a believer and an eyewitness to the life of Christ, Joseph of Arimathea naturally shared the Gospel with the people he found in England. A church was started there as a result. Now, whether or not Joseph had the special cup that Jesus drank from is speculation. If he did, the Holy Grail managed to disappear for hundreds of years!

However, according to legend, there was a nun who believed she received a vision of the Holy Grail. She shared this vision with the knights of King Arthur's Round Table. Believing the Holy Grail held special powers, the knights made it their mission to find it. This started what became known as "the quest for the Holy Grail."[2] Supposedly, whoever found it would receive eternal life! Interestingly, the Irish legend of Dagda has a similar storyline.

I hope you understand the difference between the story of the quest for the Holy Grail and the real blood that Jesus shed on the cross for our sins. These aren't the same things. Though many of the knights were Christians, they set their sights on the wrong thing for eternal life. Finding a sacred cup or Holy Grail is not a means for getting into heaven. The Bible says, *"If you confess with your mouth the Lord Jesus and believe in your heart that God has raised Him from the dead, you will be saved."* (Rom. 10:9) Faith in Christ is our means for salvation.

Nonetheless, countless stories, dramas, songs, and poems have been dedicated to the search for the Holy Grail. In literature, three of Arthur's knights—**Sir Galahad, Sir Percivale,** and **Sir Bors**—supposedly find the Holy Grail! But it seems to just be a story.

Guinevere and Lancelot

The other stories of Arthur involve more personal tragedies in his life. His beautiful wife, **Queen Guinevere,** fell in love with one of his best knights, **Sir Lancelot.** Though both Guinevere and Lancelot loved Arthur, they sinfully loved one another, too. When caught betraying the king, Guinevere was sentenced to burn at the stake! But as only a knight in shining armor could do, Lancelot rescued the queen from her fiery execution.

In the end, Guinevere and Lancelot repented of their immorality, and the remorseful queen left Lancelot to live among the nuns. Despite their repentance, there were steep consequences for the couple's sinful actions. The knights wanted war against Lancelot, thus shattering Arthur's dreams for a peaceful kingdom. He had worked so hard to "civilize" his men through a fair legal system. He never wanted them to shed blood out of revenge. Now, the ever loyal and just King Arthur was left torn between love for his queen and love for his kingdom. He couldn't have them both. Many tearful plays and movies have been made about this dramatic story.

The chapel of a medieval castle would contain stained-glass windows wide enough to let light in but narrow enough to keep enemies out.

To add to Arthur's broken heart, his only son **Mordred** tried to take over his kingdom. Arthur was forced to fight against his son—and in the end, Mordred was killed in battle. Arthur was supposedly wounded and carried away to the **Isle of Avalon** for healing. Myths say that he never died and will return one day to rule over England again. (Of course, that is just a myth.)

As you can imagine, it's difficult at times to discern between fact and fiction in fanciful stories like these. As time goes by, it is as if Arthur is recreated and stories of him retold to fit the timeless need we have for a hero. But with such devotion to Arthur, many of the legends of him are exaggerated, if real at all. Who knows for sure the origin and reality of the tales of Merlin, dragons, the Holy Grail, or the round table? But more than likely, there was a real Celtic war chief named Arthur who successfully fought against invading Saxon tribes. And I suspect he was a noble character. That seems to be what Arthur is *most* noted for, and that to me is a legend worth remembering!

---

2. David Day, *King Arthur.* New York: Barnes & Noble Books, 1999; p. 127.

ACTIVITIES FOR LESSON 23

23A—Younger Students

1. Dress in "shining armor" for lunch or dinner at a Round Table. To create armor, I suggest wrapping sheets of foil over your clothing on your arms, legs, and torso. Secure with rubber bands, string, or silver duct tape. A bike or football helmet may serve as a headpiece. Use tape to decorate the helmet with streamers "sprouting" from the top. Take a photo and file it under "Europe: England" in your Student Notebook.

2. Have your teacher hide a cup or goblet in your house. Go on a "quest" to find it!

3. Research the look of an English castle from the Early Middle Ages. Obtain black-and-white pictures of real castles from the Internet or photocopy them from your favorite picture book. Color your pictures. Place them in your Student Notebook under "Europe: England."

4. Listen to Celtic music. One suggestion would be music by Christian artists using Celtic tones (e.g., Michael Card, Ceili Rain).

23B—Middle and Older Students

1. There is so much great literature about King Arthur and the Knights of the Round Table. Read any of the modern translations from the library to learn of the tales of Sir Lancelot, Sir Percivale, and Sir Gawain. Most stories are based on *Le Morte D'Arthur,* compiled by Sir Thomas Malory.

2. Research the steps to becoming a knight. On a sheet of paper folded twice (vertically or horizontally), create space for writing three paragraphs. Write one paragraph on the duties of a **page,** one on the duties of a **squire,** and one on becoming a **knight.** Mount your paper on three-ring paper to insert it into your Student Notebook under "Europe: England."

3. Research another great Celtic king named **Vercingetorix.** In 52 B.C. he fought the Romans but was forced to surrender!

23C—Older Students

1. Choose to read at least one of the following pieces of literature, if not several.

   a. Read *The Seafarer,* an Anglo-Saxon poem describing the life of the men who sailed the seas to invade England.

   b. Read Alfred, Lord Tennyson's "Holy Grail," a poem in *Idylls of the King.*

   c. Read Tennyson's "The Lady of Shalott," based on the tale of Lady Astolat who loved Lancelot but could not win his affection. She died of a broken heart.

   d. Read *A Connecticut Yankee in King Arthur's Court,* a novel by Mark Twain.

2. With parental permission, view the 1967 musical *Camelot* (rated G), starring Richard Harris as King Arthur. Though the movie appears to glamorize the unfaithfulness of Guinevere and Lancelot, it concludes with the devastation brought by immorality. An all-time personal favorite!

JUSTINIAN I AND THEODORA, RULERS OF THE BYZANTINE EMPIRE

LESSON 24

Before I can tell you about an interesting couple that ruled the Byzantine Empire, you must first know what the **Byzantine** was. The name is a little confusing, so we'll start there.

The Byzantine Empire was the name given to the ***Eastern* Roman Empire.** Now you may be wondering where the Eastern Roman Empire came from since we recently studied the fall of the *Western* Roman Empire. Well, as you may recall, the Roman Empire was first divided into the east and the west under **Diocletian** in A.D. 284 (Lesson 13). Then it was put back together as *one* empire under **Constantine the Great** in 324 (Lesson 14). Constantine is the one who moved the capital of Rome to the ancient city of **Byzantium** and renamed it **Constantinople.**

Well after Constantine died, the Roman Empire split *again* in 395. This time, the Eastern Roman Empire acquired the name of the "Byzantine Empire" because of the ancient city of Byzantium. So there—that explains the name given to the Byzantine Empire. Did you follow all of that? I hope so. Of course the Western Roman Empire did collapse in 476 from all kinds of problems and invasions. But, there were thousands of Romans who remained in the Eastern Roman Empire, or the Byzantine. Unlike the Western Roman Empire, the Byzantine was strong and healthy, and it remained so for centuries to come.

Now, with that bit of geography behind us, let's look at **Justinian I** and **Theodora.** These are the names of a Byzantine king and queen who ruled the empire for almost 40 years, from **527–565.** Because of their backgrounds, both were fortunate to *ever* have become royalty.

Justinian I

Justinian was born of a peasant family with hardly a thought for one day becoming a king. But Justinian's uncle happened to be one of the Western Roman Emperors before that empire collapsed.

He had no sons to replace him. So, as a youth, Justinian was taken to the emperor's court to be trained as a ruler. With Rome falling apart, Justinian's future was uncertain. But the way things worked out, he was moved east and declared Emperor of the *Eastern* Roman Empire, or the Byzantine.

When it came to learning, Justinian was a very disciplined young man. He loved to study. Without eating or sleeping, Justinian would sometimes read for hours into the night and still rise early to conduct

Justinian I and his wife, Theodora, were two of the most prestigious of all Byzantine rulers for contributing strong laws and great luxury to the empire.

business. His interests were in law, poetry, architecture, theology, philosophy, and music—all great things for a king to know.

Justinian was even disciplined in what he ate. Unlike most kings, who could indulge on almost anything they wanted, Justinian's diet was mainly that of a vegetarian. He also fasted for periods of time throughout his life. That means he would choose not to eat at all in order to dedicate himself to prayer and meditation.

Though Justinian was certainly to be admired for his self-discipline, not everyone respected him as a king. His critics accused him of being "wishy-washy" on political matters. That means he would sometimes say one thing but do another. And he seldom if ever went to the battlefield, which made him appear weak and cowardly.

Theodora

This modern-day bear trainer in the famous Russian Circus reminds us that some things haven't changed much from the Middle Ages.

Probably one of Justinian's greatest strengths turned out to be his wife, Theodora. She was a good queen and very involved in the running of the empire. It is amazing though that she ever became a queen. Theodora was born on the island of **Cyprus** as the daughter of a bear trainer in a circus. After years of unsettled circus life, she went into acting. Unfortunately, she also led a rather lewd and immoral life as a young woman. Though she wasn't married, Theodora gave birth to a child. In time, however, Theodora settled down. She made a meager but respectable living spinning wool in the city of Constantinople.

As fate would have it, Justinian somehow met the poor, hardworking Theodora. Though she was an unlikely candidate for queen, he fell in love with her. Like a fairy tale come true, there is no doubt that Theodora's beauty and charm changed the course of her life. The historian **Procopius** said this of Theodora when describing a statue of her, "It is beautiful, but still inferior to the beauty of the Empress; for to express her loveliness in words, or to portray it as a statue, would be altogether impossible for a mere human being."[3] I think you might get the picture. Theodora must have been gorgeous, which helped her to catch the eye of the king. The story is a bit like that of Cinderella.

The Nika Riot

Theodora was not only a beauty—she was apparently brave and smart as well. Early in Justinian's reign, a riot broke out in Constantinople in 532. Theodora helped to settle it. It seems there was fighting in the streets between the "Blues" and the "Greens." Those were the names of groups that developed from people dressing in the color of their favorite jockeys. (Jockeys were horse racers, and yes, there were riots over sporting events even way back then!)

The rioting got so bad that fires broke out; a famous church named **Saint Sophia** was destroyed; and the emperor's palace was attacked! People ran through the streets yelling "Nika!" which meant "Victory!" So the incident has been remembered as the **Nika riot.**

Well, it was in Justinian's feeble character to hide in the palace and try to escape the rioting crowds. Remember that he wasn't the kind of king that spent time on the battlefield. It was the more courageous

---

3. Will Durant, *The Age of Faith.* Vol. IV of *The Story of Civilization.* New York: Simon and Schuster, 1950; p. 106.

Theodora who persuaded Justinian to remain in Constantinople and take control of the situation. Justinian listened to her advice and put his best general, **Belisarius,** on the job. To gain back the city, Belisarius had 30,000 people killed in a public arena! It was a terrible massacre that ended the rioting.

With the Nika riot behind them, Justinian and Theodora proceeded to rule the Byzantine Empire with great confidence. They started with repairing buildings damaged from the riots. Justinian poured himself into making Constantinople one of the most spectacular cities in the world.

Of most significance, Justinian claimed that he would rebuild the cathedral of Saint Sophia to be even more glorious than Solomon's Temple. He just about did it, too! Saint Sophia is one of the greatest works of **Byzantine architecture** ever constructed. With walls of marble, numerous mosaics, and precious stones placed in the decor, the cathedral rises toward the sky in the shape of a cross. It is covered by huge, majestic domes measuring 185 feet high and 100 feet in diameter! When the cathedral was completed on December 26, 587, Justinian walked to the pulpit of the magnificent structure and said, "Glory be to God who has thought me worthy to accomplish so great a work! O Solomon! I have vanquished you!"[4] Though full of pride, he knew he had done a great thing.

Both Justinian and Theodora loved the wealth and splendor of being king and queen—maybe because they grew up with so little. They were well known for dressing extravagantly with pearls, jewels, crowns, and robes. Justinian enjoyed the ceremony of entering and exiting events with a great show. He went so far as to require his guests to kiss the hem of his long purple robe or to kiss his toes!

From the influence of Justinian and Theodora, Byzantine architecture is still prevalent in Eastern Europe.

The Justinian Code

Despite being showy, Justinian proved to be a capable leader. He is best remembered for updating a code of laws. These laws bear his name and are called the **Justinian Code.** They were basically an updated version of earlier Roman laws. Some of the laws were good ones that helped people, such as slaves and women, to have better legal rights. Theodora had a lot to do with the recognition and education of women. Many of the laws reflected Justinian's own belief in Christianity. For example, it became law that judges were to swear an oath of honesty on a Bible before every trial. We see a similar procedure in courtrooms today.

However, the penalties for breaking some of the laws were harsh and over time were ignored for being extreme. For example, adultery was punishable by death, as was homosexuality, sorcery, and desertion from the army. A particularly cruel penalty was that of bodily mutilation. People could lose a nose, hand, tongue, or their eyes for certain crimes!

As you can see, the Justinian Code was strict and conservative. But Justinian was wise when he wrote that a ruler should "be armed with law as well as glorified with arms [weapons], that there may be good government in times both of war and of peace."[5] (Word in brackets is mine.) In other words, Justinian saw that a *civilized* government was as valuable as a *strong* army. In a time of much fighting and feudalism in Europe, this concept made the Byzantine Empire a special place and provided much stability for its citizens.

---

4. Ibid., p. 130.
5. Will Durant, *The Age of Faith*. Vol. IV of *The Story of Civilization*. New York: Simon and Schuster, 1950; p. 111.

Well, now you know about the lives of two more famous people, Justinian I and Theodora. Though an unlikely pair for king and queen, they greatly shaped the Byzantine Empire with their style, their beliefs, and their laws. The solid foundation they laid probably helped the Byzantine Empire remain intact for centuries to come.

ACTIVITIES FOR LESSON 24

ALL STUDENTS

Make your Memory Cards for Lessons 22–24.

24A—Younger Students

1. Theodora grew up in a circus. Her father was a bear trainer. Using stuffed bears, put on your own mini-circus for friends or your family. To make it more lifelike, research just what kinds of things trained bears can do! Take a picture of your event and file it in your Student Notebook under "Asia: Turkey (the Byzantine Empire)."

2. Dress up as a king or queen. Use robes, jewels, and crowns. Make a list of laws, or codes, for your kingdom.

24B—Middle Students

1. GIRLS: Give a dramatization. In the Activity Supplement, you will find a translation of the speech that Theodora gave to Justinian to persuade him to resist the Nika riot. Practice reading this as a persuasive speech. Videotape yourself!

2. Research the cathedral of Saint Sophia in Istanbul (also called "Hagia Sophia") to find the answers to these questions. (Be careful—there are many cathedrals named Saint Sophia.) What is so unique about this structure? What does the name Hagia Sophia stand for? What other religious group owned it for some time? What is it used for today? Photocopy a picture of it and file it in your Student Notebook under "Asia: Turkey (the Byzantine Empire)."

24C—Middle and Older Students

1. *Creative writing project for girls:* Pretend you are Theodora. Create a page of her diary on the day before she married the king. Imagine her change of status from that of one who spun wool to that of queen! Make your diary page appear aged following directions from Activity 8A or 11B. File your page under "Asia: Turkey (the Byzantine Empire)" in your Student Notebook.

2. *Creative project for boys:* Pretend to be a sports announcer. On a tape recorder, report on the rioting between the "Blues" and the "Greens." Use your imagination to add to the story as needed!

3. Search for a copy of the Justinian Code. Read a few selections and compare these to laws in your community today. Do you consider some of them to be harsh? Discuss the benefit and the drawback of strict laws. In comparison, what is the benefit and drawback to laws that are not strict enough? Photocopy or print the code and add it to your Student Notebook under "Asia: Turkey (the Byzantine Empire)."

Wall of Fame

1. *Daily Life in the Dark Ages (c. 500–1000)*—Draw and cut out a little house. Now rub dirt on it to depict the harsh conditions of the time period. **With parental supervision,** burn the edges slightly to depict the many dangers of the time, such as fire! [There is no corresponding figure available from *History Through the Ages*.]

2. *King Arthur (503)*—Depict a man with a crown on his head and a long sword in his hand. Write "Excalibur" on the sword. [From *History Through the Ages,* use *King Arthur*.]

3. *Justinian I and Theodora (527–565)*—Create a very fancy king and queen with scraps of fine fabric and gold trim. [Use *Justinian I* and *Theodora*.]

SomeWHERE in Time

1. Using Outline Map 11, "Byzantine Empire", c.568:

   a. Color the shaded area purple to show the large size of the Byzantine Empire under Justinian I and Theodora.

   b. Mark the city of Constantinople.

   c. Label the Mediterranean Sea, the Black Sea, and the Atlantic Ocean. Color them each a different shade of blue.

   d. Label the present-day countries of Spain, France, Italy, Greece, and Turkey, and the continent of Africa.

2. Knights lived for excitement. For the sake of adventure (and to work on your understanding of mapmaking), create a treasure map of your backyard, city block, or apartment. Consider what your home or yard would look like from the sky if you were a bird looking down at it. This is the perspective from which maps are usually drawn. Start by drawing your bedroom. Then go from there with surrounding rooms and halls. Keep going to the outdoor region surrounding your home. Think about how you can depict the top of a tree or bush compared to the top of a trashcan. Be creative and colorful. It may be necessary to create a legend or key in order to read your map.

   Somewhere in the map, draw a "treasure" for someone else to discover using your map. Have fun!

   File your map in your Student Notebook under the country and continent in which you live.

Crossword. Complete the crossword puzzle on the next page. Remember, you may look in your book for the answers. (To help you know where to look, the lesson number is in parentheses.)

ACROSS

1. Arthur removed this from a stone (23)

4. Roman festival of love (12)

5. Number of Paul's journeys (3)

6. Played the lyre (4)

9. Vanished from Mexico centuries ago (16)

10. Means "victory" (24)

12. Exiled to Patmos (5)

13. Symbol of the Trinity (19)

15. Jewish fortress for a time (7)

16. Also called Paul (2)

19. Jewish historian (6)

20. Edict of _____ (14)

DOWN

1. Attila—the "_____ of God" (20)

2. Buried by Mt. Vesuvius (9)

3. Called himself "Dominus Noster" (13)

7. Indian fabric (15)

8. Led Second Jewish Revolt (10) [Be sure to include the hyphen in this name.]

11. City where St. Augustine was a bishop (17)

14. Invaded the city of Rome (21)

17. Performed bloodletting (22)

18. Latin Bible (18)

21. Means "universal" (11)

22. Means "fifty" (1)

23. Dead _____ Scrolls (8)

WHAT DO YOU KNOW?

PRETEST 9

Scramble! Unscramble the words to fill in the blanks. Use the word bank below.

1. Although Columba had a bad temper, his name meant ("voed") _____.

2. After causing a bloody battle, Columba left Ireland to win souls for Christ in (tocSdanl) _____.

3. Mount (juiF) _____, one of the most picturesque mountains in the world, is nestled in the islands of Japan.

4. (Stoihn) _____, the earliest religion of the Japanese, requires complete devotion to the emperor and the country of Japan.

5. Prince Shotoku has been called the (doerfun) "_____ of Japanese civilization."

6. Gregory the Great was one of the most admired (spoep) _____ of the Middle Ages.

7. Because Gregory was quite humble, he preferred to dress and eat like a common (komn) _____.

8. Gregory the Great was dedicated to serving the (orop) _____ and the (kics) _____ of Rome through charity and letters of encouragement.

WORD BANK

Shinto	monk	dove	poor/sick
Scotland	founder	Fuji	popes

COLUMBA, MISSIONARY TO SCOTLAND
LESSON 25

Have you ever known the Lord to take something bad and use it for good? I think you will agree with me that this is exactly what happened in the case of **Columba.** Columba—a fiery Irishman—had a hot temper that sometimes got him into trouble. And that's a bad thing. But the Lord used it to inspire him to take the Gospel of Christ to **Scotland.** And that's a good thing!

Columba was born of a Christian family in **Ireland** in 521. Being a good student and a strong Christian, Columba went to schools called **monasteries** that had been set up by Christian monks. He was such a good scholar that in time Columba set up several of his own monasteries across Ireland.

Even though Columba's name meant "dove," he didn't always behave like one. One time Columba had a terrible dispute with a local chieftain in Ireland. This dispute led to a gruesome battle in which 3,000 men were killed! Columba was devastated at what had taken place. As a man of God, he was truly sorry for what *he* felt he had caused. Though he knew God was capable of forgiving him, Columba wanted to make up for the tragedy. He resolved to convert as many men to Christ as had died in battle. That means he hoped for at least

The term "monastery" comes from the Greek word "monos," which means "alone." Early monks spent a lot of time alone studying and copying the Bible. (Pictured is a monastery in Etal, Germany.)

3,000 souls to come to know Jesus! He also vowed *never* to return to Ireland so that he might not cause such trouble there again.

Columba decided on Scotland as the place where he would fulfill his mission and spend the rest of his life. He made a beautiful choice, too. Scotland is lush, green, and mountainous. Though the skies are often heavy with rain and clouds, ocean winds blow them away to reveal crystal blue lakes and fields of purple flowers underneath. Glens and valleys cut through the mountainous highlands of the north, and sea lochs carve narrow bays along the rocky coasts. In keeping with their customs, the Scottish are the ones still known today for wearing kilts (which look like plaid skirts) and playing the bagpipes.

Columba didn't have to travel far to get to Scotland. Only a small channel of water separates Scotland from Ireland. As part of Great Britain, Scotland is actually on the same island as the countries of England and Wales.

Columba Sails to Scotland

It was **563** when Columba left the coast of Ireland for good with 12 of his friends. They sailed in what the Irish call a **currach,** which is a hide-covered sea vessel. They landed on **Iona,** a tiny island off the western coast of Scotland.

These dedicated men immediately set up homes and a church in Iona. Their hope was to befriend a neighboring tribe that they referred to as the **Picts.** The name of the Picts came from the Romans. It meant the "painted people" because, quite simply, they liked to paint their bodies!

Painted or not, the Picts had a reputation for being fierce. Other Scots living in the land feared them and hoped that Columba and his men would convert them to Christianity and bring peace to the land. However, the Pict's chief leader, a daunting man named **Brude,** wanted nothing to do with Columba, his men—or their faith. He bolted his village gates to keep them out.

A story has been handed down which says that Columba made a sign of the cross on the locked gates—and they flew wide open in a miraculous display of God's power! Though it wasn't the parting of the Red Sea, it was enough to get the attention of a tough guy like Brude. With a change of heart, he listened intently to the men and their message. Within years, Brude—and nearly the entire community of Picts—became followers of Christ.

Columba kept his commitment to try to save souls in Scotland. As he had done in his homeland of Ireland, Columba set up monasteries for teaching and serving the Scottish. His greatest influence was through serving as the abbot of a large monastery in Iona. Iona was so changed that this tiny island became a significant center for learning and evangelism. The Scottish monastery became a model for other monasteries across the continent of Europe. So fine was the reputation of Iona that over time 46 Scottish kings wanted to be buried there, as was Columba.

One of the most important services of the monasteries was to preserve the writing of books. At a time when many people were illiterate (which means they couldn't read or write), monasterial monks were busy copying books— particularly the Bible. Because the printing press had not yet been invented, books could only be copied by hand. It was very tedious work. But the monks made a beautiful and valuable art of it, using brilliant colors and **illuminated letters.** (An illuminated letter is usually the first one on a page and stands out from the rest by size and elaborate decoration. These letters are truly beautiful.)

With deep devotion to God, Columba did much to spread the Gospel of Christ to Scotland.

Through years of dedication and the writing of some of his own books, Columba was eventually responsible for sending out many preachers and missionaries into the world. Though Scotland was a small country, it became an influential one. The Christians of Scotland became serious about sharing the good news of Christ with the world.

Perhaps through his Christian influence, Columba did live up to the meaning of his name. Despite his bad temper, he was like a "dove" bringing a message of peace to the world. By the end of his life, Columba had influenced *at least* 3,000 people for the kingdom of God, which was his inspiration for going to Scotland in the first place.

ACTIVITIES FOR LESSON 25

ALL STUDENTS

Turn to the Activity Supplement in the Appendix for a beautiful sample of an illuminated letter. Photocopy and color as you desire. File it in your Student Notebook under "Europe: Scotland."

25A—Younger Students

1. Have you ever heard bagpipe music? Look for a recording on the Internet or at your local library. The bagpipe is considered the national instrument of Scotland. You might also look in an encyclopedia for information on bagpipes. Photocopy or print a picture of bagpipes and file it under "Europe: Scotland" in your Student Notebook.

2. Decorate yourself like the Picts.

Materials: Nontoxic body paints. (An alternative would be to add food coloring to hand or body lotion. Use caution with red, as it is difficult to remove!)

With teacher approval, decorate yourself with body paint. (Make sure it is nontoxic and designed for use on your body.) Make interesting patterns on your arms and legs. Take your picture and file it under "Europe: Scotland" in your Student Notebook.

3. To appreciate the dedicated work of the monks, copy a verse of the Bible by hand. I have been told that if a child were to begin copying the Bible at age 5 or 6, it could be completed by the time he or she graduated from high school. It would also create a meaningful record of growth in penmanship over the years that would hopefully correspond to the student's spiritual development. Consider beginning this tremendous undertaking of copying the entire Bible or the New Testament.

25B—Middle Students

Play "Toss the Caber."

Materials: Heavy-duty gloves, one medium-sized log, tape measure

As a test of strength, the Scottish hold an athletic event called "Toss the Caber." In this event, men pick up a wooden beam about the size of a telephone pole and toss it as far as they can. Some beams weigh as much as 180 pounds and are thrown about 80 feet!

For your event, draw a line in an open place such as your backyard or a playground. Using gloves, have each contestant or class member take a turn standing on the line and tossing a medium-sized log underhand as far as he or she can. (Play this carefully!) Mark the landing place of each player's log and record the winner's distance in feet or meters.

If you want to really stay in character with the Scottish, do this wearing something resembling a plaid kilt! Take a photo and file it under "Europe: Scotland" in your Student Notebook.

25C—Older Students

1. Calculate your handwriting speed.

Materials: A Bible, paper, pen, clock, calculator

How many hours might it take you to copy the Bible by hand? A few hundred? A few thousand? Find an approximation using this calculation. In minutes, time how long it takes you to copy one column of one page of the Bible. Take this number and multiply it by two. This new number tells you how long it will take you to copy one full page of the Bible, assuming you write at the same pace. Take that number (still in minutes) and multiply it by the number of pages in your Bible. Now, divide that number by 60 to calculate the number of hours it would take you to copy the entire Bible by hand.

The tedious work of the monks is to be greatly admired! File your sample under "Europe: Scotland." Title it "Scottish Monks Help Preserve the Bible."

2. Research the **Book of Kells.** Handwritten by the monks of Iona, it is one of the most beautiful, handwritten copies of the Bible ever preserved. It is

The Book of Kells is known for its beautiful-artistic detail and interlaced designs.

kept today in the library of Trinity College in Dublin, Ireland. Print a copy of it and file it in your Student Notebook under "Europe: Scotland."

3. Research the **Lindisfarne Gospels.** Like the Book of Kells, this too is a well-preserved handwritten copy of Scripture. Its writing was inspired by a missionary from Iona who took the Gospel to Ireland! Consider the ripple effect of the life work of Columba. Obtain a picture of the Lindisfarne Gospels and note the Celtic style of it. File a copy of it in your Student Notebook under "Europe: Ireland."

573

EARLY JAPAN AND PRINCE SHOTOKU
LESSON 26

If you had to choose, where would you rather live—by the mountains or the ocean? I think both are beautiful! Well, if you lived in Japan, you could enjoy the mountains *and* the ocean at the same time because every city in Japan is within 100 miles of the coast. And about 70 percent of Japan is made up of mountains! In fact, **Mount Fuji,** one of the most picturesque mountains in the world, is nestled in the islands of Japan. Today we'll look at this beautiful country and its early history.

Japan is actually an **archipelago,** which is a fancy name for a chain of islands. The islands of Japan are located in the Pacific Ocean just off the eastern coast of China. Look at them now on a map or globe. What you'll see is that there are four main islands that make up Japan. They are named **Hokkaido** (huh KI do), **Honshu** (HON shoo), **Kyushu** (KYOO shoo), and **Shikoku** (shi KO koo). But what you can't see very easily on a map or globe is that there are actually 4,223 tiny islands that make up Japan! (Only 600 of them are inhabited, that is, have people living on them.)

According to mythological legend, a brother and a sister in the heavens were commanded by their elders to create Japan. From a bridge in heaven they drew a jeweled sword out of the ocean and every droplet of water that fell from the sword became an island. The Japanese call these sacred islands ***Nippon*** (nee pone), meaning "source of the sun." We call them *Japan* because it is a shortened version of the name **Cipango** (si PAHNG go). That's the name the explorer **Marco Polo** used for the islands. (We'll learn more about him later.)

At 12,388 feet, Mount Fuji stands as the highest and most awe-inspiring peak in Japan. Thousands of Japanese climb to the top of the mountain, which holds an inactive volcano crater.

The first inhabitants of Japan didn't look at all like "modern" Japanese people—nor do they now. These early island dwellers, who still live in northwest Japan, are the **Ainu** (I noo) people. The Ainu are short, stout people with white skin, circular eyes, thick noses, and lots of hair. In comparison, the modern Japanese person is taller and thinner with almond-shaped eyes, a slender nose, and very little body hair. So what happened? Well, one theory suggests that sometime in the early history of the world, people from China and Korea migrated to Japan, pushing the Ainu people to one corner of the country. Since then, the Chinese, Korean, and Indonesian races have blended to make up the Japanese people we know today.

There is not much documented history of early Japan. But it seems that one of the first emperors was named **Jimmu Tenno** and lived about 600 years before Christ. According to Japanese myth, Tenno was a descendant of a sun goddess. Although there was an emperor in existence that long ago, most of Japan was ruled by scattered clan leaders who often fought against one another. That is, until about the year 400. At that time, the **Yamato clan** gained some control over all the other clans. Ever since then, the imperial rulers of Japan have claimed to be descendants of the Yamato clan—even still today.

Shinto

The earliest religion of Japan is called **Shinto.** It means "way of the gods." Shinto is one of the oldest religions of the world. It holds that **Kami** is the sacred energy behind everything, be it the gods, nature, or the emperor. Followers offer gifts to appease the forces of nature and countless numbers of spirits. Shinto has no formal doctrine, no fancy rituals, no priests, and no teachings of heaven or hell. It is not so much a set of beliefs as a way of life.

Though Shinto has no doctrine to believe in, it does require *complete* loyalty to Japan and its emperor. This makes Shinto like no other religion. No other country in the world has adopted Shinto because it claims that Japan *alone* was created a sacred place and that the Japanese *alone* are sacred people! Nothing has ever proved the patriotic teachings of Shinto more than the World War II **kamikaze pilots** who died for their emperor and country. (A kamikaze pilot is one who kills himself by flying his plane into the enemy.)

As admirable as it is to die for one's country, Shinto fails to address the real spiritual needs of the Japanese people. By believing in the superiority of the Japanese, it would appear they have no need for salvation from sin.

Prince Shotoku is considered the "founder of Japanese civilization" for writing a constitution for Japan.

However, the Bible says, *"For all have sinned and fall short of the glory of God."* (Rom. 3:23) The word *all* in this passage means even the people of Japan. The good news is that the Bible also says, *"For God so loved the world that He gave His only begotten Son, that whoever believes in Him should not perish but have everlasting life."* (John 3:16) The word *world* in this passage refers to everyone in the *world,* including the Japanese people—for whom God offers eternal life through Christ.

Now you may be wondering if the Shinto religion still exists in Japan. To some degree it does. There are still many public and private temples where the Japanese worship in Shinto style. However, there was born a prince in **573** who brought a new religion as well as many other ideas into Japan. The prince's name was **Shotoku Taishi** and the new religion was **Buddhism.**

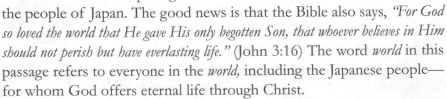

Apart from the knowledge of Jesus Christ, many are still drawn to worship at Buddhist temples.

Prince Shotoku

Shotoku spread his belief in Buddhism all across Japan by supporting Buddhist monasteries and building Buddhist temples. His exposure to

Buddhism probably came from China. As Shotoku promoted Buddhism, many Japanese kept their Shinto beliefs but added Buddha's teachings to them. Because Buddhism is considered a religion of great compassion, Shotoku was considered a great humanitarian by his people and was widely respected.

Prince Shotoku not only introduced Buddhism to Japan, but he also wrote history, painted pictures, and oversaw the building of the **Horiuji Temple,** one of the greatest masterpieces of early Japan. Even more significant is that Shotoku wrote a *constitution* for Japan. With it he started the idea of there being a central government in place. (This idea also came from China.) For all these new ideas, Prince Shotoku has been named the **"founder of Japanese civilization."** When he died, the Japanese grieved deeply over him.

Even after his death, Shotoku continued to influence Japan. A Great Reform called the **Taika** took place in the government in 621 as a result of what Shotoku had started. Through the Taika, the emperor became the owner of *all* the land of Japan, and taxes were paid directly to him. This kind of imperial rule lasted for centuries. And by 747 there was evidence that the Japanese would continue to embrace the practice of Buddhism that Shotoku started as they built a huge monument to Buddha called the **Daibutsu** (die BOOT sue) in the city of Nara. The Daibutsu stands 53 feet tall and contains over a million pounds of metal. (The little finger of the statue is about the size of a man!)

As pictured here, the Japanese built another Daibutsu, or "Big Buddha," in the city of Kamakura in 1252. At 31 feet high, the statue towers over tourists much like the one in Nara.

Of course, like Shinto, the teachings of Buddhism and the building of great shrines fail to address the real spiritual needs of the Japanese. Buddhism may provide moral teachings for the Japanese, but it does not introduce them to the Savior. Jesus said of Himself, *"I am the way, the truth, and the life. No one comes to the Father except through Me."* (John 14:6)

Well, as I said in the beginning, Japan is a beautiful place and its history is interesting. As you can tell, Japan has been greatly influenced by its religions and its leaders. We will come back to the development of Japan in the third quarter when we learn about the ***samurai.*** I think you'll find them intriguing!

ACTIVITIES FOR LESSON 26

ALL STUDENTS

Sushi, a Japanese rice and fish dish, has become increasingly popular in the United States. Rice and fish are the main staples of a Japanese diet. Try sushi at a Japanese restaurant in your area or look to make your own by visiting this Japanese *Cookbook for Kids* site on the Internet:

> http://web-jpn.org/kidsweb/cook.html

Then click on "Sushi" for a variety of recipes. Check out the other links as well!

(The "home" site for this cookbook is Web Japan. Its Web site is:

> http://web-jpn.org

Click on "Kids Web Japan" and click on "Cookbook for Kids" to access the cookbook. There are also many additional Japan-oriented links for children. As always, **adult supervision** is advised!)

26A—Younger Students

1. Research Mount Fuji on the Internet, at the library, or in an encyclopedia. Find out how tall it is and what island it is on. Write these two facts down on paper. Photocopy a picture of Mount Fuji and glue it to your page of facts. Place this paper in your Student Notebook under "Asia: Japan."

2. Using picture books from the library, look for examples of traditional Japanese clothing. Photocopy your favorites in black and white. Cut them out, color them, and glue them on paper. Place these colorful samples in your Student Notebook under "Asia: Japan."

26B—Middle Students

1. Japan has a history of many terrible earthquakes. One dates as far back as 599. Other significant dates include the years 1703 (32,000 died in Tokyo), 1885 (thousands died), and 1923 (100,000 died in Tokyo and 37,000 in Yokohama). I read that some children in Kamakura still went to school the next day using broken plaster for pencils and broken tiles for slates! Research what causes earthquakes and why some countries are more prone to them than others. Write one to three paragraphs on paper. Photocopy pictures of earthquake devastation and add these to your report. File this in your Student Notebook under "Asia: Japan."

2. Research kamikaze pilots. Though we're jumping ahead in history here, the role of kamikaze pilots was significant in the bombing of Pearl Harbor in World War II. Search out the estimated number of pilots who gave their lives in this manner based on their religious beliefs. File your conclusions in your Student Notebook under "Asia: Japan."

26C—Older Students

As we did with the religions studied in Volume I of *The Mystery of History,* research and compare Shintoism to Christianity. (If you have not previously done this for Buddhism, then include it also in your comparison.) I highly recommend the resource, *Handbook of Today's Religions* by Josh McDowell and Don Stewart. (Answers are provided in the Activity Supplement.)

1. The founder of the religion and date of origination.

2. The source of authority (written works of the religion, visions, prophecy).

3. The doctrine of God (believing there is one God or many gods).

4. The doctrine of Jesus Christ (believing Jesus was God in the flesh or just a prophet).

5. Their belief in sin.

6. The doctrine of salvation. (On what basis is sin forgiven or accounted for?)

7. The doctrine of things to come. (Is there a belief in life after death or in a coming judgment of the world?)

8. What draws people to this religion (lifestyle, ritual, heritage, etc.)?

GREGORY THE GREAT

LESSON 27

Have you ever heard of the **pope**? I mentioned him briefly in Lesson 22 when discussing the importance of the church in the Dark Ages. Depending on your religious background, you may or may not know much about him. For those of you who don't, I'm going to explain who the pope is because the man we're studying today, **Gregory I**, was a pope in the Early Middle Ages. He was a very good one, too, which is why most people remember him as **Gregory the Great**.

The story of the pope goes way back to the Early Church. Members of the present-day **Roman Catholic Church** believe that Jesus started the position of the pope when he said these words to **Peter**:

> *"And I also say to you that you are Peter, and on this rock I will build My church, and the gates of Hades shall not prevail against it. And I will give you the keys of the kingdom of heaven, and whatever you bind on earth will be bound in heaven, and whatever you loose on earth will be loosed in heaven."* (Matt. 16:18–19)

From this passage, the Roman Catholic Church believes it is the one true church started by Jesus through Peter. That would make Peter the first "pope" of the Roman Catholic Church, though he wasn't called that during his lifetime. The word *pope* in Latin simply means "papa" or "father." Like a father is the head of a family, so the pope is considered by Roman Catholics as the "visible head" of the Roman Catholic Church, and Christ is considered the "invisible head."

However, there are many Christians who interpret the Bible differently than Roman Catholics do and who don't believe in the position and authority of the pope. They would say that Peter only considered himself an "elder" of the church, as stated in 1 Peter 5:1–4. In that passage, too, Peter says he is an example to the flock, not a lord. We will be learning more about that in another volume when we cover the **Reformation**. That's the time in history when lots of people tried to "reform," or change, the teachings of the church in regard to the pope and other matters. These reformers became known as **Protestants** for protesting against the church. You may want to discuss with your teacher now whether your family is Protestant, Roman Catholic, or some other faith.

The tradition of the Roman Catholic Church has remained strong and powerful for over 2,000 years. According to them there has been a pope ever since Peter lived. Not once has the chain been broken. (Although there were times when more than one man claimed to be pope, but that's another story!) This kind of long tradition naturally brings with it great power.

As I mentioned in Lesson 22, the first men who followed Peter as leaders of the church called themselves **bishops**. It wasn't until the fifth century, after the fall of the Western Roman Empire, that the word *pope* was used instead. It was used to designate the head of all the other bishops, or the bishop of Rome. You will also hear the terms *pontiff* and *papacy* to describe the pope and his ruling system.

Pope, pontiff, and papacy are all terms used to describe the pope and his ruling system.

Somewhere along the way, the men who were chosen to be pope began to change their names. On becoming pope, they would rename themselves after a saint or a former pope whom they admired. That explains why so many of the popes' names are the same. For example, Gregory was the name of 16 different popes. The name became popular because the very first Gregory was truly a great man, as his name implies. Let's examine his life now and learn how he developed such a good reputation.

Gregory the Great

Gregory was born of a wealthy family. He inherited a lot of money from his parents as well as a palace of his own. At age 33 he became the mayor of Rome. But after one term, Gregory learned that he disliked politics a great deal. The evil things he saw around him convinced him that the world was soon coming to an end. Though he was wrong about the world ending then, he was right about how hard life was around him. It was, of course, the period called the Dark Ages when people were still struggling to survive after the fall of the Roman Empire.

Being a man of great compassion for the poor and having concern for the lost, Gregory did a most incredible thing. He turned his luxurious palace home into the **Monastery of St. Andrew** and took the lowly vows of a **monk.** Now think about that for a minute. If you were rich and owned a mansion, would you want to give it away to serve your community and live like the poor? Not many people would. It was this kind of charitable gesture that characterized the rest of Gregory's life and caused others to admire him.

One of Gregory's greatest passions was to travel and share the Gospel of Christ. In other words, he wanted to be a missionary. However, Gregory was so valuable to the church in Rome that he was never given permission to leave. Gregory said later that some of the happiest days of his life were those he spent serving as a monk in Rome. He was glad that he had stayed there after all.

As the years went by, Gregory grew in wisdom. When **Pope Pelagius II** died in **590,** Gregory was naturally the most likely monk to fill the empty position. But, you know what? He didn't want to be pope! At age 50, Gregory cherished his life as a monk. If he were to accept the position of pope, he would inherit great duty, tremendous power, and even wealth. Becoming a pope in those days was practically like becoming a king. Gregory greatly struggled with the idea of this.

To solve the dilemma, Gregory decided to take the position of pope but *only* under the condition that he would keep the simple lifestyle of a monk. That meant that he would continue to dress in plain robes, live in simple quarters, and eat basic foods. Gregory fulfilled all of this. As an example, he lived mostly on raw fruits and vegetables and fasted for long periods of time. To deal with the wealth of the Western Church, Gregory gave most of it to the poor.

Though Gregory chose to live a simple life, the legacy he left as a pope was hardly simple at all. Gregory I, as I will now refer to him, was a brilliant leader. He made tremendous decisions and advancements for the Western Church. His authority was well established and respected throughout the Christian world.

Gregory I even got back into politics to some degree. He did so because the **Lombards** were invading Rome. Gregory I turned to the Byzantine Empire for help but was refused. So, Gregory I used rent money from the church to support an army that fought the Lombards. For this, Gregory I gained great respect as a *civil* leader as well as a religious leader.

Gregory had great compassion for the poor, the sick, and the lost. Though he became a powerful pope, Gregory kept the simple lifestyle of a monk until his death.

Even with this great power, Gregory the Great's heart remained pure to his passion for the lost. There is a story about him that goes like this: While passing through the market in Rome one day, Gregory I saw a group of slaves being unloaded from England. He was struck by their light-colored hair, blue eyes, and fair skin. Gregory asked if these beautiful people knew anything of Christianity. He was told no, and that these people were **Angles** from a pagan land. With compassion, Gregory said of them that they looked like "angels," not Angles. And though he could not leave Rome to preach the Gospel to them, he sent **Augustine of Canterbury** to do the job.

Augustine of Canterbury and other Benedictine monks invested their lives in converting many Angles, Saxons, and Jutes in England to Christianity. Gregory I also sent missionaries to Sicily, Sardinia, and Lombardy. Seven monasteries were founded as a result of Gregory the Great's concern for the gospel. In every situation, he gave priority to the poor and the oppressed. He also made sure that, whenever possible, the church paid to free prisoners of war.

Gregory I was so dedicated to the poor in Rome that the destitute of the city received a month's portion of food, clothing, and money. If people were too sick to get their food, it was delivered to them. And, Gregory I personally wrote hundreds of letters of encouragement to those who were in great need of counsel or healing. He was considered to be a true pastor to his people, a caring shepherd to his flock. He was so humble that he called himself *servus servorum Dei,* which is Latin for "the servant of the servants of God."[1]

Though born in Italy, Augustine of Canterbury has been called the "Apostle to the English" for sharing Christ with thousands of Saxon people.

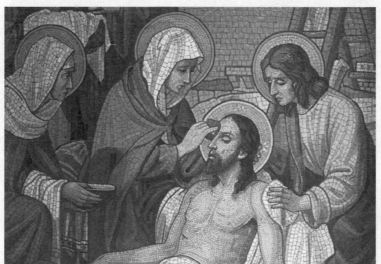

In great humility, Pope Gregory referred to himself as "the servant of the servants of God."

To keep his legacy of servanthood alive, Gregory I wrote training manuals for other bishops to learn from. He wrote, "Every preacher should give forth a sound [he should provide a model] more by his deeds than by his words, and rather by good living imprint footsteps for men to follow than by speaking show them the way to walk."[2]

Gregory I wrote lots of other books, too. He was very intrigued by the supernatural activity of angels and demons and wrote a lot about them. These writings greatly influenced the theology of the Western Church and the use of holy relics in worship. He wrote also of the life of Job, a character in the Old Testament who suffered much hardship in life. The famous **Gregorian chant**, a special kind of soothing music, is

1. Will Durant, *The Age of Faith.* Vol. IV of *The Story of Civilization.* New York: Simon and Schuster, 1950; p. 521.
2. James A. Corrick, *World History Series: The Early Middle Ages.* San Diego: Lucent Books, 1995; p. 35.

named after Gregory I although he probably didn't create it. (Monks were known for spending hours in prayer and meditation. Chanting and singing were part of the worship process.)

While Gregory the Great's spiritual influence grew over the years, his physical strength slipped away. As Gregory I grew older, his body became more and more fragile. His last years on earth were spent in much pain and physical weakness. In 599 he wrote, "I have rarely been able to leave my bed. I am tormented with gout and painful anxieties that . . . every day I look for the relief of death."[3] In 604 he died peacefully, as was his desire.

As you can tell by now, Gregory I is one of those men who rightfully have been remembered as "great." As one of the most outstanding popes of medieval times, Gregory I demonstrated a true servant's heart. It is no wonder that many popes who followed him would choose the name of Gregory.

ACTIVITIES FOR LESSON 27

ALL STUDENTS

1. **Make your Memory Cards for Lessons 25–27.**

2. Sing the hymn, "When I Survey the Wondrous Cross." Though Isaac Watts is credited with writing the hymn, it is based on a Gregorian chant. (If you don't know the words or music, go to www.cyberhymnal.org and search on the title.)

27A—Younger Students

1. Dress like a monk. (Sort of!)

Materials: Large brown paper bag for lawn and garden waste (use a self-standing large paper bag, 16 by 12 by 35 inches; see Photo 1), a 2- to 3-foot cord or piece of rope, pencil, scissors

Place the large bag over your head and body with any lettering on the back side. (Please note this will only work with a very large paper bag. Never place a plastic bag over your head!) With your teacher's help, determine the approximate location of your arms and head. Use a pencil to mark this from the outside. (See Photo 2.) Remove the bag from your head. Use the scissors to cut a hole for each arm and for your head. Place the bag back over your head, inserting your head and arms through the holes. Tie a cord or rope around your waist. (See Photo 3.)

Though obviously monks did not and still do not wear paper bags as clothes, consider the *simplicity* of what you have on. What spiritual, emotional, and financial benefits are there to simplifying one's life? (Discuss what *spiritual, emotional,* and *financial* mean.) Take a photo and file it under "Europe: Italy" in your Student Notebook.

| Photo 1 | Photo 2 | Photo 3 |

3. Will Durant, *The Age of Faith.* Vol. IV of *The Story of Civilization.* New York: Simon and Schuster, 1950; p. 524.

2. Have your teacher find the sound of a Gregorian chant. (I recommend using a computerized encyclopedia with CD-ROM capabilities or the library.) Listen to the soothing sounds and discuss with your teacher how it makes you feel. Why do you think the monks used this kind of music for meditation and worship? Talk about modern praise music used in worship. Do you have a favorite praise song?

(*Note to Teacher:* My historical editor recommends a CD by Spanish monks appropriately titled *Chant.*)

27B—Middle Students

Gregory I wore plain brown robes like those of a monk even after becoming pope. To appreciate this, consider what he could have worn as pope.

The pope usually wears a white robe with an ornamental clasp made of precious jewels. Around his waist he wears a *pallium,* which is a woolen band embroidered with crosses. His shoes are red with an embroidered cross on each. The pope has a golden cross necklace that is said to have part of the true Cross in it. He also wears a ring called the *fisherman's ring* because Peter had been a fisherman. The pope often wears a small cloth on his head like a beanie. In processions, he might wear a large cone-shaped triple crown called a *tiara.*

Photocopy pictures you find of the pope in an encyclopedia or reference book (or print them from the Internet). Then try to find a picture of a monk from the Middle Ages. Glue these photos on the same page. Title your page "Gregory I, the Pope Who Dressed Like a Monk." File it under "Europe: Italy" in your Student Notebook.

27C—Older Students

1. Research the present home of the pope, which is the Vatican Palace in the Vatican City. (The Vatican City is an independent state within the city of Rome.) Research the most famous painted ceiling in the world, the Sistine Chapel, located at the palace. Photocopy or print it from the Internet. Place it in your Student Notebook under "Europe: Italy." Title it "The Home of the Pope."

2. Investigate the Ruthwell cross. It was carved in the eighth century as a creative means to tell the Gospel. In what similarly creative way can you share the Gospel? Present your ideas to your class or family using modern imagery, artwork, or symbolism.

TAKE ANOTHER LOOK!

REVIEW 9: LESSONS 25–27

Wall of Fame

1. **Columba (563)**—To remember that Columba was a missionary to Scotland, the land of kilts and bagpipes, color a plaid skirt on the figure. [From *History Through the Ages,* use *Columba*.]

2. **Prince Shotoku (573)**—Create a smiling man (to depict his being a good humanitarian) holding the title "Founder of Japanese Civilization." [Use *Prince Shotoku*.]

3. **Gregory the Great (590)**—Since Gregory dressed as a humble monk rather than as a highly decorated pope, color or place a brown robe over him with a piece of string for a belt. [Use *Pope Gregory the Great* and *Augustine of Canterbury*.]

SomeWHERE in Time

1. The people of Scotland speak the language of "Scot." (Though once considered only a dialect of English, Scot has in recent years been officially recognized as a language of its own.) While Scot is similar to English, it contains many words unique to the landscape and customs of the Scots. In an English dictionary, look up the following Scottish words that describe special geographical features common in Scotland. Match them to the definitions. (Answers are given at the end of this review section.)

_____1. Loch	a.	The ground along a winding waterway; a sandhill
_____2. Glen	b.	Flat, wide river valley or the grassland along it
_____3. Strath	c.	Bay opening to the sea
_____4. Moor	d.	Lake or bay
_____5. Links	e.	A boggy area of wasteland, sometimes grassy
_____6. Sea loch	f.	The place where an ocean tide meets a river; an estuary
_____7. Firth	g.	Valley

2. To remember the four main islands of Japan, I want you to create a hanging mobile. (I suggest you read the directions one time through before assembling the mobile. This project may be too tedious for some students and thus will require teacher assistance.)

   Materials: Outline Map 12, "Japan"; Outline Map 13, "Honshu"; and Outline Map 14, "Hokkaido, Shikoku, and Kyushu"; poster board; glue; scissors; colored pencils; bold marking pen; a clothes hanger; yarn or string; ruler; hole punch. You will be using Map 12 for reference and cutting out Maps 13 and 14.

   a. Using colored pencils of your choice, color each of the four main islands of Japan a different color. (See Photo 1.)

   b. Using a bold marking pen, label each island with its proper name in large letters. The island names are indicated on your maps as **Honshu, Shikoku, Kyushu,** and **Hokkaido.** (See Photo 2.)

   c. Glue Map 13 and Map 14 each onto a piece of poster board, making sure that you have applied glue to the back side of each island.

d. Cut out each island (cutting the poster board at the same time). It is not necessary to cut out every intricate detail of the coastlines, but cut as close as you can to keep the general shape of the islands. (See Photo 3.)

e. Cut two pieces of yarn or string, each about 6 inches long.

f. Take the small northern island of **Hokkaido** in your hands. Use a hole punch to create holes at the places marked A, B, and C. (See Photo 4.)

g. Tie the 6-inch pieces of string to the island at holes A and B. (Leave hole C blank for now.) Attach the loose ends of the strings to the farthest right-hand corner of your hanger. (See Photos 5 and 6.)

h. Take the large island of **Honshu** in your hand. Punch five holes in it for hanging. They are labeled D, E, F, G, and H.

i. Cut another piece of yarn or string 6 inches long. Tie and attach this yarn from point C on the island of **Hokkaido,** to point D on the island of **Honshu.**

j. I recommend at this point that you view Map 12, the overall map of the four islands of Japan. Notice the relationship of each island to the other. You will be recreating this relationship by the way you hang the islands from each other and from the hanger. Now proceed. (See Photo 7.)

k. Lay the hanger flat on your working surface with the island of **Hokkaido** straightened out and the island of **Honshu** suspended from it by one piece of yarn. Measure a new piece of yarn long enough to allow you to tie yarn from point E on **Honshu** to the middle of the hanger. Straighten the island as you go, keeping it proportional to the overall map of the islands of Japan. (See Photo 8.)

l. Repeat this step, tying a long piece of yarn from point H on **Honshu** to the left end of the hanger.

m. You should now have two islands of Japan hanging from your mobile. It is time to add another. Pick up **Shikoku.** Punch holes where indicated at points I and J.

n. Using very short pieces of yarn, tie and attach the island of **Shikoku** by connecting point F on **Honshu** with point I of **Shikoku.**

o. Tie and attach point G on **Honshu** to point J on **Shikoku.** This island sits very close to **Honshu.** (See Photo 9.)

p. You should now have three islands of Japan hanging from your mobile. Before proceeding, check your overall map to make sure your islands are hanging in the proper direction. It may be necessary to retie the pieces of yarn and use slightly different lengths to accomplish the proper orientation of one island to another. (See Photo 10.)

q. It is time to attach the fourth and last island. Pick up **Kyushu.** Punch a hole at point K as indicated.

r. Using a very short piece of yarn, tie and attach the island of **Kyushu** to the large island of **Honshu** by connecting point H on **Honshu** (this hole is being used twice) with point K on **Kyushu.**

s. After following these tedious directions, you should now have a finished product that looks something like Photo 11. My intent is that you will be much more familiar with Japan and the names of its islands after handling them as you just have. I don't think this mobile will fit into your Student Notebook, so I suggest you take a photo of it and place that in your Student Notebook under "Asia: Japan."

Photo 1

Photo 2

Photo 3

Photo 4

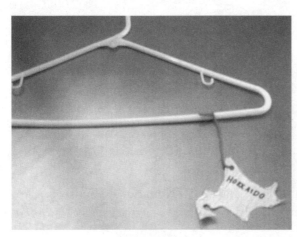

Photo 5

Photo 6

Photo 7

Photo 8

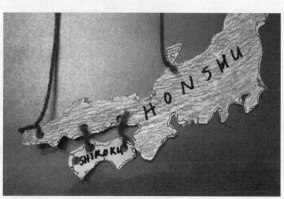

Photo 9

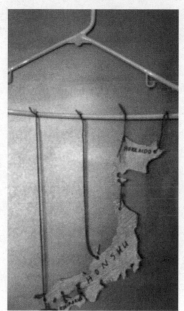

Photo 10

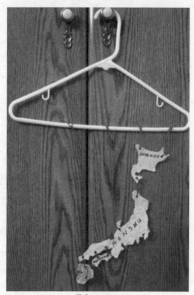

Photo 11

WHAT DID YOU LEARN?
WEEK 9: QUIZ

I. Fill in the Blanks. Using a word from below, fill in the blanks.

1. Pope Gelasius declared February 14 as Saint _____ Day to try to replace Lupercalia on February 15.

2. To make the Roman Empire more manageable, Diocletian neatly divided it into 120 _____ .

3. After a spiritual experience at the Battle of Milvian, Constantine wore the symbol of the _____ and the letters *chi* and *rho* on his armor.

4. Hinduism is based on ancient hymns and writings called _____ .

5. The Maya built tall step _____ to try to reach the gods of nature.

6. St. Augustine of Hippo was gifted in _____, the art of speaking and writing.

7. In translating the Bible, Jerome compiled the books of the _____ , which were not included in the Bible because they did not meet the necessary criteria.

8. As a slave in Ireland, young Patrick was forced to work on a _____ farm.

WORD BANK

cross	rhetoric	pig	Valentine's
provinces	*Vedas*	pyramids	Apocrypha

II. Matching. Match the following items by placing the correct letter next to the number.

_____1. Huns

a. A lowly peasant

_____2. Angles, Jutes, and Saxons

b. Beloved Celtic king; fought the Saxons

_____3. Serf

c. "Founder of Japanese civilization"

_____4. King Arthur

d. Scarred their children's faces

_____5. Justinian

e. Missionary to Scotland; name means "dove"

_____6. Columba

f. Invaded England at the fall of the Western Roman Empire

_____7. Prince Shotoku

g. King of the Byzantine Empire; married Theodora

_____8. Gregory the Great

h. A humble pope who cared for the poor and sick

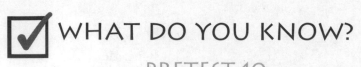

WHAT DO YOU KNOW?

PRETEST 10

True or False? Circle your answers.

1. The Grand Canal, built under the Sui dynasty, is the largest man-made waterway in the world.   T F

2. Li Yuan started the Tang dynasty and ushered in the "Golden Age of China."   T F

3. Li Shi Min, the son of Li Yuan, converted to the Jewish faith.   T F

4. Mohammed, the founder of Islam, grew up in Spain.   T F

5. In the "Hegira," Mohammed fled for his life from Mecca to Medina.   T F

6. Mohammed taught others to believe in hundreds of gods.   T F

7. The name Islam means "submission to God."   T F

8. Like Jesus, Buddha is considered a great prophet in the Islamic faith.   T F

THE SUI AND TANG DYNASTIES OF CHINA
LESSON 28

Zhongguo. That is what the early Chinese called the land of China. It means *Middle Kingdom* because the Chinese believed that their country was in the *middle*, or the very *center*, of the civilized world. If you studied Volume I of *The Mystery of History*, then hopefully you learned many things like this about **China.** But for this volume, it is our first look at this enormous country. We'll begin to learn today at least a few things that were going on in faraway China while Europe was struggling through the Dark Ages.

The last we looked at China in Volume I it was being ruled by the **Han dynasty.** A **dynasty** is a powerful group or family that rules a country for a long period of time—perhaps even for hundreds of years. In her history, China has been officially ruled by 11 different dynasties. The first five, which bring us up to the time period of this lesson, were the **Xia** (shee a), the **Shang,** the **Zhou** (joh or joe), the **Qin** (chin), and the **Han** (hahn) dynasties.

The Han dynasty lasted a very long time—from about 200 years *before* Jesus lived to about 200 years *after* He lived. That would be about 400 years altogether. Because of this long reign, most of the one billion residents of China today are descendants of the Han people. When the Han dynasty did collapse in A.D. 221, there wasn't another family strong enough to keep the country united. Instead, the states of China fought and struggled against each other for 370 years. That's a long time to struggle without a leader.

The Sui Dynasty

But finally there arose a man capable of bringing China back together. His name was **Yang Jian.** In **589** he started the **Sui dynasty.** Yang Jian bravely took the throne of northern China; then he crossed the Yangtze River and conquered southern China, too. To understand how important that was, you might want to look at China this way—just as the Roman Empire was once split between the east and the west, China was divided between the north and the south. So, it was a remarkable accomplishment by Yang Jian to bring the two regions together.

Yang Jian did at least two really smart things to help make the country more stable. He lowered the taxes that were way too high, and he allowed men to serve in the army for shorter periods of time. In that way men could keep more of their income and spend more time with their families. It produced a healthier nation.

To further add to the health of China, the next Sui emperor—named **Yang Guang**—oversaw the building of the **Grand Canal.** It is the largest man-made waterway in the world! It took over a *million* people to build it. The canal connected over 1,200 miles of small rivers across China, from the city of **Hangchow** in the south to **Peking** in the north. It is pretty incredible still today.

In 589 Yang Jian started the Sui dynasty and united northern and southern China.

Barges and boats of all shapes and sizes carry goods and people through thousands of miles of canals and waterways in China.

Unfortunately, though, Yang Guang had another idea that wasn't so smart. He expected people to pay their taxes *10* years ahead of time so that he could build nice parks and palaces with their money! Needless to say, this idea didn't go over very well. The people of China rebelled and had him killed. By 618, the Sui dynasty fell apart, leaving China in chaos once again.

The Tang Dynasty and Li Shi Min

However, there was one Chinese official under the Sui dynasty who was glad for the chaos. He saw it as an opportunity to rise to power and lead China back to its greatness. His name was **Li Yuan.** In **618,** with the Sui dynasty crumbling, Li Yuan started what is called the **Tang dynasty.** Unlike the short-lived Sui dynasty, the Li family kept its rule for about 300 years and ushered in what historians would call the **Golden Age of China.**

One of the more interesting rulers of the Tang dynasty was Li Yuan's son. His name was **Li Shi Min** (627–650). Like most kings, Li Shi Min started his reign trying to conquer surrounding nations through battles and bloodshed. But unlike most kings, he grew tired of war. In the same way that **King Asoka** (a SHO ka) of India (Volume I) left the battlefield to study the peaceful teachings of **Buddha,** Li Shi Min also left the battlefield to seek a more peaceful way of life. He found it in the teachings of **Confucius.**

Li Shi Min read and reread the volumes of Confucius. Finding them incredibly valuable, he had them republished. The humble teachings of Confucius were a powerful influence on him. Though he was a king, Li Shi Min followed Confucius in living modestly, ruling fairly, and turning down many of the luxuries that were available to him.

As an example of his fairness, Li Shi Min did something remarkable during his reign. He was told that he needed to make tougher sentences for criminals. But, he came up with another idea. He said, "If I diminish expenses, lighten the taxes, employ only honest officials, so that the people have clothing enough, this will do more to abolish robbery than the employment of the severest punishments."[1]

To test out his new idea for reform, Li Shi Min took 290 men who were condemned to die and asked them to go into the work fields and do their work without any supervision—*if* by their word they promised to return. That means they were trusted to not escape though not a single guard was placed to watch them. Do you want to guess what happened? At the end of the day, every one of the men came back to the prison—as they had

Started by Li Yuan in 618, the Tang dynasty ushered in "the Golden Age" of China through magnificent art, invention, and trade.

---

1. Will Durant, *Our Oriental Heritage.* Vol. I of *The Story of Civilization.* New York: Simon and Schuster, 1954; p. 702.

promised! Li Shi Min was so delighted with the honor of the criminals that he freed all of them. After that, he declared that no king should ever give the death sentence to a criminal unless first the king had fasted for three days.

Though Li Shi Min remained faithful to the teachings of Confucius all his life, he was very open to the philosophies of other religions. (If you studied Volume I, you may recall that Confucianism is not really a religion in and of itself, but rather a set of moral teachings.) So, Li Shi Min welcomed **Christians, Buddhists,** and **Muslims** along with their ideas into his kingdom. In fact, one of the oldest mosques in the world is in China. (A mosque is a place of worship for Muslims. We'll learn who they are in our next lesson.)

As is probably evident, Li Shi Min was a good king for keeping China stable. When he died, the whole country grieved for him. His reign helped pave the way for China to be on top of the world. The beautiful capital he built in **Chang'an** (which is now the city of **Xi'an**) attracted great scholars, artists, scientists, poets, and musicians from all over the world. The city had its own banking system and well-laid-out streets. While Europe was groping through the Dark Ages, China was most definitely in her Golden Age.

I might add here that Li Shi Min employed one of China's most amazing women to be one of his concubines. (A concubine is a romantic companion or mistress.) Her name was **Wu Zetian.** After Li Shi Min's death, Wu Zetian managed to become the only female ruler that China ever had! But her story is so fascinating that I'm saving it for Lesson 31. You'll just have to wait.

Though now an industrial center, Xi'an was once considered the Rome of the East for its beauty, popularity, and importance during the days when it was Li Shi Min's capital city of Chang'an.

China was so advanced during the Tang dynasty that a historian named Murdoch said it was "the most progressive, and the best-governed, empire on the face of the globe."[2] What made China so brilliant? Many, many things made her the envy of the world. For one, the Chinese were comfortable. At least in their clothing they were. With all the silk that was available in China, even the common man's clothes were soft and luxurious. Besides that, the Chinese had learned to heat their homes with coal and gas. Warmth in the winter makes almost everyone feel more comfortable!

Furthermore, due to the success of trading things such as silk, corn, rice, and spices, wealth was abundant during the Tang dynasty. This allowed even ordinary families to spend a little money on recreation and entertainment. Some people had boats just for the pleasure of traveling up and down the endless riverways of China. For real amusement, the Chinese figured out how to use gunpowder to make **fireworks**! (Aren't we glad for that?) In fact, fireworks were added to the Chinese New Year during the Tang dynasty. During this fun festival, a giant man-made dragon is led through the streets with firecrackers popping because of the superstition that this will scare away evil spirits for the next year!

---

2. James Murdoch, *A History of Japan*, Vol. 1 (1925), p. 146. As quoted in Will Durant, *Our Oriental Heritage*. Vol. 1 of *The Story of Civilization*. New York: Simon and Schuster, 1954; p. 703.

While in Europe the common man at this time was drinking a weakened form of beer or ale, the Chinese peasants were enjoying fine **tea.** With fancy porcelain cups and plates, the Chinese were beginning to treat the serving of tea like a beautiful form of art. And it has remained so for centuries.

Additionally, creative poets, painters, jewelers, and inventors flourished in the big cities of China. Artists had enough resources to carve statues out of pure rubies. (Fine gems were so plentiful that sometimes even the dead were buried on expensive beds of pearls.) The famous Chinese artist named **Wu Tao-tze** painted over 400 frescoes during the Tang dynasty. Though most have since been destroyed, his works are said to have been comparable in their beauty to those of Michelangelo. And long before the Europeans, the Chinese built hydraulic bridges and refined the business of printing. They also began the important task of writing medical encyclopedias.

As you can tell, this really was a golden time for China. However, the Tang dynasty did reach its end in 906. Warring neighbors eventually weakened it. But, for the three hundred years that it ruled, it ruled very well. The Chinese can be proud of their strong heritage and of the era when they were the greatest empire in the world.

ACTIVITIES FOR LESSON 28

ALL STUDENTS

The Chinese Moon Festival dates back to the Tang dynasty or earlier. It takes place on the fifteenth day of the lunar month and is sometimes called the Mid-Autumn Festival. This festive occasion celebrates the harvest moon, or the largest and brightest full moon of the season. There are many versions of mythological legends behind the Moon Festival. Modern Chinese families still enjoy celebrating the Moon Festival by eating "moon cakes," gazing at the moon, and joining in dragon and lion dances. Research the Internet at www.newton.mec.edu/Angier/DimSum/china__dim_sum__moon_festi.html to find out more about the Moon Festival and a recipe for moon cakes.

Note to Teacher: The lengths of the underlines vary in this Internet address, and it is important to make the lengths as follows: two underlines after "china"; one underline after "dim"; two after "sum"; and one after "moon."

28A—Younger Students

1. Have a Chinese Tea Party.

   Purchase a brand of Chinese tea from the grocery store. Sit on the floor for your tea-drinking ceremony. Use tiny teacups that do not have handles. Keep tea leaves loose in the teapot, instead of in a tea bag. If you only have tea bags available, tear them open and place the tea leaves in your pot. The Chinese do not add sugar, cream, or milk. And lastly, don't use metal spoons. Though there is much more to a Chinese tea party, following these few rules should make for a fairly authentic event. Take a picture of your tea time and place it in your Student Notebook under "Asia: China."

2. Eat with chopsticks.

   Follow two simple rules when using chopsticks: Never allow the sticks to touch your mouth, and do not allow the sticks to cross when laying them down on the table.

28B—Middle Students

For centuries, women were generally looked down on in China. They were most often treated as servants. Turn to the Activity Supplement in the Appendix to a song written about the sad state of being a woman in China. Read and discuss it with your teacher. How does it make you feel? How did Jesus treat women in the Bible? Find examples.

28C—Older Students

1. As further research to the activity listed in 28B, investigate and discuss the *modern* treatment of women in China. In particular, consider the issue of mandatory abortion imposed in some parts of China.

2. There are many religious cults in our world today. It may surprise you to know just how far back in history Christian cults developed. Research the Nestorians from Persia to discover what beliefs they had that would classify them as a Christian cult. They are one group that particularly got the attention of Li Shi Min. He ordered that the Nestorian scriptures be translated to Chinese for him to read. In 635 he found the writings to be satisfactory and allowed them to be preached throughout his kingdom. A Nestorian monastery and church were started in China as a result. There still stands in China today a monument to the Nestorians dating back to 781. In light of this story, discuss with your teacher or class the significance of sound doctrine.

3. Research the sad love story of Emperor Ming Huang and the beautiful Yang Kwei-fei. Ming Huang was called the "Brilliant Emperor" of the Tang dynasty (713–756). Learn how the death of Yang Kwei-fei led to a rebellion.

4. If you are new to *The Mystery of History*, begin now a HANDWRITTEN running list of Chinese dynasties to be filed in your Student Notebook under "Asia: China." (If you have previously done this activity in Volume I, then simply add to the list you already created. Your "Special Notes" may be different from mine.)

Your list should be set up like the one below. (I'm including the information from Volume I.) For future lists, I will provide only the dates and names of the dynasties. I will ask you, the student, to then provide the Special Notes by reviewing the lesson. Today I'll give you "Hints" of what to include.

The Dynasties of China

Date of Power	Years Ruling	Name of Dynasty	Special Notes
c. 2000–1600 B.C.	c. 400 yrs.	Xia	Evidence of cities, bronze in use.
c. 1600–1066 B.C.	c. 534 yrs.	Shang	Developed writing, harvested silkworms.
c. 1122—256 B.C.	c. 866 yrs.	Zhou	Founded by King Wen, divided into Eastern and Western regions, large cities, farming, and iron abundant, **Confucius** lived.
221–206 B.C.	15 yrs.	Qin	The First Emperor of China, Shi Huang Ti, built the **Great Wall** and was buried with 7,500 terra-cotta soldiers.
202 B.C.–A.D. 220	422 yrs.	Han	Expanded under Emperor Wu Ti, horses imported, the "Silk Road" established, paper invented, **Jesus Christ** lived.

| A.D. 589–A.D. 618 | 29 yrs. | Sui | (Hint: Consider including the founder's name, the unification of the north and and south, the Grand Canal.) |
| A.D. 618–A.D. 906 | 288 yrs. | Tang | (Hint: Don't forget the Golden Age, Li Shi Min, Empress Wu Zetian, and fireworks!) |

622

MOHAMMED AND
THE BIRTH OF ISLAM
LESSON 29

In our last lesson, I mentioned a group of people called **Muslims.** They are also called **Moslems** or followers of the **Islamic faith.** Today I'm going to introduce you to the man who started the Islamic religion. His name was **Mohammed** (sometimes spelled Muhammad). Because of the huge influence that Mohammed has had on the world, I believe he is a very significant man to study. And because so many problems in our world today stem from conflict *between* Islam, Judaism, and Christianity, I believe it is wise to *try* to understand Mohammed, the founder of Islam.

Mohammed was born about 570 in the hot, dry city of **Mecca** on the peninsula of **Arabia.** (We call it Saudi Arabia now.) A **peninsula** is a piece of land almost completely surrounded by water. Saudi Arabia happens to be the largest peninsula in the world. Though surrounded by water, at least one-third of it is a scorching desert. In fact, the word *Arab* means "arid," or dry.

The city of Mecca where Mohammed was born was so hot that little could grow there. But Mecca grew large because it was a great stop for **traders.** It sits near the shore of the Red Sea where ships can easily come and go with their goods.

Mohammed was raised in a poor family by his uncle. His uncle was a tribal chief, better known as a **sheik.** Most families lived in tribes under the protection of a sheik since there was not a strong government in Arabia. Like most Arab boys, young Mohammed spent much of his youth tending sheep and camels and never learning to read or write. But one thing he liked was the chance to join caravans of traders who would pass through his city. He enjoyed hearing stories from far-off places. He was especially influenced by the Jewish and Christian traders who told him stories about there being just one God.

You see, in that time in Arabia, hundreds of gods were worshiped instead of just one. A black, square temple had been erected in the city of Mecca called the ***Kaaba*** where, in fact, *360* gods were worshiped! As seen in many cultures, the Arabs left offerings and goods at the Kaaba to seek the favor of the gods. Worshipers marched around the temple in crowded circles, chanting and praying. The most devoted would kiss a special black stone that was embedded in the wall of the Kaaba. The stone supposedly fell from heaven and was once white. (Some think it was a meteorite.) The Arabs believed that, over time, it was the sins of the people that made the stone turn black. This was the spiritual world that Mohammed was raised in.

When Mohammed was 20, he got a job helping a widow with her estate. Her name was **Khadijah.** She was about 15 years older than Mohammed. But in just a few years, they married. Despite their age difference, they were very happy together. They had three children of their own and adopted a son after their twin boys died.

Mohammed Claims to Have Visions

When Mohammed was 40 years old, he claimed to have some unusual things happen to him. He thought he was hearing an angel. At first he wondered if he was hearing things from the **jinn** or **jinni.** The jinn were believed to be both good and bad and something between an angel and a man (from where we get the notion of genies). But after some time, Mohammed believed he was receiving revelations about god from the **archangel Gabriel.**

This angel supposedly told Mohammed that there was only one god and that his name was **Allah. Allah-Taala** was the name already given to one of the gods worshiped at the Kaaba who was thought to be the ruler of the universe—but not very interested in man. So, the idea of "Allah" probably did not originate with Mohammed. But Mohammed was the first to claim that Allah[3] was the "only" god.

Over the next several years, Mohammed continued to claim revelations from Gabriel. Mohammed himself never wrote down any of these revelations because he couldn't read or write. But he said that he memorized the revelations by repeating them back to Gabriel word for word. It was after Mohammed's death that his followers

Pictured here is decorative Arabic script for "Mohammed," the founder of Islam.

wrote down these revelations in what is called the **Koran.** The Koran (sometimes spelled Quran) is the Holy Book of Islam. But I'm getting way ahead in the story here. The Koran wasn't written until after Mohammed's death.

Mohammed's father-in-law, Abu Bekr, was one of the first converts to Islam.

Mohammed shared his early revelations with his family and friends. They immediately believed him. His first converts were his wife Khadijah, his cousin **Ali,** his servant **Zaid** (whom he later freed), and his friend named **Abu Bekr** (who was also his father-in-law). Abu Bekr convinced five of his friends to convert to the teachings of Mohammed. Together the six men became known as Mohammed's "Companions," who later helped establish the Islamic faith.

But the merchants and leaders of Mecca were not so easy to convert. They were hesitant to think that there was only one god because it threatened their business. You see they made a lot of money from visitors wanting to buy sacrifices for their numerous gods. For this and other reasons, Mohammed and his followers were very unwelcome in Mecca.

---

3. Though in English it is common to write *Allah* as a proper name for their god, this is inappropriate and appalling to Muslims. They feel that the use of this term for "god" creates the impression that Allah is *different* from the God of the Bible. They believe their god is the same as the God of the Bible, though Jews and Christians strongly disagree with this.

As more and more people began to follow Mohammed, the Arabian leaders got nervous, particularly those who were of the Quraish tribe. Because *their* way of thinking was being challenged, they soon became enemies to Mohammed. They offered to pay Mohammed to see a doctor if it would cure him of his madness! Mohammed refused. The Quraish desperately wanted to run Mohammed and his new converts out of town, but they couldn't do so without starting a war. So instead they tortured the poorer converts, who were slaves, by exposing them to the boiling desert sun. Mohammed's friend, Abu Bekr, bought the freedom of as many of the slaves as he could afford to prevent this kind of persecution.

Things grew worse for Mohammed and his followers. Many of them fled to nearby cities and were separated from their tribes and clans. To make matters even more difficult for Mohammed, both his wife and a good friend died in the same year. In his grief, Mohammed tried to move to a nearby village but was stoned and forced out. Mohammed returned to his home in Mecca and married *two* new wives.

During this chaotic time, Mohammed believed he received more and more revelations from Gabriel about Allah. He claimed, too, that one night he was taken from his sleep on a winged horse and flown to the city of **Jerusalem.** He believed he was somehow "transported" to the **Wailing Wall** of the Jews— the last wall that existed from the sacred Jewish temple. Mohammed claimed that on that same night he was returned to his bed in Mecca. From that experience, Mohammed considered Jerusalem a holy site for Muslims. This is a very important fact to know because Jews and Muslims are still in dispute over this sacred place today.

It was also during this time that Mohammed frequently visited a city named **Medina** (muh DEEN uh) to teach and preach his revelations. Unlike the dry, barren city of Mecca, Medina was green and lush. It was about 200 miles north of Mecca. Many Jews lived there. The merchants of Medina liked Mohammed and invited him to come and live there. Even the Jews in Medina thought Mohammed to be a decent man. They agreed with him that there was only "one god" and didn't think Mohammed would ever be a threat to the Jewish people. (They were, of course, quite mistaken about that!)

Though the offer from Medina was appealing, Mohammed put off the invitation to move there and stayed in Mecca for another two years. However, most of his followers did

The Wailing Wall (or Western Wall) is all that remains of the Jewish Temple. Though Muslims and Jews both consider the area sacred, the Jews have held control of the wall since 1967.

move to Medina for safety. In time, the leaders in Mecca grew even more intolerant of Mohammed and his teachings. They plotted to murder him in the middle of the night. Somehow Mohammed learned of the plan and escaped. Instead of fleeing north where the Quraish expected to find him, Mohammed and his friend Abu Bekr headed south. They hid in caves until the way was clear to flee north to Medina.

Tradition tells the story that while hiding in a cave, Mohammed had a unique experience that helped save his life. Supposedly his enemies looked into a cave where he was hiding, but a spider had spun a web that covered the cave's entrance. Because the web was undisturbed, the Quraish didn't think Mohammed was there and they left. To this day, a spider is one of the sacred symbols of Islam.

The Hegira

The dangerous trip that Mohammed made from Mecca to Medina in **622** has been called the **Hegira** (hee JI re), which means "flight." For Mohammed it was a flight to safety. When Mohammed finally made it to Medina, he was welcomed like a hero by the leaders of the city and hundreds of his own people. The date of the Hegira is very important to Muslims. That was the official beginning of the new Islamic faith.

With a new religion coming to life and a group of people to lead, Mohammed became a very powerful man. He enjoyed his new position but for the most part remained a simple man. He was a hard worker and seldom used wealth on himself or his family. He gave most of his money to the poor. Toward his own people, Mohammed was said to be kind, generous, and compassionate. Mohammed had several wives by this time and split his time equally among them by sleeping at each of their different apartments (though there were occasional disputes and jealousies among them). While at his various homes, Mohammed helped with chores such as mending, sweeping, and the like. He also enjoyed children.

The Hegira, which means "flight," marks the date of Mohammed's flight for safety from Mecca to Medina in 622.

Despite his simple lifestyle, Mohammed was a cunning political leader. When it came to protecting his new movement, he was ruthless. For example, Mohammed saw to it that any caravans coming through Medina were attacked and robbed. The spoils went to feeding his people. He also found it necessary to fight against bands of citizens from Mecca who were still upset with him. When his followers in Medina asked him what their reward would be for fighting for him, Mohammed promised them **Paradise**! This is very important to know because Muslims are still willing to die for Mohammed's cause with the belief that they will receive entry to Paradise.

The First Jihad

Though things were going well in Medina, Mohammed wanted to make peace with his home city of Mecca, from which he had been forced to flee. As attacks from Mecca continued, Mohammed built a trench around Medina to keep out his enemies. The strategy worked, and the Meccan army of 10,000 warriors left him alone. This led to the signing of a 10-year peace treaty between Mecca and Medina.

But Mohammed broke the treaty after only two years. He wanted so badly to have Mecca under his power that he marched through the city against the rules of the treaty. This was Mohammed's first **jihad** (ji HAHD), or "holy war," and it took place in 630. Surprisingly, there was no war at all. Mohammed stormed through Mecca with such control over his men and was so strong a leader, that most of the people of Mecca switched their loyalties to him that day! They either believed in his cause or were in complete fear of Mohammed. Regardless of why the people of Mecca submitted, they did so without a fight.

In bold triumph, Mohammed publicly declared at the Kaaba in Mecca that there was only one god and that his name was Allah. He forbade the worship of any other gods or idols. He did, however, permit people to continue the tradition of worshiping and kissing the black stone at the Kaaba. (Because of their own beliefs against idol worship, the Jews were very critical of Mohammed for allowing this type of worship.) Mohammed also declared that from that point on Muslims should face Mecca when they prayed and that no unbeliever should ever set foot in the sacred city. These traditions are still followed today.

With Mohammed's strong declaration of beliefs at the Kaaba, the Jews in Medina grew worried. How could they allow this blasphemy against God? Mohammed at one time even claimed to be their awaited Messiah! This infuriated the Jews even more, and they soon became enemies to the Arab leader. When they were told to either convert to Islam or die, many Jews chose death! At least 600 Jewish men were killed by Mohammed and his army and buried in the marketplace of Medina. The surviving women and children were taken as slaves. Mohammed forced one of the more beautiful Jewish girls to become his mistress.

Mohammed As a Military Leader

Mohammed's last years were characterized by this type of brutal, **militant rule.** If someone wrote something bad about Mohammed, he had them executed. In the last 10 years of his life, Mohammed oversaw 65 military raids in Arabia and surrounding areas. Twenty-seven of these he led on his own. By his death, all of the Arabian Peninsula was Islamic. You see, Mohammed had become far more than a religious leader to the Arabs. He was a powerful military leader. It was probably his abilities as a general that gave Islam its strength in such a short time. The loosely scattered Arab tribes seemed to need the leadership that Mohammed offered.

Through holy war, or jihad, the Islamic faith spread to neighboring countries, extending its military might and belief system.

Interestingly, the people who admired Mohammed's power the most began to idolize him. They saved pieces of his hair, his spit, and the water that he washed with in the hope that these items would bring about **miracles.** But you know what? Mohammed never claimed to perform miracles. Neither did he try to predict the future. In fact, he claimed only to be a mortal, fallible "messenger." However, Mohammed did practice something that gave him supernatural status. That is, he offered Paradise to those who would die for Allah! We will discuss this and other details of Islam in the next lesson. In light of terrorism in the world today, it is very important to understand this belief.

By his late fifties, Mohammed began to show signs of his humanness. He suffered terribly from bad fevers. He believed they were the result of eating poisoned meat. It has never been proven. Three days before he died, he sat in the mosque at Medina to listen to the teachings of his old friend, Abu Bekr. I wonder what he thought about the religion that he had started. It has been written of him that he wanted the Arab people to have a strong religion like the Jews and the Christians that he had known as a boy. He had been especially impressed with their Holy Scriptures. Of course he created his own scripture through the dictation of the Koran. It's just something to think about.

On June 7, 632, at the age of 62, Mohammed died at the side of his favorite wife. Mohammed died not only as the founder of the Islamic faith but also as the founder of a whole new way of life for many nations. Historians would agree that because of the widespread influence of Mohammed, his life was one of the most phenomenal of the Middle Ages.

ACTIVITIES FOR LESSON 29

ALL STUDENTS

The birth of Islam (622) is a date to memorize.

29A—Younger Students

What do you know about desert life and camels? They are perfect animals for the Arabian Desert because they can go as long as 5 days without water in the summer and up to 25 days in the winter. A person will die without water in 7 to 10 days! Camels can provide milk, tender meat, and hide for clothing and tents. Even their waste products of dung and urine can be used for fuel and making an insecticide!

Pretend to be a camel today by getting on your hands and knees and allowing your teacher to tie a pillow on your back. Give "gentle" camel rides to your stuffed animals or younger brothers and sisters. Take a photo. File this under "Asia: Saudi Arabia" in your Student Notebook.

29B—Middle Students

Calculate the year according to the Muslim calendar. They consider July 16, 622 (the estimated date of Mohammed's flight), as the start of year 1, and their calendar is 354 days. To convert from a Christian year to a Hegira year, subtract 622 from the Christian year. Then multiply that by 1.031. To convert from a Hegira year to a Christian year, divide the Hegira year by 1.031. Then add 622 to your number. Thus, A.D. 1900 is 1317 A.H. (after the Hegira). Using this formula, convert the present year of the A.D. calendar to the Muslim calendar and file your answer under "Asia: Saudi Arabia." Check your work at the following Web site (and compare January 1 to December 31 of the same year):

www.islamicfinder.org/dateConversion.php?lang=english

29C—Older Students

1. Research the Kaaba. Look for answers to these questions. (Answers are also provided in the Pretest Answer Key in the Appendix.) File your answers in your Student Notebook under "Asia: Saudi Arabia."

   a. What are the dimensions of the Kaaba?

   b. What is the name given to the Islamic pilgrim who goes to Mecca?

   c. How many times does an Islamic pilgrim march around the Kaaba?

   d. In what months do the pilgrims march?

   e. How many times has the Kaaba been rebuilt?

   f. Who built and rebuilt the Kaaba (according to the Muslims)?

   g. You can find many pictures of the Kaaba on the Internet by going to www.google.com and clicking on "Images," then typing in "Kaaba."

2. Review the tragic collapse of the World Trade Center Towers in New York City on September 11, 2001. What was the message of the suicide pilots? What was the response of their families? Why were these men considered "martyrs" for their faith? How much influence on the world does Mohammed still have? Discuss these matters with your teacher, particularly the belief of gaining a place in Paradise by dying for Allah. Photocopy or clip newspaper and magazine articles depicting this tragedy. File them in your Student Notebook under "Asia: Saudi Arabia."

THE SPREAD OF ISLAM
LESSON 30

As you learned in our last lesson, **Mohammed** changed the way of life for many nations with the founding of **Islam.** Before we get into just how Mohammed changed things, let's review the way of life in Arabia *before* Mohammed. Muslims would refer to this time as *al-Jahiliya,* meaning **"the Age of Ignorance."**

Ancient Arabia was ruled by a mixture of Babylonians, Persians, Romans, and Jews. The peninsula has always been a center of trade because it sits between the three continents of Africa, Europe, and Asia. In ancient days, nearly five-sixths of Arabs were nomads called **Bedouins** (BED oo inz). A nomad is a person who travels from place to place for growing crops or raising animals.

The nomadic Bedouins and most Arabs are descendants of **Ishmael** from the Old Testament. Because Ishmael was the son of Abraham through Hagar, most Arabs consider themselves "Children of Abraham." They are a proud people. In ancient times, they lived to fight the scorching desert and the threat of other tribesmen. With hours to spend around a campsite, the Bedouins became masters at telling stories of adventure and love.

In fact, elaborate storytelling was so important to the Arabs that month-long contests were held in honor of the composers. And nothing was prized more than the transformation of the Arabic language into beautiful works of poetry. Winning poems were written down in exquisite print for all to admire. The greatest of all the Arabic poems were inscribed on Egyptian silk in golden letters and hung on the walls of the **Kaaba.** (Remember, the Kaaba is the black square temple in Mecca considered the most sacred of temples by the Muslims.) The poems were called the **Muallqat,** or "Golden Songs." Seven of them remain intact today.

Bedouin girls were sometimes married as young as 8 or 9 years of age! They were loved for their beauty and their ability to provide warrior sons to their husbands. But boys were so much more important to the Arabs that baby girls were sometimes buried alive and left to die! It was also common practice when a man died that his camel be put to death in case it was needed in the afterlife. The camel was tied to his owner's grave to suffer slow starvation.

But that was all before Mohammed. After his death in **632** and by the late 600s, the teachings of Mohammed were growing in their appeal to the nomads of Arabia. For one, he taught them to treat one another more fairly, especially servants and women (though not seen today). This created more equality between the classes. Mohammed promoted the idea of an honest brotherhood between all Arabs and the deep respect of one's parents.

The beautiful and artistic language of Arabic is read from right to left.

He forbade his people to ever kill baby girls or force a camel to die with its master. Mohammed taught good hygiene and the protection of the weak and the sick. He also discouraged the drinking of alcohol. From all of this, Islam brought much stability to the warring tribesmen and women of the desert.

The Duties and Beliefs of Islam

The name Islam actually means **"submission to God."** People's lives were changed as they "submitted" to the teachings of Mohammed, which he claimed were of Allah. In fact, the term *Muslim* means "submissive one."

So what did people actually submit to? Well, Muslims would say they are "submitting to the will of Allah" by keeping at least these five duties. According to Josh McDowell and Don Stewart in *Handbook of Today's Religions,*[4] the duties are:

1. Praying five times a day
2. Reciting the creed, "There is no god but Allah, and Mohamed is his prophet," at least 125,000 times in one's lifetime
3. Giving to the poor
4. Fasting from sunrise to sundown in the holy month of Ramadan
5. Making at least one trip to Mecca (if able)

Furthermore, Muslims believe that there is either Paradise or a burning inferno waiting for each person after death. They believe their fate is determined by Allah and based entirely on how well they fulfilled their duties. Muslims may never really know if they have done enough to enter into Paradise, but it is their desire. In other words, a Muslim seems to have to *work* for his entrance into Paradise by being good and keeping the strict duties I mentioned above. It is no wonder then that some would hope to "earn" Paradise through being a martyr instead.

In contrast, Christianity teaches that no one by his or her own goodness can earn salvation, or Paradise. Romans 3:10 says, *"There is none righteous, no, not one."* But Christians *also* believe that Jesus Christ's death on the cross, His sacrifice, takes care of man's sin—the very thing that makes us not worthy of heaven! Salvation then, or Paradise, is considered by Christians as a *gift* from God. Ephesians 2:8–9 explains it this way, *"For by grace you have been saved through faith, and that not of yourselves; it is the gift of God, not of works, lest anyone should boast."* This belief greatly divides Christian thought from Islam.

The inside of a mosque contains no chairs or pews but rather, Persian-style rugs for worshipers to kneel on and pray.

As in most religions, there are different factions and groups within Islam who vary in their beliefs from one another. But, according to the authors of *Civilization Past and Present,*[5] most Muslims would agree to the following list of beliefs:

1. There is no god but Allah.
2. There are angels that intercede for men.
3. The Koran is the last testament given by god.
4. There were several prophets of Allah including Noah, Moses, Abraham, Jesus, and Mohammed.
5. There is judgment for all mankind.
6. There are divine decrees to follow in this life as dictated by Mohammed in the Koran.

---

4. Josh McDowell and Don Stewart, *Handbook of Today's Religions.* Nashville: Thomas Nelson Publishers, 1996; p. 391.
5. T. Walter Walbank and Alastair M. Taylor, *Civilization Past and Present.* Chicago: Scott, Foresman and Company, 1949; p. 271.

The **Koran,** Islam's holy book or book of "recitations," was first ordered to be written by Mohammed's good friend, **Abu Bekr.** It was recorded about a year after Mohammed's death. Other teachings of Mohammed were later written down, but to the Muslim, none are as sacred as the Koran. There are 114 chapters, or **suras**, in the Koran, which are arranged according to their length. The longest chapters are first. Each chapter is a separate message in itself and the principal speaker is supposedly Allah. As is common to the Arabic language, the writings are very poetic and use lots of imagery.

Most copies of the Koran are in Arabic because devout Muslims disapprove of seeing it in any other language than the original.

Interestingly, the Koran speaks of both Jews and Christians. According to Muslims, Jews and Christians would be considered "Peoples of the Book" since **Moses** and **Jesus** received books of revelation. **Buddha** is never mentioned. I will add here, however, that the teachings about Jesus in Islam are very different from Christianity. Muslims may say they "believe" in Jesus, but they don't mean it the way a Christian does. Their belief in Jesus is that He was a wise man and a prophet. They don't believe Jesus was the divine Son of God who died for the sins of the world and rose from the dead. Muslims don't look to Jesus as a Savior, nor do they understand Him to be a Redeemer.

I will also add about the Koran that, unlike the Bible, it contains no **prophecy** to validate it as truth. In contrast, the Bible contains hundreds of predictions in both the Old and the New Testament that came true to prove it was the word of God! The Koran lacks this supernatural feature.

Furthermore, the Koran was dictated by Mohammed *alone* during a 22-year span of his life. It came together through one man, one language, one place, and one time period. No one else in history has ever backed up Mohammed's teachings with similar revelations. Mohammed boldly proclaimed to be the last true prophet and that his revelations were the *only* accurate ones.

In comparison, the Bible was written by over 40 different people from all walks of life, covering three continents and using three languages. The Bible was written over a 1,000-year span with every writer in agreement to the same teachings of God.

Mohammed believed that Allah was the same god as in the Bible even though his teachings about Allah do not fit with the Bible. To make sense of it, Mohammed taught that the Bible was distorted, not his teachings. Neither Jews nor Christians believe Allah to be the same god as the God of the Bible. This huge difference in beliefs has led to unbelievable strife between Islam and these other religions that still exists today!

Angels, Worship, and Islam Today

Of **angels,** Muslims believe that they exist to intervene for mankind. They also believe that 8 angels guard the throne of Allah and 19 angels guard Hell. Muslims also believe in the existence of **jinn** or **jinni,** which are thought to be spirits between angels and mankind. Some jinn are considered good, and some are believed to be wicked. The most powerful is thought to be the devil, called **shaitin** in the Koran from the Hebrew word *Satan.*

Christians believe, too, that angels are special beings created for ministering to God and man. But Satan, which means "adversary," is thought to be a fallen angel (not a jinni) whose mission is to oppose God and man. Demons are other fallen angels used by Satan to misguide and lure mankind from the truths of God.

A Muslim place of worship is called a **mosque.** At the first mosque built in Medina, Mohammed bowed three times before Allah as a symbol of his submission. This practice is still followed today. Though Mohammed is respected as a prophet and his behavior is modeled, he is not worshiped—but rather Allah. And in Islam there are no priests or pastors.

When Mohammed died in 632, there was the question of who would follow after him in leading the new religion and theocracy. A **theocracy** is a civil government ruled by religious leaders who believe they are representatives of god. For that reason, some Muslims thought the next leader should be a blood relative of Mohammed. Others thought

Arched doorways, domed rooftops, and towering minarets are common features of a mosque, a Muslim house of worship. From high in a minaret (photo at right), a man known as a muezzein ("crier") calls Muslims to prayer five times a day.

the next leader should be voted in. Though Mohammed had 10 wives, he didn't have any sons who survived to take over his rule. He did have a daughter named **Fatima** who married his adopted son and cousin, **Ali.** Ali wanted to be the first **caliph.** (Caliph comes from the Arabic word *khalifa*, which simply means "successor.")

But, as it turned out, Abu Bekr, Mohammed's father-in-law and longtime friend, took the position of the first caliph. Unfortunately, the disagreement over leadership between Ali and Abu Bekr led to years of war and ultimately to a division between Muslims that still exists today.[6] For a time, Ali also became caliph, but after five years he was assassinated.

Despite the turmoil over leadership, Islam spread like a wild fire to neighboring countries such as India and Egypt and to some nations in Europe. In 638 Muslims troops conquered the city of Jerusalem, causing all kinds of problems that still exist there. Today, Islam is primarily located in the Middle East, northern Africa, and parts of Europe and Asia. The names of some of these countries are Sudan, Pakistan, Indonesia, Bangladesh, Yemen, Iran, Nigeria, Tunisia, Egypt, and Tajikistan. Less than 1 percent of the Muslim population lives in America, though that figure is growing.

As you can imagine, it is difficult for me as a Christian to write about Islam because some Muslim groups in the world are persecuting Christians. That means they are killing people of my faith for not being of the Islamic faith. Militant Muslims are also responsible for killing thousands of Jews in Israel through suicide bombings and other forms of terror. Persecution is a sad truth and a very difficult matter to understand.

I don't believe it would be right to despise the Muslim *people* for persecution and acts of terrorism, but I believe we can despise the *deception* behind the acts as well as the acts themselves. I hope that by understanding the history of Islam, you will be better equipped to share God's love with Muslims as well as with others around the world.

---

6. Later descendants of Ali identified themselves as *Shiites* (SHEE iyts). They still hold to the belief that Ali was the rightful successor to Mohammed. Shiites presently make up about 10 percent of the Muslim population and are primarily located in Iran, where Shiism is the state religion of the Islamic Republic.

ACTIVITIES FOR LESSON 30

ALL STUDENTS

Make your Memory Cards for Lessons 28–30. Remember to highlight the birth of Islam (622) as a date to memorize.

Teachers and Parents

Please discern the spiritual maturity of your student(s) to determine suitable activities for them. My hope is that a well-grounded student would explore the claims of Islam for a greater appreciation of the Gospel of Jesus Christ. For those who may not be comfortable with this, the younger-student activities can be adapted to any age.

30A—Younger Students

1. Look in an encyclopedia at flags of the world. Look for flags with one star and a crescent moon next to each other. These two symbols together represent a country that is Islamic. The flags of Algeria and Libya are two examples. How many flags can you find with that symbolism? Does the flag of Saudi Arabia use these emblems?

2. Islamic art is known for being geometrical. It is also called "arabesque," meaning "done in the Arab way." Mohammed forbade the drawing of people in art for fear it would lead to idol worship. Find examples of Arabic art and try to create your own using straight lines and shapes about the same size. File your artwork in your Student Notebook under "Asia: Saudi Arabia."

30B—Middle and Older Students

As was done when we studied the Shinto religion of Japan, answer the following doctrinal questions about Islam. Answers are given in the Activity Supplement, but see how far you can get on your own research from this lesson and the use of other reference books.

1. The founder of the religion and date of origination.

2. The source of authority (written works of the religion, visions, prophecy).

3. The doctrine of God (believing there is one God or many gods).

4. The doctrine of Jesus Christ (believing Jesus was God in the flesh or just a prophet).

5. Their belief in sin.

6. The doctrine of salvation. (On what basis is sin forgiven or accounted for?)

7. The doctrine of things to come. (Is there a belief in life after death or in a coming judgment of the world?)

8. What draws people to this religion (lifestyle, ritual, heritage, etc.)?

30C—Older Students

1. For a better understanding of Islam and the world that we live in today, research the two main divisions of the Islamic religion: the Sunnis (SUN eez) and the Shiites (SHEE iyts). Find the answers to the following questions and more. (Answers are also provided in the Pretest Answer Key.)

   a. Which group comprises about 85 percent of Islam today?

   b. Which group includes the subdivision of leadership under the Imamis (or Twelvers)?

   c. Which group considers itself more "orthodox," or true to the teachings of Mohammed?

   d. Which group represents about 10 percent of Islam today?

e. What does *sunnah* mean?

f. What does *shia* mean?

2. Obtain a map of the world that expresses where Christian persecution exists. (As a resource, I recommend *Voice of the Martyrs*, listed below.) A great amount of persecution occurs in Islamic countries. Pray for the leaders of these nations. Pray for the persecuted church under this oppression. The persecution of Christians is a very serious problem in our world, but it rarely receives the attention of the media. Look for examples of it in the news.

The Voice of the Martyrs
P.O. Box 443
Bartlesville, OK 74005-0443
Or call at 918-337-8015
Web site: www.persecution.com

TAKE ANOTHER LOOK!

REVIEW 10: LESSONS 28–30

Wall of Fame

1. ***The Sui and Tang Dynasties (589, 618)***—Make two figures to represent the two dynasties. For the Sui, create a rectangle. Write on the top of it "Sui Dynasty." Below, draw a waterway and label it the Grand Canal. For the Tang dynasty, create a rectangle on gold paper (or color the paper gold). Write on it "Tang Dynasty." Underneath the title, write "Golden Age of China" and draw fireworks over it. [From *History Through the Ages,* use *The Sui dynasty* and *The Tang Dynasty.*]

2. ***Mohammed and the BIRTH OF ISLAM (622)***—Create a man and write on him "The Founder of Islam." **Remember, the birth of Islam (622) is a date to memorize.** [Use *Mohammed, Abu Bekr,* and *The Hegira.*]

3. ***The Spread of Islam (632)***—To represent the "holy wars" fought to spread the ideas of Islam, create a book with a sword drawn on it. Write on it "The Koran." [Use *The Arab-Muslim Sweep.*]

SomeWHERE in Time

1. Using Outline Map 7, "East Asia," follow the directions below only as far as the student is able. Use an atlas or globe as a resource.

   a. Label and color the large country of modern China. Under the Tang dynasty, China was only about half the size that it is today.

   b. Label and color these larger bodies of water: Sea of Japan, Yellow Sea, South China Sea, Bay of Bengal, and Arabian Sea.

   c. Find and label these Chinese cities: Beijing (capital), Shanghai, Hong Kong, and Chongqing.

   d. Find, label, and color the neighbors of modern China. There are many! We will start in the north and work east around the country in a circle. Mongolia, Russia, North Korea, Japan, Taiwan, Vietnam, Laos, Burma, India, Nepal, Pakistan, Afghanistan, Tajikistan, Kyrgyzstan (it is tiny), and Kazakhstan. (Younger students may want to simply hunt for these countries on a globe or in an atlas.)

   e. Find and label these geographical regions: Altai Mountains (a border between Mongolia and China), Himalaya Mountains (border to Nepal and India), Takla Makan Desert, Gobi Desert, Plateau of Tibet, Huang He or Hwang River (also called the Yellow River), and Yangtze River (the third longest river in the world after the Nile and the Amazon).

   f. Bonus for map lovers: On a fresh copy of Outline Map 7, "East Asia," find and label the capital cities of each of the neighboring countries of China that are listed above. (The answers are at the end of this Review section.) In random order, these are the names of the capitals: Viangchan (formerly Vientiane), Islamabad, Ulan Bator, Tokyo, Kabul, New Delhi, Dushanbe, Taipei, Astana, Hanoi, Pyongyang, Rangoon, Kathmandu, Moscow (off the map), and Bishkek.

2. Create a "sand" map of Saudi Arabia. (This might get messy!) It won't keep but it will be fun to make and you will become more familiar with the region.

Materials: Outline Map 15, "Saudi Arabia"; Outline Map 16, "Review 10 Answer Key"; large rectangular plastic tub or food container (approximately 8½ by 11 inches); blue crayon (or pencil or marker); pen or pencil; mixing bowl; sand; water; spoon; paper; pen; tape; scissors; toothpicks; yarn or string just a few inches long; black marker; small scrap of paper

(Younger students may opt to skip a. and b. and move on to c.)

a. On your map of Saudi Arabia, label and color blue the Red Sea, the Arabian Sea, and the Persian Gulf.

b. Starting northwest of Saudi Arabia and moving east, label the countries neighboring Saudi Arabia in this order: Jordan, Iraq, Kuwait, Qatar, United Arab Emirates, Oman, and Yemen.

c. Lay the map of Saudi Arabia flat in the bottom of your plastic container.

d. Place sand in a mixing bowl. Slowly add just enough water to make it easy to sculpt or build with (the texture you might find on the beach). Do not make it too soupy.

e. Use a spoon to carefully lay the sand over the country of Saudi Arabia. Do not cover the seas or neighboring countries.

f. Using paper, pen, scissors, tape, and toothpicks, create flags of the following places: a large flag for Saudi Arabia, small flags for the cities of Medina and Mecca, a flag with a star on it for the present-day capital city of Riyadh.

g. Using a piece of string or yarn, create a line from Mecca to Medina. This indicates the Hegira, the escape Mohammed made from his home city to Medina in 622.

h. Draw a small square on a piece of paper. Color it black and cut it out. Lay this small black square on the city of Mecca to indicate the location of the Kaaba, the Muslim's sacred temple.

i. Take a photo of your map project and file it in your Student Notebook under "Asia: Saudi Arabia."

3. Middle and Older Students: Research on the Internet the present-day countries that are predominantly Muslim. Transfer this information to a map of the world and file it under "Miscellaneous" in your Student Notebook. Use it as a prayer guide.

Answers to 1(f):

Mongolia – Ulan Bator	Vietnam – Hanoi	Pakistan – Islamabad
Russia – Moscow	Laos – Viangchan	Afghanistan – Kabul
N. Korea – Pyongyang	Burma – Rangoon	Tajikistan – Dushanbe
Japan – Tokyo	India – New Delhi	Kyrgyzstan – Bishkek
Taiwan – Taipei	Nepal – Kathmandu	Kazakhstan – Astana

Fix 'Em! The sentences below are false. Using your textbook, make them true by crossing out the wrong information and writing in the new. I have provided an example. The sentences are in the order of Lessons 13–30.

1. When Diocletian divided his kingdom, he gave half of it to ~~Jupiter.~~ Maximian.

2. At the Council of Nicaea, church leaders wrote the Apostles' Creed, which stated that Jesus was God, not just similar.

3. The ruling family of the Golden Age in India was the Shotoku clan.

4. After the Old Testament Flood, the Maya and other early Americans crossed to the new continent when a natural land bridge existed at the Gibraltar Strait.

5. St. Augustine changed his view on faith when introduced to the wise bishop of Milan named Attila.

6. In 393 church leaders met in Pompeii to standardize the New Testament.

7. At age 16, Patrick was kidnapped by Bar-Kokhba, sold as a slave, and forced to work on a pig farm.

8. The Huns were known for scourging the plains of Europe and Asia on elephants.

9. The last Roman emperor to hold the throne before being ousted by a German war chief was Nero.

10. For common people in the Dark Ages of Europe, pie was the main staple served morning, noon, and night.

11. Merlin, the "magical" mentor of King Arthur, suggested that he build a great triangular table for the knights.

12. Theodora, who became the queen of the Byzantine Empire, grew up in a musical family.

13. Columba, whose name means "duck," set up many important monasteries in Scotland.

14. The Japanese refer to their homeland as *Samurai,* meaning "source of the sun."

15. Out of a desire to serve, Gregory the Great transformed his palace into the Market of St. Andrew.

16. Yang Guang, an emperor of the Sui dynasty, oversaw the building of the Taj Mahal as the world's largest man-made waterway.

17. Remembered as the Hegira, or "flight," Mohammed fled from Mecca to the city of Byzantium.

18. According to Muslims, the time period before Mohammed was born is called "the Age of Prophecy."

☑ WHAT DO YOU KNOW?

PRETEST 11

Circle Sense. In the sentences below, *circle* the word that makes the most *sense*.

1. Wu Zetian became the only (empress, seamstress) to rule over China.

2. Wu Zetian sponsored the building of many beautiful (ships, shrines).

3. In the epic poem of *Beowulf,* the king fights and kills a snarling (snail, monster).

4. Beowulf wrestles Grendel to death by breaking off his (tongue, arm).

5. Tragically, Beowulf is mortally wounded by a fire-breathing (dragon, tarantula).

6. Ancient peoples called the Rock of Gibraltar in Spain one of the "Pillars of (Cupid, Hercules)."

7. The Moors invaded Spain from nearby (Africa, Australia).

8. The Moors brought great (monsters, wealth) to Spain in the Middle Ages.

WU ZETIAN, THE EMPRESS OF CHINA
LESSON 31

Today I am going to break one of my own rules. Instead of teaching you the history of China through one of its dynasties, I'm going to tell you the story of one extraordinary Chinese woman. On her own merit, she *made* history by being the only woman to ever rule over China! Her given name at birth was **Wu Zhao.** At 14 her name was changed to **Mei-Niang,** meaning "charming or sultry lady." It described her ability to charm men. But she renamed herself **Wu Zetian** (Wuuz zet ee UN) meaning "ruler of the sky" in honor of her own achievement at becoming an empress! Here is her remarkable story.

Wu Zetian was born into a rich, noble family. With her wealth she gained an excellent education. She knew music, history, literature, and politics. Besides that she was witty and beautiful. With all these attributes, she was considered by Chinese standards to be the perfect candidate for personal service to the emperor. By the young age of 14 she was recruited to be his concubine, or mistress. You've already learned about the emperor who employed her. It was **Li Shi Min** from Lesson 28. (I told you in that lesson that I would give Wu Zetian her own place in this book. This is it.)

For years Wu Zetian served Li Shi Min and she undoubtedly was one of his favorite companions. But when Wu Zetian was just 27 years old, Li Shi Min passed away. The entire nation grieved, but probably none more than Wu Zetian. For it was Chinese custom that former concubines of the emperor live out the rest of their lives in a Buddhist nunnery! They were never to marry.

This idea didn't go over very well with Wu Zetian. Though she moved into the nunnery, Wu set her sights on capturing the heart of the new emperor and setting herself free. The new emperor was Li Shi Min's son. His name was **Li Zhi.** He was known to be captivated by Wu Zetian's charms and visited her for years at the nunnery. To lure him with her beauty, Wu Zetian decorated her shaven head with jewels and cloth. (Buddhist nuns were required to wear short, shaven hair.)

Though ruthless in her means, Wu Zetian became the only woman ever to rule China on her own.

Wu's schemes were successful. Against all tradition, she was invited to leave the nunnery and live in the emperor's palace as his concubine. Wu gladly accepted although it was an outrage to the Chinese. But being a concubine just wasn't enough for her. Even after giving Li Zhi two sons—sons who would probably become emperors—Wu Zetian wanted more. She wanted to be Li Zhi's *official* wife and the empress of China! She came up with a most awful plot to get rid of the true wife of Li Zhi. Her name was **Empress Wang.**

As the tragic story goes, Wu Zetian accused Empress Wang of murdering Wu's new baby girl. The child was really killed by Wu herself! The trickery worked as far as Wu was concerned. Empress Wang was abolished by her husband for the supposed murder. In time, Wu Zetian got what she sacrificed her daughter for. With Empress Wang out of her way, she was able to marry Li Zhi and become his empress! Her position was the highest a woman could have in China. (Although it was still not enough to satisfy Wu!)

For several years Li Zhi and Wu Zetian, emperor and empress of China, ruled together. However, Wu's power grew and grew. She convinced her husband to make many reforms in the government despite the counsel of others. Those who opposed her were fired from their positions.

But things got far more serious than that. Li Zhi suffered a terrible stroke in 660 that left him unable to handle his affairs. As you can guess, Wu Zetian took this opportunity to *act* as the sole emperor over China though she was not officially recognized for it. Confucius had once written that having a woman rule over China would be as unnatural as "a hen crowing like a rooster at daybreak."[1] Well, Wu Zetian crowed rather loudly. Those who tried to oppose her were executed or forced to commit suicide! She spared no one—not even her own family members. Despite Wu's ruthless measures to keep power in her hands, she was an effective ruler.

In 683, Emperor Li Zhi passed away. For the sake of formality, and because it was not yet considered feasible that a woman would really be an emperor, Wu Zetian's sons were made emperors, one after the other. But Wu ruled over them completely and retained her mysterious power.

Sole Ruler of China

Finally, in **690,** Wu Zetian grew weary and impatient of ruling China through her son. She deposed him from the throne and declared herself to be the one and only true emperor of China. And it worked! After all the power-hungry years she connived and manipulated for the position of emperor, it was hers alone. For 15 glorious years, Wu Zetian lived her dream.

During her reign, Wu managed to improve agriculture, lower taxes, improve public works, and raise the standard for serving in the court. Though cruel in her methods for gaining power, Wu proved to be fair and just in the treatment of her loyal subjects and the masses. She greatly raised the status of women in general and insisted upon the writing of several biographies of Chinese women—lest anyone forget their contribution to Chinese culture.

Toward the end of her life, Wu mellowed somewhat in her ways. Perhaps to cleanse her conscience from former crimes, she held closely to the peaceful teachings of **Buddha.** (Although Buddhism does not offer to cleanse us from sin as the blood of Christ does. It challenges people to live "better" lives.) Chinese Buddhism rose to its height during Wu's lifetime as she sponsored the building of numerous Buddhist temples and shrines. **Pagodas**—tall, decorative structures found near Buddhist temples—became fashionable under Wu's influence. She perhaps downplayed the teachings of Confucius during her lifetime because of his negative viewpoint toward women in leadership.

By promoting the literature and achievements of women, Wu Zetian did much to improve the status of women in China.

Before Wu Zetian died, she was pressured to give her position as emperor to one of her sons. She did so in 705 and died the same year. Interestingly, Wu Zetian wanted to keep her tomb free of any written words about her. I think she hoped that future generations would come up with their own words for her. And of course, they have. Some call her the most ruthless woman ever to rule because of the trail of murders that followed her to the throne. Others hail her as one of the most brilliant women ever to rule for her ability to rise above thousands of years of male tradition. I find that

---

1. "Empress Wu Zetian," (Female Heroes of Asia: China). Accessed on Web site of the Women in World History Curriculum; Lyn Reese, director, at: www.womeninworldhistory.com/heroine6.html.

Wu Zetian reminds me a lot of Cleopatra of Egypt who lived about 700 years before her. Like Wu, Cleopatra was ambitious, powerful, and at times ruthless in getting what she wanted. What would you say about Wu Zetian? As the only woman to ever serve as an emperor over China, she has certainly earned the right to be remembered—be it good or bad!

ACTIVITIES FOR LESSON 31

31A—Younger and Middle Students

1. Practice your balance.

   Architecture is a word that refers to how people build things. Landscape refers to the way people plant shrubs, trees, and gardens. Both Chinese architecture and Chinese landscaping are well known for expressing

   The building of tall, eight-sided pagodas became more fashionable under the influence of Wu Zetian.

   balance. A tall pagoda, for example, appears well balanced. It has equal sides and looks like each layer is just resting on top of the other. Discuss "balance" and "imbalance" with your teacher. Just for fun, practice balance today by placing a book on your head and trying to walk across a room. Can you walk with more than one book on your head? Like a pagoda, place the larger books on the bottom and the smaller ones on top! Carefully see how many you can balance before they fall! (You might want your teacher to take a picture of your accomplishment. File it under "Asia: China" in your Student Notebook.)

2. Build a pagoda birdfeeder.

   See the directions for this fun project in the Activity Supplement in the Appendix. It is simple to build, attractive, and practical. Estimated time to complete: 30 minutes.

31B—Middle Students

1. Though panda bears are not directly related to our lesson, they are beautiful animals unique to China. Research the panda bears that were given to the United States as a gift from China. What are their names? What made them a special gift? How old are the bears? What do they eat? Have they reproduced? File your mini-report with pictures under "Asia: China" in your Student Notebook.

2. Research the Dunhuang caves in northern China where there are thousands of images of Buddha carved out of stone. Some are as high as 56 feet! Within nearly 500 caves, there are 2,000 carvings. Find pictures to photocopy or print. File these under "Asia: China" in your Student Notebook. Title the page "Buddhism Grows During the Tang Dynasty."

31C—Older Students

1. Learn more about the famous Three Pagodas in Dali, China. They were built during the Tang dynasty. For a visual and brief history, I recommend visiting the following Internet site. Click on the image shown for a larger view of the three pagodas, then print the image and file it in your Student Notebook under "Asia: China."

   http://chinaguides.shanghai-window.com/destination/yunnan/dali/3pagodas.asp

2. It was important for Wu Zetian to publish numerous biographies of Chinese women. Find three biographies of women who represent your own culture and ethnicity. Write a short synopsis of each. File this in your Student Notebook under the continent and country in which you live.

3. At the time of my writing this lesson (late 2003), there is debate in China over opening the tomb of Wu Zetian. There obviously would be great historical value to opening the undisturbed tomb, but some are concerned that technology is not yet in place to preserve the findings. Research the status of the debate.

THE EPIC OF BEOWULF
LESSON 32

Do you believe in monsters or fire-breathing dragons? Most of our ideas of these scary creatures come from medieval fairytales. The epic of ***Beowulf*** (BAY oh wolf), our subject today, is believed by some to be just that—a fairytale about monsters and dragons. But upon closer examination, Beowulf may very well be a true story, "monsters" and all!

First of all "Beowulf" is the name of both a king *and* an epic poem. The poem titled *Beowulf* is the oldest English poem in existence. A copy of it from about the year 1000 can be found in the British Museum.

Beowulf was composed in the **early 700s** by an unknown author. It was written in the language of the **Anglo-Saxons** in England, but the story takes place in **Sweden** and **Denmark** in the 500s. The reason for our interest in the poem has something to do with a Christian worldview. Let me summarize the poem for you first, and then I'll discuss its relevance to us today.

The exciting but gruesome poem opens with the story of a monster named **Grendel.** The monster has attacked and eaten 30 men at a local dining hall in Denmark. The countryside is alarmed, and news of the attack travels to Beowulf, a warrior who lives across the sea in southern Sweden. Upon hearing the trouble with Grendel, Beowulf and 14 other brave men volunteer to fight this terrible creature. Along with Beowulf's offer to slay Grendel, he gives the local people this little bit of consolation—should he die in his effort to free them from the beast, they won't need to bother "burying" him, for surely his body will be eaten by the monster!

As expected, the snarling Grendel attacks Beowulf. But what's not expected is the manner in which Beowulf fights back. Rather than fight the

The setting of the epic of Beowulf is Denmark, but Beowulf himself was a king from Sweden. Since the Middle Ages, it has been customary in Sweden to celebrate Midsummer's Eve with dancing around a Maypole.

creature with a sharp weapon, sword, or knife, Beowulf wrestles the beast with his own strength. Now here is the gory part: Beowulf manages to twist and rip off the arm of the creature, forcing Grendel to hobble back to his home in the misty swamp where he bleeds to death.

But the story isn't over yet! Apparently Grendel was but the youngster of a monster and when the mother monster discovers the fate of her son, she attacks Beowulf in revenge. Her wrath is like that of a mother bear who has lost her cub! Though not an easy task, Beowulf manages to trounce Grendel's mother as well, and he becomes a hero to the Danish people.

After the victory, Beowulf returns to his homeland in Sweden to rule as king of the **Geats** for 50 years. But the Geats are not free of monsters in their land either. In his old age, Beowulf courageously fights for his own people against a "fire-breathing" dragon. Beowulf and his friend **Wiglaf** succeed in slaying the beast by cutting it in two. But in the scuffle, Beowulf receives a fatal wound to his throat. At this point in the poem, Beowulf sums up his life in these dying words[2]:

> *This land I have ruled*
> *Fifty winters. No folk-king dared,*
> *None of the chiefs of the neighboring tribes,*
> *To touch me with sword, or assail me with terror,*
> *Of battle-threats. I bided at home,*
> *Held my peace and my heritage kept,*
> *Seeking no feuds nor swearing false oaths.*
> *This gives me comfort and gladdens me now,*
> *Though wounded sore and sick unto death.*

According to the epic poem, in his old age Beowulf fights a fire-breathing dragon back in Sweden and both die from their wounds.

Though brave to the end, Beowulf dies from the wound inflicted by the now dead dragon. The poem concludes with these words about our hero[3]:

> *His hearth companions*
> *Called him the best among kings of the earth,*
> *Mildest of men, and most beloved,*
> *Kindest to kinsmen, and keenest for fame.*

Now that you have the gist of the story, what might it mean to us today? Well, it tells us lots of things. For one, the poem sheds light on the language of the Anglo-Saxons who wrote the poem. (Okay, not very exciting.) Second, the poem tells of heroic virtues upheld by the Swedes and the Danes. (That's "nice.") But far more fascinating is the existence of the monster creature named Grendel, his revenging mother, and the fire-breathing dragon! And here is why . . .

Modern scientists would lead us to believe that mankind and dinosaurs never existed at the same time. There is widespread belief that the earth is millions of years old and that *that* is when the dinosaurs roamed our planet. This thinking is contrary to that of the Creation story of the Bible, which claims that *all* animals, including dinosaurs, were created on the fifth and sixth days of Creation—the same time as man. (See Gen. 1:20–31.) So when we have accounts like these of Beowulf's "monsters," it can only make you wonder about the co-existence of dinosaurs and mankind!

2. Rewey Belle Inglis, Donald A. Stauffer, and Cecil Evva Larsen, *Adventures in English Literature* (Mercury Edition). New York: Harcourt, Brace and Company, 1949; p. 58.
3. Ibid., p. 58.

If you take the epic of *Beowulf* to be literal, then it demonstrates that men at one time fought for their lives against large creatures, like Grendel and the dragon. We apparently don't have animals exactly like these around today. Are there records of other such creatures in old world literature? Absolutely! Tales of dragons, sea monsters, and other large creatures abound in China, Japan, and medieval Europe. The legend of **St. George** tells of a knight who gave God the glory when he saved a village from a terrible dragon. St. George really lived between A.D. 250 and 300. The Bible tells stories of great animals like **Leviathan** and the **behemoth.** (See Job 40:15, 41:1; Ps. 74:14, 104:26; Isa. 27:1.) And **Nebuchadnezzar** of Babylon had dragons engraved on his city gates.

Could dragons really breathe fire? There is that possibility. We see amazing defense mechanisms in animals today—consider the skunk, the octopus, and the electric eel. There is a little bug called the **bombardier beetle** that spits fire from a two-part chamber in its body to ward off predators. The vapor it spits reaches 212 degrees. Imagine if a large dragon-sized animal had the same defense system! That would be some serious smoke.

But, besides the stories of dragons and monsters that have circulated for centuries, there are two ancient pictures in existence today of an animal that fits the description of Grendel. One picture is part of a stone carving in England. The other is on a cylinder seal all the way from Babylonia. What is most amazing is that the cylinder seal seems to portray a man trying to twist the arm off the animal! Maybe it was a common form of defense back then to break the arms of the Grendel-type species because it was too difficult to pierce it with a sharp weapon. Hmmmm!

Is there any reason to think that Beowulf is not a true story? Not from a historical perspective. According to Bill Cooper, the author of *After the Flood*, every character in the poem IS real. Every king, place, and event in the poem line up with documented histories of Sweden and Denmark. So it is very probable that the epic poem of *Beowulf*, as recorded in about the year 700, is a true-life story from the Dark Ages.

If *Beowulf* is historically accurate, then it supports the Christian worldview. And that is very important to know. A Christian worldview is having the perspective that the things of the Bible are true, including the Creation story that places dinosaurs and mankind on earth at the same time! Remember, the *mystery of history,*

Though it doesn't entirely prove their existence, numerous tales of dragons and sea monsters are found in Old World literature.

according to this author, is God revealing Himself to man. Isn't it thought-provoking that even in the ancient poem of *Beowulf,* we quite possibly have testimony of God's creation?

ACTIVITIES FOR LESSON 32

32A—Younger and Middle Students

Make a cool shield and sword to fight off dragons! Directions are in the Activity Supplement.

32B—Younger and Middle Students

At the library, check out picture books of monsters, dragons, and dinosaurs. Compare the pictures you find to what Grendel might have looked like. Can you find any similarities to modern-day species? Photocopy your favorites and file them in your notebook under "Europe: Denmark."

1. Bill Cooper, the author of the book *After the Flood,* spent 25 years researching the genealogies of people in Europe who trace their roots back to the sons of Noah! This is incredible information that gives great support to the Christian worldview in regard to Creation, the Table of Nations in Genesis, the Flood, and the age of the earth. I highly recommend that you read the book! Write down at least five things you learned. Memorize them and give an oral report to your teacher or class. (You can read the entire book online at www.ldolphin.org/cooper.)

2. Have you ever heard of a Christian band named *Caedmon's Call?* They named their band after a monk by the name of Caedmon who believed he received a special call from God to write music containing Scripture. He lived at the same time period as Beowulf. Research this monk. Another English monk and historian by the name of Bede (672–735) wrote about Caedmon's experience.

711

AL-ANDALUS: "THE ORNAMENT OF THE WORLD" IN MEDIEVAL SPAIN

LESSON 33

Once upon a time, in the heart of the Middle Ages, there was an Islamic place where Jews, Christians, and Muslims lived together in amazing harmony. For reasons that are hard to explain, these three very different faiths shared the same rich culture. Where was this extraordinary place? It was southern **Spain.** To the Muslims it was called **al-Andalus.** To the Jews it was **Sefarad.** To the Christians it was the kingdom of **Cordoba,** or home of the **Moors.** Whatever the name, this unusual place on earth was nicknamed **"the ornament of the world"** for the way it shone in the midst of the dark Middle Ages. Before I explain the fascinating culture of al-Andalus, let me take you back to earlier times in Spain— back to its ancient roots—back to a time before Islam appeared there.

If you were to look at Spain on a map or globe, you would see that it lies at the entrance to the beautiful Mediterranean Sea. It shares the **Iberian Peninsula** with the small country of **Portugal.** As part of the Iberian Peninsula, Spain has oceans on three sides and is attached to France at the **Pyrenees Mountains.** Can you find them on a map or globe? Look for the Strait of Gibraltar, too. It is a narrow strip of water between Spain and Africa. You will want to remember it for later.

The earliest recorded people in Spain were the **Iberians,** from which we get the name of the Iberian Peninsula. Not much is known about them, but we do know a lot about the first *settlers* in Spain. They were the **Phoenicians.** The Phoenicians, as I wrote in Volume I, were a sea-loving people who lived on the other end of the Mediterranean Sea. They were famous for a beautiful, but stinky, purple-red dye that came from snails. The dye was popular enough to give the Phoenicians something to trade on the coasts of Europe and Northern Africa. In doing so, they started many new cities on the coast of Spain. In fact, it is believed that the *oldest* city in Europe—**Cadiz,** Spain—was founded by the Phoenicians in 1130 B.C. That was a long time ago.

But the first people to *conquer* the entire Iberian Peninsula were the **Romans.** That's probably not surprising if you remember anything about the Romans. Hannibal tried to stop them during the Punic Wars 200 years before Christ—but he failed. Spain, like most of Europe, became a major Roman center. Spain's name comes from what the Romans called the land, which was **Hispania.** It's Latin. Along with parts of their language, the Romans contributed great architecture and politics to the Spanish.

Though for centuries the Western Roman Empire dominated Europe, it eventually collapsed. We've already studied that. Like elsewhere in the Roman Empire, Spain was invaded by the **Vandals** and the **Visigoths** around 400. It was the Visigoths who last held Spain until Muslim armies from northern Africa invaded in **711.** That's the year where today's lesson begins.

Tariq and the Invasion of the Moors

The Muslim armies that invaded Spain in 711 called themselves the **Berbers.** However, the Romans nicknamed them the **"Moors"** from the name of the white-skinned **Mauri** tribe, which was a segment of the Berber people. (Though the term *Moor* is unpopular among the Arabs, I will refer to them as such because it is still common in the English language.) What is most important to know about the Moors is that they were Islamic. Sometime after **Mohammed** lived, the **Islamic faith** spread from Arabia all the way to the Berbers and Moors of northwestern Africa.

The first Moorish army to invade Spain was led by a man named **Tariq.** (Stay with me here, this is going to get more interesting!) When Tariq sailed to Spain from Africa, he landed at the point where the two lands almost meet. Tariq came to a huge limestone rock. It jutted some 1,500 feet into the sky! The ancients called this enormous rock one of the **Pillars of Hercules.** Tariq claimed the breathtaking rock for himself, and it has carried his name ever since—the "rock or mountain of Tariq" or in Arabic, **Gebel al-Tariq.** To us, it's the familiar name of **Gi-bral-tar** (dropping the "iq" in Tariq). This name is still used to describe the huge rock as well as the strait of water between the continents of Europe and Africa. (I find it interesting to connect present-day names with the past.)

After Tariq pushed past Gibraltar, the Moors poured into Spain to stay. And they stayed for almost 800 years! But there is much more to the story than that. Let me tell you about an intrepid young prince who ran away from home to save his life. (*Intrepid* means he was brave.) The prince's exciting escape had much to do with the incredible formation of al-Andalus, the "ornament of the world" in the Middle Ages.

Prince Abd al-Rahman and the Formation of al-Andalus

In the city of Damascus—in Syria—there lived the ruling family of the Islamic empire. They were the **Umayyads. Abd al-Rahman** was a teenage prince of the Umayyad family. He was fully expecting to one day be the ruler of the entire Islamic empire. However, he had

The magnificent Rock of Gibraltar juts some 1,500 feet into the sky on the coast of southern Spain.

enemies. In Damascus in 750, the rival **Abbasids** killed everyone in the prince's family and took over the empire! To save his life, Abd al-Rahman swam the Euphrates River and fled.

So where does a young prince flee in terrible circumstances such as these? Well, Abd al-Rahman's mother had been a Berber. So, he escaped to *her* people in northwestern Africa. (We're getting closer to Spain here!) It was a long journey that took him five years to make, but it proved to be worthwhile.

What Abd al-Rahman found among the Berbers was the opportunity to cross into Spain and keep the ruling power of the Umayyad's name alive! Because he was part Berber himself, he easily gained the respect of his kinsmen. But additionally, he was an intelligent Arab prince through and through. Though the Abbasid family was still ruling the Islamic empire in the East,[4] Abd al-Rahman resurrected the Umayyad dynasty in the West. And he did it very well!

Abd al-Rahman centered his new dynasty in the city of Cordoba. From there, the brilliant influence of the prince radiated through southern Spain—or al-Andalus as it was affectionately called by the Arabs. Abd al-Rahman gave incredible stability to the region through fair taxes, well-policed towns, organized laws, and strong marketplaces. In the capital city you could find hundreds of baths, thousands of mosques, and millions of shops. The civilization that developed under the new Umayyad family was one of the most advanced of the Middle Ages—as well as one of the most unusual!

As the last royal survivor of the Umayyad dynasty, Abd al-Rahman escaped from Damascus to re-establish his dynasty in southern Spain.

Under the Umayyads, wealth overflowed in al-Andalus. There was endless industry of gold, silver, copper, and iron. The coast produced exotic coral and pearls for trading; the city of **Toledo** made famous swords; Cordoba crafted shields, leather, and volumes of books; and beautiful handcrafted linens were made in every corner of southern Spain. Wealth trickled down to the common man and nearly every family could at least afford a donkey. Enormous aqueducts, built earlier by the Romans, provided fresh water for homes, decorative gardens, and ornate fountains. Giant waterwheels irrigated crops. Sidewalks were raised to keep them clean, and the streets were paved and lit at night! Imagine that—streets that were lit in the Dark Ages!

Of course, luxury has a way of attracting people—all kinds of people. Great thinkers, scientists, builders, doctors, artists, and musicians made their way to the great cities of al-Andalus where there was much opportunity. With at least 400,000 volumes of books in the palace library, there was enormous opportunity to learn. And though most of the scholars who were drawn to the region were Islamic, there were great numbers of Jews and Christians who were equally drawn to the great schools and libraries of this culture. That is what made al-Andalus so unusual! Muslims, Jews, *and* Christians shared in learning all kinds of things together—and most of this was accomplished through the Arabic language.

Adoption of the Arabic Language and Other Accomplishments

Though other languages have since taken hold in Spain, Arabic was the rage during the Middle Ages. Jews and Christians learned to speak it, to read it, and to write it. Christian mothers sang Arabic lullabies to their young children. Churches were decorated with Arabic on the walls and ceilings. The "Arabized" Christians were called the **Mozarabs.** One explanation for this transformation is the fact that Latin was becoming obsolete in Europe. When the Western Roman Empire fell, the Latin language of the Romans fell with it. Besides that, Arabic proved to be much more artistic and poetic than Latin. Jews and Christians alike discovered Arabic to be a beautiful language for expressing deep love, romance, and philosophy. And so they wrote it, they sang it, and they thought in it. Eventually, the Biblical books of the

---

4. In conquering the Umayyad family in Damascus, the Abbasid family moved the capital of the Islamic empire to the city of Baghdad in present-day Iraq.

Pictured are two authentic swords from Toledo, Spain, where the tradition of making some of the finest swords in the world continues.

prophets and the gospels were written in Arabic. The Greek and Roman classics had already been translated into Arabic long before and were available to all who could master the popular Arabic language.

But there was more to al-Andalus than its poetic language. The list of accomplishments is varied. One man in Cordoba invented **spectacles** and a **flying machine**! The Moors learned to breed Arabian and Spanish horses to create some of the best horses in the world. We still call them **Arabian horses.** A **postal service** was put in place and new **coins** went into circulation. Both boys and girls went to school, and there were at least 70 **libraries** across the region. At a later time in the kingdom, new waves of music swept the courts through **ring songs,** creating festive dances and merriment. Unbelievably extravagant palaces and mansions were built for royal families, with columns of marble, walls of gold, and doors inlaid with jewels.

It was a nun by the name of **Hroswitha** who described this magnificent Andalusian culture as "the brilliant ornament of the world."[5] From her humble convent, she undoubtedly saw this multicultural hub as a shining example of achievement in the otherwise dreary Middle Ages.

The Great Mosque of Cordoba and the Death of Abd al-Rahman

As for Prince Abd al-Rahman, he waited until nearly the end of his life before launching his greatest achievement. Most would say it was the building of the **Great Mosque of Cordoba.** Though started by Abd al-Rahman, the mosque was not completed until 200 years later. You can only imagine its beauty with the blend of the best of Islamic, Roman, and Gothic architecture. Nonetheless, it clearly stood as a Muslim place of worship with endless rows of red and white striped horseshoe arches, towering columns, and countless prayers to Allah.

And yet, as traditional as the Great Mosque still is, it is completely out of the ordinary in one interesting way—it does not point its worshipers toward the direction of Mecca during prayer (as do all other mosques). Why did Abd al-Rahman build it this way? Quite simply, he was so homesick for Damascus—the city of his youth—that he built the Great Mosque of Cordoba to sit in the *exact* direction that the mosque of his childhood in Damascus faced. And that was south.

You see, despite all the success that Abd al-Rahman experienced, and despite all his achievements, he was never quite satisfied. His homeland was Damascus. His heart was where his family had died. In an effort to ease his homesickness, he also built the palace retreat of **Rusafa** to resemble the home he grew up in. He even imported palm trees, plants, and animals from Syria to give his children and grandchildren the sounds and smell of "home." It's rather touching. In 788 Abd al-Rahman died there, among his precious palm trees.

The Rise of Persecution

I would prefer to end this lesson here, with the close of Abd al-Rahman's life. But I just can't. For unfortunately, there was at least one dark side to al-Andalus. Though three faiths lived there under certain harmony, there did exist some misunderstanding over religion. This confusion led to problems— serious problems, although they didn't start right away. You see, when the Moors first invaded, they

5. Maria Rosa Menocal, *The Ornament of the World.* New York: Little, Brown and Company, 2002; p. 32.

allowed the Spanish to keep their customs and religions. This was good. The Muslims referred to Jews and Christians as the *dhimmi,* meaning "the covenant people" or "the Peoples of the Book." For centuries the three faiths lived in reasonable peace with one another under the covenant of the Muslims. Christians and Moslems sometimes married and it was common for the faiths to share the same buildings for worship. Jews were able to trade freely and to prosper. In fact, the Jews fared better under the Umayyads in Spain than they did in other parts of Christian Europe where they were often unwelcome.

So what happened? Well, it's difficult to describe. On one hand, there *was* religious freedom under the Umayyad family. Christians and Jews alike were allowed to meet freely for worship. But on the other hand, if a Jew or Christian were to *publicly* speak against Allah or the prophet Mohammed, they could be killed. And unfortunately, this is what began to happen to many of the Mozarabs.

It may have started with **Pelagius** (puh LAY jee us). He was a 13-year-old boy who was asked to denounce Christ by a Muslim king. Pelagius refused and was severely tortured and killed by losing his limbs, one by one. Or it may have started with **Flora,** a pretty young girl whose father was a Muslim and whose mother was a Christian. Upon her father's death, Flora declared her faith in Christ. But her brother gave her over to the authorities. Flora hid in Christian homes and convents until she and a friend named Mary were caught, jailed, and beheaded.

In Flora's defense, a godly saint by the name of **Perfectus** spoke out about his faith. He publicly declared Mohammed "the servant of Satan and an imposter."[6] In 850 it cost him his life. The death of Perfectus inflamed the devout believers. It started a chain reaction of martyrdom as one Christian after the other decided to express how they really felt about the teachings of Mohammed. Every priest, monk, deacon, or woman who spoke against Islam was beheaded! At least 50 martyr deaths of the Mozarabs have been recorded. The faithful were led by a zealot named **Eulogius** who encouraged these heroic acts. But many Christians objected to the voluntary bloodshed because they *were* allowed the freedom to worship the God of the Bible. They were just not allowed to speak *publicly* against Allah. It was a difficult time for believers.

To complicate matters more, there were thousands of Christians in Spain who weakened in their faith under such persecution and chose to convert to Islam. They were called **renegades,** or traitors. For some, it must have seemed easier to convert than to go against the government. It certainly was good for slaves. For if a slave converted to Islam, he was granted his immediate freedom! And so, the religious climate of al-Andalus, though harmonious at times, was tainted both by freedom of speech and freedom from slavery. In response to the misunderstanding, a scholarly Muslim by the name of **Ibn Hazm** wrote one of the first books that compared religions. In his inability to grasp the Trinity, he wrote this about Christianity:

> "They [Christians] believe that one is three and three are one; that one of the three is the Father, the other the Son, and the third the Spirit; that the Father is the Son and is not the Son; that a man is God and not God; that the Messiah has existed from all eternity, and yet was created...that the Creator was scourged, buffeted, crucified, and that for three days the universe was without a ruler."[7] (Word in brackets is mine.)

I hope you found Hazm's comments interesting as well as alarming. Even more, as Christians, I hope we are saddened at the misinterpretation that Muslims have of who Jesus claimed to be. It reminds me of the passage in 1 Corinthians 1:18 that says, *"For the message of the cross is foolishness to those who are perishing, but to us who are being saved it is the power of God."* I hope that lessons such as this one will inspire you to share the message of the cross. For it is the power of God!

---

6. Will Durant, *The Age of Faith.* Vol. IV of *The Story of Civilization.* New York: Simon and Schuster, 1950; p. 300.

7. Ibid., p. 305.

ACTIVITIES FOR LESSON 33

ALL STUDENTS

Make your Memory Cards for Lessons 31–33.

Field Trip Possibility

With proper discretion, consider a field trip to a mosque in your community, or to a museum, to view Islamic art and architecture.

33A—Younger Students

1. In an encyclopedia or on the Internet, look up Arabian horses. What is your favorite breed of horse? Create a poster of different breeds of horses, using photocopies, prints, or pages from a coloring book. Be sure to include the Arabian horse. Take a picture of your poster and file it in your Student Notebook under "Europe: Spain."

2. How high can you count? Did you know that the numbers you count with came from the Arabs? Actually, the Arabs borrowed them from the people of India. But we call our numbers "Arabic" numbers. Before Arabic numbers were used, there were Roman numerals. We still use these today for clocks, page numbers, outlines, and dates of films. Explore your home today and find other places where Roman numerals are used.

   Fold a piece of paper in half lengthwise. In one column, write down 1–10 in Arabic numbers. In the other column, write i–x in Roman numerals. Your teacher should be able to help you. File your paper under "Europe: Spain."

33B—Younger and Middle Students

1. As stated in the lesson, written Arabic is very artistic. Practice drawing Arabic letters using the guide in the Activity Supplement. By carefully connecting the letters, try to write your name in Arabic. File it in your Student Notebook under "Europe: Spain."

2. The farmland in Spain is just right for growing grapes and olives. The Spanish are known around the world for their wine and olive oil, which come from refined grapes and olives. Just for fun, experiment with grape juice and olive oil.

   Materials: Grape juice, olive oil, liquid soap, glass jar, eyedropper

   Fill your jar with grape juice; add olive oil one drop at a time with an eyedropper. What happens and why? Stir the mixture and allow it to settle. Add liquid soap. What does it do? Have fun creating concoctions to remember the products of Spain!

33C—Middle and Older Students

1. Though this is a long lesson, I still was unable to include all that I had wished! There are many more interesting characters and places in the story of al-Andalus. I have listed some of these below. On your own, research one several of them. (One suggested resource: *The Ornament of the World* by Maria Rosa Menocal, a 2002 book.)

   a. Hasdai—the astounding Jew who became the vizier, or right-hand man, to the Islamic caliph of Cordoba in 949.

   b. Samuel ibn Nagrila—another astounding Jew and poet who became the vizier to the caliph of Granada in 1038.

Surrounded by gardens, Alhambra is beautiful both inside and out.

c. The magnificent Alhambra, or great "red castle," built in Granada.

d. The Church of San Roman, built in 1085 in Toledo to honor the God of the Bible but with much Arabic style and architecture.

e. Petrus Alfonsi (1106)—the Andalusian who moved to London and spread a wealth of Arabic knowledge in Great Britain.

2. Create a visual mini-report of Islamic art and architecture. See the Activity Supplement for directions.

TAKE ANOTHER LOOK!

Wall of Fame

1. *Wu Zetian, the Empress of China (690)*—Create a figure to resemble a Chinese woman with a crown. [From *History Through the Ages*, use *Empress Wu Zetian*.]

2. *The Epic of Beowulf (Early 700s)*—Create a little "monster-looking" dragon with the name Grendel. Create also a king with a sword to depict Beowulf. [Use *Epic of Beowulf*.]

3. *Al-Andalus: "The Ornament of the World" in Medieval Spain (711)*—Using permanent marker on a small diamond-shaped piece of foil (to look like an "ornament"), write the title of the lesson and the date of the Muslim invasion. [Use *Umayyad Dynasty*.]

SomeWHERE in Time

I want to review with you the following information about longitude and latitude that I first presented in Volume I of *The Mystery of History*, Review 25. The first two activities here are based on this background.

"The ancient Greeks developed a system of imaginary, intersecting lines that form a geographic (or global) grid around the earth. This grid uses lines of latitude and longitude, and it helps us to correctly find any location in the world. Think of it as a worldwide "address book"! Let me explain.

"Lines of latitude (also called parallels because they run parallel to the Equator) run east and west around the globe and measure location north or south of the Equator. The Equator is 0° latitude.

"Lines of longitude (also called meridians) run between the North Pole and the South Pole and measure location east or west of the prime meridian. The prime meridian runs through Greenwich, England, and is 0° longitude.

"The latitude or longitude of a point on the earth is called its coordinate. If you know both coordinates, you can locate any point on our planet. When giving coordinates, list the latitude first, followed by the longitude."

1. Use a globe and find the small country of Denmark. You should be able to see that it is located about halfway between 45° and 60° north on the lines of latitude (north here is referring to north of the equator) and between 0° and 15° east on the lines of longitude. Your mapping assignment today is to find the **approximate** latitude and longitude of *your* home. When you have it, write it down and file it under the continent and country in your Student Notebook.

   You can check your answer by going to www.confluence.org and using the search engine to type in the two numbers you decided upon. This is an incredible site. The goal of the Confluence Project is to have people visit each of the latitude and longitude integer degree intersections in the world and then take pictures at each location. The pictures and travel journals are then posted. You can participate! Read more about it.

2. Use a globe to find Saudi Arabia, North Africa, and Spain. Trace with your finger the spread of Islam from Saudi Arabia, to Northern Africa, to Spain. Find the Strait of Gibraltar off the coast of Spain. What is the approximate latitude and longitude of this body of water named after Tariq or Gebel al-Tariq in Arabic? (See the answer at the end of this review section.)

3. Create a symbol map.

   Materials: Outline Map 17, "Spain"; colored pencils; photocopy of map symbols found in the Activity Supplement; scissors; glue

a. In Lesson 33, I told you of several industries, inventions, and institutions that helped make southern Spain wealthy and luxurious during the Dark Ages. I would like you to cut out symbols of these items (as provided in the Activity Supplement) and glue them onto Outline Map 17, "Spain."

b. Younger Students: I suggest that you color the map with colored pencils and then glue the symbol pieces randomly across southern Spain.

c. Middle and Older Students: I suggest that you color the map with colored pencils and then follow Lesson 33 carefully to try to place the symbols near the regions or cities that are specified. For example, Toledo was known for making swords. Place the sword symbol near that city. The coast was famous for producing coral and pearl. Place these symbols along the southern coasts of Spain. Many symbols will be centered near Cordoba. Surround it as best as possible because the many symbols will help portray just how remarkable Cordoba was. A large number of symbols will not have any specific location mentioned in the lesson. Scatter them randomly throughout southern Spain to reflect the general wealth of the masses.

d. All Students: Place your map in your Student Notebook under "Europe: Spain."

Answer: 36°N, 6°W

WHAT DID YOU LEARN?

WEEK 11: QUIZ

I. Who Did It? Using colored pencils, connect these famous people with what they "did."

1. Preached at Mars Hill

    a. Trajan

2. Killed his mother, wife, half
   brother, and chief officer

    b. Bar-Kokhba

3. Threw Ignatius to the lions

    c. Jerome

4. Claimed to be the Messiah and
   "the prince of Israel"

    d. Justinian

5. Saw a cross in the sky

    e. Paul

6. Calculated the diameter of the moon

    f. Constantine

7. Translated the Vulgate

    g. King Arthur

8. Defended his homeland against the Saxons

    h. Nero

9. Rebuilt Saint Sophia after the Nika revolt

    i. Indians

II. People and Places. Match the following people and places by placing the correct letter next to the number.

_____1. Guinevere   a. China

_____2. Theodora   b. Scotland

_____3. Columba   c. Mecca

_____4. Prince Shotoku   d. Denmark

_____5. Gregory the Great   e. Spain

_____6. Li Shi Min   f. Byzantine Empire

_____7. Mohammed   g. Camelot

_____8. Beowulf   h. Japan

_____9. Umayyad dynasty   i. Rome

✓ WHAT DO YOU KNOW?

PRETEST 12

Match Me! Connect the words on the left to the definitions on the right. (Using different-colored pencils may make it more fun to do and easier to grade.)

1. St. Boniface

a. Mayor of the Franks

2. Evergreen tree

b. Means "image breaker"

3. Freisland

c. An exiled empress

4. "Iconoclast"

d. Nickname of Charles

5. Irene

e. A symbol of "everlasting" love

6. Charles

f. Apostle to Germany

7. "The hammer"

g. An important victory for Europe

8. Battle of Tours

h. German town where Boniface was killed

ST. BONIFACE, APOSTLE TO GERMANY
LESSON 34

We have already learned in this book that St. Patrick took the Gospel to Ireland and that Columba was a missionary to Scotland. I find it inspiring to learn of men so bold as these—men willing to risk their lives to proclaim Christ. Today we're going to focus on another great missionary. His name was **Winfrid.** But most remember him as **Boniface,** the name given him by the pope. Boniface desired to share Christ with the people of **Germany.** In doing so, Boniface helped to start a Christmas tradition still celebrated today.

Winfrid was born in **Wessex, England.** He was Anglo-Saxon. At a young age Winfrid proved to be a smart student. He knew by the age of 5 that he wanted to be a monk. He was taught and trained in a Benedictine monastery.

Boniface, whose original name was Winfrid, was born in England but became known as the "Apostle to Germany."

Winfrid was ordained at the age of 30. His first assignment, in **718,** was to go and preach to a resistant group of pagans in **Freisland,** Germany. (Presently, Freisland is in the Netherlands, a country neighboring Germany.) The problem in Freisland was the king. His name was **Radbod.** Though King Radbod heard the Gospel from Winfrid and other missionaries, he would not embrace it. Sadly, Radbod concluded that if his ancestors weren't going to heaven because of their pagan ways, he didn't want to go to heaven either! Very disheartened, Winfrid went back to England feeling as if he failed the people of Freisland. His negative experience would prove later to change the course of his life.

A few years later, Winfrid was commissioned to go again to Germany. This time he went to **Hesse,** a place much like Freisland where people were difficult to reach with the Gospel. But this time Winfrid was more prepared.

As the story goes, there were people in Hesse who were worshiping at what they believed to be a sacred oak tree. It was huge. Some say they were honoring the thunder god named Donar. Others claim the site was used to worship the Viking god Thor (from whom we get the name Thursday). Either way, it was not uncommon in those days for pagans to gather for worship at a tree. Winfrid was aware of this practice and had forewarned the pagans that he could overcome their false gods.

One day, Winfrid was traveling when he came upon a group of pagans who were about to sacrifice a young prince at the oak tree. That means they were going to kill him! With great fury, Winfrid intervened to rescue the poor little prince. He then raised an axe to the giant tree to demolish it for good. The trunk of the tree was nearly 6 feet across! So cutting it down was no small job.

After the oak thundered to the ground, Boniface announced to the pagan crowd, "How stands your mighty god? My God is stronger than he."[1] The awestruck crowd was speechless, as they saw no way for

---

1. See the information about Boniface on the Catholic Community Forum Web site: www.catholic-forum.com/saints/saintb15.htm.

their god to restore the dead tree. Nearby, however, there was a small fir tree shooting up. Boniface saw the tender evergreen as a perfect analogy of God. I don't know exactly how he said it, but I suspect he compared the "ever" green look of the fir tree to the "ever" lasting love of God.

Does that sound familiar to you? It should. Millions of people every year place an evergreen tree in their homes at Christmas to symbolize everlasting life! Though other cultures also helped to shape the tradition of the **Christmas tree,** most would credit Winfrid with the original symbolism.

Tradition further says that Winfrid took the wood of the giant oak tree and used it to build a church in a nearby village. He dedicated the new church to the apostle Peter. (How appropriate that was because these two men shared the same zealous personalities!) Another tradition says that Boniface used a simple game made up by the local people to help explain spiritual matters. In the game, a person threw large sticks called *kegels* against smaller sticks called *heides*. Boniface described demons as being like the heides, which were easy to knock down through the power of the Holy Spirit. It is a great word picture of a spiritual truth.

Year after year, Christmas trees are beautifully decorated as sentimental reminders of the everlasting love of God.

Winfrid Is Named Boniface

In 723 Winfrid went back to Rome where he was consecrated a bishop by the pope. It was then that the pope renamed him Boniface. Boniface continued to be a bold witness for Christ wherever he served. And wherever he went, he set up monasteries to continue his good work, his most famous being the **Abbey of Fulda.**

Boniface not only ministered to the masses through his work at the monasteries, he also ministered to kings and emperors. Perhaps with memories of trying to reach King Radbod, Boniface shared boldly with leaders of nations and empires. He was eventually raised to the position of archbishop of **Mainz** (minz). If you remember, an archbishop was of even higher rank than a bishop in the structure of the Medieval Church. For 30 years Boniface preached and taught the people of Germany the things of God. For that he has been called the "Apostle to the Germans."

As if to remember St. Boniface, this small German church has a beautiful evergreen growing right next to it.

But there was one last mission for Boniface that he couldn't quit thinking about. He had heard that the people back in Freisland were still not strong in their faith. King Radbod had long since died. Though Boniface was now 70 years old, he wanted to go back there to finish what he had once started.

It was a great idea. About 50 other monks and nuns went with him. The ministry was going well and many were coming to Christ. But a sad thing happened one Sunday afternoon. It was June 5, 754, to be exact. While preparing to baptize a group of new converts in the river, Boniface and his helpers were attacked by a hoodlum gang of pagans. It was a brutal thing to do.

With the gentleness of the Savior, Boniface chose not to fight back at his attackers. With these words Boniface pleaded with his followers, "Cease, my children, from conflict. . . . Fear not those who kill the body but cannot kill the immortal soul. . . . Receive with constancy this momentary blow of death, that you may live and reign with Christ forever."[2] And with that, Boniface and most of his clergy died at the hands of the pagan mob.

Though he died a tragic martyr's death, Boniface was an incredible man. In both boldness and gentleness, he shared God's love with countless numbers of Germans. It has been said of Boniface that he "had (a) deeper influence on the history of Europe than any Englishman who ever lived."[3] He definitely influenced the world with the symbolism of a beautiful evergreen as seen around the world at Christmastime.

ACTIVITIES FOR LESSON 34

34A—Younger Students

Make a "Candy Countdown Christmas Tree."

Materials: One piece of yellow construction paper, 20 pieces of green foil-wrapped chocolate candy, 5 pieces of red foil-wrapped chocolate candy. (If green and red candies are not available, you may substitute with silver foil-wrapped candies. I then recommend green construction paper instead of yellow to keep with the green theme of the evergreen tree.)

1. Lay a piece of yellow construction paper vertically in front of you.

2. Arrange candy pieces in the following pattern using a red piece where indicated with the letter "R" and a green piece of candy where indicated with the letter "G." Lay each piece of candy on its flat side. Use the exact number of pieces shown here.

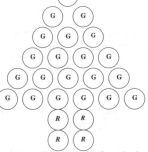

3. Once your pieces are arranged, carefully pick up one at a time and glue it in place on your paper.

4. At the bottom of your paper, write the title "The Evergreen of St. Boniface."

5. Hang your Candy Countdown Christmas Tree on a wall, your bedroom door, or your refrigerator door.

6. Beginning on December 1, eat one chocolate per day until Christmas. (There are 25 pieces of candy.) I hope it is a fun way to anticipate the celebration of Christ's birth as well as to remember St. Boniface.

34B—Middle Students

Experiment with sprigs of evergreen.

Background Information: The leaves, or needles, of an evergreen tree do not remain green throughout the year, as some would presume. Rather the evergreen tree as a whole remains green throughout the

2. A. Kenneth Curtis, J. Stephen Lang, and Randy Petersen, *The 100 Most Important Events in Christian History.* Grand Rapids, MI: Fleming H. Revell, 1991; p. 60.

3. From Chris Dawson, *The Making of Europe* (pp. 210–211). As quoted in Joseph A. Dunney, *Church History in the Light of the Saints,* (1945), Ch. VIII, "Saint Boniface: Tamer of Tribes." Accessed on the Catholic Information Network Web site: www.cin.org/books/dunney8.html.

year. How does it do this? New green leaves, or needles, grow on an evergreen before the old ones fall to the ground. Thus, the tree appears to remain green all year. Besides that, the leaves, or needles, of an evergreen are tougher, stronger, and have less surface area than ordinary leaves making them more durable in severe climates.

Cut three small sprigs from a live evergreen tree. Place one sprig in water, one in a freezer, and leave one out on a windowsill. Observe the sprigs over time to see which one remains green the longest. Do they retain their green color for the same amount of time? What is the name of the matter that makes the branches green? Write a paragraph to answer these questions and describe the results of your experiment. File it under "Europe: Germany" in your Student Notebook.

34C—Middle and Older Students

Create an object lesson. Boniface used what we would call an "object lesson" when he used an evergreen to symbolize a spiritual truth. Brainstorm other objects from around your home or classroom that could be used to teach a spiritual truth. For example, a lightbulb, a candle, or a flashlight could symbolize Christ saying, *"I am the light of the world. He who follows Me shall not walk in darkness, but have the light of life."* (John 8:12) Present a short devotional to your family or class using an object and a Bible passage to teach a spiritual truth.

726

THE ICONOCLAST CONTROVERSY
LESSON 35

We've studied a lot about religious persecution in this book. In most cases it involved people of *different* faiths attacking each other. For example, Saul persecuted the early Christians because he was a devout Jew. Tribes in Arabia tortured the early followers of Mohammed. And militant Muslims killed both Jews and Christians for speaking against Allah! Well, if it's not terrible enough that people of one faith would persecute people of *another* faith, you'll learn today that some faiths even persecuted their own! This is never clearer than during the **Iconoclast Controversy.** This is a tragic time in history when Christians fought against other Christians over the issue of **idolatry.** Some were tortured and killed in the dispute! Let me explain.

Long before Christianity spread to Europe, people practiced idol worship. In fact, the worship of idols was prevalent in the very earliest of time. The first clear example of it in the Bible is found in Genesis 31:19, when **Rachel** stole her father's household gods. They were actual objects that people worshiped. In the Old Testament, the Lord instructed the Israelites *not* to worship idols. He said through **Moses** in the **Ten Commandments**:

> *"You shall have no other gods before Me. You shall not make for yourself a carved image—any likeness of anything that is in heaven above, or that is in the earth beneath, or that is in the water under the earth; you shall not bow down to them nor serve them. For I, the LORD your God, am a jealous God . . . "* (Exod. 20: 3–5)

Well, despite God's commandments, many people over the ages worshiped idols, including the Jews, who were forbidden to do so. The **Greeks** and **Romans** were especially known for idolatrous

The word Iconoclast comes from two Greek words that together mean "image breaker," referring to the destruction of icons used in the church in the Middle Ages.

pagan practices and superstitions. That means they would treat with reverence or worship "things" that were symbolic of their many mythological gods and goddesses. Rome and Greece were full of temples and shrines that reflected these beliefs.

As Christianity spread throughout Europe in the Dark Ages, the pagan beliefs of the Romans and Greeks were challenged. In choosing to follow Christ, many new converts to Christianity gave up pagan idol worship. Jesus said He came to fulfill the Law, and the Law clearly said not to worship idols! So the new believers didn't.

But, over time, the issue of idolatry became fuzzy. Some Christians wondered if they ought to not have *any* statutes, paintings, or even crosses hanging in their churches. They called these types of items **icons.** Sincere believers weren't sure if the placement of icons in the church wasn't becoming a form of idolatry. Or, they wondered, were these sacred images just *symbols* to remember Christ by? Were people beginning to pray to the icons instead of to God? These were the concerns of church leaders. Believers were confused and divided over the issue. What was the right way for the church to interpret what the Lord intended with the Ten Commandments in regard to idol worship?

Well, I'm not going to try to answer that question because to some extent churches still don't agree on the matter. But I am going to tell you what happened in some churches during the early Middle Ages. It was a real mess. We call it the Iconoclast Controversy from the Greek words *eikon* meaning "image" and *klastes* meaning "breaker." The Iconoclasts were basically "image breakers," or destroyers of religious images. Here's why.

By the eighth century, there were many people who appeared to be praying to icons or sacred statues and paintings in their churches. Icons of **Mary,** the mother of Jesus, and images of the **saints** were abundant in the Western and Eastern churches. ("Western churches" refers to those in the old Western Roman Empire; "Eastern churches" refers to those in the Byzantine Empire.) People were known to bow before these images, kiss them, leave flowers at them, and burn candles and incense in front of them. It gave the impression to some church leaders that people were begging and bartering for miracles from their favorite saints!

Of even greater concern to church leaders was the custom of people carrying **trinkets** that were symbolic of the Christian faith as if they were good luck charms! In the Greek cities, where paganism once flourished, homes, shops, furniture, and even clothes were decorated with Christian relics for "good luck," so to speak. They were used to pray for protection against famine, floods,

Roman Catholic churches commonly revere Mary, the mother of Jesus, in the form of statues, paintings, and mosaics, as pictured here.

war, and disease. The lower church leaders claimed these were innocent images and not idols. But the common people may not have understood the difference between their practices and the Greek pagan practices around them.

Leo III Issues an Edict

Well, a certain Byzantine emperor named **Leo III** thought that all this imagery was quite superstitious and completely irreverent. And he decided to do something about it! In **726** he ordered, through an

edict, that all the statues in the churches be removed and that pictures of the saints be painted over with whitewash! (He did allow a plain cross to hang where the paintings and statues had been.) Though his actions may have stemmed from genuine concern, to some Christians this was outright persecution! Though high church leaders agreed with Leo, the lower church leaders, like the monks, were furious with Leo for his order. They felt they were being deprived of their freedom to worship. Rioting broke out in Constantinople, and some officials who were working on the removal of the images were trampled to death. Troops were called in to quiet the rioters. Those who interfered were killed! It was a terrible episode of Christians hurting other Christians.

Riots also broke out in Greece and Italy over the Iconoclast Movement. The Greeks went so far as to send a fleet of warships to the capital in protest of the Iconoclasts! Leo had the fleet destroyed, and he imprisoned the Greeks who were behind the protest. When Leo died in 741, most churches ignored the edict and went back to having their icons. But tension rose again when Leo's son **Constantine V** picked up where Leo left off.

The force that Leo had shown in issuing his edict was mild compared to what Constantine V did. It seems that Constantine V was ruthless over the matter. If he found that monks were resisting the edict, he had them tortured. Monks had their eyes torn out, their tongues removed, and their noses cut off! At least one patriarch was beheaded. By 767, Constantine V shut down most of the churches and monasteries altogether. He used the buildings for secular offices instead.

Empress Irene

This breakdown and suffering in the Eastern Church lasted for centuries to come—all because of the controversy over icons. Both sides appeared to be sincere in wanting to honor the Lord in worship. But they could not agree on how that should be done. It was awful! Some relief finally came though. Constantine V's grandson took the throne at a young age, forcing his mother, **Irene,** to serve as a regent. (That means Irene really ruled as empress until her son was old enough to take over.) During her reign, she smoothed over the controversy better than anyone else had. She allowed images to be used in worship *if* it was recognized that they were different from God Himself.

But do you know what happened when Irene's son became old enough to rule? In 790 he had his mother exiled! Irene retaliated and had *him* thrown in prison. Irene ruled for the next five years, and she ruled quite well. She lowered taxes, raised money for charity, and beautified the capital. The people loved her. But the army didn't, and Irene was eventually banished for good. She spent the last nine months of her life on the island of **Lesbos** working as a seamstress. The church later named her a saint for the suffering she endured and the good she had done.

But what about the icons? Whatever happened to the tradition of using images in the church? Well, just as the church in the East eventually split from the West (there was a major division in 1054), so there arose differences between the two. The Eastern Church went back to having images that were considered "symbols" of worship rather than idols. The Western Church didn't, at least for a long time.

In the Byzantine Empire, Empress Irene smoothed over the Iconoclast Controversy by allowing icons in the church if they were regarded only as symbols.

Later in history, after the Middle Ages, a time called the **Renaissance** began. This was a time when painting and sculpting became the rage in Western Europe. And, much of the art was centered on images of the life of Christ! Were these paintings and statues worshiped? I don't think so. To most, they were, and still are, beautiful expressions of remembering what Christ had done. At the same time, I can certainly understand the conviction of the Iconoclasts. I imagine many were sincere in trying to prevent disobedience to God by those who appeared to violate the second commandment. Regardless of their efforts, if you visited a wide variety of churches today, you would see that there are still some differences in opinion as to what should hang on the walls!

ACTIVITIES FOR LESSON 35

35A—Younger Students

Our language and culture use many symbols to represent things. Just for fun, can you name what the following images are symbolic of? (The answers are provided in the Pretest Answer Key in the Appendix.) Can you think of others?

?   ♥   ©   %   ☺

™   #   ♣   &

35B—Younger and Middle Students

Make a decorative cross.

According to *World Book Encyclopedia*, the cross "is a sacred emblem of the Christian faith. It is a symbol of redemption, signifying Christ's death on the cross for man's sins."[4] The use of the cross dates back as far as the first century. During the Middle Ages, crosses began to be used as grave markers for bishops, kings, and heroes. Turn to the Activity Supplement in the Appendix for directions on making a decorative cross.

35C—Middle and Older Students

The history of the Eastern Orthodox Church is complex. It is difficult to put a single date on when it split away from the Western Roman Church because several divisions and several unifications occurred between the fall of the Western Roman Empire and the fall of Constantinople. To get a better picture of the Eastern Orthodox Church and where it stands today, watch the following video clip from a *60 Minutes* program on CBS. (*Caution*: This video clip may contain an inappropriate commercial that cannot be fast forwarded. I recommend muting it or starting the clip after the commercial.) This clip is a fascinating depiction of "living history," featuring an interview with the present-day patriarch of the Eastern Orthodox Church, Bartholomew I, who continues to live in Istanbul (formerly Constantinople). The clip can be found at:

www.cbsnews.com/video/watch/?id=6754652n&tag=related;photovideo

35D—Older Students

In Volume I of *The Mystery of History*, we looked at the details of how Christ physically died on the cross. I believe it is so valuable for us to remember how He died that I thought I would include this description in Volume II as well. Turn to the Activity Supplement to read this portion on the death of our Savior. I feel it gives new and deeper meaning to the symbol of the cross.

---

4. *World Book Encyclopedia*, 50th Anniversary ed., s.v. "cross." Chicago: Field Enterprises Educational Corp., 1966.

CHARLES "MARTEL" AND THE BATTLE OF TOURS
LESSON 36

As you know by now, the Islamic faith became very powerful in the Middle Ages. Starting in Arabia under Mohammed in 622, Islam spread at a phenomenal rate. By 636 the Muslims had conquered Syria and Palestine. By 642 Alexandria, Egypt, was Islamic. By 646 the Muslims ruled Mesopotamia. By 697 the city of Carthage in North Africa was dominated by Muslims. And, as you learned earlier, the Islamic Moors invaded Spain in 711 (Lesson 33). Today you are going to learn how the rapid spread of Islam to Europe was abruptly stopped. It happened at the **Battle of Tours** through **Charles "Martel."** It was a major turning point in history!

Charles was a **mayor** in the palace of the **Franks.** The Franks were one of many Germanic **tribes** that had invaded the Western Roman Empire. They eventually set up what is now the country of **France.** Franks – France. I think you can see the connection. By the Middle Ages this region was primarily Christian. Its Christian roots can be traced back to a king named **Clovis.** He had converted to Christianity. As for Charles, I'm not sure if he was a Christian or not. For although he supported missionaries like St. Boniface going to Germany, it appears he was more concerned about spreading his Frankish power than about spreading the Gospel. It also appears that he corrupted the church from time to time for political reasons.

Whether Charles was a genuine Christian or not, it seems that the Lord greatly used him in history to accomplish His purposes. Charles's desire for political power and God's sovereign hand led him into a war to stop the Muslims, who were quickly moving toward Europe.

As you may remember, southern Spain had become largely Islamic with the invasion of the Moors.[5] Well, Spain happens to connect to the rest of Europe at the place where it meets France. This is the place where Islamic forces were eager to rush in. If they could have northern Africa and Spain, why not southern Europe? A general in the Muslim army of Spain attempted to lead his troops into Frankish territory with hopes of a great victory. But he didn't realize how strong his opposition was! Charles and his army went up against the Islamic forces at a place in France between the towns of **Tours** and **Poitiers** (pwah TYAY). For seven days they faced one another without fighting. It was a stare-down that intimidated both sides.

Finally, on a Saturday in October in the year **732**, the battle began. It's been remembered as the Battle of Tours. (Some history books call it the **Battle of Poitiers.**) The Franks under Charles are said to have stood like an "immovable wall." Others described them as a "rock of ice." Eyewitnesses report that hundreds of Muslims were lost in the series of battles fought near Tours. When it was all done, the Franks had easily run the Muslim army back to Spain, where they came from.

From this victory, Charles earned the nickname of **"the hammer"**—which is *Martel* in French. Just as a hammer is used repeatedly to drive a nail, so Charles "Martel" repeatedly drove the Muslims out of France and stopped the spread of Islam in Europe. And you know what? That's pretty important to those of us living in the United States because it was the Europeans who later settled the Americas!

---

5. The Battle of Tours (732) took place before the formation of al-Andalus under Prince Abd al-Rahman.

What if the Muslims had not been stopped at the Battle of Tours? What if the rest of Europe had become Islamic at the same phenomenal rate as other countries? One author thought the victory at Tours was so significant that he said this, "If it weren't for Charles Martel, we [Americans] might all be speaking Arabic and kneeling toward Mecca five times a day."[6] (Word in brackets is mine.)

These questions and statements are just for thought. The Bible makes it clear that God has a providential hand in history. The word providential means with "divine guidance." Acts 17:24–26 says:

Charles, nicknamed "Martel" ("the hammer"), put a stop to the Arab invasion of Europe at the Battle of Tours.

"God, who made the world and everything in it . . . gives to all life, breath, and all things. And He has made from one blood every nation of men . . . and has determined their preappointed times and the boundaries of their dwellings."

Also, Daniel 2:21 says, *"And He changes the times and the seasons; He removes kings and raises up kings . . . "*

These are just a few verses that demonstrate how God is the true author of history regardless of our perspective!

ACTIVITIES FOR LESSON 36

ALL STUDENTS

Make your Memory Cards for Lessons 34–36. The Battle of Tours (732) is a date to memorize. Highlight the card accordingly.

36A—Younger Students

Create a "rock of ice." The army of Charles Martel was said to stand like a "rock of ice." Follow these directions to make your own.

Materials: About two dozen plastic army men, an ice-cube tray

1. Fill an ice-cube tray with water.
2. Carefully stand two army men upright in each cube section. (Or as many as will fit.)
3. Place your tray in the freezer.
4. When it's frozen, play with the tray as an "immovable wall." On a kitchen table, have an opponent try to sneak a dozen "loose" army men past the men in the tray. It should be difficult!

36B—Middle Students

Materials: Pencil; one 2-by-4-inch block of wood approximately 1 foot in length; 60 to70 medium-sized nails; hammer

---

6. A. Kenneth Curtis, J. Stephen Lang, and Randy Petersen, *The 100 Most Important Events in Christian History*. Grand Rapids, MI: Fleming H. Revell, 1991; p. 62.

How good are you at hammering nails? Just as Charles "hammered" his opponent, practice your expertise at hammering nails into wood. Using a pencil, write the name M-A-R-T-E-L in easy-to-read letters. Hammer nails into the letters using about 10 nails per letter. This activity is just for fun, but it should help you remember this historic event. Take a photo of your work and file it under "Europe: France" in your Student Notebook.

36C—Older Students

God's sovereignty in history is a profound concept. According to the authors of *America's Providential History,* the Declaration of Independence makes reference to God in these words, "And for the support of this Declaration, with a firm reliance on the Protection of Divine Providence, we mutually pledge to each other our Lives, our Fortunes and our Sacred Honor."[7] George Washington, in a Thanksgiving Proclamation in 1789, said this: "It is the duty of all nations to acknowledge the Providence of Almighty God, to obey His will, to be grateful for his benefits, and humbly to implore His protection and favor."[8] Study the verses below to draw some of your own conclusions. Discuss these as a group or family.

Job 12:23 Psalms 22:28 Daniel 4:17, 26

7. Mark A. Beliles and Stephen K. McDowell, *America's Providential History*. Charlottesville, VA: The Providence Foundation, 1989; p. 6.
8. Ibid., p. 7.

Wall of Fame

1. *St. Boniface (718)*—Make a little Christmas tree with the title "Boniface, Apostle to the Germans." [From *History Through the Ages,* use *Boniface.*]

2. *The Iconoclast Controversy (726)*—Create a little picture of a statue of a saint. Now tear your paper in half. Glue these two pieces on another small piece of paper and write the title of the lesson beneath. [Use *The Iconoclast Controversy.*]

3. *Charles Martel and the BATTLE OF TOURS (732)*—Create a man holding a hammer. Write the "Battle of Tours" and his name on the paper. **Remember, the Battle of Tours (732) is a date to memorize.** [Use *Charles Martel.*]

SomeWHERE in Time

1. Though Boniface is considered the Apostle to the Germans, "Germany" as we know it now was not yet established. Freisland, for example (where Boniface was martyred), is presently in the Netherlands. So we will not map Germany extensively just yet. Instead, locate present-day Germany on a globe or map. Find and name the countries that surround it. How close to Germany do you live? Use a scale, or map measurement, to estimate the distance from Germany to where you live. (Maybe you live in Germany!)

2. Build a "wall of ice." Using Outline Map 18, "France and Spain," label Spain and color it orange. Label France and color it green. Find and label the city of Tours. Now, take three to six ice cubes and stack them between Spain and France near Tours. Before the ice melts, take a picture for your Student Notebook. File it under "Europe: France." Imagine how the army of Charles Martel was like a "wall of ice" blocking the Islamic Moors from invading other parts of Europe.

Beat Your Own Time! This is a game you can play against yourself. After putting the events of Group I in order as quickly as you can, you have three chances to beat your own time. Using a timer, the Contents section of this book, a timeline, your Memory Cards, and your *own* good memory, your challenge is to mark each group of sentences in the order in which they happened. Time each section individually to check for your improvement.

Group I

_____ a. **Pompeii** is buried by Mt. Vesuvius.

_____ b. **Bar-Kokhba** leads the Second Jewish Revolt.

_____ c. **Paul** travels on his missionary journeys.

_____ d. **Josephus** lives and writes of the history of the Jewish people.

_____ e. The Holy Spirit descends on the apostles at **Pentecost.**

TIME: _____

Group II

_____ a. **Jerome** translates the Bible into the Latin Vulgate.

_____ b. **St. Valentine** is martyred for his faith.

_____ c. **Attila** leads the Huns to ravage parts of Europe.

_____ d. Constantine issues the **Edict of Milan.**

_____ e. The **Western Roman Empire** collapses.

TIME: _____

Group III

_____ a. **Prince Shotoku** founds the Japanese civilization.

_____ b. **Justinian** codifies Roman law in the Justinian Code.

_____ c. **Mohammed** founds the Islamic faith.

_____ d. **Gregory the Great** becomes pope.

_____ e. **Columba** shares the Gospel in Scotland.

TIME: _____

Group IV

_____ a. **The Moors** invade Spain.

_____ b. **Charles Martel** fights the Battle of Tours.

_____ c. **Boniface** spreads the Gospel to Germany.

_____ d. Riots break out during the **Iconoclast Movement.**

_____ e. **Wu Zetian** becomes the empress of China.

TIME: _____

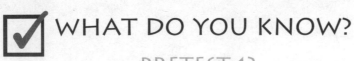

✓ WHAT DO YOU KNOW?

PRETEST 13

Jeopardy. Just as they do on the *Jeopardy* television game show, I have provided the "answers." You find the right "questions" from the bottom of the page.

1. A gift of land given to the pope by Pepin the Short.

2. "Charles the Great" in French.

3. A treaty to divide the kingdom of Charlemagne among his grandsons.

4. The capital of the Abbasid dynasty.

5. Two hundred fun and fanciful Arabic stories.

6. A Chinese boy who steals a genie-filled lamp.

7. The countries of Norway, Sweden, and Denmark.

8. The name of a Viking combat knife.

What is *The Thousand and One Nights?*
What is the Treaty of Verdun?
What is Scandinavia?
Who is Aladdin?
What is Baghdad?
What is a scramasax?
What are the Papal States?
What is the meaning of *Charlemagne?*

CHARLEMAGNE

LESSON 37

As you learned, **Charles**—the mayor of the Franks—was nicknamed **"the hammer."** We remember him as **Charles Martel**. Through a series of battles near the town of Tours, he drove Muslim troops back to Spain, where they came from. Well, the strength of the Franks didn't end with Charles Martel. His son **Pepin the Short** was a strong leader, too. But stronger than either of these men was the *grandson* of Charles Martel. His name was also Charles. But most people know him by the French version of his name, which is **Charlemagne** (SHAHR luh mayn). It means **Charles the Great**. Here is his story—starting with how his father, Pepin, became king.

The Crowning of Pepin the Short

When Charles Martel died, his son Pepin became the next mayor in the palace of the Franks. Believe it or not, neither Charles nor Pepin was the "king." The official king of the Franks was from a line of rulers called the **Merovingians**. The Merovingians possessed the true crown of France and Germany, but they had no real power or respect from their people. As rulers, the Merovingians were weak. Pepin, on the other hand, who was only a mayor, possessed great power and respect. Naturally, he believed he should be the king.

Pepin decided to go to the pope of the Western Church to get his opinion on the matter. Pepin asked him who should really be the king of the Franks—the man with the crown, or the man with the power. The pope thought it should be the man with the power. So, in 751, the Merovingians were forced out. In 754 Pepin the Short was crowned the true king of the Franks. Pepin started what was called the **Carolingian** line of rulers.

Now, you may not think that's a very big deal. But it really was. You see, the fact that the pope of the Western Church stepped in to decide who ought to be king was huge! It gave the Western Church certain *political* power it had never had before. To make the Western Church even more powerful, Pepin gave the pope a large gift of land for making him king. The gift was called the **Donation of Pepin**. The land was later called the **Papal States**. (*Papal* is a form of the word *pope*.) Now, for the first time in history, the Western Church owned land as if it were a small country. This arrangement eventually led to problems, which we will get to later.

Pepin, the son of Charles Martel, started the Carolingian line of rulers in France. He was crowned king of the Franks by the pope.

As for Pepin, he served as king until his death in **768**. His son Charlemagne, the main subject of our lesson, inherited the Frankish Empire the same year his father died. He was blonde, six-foot-four, handsomely built, and very ambitious. And for reasons other than his regal looks, some would say that Charlemagne was one of the greatest kings of the entire Middle Ages! He certainly was responsible for many good things.

Charlemagne was very concerned with **education.** I imagine it had to do with the fact that he didn't learn to read until he was an adult. And though he tried very hard, he always struggled with learning to write. So in the hope that others would be better educated than he was, he issued a decree in 789 that every monastery and abbey was to have a school. He may be one of the first to insist that education be "free." And it was under Charlemagne that "Carolingian handwriting" was taught to replace cursive in the Bible. The new handwriting style was supposed to be easier to read and write. In fact, the basis for our modern handwriting comes from this Carolingian handwriting.

As a true lover of knowledge, Charlemagne made himself a student at his own palace. His palace, **Aix-la-Chapelle** (EKS la sha PEL), was the capital of the Frankish Empire in western Germany. (Know that at this point in history, France and Germany were not separate countries as they are today.) Aix-la-Chapelle was a great center for learning and much needed in Europe after the fall of the Western Roman Empire. With the help of Anglo-Saxon and Irish scholars, Charlemagne did much to preserve the Scriptures and manuscripts through the schools. Most of this language work was in Latin, though Charlemagne's successors later drifted from this.

Charlemagne was also a successful **administrator.** He governed his ever-growing empire with great skill. To use his time well, Charlemagne went to the extreme of conducting business while getting dressed in the morning and putting his shoes on! He regularly sent out envoys to inspect his lands, and he developed a justice system that included a jury and a verdict. (These were new concepts in the Middle Ages.) For creating this kind of law and order, Charlemagne was nicknamed **"the civilizer."**

Charlemagne was smooth in politics as well. To keep peace with the neighboring Byzantine Empire, Charlemagne made a very interesting marriage proposal. Do you remember the empress **Irene** from our lesson on the Iconoclast Movement? She was the Byzantine ruler who helped calm down the Iconoclast problem. Well, Charlemagne offered to marry the empress thinking it might keep things harmonious between the Franks and the Byzantine Empire. It was a good gesture on Charlemagne's part, but Irene turned him down. (I'm not sure why!)

Even without the help of the Byzantine Empire, Charlemagne was a very successful **conqueror.** He managed to expand his empire to a size that was not duplicated until a thousand years later during the time of **Napoleon Bonaparte.** Charlemagne had control over France, Germany, Switzerland, and northern Italy. It was not nearly the size of the old Roman

Charlemagne—whose name means "Charles the Great"—has been nicknamed "the civilizer" for his able leadership and promotion of education, law, and order.

Empire, but it was still big. Besides conquering the Lombards in Italy, one of Charlemagne's greatest military accomplishments was defeating the pagan Saxons. It took 30 years of fighting and over 20 campaigns to subdue them. But in the end, he did.

Charlemagne Versus Abd al-Rahman

Now, this story of Charlemagne's conquests would not be complete without mentioning one of his southern rivals. That would be **Abd al-Rahman,** the prince of the Umayyad dynasty in Spain! Each of these equally ambitious men dreamed of expanding his borders beyond the Pyrenees Mountains. But it was someone else who instigated warfare between them. You see, there were some Muslims in Spain who did *not* want to be ruled by Abd al-Rahman. One of these was the governor of **Barcelona, Spain,** whose name was **Ibn al-Arabi.** It was Ibn al-Arabi who came to Charlemagne to ask for help against the ever-growing Andalusians. And so fighting began between the Franks and the armies of Abd al-Rahman when Charlemagne crossed the Pyrenees Mountains to help the governor of Barcelona. (Many history sources refer to the Spanish Muslim armies as the **Saracens.** This name may possibly come from the city of **Saragossa,** which was involved in the fighting.)

As strong as Charlemagne's army was, it was not strong enough to conquer Abd al-Rahman's men. With the need to fight the aggressive Saxons back home, Charlemagne retreated. He led his troops back across the Pyrenees—defeated and in single file.

Though this event has not received much publicity in history, the story that soon follows has. It seems that on the long trip back home through the difficult mountain passes, the rear division of Charlemagne's army was cut off and ambushed by yet another group of fighting Muslims! Nearly every Frankish man was slaughtered—including the nephew of Charlemagne. His name was **Roland.** One of the most famous poems of the Middle Ages—titled the ***The Song of Roland***—was written to honor the death of this war hero. The epic poem stirred the imagination of Europeans for centuries and fueled their dislike for the Muslims. In later years, Charlemagne returned to the area and was far more successful, though he never took Spain as a whole.

Unfortunately though, there was a dark side to some of Charlemagne's victories. It seems he had a ruthless ambition to spread the *power* of the Western Church. So, as he went about conquering new lands, he forced many people to convert to Christianity or be killed! I wouldn't call that "civilized" behavior. In fact, Charlemagne went so far as to give the death sentence if someone disobeyed "fast days," ate meat on Fridays, or refused baptism. On one occasion he was known for massacring 4,500 of his enemy *after* they had already surrendered!

Charlemagne had another weakness that reflected poorly on the church. Though he promoted Christianity, he failed to follow the moral guidelines of the New Testament when it came to marriage. Charlemagne had at least four wives and many mistresses, or girlfriends, who gave him children. Though he was greatly loved by his family and was a caring father, his lifestyle was very inconsistent with the Christian faith that he "forced" on others.

Charlemagne Crowned Emperor of Rome

Despite Charlemagne's character flaws, the pope was fond of him. Supposedly without Charlemagne's knowing it was going to happen, **Pope Leo** placed a glittering crown of gold on Charlemagne's head while he was bowed for prayer at church! Pope Leo then anointed Charlemagne's head with oil and saluted him. The day was December 25—Christmas Day. The year—800. The place was St. Peter's Cathedral in Rome. At that given moment in time, the pope publicly declared Charlemagne to be **Emperor of Rome**! This was a big step up from being just the king of the Franks. It was as if the old Roman Empire was being resurrected. It led to what was later called the **Holy Roman Empire.** The people loved it. They chanted, "Hail to Charles the Augustus, crowned by God the great and peace-bringing Emperor of the Romans."[1]

Becoming the emperor of Rome was a great honor for Charlemagne. He carried himself with enormous dignity in his new role. Like the sophisticated rulers of the Byzantine,

On Christmas Day in 800, Charlemagne was crowned Roman Emperor by Pope Leo III. This act led to the later formation of the Holy Roman Empire.

---

1. Will Durant, *The Age of Faith.* Vol. IV of *The Story of Civilization.* New York: Simon and Schuster, 1950; p. 469.

Charlemagne dressed with great formality on special occasions. He wore embroidered robes, a golden buckle, jeweled shoes, and an ornate crown made of gold and gems. Visitors were expected to kneel before him and kiss his foot or knee.

In his old age, Charlemagne recognized the need to divide his kingdom among his three sons. He thought if he divided it up ahead of time, it would keep them from fighting over the empire. He was wise to do so. In 814, at the age of 72, Charlemagne died of a high fever. Twenty-nine years later, in 843, the Frankish Empire was redivided by three of Charlemagne's grandsons at the **Treaty of Verdun.**

But none of the grandsons, or their descendants, ever served as effectively as Charlemagne did. There was never another Charles "the Great." Among other Carolingian kings was one nicknamed the Simple and one nicknamed the Lazy—not exactly promising terms for a ruler! As for the land, France and Germany became separate countries after the Treaty of Verdun. They were never to be united again. For years they fought over some of the surrounding lands. It goes to show that not just anyone is capable of running a large empire! Perhaps Charlemagne, even with his flaws, was one of the few "greats" worthy of the name.

ACTIVITIES FOR LESSON 37

37A—Younger Students

You may or may not have learned cursive handwriting yet. It's certainly very different from print. Practice reading and writing your favorite Bible verse in cursive. Compare it to reading and writing the same verse in print. Which do you find easier? Charlemagne liked print better than cursive, but he still struggled with writing his entire life. Place your print and cursive Bible verses in your Student Notebook under "Europe: France."

37B—Middle and Older Students

Are you familiar with courtroom terminology? Under Charlemagne, the concepts of a jury and a verdict were refined. Using a dictionary or encyclopedia, define the following terms that you are not already familiar with—they are common in courtrooms today. For fun, run a mock trial. If you have enough participants to make teams, earn points for using as many of the words below as possible.

Officers:		Procedures:	
	Bailiff		Affidavit
	District Attorney		Appeal
	Judge		Arraignment
	Justice of the Peace		Bail
	Lawyer		Evidence
	Public Defender		Fine
			Indictment
			Oath
			Sentence
			Subpoena
			Summons
			Warrant
			Witness

37C—Older Students

1. When Charlemagne became the new emperor of Rome, he took on more and more authority. But his increase in power led to some potential problems when it came to the church. Charlemagne used his role as emperor to choose who would be a bishop in the church. Just as the pope crossed

lines between the church and state when he anointed Pepin a king, so Charlemagne crossed lines between church and state when he began to choose bishops for the church.

Discuss with your teacher or class the implications of the separation of church and state. What does it mean? Discuss the Scripture, *"Render therefore to Caesar the things that are Caesar's, and to God the things that are God's."* (Matt. 22:21) Use a commentary to better understand the passage. Consider the threat to religious freedom that comes from high government involvement in the church.

2.   Research to find a copy of *The Song of Roland.* As stated in the lesson, this lengthy epic poem tells the story of Charlemagne's nephew, Roland, who dies in battle in the year 778. The story reveals that Roland fought bravely until the end. Too proud to ask for help, he fought until he was nearly the last of his men to stand. It was then that he sounded a horn for Charlemagne to come. Roland was found dead, facing the fleeing enemy. Note that little is left of historical accuracy in the poem. Much liberty was taken in the retelling of the event.

THE THOUSAND AND ONE NIGHTS: TALES FROM ARABIA

LESSON 38

Have you ever wanted a magic genie that could grant you all your wishes? Have you ever dreamed of sailing through a moonlit sky on a flying carpet? How about opening a secret cave door by chanting "Open sesame"? Whether you've secretly wanted any of these things or not, you've probably heard of such adventures as these. Magic lamps, enchanting genies, flying carpets, and secret caves! All these mysterious things are from Arab legends written during the **Abbasid dynasty** (uh BASS id). Today we will look at this lighter side of the Arabic world and at the origin of these stories.

In 750 the Abbasid family gained control of the eastern Arab world. (They were the ones who killed and overthrew the Umayyad family of Abd al-Rahman.) The Abbasid dynasty ruled successfully for a very long time—that is, until 1258. They were descendants of Mohammed's uncle, **al-Abbas.** The Abbasid family moved their capital from **Damascus,** Syria, to **Baghdad.** (Baghdad is presently the capital of Iraq.) From this new capital, the Abbasid family created an elaborate community. Much like Cordoba in Spain, Baghdad was bustling with trade, learning, and wealth of its own. It quickly became one of the largest and most amazing cities in the world—second only to Constantinople, its Byzantine neighbor.

The most famous of all the caliphs in the Abbasid family was most certainly **Harun al-Rashid** (Hah ROON al ra SHEED). By **786** he was the fifth caliph (or king) of the Islamic Empire in the East. Though Harun al-Rashid was a powerful military leader—fighting

The Abbasid family moved the capital of the Islamic empire from the city of Damascus to the city of Baghdad. (It is now the capital of Iraq.)

Harun al-Rashid, the fifth caliph of the Islamic Empire in the East, promoted art and literature while expanding his empire.

successfully against the Byzantine Empire and Tunisia—his real claim to fame came from being a gentleman of sorts. Harun distinguished himself from others by his passion for learning and his love for the arts. He disguised himself from time to time as a commoner just to experience the daily life of his own people—while at other times he mingled with the highest of kings. To Charlemagne he gave the gift of a water clock made of fine leather and brass. It contained tiny doors that opened and closed each hour with the ringing of delicate chimes. It was in this imaginative environment of the great palace of Harun al-Rashid that the stories of *The Thousand and One Nights* came to life. They are sometimes called *The Arabian Nights*.

The Arabian Nights

Legend has it that a queen named **Scheherazade** (shuh HER uh ZAHD) made up the stories of *The Arabian Nights* as a clever way to keep herself alive. As the tale goes, Scheherazade was engaged to marry a Persian king, or sultan, named **Shahriyar.** Shahriyar had a strange and wicked custom. He made it a law that every one of his new brides be killed the morning after their wedding! In fear for her life, Scheherazade decided to tell a fascinating story to her new husband on their wedding night—but to stop it at the most exciting part! Her hope was that he would keep her alive until the *next* night to hear the rest of the story.

According to tradition, Scheherazade's plan worked! Not only did the sultan keep Scheherazade alive for one more night, he kept her alive for at least "a thousand and one nights" as she told her suspenseful tales. In time the sultan fell deeply in love with Scheherazade, and he changed the law of killing his brides. As a result of the queen's cleverness, we have what is called *The Thousand and One Nights*, or *The Arabian Nights*, a collection of 200 fanciful, entertaining stories of love, life, and adventure. Though the stories were first written in Arabic, they come from places like China, India, Egypt, Mesopotamia, and Persia. Let me tell you about the three most well-known stories. Chances are you've heard them before.

Aladdin

The first tale is about a young Chinese boy named **Aladdin.** It seems that Aladdin was hired by a magician to go into a cave to retrieve a magic lamp. Aladdin went in as he was hired to do, but once he was there, he refused to give up the lamp. For this, the magician locked Aladdin in the cave! Aladdin clung to the lamp and affectionately rubbed it. What he didn't know was that in rubbing the lamp he would awaken a magical genie! The genie exploded out of the lamp to announce his lifelong dedication to Aladdin for freeing him. The genie promised to give Aladdin anything he ever wished for!

Rather than ask for riches or gold, Aladdin wished first to marry the sultan's beautiful daughter and to give her a lovely palace to live in. Much to his delight, he received them both. But the evil magician who had lost his lamp wanted revenge on Aladdin. He played a trick on Aladdin's young bride to get the lamp back, and he transported the entire palace to another country! But the story has a good ending. For the love of his bride, Aladdin followed the magician, rescued the princess *and* the lamp, and returned his palace to where it belonged. The story is a classic filled with adventure and romance!

Ali Baba and the Forty Thieves

The next tale is the one about **Ali Baba.** He is the main character of the story called "Ali Baba and the Forty Thieves." In this story, Ali Baba lived in Persia. In traveling along one day, he came upon 40 thieves. He saw that they were able to open a secret passageway of a cave by saying the magic password, "Open sesame." In fascination, Ali Baba secretly watched the thieves until they left. At the first opportunity, he tried the password himself. "Open sesame!" Ali Baba chanted. The magic worked and Ali Baba entered the thieves' cave with great anticipation.

What Ali Baba discovered was a cave full of gold! He shared this secret with his brother. His brother also tried the password and managed to get into the cave. However, on his way out, he forgot the magic words! Ali Baba's brother was trapped in the cave when the thieves returned. When they found him, the angry thieves killed Ali's brother. Suspecting there were other intruders, they next went after Ali Baba.

Thinking they were clever, the thieves conspired to ambush Ali Baba by hiding in giant oil pots. There, they secretly waited for a chance to attack. But, as fate would have it, a slave girl named Morgiana poured hot oil into the pots, thus freeing Ali Baba from the plot against his life! And of course, to end the story, Ali Baba inherited all the gold that he had found.

Sinbad the Sailor

The last tale I will share here is the one about **Sinbad the Sailor.** He is a rich storyteller in *The Arabian Nights*. Sinbad overhears that a poor beggar is jealous of his fortune. To lessen the beggar's pain, Sinbad invites him to listen to seven adventure stories of how Sinbad came to be rich. It becomes clear from the danger of each and every story that getting rich isn't easy and that it requires much bravery and cleverness.

For example, Sinbad tells of when he was forced to poke out the eyes of a giant ogre so he wouldn't be eaten alive. He describes an episode when he saved himself from the jaws of a snake by building wooden armor. Sinbad shares, too, how he rode a giant bird through a valley of death to snatch diamonds. He tells of how he was buried alive in a tomb full of skeletons and riches but how he wriggled away through the tunnel of a badger with pockets full of jewels.

In each instance, Sinbad the Sailor remained a brave and honest man, which led to great wealth and rewards from the kings who knew him. In the end, Sinbad the Sailor shares his wealth with the poor beggar and they become friends for life.

As you can tell, most of the stories of the Arabian Nights are pure fun and fiction. They are full of fanciful characters like genies, giants, and ogres. However, the tales give us a colorful glimpse into the fantasies of the Arab world. It's like peeking into the rich imagination of another culture.

ACTIVITIES FOR LESSON 38

38A—Younger Students

Re-enact parts of the story of Ali Baba and the forty thieves. Create a secret password to get in and out of a special room in your house. Say it out loud as you enter and exit but tell no one what it is! Insist that your family figure out the password to gain access to the room. They may have to spy on you to learn the word!

38B—Middle Students

Try some creative storytelling.

Using a tape recorder, create a suspenseful story that doesn't end! We call that a "cliffhanger." Play your story to your family at bedtime and make them wait until the next night for the conclusion. Play as often as your family might enjoy this form of storytelling.

38C—Older Students

Research at your library or on the Internet various versions of *The Thousand and One Nights*. Notice references to the culture from which the stories came. For example, the notion of genies stems from the Islamic belief that there are both good and bad jinn or jinni, which are thought to be something between an angel and a man. In your opinion, do these tales exemplify virtues such as honesty, forgiveness, and self-control? Discuss the differences and similarities between these tales, *Aesop's Fables*, the parables of Jesus, and other famous collections of stories.

793

INVASION OF THE VIKINGS

LESSON 39

"God, deliver us from the fury of the Northmen!"[2] This was the literal prayer of countless souls in Europe during the fearsome age of the **Vikings.** The Vikings (also called **Northmen** or **Norsemen**) were savage raiders who plundered and destroyed endless numbers of villages across Europe for about 300 years. Why were the Vikings so cruel? To them it was, in part, a matter of survival!

The Vikings were people who originally lived on the coasts of **Norway, Sweden,** and **Denmark.** (These are also called the **Scandinavian countries.**) The term *Viking* probably comes from the Norse word ***vik,*** which means "inlet" or "bay." It describes the watery coast where most of the Vikings lived. If you were to look on a map, you would see how close together the Scandinavian countries are. You will also notice how far north they are! It is both the *location* and the *terrain* of these countries that contributed to the desperation of the Vikings.

You see, each of these countries has certain difficulties when it comes to farming. *Norway* is a glistening land of hills, snow-covered mountains, and **fjords** (a fjord is a valley of water with steep hills on either side). Though breathtaking, this terrain doesn't offer much open space for crops. *Sweden*, on the other hand, has fewer mountains and more farmland—but sometimes weeks can go by without the sun shining there! (Because of how the earth tilts on its axis, the sun hides during some seasons in the far North Pole regions.) Without year-round sunshine, farming is obviously a challenge. *Denmark*, which is further south than Sweden, has exposure to the sun every day of the year but much of the country is made up of tiny islands—500 tiny islands that is! So, like Norway and Sweden, Denmark too is a tough place for farming.

Are you beginning to see the pattern here? As people grew in numbers in Scandinavia, they became hungry and desperate for more farmland and ways to support their families. And desperation, apart from the Lord, can lead to cruel measures. Hopefully, this sheds some understanding on the beginning of the Viking reign of terror.

---

2. *World Book Encyclopedia*, 50th Anniversary ed., s.v. "Vikings." Chicago: Field Enterprises Educational Corp., 1966.

So what did the Vikings do to try to survive? Well, first they built great ships so they could travel away from their lands and raid new ones. In fact, the Vikings built the best ships known in the Mediterranean world. These masterful ships, built 100 feet long, were sturdy, maneuverable, and made with layers of flexible wood. The flexible layers prevented harsh ocean waves from breaking up the boats at sea.

This photo was taken about midnight, when the sun was just beginning to set in Sweden, which is why it is literally called "The Land of the Midnight Sun."

Then, with these reliable vessels, the Vikings set out to capture, pillage, and plunder just about anything and everything they could find. They would sneak into a port, hide their boats, and pounce on their victims before anyone knew what was happening! The most profitable targets were the numerous monasteries that dotted the shores of Europe. The first documented raid of this kind was in **793** on **Lindisfarne,** a small island off England. In 802 the Vikings hit the church of St. Columba on a Scottish island. (Remember St. Columba?) Monasteries like these were usually well stocked with provisions and lightly guarded by monks and nuns. Without concern for these peaceful people, the Vikings stole their goods and burned down their dwellings! There was little mercy given to the victims. Many were killed or taken as slaves. The *Anglo-Saxon Chronicle* describes it this way:

"They lay waste everything in sight. They trample the holy relics under foot. They seize the treasure of the holy church. Some of the monks they kill outright. Others they carry away with them. A great many they insult and beat and fling out naked. Others they drown in the sea. They depart, boasting about their plunder and their wicked deeds."[3]

Smooth but sturdy, Viking ships were sometimes called "dragon boats" for the dragonhead that decorated the front bow.

Though these ruthless Viking warriors are often depicted with animal horns on their helmets, there is not much evidence that these were actually worn by the Vikings. However, it was common for Viking warriors to have helmets of leather or iron that covered the nose. Wealthy warriors had tiny rings of iron made into armor or "chain mail." Less wealthy soldiers had only thick leather coverings.

Viking weapons included **longswords, battle-axes** (for cutting through their enemies' helmets), and a single-edged knife called a **scramasax.** These were used for hand-to-hand combat. Unfortunately for their victims, this up-close combat was the most common and bloody method of fighting the Vikings used. They were rather fearless!

Some Viking warriors patterned themselves after legendary heroes called the **Jomsvikings** and the **Berserks.** The Jomsvikings were so fearfully rugged and masculine that they refused to keep women in their homes. The Berserks were even more savage. For battle they dressed in animal skins, if they wore any clothing at

---

3. Peter Speed, *Life in the Time of Harald Hardrada and the Vikings.* Austin, TX: Raintree Steck-Vaughn Publishers, 1993; p. 29.

all! They then worked themselves into a wild rage and howled like animals. The term "going berserk" comes from these crazed Vikings!

For centuries Viking raiders viciously attacked the coastlands of Europe. Viking men would pillage across the seas for a season and then travel home to their families in Norway, Sweden, and Denmark. When their supplies ran low, the raids would start all over again. But, over time, this kind of plundering wasn't enough to support Viking families. They needed new lands to settle. And so the Vikings spread throughout Europe, conquering as they went.

The Conquering Vikings

The **Swedish** Vikings traveled to and conquered the land of present-day **Russia.** They eventually made **Kiev** their capital city. They were known there as the **Varangians.** In fact, the name "Russia" probably comes from a Varangian tribe known as the "Rus" or "Rhos." (It may have described people with red hair, a common trait of these Vikings.) The Varangians were such good soldiers, that some were recruited to be the personal bodyguards for the king of the Byzantine Empire!

The **Danish** Vikings ("Danish," or "Danes," means people from Denmark) sought to conquer parts of **England, France,** and **Spain.** In England, they successfully ruled an area called **York.** They kept it a stronghold for roughly 300 years! In France, the Danish Vikings sailed inland along the Seine River to reach and destroy **Paris.** They sacked it three times— in 845, 856, and 885. Finally, the king paid them large sums of money in the form of **Danegeld** to leave! It worked, too. In fact the payment of Danegeld became a common method of taming down savage Viking attacks.

In the modern city of Kiev in Ukraine, there is not much evidence that it was once the capital of invading Vikings.

The Danish Vikings later settled a province named **Normandy** along the northern coast of France. In 911 the king of the West Franks agreed to give them this strip of land to bring some sort of peace to his country. He appointed a Viking named **Rollo** to be the Duke of Normandy. Interestingly, Rollo converted to Christianity near this time. In doing so, he pledged to keep peace with France. And he did! By the way, Normandy is the location of the famous beach that the Allies invaded in **World War II** to drive back the Germans. It was also the home of William the Conqueror, who we will study later. Lots of history comes from this Viking settlement.

The third group of Vikings, the **Norwegian** Vikings, headed in yet another direction. They settled places like **Greenland, Iceland, Scotland,** and **Ireland.** In fact, **Dublin,** the present-day capital of the Republic of Ireland, was originally a Viking town. The Norwegian Vikings also went exploring as far as **North America.** They called it **Vinland.** But that's such a good story I'm saving it for a later lesson (Lesson 52 on Leif Ericsson).

In closing, you are probably thinking that the Vikings were pretty terrible people. And from the way they raided and conquered villages of unprotected, innocent people, they were. But there is, of course, another side to the Scandinavian people. There is the side of them that cared for their families, their homes, and their faith. We'll look at this domestic side of the Vikings in our next lesson. Among their own people, the Vikings weren't nearly so dreadful as their enemies believed them to be. In fact, back in their homelands, the Vikings weren't all that different from the Europeans who prayed "deliver us from the Northmen!"

ACTIVITIES FOR LESSON 39

ALL STUDENTS

Make your Memory Cards for Lessons 37–39. The invasion of the Vikings (793) is a date to memorize. Highlight the card accordingly.

39A—Younger Students

1. Create a mask to resemble the front of a Viking helmet. See the Activity Supplement in the Appendix for a pattern and directions.

2. Dress in animal skins and/or the mask of the Viking helmet from the above activity. Within reason, pretend to go "berserk" as a Viking warrior might do to intimidate his enemies! Take a photo and file it in your Student Notebook under "Europe: Sweden, Norway, *or* Denmark."

39B—Middle Students

1. Research the change of sunlight hours in the course of a year in the regions above the Arctic Circle. Imagine the difference it would make in your life to have darkness during daytime hours and daylight during the night hours! Write down 10 things that would be different at various seasons. For example, driving with headlights on at noon during one season; going to bed with the sun shining at midnight at another season. File your list under "Europe: Sweden" in your Student Notebook.

2. Middle Students and Up: Obtain a video copy of the *Nova* documentary on Vikings.

39C—Older Students

1. Research the Christian conversion of Rollo, the Viking. Retell the story in your own words and include it in your Student Notebook under "Europe: France."

2. Research the events that took place on the beach of Normandy during World War II. Write a few paragraphs to describe it. File this paper under "Europe: France" in your Student Notebook.

TAKE ANOTHER LOOK!

REVIEW 13: LESSONS 37-39

Wall of Fame

1. *Charlemagne (768)*—Tall, blonde, and handsome. Depict Charlemagne with these features, adding a crown. Write underneath, "The Civilizer." [From *History Through the Ages,* use *Pippin (Pepin) III* and *Charlemagne.*]

2. **The Thousand and One Nights:** *Tales From Arabia (786)*—Cut a small piece of fabric for a flying carpet. Glue it onto a piece of paper. Write the name of *Harun al-Rashid* underneath and *"The Thousand and One Nights."* [Use *Abbasid Dynasty* and *Harun al-Rashid.*]

3. *INVASION OF THE VIKINGS (793)*—Draw a man with a helmet (made of foil) holding a burnt match (to portray their burning of villages) and a toothpick (for a spear). Glue or tape these pieces to a paper and write underneath, "The Fury of the Northmen (Vikings)." **Remember, this is a date to memorize.** [Use *Viking Invasions.*]

SomeWHERE in Time

1. Tracing can be fun. I would like you to trace the extent of Charlemagne's empire following these directions.

   Materials: Outline Map 19, "Charlemagne's Empire"; tracing paper; tape; pencil; colored pencils; a sunny window

   a. Lay one piece of tracing paper over Outline Map 19. Gently tape the corners of the two pieces of paper together (gentle enough that you can easily separate the papers later).

   b. Hold these two papers up to a sunny window and tape them at a height that you can easily reach. You should be able to view Charlemagne's empire through the tracing paper with the help of the sunlight.

   c. Use a pencil to trace the outline of Europe and the areas surrounding the Mediterranean Sea.

   d. Now trace the border of Charlemagne's empire.

   e. Remove your maps from the window.

   f. Use colored pencils to color in the boundaries of Charlemagne's land. Label them as far as you are able.

   g. File your traced map in your Student Notebook under "Europe: France *or* Germany."

2. The Abbasid dynasty moved their capital from Damascus, Syria, to Baghdad (presently in Iraq). Find these cities on a globe or map. Trace the route with your finger. Pray for the citizens of Baghdad.

3. To distinguish the conquering Vikings from one another, make a yarn map.

   Materials: Outline Map 20, "Viking Voyages"; colored pencils; yarn in three colors (only a few inches needed of each); glue

a. Using a black pencil for labeling, and colored pencils for shading, label and shade the countries of **Sweden** and **northwest Russia** (color as far south as the city of Kiev) in yellow.

b. Label and shade the countries of **Denmark, England, France** (Normandy), and **Spain** in orange. (Normandy is a province in present-day France.)

c. Label and shade the countries of **Norway, Greenland, Iceland, Scotland, Ireland,** and the **northeast coast of North America** in green.

d. With strands of yarn handy, create a thin line of glue from **Sweden** to **northwest Russia** (follow the path of the Gulf of Finland into Russia as far south as Kiev). Lay a piece of yarn over the glue to connect the two countries.

e. Repeat the above step using glue and a *second* color of yarn to connect **Denmark** to **England** (York), **Denmark** to **France** (Normandy), and **Denmark** to **North America.**

f. Repeat the same step using glue and a *third* color of yarn to connect **Norway** to **Greenland, Norway** to **Iceland, Norway** to **Scotland, Norway** to **Ireland,** and **Norway** to the **northeast coast of North America.**

g. Allow to dry and place this map of the Viking invasions in your Student Notebook under "Europe: (your choice of Scandinavian or European countries used in this exercise)."

 # WHAT DID YOU LEARN?
WEEK 13: QUIZ

Circle Sense. In the sentences below, *circle* the word that makes the most *sense*.

1. According to legend, to persuade Brude and the Picts to Christ, Columba drew the symbol of a (dragon, cross) on the gates of the city and they flew open.

2. The archipelago of Japan is really made up of 4,223 (volcanoes, islands).

3. Though selected to be a pope, Gregory the Great preferred to dress and eat like a (monk, barbarian).

4. During the (Gupta, Tang) dynasty, Li Shi Min reinstated the ancient teachings of Confucius.

5. Mohammed declared Allah the one true god but allowed the Meccans to continue to (worship, fight) at the Kaaba.

6. After Mohammed died, Abu Bekr oversaw the writing of the (Ramayana, Koran).

7. Wu Zetian, the empress of China, sponsored the building of many (mosques, shrines).

8. In the epic of *Beowulf,* Beowulf kills (Leviathan, Grendel) by twisting and ripping its arm off.

9. Gebel al-Tariq entered Spain through what the ancients called the Pillars of (Hercules, Pelagius).

10. St. Boniface helped shape the Christmas tradition of a (tree, stocking).

11. Iconoclast means "image (maker, breaker)."

12. Charles Martel was nicknamed "the (hammer, genii)" for driving back the Muslims at the Battle of Tours.

13. The name Charlemagne means "Charles the (Simple, Great)."

14. Under the Abbasid dynasty, the capital of Islam was moved from Damascus to (Baghdad, Rome).

15. Scandinavia is composed of these three countries: Norway, Sweden, and (Germany, Denmark).

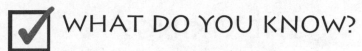

WHAT DO YOU KNOW?

PRETEST 14

Fill in the Blanks. Using a word from the bottom of the page, fill in the blanks.

1. Viking women used decorative _____ to fasten their clothes and carry important things like keys.

2. A lazy Viking child was nicknamed a "_____" for sitting around the fire.

3. Thursday is named for the Viking god _____.

4. The Slavic tribe known as the Bulgars settled what is present-day _____.

5. Methodius and Cyril helped develop an entire _____ to share the word of God with Slavic-speaking people.

6. Alfred the Great learned to _____ before any of his brothers, even though he was the youngest boy in his family.

7. Showing great wisdom, Alfred the Great based the common laws of England on the _____ _____.

8. To record the history of England and to promote patriotism, Alfred the Great started what was called the _____.

WORD BANK

| Bulgaria | brooches | Ten Commandments | Thor |
| alphabet | charcoal chewer | *Anglo-Saxon Chronicle* | read |

THE VIKINGS:
THEIR FAMILIES, THEIR HOMES, AND THEIR FAITH
LESSON 40

As we just learned, the **Vikings** were at times a cruel and ruthless people. For the sake of their own survival, they stole from others and invaded new lands for nearly three centuries (from the **800s to the 1100s**). But back home in **Norway, Sweden,** and **Denmark** they lived much like the very people they attacked. Today we'll look at Viking families, homes, and faith. In an interesting way, they remain an influence on us every day of the week.

Viking Families

Viking families often included grandparents, aunts, and uncles as well as mothers, fathers, and their children. When a baby was born into a Viking family, it was the father who decided if it should live or die depending on how healthy the infant was! The Vikings had no last names to pass on to their children, but they almost always had descriptive nicknames, like Eric "the Red" for example. He had red hair.

Viking families were very self-sufficient. They made for themselves almost everything they needed—especially **food** and **clothing.** Since most clothes were made at home, they were kept simple and practical. Men wore tight woolen pants that were scratchy but warm and long lasting. Women wore long-sleeved dresses made from softer linen. Married women wore scarves over their hair and children wore clothes just like their parents. Everyone wore warm leather shoes to survive the cold winter weather.

The Vikings also wore warm woolen tunics to fight the cold. With no buttons or zippers, the Vikings used decorative **brooches** to attach the tunics at the shoulder. From these brooches, it was common for a woman to hang her keys or a comb. (It was like wearing the things that women today would carry in a purse.)

For work, most of the Vikings farmed their own land. But there were also craftsmen who specialized in making items of **leather, wood, glass, bone,** and **antler.** In fact, the Vikings carved beautiful pieces of bone and antler into ornate combs and belt buckles. Iron ore was abundant in Viking regions, so **blacksmithing** was a common trade. Blacksmiths made crude **nails, locks, horseshoes, weapons,** and **tools.**

Viking craftsmen carved intricate designs in wood, glass, bone, and antler.

When the Vikings weren't hard at work, they loved to play games. At home they played **board games** and **chess** and threw **dice.** Some of the Vikings must have been cheaters because dice have been found with secret weights inside of them, which make the dice fall a certain way! The game of chess was picked up from the Arabs, whom the Vikings sometimes traded with.

For entertainment, the Vikings held horse fights, trained dogs to do tricks, and learned to jump from one oar to the next around the outside of a Viking ship! They made ice skates from cattle bones, created riddles, juggled, and held two-week-long feasts three times a year. At every occasion there was much eating, drinking, and storytelling. Typically a large horn of ale was passed around at feasts until everyone had drunk from it. It had to be shared this way because the drink would spill if it were set down!

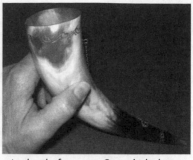

A drink from a Swedish horn like this would spill if it were set down!

Viking poets were called **skalds.** Though there was a written language made up of **runes**—very straight up and down letters—very few Vikings could read or write. So skalds memorized stories and legends of Viking gods and warriors. Some of these sagas were written down in the thirteenth century. Many can still be read today. They are a great source of knowledge about Viking beliefs and traditions, as are rune stones—great slabs of stone carved in runes as memorials and markers.

Carved rune stones similar to this can be found in parts of Europe as reminders of the once fierce Vikings.

Viking Homes

The most common Viking home was a **longhouse.** These rectangular structures *were* long, measuring 100 feet in length. They were made of logs and thatch. Walls made of packed dirt were up to 6 feet thick just to help keep in the warmth. Some homeowners grew grass on the top and sides of their house to keep it even warmer. Remember, it was cold in these far northern lands!

Inside a longhouse you would find a fire going almost all the time right in the center of things. There were no windows—just a small hole in the roof for smoke to escape. A giant iron pot, or **cauldron**, was suspended over the fire for cooking and heating water. Along the walls, the Vikings built benches for sitting and working at during the day and for sleeping on at night. The hard benches were made cozier for sleeping with layers and layers of animal skins. The only other furniture in a longhouse might be a table for food preparation.

Wealthier homeowners had separate rooms in the longhouse that were used for storage, stables, drying fish, or as a bathroom. It was nice to keep these rooms separate because of the smell! The Vikings created steam baths by pouring water over fiery hot rocks. It was like having a sauna in your own home! Afterwards, they would beat themselves with bunches of twigs to improve their circulation and then run outside and roll in the cold snow! Sounds painful to me.

In the middle of the summer, it was common for families to move to small homes in the mountains called **shielings.** The purpose of their move was to follow their cattle to better grazing grounds. This season also kept Viking families busy making milk, butter, and cheeses to store for the winter.

Viking children never went to school but instead worked with their parents. And a lot of hard work was needed around a Viking home. A child who appeared to be lazy was called a **"charcoal chewer."** It meant that the child sat around the fire too long doing nothing. (It's probably similar to our expression of being a "couch potato"!)

One of the greatest areas of work in a Viking home was in meal preparation. Food items had to be grown, harvested, stored, and of course cooked. Everyone in the family had some part in getting food on the table. Vikings ate wild animals that they hunted, domestic animals that they raised, fish that they dried, bread that they baked, and dairy products that they made. It was hard work just to eat, which is probably why the Vikings had only two meals a day.

Much like the ancient Greeks and Romans, the Vikings placed their faith in dozens of mythological gods. They believed there were two families of gods, the **Aesir** and the **Vanir.** Both supposedly lived in a place called **Asgard,** which was joined to the earth by a rainbow bridge. In Asgard, supposedly, there lived 12 gods and 12 goddesses. The Earth was thought to be flat like a pancake and surrounded by deep oceans of monsters! It was believed that beyond the oceans were the **Frost Giants,** who were enemies of the gods. Even stranger, the Vikings thought that if they died in bed, they would be taken to the enemy in a boat full of toenail clippings! Ooh!

Like the ancient Egyptians, the Vikings believed that they needed to prepare themselves for the afterlife. Wealthier people were buried in ships with everything they might need in the future—food, clothing, tools, weapons, and sometimes even their slaves. A Viking ship was either buried with its owner or set aflame and sent out to sea. The sight of flaming torches hitting the sail must have been heart-wrenching for loved ones left behind.

Of great significance to the Vikings was a legendary place called **Valhalla.** It was like heaven to them. Viking warriors believed that if they died in battle, they went straight to Valhalla on the back of an eight-legged horse named **Sleipner.** Valhalla was a great hall with 140 doors, each wide enough for 800 men to enter at once! At this great hall, men could eat, drink, and fight endlessly while being served by beautiful young women!

The god of greatest importance to the Vikings was **Odin.** He was supposed to own Valhalla. By Viking tradition, Odin was the god of kings, poets, and warriors. He was thought to be very wise and the creator of the rune alphabet. As payment for his wisdom, he supposedly lost an eye at the **World Tree** where Odin sacrificed himself and came back to life. The English called Odin, **"Woden."** It is from this name that we get the day **Wednesday!** It meant "Woden's Day." (Now you know why Wednesday has a silent "d" in it! It's from Woden's name.)

Another important god to the Vikings was **Thor.** It is from his name that we get **Thursday** (Thor's Day)! Thor was very popular as a big, strong god. He was supposed to have a bright red beard and a quick temper. But tradition says he laughed a lot, too. Thor was considered the god of the sky, and he had a magic weapon. It was a hammer. To remember and honor Thor, the Vikings made little hammer-shaped charms to carry and trade.

Frey was the name of another Viking god. He was supposed to be responsible for peace, crops, cattle, and marriage. It was thought he could control the rain and the sun for the farmers. You would think that Friday was named after him. But **Friday** actually comes from the Viking goddess named **Frigg.** Frigg was supposedly the wife of Odin and the Viking goddess of love and fertility. **Tuesday** comes from a Norse god named **Tiw.** He was thought to be the god of war.

Though the Vikings had their gods and customs, they also had the chance to hear the Gospel of Jesus Christ. After several decades of interacting with the Europeans, the Vikings were exposed to the one true God. Many missionaries shared with the Vikings in the 800s and the 900s. And you know what? It made a difference! It appears that in learning about the Lord (and in losing many battles), the Vikings eventually abandoned their savage ways. The looting, the raiding, the pillaging, and the plundering finally ceased for more peaceful means of survival. The Vikings went from ruthless pirating to trading and production of commerce. Of course, some Vikings only converted to Christianity by name so they would be better accepted among the European traders. But many became sincere Christians.

The Vikings remained in their Scandinavian homelands and in their new settlements across Russia and Europe. Over time, the Vikings weren't called Vikings anymore. They adopted the names of the countries in which they lived. However, every week of every month of every year, those who speak English have four days to remember the Vikings by—Tuesday, Wednesday, Thursday, and Friday! I find it astounding that the Vikings still have that influence over us!

ACTIVITIES FOR LESSON 40

40A—Younger Students

1. Make a longhouse out of a shoebox. Lay a shoebox on its side. Create benches along the walls out of cardboard. Lay furry fabric over the benches to make beds. Make a pretend fire out of a pile of sticks. Using reference books from the library for ideas, add other assorted household items that the Vikings might have used. Cover your box with thick mud and grass to keep it insulated. You may want to sprinkle grass seed on the mud to grow over time. (You will have to keep the mud moist.)

2. Make butter. Place heavy whipping cream and a pinch of salt in a closed container. Shake it until it firms up like butter. It takes a long time!

3. Make a Viking woman's brooch. Take a decorative jeweled pin; attach a comb and some keys to it. Attach the brooch with these items to an outer garment.

4. Sleep in layers of "animal" skins. Perhaps use leather jackets or a fleecy woolen blanket. Be creative!

Take pictures of these activities and file them in your Student Notebook under "Europe: Sweden, Norway, *or* Denmark."

40B—Middle Students

1. With parental approval, try to whittle a bone (chicken or beef) into a sharp tool. Imagine carving the bone into something beautiful!

2. Carve a rune stone. A rune is a character of the alphabet used by the Teutonic peoples of Europe. *Rune* is a Gothic word that means "secret"; very few people understood the meaning of the runes, which were typically made of straight lines. They may have originated with the early Greeks and Romans and then been carried to the Scandinavian countries.

   Materials: Plaster of Paris, small box, screwdriver, hammer, sample of rune letters provided in the Activity Supplement in the Appendix

   a. Mix enough plaster of Paris to fill a small box.

   b. Allow the plaster to harden overnight.

   c. Examine the sample of runes found in the Activity Supplement. (Observe the straightness of the characters.)

   d. Use a screwdriver and hammer to "chisel" runes into the plaster of Paris, forming words if you can. You will quickly understand why runes were straight and not round. It is very difficult to chisel rounded letters.

   e. Take a photo of the rune stone you created, and file your photo under "Europe: Sweden, Norway, *or* Denmark."

40C—Older Students

1. Practice juggling just for fun.

2. With parental approval, watch the 1958 movie *The Vikings* (not rated) starring Kirk Douglas and Tony Curtis. Look for historical accuracy and reference to the Viking gods. (True to history, rape and other sexual misdeeds by the Vikings are implied in this film, though not portrayed graphically.)

METHODIUS AND CYRIL, MISSIONARIES TO THE SLAVS
LESSON 41

How important is a written language? In sharing the Word of God, it's very important. At least that's what two dedicated brothers discovered to be true. Today you'll learn about **Methodius** (meh THO dee us) and **Cyril** (SIR il), missionaries and brothers who helped influence **Slavic nations** for Christ. They gave them the Word of God in their *own* language. Here's the remarkable story.

The people known as the Slavs were originally scattered across parts of Europe. In the eighth century they finally settled in southeastern Europe and western Russia. The first Slav state was ruled by the **Bulgars.** (The country of Bulgaria later developed from this.)

Well, the Bulgar Slavs were not very friendly with their neighbors. They were especially hostile to the Byzantine Empire. The Bulgars attacked **Constantinople** in 811 and killed the emperor of the Byzantine world! This attack sent waves of fear through the region. Other Slavs in the area, named the **Moravians,** were afraid it was the beginning of war. (Moravia, by the way, is the modern-day **Czech Republic.**)

A **Moravian king** named **Rostislav** came up with a plan that demonstrated great faith on his part. Rather than prepare for war, King Rostislav asked the next Byzantine emperor to send Christian missionaries to the Slavic nations. He believed that the Gospel of Christ could do more to bring peace to the troubled area than anything else!

Now here is where Methodius and Cyril enter our story. In **863** these two brothers heard about King Rostislav's call for missionary help. They were Greeks from **Thessalonica** (the city associated with the New Testament books of 1 and 2 Thessalonians). Methodius was the abbot of a Greek monastery. Cyril was a teacher of philosophy in Constantinople. Together they had already been missionaries to people living near the **Black Sea.** They were perfect candidates for the job.

Though now called the Czech Republic, Moravia was at one time named Czechoslovakia. Pictured here, the city of Prague in the Czech Republic is one of the most beautiful cities in Europe.

But, as Methodius and Cyril became acquainted with the Slavs, they came across a serious problem. The Slavic people had no written language of their own in which to learn the Bible. They didn't know **Latin** or **Greek,** which were the *only* languages that the New Testament was written in. What were the brothers to do to effectively share God's word?

The Cyrillic Alphabet

Methodius and Cyril decided to create a written language especially for the Slavic people. The Slavs best understood and spoke **Slovak.** It was their native tongue. To put it into written form, Cyril invented a whole new alphabet. It became known as the **Cyrillic alphabet.** It was similar to Greek but it included special symbols that expressed sounds unique to the Slavic people. The Cyrillic alphabet also became the foundation for the **Russian alphabet** that is used today.

Methodius and Cyril— brothers dedicated to the Gospel—not only helped evangelize Slavic nations but also created the Cyrillic alphabet to promote the reading of God's Word.

With this new alphabet, Methodius and Cyril poured themselves into translating portions of the Bible and other church writings. As it turned out, the brothers were really creating a new language. In particular, Cyril translated the entire Old Testament from the Greek Septuagint into what was called **Slavonic.** It was a remarkable feat. Unfortunately, Cyril died in 869 just a short time after taking vows to be a monk.

As for Methodius, he continued his work in **Moravia** as a bishop in the church. Besides that, he had other talents that helped him in his efforts to evangelize the Slavic people. He was a gifted painter. There is a story that Methodius once painted such a beautiful picture of the Last Judgment of Christ that **King Boris of Bulgaria** was converted to the Christian faith upon just seeing it! It must have been spectacular.

Despite the remarkable work of Methodius and Cyril, over time other written languages crept into the Slavic nations and churches. The churches of **Moravia, Bohemia, Slovakia, Hungary,** and **Poland** all eventually used Latin in their services. They patterned themselves after the Western Church. But **Bulgaria, Serbia,** and **Russia** kept the Slavonic language and alphabet as created by the missionary brothers. These churches also adopted the rituals of the Eastern Orthodox Church. It's just kind of interesting how it all panned out.

Towering spires and pointed arches were typical of the Western Church of the Middle Ages.

As for King Rostislav's vision for peace among the Slavs, it took awhile for that to happen. Slavic nations quarreled with their Byzantium neighbors until they were defeated in 1014. But at least through the missionary work of Methodius and Cyril, the Word of God was available to the Slavs in their very own tongue.

ACTIVITIES FOR LESSON 41

41A—Younger Students

1. Methodius used his talent as a painter to portray a scene from the life of Christ. It had a powerful effect upon the king of Bulgaria. Try your hand today at painting something from the life of Christ. Consider finger paint or watercolor. I suggest you get ideas from an illustrated children's Bible. Perhaps the Lord could use your painting to influence someone to believe!

2. (A student of any age might find this fun.) Methodius and Cyril created new letters to match the sounds unique to the Slavic people. Just for fun, listen around your home for interesting sound effects, such as a door slamming, a floor creaking, a baby gurgling. Then create a new letter or symbol for this sound. Use it in a sentence. Now unless you teach the new letter to others, it won't make any sense at all. Imagine the huge task set before the missionaries who created a whole new alphabet so that others might read the Word of God!

With golden domes and multisided towers, this church in Kiev, Ukraine, is patterned after the Eastern Church of the Middle Ages. (This church is named Saint Sophia after the one built by Justinian in Constantinople.)

Turn to the Activity Supplement to view some of the unusual characters in the Cyrillic alphabet. Try to write your name using the guide provided. File your paper under "Europe: (your choice of Slavic country—Hungary, Bulgaria, Czech Republic, Slovakia, etc.)."

41C—Older Students

1. To familiarize yourself with the countries mentioned in this lesson, find the capital city of each. Here is a list of each country as they appeared in the text:

> Russia, Bulgaria, Czech Republic, Slovakia, Byzantine Empire,
> Greece, Hungary, Poland, Serbia

2. Familiarize yourself with nations that today are still lacking the written word of God in their language. Pray for them!

871

ALFRED THE GREAT, KING OF ENGLAND
LESSON 42

Of all the kings that have ever reigned in **England,** only one has been called "the Great." His name was Alfred. We'll look at **Alfred the Great** today and consider why he developed this noble reputation. But first, let's review England. For being such a small country, it has had a great influence on the world! For that reason, I feel England is worthy of a little more attention here.

English history is complex. Many different people groups have called it home. If we were to go as far back as 2700 B.C., we would find the amazing people who built **Stonehenge** in Wiltshire, England. Stonehenge is a huge stone structure, still standing today, that clocks the seasons. (I wrote about it in Volume I of *The Mystery of History*.) Though we don't know exactly who the people were that built Stonehenge, they left us the phenomenal stones to remember them by.

The builders of Stonehenge remain a mystery, but they will always be remembered by the huge stone structure they left behind.

But in this volume, you learned first of the **Celts** (keltz) who occupied England around 600 B.C. They remained separated from the rest of Europe until a rather famous Roman invaded in 55 B.C. His name was **Julius Caesar.** (His interesting life story is in Volume I as well.) The Romans stayed in England for 300 to 400 years, living side by side with the Celts. The Celts never left.

So, follow along with me. We have first in ancient times, the builders of *Stonehenge*. Then the *Celts* arrived. Then the *Romans* invaded under Julius Caesar.

Julius Caesar, the first of many "caesars" in Rome, conquered vast parts of Europe, including England.

Well, you may remember that the **Western Roman Empire** collapsed in 476. It didn't fall apart only in mainland Europe; it collapsed in England, too. As the Roman Empire toppled, there were three tribes of people who invaded England. They were the **Angles**, the **Saxons**, and the **Jutes.** When they arrived, the Romans left! The Celts stayed.

The most famous Celt who stayed to stop the Saxons was, of course, **King Arthur.** He is best known for his **Knights of the Round Table** and the search for the **Holy Grail.** Fabulous tales exist about King Arthur.

So, follow along with me again (we're getting to Alfred eventually!). The ancient people in England built *Stonehenge*. Then the *Celts* moved in. Then the *Romans* invaded under Julius Caesar. Then the *Jutes, the Angles, and the Saxons* invaded. The Romans left and *King Arthur*, a Celtic king, fought the Saxons.

Now, despite King Arthur's many successes, the Angles, the Saxons, and the Jutes together set up seven kingdoms in England. And they set them up to stay. Unlike the Romans who left after 300 years, these tribes dug deep roots in England. Even the name England comes from the Angles (*Angle-land*). It was during this period too that **Christianity** was brought to England. Under the leadership of **Gregory the Great**, **St. Augustine of Canterbury** and many others *evangelized* the Angles, the Saxons, and the Jutes. (To evangelize means to share Christ.)

But, peace was not to last among these tribes. There was yet another people group that invaded England. These were the **Danish Vikings** (Vikings from Denmark). I'm sure you remember learning how the Vikings savagely attacked and plundered the places they wanted. They certainly did so in England in 787.

So, one more time, a quick review of England looks like this. You fill in the blanks! Some ancient people built _____ (*Stonehenge*), then the _____ (*Celts*) settled there, then the Romans invaded under _____ (*Julius Caesar*), then the Angles, the _____ (*Saxons*), and the Jutes moved in. King _____ (*Arthur*) tried to stop them. Christianity was brought by _____ (*Gregory the Great*) through St. Augustine and others. Then the Danish _____ (*Vikings*) attacked.

This brings us up-to-date. I know that was a long review. But in understanding the history of England, you know far more history than most. Also, in knowing this background, you will better appreciate the very good king that Alfred the Great became. So let's finally look at him.

Alfred, the King of Wessex

Alfred was born the youngest of five boys in **Berkshire, England.** A story is told that his mother created a contest for her many sons. She would award a prize to the one who could learn to read first. Against all odds, Alfred beat every one of his older brothers in learning to read first! His mother awarded him a book of Anglo-Saxon poems. Before he was 7, Alfred had visited **Rome** twice and was confirmed by the pope. These trips to Rome gave Alfred a taste of civilization that would later influence him as king.

In **871** Alfred became the king of **Wessex,** the western kingdom of the Saxons. Alfred was only 22 years old. He was graceful, wise, a good hunter, and handsome. But Alfred faced a great challenge in ruling Wessex. His challenge was war with the Danish Vikings! I'm sure you remember how dreadful the Vikings were. In Alfred's *first* year as king, he had to fight nine battles against the Danes to try to stop them from raiding churches and monasteries. He wasn't always successful.

Legend says that on one occasion—when the Danes seemed to be winning the war—King Alfred disguised himself as a minstrel (or entertainer) and snuck into the Danish camp. There, while performing in front of **Guthrum,** the Danish chieftain, Alfred secretly learned of the plans and strategies of his enemy. His spying worked, and by springtime King Alfred was able to rally his troops together and force Guthrum and the Danes back into submission.

As sweet as this victory was for King Alfred, he feared it wasn't lasting. So, in 878, Alfred devised a more sacred plan for peace between the English and the Danes. King Alfred proposed that Guthrum and 30 of his most honorable men embrace the Christian faith. And you know what? They did! Guthrum, the once-savage Danish chieftain, was baptized as a Christian with King Alfred standing as his godfather. In honor of the occasion, Alfred hosted a 12-day feast for all the men involved!

If that wasn't unusual enough, King Alfred invited the converted Danes to stay in England under a peace treaty—a treaty that bound them together under the Lordship of Jesus Christ. For a time this arrangement worked well. Guthrum and Alfred fought side by side against other Viking raiders to protect their Christian land.

Unfortunately though, more aggressive Danish warriors invaded a few years later. They broke the peace and ravaged the English countryside just as they had done in the past. This pushed Alfred to drastic measures. More determined than ever to end the strife, Alfred took the city of **London** in 886. In doing so, he subdued the Danes at last! They were pushed to an eastern region of England named the *Danelaw.* For at least a hundred years, the Danish Vikings stayed put in Danelaw and left the Anglo-Saxons in peace.

With that great victory, most of the English people, not just the people of Wessex, acknowledged Alfred as their king. Freedom from the Danes was that significant. It's no wonder Alfred was considered "great." To keep England safe, Alfred reorganized the army and built a navy to protect the coast. He worked hard at rebuilding the towns and villages that the Vikings had ransacked and fortified them against further attacks.

Alfred's Great Contributions

To help keep peace between the seven different kingdoms in England, King Alfred created **common laws** for them to follow. That means he took all the laws of differing tribes and codified them. These common laws were a big deal because Alfred funneled each and every one of them through the grid of the **Ten Commandments** from the Bible. In great wisdom, he acknowledged God's laws as the best ones for mankind and placed them in the front of the English law code. Furthermore, Alfred gave legal protection to the poor and promised one-eighth of the revenue of his kingdom to help the needy. I'm sure *those* people thought Alfred was great!

But Alfred did even more to earn his "great" reputation. He worked to restore the educational system of England that was lost to the Danes. The following is a quote by Alfred painfully remembering this from his boyhood:

In great wisdom, King Alfred based English common law on the Ten Commandments of the Old Testament.

> "the churches stood filled with treasures and books . . . before they had all been ravaged and burned (by the Danes). . . so clean was learning decayed among English folk that very few there . . . could understand their rituals in English, or translate . . . Latin."[1]

---

1. Will Durant, *The Age of Faith.* Volume IV of *The Story of Civilization.* New York: Simon and Schuster, 1950; p. 484.

Alfred the Great—a man of strong faith in God— was considered one of the finest kings of England for restoring education, strengthening the laws of England, and subduing the Danes.

It bothered King Alfred a great deal that so few English were well taught after the Danes destroyed their centers of learning. Do you remember how fond he was of reading as a child? He was so hungry for knowledge that he was known to hire men to read to him to keep him satisfied. Alfred set up a palace school and brought in teachers from Europe and northern England. He gave one-eighth of the money of his kingdom to education.

But even beyond that, Alfred worked personally on translating important literary works from Latin into the Anglo-Saxon language. This included the four Gospels of the New Testament. The language of the Anglo-Saxons is sometimes called **Old English.** Nearly half of modern English is derived from it!

To help the English keep track of their complex history, King Alfred began what was called the ***Anglo-Saxon Chronicle.*** It was a running account of current events that was published for centuries. Alfred also gathered songs that captured the customs and history of England and taught those to children—he felt it was important for the English to develop some kind of identity after so many years of changing leadership.

I think Alfred the Great was wise to bring Englishmen together this way. But others thought he was wise, too. **Voltaire**, a famous French philosopher, said this of Alfred the Great, "I do not think that there ever was in the world a man more worthy of the regard of posterity than Alfred the Great."[2] (Posterity refers to all future generations.) Through laws, education, literature, and songs, King Alfred *greatly* helped shape the nation of England.

However, what Alfred didn't know was that what he accomplished was not altogether permanent. He didn't know that England was to be conquered by yet another outside group—the **Normans.** The Normans would also greatly shape the heritage of the English. But we'll learn about them in a few weeks.

ACTIVITIES FOR LESSON 42

ALL STUDENTS

Make your Memory Cards for Lessons 40–42.

42A—Younger and Middle Students

1. Have a reading contest. Set appropriate goals for each student or family member. Whoever reaches his or her goal first receives a prize! Since Alfred received a book of poems for his prize, you may want to receive something similar to that, such as a favorite book or a book from a series.

2. Alfred taught songs to children that told of English customs and history. Review the words of familiar patriotic songs for your country. Do they help tell the story of your nation?

3. Make an Anglo-Saxon helmet. The British Museum Press (1993) created a colorful instruction book on how to make your own beautiful Anglo-Saxon helmet. It is recommended for students age 7–11. The title is *Anglo-Saxon Helmet*, and the ISBN number is 0714116734.

42B—Middle Students

1. If students in the United States are not aware of the history surrounding the writing of "The Star-Spangled Banner" by Francis Scott Key, this would be a good time to research it.

---

2. Ibid., p. 485.

2. A good amount of modern English is derived from the Anglo-Saxons. Here are a few examples[3] to copy and place in your Student Notebook under "Europe: England." Title it "Language of the Anglo-Saxons."

Anglo-Saxon (Old English)	Modern English
Baec	back
Cynd	kind
Disig	dizzy
Flod	flood
Foda	food
Fyllan	fill
Geolu	yellow
Ham (e.g., Nottingham)	home
Lang	long
Lond	land
Reef	king's agent
Shire (e.g., Wiltshire)	county
Shire + reef	sheriff
Standan	stand
Ton (e.g., Edington)	town
Under	under (no change)
Wascan	wash
Windige	windy
Wyrd (meaning fate)	weird

42C—Older Students

1. I mentioned in the lesson that Alfred helped to translate several important literary works into English. The titles follow. Familiarize yourself with any one of these works.

   • *Consolation of Philosophy* by Boethius
   • *Pastoral Care* by Gregory
   • *Universal History* by Orosius
   • *Ecclesiastical History of England* by Bede

---

3. These examples are taken from *Webster's Seventh New Collegiate Dictionary*. Springfield, MA: G&C Merriam Company, 1971; various pages.

2. Examine more closely the history, or *etymology*, of the English language through a detailed dictionary. Look at the example below.[4]

Yearn \'yern\ *vi* [ME *yernen*, fr. OE *giernan*, L *hortari* to urge, encourage, Gk *chairein* to rejoice]
1: To feel a longing or craving 2: to feel tenderness or compassion

In this example, the initials ME stand for Middle English; OE stands for Old English; L for Latin; and Gk for Greek. Each is followed by the original word in that language.

For our purposes of understanding the evolution of modern English from Old English and Middle English, look at the example above again at the letters *fr.* These two letters simply stand for *from* and mean that the Middle English version of the word came *from* the Old English version of the word. Old English is technically the language of the Anglo-Saxons. Middle English came later after the Norman Conquest. A good dictionary is full of notes like these that you might not have ever understood before!

Comb through the dictionary to find five good examples of modern English words that have Old English as their root. Write these down with their complete etymology. File them in your Student Notebook under "Europe: England." Title the page "Old English—One Contribution of the Anglo-Saxons."

---

4. Ibid., p. 1036.

TAKE ANOTHER LOOK!
REVIEW 14: LESSONS 40-42

Wall of Fame

1. *The Vikings: Their Families, Their Homes, and Their Faith (c. 800–1100)*—Sketch a rectangular house. Tape some dry grass on the roof. Write "Vikings" on the side. [There is no corresponding illustration in *History Through the Ages*.]

2. *Methodius and Cyril (863)*—On a tiny book, write "Slavonic Bible." Add the names of Methodius and Cyril on the bottom. [*Use Methodius and Cyril.*]

3. *Alfred the Great (871)*—Depict a man holding a book in one hand (to represent English law) and a Bible in the other. [*Use Alfred the Great.*]

SomeWHERE in Time

1. Make a map highlighting Slavic nations and the Byzantine Empire, c. 888.

   Materials: Outline Map 21, "Slavic Nations and the Byzantine Empire, c. 888"; pencil; yellow, pink, green, and blue highlighters

   On Outline Map 21, label Moravia (using a pencil) and highlight the region in yellow. Label the Bulgar state and highlight it in green. Label the Byzantine Empire and highlight it in pink. Label the Mediterranean Sea and the Black Sea and highlight these in blue. File your map in your Student Notebook under "Europe: Slovakia."

2. Go on a Latin hunt!

   a. As evidence of the Roman Empire's influence over England and the United States, the names of several cities in these countries today have a Latin base. (Latin was the language of the Romans.) On a map of England and of the United States, search for cities ending in the suffix of -ester or -aster. For example, Manchester, Lancaster. These are great examples of Latin because "castra" is Latin for "camp." (In time, *castra* evolved to the abbreviated suffix of -ester or -aster.) The early Romans set up these "camps" that grew into towns. The English brought the names of these towns to the United States although the Romans were the ones responsible for these names.

   b. Older Students: Make two lists of these cities. One list, containing cities in the United States, can be filed in your Student Notebook under "North America: United States." A second list—of English cities—can be filed under "Europe: England."

PUT IT ALL TOGETHER
WORKSHEET 2: LESSONS 22-42

We have covered 21 lessons in the second quarter of this history course. It's time again to "Put It All Together." Using your textbook, Memory Cards, maps, and timeline, go through this worksheet and answer the questions from Quarter 2. This worksheet, along with Worksheet 1, will help prepare you for the upcoming Semester I Test. So take your time. Use this review to your advantage.

I—Dates to Memorize

Write out the names and dates that I have asked you to memorize four times each on the lines below for practice.

Birth of Islam   622

1. _____

2. _____

3. _____

4. _____

Battle of Tours   732

1. _____

2. _____

3. _____

4. _____

1. _____

2. _____

3. _____

4. _____

II—Fill in the Blanks. Using Lesson 22 in your textbook as a guide, fill in the blanks below about daily life in the Dark Ages.

1. In ordinary homes, "Furniture was made of hard _____, mattresses were of prickly _____, and blankets were made of scratchy _____."

2. "_____ was the main _____ served morning, noon, and night."

3. "For the poor, formal _____ in a classroom was _____."

4. "The serfs were the lowest of these peasants. . . . Just above the serfs were the _____."

5. "Doctors would use _____, a _____-sucking worm, to literally suck _____ from patients."

6. "The church was responsible for teaching _____, _____ children, performing _____, and _____ the dead."

III—Three-Way Tie. We have learned about several famous pairs in this quarter. First, connect the pairs by drawing a line from one to the other with colored pencils. Second, continue the line to the matching location. I have provided you with one example.

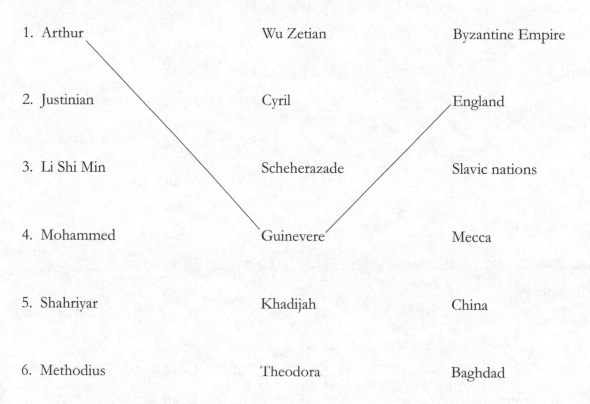

1. Arthur   Wu Zetian   Byzantine Empire

2. Justinian   Cyril   England

3. Li Shi Min   Scheherazade   Slavic nations

4. Mohammed   Guinevere   Mecca

5. Shahriyar   Khadijah   China

6. Methodius   Theodora   Baghdad

IV—Match the Messenger. Match the messenger of the Gospel to his location of influence by placing a letter to the left of the number. The lesson number is in parentheses.

_____1. Joseph of Arimathea (23)   a. Spain

_____2. Columba (25)   b. Scotland

_____3. Gregory the Great (27)   c. Germany

_____4. Eulogius (33)   d. England

_____5. Boniface (34)   e. Slavic nations

_____6. Methodius and Cyril (41)   f. Rome

V—China or Japan? From a Western perspective, some cultures from the Far East may appear similar when in fact they are quite distinct from one another. By circling the correct answer, identify the items below as being representative of China or Japan. There should be seven for each culture. As a reference, you may look at Lessons 26, 28, and 31 in your textbook.

1.	Mount Fuji	China	Japan
2.	Han dynasty	China	Japan
3.	Chang'an	China	Japan
4.	Grand Canal	China	Japan
5.	Nippon	China	Japan
6.	Confucianism	China	Japan
7.	Shinto	China	Japan
8.	Pagodas	China	Japan
9.	Ainu people	China	Japan
10.	Horiuji Temple	China	Japan
11.	Fireworks	China	Japan
12.	Daibutsu	China	Japan
13.	Taika	China	Japan
14.	Empress Wu Zetian	China	Japan

VI—Matching Square. This quarter tells many stories containing interesting objects. Using different-colored pencils, draw a line from the objects on one side of the square to their matching story on the opposite side of the square. I suggest you go clockwise from the top left. If you answer correctly, you should get an interesting pattern. One example has been done for you.

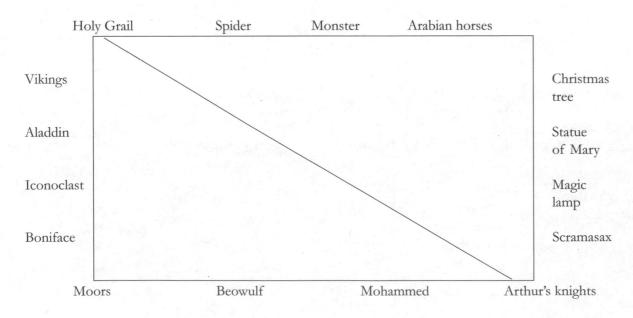

VII—The Koran vs. the Bible. It is an unavoidable fact that the doctrines and structure of the Koran and the Bible are different from one another. Sort through the facts below and place them in the appropriate boxes. You may abbreviate your answers using the words in bold. Answers can be found in Lessons 18 (Quarter 1) and 30. An example is provided.

▶▶ Contains 114 **suras**

▶▶ Contains 66 **Old & New Testament books**

▶▶ Written by **40 authors**

▶▶ Composed by **one author**

▶▶ Covers about a **1,000-yr. time span**

▶▶ Covers a **22-yr. time span**

▶▶ Contains **no prophecy**

▶▶ Contains **hundreds of prophecies**

▶▶ Uses **three** original **languages**

▶▶ Uses **one** original **language**

▶▶ Originates from **one place**

▶▶ Originates from **three continents**

▶▶ Speaks of **Jesus as God**

▶▶ Speaks of **Jesus as a prophet**

▶▶ Teaches **Allah is** the one true **god**

▶▶ **Allah not mentioned**

▶▶ Teaches **Mohammed is a prophet**

▶▶ **Mohammed not mentioned**

KORAN
1. suras
2.
3.
4.
5.
6.
7.
8.
9.

BIBLE
1. Old & New Testament books
2.
3.
4.
5.
6.
7.
8.
9.

VIII—Duties of Islam. Using Lesson 30 as a reference, fill in the blanks below to complete the duties of Islam.

DUTIES OF ISLAM

1. *Praying* _____ *times a day*

2. *Reciting the creed, "There is no* _____ *but Allah, and*

    _____ *is his prophet," at least 125,000 times in one's lifetime*

3. *Giving to the* _____

4. *Fasting from* _____ *to sundown in the holy month of*

    _____

5. *Making at least one trip to* _____ *(if able)*

IX—Bonus: Victorious Vikings. Using the words below, write a paragraph describing the invasion of the Vikings. Earn half a point for every word you can use.

| Norsemen | Scandinavia | Lindisfarne | farmland |
| raid | battle-axes | scramasax | Berserks |

_____

_____

_____

_____

_____

_____

_____

_____

_____

_____

_____

_____

_____

_____

_____

_____

SEMESTER I TEST

LESSONS 1–42

Much like the biweekly quizzes you have been taking throughout Quarters 1 and 2, this semester test will challenge your ability to recall information learned from the beginning of this book. I suggest you study beforehand using your textbook, Memory Cards, former quizzes, and worksheets. You can expect to find one question from every lesson in Semester I plus a bonus essay question worth 2 points. I will not test you on any dates other than those six that I specifically challenged you to memorize in this semester.

Note to Teacher: Younger students or those with special needs may require teacher assistance, may choose to do this as an open-book test, or may skip this test entirely to move on to more great stories of the Middle Ages!

I—Memory Lane. Match the event on the left with one of the dates on the right.

_____1. Birth of Islam   a. 732

_____2. Edict of Milan   b. c. A.D. 33

_____3. Battle of Tours   c. 622

_____4. Pentecost   d. 313

_____5. Invasion of the Vikings   e. 793

_____6. Fall of the Western Roman Empire   f. 476

Note to Teacher: From this point on, the number of each question corresponds to the number of the lesson in the textbook.

II—True or False? Circle your answer.

1. Before John the Baptist went to heaven, he said that he would send the Holy Spirit.   T   F

2. Saul was a devout Jew and the son of a Pharisee.   T   F

3. In the city of Bethlehem, Paul and Barnabas were commissioned as the first missionaries of Christ.   T   F

4. Nero, one of the least favorite of all Roman emperors, was killed by an angry mob of Christians.   T   F

5. It was Tertullian who wrote, "The blood of the martyrs is the seed of the church."   T   F

6. Josephus, the great Jewish historian, adopted the family name of Flavius from Titus, a Roman.   T   F

III—Multiple Choice. Choose one answer for each question or statement.

7. Masada is the name of

   a. a volcanic mountain.

   b. a fortress where Jews hid themselves from the Romans.

   c. an edict signed by Constantine.

   d. a Jewish midwife.

8. The Dead Sea Scrolls were written and stored near the Dead Sea by
    a. the Bedouins.
    b. the Romans.
    c. the Essenes.
    d. the Sadducees.

9. In A.D. 79, the city of _____ was buried by the volcanic blast of Mt. Vesuvius.
    a. Atlantis
    b. Constantinople
    c. Nazareth
    d. Pompeii

10. To many, Bar-Kokhba was a hero of the
    a. Battle of Milvian Bridge.
    b. First Jewish Revolt.
    c. Battle of Tours.
    d. Second Jewish Revolt.

11. The Latin word *credo* (from which we get the Apostles' *Creed*) means
    a. "I believe."
    b. "I repent."
    c. "I love."
    d. "I saw."

12. Pope Gelasius hoped that Saint Valentine's Day would replace the Roman festival of
    a. Lights.
    b. Love.
    c. Lupercalia.
    d. Leprechauns.

IV—Fill in the Blank. Fill in the blank using the most appropriate word from the word bank below.

13. Diocletian called himself "Dominus Noster" meaning _____.

14. At the Battle of Milvian Bridge, Constantine believed he saw the symbol of a _____ in the sky.

15. During the Golden Age in India, _____ was one of the most beloved rulers for supporting art, science, literature, and religion.

16. From the forests of Mexico and Guatemala, the _____ built tall step pyramids, created a unique form of writing, and developed the concept of zero.

17. St. Augustine, born in _____, was converted to Christianity through the influence of Ambrose, the intelligent bishop of Milan.

18. The Greek Septuagint was the only translation of the Old Testament that existed until Jerome translated it into the _____.

V—Who Am I? Using different-colored pencils for easier grading, connect the names on the left with clues about them on the right.

19. St. Patrick	a. Sacked the city of Rome
20. Attila the Hun	b. Missionary to Ireland
21. Vandals	c. King and queen of the Byzantine Empire
22. An "apprentice"	d. Celtic war chief and his wife
23. King Arthur and Guinevere	e. An unpaid guild worker
24. Justinian and Theodora	f. Nicknamed the "scourge of God"

VI—Circle Sense. In the sentences below, *circle* the word that makes the most *sense*.

25. Columba, an Irishman, set up many (monasteries, mosques) in Scotland to fulfill his pledge to spread the Gospel.

26. Prince Shotoku was considered the "founder of Japanese civilization" for writing a (religion, constitution).

27. In great humility, Pope (Pelagius, Gregory) called himself "the servant of the servants of God."

28. Li Shi Min, one of the more interesting emperors of the Tang dynasty, reinstated the teachings of (Confucius, Wu Zetian).

29. The birth of Islam is dated from Mohammed's famous flight from Mecca to Medina called the (Jihad, Hegira).

30. The (Koran, Kaaba) in Mecca is considered the most sacred of temples by the Muslims.

VII—People and Places. Match each place listed below with the person or event most likely to be associated with it.

_____31. China	a. St. Boniface
_____32. Denmark	b. Iconoclast Controversy
_____33. Al-Andalus	c. Charles Martel
_____34. Hesse, Germany	d. Wu Zetian
_____35. Byzantine Empire	e. Abd al-Rahman
_____36. City of Tours	f. Beowulf

VIII—Who Did It? From the word bank on the next page, choose the correct answer for each question and write it in the blank provided.

37. I promoted education in the Holy Roman Empire. _____

38. I told suspenseful tales to save my life. _____

39. We raided monasteries and villages on the coasts of Europe. _____

40. Mythology says that I owned a heavenly place called Valhalla. _____

41. We created a written language for Slavic nations. _____

42. I incorporated the Ten Commandments into English common law. _____

WORD BANK

Alfred the Great	Charlemagne	Odin
Methodius and Cyril	Vikings	Scheherazade

IX—Bonus Essay. Earn two extra points for using complete sentences to answer the following question: Why have the early Middle Ages been called the "Dark Ages"?

X—Older Students (Or those who dare!): If you completed Volume I of *The Mystery of History*, then give yourself the ultimate bonus by taking the "Semester I Test" from Volume I. I suggest that it be done as an open-book test for extra credit. Consider it a trip back in time to see what you remember of Stonehenge, the Trojan War, King David, and more!

Semester II

The Middle Ages

CONTENTS

QUARTER 3   The Fire Grows: 874 to 1192

Pages

Around the World   249–251
Weeks 15–21   253–361
Put It All Together (Worksheet 3)   362–368

QUARTER 4   The Fire Shines: 1210 to 1456

Around the World   369–371
Weeks 22–28   373–490
Put It All Together (Worksheet 4)   491–496

SEMESTER II TEST   497–501

THE FIRE GROWS:
874 TO 1192

Let's think about "fire" for a minute. Fire can be good when used properly—say, for cooking and staying warm. But fire can also be deadly. When out of control, it can destroy and consume. For this reason I think that "fire" is a good word picture for the practice of Christianity during this time period. Let me explain.

On the good side, genuine Christianity grew during the Middle Ages. We will see this in our lessons about *Good King Wenceslas*, who had compassion for the needy; about *St. Simon*, who had enough faith to "move a mountain"; and about *Leif Ericsson*, who took the Gospel to Greenland. We will also see true faith when we learn of the *Petrobrusians* and the *Waldensians*—men and women devoted to teaching the Word of God.

But on the negative side, some misused the name of Christ in the Middle Ages and distorted Christianity. For example, we will learn about *Otto I*, who actually *forced* people to convert to Christianity to unite his kingdom. We will also learn about the *Crusades*. Through the tragic Crusades, thousands of people went on a killing spree in the name of Christ to capture the Holy Land. Though some were devout believers concerned with persecution in Jerusalem, many crusaders were misled by selfish ambition or the promise of reward. Like a fire out of control, crusaders used the name of Christ to destroy and consume. It's a tough topic to study.

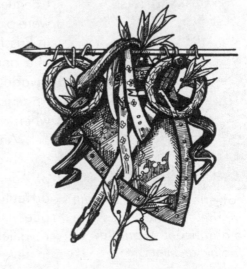

Under poor leadership and out of control, thousands of zealous crusaders marched on the Holy Land during the Middle Ages.

On the lighter side, in this quarter we will travel to some remote corners of the world that were unaware of the troubles in the Holy Land. We will visit *Iceland*, *Greenland*, *New Zealand*, and *Zimbabwe*. We will also visit the distant lands of *China* and *Japan*. Each country is fascinating in its own way and teaches us something about culture. Culture can be defined as the unique characteristics of a group or class of people. Culture can be found in little things, like *kiwi birds* and *lily feet*, or found in spectacular things, like the dress of the *samurai warrior* and the dance of the *Maori*. All these things help to give people a sense of identity. We all reflect some sort of culture. It just looks different around the world!

And did you know that "piggy banks" originated in the Middle Ages? Since metal was hard to come by, people used a dense orange clay called *pygg* to make everyday household items. Naturally, money was stored in containers made of pygg. They became known as "pygg jars." It was later, in the eighteenth century, that craftsmen literally shaped the jars into the image of a pig as we commonly see them now.

The making of money jars from pygg clay in the Middle Ages led to the creation of "piggy banks."

In this quarter will also meet men of legendary status—that is, men who left such a mark in history that they have become the main characters of poems, plays, and operas. These men would be *Macbeth*, *El Cid,* and *Robin Hood*. I imagine you have heard of Robin Hood and his "merry men," but the other guys may be new to you. We will sift through the facts and fiction surrounding all these characters.

Towering cathedrals built in the Middle Ages are magnificent examples of Gothic architecture.

As for kings and queens of the Middle Ages, our study wouldn't be complete without addressing a few of them. This quarter we will learn of *Vladimir of Russia* and *William the Conqueror*. Strangely, both kings were of Viking blood. But one lived in Russia and the other in France. The one in France proceeded to invade England at the *Battle of Hastings*! We will get it all straight when we get to him.

Another interesting life to sort through will be that of *Eleanor of Aquitaine*—one of the most adventurous, colorful, and daring

Flying buttresses add strength and beauty to this Gothic structure.

queens of the Middle Ages. Personally, she is one of my favorite royalties, as is her son *Richard the Lionhearted*. His name appears in several lessons in this quarter where the adventure of one story overlaps into the next. I love it when that happens!

As I've mentioned in previous lessons, Gothic architecture was transforming the look of Europe. As builders sought to create bigger churches with higher ceilings, they were forced to be more inventive. You see, for a structure to be built higher, it has to also be built stronger underneath (so it doesn't fall down!). Architects solved this problem with the invention of "flying buttresses." These are broad, arching beams that are added to the outside of a building to strengthen it. In adding these, architects were able to go higher and higher with walls, spires, and towers. The buttresses themselves became works of art with sharp points, gargoyles, and crosses topping them off. (A gargoyle is a scary-looking little statue. Though just a myth, it was believed that they would keep evil spirits away!)

The high, vaulted ceilings of a Gothic cathedral naturally draw a worshiper's attention upward to heaven.

And on the inside, these great Gothic structures were reinforced with equally great "vaulted ceilings." The enormous vaulted beams in these ceilings were like ribs designed to add even more strength to the buildings. With their added height, cathedral walls became even more perfect for large works of stained glass. It is no wonder that it took decades and generations of builders to complete these Gothic masterpieces.

On a more somber note, we will learn in this quarter of some serious struggles in the Middle Ages. There was a huge power struggle between *Pope Gregory VII* and *Henry IV* that was never really solved. It was called the *Investiture Controversy*. And there were ongoing struggles for the *Jews of the Middle Ages*, who faced persecution from Christians *and* Muslims. That lesson was a tough one for me.

Now that you're halfway through this volume, I hope you are absorbing the importance of history. It is a rich subject. From it we learn more than just the names of people who lived long, long ago; we learn of a God who still lives and seeks to reveal Himself to mankind. Remember that as we proceed. I believe God *is* the mystery that holds all the pieces of history together.

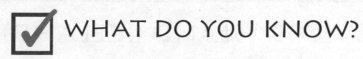

☑ WHAT DO YOU KNOW?

PRETEST 15

Who/What Am I? Choose the best answer from the list below.

1. I am an imaginary line around the globe marking things far north. What am I?

2. I am nicknamed the "Land of Fire and Ice." What am I?

3. Frustrated over the cold weather, I am the Viking who named the island of Iceland. Who am I?

4. We left Polynesia to settle the beautiful islands of New Zealand. Who are we?

5. I am the name of a brown, furry bird and a brown, fuzzy fruit from New Zealand. What am I?

6. I am a constellation seen only in the Southern Hemisphere. What am I?

7. My name means "houses of stone." What am I?

8. I helped to make Great Zimbabwe one of the greatest trade centers in Africa. What am I?

WORD BANK

Maori	Iceland	Zimbabwe	Floki Vilgerdarson
Southern Cross	Arctic Circle	gold	kiwi

LYDVELDID ISLAND (ICELAND)

LESSON 43

If you just learned that you inherited an island, would you want to go there? A Swedish man named **Gardar** did. Around 860, Gardar went to claim **Hebrides** (HEHB ruh deez)—a small island about 500 miles west of **Sweden**—because it belonged to his new Norwegian wife. Hebrides was willed to her by her father. A funny thing happened, though, on Gardar's way to inspect the tiny island. He got lost in a storm and happened upon *another* island—one much bigger than Hebrides. Gardar discovered what many would now call **Iceland**! Icelanders call it **Lydveldid Island** (or *Republic of Iceland*).

What Gardar found was a land of great beauty. The mysterious new island was full of icy mountains, frozen waterfalls, rocky cliffs, and a long, flat coastline. Gardar spent the winter in a location just about 40 miles south of the **Arctic Circle.** When spring came, he set sail to circle the entire island. (It is about the size of Kentucky.) Gardar was very pleased with what he found and so named the land after himself. He called it **Gardarsholm.** This new land remained nothing more than an adventure story though, for after the exciting discovery Gardar headed back to Sweden to live.

With its rugged, rocky coastline, Iceland is about the size of the state of Kentucky.

A few years later, however, a similar thing happened to another Viking. His name was **Naddod.** He was fleeing to the **Faeroe Islands** to avoid his many enemies. As Naddod put it, he was leaving "for the good reason that he had nowhere else he would be safe."[1] But on his way, he was also blown off course in a bad storm! Like Gardar, Naddod stumbled upon Iceland. He found it full of snow, so he named it **Snaeland,** or "**Snowland.**"

Naddod went back to Scandinavia full of his own adventure stories. He made Snowland sound so amazing that it inspired yet another Norseman to set sail. But this Viking, **Floki Vilgerdarson,** set out to intentionally explore Iceland. And that he did.

Floki Vilgerdarson Names Iceland

Floki Vilgerdarson loaded his ships with far more than tools for exploring. He took with him livestock and homesteading supplies—fully hoping to settle the new island. Legend says that Floki also took three ravens with him aboard his ship. Much like Noah on the ark testing for dry land, Floki set his birds free one at a time. The first and second birds came back to the ship. But the third raven flew on to land. Floki followed and the curious island was found again!

Because Floki and his men first arrived in Snowland in the summer, things were great in the beginning. There was beautiful green pastureland for the livestock and plenty of fish and seals to keep Floki and his men well fed. However, winter hit them much harder than they expected. Ice and snow covered the interior of the island—the cattle starved to death. Because of such bad weather, Floki and his men were

---

1. Charman Simon, *The World's Great Explorers: Leif Eriksson and the Vikings.* Chicago: Children's Press, 1991; p. 31.

prevented from sailing back to Norway! They were forced to spend two difficult winters there. With great discouragement Floki came up with another name for Snowland while staring at the frozen ice lining the miles of fjords surrounding him. He called it "Iceland."

Viking Cousins Settle Iceland Permanently

Despite the bad stories about Iceland that Floki had to share back home, there were still more Vikings who seemed lured to it. Two adventurous Viking cousins from Norway, named **Ingolf Arnarson** and **Hjorleif,** wanted to settle Iceland permanently. They weren't the simple farming kind of Vikings. These were the tough raiding kind of Vikings! To help them afford the trip to Iceland, Hjorleif plundered villages in Ireland and took 10 Irish slaves into captivity! With family problems to drive them away from home and with a warrior mind-set, the cousins were unstoppable. By **874,** they achieved their goal of making Iceland a home for themselves, their families, and their slaves.

According to Icelandic folklore, Ingolf founded the present capital of Iceland, **Reykjavik.** But his method was a bit odd. He vowed to the Norse god **Thor** that wherever the pillars to his special high seat washed ashore, there he would settle. The pillars were not found at first. And so Ingolf spent his first winter on the southern coast. The next spring, however, Ingolf's slaves found the pillars washed ashore at the place where the capital now sits. Ingolf named the site Reykjavik, which means **"smoky bay."** He gave it this name because of the steam that rose from hot springs in the area. (This smoky bay has since been harnessed as a great source of heat for Iceland, greatly reducing the need for pollution-causing fossil fuels on the island.)

When hot water rises from deep within the earth and hits cold air, spooky steam forms and hovers above the ground.

Within 60 years of Ingolf and Hjorleif's first settlement, hundreds more Norwegians followed. In that short time, almost all the good farmland was inhabited. Why did they come? Some Norwegian Vikings were simply looking for adventure. Others needed pastureland for their cattle. Many were fleeing the tyranny of an unpopular king back in Norway. Regardless, once the Norwegians came, they stayed. Iceland became a true settlement. By 930 there were over 20,000 people living in Iceland.

Unlike neighboring countries, Iceland never had a king. As the population grew, the people voted instead to set up regions called ***things.*** Each *thing* had a chief who helped to settle disputes. In time, the regions came together to form one of the world's first **parliaments.** A parliament is a lawmaking body. They called it ***Althing*** because it included *all the things!* It is still in existence today!

Interestingly, there were a few people who lived in Iceland before the Vikings ever set foot on it. Apparently there were some gentle monks in Ireland who traveled to Iceland to get away from corruption in their homeland. They lived in tiny caves nestled in the high cliffs of the coast of Iceland. When the heathen Vikings began to move in, the peaceful monks moved out! According to the *Book of the Islanders:*

"There were Christian men here then whom the Norsemen call 'papar.' But they went away because they were not prepared to live in the company of heathen men. They left behind Irish books, bells, and crosiers [staffs], from which it could be seen that they were Irishmen." [2]

2. Ibid., pp. 42–43.

The Land of Fire and Ice

Though Lydveldid Island (or Iceland) is home to many even today, it's not without its challenges. On the one hand, a third of the island is actually ice! On the other hand, this island has more volcanic activity than any other island in the world. At least one volcano erupts every five years! These eruptions give way to multitudes of hot springs and **geysers.** A geyser is a spring that erupts hot, steamy water from time to time. For this contrast of hot and cold, Iceland has been nicknamed the **"Land of Fire and Ice."**

And because of its far northern location on the earth, Lydveldid Island has days in the summer when the sun shines all but a few hours, as well as days in the winter when the sun hardly shines at all. This makes for some difficult patterns of work and sleep! It is also challenging for the people of Iceland to be completely independent. As a small island, Iceland depends on its neighbors for grain and many other products.

Despite these less desirable features, Lydveldid Island remains a prosperous, beautiful, and comfortable place to live. Though you would expect "Iceland" to be extremely cold, it really isn't—at least not around the perimeter where most people live. In January, the average temperature in the capital city is 31 degrees Fahrenheit. In July, it reaches 52. How little did Gardar realize what an interesting and magnificent land he stumbled across so very long ago.

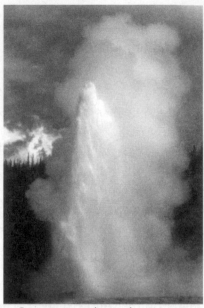

Geysers, such as this one in Yellowstone Park, are named after Great Geysir, which is near Reykjavik, Iceland. A large geyser can shoot hot water and mist up to 200 feet in the air!

ACTIVITIES FOR LESSON 43

ALL STUDENTS

Choose any of these popular Icelandic meats for creating a family meal: mutton, lamb, cod, salmon, trout, halibut, or raw pickled salmon. For what obvious reasons might fish and sheep be plentiful in Iceland?

43A—Younger Students

The people of Iceland have an unusual custom in making names. They place a greater emphasis on first names than on last names. (In a phone book, names are listed alphabetically by first name, not by last.) For a last name, a child takes the first name of one of his parents and adds either "sson" to it if the child is a male or "dottir" if the child is a female. For example, my name is Linda Hobar. My son could go by Kyle Lindasson. My daughter could go by Ashley Lindadottir. Or if they chose their father's name (Ron), they could go by Kyle Ronsson and Ashley Rondottir. Just for fun, what might your last name be if you were a resident of Iceland? Write it down and file it under "Europe: Iceland" in your Student Notebook.

43B—Middle Students

The Icelandic people speak a Germanic language and always shake hands when greeting one another. Practice the following sayings while shaking hands:

Goden daginn (Good day)

Gott kvold (Good evening)

Bless (Goodbye)

Research the formation of geysers. What causes them? Where are they located? Are they dangerous? Write a few paragraphs on geysers, then file this research in your Student Notebook under "Europe: Iceland."

C. 900

THE MAORI OF NEW ZEALAND
LESSON 44

Have you ever seen birds that can't fly, heard geysers hiss, or watched someone's face get tattooed? These may not be common where you live, but if you lived in **New Zealand** during the Middle Ages, you would know these things well. Today we'll look at life on the other side of the world from our last lesson. There we will meet the **Maori** (im OW ree) people, which means "native" in their language. They're the first people known to have inhabited the beautiful islands of New Zealand.

Do you know where New Zealand is? Using a globe, if you were to place your finger on Iceland, then New Zealand would be on the exact opposite side of the earth and almost as far south as one can travel before hitting Antarctica. Much like Iceland, New Zealand's extreme location is important in understanding its history and uniqueness. New Zealand is actually a cluster of islands located in the **South Pacific Ocean.** These islands are roughly 1,200 miles southeast of **Australia.** (Though they are neighbors, New Zealand is not considered part of the continent of Australia.)

The Pacific Ocean, which completely surrounds New Zealand, is the largest and deepest ocean on earth. Pacific means "peaceful."

The Maori first arrived in New Zealand sometime between **900** and 1300. I find it quite interesting that both Iceland and New Zealand were being founded about the same time, though at two completely different ends of the earth. According to legend, an explorer by the name of **Kupe** was the first to arrive. He named the island **Ao-tea-roa** (ah-oh-tay-ah-RROH-ah), meaning "Land of the Long, White Cloud." Why? I don't know. Perhaps the long white clouds were a description of the many geysers in New Zealand. Regardless of the name, it seems that Kupe and many others traveled by canoe from other **Polynesian Islands.** They brought with them dogs, rats, and edible plants like the sweet potato. But where are the Polynesian Islands, you ask? Let me explain them to give you the big picture of the South Pacific.

Islands of the South Pacific (Oceania)

The South Pacific Ocean, the large body of water between North America and Asia, is home to more than 30,000 islands. As a whole, they are sometimes called **Oceania** (oh she AN ih uh). The islands of Oceania are generally divided into three groups. They are the **Melanesia** (mehl un NEE zhuh), the

Micronesia (my kroh NEE zhuh), and the **Polynesia** (pahl uh NEE zhuh). These names help to classify the islands by people groups *and* location. The Polynesians are the tallest of the Oceania population and have the lightest skin color. The Polynesian Islands are the largest of the three groups. They stretch as far north as to include Hawaii in the United States, as far east as to include islands off South America, and as far south as to include New Zealand itself. To the west of them is Australia. (New Zealand is considered one of the Polynesian Islands.)

Considering the small size of most of the Polynesian Islands, the early Maori who first discovered New Zealand must have thought they struck gold! It is by far the largest of all the Oceania islands and is particularly rich in resources. New Zealand is about the size of Italy and is composed of three main islands: the **North Island,** the **South Island,** and **Stewart Island.** Each of the islands is warm and lush at sea level, and mountainous through the middle. But the North Island definitely attracts more residents because of its special beauty and climate:

One of the many things the Maori discovered in coming to New Zealand was a rather large bird that had no wings. It was called a ***moa.*** A moa could grow up to 13 feet tall! It might have been the largest bird on earth at that time, and it had a powerful kick. But, without wings, it was easy to hunt. Maybe it was too easy because by the 1800s, the moa was extinct. For centuries before that, the bird was the main source of meat for the Maori.

The green rolling hills of New Zealand are ideal for farming and raising sheep.

Another flightless bird unique to New Zealand is the ***kiwi.*** He was named by the Maori for the sound he makes, which is like "kee wee." He's a cute little bird that looks like a brown fur ball with a beak. The kiwi is the national symbol of New Zealand.

As a side note here, the name "kiwi" has further been used to describe a little round, brown, fuzzy fruit—probably because it looks like the bird! Though kiwi fruit is not originally from New Zealand, it grows very well there and is exported to all parts of the world. (It's quite delicious and very high in Vitamin C.) As if using the name kiwi wasn't enough for birds and fruit, some New Zealanders today refer to *themselves* as "Kiwis." It's like a modern-day nickname for the nationals.

The Maori also found that, besides being home to birds that can't fly, New Zealand was a land full of hissing geysers and incredible scenery. Much like Iceland (Lesson 43), New Zealand has many of these spectacles of nature, which makes sense because most of the islands of Oceania were formed by volcanic activity. Violent forces under the earth's surface helped to form the majestic mountains, sharp waterfalls, and deep fjords that cut into the coastline of the islands. All of these help to make New Zealand one of the most beautiful places in the world!

Black and white sands blend together on the beaches of New Zealand, making them some of the most beautiful beaches in the world.

When the Maori migrated to New Zealand, they naturally brought with them their customs and traditions. One of those involved the art of tattooing elaborate patterns of spirals and curves on the face. This practice is called **moko** (MOH koh). Moko was used not only for beautification but also for quick and easy identification. For example, adult members of a family or people of the same trade might all have the same moko. A tribal chief would most certainly have the most elaborate moko in the community to distinguish his authority. On the other hand, a servant woman's moko was usually painted right on top of her nose.

A moko artist was considered to be far more than a craftsman. He was more like a priest. It was part of his job to chant and pray to the gods while he worked. (The Maori worshiped many gods of nature.) Because sharp bones were needed to pierce the skin, the ritual was painful to receive and could only be tolerated in short segments of time. Some moko were so elaborate they took years to complete. Though most Maori today no longer apply permanent tattoos on their faces, many paint temporary symbols on themselves for special festivals and dances.

I might add here that at a modern-day festival of Maori, it would be common to see men and women dressed in traditional skirts made from **hemp** and competing in dancing and singing. Women's and children's tops and headbands are woven into distinctive red, white, and black geometric patterns. Women's dances include the graceful twirling of the **poi,** a ball on a string. When the men perform war dances (called **Haka**), they stick their tongues out as far as they possibly can and bulge their eyes as wide as possible to intimidate their enemies! These scary faces are traditionally carved into wood and are still visible all over New Zealand. Woodworking is a favorite Maori pastime.

Moko, the art of facial tattooing, was used by the Maori for identification as well as for beautification.

Another unique tradition the Maori started was the carving of greenstone, or **pounamu** (poo-NAH-moo). Pounamu literally means "green-colored stone." It's the Maori name for jade. This stone is both useful and decorative. Jade is so hard in texture that it can be carved to make extremely sharp tools or weapons. Greenstone is so beautiful that it makes valuable jewelry. Gathering the greenstone required long and difficult expeditions on the South Island that sometimes lasted for months. In search of this treasure, the Maori of the past blazed numerous trails through mountain passes that still exist today. Hikers, or "trampers" as the New Zealanders call them, can presently spend weeks at a time exploring New Zealand on these old trails.

Maori of the past and of modern times are very close to their families and communities. That might explain their traditional greeting of touching foreheads and noses! Maori value taking care of one another and sharing what they own. A special meeting place for the Maori is called a **marae.** It is a piece of land that includes a meetinghouse. All important events, such as weddings and funerals, take place there. Maori children are expected to be on their best behavior while at the marae.

As for the uniqueness of New Zealand itself, it is a place of many rare species of plants that don't grow anywhere other than these islands. In fact, there are 1,500 species unique to New Zealand! For example there are bushes called the **mamku** and the **whekiponga.** There are trees called the **kauri rimu** and the **toatara.** Have you ever seen or heard of these? Unless you are from New Zealand, I doubt it.

You might want to know too that the seasons of countries south of the equator are the exact opposite of those in the Northern Hemisphere. So when the New Zealanders celebrate Christmas in December, it's usually a warm month for them. On the other hand, it would be common for them to snow ski in July. That's their winter season. I find it interesting how that works. Also, because of the tilt of the earth, water flowing down a drain swirls to the left if you live in the Southern Hemisphere. It swirls to the right if you live in the Northern Hemisphere. (Try it sometime!)

But back to the Maori . . . we might know more about them if they had kept written records of their history. But they didn't. Instead, the Maori told stories of their people that were passed down from one generation to the next. Had it not been for European explorers, we might still not know of the Maori. New Zealand was completely unknown to the Europeans until 1642. That's only about 400 years ago. It was then that a Dutch explorer named **Abel Tasman** came upon the island. He named it **Nieuw Zeeland** after the **Zeeland province** in the Netherlands. However, Tasman was terrified of the fierce look of the Maori and never actually landed on the island! (It might have been the warriors' bulging eyes and protruding tongues that scared him off!)

Over a hundred years later, though, **Captain James Cook** (a British navigator) made maps of the island from his explorations. A fun fact to know here is that Captain Cook brought something over with him from England that was completely unknown to the Maori. He brought pigs. To this day, pigs in New Zealand are referred to as **"Captain Cookers"**! They are hunted for sport and for food.

Captain Cook's explorations opened the door for curious pioneers to flood in. By the 1800s, thousands of Europeans moved to New Zealand to stay. The Maori call the Europeans *pakeha* (pah-KEH-hah). As in the history of the United States, the new European settlers quickly outnumbered the original inhabitants. Today only 6 to 10 of every 100 New Zealanders are of Maori descent. Seventy-five percent of the population is European, or pakeha.

New Zealand makes great strides today to try to protect the heritage of the Maori. Nonetheless, as a minority group, the Maori still experience some degree of prejudice against them. An important treaty was signed between the Europeans and the Maori in 1840. It was called the **Treaty of Waitangi**. It was supposed to keep the Maori safe from European invasion. But it failed to do so. Fighting went on for years between the Maori and the pakeha, both wanting to claim New Zealand as their home.

The good side of the story is that in God's sovereignty, the Europeans brought at least one special thing to the Maori and that was the Gospel. The Maori, who were once isolated from the rest of the world, were exposed to the teachings of Christ

These modern Maori demonstrate the ceremonial dance of their ancestors. Notice the wide-eyed look on one dancer's face.

through missionaries and believers who made New Zealand their new home.

Tradition tells an interesting story of the Maori as God prepared them to hear the Gospel of Christ. It is believed that long before missionaries came to tell of the Christ child, a Maori artist made a carving of a baby in the arms of its mother. But—and this is the amazing part—unlike other Maori babies, this baby carved in the wood was bulging its eyes as a warrior and was decorated with an elaborate moko on its face! It appeared to tell the story to the Maori that there would one day be born a child who would have victory over the enemy of death and that this child would have the authority of a king. I hope you recognize how much this baby describes the Lord Jesus.

Besides that, it may also be interesting to know that the Maori and Europeans alike in New Zealand have something in the sky to remind them of the Gospel. That would be the **Southern Cross.** It is a constellation of stars in the shape of a cross that can be seen clearly only from countries south of the equator. God has many ways to reveal Himself to mankind.

ACTIVITIES FOR LESSON 44

44A—Younger Students

1. Make a kiwi bird out of kiwi fruit. (Approximate time needed: 5–10 minutes)

   Photo 1

   Materials: Photograph of a kiwi bird, one piece of kiwi fruit, a permanent marker, toothpick, scissors, an emery board, glue

   a. Use your photograph of a kiwi bird as a model. Insert a toothpick into the end of your fruit at an angle slightly sloping down. It should resemble the beak in your photo. (See Photo 1.)

   b. With a marker, draw eyes on your fruit.

   Photo 2

   c. Cut two pieces of emery board to the length of 1¼ inches. Using scissors, cut two little triangles into the edge of the emery board to create little pointed feet. (See Photo 2.)

   d. Glue the feet onto the base of your fruit.

   e. Take a photo of your kiwi (see Photo 3) and file it under "Australia: New Zealand"³ in your Student Notebook.

2. Make scary war faces in the mirror like the Maori by bulging your eyes and sticking out your tongue as far as possible. Take your picture. File it under "Australia: New Zealand" in your Student Notebook.

   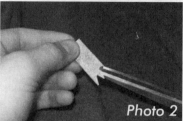
   Photo 3

3. Using a long tape measure, mark 13 feet on a high wall in your home or classroom. Imagine the height of the now extinct moa bird! Would you have been able to jump up to his head? Practice jumping to see how high you can reach.

44B—Middle Students

1. One of the longest words in the world is from the Maori language. The word is a name meaning "the hilltop where Tamatea Polai Whenua played his flute to his loved one." Practice trying to pronounce the following word. Copy it on paper and file it in your Student Notebook under "Australia: New Zealand."

   Taumatawhakatangihangakoautamateapokaiwhenuakitanatahu

   If you have a computer with a spell-checker feature, it might be fun to type this word, then "add" it to the spell-checker dictionary. Retype the word with a slight misspelling. Then allow your spell checker to correct it! Your computer will appear really smart (but actually you are!).

2. Search the Internet or an encyclopedia for a picture of the Southern Cross. Print or copy and file it under "Australia: New Zealand" in your Student Notebook. If you live in the Southern Hemisphere, enjoy stargazing with your own eyes on a clear night!

3. Modern-day New Zealanders enjoy hiking, or "tramping" as they call it. Create your own hike today to explore your local area. Observe wildlife and vegetation that is unique to your region.

---

3. New Zealand is not considered part of the continent of Australia. But for convenience, we will file our activities under Australia because it is the nearest continent to New Zealand.

1. New Zealand was one of the first countries to allow women the right to vote. Research the women behind the movement, when it occurred, and the significance of the issue.

2. What specific things are being done in New Zealand to help preserve the heritage of the Maori? Discuss with your teacher the complex issue of preserving the heritage of a culture (i.e., respecting language, dress, customs, etc.) without endorsing pagan practices (i.e., idol worship, sacrifices to the gods, etc.). Discuss the meaning of Romans 2:14–15 and how it applies to the Maori of long ago. How did they demonstrate that the Law was written in their hearts even though they knew not the Law?

3. During the land wars between the Europeans and the Maori, several Maori cults were started, mixing traditional beliefs of the Maori with Christianity and Judaism. Research any of the following and file your information in your Student Notebook under "Australia: New Zealand."

   a. The Pai Marire, or Hauhauism. (The word *hauhau* comes from the sound of a Maori battle cry.)

   b. The Ringatu Church, started by Te Kooti Riokirangi, a guerrilla leader.

   c. The Ratana Church, started by Tahupotiki Wiremu Ratana, a Maori farmer who placed great emphasis on visions, prayer, and healings.

C. 900

THE GREAT ZIMBABWE OF AFRICA
LESSON 45

The world is a big place. And we've studied a lot of it so far. But we've not yet looked at the greater parts of **Africa.** If you were to put Europe, China, and the United States all together, Africa would still be bigger! This enormous land of 53 nations falls into two **hemispheres.** (A hemisphere is a division of half the world by either North and South, or East and West.) Today we are going to look at the beginnings of just one country in Africa. It's **Zimbabwe.** But before we do, let's consider a little of the history of Africa.

The most famous land of ancient Africa would undoubtedly be **Egypt.** This land of mysterious pyramids, pharaohs, and mummies has quite a reputation. But Egypt takes up only one little corner of Africa. There's much more to Africa than that! It may interest you to know that the **Sahara,** which is the world's largest desert and is located in north central Africa, was not always a desert. About 2,500 years before Christ, this area was lush and green. Naturally, people lived there. But, as the area dried up, people moved.

The plains of Africa are home to many exotic animals such as the giraffe pictured here.

The Kingdom of Kush (Nubia) and the Nok

Besides settling in Egypt, the early people of Africa moved to a place just south of Egypt. It was called the **Kingdom of Kush.** (The Kushites are sometimes referred to as the **Nubians.**) This ancient kingdom was located along the **Nile River** where modern **Sudan** lies today. The main city was **Meroe.** It was actually called the "Island of Meroe," but it wasn't really an island at all. Meroe was a city situated right where the Nile River divides into smaller rivers. It was like an "island" because it was almost surrounded by water from nearby rivers.

The long and winding Nile provided plenty of water to the Kushites for crops and made trading with other countries easier. The Kushites could easily trade with anyone else who could reach the **Mediterranean Sea.** (That's because the Nile spills into the Mediterranean Sea.) It is evident from archaeological finds that the Kushites did trade with people as far away as **China**! They certainly traded gold and ivory with people in far West Africa although they were more than 2,000 miles away.

Much like the well-known Egyptians, the Kushites were rather amazing people. During their thousand-year history, these dark-skinned people built a few pyramids themselves and at one time even ruled over the wealthy Egyptians. One of their palaces revealed an ornate brick-lined swimming pool that was supplied by a complicated water system. It was decorated with carved waterspouts shaped like lion heads. How cool—a fancy swimming pool in the middle of ancient Africa! The Kush are also thought to have been the first to train elephants for use as weapons in war, and they were quite advanced in ironmaking. But, as many cultures have done in the past, the Kush died out for reasons no one really knows. By A.D. 250, they all but disappeared. More would be known about the Kushites if their writings could be deciphered. But no one has figured out their language yet!

Another ancient people group of Africa was the **Nok.** They emerged in history sometime between 1000 and 500 B.C. in the area now known as **Nigeria.** The Nok culture was located west of the Kush kingdom and south of the Sahara. Like the Kushites, they too were dark-skinned and good at ironmaking. But they were also artistic. They left behind distinct terra-cotta sculptures of faces of the Nok people. Since there were obviously no cameras back then, it's very special that we have a record of the looks of these people from so long ago. Not a whole lot of other information is known about the Nok culture. They too seemed to disappear around A.D. 250.

Like her ancestors, the Kushites and Nok, this young African girl is dark-skinned. Notice how skillfully she balances goods on her head to sell at the market.

Zimbabwe

Now, let's look at the country of Zimbabwe. Modern Zimbabwe is located in the southeast corner of Africa. On a map, it is kind of oval shaped. The country is 500 miles from top to bottom and about 400 miles from side to side. Three different rivers help to shape its borders.

But let's go back to the year **900.** That's about the time that a great civilization began to arise in Zimbabwe. We know a lot about the early residents because of what they left behind. Let me explain. Between the years 900 and 1100, the people of Zimbabwe began to build some rather amazing brick buildings. They're amazing because they still stand today without the help of any **mortar**! These buildings were so important to those who lived there that the name of the city and the country came from them. You see, the word **zimbabwe** means **"houses of stone."** The term ***Great Zimbabwe*** can be interpreted as **"great stone house."** Both names refer to the intricate brick buildings that set Zimbabwe apart from its neighbors.

There are three distinct sets of stone buildings that make up Great Zimbabwe. Together they cover a 99-acre area. The northernmost group of stones is called the **Hill Ruins.** They stand more than 300 feet above the rest. The Hill Ruins contain many small rooms and walls. There is also a natural cave there; if someone shouts in it, they can easily be heard in the valley below! Archaeologists think the complex was built around this marvelous cave as a religious shrine of some sort.

South of these ruins is the **Elliptical Building.** Shaped like an irregular oval more than 1,800 feet around, this structure was probably home to a king and other leaders. Its walls are nearly 32 feet high and 16 feet thick in some places. It was probably meant to keep someone important safe on the inside! The most unique structure of all the ruins is located in the Elliptical Building. It is a very tall, cone-shaped tower. Its curved and tapered shape makes it extraordinary and would have been difficult to construct out of cut stones.

Without mortar, the tall cone-shaped tower illustrated here would have been very difficult to build from cut granite stone.

In between the Hill Ruins and the Elliptical Building stands the **Valley of Ruins.** There are 10 distinct structures here that probably housed less important community leaders. ***Dagas***, or mud huts, would have covered the entire area in the Valley of Ruins where most of the population of Great Zimbabwe lived.

At each location, the stone ruins of Great Zimbabwe were made of granite and cut precisely enough to lie just right without the need for any mortar. All of the walls were slightly curved and some contained narrow doorways. Though very impressive, the structures were not perfect enough to allow for roof coverings! The walls were too far apart and irregular to have properly supported a roof.

On a decorative note, these early builders left behind eight uniquely carved birdlike statues. They were made of soft soapstone and were only about 15 inches high. It's thought that these birdlike figures might represent the spirits of past kings. They are now seen as symbols of Zimbabwe on the country's flag, coins, and national coat of arms.

Of course, a group of bricks like those of Great Zimbabwe wouldn't be special at all except for what they teach us about people from long ago. From the arrangement of these stones and the great work of archaeologists, we have some good ideas of what life was like in this part of Africa more than a thousand years ago. If nothing else, we know it was busy!

Most of the 10,000 residents appear to have been farmers who supported the local population. But there is much evidence of a strong trade route through Great Zimbabwe giving jobs to merchants, craftsmen, and traders. Gold was plentiful and highly prized as a trade item, as were iron and copper. As one historian put it:

"A unique hoard of the most diverse and bizarre goods was unearthed in 1902 . . . just outside the largest ruin . . . There was a great quantity of coiled wire of iron, copper, bronze and gold; sheets and bead of gold; ingot of copper; and copper jewelry. Three iron gongs . . . were found. These are characteristic of musical instruments of West Africa . . . There were also tens of thousands of glass trade beads..."[4]

Well, in our study of Volume II, we have now studied at least some of the history of three of the seven continents—Europe, Asia, and Africa. The world really is a big place! Little by little, we'll get to the rest of it.

---

4. Quote from *The Kingdoms of Africa* by Peter Garlake. In Louise Minks, *World History Series: Traditional Africa*. San Diego: Lucent Books, 1996; p. 32.

ACTIVITIES FOR LESSON 45

ALL STUDENTS

Make your Memory Cards for Lessons 43–45. Remember that with the start of this second semester, we are using gray markers on the front side of the cards to distinguish them from the first semester's cards.

45A—Younger Students

1. Go on a gold hunt.

   Materials: Several nuggets of "fool's gold" or similar material (gold foil-wrapped chocolate coins might add to the enthusiasm of the search!)

   Have you ever searched for gold? Gold was an important trade item for the people of Zimbabwe. Have your teacher hide gold nuggets around your yard or inside your home. See how much "gold" you can discover.

2. Play "gongs" like those discovered in 1902. Using the metal lids of pots from your kitchen, crash them together to make music. It may sound best alongside drumbeats!

45B—Middle Students

1. Visit a local craft shop and buy some beautiful glass beads. String them together in honor of this ancient African tradition.

2. In an encyclopedia or on the Internet, find a picture of **Victoria Falls** in present-day Zimbabwe. It is a beautiful example of God's creation. Photocopy or print the falls and file them in your Student Notebook under "Africa: Zimbabwe."

45C—Older Students

The nations of Africa are diverse and sometimes complicated. Research present-day Sudan, Nigeria, and Zimbabwe—the three countries represented in our lesson. Search for the following basic facts about each. (Place your answers on separate pieces of paper.)

1. Type of government
2. Capital city
3. Population
4. Official language
5. Primary religion
6. Chief products

Photocopy a map of each country to add to your report. File your answers in your Student Notebook under "Africa: Nigeria," "Africa: Sudan," and "Africa: Zimbabwe."

TAKE ANOTHER LOOK!

REVIEW 15: LESSONS 43–45

Wall of Fame

1. *Lydveldid Island (Iceland) (874)*—Create and label a small map of Iceland. Dot the island with glitter glue and **(with adult supervision!)** gently burn the edges to remember the "Land of Fire and Ice." [From *History Through the Ages*, use *Iceland*.]

2. *The Maori of New Zealand (c. 900)*—Create a smiley face. On it, draw symbolic moko. [Use *The Maori*.]

3. *The Great Zimbabwe of Africa (c. 900)*—Sketch a cone-shaped building. Write on it "Great Zimbabwe." Color over the structure with a gold crayon to remember the gold trade of Africa. [Use *Great Zimbabwe*.]

SomeWHERE in Time

Make a balloon globe.

Materials: A round balloon, a permanent marker, a globe or an atlas

Background Information: The word *hemisphere* comes from the Greek word *hemisphairion*, which means "half of a sphere." The earth is in the shape of a sphere. It has imaginary lines around it to divide it into four hemispheres. They are called the *Northern Hemisphere, the Southern Hemisphere, the Eastern Hemisphere*, and *the Western Hemisphere*. The *equator* divides the earth into the Northern and Southern hemispheres. A *meridian line* at approximately 20 degrees west longitude and 160 degrees east longitude divides the earth into the Eastern and Western hemispheres.

1. I have one simple activity today for young and old that is applicable to every lesson of the week. Blow up and tie off a round balloon (not too big or it will lose the shape of a sphere). I will refer to this as your "balloon globe" to distinguish it from a real globe that you will be handling as well.

2. Hold your balloon globe with the knot on the bottom. Using a permanent marker, draw a line all the way around your balloon globe to represent the equator. (Younger students will need help getting this line straight!) This line will divide your balloon globe into the Northern Hemisphere and the Southern Hemisphere. Can you see it clearly?

3. Now draw a line all the way around your balloon globe from top to bottom. This line will divide the earth into the Eastern Hemisphere and the Western Hemisphere. Can you see it?

4. Now I would like you to handle a real globe (or an atlas). Find the continents of *Europe, Asia, Africa,* and *Australia*. These four continents are found, for the most part, in the *Eastern Hemisphere*. These continents are sometimes called the *Old World*. You will see that Europe and Asia are in the Northern Hemisphere. Australia, sitting below the equator, is in the Southern Hemisphere. Africa falls in both the Northern and the Southern hemispheres.

5. Find now the continents of *North America* and *South America*. These two continents are found in the *Western Hemisphere*. They are sometimes called the *New World*. North America sits above the equator in the Northern Hemisphere. Like Africa, South America has some countries above the equator in the Northern Hemisphere—but most of the continent lies in the Southern Hemisphere.

6. There is still one continent unaccounted for. Do you know which one it is? It would be *Antarctica*. It is found at the very bottom of the *Southern Hemisphere*.

7. With the above information, I want you to try to draw each continent in its proper hemisphere. Don't worry if the shapes of your continents are not very accurate. It will be difficult to get them just right. The important thing is that they are in the proper quadrant of your balloon globe. Remember that Africa and South America will each fall into two hemispheres by sitting above *and* below the equator. Label each continent with your marker.

8. I would now like you to find *Iceland* on a globe or in an atlas. Notice that the meridian line that divides the Eastern Hemisphere from the Western Hemisphere (20 degrees longitude) runs practically right through Iceland! Use your marker to draw an island on this line. Of course, Iceland is well *above* the equator and found in the Northern Hemisphere.

9. Search now for *New Zealand* on a globe or in an atlas. You will find it on the complete *opposite* side of the world from Iceland. New Zealand is far *below* the equator and found in the Southern Hemisphere. It, too, lies very close to the continuous meridian line dividing the Eastern Hemisphere from the Western Hemisphere. (It is just east of the line by about 5 degrees.) Use a permanent marker to draw New Zealand on your balloon globe in its approximate location.

10. Take a photo of your balloon globe. File it in your Student Notebook under "Miscellaneous."

WHAT DID YOU MISS?

Each student should have a photocopy of this page. Using the Contents section in this textbook as a guide, fill in the missing events that were important in the history of the church. When finished, cut on the dotted lines (imagine the dotted lines extending to the far right side of the page). Carefully fold back *to the left* every other strip you have created to "hide" half the events in your list. (Fold the strips back to the solid line so they cover the dates as well.) Can you remember the "hidden" events? Unfold the strips to check your answers. Do this self-check several times to remember these important events of the Early Church.

   Middle and Older Students: Unfold the strips to their original positions. Repeat this self-check by folding the *alternate* strips back to the left. Test yourselves on these several times as well.

1.	c. A.D. 33	Pentecost
2.	c. A.D. 35	
3.	c. A.D. 46–66	Paul takes missionary journeys
4.	c. A.D. 64–257	
5.	A.D. 2nd–7th Centuries	The Apostles' Creed
6.	313	
7.	354–430	St. Augustine lives
8.	382–405	
9.	c. 389–461	St. Patrick goes to Ireland
10.	563	
11.	718	St. Boniface evangelizes Germany
12.	863	

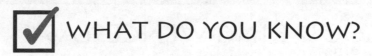

WHAT DO YOU KNOW?

PRETEST 16

Scramble! Unscramble the words to fill in the blanks. Only use the word bank below if you need to!

1. "Good King Wenceslas" is a popular (samtsriCh) _____ carol based on a true kind-hearted duke from the Middle Ages.

2. Wenceslas and his page trod through the (wons) _____ to deliver a meal to a poor man.

3. Wenceslas's own (rotbreh) _____, Boleslav, attempted to murder him on the steps of a church.

4. Otto I was crowned "Roman Emperor of the (seWt)" _____ in 962.

5. Otto's kingdom became known as the (yoHl) _____ Roman Empire even though it was mainly German.

6. The great trade cities of Russia were invaded by (singVik) _____ in the 800s.

7. Vladimir I, a descendant of the Vikings, did much to shape the religion of (saisuR) _____ for centuries to come.

8. Vladimir I, who learned about God through his grandmother, brought the highly decorated Eastern (dorthOxo) _____ Church to Russia.

WORD BANK

Holy	Orthodox	brother	snow
Vikings	Christmas	Russia	West

"GOOD KING WENCESLAS"
LESSON 46

"Good King Wenceslas looked out on the Feast of Stephen,
When the snow lay round about, deep and crisp and even.
Brightly shone the moon that night, though the frost was cruel,
When a poor man came in sight, gathering winter fuel." [1]

Have you ever sung this familiar Christmas tune? Though written in the 1800s, this traditional carol describes a tender scene straight out of the Middle Ages—at the exact place that we are in our chronological study of history. The carol is a beautiful tribute to a kindly *young* saint named **Wenceslas.** Let's look at his life and, more particularly, his unfortunate death.

We must first backtrack to our lesson on two missionary brothers—**Methodius** and **Cyril.** Do you remember them? They were responsible for creating a written language for the Slavic people. In the midst of their work, they visited **Czechoslovakia** (presently the Czech Republic). While there, the zealous missionaries were able to share the Gospel with the prince of Czechoslovakia and his wife, **Ludmilla.** They became strong believers as a result.

Now, you may be wondering what the prince of Czechoslovakia and his wife, Ludmilla, have to do with Wenceslas. Well, they were his grandparents. And, more than likely, it was *their* strong Christian faith that helped shape the good heart of Wenceslas while he was still in his youth. You see, when Wenceslas was just 13 years old, his father—the **Duke of Bohemia**—was killed in battle. (Bohemia was a province in former Czechoslovakia.) With his father gone, Wenceslas moved in with his grandparents. It was Grandmother Ludmilla's idea. She wanted her dear grandson to grow up under her influence in the knowledge of the Lord and to become a strong Christian ruler. And you know what? He did!

As one example of how dedicated Ludmilla was to her grandson, there is the story of a tree she planted in his name. Ludmilla planted the seedling when Wenceslas was just a baby. His caretakers watered the tree with his own bathwater! It supposedly made the tree grow unusually strong. It still stands today even though it's over 1,000 years old!

Methodius and Cyril influenced many with the Gospel in the Czech Republic. This beautiful church stands there today in the city of Prague.

Drahomira

Well, unfortunately, this tender arrangement between grandmother and grandson wasn't to last very long. You see, there is another character in this story that I have not yet introduced you to. That would be the *mother* of Wenceslas. Her name was **Drahomira.** It seems that Drahomira didn't like the special treatment *or* the Christian upbringing that Wenceslas was receiving from his grandparents. Drahomira

---

1. Lyrics from The Cyber Hymnal Web site, www.cyberhymnal.org.

was from a strong *pagan* background. Her difference of faith caused a lot of tension between the royal families.

To add to the tension, Drahomira was ruling Bohemia until Wenceslas was old enough to take his father's place as the duke. The nobles who surrounded her were pagan in their beliefs, too. It may be that they influenced Drahomira to do something that was dreadfully wicked. To get Wenceslas out from under his grandmother's influence, Drahomira arranged for Ludmilla to be strangled to death! It was murder!

After Ludmilla's death, Wenceslas was brought back under his mother's care where she involved him in her pagan traditions. But Wenceslas could not be swayed in his beliefs. As a young man under his grandparents' guidance, he had grown to have a strong, genuine faith in Jesus Christ. He continued to worship the Lord in secret! It must have been a difficult thing to do.

Wenceslas Becomes Duke of Bohemia

But Wenceslas was soon spared from this trying situation and justice was done. In 922 Drahomira was banished by the authorities for Ludmilla's murder! With Drahomira gone, Wenceslas became the rightful duke of Bohemia when he was just age 18. And as his grandmother had prayed, he became a strong Christian ruler!

As a demonstration of his Christ-like character, do you know what one of Wenceslas's first acts of kindness was as the new duke? In response to the scripture to "honor your father and your mother" (Exod. 20:12), Wenceslas brought his mother out of banishment and back to his castle. He forgave her for the murderous plot that killed his dear grandmother! That was just the beginning of the gracious behavior Wenceslas modeled while Duke of Bohemia.

Wenceslas's kindness and generosity extended to rich and poor alike. He was greatly dedicated to giving clothes to the needy and shelter to the homeless and to buying the freedom of slaves—especially the freedom of children caught in slavery. In an effort to spread Christianity further, Wenceslas invited missionaries to Bohemia from Germany. And on at least one occasion, to settle a dispute, Wenceslas courageously faced an opponent in an open duel rather than have his own troops go to battle. Many lives were spared by his bravery!

When Drahomira was banished for her crime, Wenceslas became the duke of Bohemia. He was just 18.

Then of course there is the story of "Good King Wenceslas" from the traditional Christmas carol. (The song refers to Wenceslas as a "king" although he was really a "duke.") It describes a scene from the life of Wenceslas that gives a touching glimpse into the heart of this man. The carol tells of a cold bitter night when King Wenceslas and a **page**, or helper, notice a poor man gathering firewood. The kindhearted king asks the page where the man lives. When learning that the poor man lives against a faraway fence, the king instructs the page that they shall go to his dwelling that very night and provide the man with a meal.

As they trod off into the snow, the page complains of how cold his feet are. Wenceslas suggests that the page walk in his warm footsteps to lessen the pain of the cruel snow. The song implies that Wenceslas was so warmhearted that there was heat in the footsteps he left behind for the young! And so the two, the king and the page, travel on to bless the poor man with a meal.

With this kind of servant-leader reigning in Bohemia, all should have been well in the kingdom. But unfortunately, not all the nobility appreciated the generous heart of Wenceslas. In fact, some considered it a weakness. Wenceslas's own pagan brother, **Boleslav**, thought it "unfitting" for a king to mingle with peasants and the poor. He was also jealous that Wenceslas had a son who might rule as the next duke instead of him.

As the sad story goes, Boleslav invited Wenceslas to celebrate a feast at church. Wenceslas was warned ahead of time that his brother *might* be plotting against his life, but in good faith, he attended anyway. Perhaps he should have been more cautious! For, on September 28, **929**, Boleslav raised his sword against his brother Wenceslas to slay him. With great mercy, Wenceslas forgave Boleslav on the spot for the offense. But as he turned up the steps of the church, other members of the nobility attacked Wenceslas. One struck him in the arm, two beat him, and another pierced him in the side! Wenceslas died right there. He was only 25 years old.

"Good King Wenceslas" was buried at the church of St. Vitus in Prague, Czechoslovakia. Thousands of mourners visited his tomb in the Middle Ages to honor the humble saint. For years there were stories of miracles occurring near and around his grave. A statue in his memory still stands in the Prague city square that bears his name.

Pictured here is the ornate entryway to St. Vitus, the church where Wenceslas was buried.

And September 28 is dedicated as St. Wenceslas Day. Isn't it fitting that we would remember a man of such generous character in a Christmas carol?

ACTIVITIES FOR LESSON 46

ALL STUDENTS

Follow the example of Wenceslas. Help your family deliver a meal to someone in need, donate clothing items, or provide other physical help. What Bible passages encourage us to behave in this manner? (See James 1:27 and Matt. 25:31–46 for examples.) Take a photo of your activity and file it in your notebook under "Europe: Czech Republic."

46A—Younger and Middle Students

With your teacher's help, look at this Internet site for the words and music to "Good King Wenceslas." Sing the carol together.

www.cyberhymnal.org/htm/g/o/goodking.htm

If you do not have access to the Internet, you can find the words to the carol in the Activity Supplement in the Appendix.

46B—Older Students

Title a sheet of notebook paper "The Family Tree and Godly Influences on Wenceslas." Use the information from the lesson to complete the following diagram. I have provided first letters as clues.

Though they may never have met, consider the godly influence of Methodius and Cyril on the life of Wenceslas. Consider the influence you have on others in your life. File this page under "Europe: the Czech Republic."

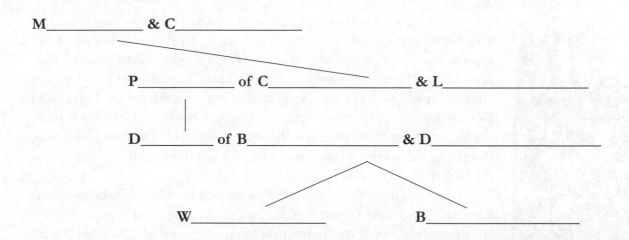

M_____ & C_____

P_____ of C_____ & L_____

D_____ of B_____ & D_____

W_____ B_____

936

OTTO I AND THE HOLY ROMAN EMPIRE
LESSON 47

From the title of today's lesson, it might sound as if the Romans made a comeback. (They never seem to go away!) But today's lesson is on the **"Holy" Roman Empire.** Interestingly enough, it was neither very "holy" nor very "Roman." Let's examine it more carefully. To do so, you'll first need to meet **Otto I.**

Otto I, sometimes called **Otto the Great**, became the king of **Germany** in **936.** His father had been a prince. Otto was a very successful conqueror. He beat out many princes from surrounding regions to establish his power.

In time, Otto further expanded Germany by fighting against the countries around him. You see, the **Slavs** of **Poland** and **Bohemia** revolted against Otto I, as did the **Magyars,** or the **Hungarians.** But in the battle of the **Lech River** in 955, Otto crushed the Magyars once and for all. This forced the Poles and the Bohemians, as well as the king of Burgundy, to come under Otto's rule.

Well, apparently all this success wasn't enough for Otto because he set his sights on northern **Italy.** But rather than go to war with the Italians, he decided to marry his way into power. And so he did. He married the widow of an earlier king from Italy. (He did have to fight other suitors who were interested in the same position!)

Otto had built up quite a reputation at this point. It was enough of a reputation, in fact, for the pope in Rome to summon his help. It seems there was an uprising in Italy that the pope wanted Otto to put down. He did so quite effectively. And then an eerie thing happened. Do you remember that one of the popes declared **Charlemagne** to be a "Roman Emperor" in the year 800, long after the Roman Empire had collapsed? Well, the same thing happened in 962. **Pope John XII** crowned Otto I, a German, as the **"Roman Emperor of the West"—Emperor "Augustus,"** to be exact! And his kingdom became known as the *Holy* Roman Empire.

Otto I, the king of Germany, was crowned "Roman Emperor of the West" and started the Holy Roman Empire.

Now think about that for a minute. Why was a German being crowned a *Roman* emperor? Well, the pope was Roman. So the term seemed to fit from that perspective. But what about the empire? Was it really Roman? Well, not exactly. The last of Charlemagne's "Roman Empire" had faded shortly after he died in 814. His sons were unable to rule it effectively. France and Germany divided after that, never to be united again. So, Otto I was really the king of Germany. More specifically, he ruled over Germany, Bohemia, Burgundy, and northern Italy. You could look at it this way: these lands *became* the Holy Roman Empire under Otto I.

However, the term *Roman emperor* remained popular with the Germans for a very long time. Up until 1806 (the time of Napoleon), every king of Germany after Otto I called himself the "Roman Emperor." The word "Holy" was officially added by **Emperor Barbarossa** in 1155. (Since then, historians refer to *all* the kings from this long line as *Holy* Roman Emperors. Some even name Charlemagne as the first of the Holy Roman Emperors, though technically he was not.)

As for the "holiness" of the Holy Roman Empire, I don't think it ran very deep. The term *holy* seemed to come from the efforts of Otto I to force Christianity on people. Not that that was a holy thing to do! Otto appears to have used the common bond of Christianity to help pull his empire together. It was a matter of unity for his kingdom. Unfortunately, the use of brute force to spread Christianity only led to a distorted expression of the faith. This will become more evident when we study the **Crusades.** Furthermore, just like Charlemagne, Otto's union with the church led to later conflicts between kings and popes. Few of them ever got along because they quarreled over who had the most power.

Despite some flaws within the Holy Roman Empire, there did exist some true strengths. From 955–1075, Germany was probably the most prosperous country in all of Europe. The ground was rich with iron, copper, and silver; Roman and German skills were blended to make beautiful crafts; the church served to give a good education to the people; and artists flourished. Considering how "dark" the Dark Ages had been in Europe, this time period in the Holy Roman Empire was refreshing. It was a little taste of what was to come later, in the era called the **Renaissance.** You've probably heard of that time before. But I'm getting way ahead of myself here.

Our focus today has been the birth of the Holy Roman Empire and the man responsible for it, Otto I. As I said in the beginning, the empire itself was neither very holy nor very Roman, but it was quite significant in the development of Europe. Over the next 900 years of history, we will see just how influential the Holy Roman Empire was.

As part of the Holy Roman Empire, Germany became prosperous during the Middle Ages. The church helped provide education as well as spiritual guidance.

ALL STUDENTS

There are many hardy foods that are distinctive to Germany. Create a dinner of beef goulash, bockwurst, and/or steamy potato dumplings. Top it off with warm and crispy apple strudel. Take a photo of your meal and file it under "Europe: Germany."

47A—Younger Students

Do you like fairy tales? Many of them originated in Germany in the Middle Ages. In the 1800s, two brothers, Jacob and Wilhelm Grimm, wrote down stories that had been told in Germany for generations and generations. These famous tales include *Hansel and Gretel, Cinderella, Snow White and the Seven Dwarfs,* and *Rumpelstiltskin.*

Choose any one of Grimm's Fairy Tales and re-enact it for your family. It might be easiest if your teacher narrates the story and you act it out using other siblings or props from around the house. Videotape your performance.

47B—Middle and Older Students

Have you ever heard of the Black Forest of Germany? In some ways, it's not really a forest at all. Research this famous region through encyclopedias or the Internet. Pretend to be a travel agent and create a brochure to depict the Black Forest. File your information in your Student Notebook under "Europe: Germany.

As pictured here, the forests are so dense in some places in Germany that they appear black.

C. 956

VLADIMIR I OF RUSSIA

LESSON 48

One country we've not really studied yet is **Russia.** There's a reason for that. Up until this time in the Middle Ages, Russia—as we know it now—was not clearly established. Certainly there were people living in the area for thousands of years. But they were only loosely organized. I will tell you a little about the ancient people of Russia and then share with you the story of one king who helped to shape present-day Russia. His name was **Vladimir I.**

As early as the seventh century before Christ, there were people from **Greece** and **Persia** who migrated into Russia and started cities there. The Persians, or **Scythians**, were probably from **Iran.** Traders lived near the edge of the **Black Sea** in order to attract business from the busy waterways. Towns grew, with names such as **Olbia, Tanais, Theodosia,** and **Panticapaeum.**

By the second century before Christ, more Iranians moved into Russia pushing the Scythians out. These were the **Sarmatians.** After them, the **Goths** moved in and then the **Huns.** Remember them? The fearsome Attila once led them! Eventually southern Russia was a mixture of several nomadic tribes. They were the **Bulgars,** the **Slavs,** the **Khazars,** the **Magyars,** and the **Mongols,** just to mention a few.

These tribes of people were so different from one another in their religious beliefs that in the capital city of **Itil** it was necessary to set up seven different courts to administer justice. What I mean is that in the city of Itil alone, there were two courts for the Jews, two courts for the Christians, two courts for the Muslims, and one court for pagans. This acceptance of so many beliefs or creeds led many to freely settle and trade near Itil. Located at the mouth of the **Volga River** and in between the **Baltic Sea** and the **Caspian Sea,** Itil became one of the largest trade cities in the world by the 700s.

The only threat to these loose tribes was the **Vikings.** I'm sure you remember them! As I mentioned a few lessons back, they worked their way into the region looking for things to steal and land to keep. They eventually found both. By the middle of the ninth century, the Vikings had looted and settled land from the city of **Novgorod** to the city of **Kiev.** They called themselves the **Rus,** which is probably how the name of Russia came to be. **Rurik,** a Viking, was their first leader. (All the Russian kings after him were thought to be his descendants.)

Vladimir—A Descendant of the Vikings

This brings us to Vladimir. Born **about 956,** he was considered the fifth **Grand Duke of Kiev** and a descendant of Rurik. But he brought more than his Viking heritage to Russia. He brought his spiritual heritage. Early in his life he learned about God and Christ through his grandmother. Though he may or may not have been a Christian himself, he helped shape the religion of Russia for centuries to come. He did so by establishing churches all across Russia. For this he was named a saint.

Vladimir I, a descendant of Vikings, was the fifth "Grand Duke of Kiev" in Russia.

There is a story that Vladimir was unclear about the differences between the **Western Roman Church** (later called the Roman Catholic Church) and the **Eastern Orthodox Church** (or Greek Orthodox Church) of the Byzantine Empire. He wasn't sure which "brand" of church to start in Russia. The confusion is understandable, as each had developed its own style of worship and rituals. Furthermore, the churches differed in their viewpoint of the pope. The Orthodox Church did *not* recognize the **pope** as having the power that the Western Roman Church gave him.

To better understand these churches, Vladimir sent representatives to each. To be more specific, he sent his representatives to Germany in the West and to Constantinople in the East. Do you remember the name of a spectacular church that was built in Constantinople? It was Saint Sophia, built by Justinian. Well, the reports that Vladimir got back were rather interesting. It seems that those who visited the Eastern Orthodox churches were far more impressed than those who visited the Western Roman churches. But it was not so much with what the churches taught or what they believed, it was with how they looked! Here is what was said:

> "When we stood in the temple we did not know where we were, for there is nothing else like it upon earth: there is truth God has His dwelling place with men; and we can never forget the beauty we saw there." [2]

Pictured here is a priest of the Eastern Orthodox Church in present-day Russia.

---

2. Roger L. Berry, *God's World: His Story.* Harrisonburg, VA: Christian Light Publications, Inc., 1976; p. 258.

In present times, Eastern Orthodox churches in Kiev remain highly decorative and ornate.

Like many buildings in the Byzantine Empire, it seems that the Eastern Orthodox churches of that time period were extremely well decorated. Like Saint Sophia, they were quite beautiful both on the inside and out. Hanging incense burners, lush tapestries, frescoes, and ornate pieces of furniture lined the cathedrals. This beauty impressed Vladimir so much that he chose the Eastern Orthodox Church as the one he wanted for all of Russia.

Vladimir called upon missionaries from **Constantinople** to build up the church in Russia. They did so very successfully. The word of God spread. But unfortunately, Vladimir became so adamant about his campaign that he also *forced* Christianity on his people. He was baptized in 988 and made his subjects be baptized as well. Byzantine priests were instructed to baptize the masses. We've seen this crime before, haven't we? Otto I of Germany was guilty, too, of attempting to spread the Christian religion by force rather than by genuine conversion.

Despite this misuse of power, Vladimir accomplished other things for Russia that are worth our remembering. He built schools, libraries, and new cities. He promoted trade with other nations while at the same time protecting Russia from its neighbors. Vladimir also established a strong connection with the Byzantine Empire by marrying a Byzantine princess. Her name was **Anna.** Anna brought to Russia the finer customs and pageantry of the Byzantine Empire. And their son, **Yaroslav the Wise,** continued in the footsteps of his parents, building a strong government and cathedrals that looked like those in Constantinople. (The **Saint Sophia Cathedral** in Kiev was built during the reign of Yaroslav.)

So, that is the story of Vladimir and the birth of Russia. As you can see, Russia was a true melting pot of cultures in the beginning. From Greeks, to Persians—from Jews, to Slavs—and eventually to the Vikings—Russia grew to be home to millions. And if you visited Russia today, you would still notice the influence of the Byzantine Empire and the Orthodox Church. It is interesting to me how much one or two people can shape a nation for centuries to come!

This beautifully detailed mural depicts Vladimir I as one who contributed to the building of the church in Russia.

ACTIVITIES FOR LESSON 48

ALL STUDENTS

Make your Memory Cards for Lessons 46–48.

48A—Younger Students

Do you know the music of the *The Nutcracker*? A famous Russian composer wrote it in the 1800s. His name was Peter Ilich Tchaikovsky. Listen to a recording today of the Nutcracker Suite. You will probably recognize the music. A suggested Internet site (requires registration) is:

www.classicalarchives.com

48B—Middle Students

To help you grasp the influence that the Byzantine Empire had on Russia, contrast the architecture of the famous sites listed below. Through the Internet or reference books, look first at Saint Sophia (Hagia Sophia) of Constantinople. Then investigate these famous sites in Russia:

- The *Cathedral of the Annunciation* at the Kremlin in Moscow (the Kremlin is a group of government buildings)
- *Saint Basil's Cathedral* in Red Square (a site near the Kremlin)
- *Saint Sophia Cathedral* in Kiev (built by Yaroslav the Wise, the son of Vladimir, specifically to resemble the cathedral by the same name in Constantinople)

Print or photocopy the sites you could find. Notice the similarities. File these in your Student Notebook under "Asia: Russia."

St. Basil's Cathedral in Red Square is one of the most recognizable Russian structures in the world.

48C—Older Students

1. Familiarize yourself with one of Russia's famous authors, Leo Nikolaevich Tolstoy. Read in an encyclopedia or on the Internet about his unusual life. You will especially want to familiarize yourself with Tolstoy's most famous work, the book *War and Peace*, written from 1868–1869. Find a synopsis of the story or perhaps read it yourself!

2. Using a dictionary, define the term *orthodox*. Can you think of other religions that use this term? What does it mean? Write it down and file it under "Asia: Russia" in your Student Notebook.

TAKE ANOTHER LOOK!

REVIEW 16: LESSONS 46–48

Wall of Fame

1. **"Good King Wenceslas" (929)**—Using dark paper and a white crayon, draw two stick figures walking in the snow. Label it "Good King Wenceslas." [From *History Through the Ages*, use *"Good King" Wenceslaus*.]

2. **Otto I and the Holy Roman Empire (936)**—Create a fancy crown with jewels and gold crayon. Write underneath it "Otto I Crowned Holy Roman Emperor." [*Use Otto I.*]

3. **Vladimir I of Russia (c. 956)**—Sketch or photocopy an ornate church cathedral. Write underneath it "Vladimir of Russia." [*Use Vladimir of Kiev.*]

SomeWHERE in Time

Connect the capitals.

The following countries (or their modern counterparts) were mentioned in this week's lessons. Using an atlas, a globe, or a set of encyclopedias, become more familiar with this central region of Europe and Asia by connecting the countries on the left to their present capital cities on the right. The answers are below.

1. Czech Republic
2. Germany
3. Poland
4. Hungary
5. Italy
6. France
7. Ukraine (formerly Russia)
8. Iran
9. Greece

a. Berlin
b. Kiev
c. Athens
d. Budapest
e. Prague
f. Paris
g. Rome
h. Tehran
i. Warsaw

Answers: (1) e   (2) a   (3) i   (4) d   (5) g   (6) f   (7) b   (8) h   (9) c

WHAT DID YOU LEARN?

WEEK 16: QUIZ

Stump the Teacher. Today's quiz is a little out of the ordinary. It is your turn to write it! I would like you—the student—to provide good quiz questions for your teacher (or parent). The quiz can be oral or written. I suggest that younger students write one question per week out of the textbook to create a 16-question quiz. Middle students should come up with two questions per week for a 32-question quiz. Older students should provide one question per lesson for a 48-question quiz!

Here is the trick though: Each student must be able to provide the answers as well! That way, everyone involved is learning and reviewing. If you are keeping a careful record of grades received and want to have a grade for this quiz, I recommend that students receive one point for every good question and answer provided out of the total suggested for the age group. (Teacher: I advise you to study!)

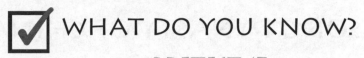 WHAT DO YOU KNOW?

PRETEST 17

True or False? Circle your answers.

1. During the Song dynasty of China, peasant farmers were considered   T   F
the *lowest* rank of society.

2. The Chinese invented porcelain, acupuncture, and compass needles.   T   F

3. The Chinese valued "lily feet" for being long and slender.   T   F

4. *Coptic* means "Egyptian."   T   F

5. Nearly every day before sunrise, St. Simon delivered cheese to the elderly.   T   F

6. In exile from his domestic problems in Iceland, Eric the Red stumbled   T   F
across Australia.

7. Eric the Red named Greenland for the green iguanas that live there.   T   F

8. Greenlanders call their island *Kallaallit Nunaat*, meaning "Land of the People."   T   F

THE SONG DYNASTY OF CHINA
LESSON 49

China fascinates me. It's huge, it's distinctive, and it's colorful! There is so much to know about China that it would be hard to learn about it all at once. And so, throughout *The Mystery of History*, I'm primarily teaching you about China one dynasty at a time. Today we will focus on the **Song dynasty.** It was established just after the **Tang dynasty,** which we learned about in Lesson 28.

The Tang dynasty, if you remember, was a Golden Age for China. Art, literature, science, and agriculture boomed for over a hundred years. The capital city (**Chang'an,** or **Xi'an** as it was later called) was one of the strongest in the world. Nearly 10,000 poets came out of the Tang dynasty. That's a reflection of its being a rather peaceful and prosperous time period. (Had it been a time of war or depression, the arts would have been pushed aside.) It was also during the Tang dynasty that the ruthless albeit successful Empress Wu Zetian seized control of China as the only female in history to do so!

But, as golden ages have a way of coming and going under the sovereign hand of God (see Prov. 8:15–16 and Dan. 4:17), the Tang dynasty collapsed by the year 906. Five different emperors tried to make China strong again. But none were successful. It's just not that easy to be an emperor of a land as large and diverse as China. (It is the third largest country in the world!)

General Zhao Kuang Yin Makes Kaifeng the Capital

However, there was a man who was finally able to pull China back together. His name was **General Zhao Kuang Yin** (927–976). He stole the throne from a 7-year-old emperor and started what is called the Song dynasty in **960.** He made **Kaifeng** his capital. It was an interesting place. Kaifeng had a natural moat around it for protection and was located in the heart of the new empire. This made it a great site for trading.

And interestingly, long before fast-food restaurants such as we have today, there were hundreds of 24-hour restaurants in the city of Kaifeng. Markets were plentiful and theaters were everywhere. The theater was home to acrobats, opera stars, and puppeteers. Festivals were held weekly at the main temple where people could buy and sell clothes, furniture, books, and pets. It was definitely an active place!

Though the military was not very strong during this time period, the Song dynasty lasted until 1279. One reason may be that the teachings of **Confucius** were reborn during this time. Confucius did not give credit or honor to God for his teachings, but his philosophies are similar to the second greatest commandment given by a Jesus: *"You shall love your neighbor as yourself."* (Matt. 22:39) Adherence to this principle brought great stability to the nation. Furthermore, unlike philosophers in Europe, Confucius believed that the poor were some of the most important people in the country and should be treated fairly. Why? Because they did most of the farming to feed the nation!

Confucius, considered by the Chinese to be a wise teacher, lived about 500 years before Christ.

So, in order of importance, the social hierarchy of China looked like this:

1. The **emperor** was above all.

2. The **shi**, or the nobles and officials, helped run the government.

3. The **nong**, or the poor peasant farmers, were necessary for the nation to survive.

4. The **gong**, or artists, enriched the nation.

5. The **shang**, or the wealthy merchants, sold goods and services.

6. The **soldiers** defended the land.

7. **Slaves** were bought and sold like property (though very little slavery existed in China because of the decent treatment of the poor).

The hardworking peasant farmers in China were considered more important in society than the artists, rich merchants, or soldiers.

This system was strange to Europeans who placed soldiers and knights second only to the king in importance. And in Europe, the poor were at the bottom of society—not in the middle! However different this system was from the West, it worked well in the Far East.

Inventions During the Song Dynasty

One way to judge how well China was doing during the Song dynasty is to evaluate the many inventions from this time. There were lots! One of those was **paper money.** Now that might not sound like a big deal at first. But think about how much more convenient and lightweight paper money is compared to coins. The Europeans didn't start using paper money until the seventeenth century. Of course the Chinese had already figured out a unique way to carry their heavy coins. They cut square-shaped holes in them so they could be strung together on a cord! How clever. I'm surprised we don't see more of these around the world. Coins strung together plus the use of paper money made trading easier in China. And the easier it is to trade, the more prosperous people are likely to become.

The Chinese were the first to invent lightweight paper money. They also placed holes in their coins for carrying them on a cord.

Another clever invention was the making of **movable type.** A man by the name of **Bi Sheng** figured out how to make individual Chinese letters, or characters, out of hard clay and then move them around to create words for printing. This one advancement in printing was probably as important to the people of the Song dynasty as the invention of computers was to us! It forever changed the way people communicated their ideas. One of the more significant publications during the Song dynasty was a book called ***The Dream Stream Essays.*** It was written by **Sheng Kuo** in 1041. He was an expert in science, math, medicine, and architecture. The duplication of his book helped to educate others in these important fields.

The Chinese of the Song period were also responsible for inventing new **explosive weapons.** You may remember that the Chinese were first to invent fireworks. Well, the Chinese of the Song period took their knowledge of explosive fireworks and applied it to warfare. They created a bow-and-arrow set that was triggered by gunpowder! The gunpowder was a mixture of saltpeter, sulfur, and charcoal. When lit, it literally "rocketed" the arrows into deadly flaming missiles. Pretty amazing! The Arabs nicknamed the terrifying Chinese gunpowder **"China snow"** for its dramatic aftereffect.

On the lighter side, it was during the Song dynasty that **porcelain** was first created. To appreciate what is involved in making this delicate pottery, let me describe the procedure to you. Porcelain is made from coal dust and a fine, white clay called **kaolin.** To make ordinary ceramics, items are designed and then baked (or "fired") at 932 degrees Fahrenheit. But to make porcelain, a sculpture needs to be baked at *2,100* degrees Fahrenheit, glazed, and baked again! This makes porcelain hard, thin, and translucent. (That means you can almost see through it in places.) These beautiful works of art were in high demand all over the world. In the **Zhejiang province** alone, there was a kiln (a place where ceramics are baked) that could "fire" up to 25,000 pots at a time!

Another unique thing to the Song dynasty was the medical development of **acupuncture.** This is the method of inserting tiny needles into the body at special points to relieve undesirable symptoms. Though not fully understood, acupuncture is a widespread practice still in use today. In fact, its use is growing in western countries.

Speaking of needles, the incredible invention of the **compass needle** came during the Song dynasty. A compass is a device that finds north and south. It does so by floating or suspending a magnetic needle. The needle is naturally attracted to the Earth's magnetic North Pole. In case you're wondering, if you visited the top of the world, you wouldn't be able to see the magnetic North Pole. Scientists think that it moves around a little bit every year and is about 70 miles below the Earth's surface. But the magnetic force is so strong that a compass points to it from anywhere in the world, helping people to find direction!

Richly decorated porcelain jars and vases are still produced in China. It is customary in the United States for young couples to receive fancy porcelain plates called "china" when they get married.

In addition to these marvelous inventions during the Song dynasty, **art** continued to flourish in this time period. Landscape paintings on silk, jade carvings, beautiful calligraphy lettering, and decorative folding fans made from feathers—all of these and more depict the artistic flare of the Chinese. **Mi Feng**, one of China's most famous artists, was known for painting with the "method of blobs." Somehow he beautifully crafted scenes from daubs of ink without the use of lines! Though his style was odd, it just seemed to reflect his character. Mi Feng was known for being a little bit eccentric.

A tragic custom practiced during the Song dynasty and beyond was foot binding. It seems that some Chinese considered a woman more beautiful if her feet were especially tiny. These tiny feet were called **"lily feet."** There was such a high value placed on this trait that the Chinese created a way to force women's feet to be smaller! Unfortunately, the method was cruel, painful, and caused great deformity. At birth, a baby girl's feet were wrapped and bound tight enough to stop normal growth. They remained wrapped for years and were unable to grow properly. By adulthood, these "lily feet" were almost impossible for women to walk on! For this reason, the practice was much more common among the rich who could afford to have servants work for them. Despite the problems it caused, this practice was carried on for centuries.

As I said in the beginning of this lesson, there's a lot to know about China. I've only been able to share a few highlights of the Song dynasty here. But I hope it is enough for you to appreciate the beauty and ingenuity of the Chinese—for both are indeed rich.

ACTIVITIES FOR LESSON 49

Field Trip Possibility

To better appreciate the fine art of making porcelain, schedule a field trip to a pottery maker, ceramic kiln, or porcelain maker. Learn about the process of "firing" ceramic pieces.

49A—Younger Students

1. Create Chinese coins. (Tracing and cutting may need to be done by your teacher.)

   Materials: One quarter, thin cardboard, pencil, scissors, foil, glue, hole punch, string

   Trace the shape of a quarter onto a piece of thin cardboard. Trace as many coins as you would like to create. Cut them out carefully. Fold a large piece of foil in half. Now trace the cardboard pieces onto the foil. Trace each cardboard coin you cut out. (By folding the foil you have made a front and a back for each coin.) Glue the foil pieces onto the cardboard coins. Use a hole punch to cut a hole in the middle of each coin. Slide the coins onto your piece of string and tie the string together to create a clever way to carry your coins!

2. Make a feathery, foldable fan.

   Materials: Ruled legal paper (preferably of a pretty color), tape, hole punch, 10–12 inches of fancy cord or string, dozens of small colorful feathers from a craft store, glue

   Starting at the bottom of the legal paper, fold it at about every other line (going opposite directions with your fold as you go up the page). Bring together one end of your paper to serve as the handle, and "fan out" the creases on the other end. Add some clear tape to the handle for strength. Punch a hole through this end and insert a fancy cord or string. Tie the cord and use it to carry the fan on your wrist. Glue decorative feathers on one side of your fan going in and out of the creases. Overlap them as needed, allowing the tips of the feathers to peak over the ends of the fan for a dainty, wispy look.

49B—Middle Students

1. Obtain a sturdy compass. Using the compass, determine the direction in which your school or home faces. Create a set of directions for someone else to find something you've hidden. For example, hide a pencil 15 steps north from the front door, 8 steps east, and 5 steps south, etc.

2. Obtain Chinese characters from a resource book or the Internet. Use a special calligraphy pen to copy a few of the letters to the best of your ability. File the characters in your Student Notebook under "Asia: China."

3. Purchase a silk-scarf painting kit at a local craft store to create beautiful designs in silk. If unable to find a kit, improvise with the purchase of a light-colored (undecorated) silk scarf and quality fabric paint. Silk is difficult to paint with detail. Consider using a watery fluid fabric paint and creating interesting colors and designs through a "tie-dye" approach. More specifically, use rubber bands to gather small bunches of the scarf. Dip these "clusters" of silk into your watery paint to create unique blends of color and design. Allow to dry, then unwrap your one-of-a-kind creation.

49C—Older Students

1. Research the modern use of acupuncture. I recommend you use discernment here and attempt to separate *practice* versus *principle*. Some activities are good and effective in their practice but are not necessarily based on proper principle. For example, the practice of stretching found in yoga may

be beneficial for the body but the principles of the exercise are based on Eastern mysticism that is contrary to biblical teachings. In much the same way, the practice of meditation can be used for either good or evil depending on what one is meditating on!

I believe there are many alternative forms of medicine today that are effective in their practice but are not necessarily based on sound principle. Research acupuncture and derive your own opinion. Seek sound medical theories that might explain the effectiveness of acupuncture and contrast these to the ancient concepts of yin-yang and Taoism, which claim to support acupuncture in principle. File your research under "Asia: China" in your Student Notebook.

2. Add the Song dynasty to the list of dynasties in your Student Notebook that you started in Volume I or with Lesson 28 of Volume II.

The Dynasties of China (cont'd)

Date of Power	Years Ruling	Name of Dynasty	Special Notes
960–1279	319 yrs.	Song	Add your own summary statements here.

979

ST. SIMON AND THE COPTIC ORTHODOX CHURCH

LESSON 50

Now I have an amazing story to tell you about God's power. It is so amazing and so hard to believe that you won't find it in the pages of most history books. Let's just say it's not every day that men move mountains by their faith! But, according to members of the **Coptic Orthodox Church,** that is exactly what happened in **979.**[1] Let me first tell you who the **"Coptics"** of the Coptic Orthodox Church are. Then we'll look at this incredible miracle of faith.

The Coptic Orthodox Church is the **Egyptian Orthodox Church.** *Copts* is a European version of the Arabic word for Egyptian, which is *kibt*. "Copt, kibt." I think you can hear the closeness of the names if you repeat them a few times.

The Coptic Orthodox Church has an interesting history. They claim that their church was started by the **apostle Mark.** I'm referring to the Mark who wrote one of the four gospels about Jesus. This New Testament church had a great impact on Egypt. As Christianity spread, the faith of the ancient pharaohs faded. The practice of mummification ceased, and the building of pyramids was abandoned. With the new belief of bodily resurrection as taught in the Bible (1 Cor. 15), there was no need for the Egyptians to prepare themselves for the afterlife as they had done over the centuries.

---

1. A printed source of this story can be found in Arabic in *St. Simon. Mokatm.* Dar Ilias El Asria: Cairo, Egypt. (April 1996) 4th printing International # 977-5529-00-X . Phone number of church 512-4080-512-36-66. There is also considerable information on the Internet. Try searching on these keywords: "St. Simon the Tanner" and "Mokattam Mountain." For my purposes, this story was translated and retold through a personal interview with Noha Zaki, a former member of the Coptic Orthodox Church.

By A.D. 300 the Coptic Church in **Alexandria, Egypt,** was one of the strongest in the world (though they later broke away from the Eastern and Western churches). By the late 500s, the Copts were famous throughout the **Byzantine Empire** for making beautiful, intricate tapestries and for building pointed archways. They had also developed their own language by combining the Greek alphabet with Egyptian words and symbols.

As Christianity spread to Egypt, the faith and customs of the ancient Egyptians faded away.

But fame and ingenuity were not enough to protect the Copts from Islamic invasion. You see, the followers of Mohammed were growing in great number and looking for new lands to conquer. Because Egypt sits so close to **Saudi Arabia** (the birthplace of Mohammed and the center of Islam), it just seemed natural that Egypt would become a target for invasion. And it did!

In fact, in 642 the Arabs invaded Egypt with such fierceness that they almost obliterated the Copts! The Muslim invaders made it difficult NOT to convert to Islam. Any slave who converted was given freedom. Anyone not converting to Islam was heavily taxed. (That means they had to pay huge amounts of money to the Islamic government, leaving barely enough to buy food!) It was a terribly difficult time for the church. It was so difficult that by the year 744, thousands of Christians outwardly converted to Islam to avoid persecution. Twenty-four thousand to be exact!

The Copts inspired the popular design of a pointed archway as pictured here.

But there was a small group of devout Christians who held out against the Muslims and refused to convert. They kept the name and identity of Coptic Christians. It was a struggle for them to maintain their faith in Christ, but they did. At times they were forced to worship in secret. Like the early Christians who were persecuted under the emperors of Rome, so the Copts were persecuted under the Islamic kings of Egypt. (Islamic kings, by the way, are called ***caliphs***.)

Moaz Hosts a Debate

Now this is where the story gets really interesting! It seems that in approximately 979 there was one particular caliph by the name of **Moaz Ladeen Allah El Fatimy** (I will call him Moaz for short), who really enjoyed listening to a good **debate** from time to time as a form of entertainment in his court. (A debate is a strong discussion between people with very different opinions.) Caliph Moaz thought it would be especially entertaining to hear a debate between a Christian and a Jew. He had no idea what kind of showdown he would be hosting!

Each of the two faiths brought in their best man for the big debate. The Christians selected a well-versed bishop by the name of **Sawiras.** The Jews brought in a well-educated scholar by the name of **Moses.** (Not THE Moses of the Old Testament, of course, but another one.) And the debate for the caliph began, with many anxious spectators.

Well, according to members of the Coptic Orthodox Church, the debate heated up very quickly. It seems that Sawiras told the caliph that the Jews were "ignorant," according to their own Scriptures! He claimed to "prove" it by reading Isaiah 1:3, which states, *"the ox knows its owner and the donkey its master's crib; but Israel does not know. My people do not consider."* (Bold italics are mine.)

At this point in the debate, the caliph laughed! Moses and his companions, however, were outraged. Feeling insulted and humiliated, Moses requested a break from the debate to work on his defense. When he returned, he thought for sure he had found a passage in the New Testament that would humiliate Sawiras. The verse Moses chose was Matthew 17:20. It reads, *"If you have faith as a mustard seed, you will say to this mountain, 'Move from here to there,' and it will move."*

"Aha!" thought Moses. Now, I don't know exactly what Moses said to himself. But it might have been something like this: "I have found a verse in their own Scriptures that will make them look foolish. For surely no man can move a mountain!"

Well, the caliph was intrigued by these powerful words of the Bible. He decided to put them to a test. Caliph Moaz issued a **decree** saying that Christians had three days to prove their scriptures to be true according to Matthew 17:20. After three days, they had these four choices: (1) Move a mountain; (2) Convert to Islam; (3) Leave Egypt; or (4) Be killed by the sword!

Needless to say, the Christians were rather shaken. Though their faith was strong, they'd never seen a mountain move—at least not literally. The **pope** of the Coptic Orthodox Church asked all church members to pray and fast for a miracle. On the third day, the pope stayed up to pray through the night at church. About 4 A.M. he believed he received a special message from God in a dream. It was something like this, "Go out and you'll find a man with enough faith to move a mountain. You will know him because he is carrying water."

Simaan El Kharaz (Simon)

Now, before I tell you about the pope meeting this man "carrying water," let me tell you who this special man was. His name was **Simaan El Kharaz.** (I will translate "Simaan" to "Simon" for easier reading.) I believe God used Simon's humble heart, his genuine integrity, and his great faith to demonstrate the power of God and His Word. Let me tell you why.

According to the Coptic Orthodox Church, Simon was a poor shoemaker who loved the Lord with all his heart. Simon was so dedicated to the pure teachings of Christ, that he once gouged out his own eye to help protect him from the sin of lust! (Lust is to have selfish, romantic desires for a man or woman who is not one's husband or wife!) Simon did this in obedience to a passage in Matthew that says:

"I say to you that whoever looks at a woman to lust for her has already committed adultery with her in his heart. If your right eye causes you to sin, pluck it out and cast it from you; for it is more profitable for you that one of your members perish, than for your whole body to be cast into hell." (Matt. 5:28–29)

What a man of conviction this Simon was! Simon also held strongly to the Lord's command to take care of widows and orphans. (James 1:27) He was known in his community to carry water to the elderly every morning at 4 A.M. before he went to work making shoes. Every day after work he took food to the poor and spent the rest of his evenings in prayer. Simon was surely a man of great humility and faith.

Did you notice something in that last paragraph that would bring the pope and Simon together? The pope was told in his vision to go out and find a man carrying water at 4 A.M.! Why that's the very hour that Simon went out to take water to the elderly. So when the pope left the church in the early morning hours, it was Simon he found—just as the Lord said he would.

With great excitement, the pope explained his vision to Simon. He told Simon that God wanted to use *his* great faith to move a mountain. Simon agreed but only on two conditions—one, that his presence would remain anonymous in the crowd of people (that means Simon would not be seen or heard); and two, that the pope would *not* speak of Simon, even by name, until after Simon had died! So humble was this man that he did not want any credit for being used by God for something spectacular.

Miracle at Mokattam Mountain

A great crowd gathered later that morning on **Mokattam Mountain.** With great anticipation, as well as some fear and trembling, Jews, Christians, and Muslims alike gathered to witness what the Lord would do. The Christians stood on one side, and the Muslims and Jews on the other. Everyone of importance was there, including Simon who was hidden somewhere in the crowd. Could the Christians "move a mountain" by their faith as the Scriptures claimed or would they be humiliated and persecuted all the more?

As you may already suspect, the Lord prevailed that day. He made Himself known through the supernatural! According to the Coptic Church, the pope prayed and the Christians chanted "Forgive us" to the Lord 400 times. Then the crowd of Christians stopped; they bowed and rose three times while the pope waved a sign of the cross in front of the mountain. With every low bow before God, the earth shook violently and the mountain just east of the crowd rose straight up into the sky! When the Christians stood back up, the mountain fell back down. According to the Coptics, the mountain rose high enough in the sky that the early morning sun could be seen shining between the mountain and the ground!

In complete astonishment the caliph shouted praises out loud to God, and he begged the Christians to stop. He decreed right then and there that all Christians would be free of persecution under his rule. The great debate was over. Only God knows the faith that may have been born in all of those who witnessed the miraculous event.

As for Simon, he disappeared from the crowd on that great day. The pope was unable to thank him for his humble faith and prayer, which God used to move the mountain, bring glory to His name, and protect the Coptic Church. The pope remained faithful to his promise to Simon and never spoke of him until after Simon's death. Simon was then named a saint.

According to the Coptic Church, a miracle occurred when Mokattam Mountain rose high enough in the sky for the morning sun to peek under it!

In honor of St. Simon, a church was built in his name on Mokattam Mountain. And do you know what this church does? It ministers to the poor and needy of the community just as Simon did. To be more specific, the church ministers today to a large population of families who live and work at a garbage dump located on the mountain. Don't you think that if Simon was still living, that is exactly the kind of ministry he would have? I think so!

ACTIVITIES FOR LESSON 50

50A—Younger Students

How heavy is water?

Materials: Three to four empty gallon-sized milk containers, bathroom scale

Simon is remembered for helping to carry water to the elderly in his community. Why do you think he needed to do that? It was probably because there was no running water in that village. And people need water every day to drink, bathe, and cook. To remember Simon's great act of kindness, I want you and your teacher to fill three to four empty gallon-sized milk containers with water. How much do you think one weighs? How much do two, three, and four gallons together weigh? Set one or more on a bathroom scale to find out. See how many you can safely hold at one time. Imagine Simon waking early every morning to carry water for those who couldn't!

50B—Middle Students

Research the size of a mustard seed. In comparison to its small size, how large does the average plant get? On a piece of notebook paper, write a paragraph about what you believe Jesus meant by having "faith as a mustard seed." (Matt. 17:20) Find a real mustard seed if you can and tape it to your notebook page or find photos of the plant. File your page under "Africa: Egypt" in your Student Notebook.

50C—Older Students

1. Research the life and problems of families who live and work at garbage sites around the world. Though unsanitary and difficult, some families can earn more income by pillaging through the garbage and selling their finds than by other means. A recommended website for further information is:

   www.unicef.org.vn/workchild.htm

2. Research the Council of Chalcedon in 451 to learn the reasons behind the break of the Coptic Orthodox Church from the Eastern and Western churches. It had something to do with a difference of opinion regarding the nature of Christ. Discuss the significance of this doctrine with your teacher. Write about it and file it under "Africa: Egypt" in your Student Notebook.

985

ERIC THE RED AND THE SETTLEMENT OF GREENLAND
LESSON 51

Have you ever heard that **Iceland** isn't icy and **Greenland** isn't green? Well, there's some truth to that. We've already learned that Iceland has lots of warm places and isn't completely made of ice. It was during a bad winter storm that one of its first explorers named it "Iceland" out of his despair with the elements. Well today you'll learn why the European discoverer of Greenland—**Eric the Red**—named the glacier-covered ice cap of Greenland to sound "green" and "warm"!

Eric the Red was born in **Norway.** He was called Eric the Red because of his distinctive red hair. The term also fit his red-hot temper! It seems he got that from his father. When Eric was just 15, his father killed a man in a dispute. The family was forced to move. They chose Iceland as their new home.

Upon arriving in Iceland, Eric's family discovered that most of the good green pastureland had been taken by other immigrants. They were forced to live further north where indeed it was much colder and icier. Eric's family had no way of knowing that they were preparing Eric for one day living in the much-colder Greenland.

Eric the Red grew to adulthood in Iceland. He met and married **Thjodhild**, the daughter of a tribal chief. While living in Iceland, they gave birth to a son named **Leif Ericsson.** (Leif grew up to be a pretty important guy. I'll tell you more about him in our next lesson.)

Eric the Red had some problems living in Iceland, much like his father had in Norway. Eric wound up in a dispute with his neighbors and killed two people! For this he was exiled from Iceland for three years. But where was he to go? His father's bad reputation for murder prevented him from returning to his childhood home in Norway. He had to go somewhere else.

As you may already have guessed, Eric the Red decided to explore an island to the west that others had only told tales of. (This island was Greenland, of course, but it hadn't been named that yet.) A Viking sailor in 900 had been blown off course from his normal travels and stumbled upon the mysterious island. He named it **Skerries.** Why not go there? It almost seemed it was Eric's destiny and in his Viking blood to explore.

On his first voyage west to the island, Eric took 30 men with him. Apparently, he liked what he found because on his second voyage there in **985,** Eric went back to stay. This time he took 25 cargo ships loaded with 40 colonists per boat and all the supplies they needed to survive. That included a lot of grain, cattle, timber, and iron products. Each ship was only 80 feet long, 16 feet wide, and 7 feet deep. It was so dangerous to carry these heavy loads that only 14 ships made it safely. Some boats turned back to Iceland, but unfortunately, many sank in the icy waters of the **North Atlantic Sea.**

Following the lead of Eric the Red, 14 of 25 Viking ships made it safely to Greenland with enough supplies and cargo to start a new settlement.

Eric the Red Names Greenland

Do you wonder how Eric the Red persuaded 1,000 people to make such a dangerous voyage? On the one hand, his job was easy. For it seems to be in the human spirit to seek new land and *migrate*. (That's where we get the word "immigrants.") Consider how many thousands of immigrants just a few generations ago braved the seas to settle America. But besides the spirit of adventure working in his favor, Eric the Red plotted another way to recruit pioneers. He did so by renaming the island to sound like a desirable place to live. And so Eric the Red named his new home "Greenland." It sounds warm and friendly, don't you think?

What the new settlers of Greenland found was indeed a suitable place to live. For one, the land may not have been as frozen as it is today. (Greenland's climate has grown colder over time.) The pioneers found enough farmland to grow barley, enough pastureland for their own cattle to graze, and plenty of local wildlife to live on. Greenland offers enormous wildlife for hunting, such as 700-pound **musk oxen**, 1,000-pound **polar bears**, 2,000-pound **walruses**, and two-ton **narwhals.** Now, that's a lot of meat to go around! Besides these, there are plenty of **caribou** (better known as **reindeer**), **arctic foxes**, **falcons, seals,** and **fish** to eat in Greenland.

But don't think it wasn't difficult to survive otherwise in Greenland. It had other challenges. The middle of the island, which is the largest island in the world, is completely uninhabitable. That means no one could possibly live there. It is uninhabitable because the ice there is from 7,000 to 10,000 feet thick! Eighty-five percent of the island is permanently covered with ice. This icy cover is called **permafrost.** You might expect there to be large amounts of snow in

One polar bear can weigh up to 1,000 pounds, providing a great deal of meat and fur.

Greenland. But actually the air is so dry from the cold that it snows only about 10 inches per year. So it is *ice* rather than snow that makes life challenging in Greenland.

Ice, in the form of giant **glaciers,** causes lots of problems. For one, it makes sea travel difficult. The famous ***Titanic*** sank because it hit a hidden iceberg in the sea! On land, huge glaciers can sometimes break and travel. Like a giant landslide, the ice stops at nothing in its path!

Then there is the issue of limited sunshine. Like other countries near the **North Pole,** Greenland tilts close to the sun for six months of the year and away from the sun for the other six months. When the sun shines all day, it is called the **midnight sun.** It's not so difficult to live through—but six months of near darkness? That's a tough assignment! This is called **polar night,** and it occurs when the sun rises only slightly as if it were twilight. In the far north there are some periods of complete darkness. It is so exciting when the sun first rises in that part of the island that the Greenlanders usually celebrate with a trip to the mountains, hoping to be the first to see the golden sun! Families celebrate together with traditional dancing and feasting.

Early Greenlanders

Now, I've told you all about Eric the Red and the people *he* brought from Iceland to settle Greenland. But did you wonder if maybe some other people were already living there? Did you think for a minute that an island of this size could not already have been discovered? Of course it was. As far back as 2500 B.C. there is evidence that the **Sarqaq** people lived in Greenland. They are thought to have traveled from **Siberia** in northern Russia, to North America, and on to Greenland when land bridges were more easily exposed between the continents. The Sarqaq were a nomadic people who hunted seals and reindeer. They disappeared about 3,000 years ago.

Around 600 B.C. the **Dorset** people migrated from **Canada** to Greenland. They survived about 800 years before disappearing! Like the Sarqaq people, they were hunters but they also built tents made of animal skins and snow houses like **igloos.** Their fuel for keeping warm was seal oil.

Next we know that the **Independence** people occupied Greenland. They were not only hunters and tent dwellers, but they were also craftsmen. They left behind bones crafted into tools and sewing instruments. These people heated their homes by burning driftwood and fatty bones.

And then, in about 900, there was a migration of people from Alaska who settled in Greenland. They are the **Thulte** people. Wait! Wasn't that about the same time that Eric the Red was settling Greenland? Yes, it was. While Eric and his pioneers were settling on one side of Greenland, the Thulte were moving in with dogsled teams on the other side! It could have been a real problem. But the two people groups lived far enough apart that they remained peaceful with one another most of the time.

The Thulte, like the groups mentioned above, were closely related to other people groups living north of the Arctic Circle. They call themselves the **Inuit** (IN you eet). It means "people." The Native Americans named these people **Eskimos,** which means "men who eat raw meat." In America, the term *Eskimo* is still widely used, but these proud people would much prefer to be called Inuit.

Though the Arctic Circle is an invisible line around the earth, in some countries it is marked with reference signs for tourists and local people. (That's my husband holding the video camera!)

Back to the Thulte—they were ingenious settlers. They created **kayaks** for easy travel around the coast of Greenland. They also built longer-lasting homes in the sides of the hills. Because of their abilities to survive the cold climate, 75 percent of Greenlanders today are descendants of the Thulte people.

Viking Settlers Disappear

But whatever happened to Eric the Red and his people? Well, after many years of leadership in the new colony, Eric the Red died in Greenland. His colony multiplied to approximately 10,000 people. But strangely enough, just 400 years after settling in Greenland, they disappeared! There are several theories as to what might have become of them. Some historians suspect that a cold spell and an invasion of **caterpillars** in the 1400s destroyed their crops and drove them to starvation. Others think that pirates may have overtaken the colonists. Still others wonder if there wasn't finally conflict between the Thulte and the Vikings that led to mass murder. No one knows for sure.

The Europeans talked of sending expeditions to find the colonists, but efforts were never made and the Viking settlement was nearly forgotten over time. The only way we even know these people existed is from the written poems they left behind. They were called **sagas.** It is from these beautiful historical poems (that still exist today) that we know so much about Eric the Red and his family. Had the other cultures that settled in Greenland left us with such good records of *their* history, then this lesson would probably have been about them instead!

As for the name of Greenland, it has lived on as designated by Eric the Red. That is, unless you ask someone who lives there. The Greenlanders, who descended from the Inuit, have their *own* name for the island. They call it **Kallaallit Nunaat** (ky lay LITE noo NA at), meaning "Land of the People." I think both names sound enchanting!

ACTIVITIES FOR LESSON 51

ALL STUDENTS

Make your Memory Cards for Lessons 49–51.

Note: All the following activities are to be filed in your Student Notebook under "North America: Greenland." But, technically, Greenland is not a country in North America. It is owned by Denmark, which is a country in Europe. But for our purposes, we will keep information on Greenland listed in North America because it is considered part of that continent.

51A—Younger Students

1. Build an igloo. (This will take more than one day to complete.)

   Materials: Disposable plastic bowl (dome-shaped like a cereal bowl) to serve as a mold, water, ice cubes, plate

   Fill your disposable bowl halfway up with water and place it in the freezer overnight. The next day, peel away the plastic. Use the dome-shaped ice as the top of your igloo. On a plate, build walls out of ice cubes to support the dome. Be sure to leave an opening on one side! Take a picture of your igloo before it melts and place it in your Student Notebook under "North America: Greenland."

2. Learn more about God's amazing arctic animals. I recommend the book *Draw Write Now: The Polar Regions–The Arctic –The Antarctic* by Marie Hablitzel and Kim Stitzer. (Book 4 in the series, it is available from www.kingsharvest.com.) Create beautiful artworks for your Student Notebook.

51B—Middle Students

1. Research dogsled teams. What types of dogs are best for dogsleds? Where are these used today? How many dogs are needed to make a team? Find answers to these questions and more. File your report under "North America: Greenland" in your Student Notebook.

2. Research polar bears. Use the following questions as a guideline for a report.

   a. Where do polar bears live?

   b. What do they eat?

   c. How big do they get?

   d. What special features does the polar bear have to protect itself? (Hint: Consider what is unique to his fur and feet.)

   Include pictures of polar bears in your report. File it under "North America: Greenland" in your Student Notebook.

51C—Middle and Older Students

1. Research the modern Inuit of Greenland, North America, and Siberia. What do these cultures have in common? (Hint: Diet, language, challenges of the cold, etc.) Describe in story form a day in the life of the Inuit. File it under "North America: Greenland" in your Student Notebook.

2. Archaeologists believe they recently unearthed the home of Eric the Red. Research this on the Internet. Print your findings and file it under "North America: Greenland" in your Student Notebook.

3. Research the amazing discovery of "mummies" in Greenland. According to the author of *Greenland Mummies*, several well-preserved bodies of ancient people have been found in Greenland. (The cold climate kept them intact.) For more information, search the library or Internet for *Greenland Mummies* (Time Travelers series) by Janet Buell, published in 1998.

4. Search the library or the Internet for original works of the Viking settlers in *The Greenlanders Saga* and *The Saga of Eric the Red*. An Internet search on "Eric the Red, saga" brought up several good sites, as did "Greenlander Saga."

TAKE ANOTHER LOOK!

Wall of Fame

1. *The Song Dynasty of China (960)*—Sketch a small compass with the markings of North, South, East, and West. Underneath, write "Kuang Yin Founds the Song Dynasty." [From *History Through the Ages,* use *Song Dynasty.*]

2. *St. Simon and the Coptic Orthodox Church (979)*—Sketch a small mountain and include the ground it rests on. Cut the mountain apart from the ground. Glue the two pieces onto another small piece of paper with a space between them. Color the sun peeking out between the mountain and the ground. Underneath, write "Simon Prays to Move a Mountain." [Use *Saint Simon (Simaan El Kharaz) and the Coptic Orthodox Church.*]

3. *Eric the Red and the Settlement of Greenland (985)*—Sketch a stick figure of a man with red hair. In a caption box over his head, place the words "Come to Greenland." [Use *Erik the Red.*]

SomeWHERE in Time

1. Younger Students: Find Egypt on a globe or in an atlas. Do you remember who lived there from this week's lesson? It was St. Simon, the humble shoemaker. It is also believed that Mark, the author of the Book of Mark in the New Testament, started a church there a long time ago. Coptic Christians, or Egyptian Christians, still live there today.

2. Younger and Middle Students: Create a 3-D model of Greenland.

   Materials: Sturdy paper plate (preferably waterproof), marker, globe or atlas, about ¼ cup of dirt, three to five ice cubes, four to five toothpicks, about ½ cup salt

   - Land:
     a. Using a marker, sketch a rough map of Greenland on the paper plate. It does not need to be exact, but using a globe or atlas for guidance may be helpful.
     b. Carefully "pour" about 1/3 cup of dirt over the island.
     c. Smooth the dirt carefully and be sure to cover the island to the edges.
   - Permafrost/ice cap:
     a. Lay three to five regular-sized ice cubes down the center of Greenland to represent the ice cap that covers 85 percent of the island.
     b. Keep the edges of Greenland free of ice!
   - People:
     a. Break four or five toothpicks into three to four pieces each. This should give you around 15 or 20 little toothpick "people."
     b. Plant the little toothpick people around the edges of the island. Place most of them along the southwestern coast of Greenland because this represents the area where the majority of residents live.
   - Snow:
     a. Sprinkle lots and lots of salt over the entire island to represent snow.

b. Have fun watching the salt penetrate the ice cubes and convert them into spiky, sparkling wonders!

Take a photo of your 3-D model of Greenland before the ice cap melts! File it in your Student Notebook under "North America: Greenland." (Recall the Note from the Activities section of Lesson 51: Technically, Greenland is not a country in North America. It is owned by Denmark, which is a country in Europe. But for our purposes, we will keep information on Greenland listed in North America because it is considered part of that continent.)

3. Older Students: In "Take Another Look," Review 10, I gave you an extensive mapping project for China. If you were unable to complete the mapping project at that time, use *this* week to finish it.

WEEK 17: EXERCISE

WHAT DID YOU MISS?

"Post and Match" Game. Today you are going to create a fun game of posting and matching 20 answers with 20 clues, using self-sticking Post-it stationery notes. This game requires at least two people.

> *Materials:* 40 self-sticking Post-it notes (or substitute with tape and 40 slips of paper, each about 3 inches by 3 inches in size), pen or pencil

1. Using pen or pencil, copy the 20 "Clues" provided below onto 20 Post-it notes. Copy one clue per note. Include the number of the clue. This task may be divided among all in the classroom.

2. Next, copy the 20 "Answers" on to the remaining Post-it notes. Copy one answer per note. Include the letter of the answer. The answers are scrambled on the list below so as not to give them away.

3. Now for the fun part. Have one or more people randomly post clues and answers all around the room. You may include the floor, the ceiling, desktops, walls, etc. Determine appropriate boundaries.

4. If playing with only one other person, take turns timing how long it takes each person to match the clues to the answers. The one who can do it the fastest wins.

5. If playing with two or more people at the same time, make a contest of who can match the most right answers to the clues within a given time period. A simple rule to follow: You cannot pick up an answer without the matching clue in your hand!

Clues	Answers
1. Means "50"	a. Iconoclasts
2. Jewish historian	b. Theodora
3. Statement of beliefs	c. Copts
4. Grew up in the circus	d. Josephus
5. Invented fireworks	e. Floki Vilgerdarson
6. Founded Islam	f. Woden
7. Killed Grendel	g. Alfred
8. Escaped Damascus	h. Mohammed

9. "Image breakers"

10. Viking god for Wednesday

11. Won a reading contest

12. Named Iceland

13. Means "native"

14. Largest desert

15 Means "houses of stone"

16. Grandmother of Wenceslas

17. Started Holy Roman Empire

18. Duke of Kiev

19. Egyptian Christians

20. Named Greenland

i.   Pentecost

j.   Abd al-Rahman

k.   Beowulf

l.   Chinese

m.   Ludmilla

n.   Otto I

o.   Creed

p.   Maori

q.   Sahara

r.   Eric the Red

s.   Zimbabwe

t.   Vladimir

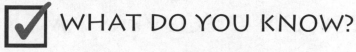

WHAT DO YOU KNOW?

PRETEST 18

Circle Sense. In the sentences below, *circle* the word that makes the most *sense*.

1. Leif Ericsson was nicknamed "Leif the (Lucky, Loser) " for rescuing people from a sinking ship.

2. Olaf Tryggvason, the king of Norway, was instrumental in exposing Leif Ericsson to (Buddhism, Christianity).

3. Leif Ericsson, a Viking, is thought to be the first known white explorer to the mainland continent of (South America, North America).

4. At the battle of Bothnagowan in 1040, Macbeth killed Duncan I to become the king of (Scotland, Zimbabwe).

5. Though not historically accurate, (Josephus, William Shakespeare) wrote a famous tragedy based on the character of Macbeth.

6. *Santiago de Compostela*, a holy site to Medieval Christians, means "St. James of the field of the (star, llama)."

7. A caballero is a term for a Spanish (knight, king).

8. El Cid, a Spanish hero, played a large role in the (revolution, Reconquista) of Spain.

LEIF ERICSSON DISCOVERS AMERICA
LESSON 52

Traditionally, Americans remember **Christopher Columbus** as the first white man to discover the **New World.** A favorite poem tells us, "In fourteen hundred ninety-two, Columbus sailed the ocean blue . . . "[1] However, according to Viking tradition, **Leif Ericsson** was the first white man to "sail the ocean blue" and land on the mainland shores of North America! And it happened about 500 years before Columbus! Today we'll look at both the facts and the folklore surrounding this significant event.

I introduced you to Leif Ericsson in our last lesson. He was the son of **Eric the Red.** As you may remember, Eric the Red had the reputation of being hotheaded. But Leif had an entirely different reputation. He was nicknamed **"Leif the Lucky."** He was thought to be lucky because he once saved a group of people from a sinking ship. (I think *they* were the lucky ones!)

In his youth, Leif wanted to meet the king of Norway. His name was **Olaf Tryggvason.** Leif was intrigued by the amazing stories he had heard of the king from traders who sailed back and forth between Greenland, Iceland, and Norway. King Olaf was known for being very tall, a strong athlete, fierce, and yet generous. Besides all of this, he had converted to Christianity. In 999, Leif sailed to Norway to meet King Olaf face to face. It was also a chance for Leif to become acquainted with his father's homeland. (If you remember, Eric the Red was originally from Norway. Naturally, Leif had strong roots there.)

In the process of mingling with King Olaf, Leif also converted to Christianity. We have no record of how genuine Leif's conversion was. Some say he may have embraced the king's faith to keep trade relations strong between Greenland and Norway. Regardless, Leif was commissioned by King Olaf to take the Christian faith back to Greenland. Leif obliged, returning to Greenland with priests and the message of the Gospel.

Leif Ericsson Takes the Gospel to Greenland

As the story goes, one of Leif's first converts was his very own mother. Her name was **Thjodhild** (as mentioned in our last lesson). She and many other Greenlanders embraced the teachings and forgiveness of Christ with ease. However, her husband, Eric the Red, was obstinate toward the new religion. Though Thjodhild built a Christian chapel right on their own property, Eric kept his distance. He remained faithful to his Viking gods the rest of his life.

Meanwhile, there was some other interesting news being circulated around Greenland. It seems that a Viking trader named **Bjarni Herjolfsson** (BYAHR nee hehr YOHLF son) was telling everyone about a wooded coastland he had seen to the west while blown off course from his travels. Bjarni sighted this land but never made it ashore. This story was naturally very intriguing to both Eric the Red and his son Leif. As a true Viking, Leif immediately wanted to explore it, but Eric was not so sure. As an old man and the leader of Greenland, he thought his days of exploring should be over.

But Leif persisted in persuading his father to go with him. With reluctance, Eric the Red agreed to accompany the expedition. However, on the morning of their departure, Eric accidentally fell from his horse. He considered this fall to be a bad omen of the gods and Eric backed out of the expedition altogether. With everything set to go, it only made sense for Leif to proceed without him.

---

1. Go to www.teachingheart.net/columbus.htm for all the words to the 1492 poem and a song for Columbus Day as well.

In and around the year **1003,** Leif Ericsson made his mark in history with the yearlong voyage he took at the age of 21. It seems that Leif bought Bjarni's ship and recruited 35 men to sail with him. Where to? They were not exactly sure. They didn't know that North America existed! They just headed northwest and to the south. The team made three significant stops.

Leif Explores North America

The first land Leif found was disappointing because it had no trees at all. It was probably the place today called **Baffin Island,** located in what is now **Nunavut,** the Inuit territory in modern-day Canada.[2] Finding it rocky and desolate, Leif named it **Helluland,** meaning "Slab-land."

The second sighting was a bit more promising. Leif probably landed on the coast of modern-day **Labrador**, a peninsula in northeastern Canada. He found some forests there, but the land was rugged, full of bears, and uninviting. Leif named it **Mark-land,** or "Forestland," and kept sailing south.

Leif Ericsson's next and final stop is the one that is of the most interest. It seems he sailed at least as far as **Newfoundland** (NOO fun land**), Canada**, and possibly to the coast of **Nova Scotia, Canada.** This makes Leif Ericsson the first known white man to visit the mainland continent of North America! Though he didn't stay long, Leif stayed long enough to get credit for it.

Leif Ericsson and his men reached the coast of Canada, making them the first known white men to explore North America.

Leif Ericsson and his men found endless resources of trees, thick grass, fresh salmon, and grapes. Some say that Leif named the location **Vinland,** or "Wineland," because of the grapes. Others say it was named Vinland because the word *vin* in Old Norse means "green grass" or "meadow." Regardless of why he named it Vinland, Leif Ericsson called it home for a time. He and his men built sturdy stone and turf shelters called ***Leifsbudir***, or "Leif's booths," and stayed for the winter.

One of the many things the men appreciated about their new home was the absence of frost on the ground. (They were so used to it in Greenland!) They also enjoyed the nearly equal periods of daylight and nighttime. This also was different to them from Greenland where the sun shines for months and then goes away for months at a time. The forests proved to be helpful for years to come by providing sturdy lumber for shipbuilding. But as lush as North America was, Leif longed for his homeland. In less than a year he returned to Greenland. Though he may have visited Vinland a few more times, he never again made it his home. However, his brother and sister both tried.

Thorvald and Freydid

In 1004, Leif's brother **Thorvald** used the same ship to sail back to Vinland. He went again in 1011 with 60 men, 5 women, livestock, and supplies. The group had every intention of staying for a while. A couple by the name of **Thorfinn** and **Gudrid** stayed long enough to give birth to a son there. His name was **Snorri.** As far as we know, Snorri was the first white child to be born in North America. Snorri spent the rest of his life in Iceland not knowing that he had made history.

---

2. In 1999 the Nunavut Territory and government, which had been approved in 1993, officially came into existence, giving the Inuit people their own self-governed territory within Canada. The name *Nunavut* means "Our Land." It was created out of land that was previously part of the Northwest Territories and includes Baffin Island, the fifth largest island in the world.

The Viking settlers fared well for a time in America. With the local natives, they traded things like dairy products and red cloth for furs and wood. They might have stayed much longer, but they began to run into some trouble. Their trouble was that the native people were becoming more and more hostile toward them. The Vikings called these dark, stocky people **skraelings.** They may have been **Inuit** or they may have been **Native Americans.** (Of course, thousands of Native Americans were in North America long before Leif Ericsson.) No one knows for sure who the local people in Vinland were. But whoever they were, they must not have been attractive to the Vikings. The name *skraelings*, as given by the Vikings, means "ugly people." With numerous incidences between the Vikings and the skraelings, Thorvald's settlers felt it best to leave. They only returned on occasion for timber.

Because tall timber was valuable for building homes and ships, it was important to the Vikings to return to North America where there seemed to be plenty of thick forests.

Some Viking sagas report that Leif Ericsson's sister, named **Freydid,** made a later attempt to settle the land. To be more accurate, she tried to make money off the New World. Supposedly Freydid took two ships back to Vinland with the promise that the crews of both ships would profit from their fur trade with the native people. But Freydid went back on her word. Like thieves in the night, she and her crew murdered the crew of the other ship so they could keep more of the profits!

If this incident wasn't enough to make Freydid sound terrifying, folklore says that Freydid once scared off hostile skraelings from her camp by wildly beating her chest with a sword and yelling loudly. I'm not sure if she was being brave or just a bit crazed! Either way, her reputation was not a good one at all, as told in the Viking sagas.

Though the sagas are full of interesting stories like those of Freydid, it's hard to know just how accurate they are since they were written down about two hundred years after the events took place. A few of the stories are told differently. For example, one saga implies that Leif Ericsson was blown off course when he discovered America. Another saga tells us that he went searching for America after Bjarni sighted it.

Either way, it seems to be true that Leif Ericsson was once in North America. As recently as 1960, archaeologists have found evidence of the Viking settlements to testify to their existence. And regardless of how Leif found America, I think it makes for interesting history.

I suppose what intrigues me the most about the whole story is that American history books would tell a different story had the Vikings decided to stay! Of further interest is the fact that in 1477, none other than Christopher Columbus sailed to *Iceland* to research legends of the *Viking* discovery of the New World. So, in an indirect way, the Vikings *did* have something to do with the famous voyage of Christopher Columbus in 1492. How about that!

ACTIVITIES FOR LESSON 52

ALL STUDENTS

This is a date to memorize: Leif Ericsson discovers America (c. 1003).

52A—Younger Students

1. You won't want to miss the beautifully illustrated storybook titled *Leif the Lucky* by Ingri and Edgar Parin D'Aulaire. Read it aloud with your teacher.

2. In remembrance of Leif Ericsson's discovery of Vinland—a land full of grapes, trees, and salmon—play hide-and-seek today with these items. Have your teacher hide grapes, paper (to represent trees), and a can of salmon. Just have fun trying to find them!

52B—Middle Students

1. You too will enjoy reading *Leif the Lucky* by Ingri and Edgar Parin D'Aulaire.

2. Research any group of Native Americans living in America at the time of Leif Ericsson's discovery. I recommend researching the Hopewell Indians living in Ohio (Fort Ancient in Lebanon, Ohio).

52C—Older Students

1. In 1898, a farmer in Kensington, Minnesota, claimed to find a Viking rune stone on his farm. Supposedly, the 200-pound stone tells the story of Vikings killed by local Native Americans. To this day, the authenticity of the stone is in question, although the Smithsonian displays it. Some believe the stone to be a fake that was carved by the farmer who claims to have found it. Research it yourself. Consider the implications if the stone is real. How and/or when might the Vikings have traveled all the way to Minnesota?

2. Research the remains of a Viking settlement discovered in the 1960s in Newfoundland, Canada. The exact place is called L'Anse aux Meadows. File your research under "North America: Canada."

3. Research the original works of the Viking sagas known as *The Saga of Eric the Red* and the *Greenlanders' Saga*. *The Saga of Eric the Red* is in two manuscripts—*Hauk's Book* and the *Skalholt Book*. The author was Hauk Erlendsson, born in Iceland about 1265. The *Greenlanders' Saga* is in the *Flateyar Book*, written in the 1380s by Jon Tordarsson, a priest. It was completed by another priest, Magnus Torhallsson. One excellent source for a partial translation of the sagas in English is the book *Land Under the Pole Star* by Helge Ingstad, published by St. Martin's Press, 1966 (Library of Congress Catalog Card Number: 66-21921).

1040

MACBETH, KING OF SCOTLAND
LESSON 53

Generally speaking, when you think of the Middle Ages, you probably think of knights in shining armor, enchanted castles, and beautiful princesses. I certainly do. But if the truth were known, the lives surrounding the kings and queens of the Middle Ages were quite often gruesome, grim, and bloody. Today's lesson is about one such medieval king whose reign started with a murder and ended with a murder—his own murder, that is. The king's name is **Macbeth.** His home was **Scotland.** Macbeth's life was so dramatic that it inspired **William Shakespeare** in the sixteenth century to create a play based on his character. It's popular still today!

The last we looked at Scotland, we learned of **Columba** (Lesson 25). He was an Irish missionary who took the Gospel to Scotland. His work was significant. Scotland became a strong center for the teaching and evangelism of the Christian faith.

But of course, not everyone in Scotland was positively influenced by Christianity. Such was the case of Macbeth. He was a greedy general. He worked under **King Duncan I** of Scotland. Macbeth wasn't content being just a general—he wanted to be king. And because his wife had royal blood in her family, he thought he *ought* to be king!

So, in the battle at **Bothnagowan** in **1040**, Macbeth faced King Duncan to steal the throne of Scotland. In the midst of the battle, Macbeth killed Duncan with his own hands. With this show of strength, Macbeth declared himself the king of Scotland. He kept the position for 17 years. Despite his brutal means of becoming king, Macbeth ruled over Scotland in a decent manner. All in all, he was considered a strong and good king.

Revenge!

Macbeth, a mere general in the army, declared himself the king of Scotland after killing Duncan I.

There was a problem though. Duncan I had a son—a son who rightfully should have been king had it not been for Macbeth. This son's name was **Malcolm III.** He wanted revenge for his father's death as well as to be the king of Scotland. So, the plot thickens. In 1054 Malcolm III teamed up with **Siward of Northumberland** in a fight against Macbeth. This happened at a place called **Dunsinane.** Technically speaking, Malcolm III and Siward won—but they were unable to remove Macbeth from the throne.

Three years later, in 1057, Malcolm III tried again. This time he met up against Macbeth at a place called **Lumhanan.** In retaliation for his father's death—and in hopes of becoming king—Malcolm III wanted more this time around than a battle victory on the field. He wanted Macbeth dead! And so Malcolm III killed Macbeth with his own hands! How ironic that Macbeth was killed by the *son* of the man Macbeth had killed!

Despite Malcolm III's victory, he still wasn't the king of Scotland yet. For a few months, Macbeth's *stepson* took the throne of Scotland in his father's place. But eventually Malcolm did gain the rightful crown of Scotland. He ousted the stepson and made himself the king.

All in all, the time period of Macbeth and Malcolm was a turbulent one. From 844 to 1057, there were 12 assassinations for the throne of Scotland! The times were violent. Besides fighting within the kingdom, the Scots were under constant attack from the Vikings. It was centuries before Scottish literature would be born, as there was no time for the arts.

Shakespeare's Macbeth

But this intriguing plot of revenge and murder has hardly been forgotten in literature. You can see where the fight for the throne makes for a great script. At least William Shakespeare thought so. He is a famous Englishman who took the story of Macbeth murdering Duncan I in order to be the king and built an incredible **tragedy** around it. A tragedy is a play that usually doesn't have a happy ending. Of course, like many moviemakers of today, Shakespeare added much to the plot. Many fictitious characters were created to dramatize the events of the story and make it even more interesting.

Therefore, if you ever read or watch a Shakespearean play of *Macbeth*, don't consider it historically accurate. It's not at all. But the play, in my opinion, truthfully depicts how easily man is sidetracked by his own ambitions, especially apart from God.

53A—Younger Students

1. Be a king (or a queen) for the day! Make a crown fit for a king (or a queen) following the directions in the Activity Supplement in the Appendix.

2. Obtain a book about castles from the library. I recommend David Macaulay's book titled *Castle*. Consider constructing your own castle out of blocks, boxes, empty paper-towel rolls, etc.

53B—Middle and Older Students

1. Write a short play. As you are probably aware, a play is written differently than a book or a story. "Dialogue" is written out for the actors to speak. Find samples of plays in books and note the layout of the text. Look for a list of actors, division of the play by acts and scenes, enter and exit notes, and narration.

   Take a familiar short story or a Bible story and adapt it to a play format, giving each character lines to speak to bring the story to life.

2. Just for interest, investigate the legend of the **Loch Ness monster**. It supposedly lives in Scotland. One suggested resource would be *After the Flood* by Bill Cooper. He has an interesting explanation of the creature.

53C—Older Students

Read or watch a performance of Shakespeare's *Macbeth*. Note the fact and the fiction of the drama.

1040

EL CID, A SPANISH HERO

LESSON 54

El Cid is a true hero according to Spanish tradition. He is remembered for helping the Spanish reclaim their land from the **Moors.** And that was no small task! But upon closer examination, I think El Cid's heroic reputation goes a little beyond his true character.

To understand this story, we'll need to review the invasion of Spain by the Moors (Lesson 33). Do you remember them? The Moors were Muslim people from northern Africa who invaded Spain in 711 at the Strait of Gibraltar. They brought with them great prosperity. Spain flourished in art, science, and architecture under the influence of the Umayyad dynasty. Serious problems existed, however, in regard to religion. Though Christians were given freedom to worship, they were also persecuted. It was a difficult time for the church.

For centuries there were faithful Christians who set up their own communities and managed to live apart from Muslim influence. A large population of these Christians lived in northeastern Spain along the **Pyrenees Mountains.** They were protected in the northeast by a French region named **Navarre.** Their southern borders, however, were completely unprotected. But they were also unnoticed! The Muslims weren't really paying attention to the growth of the Christians in the north.

What the Muslims might not have understood was that a revival of sorts was going on in northern Spain. It started with an unusual discovery. As the story goes, in 835 a shepherd was led by a star to a marble coffin in the mountains. Inside the coffin were, supposedly, the bones of **James** who wrote the

Book of James in the New Testament. (Some believe James was the half brother of Jesus.) To say the least, it was inspiring to the local Christians to have the remains of this great man and martyr in their midst. The Spanish Christians "adopted" James as their own special saint. They named the place of discovery *Santiago de Compostela*, which means "St. James of the field of the star."

This discovery—be it legend or fact—inspired thousands of Christian pilgrims to visit the area. During this era of the Middle Ages, the holy site at Santiago de Compostela was second in popularity only to the city of Jerusalem. All this to say that the number of Christians in Spain grew as a result of the renewed interest in the faith. And with this growth came renewed passion to reclaim all of Spain for Christ. Christian soldiers shouted "Santiago" and made banners of this name to lead their campaigns. Priests and knights alike rose up in arms against the Muslims.

Castillo de Gibralfaro is the name of this castle fort in Malaga, Spain.

From all this enthusiasm, and through the sovereignty of God, Christian regions in Spain began to spread. By 1037 the Christian states of **Leon** and **Castile** emerged. A little to the east of these, the Christian state of **Aragon** appeared. And later, **Portugal** was established. All along the way, fortress-like castles were built to protect these lands from the Muslims. This slow takeover became known as the *Reconquista*. (Reconquista means "reconquest" in English.) This reconquest lasted for about 450 years!

El Cid—Knight of the Reconquista

It was during this revival of Christianity in the early period of the Reconquista that our hero El Cid came to be known. El Cid was a Spanish knight, or *caballero*, admired for his skill in combat. His real name was **Rodrigo Diaz,** and he was born about **1040.** The Christians called him *El Cameador,* meaning "challenger" or "champion." The Muslims called him *El Sayyid,* which means the "lord" or "noble" in Arabic. El Sayyid was shortened to El Cid. It's interesting that El Cid is remembered in history by a version of his Arabic nickname. That might have had something to do with his mixed loyalties. Let me explain.

Though El Cid began his military adventures fighting for Christians in Castile, it seems he was less than virtuous along the way. El Cid was accused of keeping some money that he collected for the king. For this crime, he was banished from Castile in 1081. After his banishment, El Cid declared himself a **freebooter.** That means he would accept employment from *anyone* who needed his fighting skills—be they Christian or Muslim! He didn't care.

As you can imagine, El Cid and his small army of caballeros were kept pretty busy. Considering the turbulent times between the Spanish Muslims and the Christians, there were many in need of his services. For eight years El Cid worked for the Muslim emir of **Saragossa** (a city in Aragon) and extended the Muslim territory. This hurt the cause of the Christians trying to expand Aragon.

Though no longer under Muslim rule, Saragossa (or Zaragoza) remains a beautiful city in Spain. Pictured is the Basílica del Pilar.

Then in 1089, for a mere fee of 10,000 gold dinars, El Cid switched loyalties again and led 7,000 men in capturing **Valencia** *from* Muslim forces! Valencia, a large city on the Mediterranean shore of Spain, was an important port city to Muslims and Christians alike. Total possession of it was critical for either side.

To secure Valencia for good, El Cid did something more brutal than heroic. In 1094, he burned the chief justice alive. He would have killed the justice's entire family had not his own men protested. He also took the possessions of the people and divided them among his own men. Though El Cid was successful, his measures were drastic. To atone for his ruthless behavior, El Cid proceeded to govern Valencia with great justice and ability. For this he became a "hero" to the Spanish people.

It seems that El Cid's wishy-washy loyalties between the Christians and the Muslims were forgotten over time. He was remembered instead for being the bold caballero who took Valencia back from the Muslims. It was a pivotal victory in the long, agonizing Reconquista. But even more than that, El Cid is credited with reclaiming Spain for Christ, though this may or may not have been his personal ambition.

El Cid died in 1099. His wife governed Valencia for three years in his place. El Cid was buried in the town of **Burgos,** the same place he was born. His bones are revered by some as those of a saint. His fame grew in part from a poem written in his honor in 1140. It was simply called ***The Poem of the Cid.*** Though written years after El Cid's death, the poem undoubtedly helped him to forever win the hearts of the Spanish. In Spanish literature he grew to be full of holy zeal and one of the greatest Spanish heroes of all time. El Cid's adventures as caballero also inspired the writing of an opera by **Jules Massenet.**

As to the Spanish Muslims and their recollection of El Cid, I don't think he would be considered much of a hero. During the Reconquista, the Muslims were pushed farther and farther south into the region of **Granada.** Ultimately they were defeated there by **Ferdinand** and **Isabella** in 1492. Hey, isn't that when **Columbus** made his famous voyage to America? Yes, it is. But I'm getting way ahead of myself here. We won't cover that event until Volume III!

Though his loyalties were mixed, El Cid has been remembered as the Spanish caballero who led the Reconquista against Spanish Muslims.

ACTIVITIES FOR LESSON 54

ALL STUDENTS

1. **Make your Memory Cards for Lessons 52–54. Remember to highlight Leif Ericsson discovers America (c. 1003) as a date to memorize.**

2. Have a healthy discussion about genuine heroes in your culture by answering some of the following questions.

   a. Does the society you live in ever mistakenly create heroes? (Consider the past and the present.)

   b. Does your society ever confuse the appreciation of *talent* with the admiration of *courage* and *leadership*?

   c. Does the media give more attention to the lives of musical artists and athletes than to the lives of those who lead and defend your country?

   d. How did the tragic collapse of the World Trade Centers in New York City affect the appreciation of firemen and policemen in America?

   e. Who are some modern-day heroes and what ways can you think of to recognize them?

54A—Younger and Middle Students

Castles in the Middle Ages were often built as fortresses. Examine castles in reference books. Make a list of 5 to 10 components of a castle that help protect it from intruders. For example, consider the benefit of a deep, murky moat and a drawbridge! If you were going to build a castle, what would you add to deter invaders? Would you add piranhas to your moat? How about jagged rocks around the edges? Just for fun, draw or construct a castle that includes your ideas. File it under "Europe: Spain" in your Student Notebook.

As shown here, a strong castle should at least have a lookout tower to help detect the approach of an enemy.

54B—Older Students

1. Research the modern city of Santiago de Compostela as a tourist. What would you find there? Find the name of one hotel, a few restaurants, one shopping district, and one tour. Most of this information is easily obtained on the Internet. Create a two-day itinerary for your family. Type it up and file it in your Student Notebook under "Europe: Spain." Discuss with your teacher the obstacles a pilgrim would face when traveling in the Middle Ages!

2. Obtain and read a copy of *The Poem of the Cid*. I recommend *The Poem of the Cid: A Bilingual Edition with Parallel Text* (A Penguin Classic), edited by Ian Michael and Rita Hamilton. It received a 4½-star rating on Internet reviews.

3. For opera enthusiasts, research the opera *El Cid* by Jules Massenet on the Internet. The opera is available from CBS Records Masterworks (Austria, 1989). Though the opera was not popular for decades, it was recently revived by world-famous opera singer Placido Domingo, a Spaniard no less. Domingo's performance debuted in 1999.

4. View the 1961 film *El Cid* starring Charlton Heston.

TAKE ANOTHER LOOK!

REVIEW 18: LESSONS 52–54

Wall of Fame

1. *LEIF ERICSSON DISCOVERS AMERICA (c. 1003)*—Sketch a tiny map of Greenland and North America. Draw a dotted line from one to the other with the caption, "Leif Sails to North America." **Remember, this is a date to memorize.** [From *History Through the Ages*, use *Leif Eriksson*.]

2. *Macbeth, King of Scotland (1040)*—Sketch a crown with Macbeth's name on it. [Use *Macbeth*.]

3. *El Cid, a Spanish Hero (1040)*—Sketch a two-headed man. From the mouth of one, draw a cartoon "bubble" that says, "I am El Cameador." From the mouth of the other, "I am El Cid." [Use *El Cid*.]

SomeWHERE in Time

This is a multistep mapping activity to become more familiar with Canada, the northernmost country of North America. Complete as is suitable for each student. All will use the same map. (Younger students may be capable of performing steps 5 and 6 after some assistance with steps 1 through 4.)

Background Information: Canada is the second largest country in the world. It covers about two-fifths of North America and is a little larger than the United States. However, not nearly as many people live there. Canada is made up of 10 provinces and three territories. Nunavut, one of the three territories, was only recently created for the Inuit people (1993). It includes Baffin Island, the fifth largest island in the world and one of the stops of Leif Ericsson in his exploration of North America.

Materials: Outline Map 22, "Canada"; modern globe or atlas; colored pencils; black and red markers

1. Using a globe or an atlas, find and label the 10 provinces of Canada. Color each province as indicated. From west to east, they are:
   - *British Columbia* – yellow
   - *Alberta* – orange
   - *Saskatchewan* – red
   - *Manitoba* – brown
   - *Ontario* – light blue
   - *Quebec* – light green
   - *New Brunswick* – dark blue
   - *Prince Edward Island* – dark green
   - *Nova Scotia* – purple
   - *Newfoundland* – pink   (Newfoundland has two parts. One part is on the mainland; the other part is an island. Label the northern coast of the mainland *Labrador*. It is an important region in the travels of Leif Ericsson.)

2. Find and label the three territories of Canada. Color each territory as indicated. From west to east, they are:
   - *Yukon Territory* – silver (or gray)
   - *Northwest Territories* – gold   (Label *Banks Island*.)
   - *Nunavut* – turquoise   (Label *Ellesmere Island, Queen Elizabeth Islands, Victoria Island, Baffin Island,* and *South Hampton Island*—all are regions of Nunavut.)

3. Find and label *Greenland*. Color it white.

4. Now that you have labeled and colored the significant provinces and territories of Canada, we will trace the travels of Leif Ericsson. Use a black marker to put a small star on the southern coast of Greenland. Write "#1" on the coast of Baffin Island. Write "#2" on the coast of Labrador (the northern coast of mainland Newfoundland). Write "#3" on the large island of Newfoundland. Put a "?" on Nova Scotia to indicate that Leif Ericsson possibly traveled that far south.

5. Go back to the star in Greenland. Use a red marker to "connect the dots" and draw a dotted line from Greenland to Baffin Island, to Labrador, to Newfoundland, to Nova Scotia.

6. Middle and Older Students: Using information from the lesson, create a key on the side of your map giving the names that Leif Ericsson gave to the lands he found.

7. Older Students: Find and label the capital cities of each province and territory of Canada. In alphabetical order, the city names are given below. You find where they belong! (Answers are provided at the end of this Review.)

Charlottetown Edmonton Fredericton Halifax Iqaluit Quebec Regina
St. John's Toronto Victoria Whitehorse Winnipeg Yellowknife

8. Older Students: Find and label these bodies of water:

Arctic Ocean Baffin Bay Hudson Bay James Bay Hudson Strait
Ungava Bay Davis Strait Labrador Sea Atlantic Ocean

9. All Students: File your map in your Student Notebook under "North America: Canada."

Answers to capital cities:

Charlottetown – Prince Edward Island
Edmonton – Alberta
Fredericton – New Brunswick
Halifax – Nova Scotia
Iqaluit – Nunavut
Quebec – Quebec
Regina – Saskatchewan

St. John's – Newfoundland
Toronto – Ontario
Victoria – British Columbia
Whitehorse – Yukon Territory
Winnipeg - Manitoba
Yellowknife – Northwest Territories

WHAT DID YOU LEARN?

WEEK 18: QUIZ

I. Multiple Choice. Circle the correct answer for each question.

1. As a result of the First Jewish Revolt, many Jews fled to the fortress of _____ to try to escape the Romans.

   a. Pompeii

   b. Masada

   c. the Colosseum

   d. the Temple

2. Though ruins of the Maya were hidden for centuries, the Mayan people once dominated the rain forests of

   a. Zimbabwe.

   b. New Zealand.

   c. Mexico and Central America.

   d. Baffin Island.

3. St. _____ of Hippo, who was gifted in the art of rhetoric, wrote several Christian classics, including *Confessions, On the Trinity,* and *The City of God.*

   a. Augustine

   b. Jerome

   c. Patrick

   d. Valentine

4. Reasons for the fall of the Western Roman Empire would include

   a. the eruption of Mt. Vesuvius.

   b. the Second Jewish Revolt.

   c. invasions of the Angles, Jutes, Saxons, and Vandals.

   d. the disappearance of the Mayas.

5. Though born in Ireland, _____ became a missionary to Scotland, pledging to lead at least 3,000 souls to Christ.

   a. Patrick

   b. Augustine

   c. Methodius

   d. Columba

II. Who Did It?
Match the people on the left with the events on the right by placing the correct letter next to the number.

_____6. Prince Shotoku   a. Won the Battle of Tours

_____7. Li Shi Min   b. Stopped the Danes in England

_____8. Abu Bekr   c. Proclaimed himself caliph after Mohammed died

_____9. Charles Martel   d. Wrote a constitution for Japan and spread Buddhism

_____10. Alfred the Great   e. Helped China prosper under the Tang dynasty

III. True or False.
Circle the correct answer.

11. Iceland, the "land of fire and ice," is the largest of the Polynesian islands.   T   F

12. One of the amazing features of the settlements in Zimbabwe is that the
houses of stone were built without mortar.   T   F

13. Though crowned by the pope as a Roman emperor, Otto I was German.   T   F

14. During the Song dynasty, farmers were considered the lowest rank
of society.   T   F

15. Eric the Red, a settler of Greenland, was nicknamed for his red hair—a
name that also fit his hot temper.   T   F

16. After discovering North America, Leif Ericsson lived there for 32 years.   T   F

17. Malcolm III revenged his father's death and killed Macbeth to eventually
take the throne of Scotland.   T   F

18. El Cid, whose real name was Rodrigo Diaz, has been remembered as a
hero for taking Valencia in the *Reconquista* of Spain.   T   F

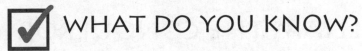

WHAT DO YOU KNOW?

PRETEST 19

Match Me! Connect the words on the left to the definitions on the right. (Using different-colored pencils may make it more fun to work and easier to grade.)

1. William the Conqueror

a. Latin word for "cross"

2. Queen Matilda

b. Holy Roman Emperor who begged forgiveness in the snow

3. Pope Gregory VII

c. City in the Holy Roman Empire

4. Worms

d. Arabs from Turkistan

5. Henry IV

e. Incompetent leaders of the earliest crusade

6. Seljuk Turks

f. Embroidered the Bayeux Tapestry

7. *Crux*

g. Excommunicated Henry IV

8. Peter the Hermit / Walter the Penniless

h. Conquered England at the Battle of Hastings

WILLIAM THE CONQUEROR AND THE BATTLE OF HASTINGS

LESSON 55

When we last looked at England, we learned about **Alfred the Great** (Lesson 42). He was the Saxon king responsible for pushing the Danish Vikings into the Danelaw. He also did much for establishing the nation of England with common laws and literature. He was a "great" king as his name states.

Let's see now if you can remember the history of England from that lesson. It went something like this: Some ancient people built _____(Stonehenge), then the _____(Celts) settled there, then the Romans invaded under _____(Julius Caesar), then the Angles, the _____(Saxons), and the Jutes moved in. King _____(Arthur), a Celtic king, tried to stop them. Christianity was brought by _____(St. Augustine) and others, then the Danish _____(Vikings) attacked but were stopped by Alfred the Great. (You older students should try this paragraph again until you can fill in the blanks!)

Notice the enormous size of Stonehenge in comparison to the tourists in the photo. (That's my mom on the left!)

Well, today we are going to add a large missing link to this chain of historic events. That would be the invasion of the **Normans** under **William the Conqueror.** It's sometimes called the **Norman Conquest** for short. Let's review first who the Normans were and then consider William. As his nickname implies, he was a true "conqueror."

William—the Duke of Normandy

Before he was known as William the Conqueror, William was the duke of Normandy in France. He was descended from the Vikings of Normandy.

Technically speaking, the Normans were descendants of the **Danish Vikings.** How is that? Well, at one time the Danish Vikings invaded France and settled the province of **Normandy.** They have been called *Normans* ever since. The Normans were sort of "given" the coastal region of Normandy as a gift for leaving the rest of France alone! Over the years, the Normans adopted Christianity and developed a taste for more civilized living. The Normans weren't nearly as barbaric as their raiding Viking ancestors were!

This leads us to William, the main character of our lesson. He was the **duke of Normandy** in France. Though Viking by blood, he was a true Norman—civilized and sophisticated. He received the position of duke when he was just 8 years old but he had to hide for a few years to protect himself from others who wanted his title. By the time he was a teenager, he came out of hiding and became a strong soldier fully capable of defending his title as duke.

William was also a cousin of and a good friend to the king of England, whose name was **Edward the Confessor.** (Edward grew up in Normandy. That's how the two came to be so close.) Edward was nicknamed the Confessor for being a religious man. He is most remembered for building the famous **Westminster Abbey.** Now, the kinship between Edward the Confessor and William is very important in this story. For according to William, Edward once promised him that he could be the next king of England—since Edward had no sons of his own. That was certainly a nice gesture and all. But do you think the people of England wanted a Norman as their king? The answer is no.

William the Conqueror and most of his successors were crowned in the famous Westminster Abbey.

The English had someone else in mind. Edward's right-hand man had a strong and capable son named **Harold of Wessex.** Most of the nobility thought that Harold should rightfully be the next king of England. Harold of Wessex claimed too that Edward, when on his deathbed, granted *him* the right to be the next king. So when Edward died in 1066, Harold declared himself the king of England!

But things got more complicated. It seems that shortly after Harold of Wessex claimed the throne of England, *another* Harold decided to invade England to become the king! This Harold was **Harold Hadrada**, the **king of Norway.** He attacked England in the North.

Three Claim the Throne of England

Let's stop and put this confusion all together. First—William (a Norman in France) was supposedly "promised" the throne of England by Edward the Confessor when they were young. Second—Harold of Wessex (a powerful Anglo-Saxon) claimed the throne for himself out of his popularity with the English. And now, third—the king of Norway (another Harold, but with the last name Hadrada) wanted the throne, too! I think you can see the problem here. Three capable men were trying to be the king of England at the same time. Somebody had to go!

The breakdown started first with Harold of Wessex. He moved north to fight off the king of Norway. He did so successfully at **York.** That helped to eliminate one of the three rivals. But while Harold of Wessex was up north, William invaded England in the south! It was a clever military move. Harold and his troops were exhausted from their battle against Harold Hadrada, the king of Norway. When they returned to face William, they had a tough assignment. They met for just one day, October 14, **1066**, at the **Battle of Hastings.** This is what happened . . . (You might want to pay attention since this battle is considered one of the 15 most pivotal of all time!)

The Battle of Hastings

At the onset of the Battle of Hastings, Harold and his troops held their own ground. They were positioned on the top of a hill near the town of Hastings. The Norman troops wearied themselves and their horses trying to scale the hill. They appeared to give up the fight and retreat in disorder. But it was only a trick! When the Normans backed down, the English naturally ran down the hill to pursue them. When they did this, the Normans surrounded them and split the English troops in half. Harold was struck and killed by a Norman arrow to his eye. After that, it was an easy victory for the Normans, and for William.

So that is how William "conquered" Harold and his English army. On Christmas Day in 1066, William was crowned the king of England. His official title became **William the First,** but he is best remembered as William *the Conqueror.* To commemorate the victorious event, William's wife—**Queen Matilda**—embroidered a spectacular tapestry that was 230 feet long and 20 inches wide! (That is very long and must have taken years to complete.) It was named the **Bayeux Tapestry** since it was made for the cathedral of the bishop of Bayeux in France. It hangs there still today.

Despite how much the English disapproved of a Norman ruling over them, William the Conqueror proved to be a very capable king. He was not a particularly nice king, but he knew how to use his authority and create stability. To keep the English from rising up against him and creating more chaos, he started the **feudal system** in England. It lasted for centuries.

The Bayeux Tapestry, embroidered by Queen Matilda, is 230 feet long! With amazing detail it depicts the Battle of Hastings.

The Feudal System

Because the feudal system became such an important way of life in Europe, it would be worth our time to better understand what it was. The feudal system was a plan that governed the way people lived. It started in Europe in the 800s. This is how it operated: A king would declare himself the owner of all the land in a region. As people would work for him, or serve him as knights, he would give them land instead of money. Since most people wanted land, it motivated them to be loyal to the king. New landowners would then turn around and loan out their lands in smaller portions to those who would work for them.

In a way, the feudal system kept almost everyone employed. People lived near the large estates and castles and were practically self-sufficient. They grew or made what they needed for the community, so little outside trading was done. Unfortunately, this also kept almost everyone poor except those at the top.

In rank order, the king was the owner of all the land. He gave large chunks of it to landowners called **barons.** The barons gave smaller portions of their land—each called a fief (feef)—to **knights,** who in turn gave smaller portions to the **villeins,** or peasants. Villeins made up the largest and the poorest group in the population.

Besides using the feudal system to maintain control over England, William the Conqueror appointed Frenchmen to replace some of the Englishmen in his court. This didn't go over very well with the English. But then, neither did the census that was taken of them in 1085. It seems that to collect more taxes, William authorized a long and detailed census to be taken of every man, woman, and child in England as well as every chicken, sheep, and pig! The thick book containing the census was later nicknamed the **Domesday Book.** Some believe it received this name for resembling in detail the Last Judgment as described in the Bible, which is often called "Doomsday." Others have simply said that the census was responsible for "dooming" everyone to pay more taxes and settle land disputes! Either way you look at it, the Domesday Book was very unpopular with the English.

Despite William's firm rule over England, he brought some good, too. Numerous castles were built under William, as were large monasteries, convents, and **cathedrals.** In fact, the famous **Tower of London** was begun just a year after William became king. These buildings are beautiful landmarks now, but in their time they served as places of protection, centers of learning, and prisons. Towns naturally grew up around them. William also encouraged the development of large forests for the sake of hunting, but he then got too serious about the sport—if someone was caught trespassing in a royal forest, his or her penalty was to lose an eye! (You will hear more about that when we study Robin Hood.)

Though William kept strict control over his kingdom, he struggled with issues of control over his family. Apparently, William argued a lot with Queen Matilda. And he quarreled with his son over ruling Normandy. He appeared to struggle with controlling his eating habits, too. Toward the end of his life, he was almost too stout to mount his own horse! It's been told that even his coffin was made too small for his large body, causing a real problem at his funeral.

As for the English people, they survived the strict Norman rule. After the Normans, there was never again a significant invasion. The customs of the Normans, and even their French language, were eventually absorbed into the Anglo-Saxon culture. The Old English of the Anglo-Saxons blended with French to make what linguists would call **Middle English.**

To their credit, the English seemed to have kept the best of the best of their heritage. Some would say they were ingenious like the builders of Stonehenge, crafty like the Celts, organized like the Romans, proud like the Anglo-Saxons, daring like the Danish Vikings, and determined like the Normans. Not a bad mix of strengths for any nation!

ACTIVITIES FOR LESSON 55

ALL STUDENTS

Memorize the date of the Battle of Hastings (1066).

55A—Younger and Middle Students

1. To better understand the feudal system, I want you to try this exercise for a day. First, consider that your mayor or governor is like a king who owns all the land in your city or town. Then consider that your teacher or parent is the major landowner, or *baron*, of the place where you live or go to school. In order for you to "own" a piece, or *fief*, of this land (your bedroom, for example), you must agree on a particular ongoing chore. You then become a *knight* and own that part of your house or school as long as that chore is getting done!

   Now, you might want to sell a small piece of your fief, or property, to a younger family member or neighbor. Consider what that person can do for you to make it worth selling (put away your dirty clothes, clean off your desk, etc.). Find a *villein*, or peasant, willing to work out this arrangement with you and then that villein, too, becomes a knight and owns a small piece of land.

   To help keep the names straight, wear nametags indicating baron, knight, and villein.

2. Re-enact the Battle of Hastings using the description from the lesson. Use army men, horses, and a hill.

3. Read the beautifully illustrated book *Cathedral: The Story of Its Construction*, by David Macaulay.

55B—Middle and Older Students

1. Like Queen Matilda, practice embroidery. If you are a beginner, consider a simple kit from a craft store.

2. Step in the shoes of a soldier with creative writing.

   Materials: Notebook paper, three to four teabags, small pot, matches, shoes, a concrete outdoor area, and clear-plastic notebook sleeve

   Write a diary page of a soldier who survived the Battle of Hastings. Describe the scene, the Normans' trick maneuver, and the outcome. Include the date. You can decide if you're Anglo-Saxon or Norman. When you've completed the page, follow the directions below to make the page appear aged. File it in your Student Notebook under "Europe: England."

   Adult Supervision Needed

   a. Take about four tea bags. Boil them in a small pan of water. Remove from heat and let steep, or sit, for at least 20 minutes.

   b. Now, crumple your diary page slightly and, using tongs, dip the whole thing into the tea solution. Let it drip-dry overnight. It should look aged.

c. To make it look older, burn the edges slightly after the paper has dried. I suggest you do this outside over a sidewalk or driveway with shoes on. You may need to stomp the paper to stop the burning! Be careful—and do this only with adult supervision please!

d. To preserve the page, keep it in a clear plastic sleeve that can go into your Student Notebook.

55C—Older Students

1. Research the location of the Domesday Book today. It is considered one of the most valuable documents in English history.

2. Research the famous Westminster Abbey, started under Edward the Confessor. Where is it? From where does it derive its name? Print pictures of Westminster Abbey from the Internet or photocopy them from a resource book. File them in your Student Notebook under "Europe: England."

3. Research the Tower of London. What famous people were imprisoned there? Print a photo and create a list of some of its unfortunate inhabitants. File this under "Europe: England" in your Student Notebook.

4. If you want more information on William the Conqueror and his many exploits, check out the Web site listed below. There is far more information on him than I could include in this lesson. Consider these two points of interest in his life: (1) His arrangement with Harold of Wessex after a shipwreck (Harold promised William he would support him as king but obviously changed his mind!), and (2) William's confessions at his death, and his decision to give his wealth to the poor and the church.

http://www.spartacus.schoolnet.co.uk/MEDwilliam1.htm

POPE GREGORY VII, HENRY IV, AND THE INVESTITURE CONTROVERSY
LESSON 56

Since the beginning of time, man has struggled with **authority.** Think back with me to the Garden of Eden. Who struggled with authority there? It was Adam and Eve, of course. By choosing to disobey God's command about the forbidden fruit, Adam and Eve were questioning the authority of God. "Who's in control here?" they seemed to ask. "Who knows what's best for us?"

Over the ages, men have continued to struggle with authority, not only with God but also with one another! We will see that very clearly in today's lesson. The issue of authority became a huge problem between the popes of the Middle Ages and the Holy Roman emperors. It was an especially big problem between **Pope Gregory VII** and **Henry IV.** Let me start by introducing the pope, then the emperor, and then their terrible conflict. It was called the **Investiture Controversy.** I'll explain those big words when we get to them.

Pope Gregory VII

Gregory VII's name before becoming a pope was **Hildebrand.** Hildebrand was rather short, a bit overweight, pasty in complexion, and stuttered. Though not impressive in stature and speech, Hildebrand possessed good people skills. As a **Benedictine monk,** he was well liked and very well respected. Hildebrand served as advisor to five popes before him.

Upon becoming pope, Hildebrand changed his name to Gregory VII. He named himself after **Gregory the Great,** a fine man whom we already studied (Lesson 27). If you remember, that's what the popes do even now. They name themselves after another pope they admire. (That's why so many of their names are the same!)

Pope Gregory VII had great ambitions. He saw many problems in the church and the government. He hoped to change them. I think he was sincere in his efforts to do so.

But even the most sincere efforts can backfire. It seems that the changes Gregory made created *other* problems. First, in an effort to purify the priesthood, Pope Gregory VII insisted that every priest in the church be unmarried. He believed that the priests could be more loyal to the church without wives and children to be responsible for. Though Gregory's intentions were good ones, it created terrible problems for the priests who at that time were *already* married. In order to comply with the wishes of the pope, the priests had to either give up their wives or give up the priesthood! It caused problems for years.

But worse than that was the problem of the government interfering with church business. You see, in most cases the Holy Roman Emperor or members of his staff were choosing the men who would serve in important church positions. Gregory saw this as a problem that he needed to solve. He firmly believed that members of the church, not the government, should select men to positions in the church. Gregory probably had the best of intentions in correcting this situation. But in doing so, he stirred up more trouble than he ever dreamed.

Henry IV

That leads us to Henry IV. He was part of the trouble! But before I fully introduce him, let me stop and explain who the **"Henry's"** were in the Middle Ages. There were so many of them that it can be confusing.

First of all, Henry was the name given to eight different kings of **England.** The first Henry happened to be the son of **William the Conqueror.** The last Henry of England was the infamous **Henry VIII.** There have been songs and nursery rhymes written about him.

In **France** there were four kings named Henry. None were so famous that I'll mention them here. But in **Germany,** there were seven kings named Henry. All but the first were considered Holy Roman emperors. It is Henry IV of Germany, one of the Holy Roman emperors, who is the focus of our lesson today. Now I'll explain who he was.

Henry IV became emperor when he was just 6 years old. His mother served as regent in his place until he was old enough to be a true emperor. By the time Henry was 19, his authority was well established in Germany. That is, except with the pope!

It seems that for years the kings of Germany, or the Holy Roman emperors, were choosing who would serve in the church. They saw this arrangement as part of the feudal system. We learned how the feudal system worked in the last lesson. The kings, as major landowners, thought they had authority over *everyone* who owned land under them—including members of the church! Because of this, the kings thought they should have the right to choose who would serve in high church positions. It became a ceremonial tradition for kings to **"invest"** these church leaders with a **sacred staff and ring** as symbols of power. So, the term **_investiture_** came to refer to the power of *kings* to appoint church leaders. Read that last sentence again and remember it!

The Investiture Controversy

Now, before I explain details of the Investiture Controversy (as the problem of investitures was called), let's back up in history a bit. I want to review something important that we already studied. Do you remember learning about **Charlemagne** (Lesson 37)? In that lesson we learned that **Pepin the**

Short, Charlemagne's father, did something that perhaps started this whole conflict between popes and emperors. Pepin asked the *pope* to help him become king. In doing so, you could say that he "transferred" power to the pope that the pope had *never* had before. It was not long after that, one of the popes actually placed a crown on Charlemagne's head and named him the Holy Roman Emperor! This was a clear time in history when a church leader *acted* with authority over an emperor. (Not that that is necessarily bad—it just led to later confusion.) I suggest you reread this paragraph and make sure you understand it.

To add to the confusion of authority, popes in the Middle Ages wore crowns very similar to those of a king.

My point in reviewing that lesson is this: For centuries after the crowning of Charlemagne, the lines of authority between the church and the state were fuzzy. (The "state" by the way just means the government.) With the pope crowning the king, it was easy to confuse who was ultimately in charge.

So back to Pope Gregory VII. Though he didn't mind the church giving guidance to the government, he did NOT like the government giving guidance to the church! He began to see the danger of ordinary and quite possibly ungodly men making spiritual decisions that influenced the church. It was far too easy for men to bribe their way into the church by performing favors for the king. I can understand Gregory's concern here. The use of investitures (reread that definition if you need to) was an unhealthy arrangement. (Many countries today, like the United States, keep the church and the state separate for this very reason.) But in an effort to defend his position, Gregory went to the extreme.

Pope Gregory VII began to teach that the church was always right about everything! He once wrote:

> "Human pride has created the power of kings; God's mercy has created the power of bishops. The Pope is the master of Emperors. He is rendered holy by the merits of his predecessor, St. Peter. The Roman Church has never erred, and Holy Scripture proves it can never err. To resist it is to resist God." [1]

With that powerful proclamation, Gregory did something that popes don't usually do. He issued a law against the king and his staff forbidding them to appoint church officials. Because he believed he could do no wrong, Gregory asserted complete authority here over the government.

This law insulted and infuriated Henry IV, the Holy Roman Emperor of the time. It made him so angry that he called a special meeting of important leaders. It was called the **Synod of Worms**. Now this meeting had nothing to do with squirmy little worms that live in the ground! *Worms* is the name of a city in Germany. (In German, it is pronounced *Vermz*.) And *synod* is a fancy name for a meeting. So the Synod of Worms was just a meeting in the city of Worms.

Now that you understand that, it was at the Synod of Worms in **1076** that Henry IV did something extreme himself. He and the other leaders ***deposed*** Pope Gregory VII. That means they fired him from his job! Or at least they tried. Henry composed a nasty letter to Gregory that started like this:

> "Henry . . . to Hildebrand, not pope, but false monk . . . you have never held any office of the church without making a source of confusion and a curse to Christian men instead of an honor and a blessing." [2]

1. T. Walter Wallbank and Alastair M. Taylor, *Civilization Past and Present*. Chicago: Scott, Foresman and Company, 1949; p. 382.
2. James A. Corrick, *World History Series: The Late Middle Ages*. San Diego: Lucent Books, 1995; p. 58.

You may notice that Henry started the letter by addressing the pope by his birth name of Hildebrand rather than his chosen name as pope. That in itself was a put-down. But worse that that, Henry ends his letter with strong words like these:

"You have attacked me, who . . . have . . . been anointed to rule among the anointed of God . . . Let another ascend the throne of St. Peter, one who will not use religion as a cloak of violence." [3]

After sending this letter, a rather ironic thing happened. In response to being "deposed," Gregory VII ***excommunicated*** Henry IV from the church and fired *him* from being the king! (To be excommunicated is to be released from membership in the church and denied all rights in the church.)

Now let's break this situation down into simple terms. It seems the king fired the pope, so the pope fired the king! How absurd is that? It became a battle of authority and a time of much confusion. It was never more unclear who was really in charge of the empire!

I wish I could say that the matter was easily solved. But it wasn't. For decades there was conflict between the popes and the Holy Roman emperors over control. But an interesting thing happened between Henry and Gregory. Henry began to lose popularity with the public after Pope Gregory excommunicated him. Excommunication is a serious matter. As stated earlier, it is an act of being completely cut off from the church. Now I'm not sure if Henry was upset over being excommunicated, or if he was upset because it threatened his throne. Regardless, Henry went begging to

Neither Henry nor Gregory respected the position of the other, and the struggle for power raged on between the Holy Roman Emperor and the pope.

the pope for forgiveness. And I really mean begging. This is the most interesting part of the story.

Henry's Penance at Canossa

In plain clothes and bare feet, Henry stood in the snow for three days, knocking on the door of a castle and begging forgiveness from the pope.

With his wife and children, Henry tried to meet up with Gregory at a castle in **Canossa** (kah NOHS ah), Italy. It was in the mountains. Though it was winter, Henry was barefoot and dressed in plain peasant clothes. He knocked at the castle doors to beg forgiveness (or penance) from the pope. Do you think the pope was quick to let him in? Not at all. For three straight days Gregory left Henry outside, barefoot in the snow, knocking on the door and pleading for forgiveness! Finally, Gregory let him in. Henry bowed down and kissed Gregory's toe; then Gregory pardoned and forgave Henry for deposing him.

Though this may sound like the end, it isn't. After receiving forgiveness, Henry IV had the nerve to stir up trouble again. You see, back in Germany the people selected another man to be their king. His name was **Rudolf.** For years, Henry IV and Rudolf fought over who was the rightful king of the Holy Roman Empire. Pope Gregory VII naturally supported Rudolf. This infuriated Henry so much that he called together another important meeting to try to depose Gregory! Again!

In the midst of the war between Rudolf and Henry, Rudolf was killed. When this happened, Henry thought it was his opportunity to declare war against Rome itself! (Rome, of course, was where Pope Gregory lived.) In

---

3. Ibid.

great fury, he headed south and attacked the city. Pope Gregory summoned his friend William the Conqueror for help. But William didn't come. So, in fear for his life, Gregory fled into exile!

For about a year, Henry got the glory he wanted. He placed another man in the position of pope who was willing to re-crown Henry as the Holy Roman Emperor. For a time, Henry was the true master of Rome and the Holy Roman Empire.

Gregory, however, died while in exile in 1085. At just 62, he was said to die from strain and bad nerves—mostly due to Henry. Pope Gregory VII said of himself, "I have loved righteousness and hated iniquity, therefore I die in exile."[4]

As for Henry, his end came when his own son rose up in rebellion against him. While preparing for battle, Henry IV died in 1106 at age 56. Because the church had previously excommunicated Henry, he was not entitled to a proper church burial. But eventually, his remains were "released" from the sentence of excommunication and laid to rest at Speyer Cathedral in Germany.

Strong and stubborn to the end, both Henry and Gregory died somewhat defeated. Neither saw in their lifetime any true resolve to their problems. They never reconciled their differences with one another. Later popes and emperors did the same kind of quarreling over the issue of authority. But few were as interesting as these two powerful men were.

ACTIVITIES FOR LESSON 56

ALL STUDENTS

To demonstrate a power struggle, like that between Gregory VII and Henry IV, play the game "tug-of-war."

Materials: Yardstick; jump rope or long cord; clothespin; at least two people

Lay a yardstick on the ground or floor. Fold the jump rope or cord in half to find the center point of it. Mark the center point with a clothespin. Lay the jump rope on the ground with the center point on the yardstick. Have one person or a team of people at one end of the jump rope and the other person or team at the opposite end. On the count of three, each team or person should pick up the rope and TUG. After one minute, whoever has the center point on their side of the yardstick wins. If your teams are somewhat equal in strength, you will probably experience a real struggle between the two. Consider the years of struggle for power that existed between Gregory and Henry. As in tug-of-war, it can be exhausting!

56B—Middle and Older Students

Henry IV went to extreme measures to ask the pope for forgiveness. Despite his pleading, it may or may not have been sincere. Do a word study on forgiveness. Use a Bible concordance to find several passages on the subject. What does the Bible say about forgiveness? Write your answers down and file them in your Student Notebook under "Europe: Germany."

56C—Middle and Older Students

Discuss and/or diagram lines of authority in your family, your community, or your nation. Is it always clear who is in charge? For example, when a disastrous tornado strikes a small town, who is in charge of the cleanup? Is it the mayor, the police, the fire department, the Red Cross, or the insurance companies? All these agencies might be involved, but without proper organization, progress might be slowed down or halted. Consider the confusion created by unclear lines of authority in other situations. Consider the stress created in the Holy Roman Empire during the Middle Ages over the issue of who was in charge.

---

4. Will Durant, *The Age of Faith*. Vol. IV of *The Story of Civilization*. New York: Simon and Schuster, 1950; p. 551.

THE EARLY CRUSADES
LESSON 57

Brace yourself. Learning about the **Crusades** of the Middle Ages is difficult. Difficult because the Crusades involved so much bloodshed. And bloodshed is never pretty! Though there were eight Crusades in the Middle Ages, we will look at just a few of them. Today I will attempt to explain the start of the Crusades and the results of the First and Second Crusades. We will learn of the other Crusades in later lessons, as each has its own complicated story.

So that you will understand the Crusades, I first need to explain what was going on in the **Holy Land.** The "Holy Land," by the way, is an expression used to describe **Israel,** the place where **Jesus** lived. As a quick review, **Palestine** (which formerly was called Israel) was under the leadership of the **Jews** and the **Romans** at the time of Christ. But 70 years after Christ, the Romans completely conquered Palestine and destroyed the Temple in Jerusalem. In A.D. 135, **Bar-Kokhba** led a revolt against the Romans, leading many to believe he was the Messiah. (I hope you remember this fascinating character from Lesson 10.) For a short time there was hope that the Jews could win back Palestine. But Bar-Kokhba died in battle, as did the hope of the Jews. The Romans, and later the **Byzantine Empire**, ruled over Palestine for the next 500 years.

Now I'm sure you remember learning about **Mohammed.** He started **Islam** in the 600s. His followers were the **Muslims,** and they created the **Arab Empire.** It was a government as well as a religion. As the Muslims grew in number, they conquered countries all around them, *including* Palestine. The Arab Empire ruled over Palestine for about 400 years.

Had the Muslims remained as they were in Palestine, there might not have been any Crusades. But in 1071 a powerful *new* group of Muslims invaded Palestine. These were the **Seljuk Turks**—ruthless warriors from **Turkistan.**

The Seljuk Turks were a problem not only to the Muslims in Palestine but to the Christians as well. You see, the first Muslims who conquered Palestine were tolerant of Christians who visited the Holy Land. That means they allowed thousands of Christian **pilgrims** to travel year after year to the special places where Jesus lived, died, and rose from the dead. You can imagine the inspiration of a trip like that. The city of Jerusalem was especially meaningful for Jews and Christians alike to visit. But when the Seljuk Turks moved in, Jews and Christians were no longer welcome there. In fact, Christians were greatly **persecuted** under the Turks. Countless numbers of Christians were tortured and killed. It is important to remember that to understand the passion of the crusaders.

Pope Urban II

It was in this hostile setting that the Crusades really began. It started with a **Byzantine emperor** who feared the nearby Seljuk Turks. They were constantly attacking **Constantinople,** the capital of the Byzantine Empire. In desperation, the emperor sent a letter to **Pope Urban II** in **Rome.** In it he described the atrocities and cruelties going on in Palestine as well as his fear of the Turks taking over the Byzantine Empire. The emperor asked the pope for help!

Now, the pope of the West and the Byzantine emperor were not good friends. So it was a big deal that one was asking the other for help. Years before, there had been a great break between the church in the East and the church in the West. But on this occasion, the two found common ground to bring them together. They both wanted to free the Holy Land from the tyranny of the Turks.

To recruit soldiers and assist the Byzantine Empire, Pope Urban II began to preach to the masses in the West about the trouble in Palestine. He pleaded with peasants and nobles alike to take action. He even went so far as to suggest that anyone who would fight for the cause of reclaiming the Holy Land would be forgiven of his or her sins and "be assured of the reward of imperishable glory in the Kingdom of Heaven."[5]   Of course, the Bible doesn't teach that we can do anything to earn more of God's love and forgiveness. (Eph. 2:8–10; Rom. 3:23–25) So the message of Pope Urban II was terribly misleading. Nonetheless, it worked. With great enthusiasm, the crowds chanted over and again, "*Dieu li volt!*"—which is French for "God wills it."

This replica of a crusader's helmet bears the image of a cross and has a small opening for the eyes to see through.

Thousands of people joined the cause to reclaim the Holy Land. It became known as the Crusades from the Latin word ***crux,*** meaning "cross." The new recruits adorned themselves with cloth crosses on their shirts. On the way to Palestine, they wore them on the front of their clothes. On the way home, they wore them on their backs. Young, old, poor, rich, the healthy, and the lame—all walks of life seemed to join in as soldiers for Christ. I imagine many went with devout hearts for God. But some people may have joined for the sheer adventure of it all. Others thought it an opportunity to make money or gain land.

Regardless of all the reasons why, the earliest Crusade, in **1096,** started a campaign against the Muslims that lasted about 200 years. It was horrible for both sides. The first group of crusaders were poorly organized under the leadership of **Peter the Hermit** and **Walter the Penniless.** It's been recorded that Peter was a mere barefoot French monk. Walter the Penniless was, I suppose, a man without much money. The names of these men are indicative of their

Peter the Hermit, a barefoot monk from France, was totally unprepared for the 15,000 crusaders who attempted to follow him to the Holy Land. Many perished as a result.

abilities. Without any plan for a way to feed 15,000 crusaders, many people died of pure starvation on the long journey to Palestine. Most were poor peasants to begin with, lacking skills and equipment for such a trip. It was a disaster. These marching peasants were so hungry that they ravaged and plundered innocent villages along the way! Before this group of make-shift soldiers ever made it to Palestine, most were slaughtered by the Turks. Their bodies were purposefully left to rot in the sun as a warning to others.

The First Crusade

The next band of Crusaders were far more prepared for their trip to Palestine. In 1099 they were led by nobles and knights trained in combat and warfare. This was considered the official **First Crusade.** Of all the Crusades, it was probably the most successful. With an army of 50,000 men, the nobles and knights conquered many Muslim lands along the way. And eventually they took Jerusalem—the ultimate prize.

But the victory wasn't without horrific actions. Like wild men on a killing spree, the Crusaders took on a mad vengeance against the Turks in Jerusalem. They killed men, women, and even innocent children. They killed some without regard as to whether or not they were even the enemy! This included the

---

5. Ibid., p. 587.

massacre of many innocent Jews. Blood in the streets was said to be so deep that it touched the reins of the horses! The massacre was brutal.

The crusaders divided the conquered land into four regions. Each was assigned a king—men who had been nobles back home. These four Christian kingdoms ruled in Palestine for nearly a hundred years. But it wasn't always easy. By 1144, Jerusalem was in trouble again and summoned help from the West.

The Second Crusade

Help didn't come this time from the preaching of the pope. Instead it came from the preaching of an inspirational monk named **Bernard of Clairvaux.** Much like Pope Urban II, Bernard challenged the masses to take action and fight to keep the Holy Land. This started what historians call the **Second Crusade.**

Both the **king of France (Louis VII)** and the **Holy Roman Emperor (Conrad III)** responded to Bernard's message. With a great sense of moral duty and mission, the two men led thousands more to march hundreds of miles to Palestine to help the cause. However, this Crusade ended almost as bitterly as did the one led by Peter the Hermit and Walter the Penniless. Though kings and emperors are more powerful than peasants, they are not unbeatable. And though Louis VII was a devout man, he wasn't much of a soldier. Before these crusaders ever reached Damascus, they were stopped by the Muslims. Great numbers died.

The official First Crusade was made up of knights and nobles. Through their efforts, Christians gained control of the Holy Land for about 45 years.

A monk named Bernard of Clairvaux inspired the masses to take part in the Second Crusade to the Holy Land. It was not a success.

I imagine it was hard for either side to forget the atrocities they saw in these awful wars. The Turks persecuted the Christians, the crusaders slaughtered the Muslims, the Muslims killed the crusaders, and the cycle went on. In a few more lessons, we will look at more of the Crusades. Though blood-filled and gory, they have much to teach us. If ever we can learn what NOT to do to repeat history, let us hope it is with the Crusades.

ACTIVITIES FOR LESSON 57

ALL STUDENTS

Make your Memory Cards for Lessons 55–57. You have two key dates to memorize this week—the Battle of Hastings (1066) and the Early Crusades (1096). Highlight both cards accordingly.

57A—Younger and Middle Students

1. Make a cloth cross.

Materials: Red cloth, pencil, ruler, scissors, safety pins

In honor of the sincere crusaders who fought for the Holy Land, make a cloth cross to pin on your clothing. Use a pencil to trace the shape of a ruler on your red cloth. Turn the ruler horizontally and trace half of it to create the shape of a cross. Cut out the cross. Pin it on the front of your clothing when traveling from your home to a destination. Pin it on the back of your clothing to travel home again. Though not all the crusaders had good intentions, remember the many thousands of sincere ones who left their homes to defend the Holy Land.

2. In remembering the difficult march of the crusaders, walk a mile today with bundles of clothing, a small amount of food, and a canteen of water. If conditions allow for it, walk the mile barefoot. Imagine going hundreds and hundreds of miles on one of the Crusades.

57B—Middle Students

What sights are there to see today in the Holy Land? Interview someone who has been there. Were they inspired by visiting the places where Christ once walked, taught, or was crucified? Photocopy out of resource books or print from the Internet pictures of significant holy sites in Jerusalem. File these in your Student Notebook under "Asia: Israel."

57C—Older Students

Research the life and hymns of Bernard of Clairvaux. Bernard has been credited with writing one of *my* favorite hymns, *O Sacred Head Now Wounded*. Write the words of the first verse and file the hymn in your Student Notebook under "Europe: Rome." Title the page "Bernard of Clairvaux, Author of Hymns, Inspires the Crusades."

TAKE ANOTHER LOOK!

Wall of Fame

1. *William the Conqueror and the BATTLE OF HASTINGS (1066)*—Depict a man with both a shield and a crown. Label your figure with the title of the lesson. [From *History Through the Ages*, use *William I and Battle of Hastings*.] **Remember, the Battle of Hastings (1066) is a date to memorize.**

2. *Pope Gregory VII, Henry IV, and the Investiture Controversy (1076)*—Depict two men in a tug of war. Glue a real piece of string between them. Label your figure with the title of the lesson. [Use *Henry IV and Pope Gregory VII*.]

3. ***THE EARLY CRUSADES (1096)***—Cut out the shape of a cross on red paper. Write on the crossbar "The Early Crusades." [Use *Urban II, Peter the Hermit, Bernard of Clairvaux,* and *The Crusades*.] **Remember, the Early Crusades (1096) is a date to memorize.**

SomeWHERE in Time

1. On a globe, trace the route of the crusaders from the Holy Roman Empire to the Holy Land (approximately Germany to Israel). What are the names of the modern-day countries that they passed through? Realize that many of the Crusaders were traveling on foot. Thousands died on the journey.

2. Map the Battle of Hastings.

   Materials: Outline Map 10, "British Isles"; atlas; colored pencils; two different shades of fluorescent highlighters

   Use an atlas to find the following sites. Label them accordingly on Outline Map 10. (Younger Students: To make this a little easier, find and label only the places listed that are in all-capital letters.)

   a. Countries: ENGLAND, NORMANDY (FRANCE), Wales, Scotland, Northern Ireland, Ireland.

   b. Cities: YORK, HASTINGS, London.

   c. Bodies of water: ENGLISH CHANNEL, Strait of Dover, Bay of the Seine, North Sea, Irish Sea.

   d. Use one fluorescent highlighter to draw an arrow from York to Hastings. Label the arrow "Harold Heads South."

   e. Use another fluorescent highlighter to draw an arrow from the coast of Normandy to Hastings. Label this arrow "William Invades England."

   f. Label the entire map "William the Conqueror Takes England at the Battle of Hastings."

   g. File this map in your Student Notebook under "Europe: England."

3. Map the widespread use of the English language. Use an atlas or globe to find, label, and color the following countries on Outline Map 3, "World":

   Canada, United States, Great Britain, Ireland, Australia, New Zealand

Though the size of Great Britain is small, consider the vast number of those who speak English as their primary language. Consider how many more speak English as a second language. Label your map "The English Language." File it in your Student Notebook under "Europe: England."

Picture This! Today will be a fun review requiring at least two people. Photocopy and cut out the boxes below. Create a pile of draw cards from these slips of paper. Lie them face down. As in the "Pictionary" board game, the first participant takes a card from the pile. He or she has *one minute* to draw a picture (or several pictures if possible) of the person, place, or thing named on the card for the rest of the group to guess. No sounds, gestures, or written words can be used by the artist—only pictures! (The category of person, place, or thing should first be given orally as a clue for those who are guessing.) The person who guesses correctly before the minute is up receives one point. If no one is able to guess correctly, the artist drawing the picture loses one point. The one with the most points wins. I suggest the use of an erasable white board for a large group.

Attila the Hun (Person)	Masada (Place)
Aladdin (Person)	Dead Sea Scrolls (Thing)
Wu Zetian (Person)	Japan (Place)

"sword in the stone" (Thing)	Kaaba (Place)
Pagoda (Thing)	Vikings (Person)
Rock of Gibraltar (Place)	Evergreen tree (Thing)
Maori warrior (Person)	Great Zimbabwe (Place)

Geyser (Thing)	St. Simon (Person)
El Cid (Person)	Holy Land (Place)
Newfoundland (Place)	Igloo (Thing)

☑ WHAT DO YOU KNOW?

PRETEST 20

Jeopardy. Just as they do on the *Jeopardy* television game show, I have provided the answers. You find the right question for each answer from the bottom of the page.

1. The followers of Peter Bruis.

2. The followers of Peter Waldo.

3. The adventurous queen of France and then England.

4. A knight well versed in poetry and music.

5. The favorite son of Eleanor of Aquitaine.

6. The favorite son of Henry II.

7. A brilliant Jewish philosopher of the Middle Ages.

8. Arab term for a Jewish leader.

Who was John?

Who were the Petrobrusians?

What is a *troubadour*?

Who was Moses ben Maimon?

Who were the Waldensians?

Who was Eleanor of Aquitaine?

What is an *exilarch*?

Who was Richard the Lionhearted?

THE PETROBRUSIANS
AND THE WALDENSIANS
LESSON 58

I believe that the most amazing events of history are the life, death, and resurrection of Jesus Christ. To think that the Lord of all things, the Creator of the universe, came to earth and sacrificed Himself for our sins is profound! You could ponder that for a lifetime and still be amazed. Well, equally amazing, in my opinion, is the Word of God. The Bible is one of the most extraordinary ways by which God reveals Himself to mankind. It is so important that many men and women have died to protect it. Today's lesson is about some of those people. They were the **Petrobrusians** (pet roh BROO zuns) and the **Waldensians** (wall DEN see unz). Their names may be uncommon, but because of their great faith and courage, I think they are worth remembering.

I'll begin with the Petrobrusians. They were named for being followers of **Peter Bruis** (Bru EE). Peter Bruis was a priest who lived in southern France in the early **1100s.** We don't know a lot about the personal life of Peter Bruis, but we do know what he taught—and that was the Bible. It seems that like most priests of his time, Peter lived a devoted life for God. But unlike most priests of his time, Peter Bruis read the Bible for himself and taught others to do the same.

There are at least two legitimate reasons why it was unusual for a priest to read and teach the Bible. For one, many people, including priests, were unable to read at all in the Middle Ages. Second, Bibles were handwritten and very expensive. Few existed to be read. But sadly, even those who *could* read were at times discouraged from doing so. Why? It seems that the upper clergy of the church were concerned with the Bible being misunderstood if read by lower clergymen or commoners. They therefore felt it was *their* responsibility to read the Bible first, and then explain it to others.

But what was perhaps not understood by these upper clergymen was that the Word of God *"is living, and powerful, and sharper than any two-edged sword, piercing even to the division of soul and spirit, and of joints and marrow, and is a discerner of the thoughts and intents of the heart."* (Heb. 4:12) I believe this passage supports the value of the Word of God in the hands of all men and women—that it might shape their very lives.

Peter Bruis believed this way, too. For twenty years he read the Bible for himself and taught others to do the same. His followers were called Petrobrusians. But, unfortunately, some members of the Medieval Church misunderstood the intentions of this group. They viewed Peter and his teachings as a threat. They were afraid that reading the Bible might lead people to question the way things were done in the church. In some cases it was an issue of control.

Sadly enough, Peter died for his beliefs and his desire to teach the Word of God. He was burned at the stake for **heresy.** Heresy is big word for teaching and preaching things different from the established church and the Scriptures.

The Waldensians

The Waldensians were another group of devoted believers who were particularly interested in the Word of God. They were named after **Peter Waldo.** Peter Waldo has an interesting life story. It seems he was a rather wealthy businessman at one time, living the high life in **Lyon, France.** But upon becoming a follower of Jesus Christ, Waldo began to study and memorize the Word of God for himself. Much like Peter Bruis, Peter Waldo developed the belief that the Bible should be the sole authority of a believer's

Peter Waldo, a dedicated follower of Jesus Christ, believed strongly in the power of the Word of God.

life, not the rules and rituals of the church. He ultimately believed he could depend on God's perfect Word to guide him rather than on the teachings of men. Waldo completely rejected the claim of the Medieval Church that ordinary men would be corrupted by reading the Bible for themselves.

Peter Waldo was so compelled to advance the reading of the Bible that he personally funded the translation of it into the everyday language of the French people. Not that that was easy. As mentioned earlier, each and every copy of the Bible was done by hand in those days! Nonetheless, Waldo's efforts were successful. Hundreds of people followed after him in reading the Scriptures—most for the first time.

The Waldensians had a clever way of introducing others to the Bible. They first went out in pairs as merchants to sell jewelry and cloth. As customers would ask if they had anything more to sell, the Waldensians would reply, "Yes, great rarities; I have one precious stone through which you can see God, and another that kindles love to Him in the heart."[1] With these words, they would bring out a Bible to share.

"The Poor Men of Lyon"

Besides sharing the Bible with others, Peter Waldo shared his money. In 1176 he decided to give his wealth to the poor. At the same time he took on a vow to live a life of poverty, purity, and obedience. Such a great number of his followers did the same thing that they became known as "the poor men of Lyon." They were described as men who went about "two by two, barefoot, clad in woolen garments, owing nothing, holding all things in common like the Apostles."[2]

Now, it was common for nuns and monks in medieval times to live lives of poverty. It was almost expected. But it was rare for common men, like the followers of Waldo, to take the life of Christ so seriously. The Waldensians were considered then a radical group of people for allowing Christ to so change their lives.

This sect of believers grew. Unfortunately, the Waldensians, like the Petrobrusians, were viewed as a threat to the Medieval Church. Because they were not priests, monks, or nuns, they were instructed *not* to teach the Bible! Waldo's response was this passage from the Bible[3]: *"We must obey God rather than men!"* (Acts 5:29) Completely disillusioned with the church, the Waldensians rejected many of its traditions, such as going on pilgrimages, following the saints' days, or collecting holy relics.

In 1184 Pope Lucius III excommunicated many of the Waldensians from the Medieval Church for disobeying the order not to preach and for working *outside* of the church. Tragically, some even died at the stake. They were thought to be guilty of heresy. Though Peter Waldo himself might easily have been accused of heresy and burned at the stake, he lived a long life and died of natural causes.

Despite the persecution, the Waldensians continued to grow. A crusade was launched against them in the 1400s, but it wasn't successful. By the 1500s they were strong in number again, and they still exist even today! At least 30,000 people consider themselves Waldensians. They live in many parts of Europe as well as in Argentina, Uruguay, and the United States. I wonder how Peter Waldo would feel about that.

---

1. George T. Thompson and Laurel Elizabeth Hicks, *World History and Cultures in Christian Perspective* (1st ed.). Pensacola, FL: A Beka Book, 1985; p. 131.
2. A. Kenneth Curtis, J. Stephen Lang, and Randy Petersen, *The 100 Most Important Events in Christian History*. Grand Rapids, MI: Fleming H. Revell, 1991; p.78.
3. Ibid.

ACTIVITIES FOR LESSON 58

58A—Younger Students

Role-play as a medieval merchant!

Dress up as a merchant of the Middle Ages. Like the Waldensians, carry jewelry, cloth, and a Bible. As you "sell" your goods, say to your customers who ask if you have more: "Yes, great rarities; I have one precious stone through which you can see God, and another that kindles love to Him in the heart." Then share the precious words of the Bible.

58B—Middle Students

Have a "Sword Drill" contest.

Have a contest to find passages in the Bible. We will call it a "Sword Drill" because the Bible says the Word of God is "sharper than any two-edged sword." Each student needs a Bible. When all are ready, the teacher should state, "Swords ready!" Students hold their Bibles shut over their heads. The teacher calls out loud the reference to a verse, and at the word "Go!" students search their Bibles for the passage. The first student to find the passage should read it out loud with the reference. Continue in this fashion until several points are earned. The student with the most points wins.

58C—Older Students

Research the beliefs and customs of the **Albigensians** in the Middle Ages. According to modern Bible scholars, they were appropriately condemned for heresy. However, their radical presence led to much confusion over who was a heretic and who wasn't.

1154

ELEANOR OF AQUITAINE, THE QUEEN OF TWO NATIONS
LESSON 59

Picture in your mind a feisty young girl, one who is not only full of life but smart and beautiful, too. In your imagination, place her in a castle filled with dancing, singing, and roaming troubadours reciting poetry. Can you see her laughing with friends, dining with royalty, and frolicking about the court? If so, you are capturing a glimpse of **Eleanor of Aquitaine** (AK wih TAYN). This young, vigorous beauty grew up to become not only the **queen of France** but also the **queen of England.** Because of her spirited personality and extravagant background, Eleanor of Aquitaine was undoubtedly one of the most influential women of the Middle Ages. Personally I find her fascinating.

Eleanor's heritage can be traced back to **Charlemagne,** the once great "civilizer" of the Frankish Empire. As our story unfolds, you may notice that the bloodline of Charlemagne's greatness seems to run through the veins of Eleanor. Eleanor's father was the duke of Aquitaine, a beautiful province in southern France. When her father died, Eleanor inherited Aquitaine as her own. As a political move to gain Aquitaine, Eleanor's first marriage was arranged when she was only 15 years old. Though the couple had never met, Eleanor married the young prince of France. His name was **Louis VII.** Shortly after becoming husband and wife, they were crowned the king and queen of France. They were only teenagers.

Through an arranged marriage, the spirited Eleanor of Aquitaine became the queen of France when she was only 15 years old. She was related to Charlemagne.

Eleanor liked being a queen. It seemed her destiny. However, she didn't care at all for her new home in **Paris.** That's where Louis lived. The castle in Paris was far colder and drearier than her estate in Aquitaine. It was also far quieter. She quickly set about decorating the walls with bright tapestries and hiring musicians to fill the emptiness. But these outward changes didn't change the coldness she felt in her heart toward Louis.

Louis VII wasn't at all like the brave and romantic knights Eleanor had grown up around. He was a shy, quiet man of God and a serious student. In his somberness, he reminded Eleanor more of a monk than of a king. She was not impressed by him or inspired to be his queen.

But Louis loved his young queen. He wished to make her proud. When he heard of the Crusades marching to free the Holy Land, he thought it a perfect way to do something lasting for the Lord *and* to win the heart of his queen.

Unfortunately, Louis VII accomplished neither. The Crusade he joined turned out to be disastrous—it was the "Second Crusade" (discussed in Lesson 57). But the disaster was not all Louis's fault. Eleanor was partly to blame. As a 25-year-old adventure seeker, she looked at the Crusade as an opportunity to see the world and leave Paris for a time. As if she were in a parade rather than a war, Eleanor packed her finest clothes and accessories and took her doting attendants along to accompany her to the Holy Land. Her baggage alone was an embarrassing mistake. Louis and his troops could hardly maneuver through the rough terrain with their battle supplies, much less with Eleanor's "stuff."

After three months of harsh traveling, the crusaders stopped in **Constantinople**, the luxurious capital of the Byzantine Empire, to visit and plan strategy with the **prince of Antioch,** who also happened to be Eleanor's uncle. With great wealth and a strong personality, Eleanor's uncle was everything she thought a king ought to be. It made her disapprove of her husband even more. But Louis began to disapprove of Eleanor as well. After making a spectacle of herself over her uncle's riches and military strategies, Eleanor was arrested by her king and escorted home on a ship! Treacherous sea conditions almost killed her. But Eleanor survived—only to find herself a hardened and humiliated queen.

To make matters worse, Louis suffered complete defeat during the Second Crusade. Eleanor's uncle was killed in battle due in part to one of Louis's poor military decisions. It was a tragic event that turned Eleanor's heart against Louis for good.

At the age of 29, Eleanor convinced the archbishop to have her marriage *annulled* based on the fact that she and Louis were actually fourth cousins who should not have married to begin with! (An annulment is a controversial practice in which the church declares a marriage null and void.) Eleanor left Louis VII and their two daughters and headed back to Aquitaine, the one place where she found great comfort.

However, there was no peace in Aquitaine. Because of her wealthy estate, she was nearly kidnapped twice! She knew she needed a husband to protect her and her land. It seems that while still married to Louis, she had noticed a rugged young prince who she imagined could be her true knight in shining armor. His name was **Henry.** As the great-grandson of **William the Conqueror,** Henry was the **duke of Normandy** and the **count of Anjou.** Even though he was 11 years younger than Eleanor, she believed his ambition and strength would surely make her proud. They married right away.

In many ways, Henry did make Eleanor proud. He convinced the king of England to make him his heir. That means that when the king of England died in **1154,** Henry became the next king of England! His official title was **Henry II** but most called him **Henry Plantagenet.** "Plantagenet" was a nickname passed on from his father who often wore a sprig of a broom plant—*planta genista*—in his hat. Henry's new title of king meant that Eleanor was again a queen. But this time she was the queen of England!

Henry II was nicknamed Henry Plantagenet for the sprig of broom plant his father wore in his hat.

The Queen of England

Eleanor's new home in **London, England,** was interesting. She saw ice-skating for the first time in her life and found the city bustling with busy merchants. But more often than not, she traveled with Henry and their children to visit the numerous territories they ruled. In the process, both Henry and Eleanor noticed that the laws in one area were completely different from the laws of the next area. It was difficult to rule the people fairly. Henry improved the situation by introducing a trial by **jury,** where 12 honest men were chosen to judge a person's crime. It became immensely popular and was a huge contribution made by Henry II and Eleanor.

Other than that, Eleanor contributed her extravagant taste and romantic ideals to the English. To make London more like her childhood home, she brought in decorators, minstrels, and **troubadours** to liven things up. (A troubadour was a knight well versed in poetry and music.) In bringing in the arts, Eleanor brought a more *refined* **chivalry** to the English.

The term *chivalry* is used to describe a code of conduct a knight would live by. Of course, knights already lived under a strict ethical code in England long before Eleanor came around. But under Eleanor's influence, a *true* knight was not only a man who was strong and courageous, he was also a man who could express tender words of love. So great was Eleanor's influence that love and admiration for women grew to new heights in the Middle Ages. Poems and love songs were written and rewritten by ordinary knights and troubadours alike to honor legends like **King Arthur, Guinevere,** and Charlemagne. Women were elevated from a dreadfully low status to one highly exalted.

Though Henry II had been upset with Thomas Becket, he was not expecting four of his knights to murder the innocent archbishop of Canterbury.

Royal Troubles

Though life was looking good for this ambitious couple, the king and queen had their problems. Henry was known for having a terrible temper. At times he would go into such a bad rage that he would shout and throw furniture! One day, Henry spoke so furiously about the **archbishop of Canterbury** that four of Henry's knights went and killed him! That archbishop's name was **Thomas à Becket.** Apparently, Thomas Becket and Henry had been the closest of friends in their younger years. Becket's senseless murder haunted Henry the rest of his life because his bad temper had spurred on the incident.

But worse than Henry's guilt was the condition of Henry's marriage. He found himself no longer in love with Eleanor. In violation of his wedding vows, he started a relationship with another woman. Queen Eleanor was devastated. How could she, the patron of romantic love and chivalry, lose her own king to someone else? What would Henry do with her? Eleanor loved Henry as much as she loved herself. But his rejection was more than she could bear. She schemed an attack of revenge—not on Henry personally, but on his power. She set his own sons against him to take the throne.

Henry may have had a bad temper, but he was no fool. He knew Eleanor was plotting against him through their sons. If he were to divorce her, he would lose Aquitaine. If he were to have her killed, he would be haunted even more than he was over the death of Thomas Becket. So, his only solution seemed to be to *seclude* this daunting woman. Henry thought first of sending Eleanor to a nunnery, but she would have nothing to do with the religious life. So instead, he locked her up in a castle in southern England for nearly 15 years! Eleanor was allowed some freedoms during her long stay at **Salisbury Castle,** but she was under constant guard and could never escape. With some mercy, Henry let her out on special occasions and Christmas.

Any ordinary person would wither in the conditions that Eleanor was forced to live under. But then, Eleanor was no ordinary person. Somehow, she became a more determined queen through her captivity. She continued to entertain from her castle prison and to encourage the love of the arts. As a result, the people still held her dear. One of her Aquitanian admirers wrote to her:

For 15 long years Eleanor of Aquitaine was locked in a castle similar to this one. Henry II let her out at least once a year to celebrate Christmas.

"Return, O captive, if you can. . . .The King of the north holds you in captivity. But do not despair; lift your voice like a trumpet and it shall reach the ears of your sons. The day will come when they will set you free and you shall come again to dwell in your native land." [4]

Fortunately for Eleanor, the day *did* finally come—because Henry II was not in good health. After attempting one of the long difficult Crusades, he died. Eleanor was immediately set free. She was 67 years old.

Freedom and Adventure!

You would think that because of her age, Eleanor would retire to a free and quiet life after all she had endured. But not Eleanor. She had had enough of the quiet life at Salisbury Castle—her prison of 15 years. Now free, she started life all over again—stronger, wiser, and far more compassionate toward the less fortunate. Eleanor had much to offer England as the "Queen mother." Her son, **Richard I** (sometimes called **Richard the Lionhearted** for his bravery), was the new king.

Richard the Lionhearted is so fascinating that I'll devote another lesson to him. But what you need to know now is that he went on a rather long Crusade to the Holy Land. In his absence he "unofficially" left England in the hands of the person he trusted most—his mother, Eleanor. She did a great job, too.

With many years to think about the more important things in life, Eleanor ruled England better than most. Despite her age, she traveled extensively and kept close contact with her people, both in England and in Aquitaine. Even at 70, she had the energy to scour all of Europe to find Richard a

---

4. Polly Schoyer Brooks, *Queen Eleanor, Independent Spirit of the Medieval World: A Biography of Eleanor of Aquitaine.* New York: J. B. Lippincott, 1983; p. 122.

suitable wife since he had never married. All the while, she kept close tabs on her other son, **John**, for fear he would fight his brother for the throne of England.

Eleanor was right about her sons' rivalry. Richard and John threatened each other for years. Interestingly, Richard had long been Eleanor's favorite and John was Henry's. Each parent wanted their favorite son on the throne. At one point, Richard found himself a prisoner of the **Germans.** It might have been John's opportunity to be king. But Eleanor was too quick and shrewd to allow this to happen. She raised a huge ransom to offer the king of Germany for Richard's release. Her ransom worked, and everyone present wept at the sight of the old queen embracing her favorite son upon his release.

But a far sadder scene was soon to come their way. Richard was shot in the neck by a **crossbow.** He died in his mother's arms. It was heartbreaking for Eleanor. In Richard, she had molded the brilliant leader, the romantic knight, and the strong king that she had always dreamed of. Now he was dead. Her other son, John, whom she found greatly disappointing, became the next king of England.

Eleanor did her best with John. Even in her old age, she continued to have a heavy hand in ruling England. And even in her last days she did much to improve it. As she traveled about and saw the damage done by royal wars and battles, she had great compassion for the common people. Eleanor granted all kinds of charters giving freedom to the citizens of small towns. They were given freedom from certain taxes, freedom from bridge tolls, freedom from military service, and the freedom to choose husbands for their daughters without a lord's approval.

I doubt Eleanor realized then what impact she was having on the world to come. These "free" citizens took far more pride and care in their communities and they prospered. For centuries to come, kings learned from Eleanor and prospered their kingdoms through freedom and a just legal system.

Though this would make a great end to the story of Eleanor, it isn't the end yet! When she was more than 80 years old, Eleanor was still powerful enough to be a threat to others. Her own distant grandson named **Arthur** captured her for an enormous ransom from John! After years of being a failure in Eleanor's eyes, John finally had a chance to prove himself to her. John rescued his dear old mother from Arthur as if she were again a young damsel in distress. He threw Arthur into a dungeon, and he was never heard from again!

With that, Eleanor finally had had enough adventure. At 82 she retired to live her final days with the nuns. They fondly said of her, "She enhanced the grandeur of her birth by the honesty of her life. . . She surpassed almost all the queens of the world."[5]

On April 1, 1204, Eleanor of Aquitaine died. She was buried at an abbey in France next to her beloved son Richard and not far from Henry. Eleanor's effigy (which is a stone replica of her body) holds a dainty book, probably to represent the poetry she so loved. Her life was one of such adventure, courage, and drama that even long after her death she inspired the writing of countless tales and poems. I think that's what she would have wanted.

ACTIVITIES FOR LESSON 59

ALL STUDENTS

Through all the years of being a queen, I imagine that Eleanor of Aquitaine enjoyed hosting large, lavish banquets with lots of food, plenty of drinks, and lively entertainment. Host your own medieval feast for your class or family. Suggestions are in the Activity Supplement in the Appendix.

---

5. Ibid., p. 164.

59A—Younger and Middle Students

1. One of the ways that Queen Eleanor brightened up the dreary castles in France was by hanging tapestries on the walls. Brighten up a drab bedroom by thumbtacking lightweight decorative blankets or sheets on the wall. Pretend it is your castle for the day. Place a photo of your décor in your Student Notebook under "Europe: England."

2. Rather than act out being locked up in a castle for 15 years, try being "locked up" in one room of your house for 15 minutes. Have very little entertainment in whatever room you choose. Imagine the feelings that Queen Eleanor built up after 15 years of such solitude!

3. Imagine the ridiculous things that Eleanor packed to join the Crusades. Fill a suitcase with completely unnecessary items for a trip. On your next trip out of the house to run errands, take this suitcase along. Discuss the meaning of "extravagance" with your teacher or class.

59B—Middle Students

1. If a younger sibling is acting out a 15 minute "lock-up" as described above, plan a dashing rescue in the spirit of knights of old!

2. Write a love poem for a family member. Sign it "Your Secret Troubadour." Place a copy of it under "Europe: England" in your Student Notebook.

59C—Older Students

1. Write an imaginary page from the diary of Eleanor of Aquitaine. Choose any season of her fascinating life. File it in your Student Notebook under "Europe: England."

2. Creative Story. Imagine you were allowed out of your home only once a year, on Christmas. Write a story about what you would do, whom you would see, and what you would miss in between. File it in your Student Notebook under "Europe: England."

3. View the video or DVD of *The Lion in Winter* (1968) starring Katharine Hepburn and Peter O'Toole. It is a very well done drama depicting the release of Eleanor one Christmas during her captivity. One of my personal favorites!

C. 12TH CENTURY

THE JEWS OF THE MIDDLE AGES
LESSON 60

Once in awhile I cry while doing research for this book. Today was one of those days. When I began to learn of the tragedies suffered by the **Jews** during the Middle Ages, I was moved to tears. I don't necessarily want to make you feel that sad as you learn about the Jews. But I hope that when you read of their oppression, you will be more grateful for your own religious freedom. That is, if you have religious freedom! Some of you may not. And that makes me sad, too.

The story of the Jews is an interesting one. They are a people with a great heritage. In Bible times they were called the Hebrews, the Israelites, or the children of Israel. The Bible says they are "chosen." (Isa. 44:1) And of course, **Jesus Christ of Nazareth** was a Jew Himself.

As you know, though, only some of the Jews believed Jesus was the Messiah. Like **Saul of Tarsus,** for example. He believed and dedicated his life to making the story of Jesus known to Jews and Gentiles alike. In time, believing Jews blended in with believing Gentiles. All were called **Christians,** which means "little Christs."

But what of those Jews who didn't believe Jesus was the Messiah? Well, they remained a large population then, and they are a large population now. But their survival has not been an easy one.

As we've already learned, the Jews were first expelled from their homeland under the **Romans.** (Older Students: In reality, the Jews *first* lost their homeland to the **Assyrians** and the **Babylonians** as a result of their disobedience to God! See Volume I.) After the Romans, the **Muslims** invaded. For a short time, the **crusaders** recaptured the Holy Land. But for the most part, the Muslims occupied the Holy Land throughout the Middle Ages. This meant that the Jews had no place to call their own. They were a people held together by a common religion, but without a common homeland.

Where then did the Jews live? Well, they lived wherever they could. Some countries welcomed them; other countries did not. Some Christians protected them; other Christians persecuted them. Some Muslims embraced them; other Muslims tortured them. The treatment of the Jews varied *between* other religions as well as *within* other religions. It was a difficult and confusing time for the Jews who weren't sure *who* their friends were.

The Muslims and the Jews

Let me start with the Muslims. During the *early* Middle Ages, the caliphs of the Arab Empire were accepting of the Jews. They were happy to allow Jews to live in Muslim lands under their own Jewish leadership. These special Jewish leaders were called **exilarchs,** a term reminding them that they were *exiled* from their homeland. The exilarch was given freedom to rule and lead the Jews of his area as long as he would "rise in the presence of the Prince of the Captivity [the caliph] and to salute him respectfully."[6] (Words in brackets are mine.) This arrangement seemed to be all right with the Jews. As long as they were free to keep their identity, they didn't mind respecting the local Muslim caliph.

In **Spain,** the Jews were particularly prosperous under the **Umayyad dynasty.** Thousands of Jews lived peacefully alongside the Muslims. They were so close that many Jews adopted Islamic dress and style. Whole villages of Jews grew strong and education flourished. For the Spanish Jews, it was a golden age. Wealth and prosperity abounded.

But, much like the Christians under the Muslims, there came a time of sudden persecution for the Spanish Jews. In 1066 there were at least 4,000 Jewish people massacred in **Granada, Spain.** Great numbers more are presumed to have suffered. Some Jews pretended to convert to Islam to save their lives. Other Jews fled to the north under the protection of the Christians living there.

The Christians and the Jews

That leads us to the Christians. As in northern Spain, there were many places in Europe where Christians were kind to Jews. In some instances, as with **Gregory the Great**, it was the popes of the Medieval Church who were best at treating Jews with dignity and respect. One Jewish historian wrote, "Had it not been for the Catholic Church, the Jews would not have survived the Middle Ages in Christian Europe."[7] The same was true of some emperors. **Charlemagne**, for example, was particularly welcoming of the Jews in his empire. He appreciated their commerce and admired their skills. Charlemagne's own personal doctor was a Jewish man.

---

6. Will Durant, *The Age of Faith.* Vol. IV of *The Story of Civilization.* New York: Simon and Schuster, 1950; p. 366.
7. S. W. Baron, *A Social and Religious History of the Jews,* Vol. II (1937), p. 85. As quoted in Will Durant, *The Age of Faith.* Vol. IV of *The Story of Civilization.* New York: Simon and Schuster, 1950; p. 389.

Unfortunately, this acceptance was not the case across the board. There were other popes and emperors who blatantly persecuted the Jews. In the fourth century, **Constantine** banished rabbis. In 581 one ruler told the Jews to convert to Christianity or they would have their eyes torn out! In 1313, at the **Council of Zamora**, the Jews were instructed to wear a **gold badge**. (A similar thing occurred later in history under **Adolf Hitler!**) In other places, they were required to mark their hats or veils. By doing this, the Jews were quickly identified and more easily mistreated. At another council it was declared illegal for Christians to use Jewish doctors or vice versa. Jews were not allowed to touch fruit in an outdoor market. Nor could they hold public office.

All these rules led to what we would call **segregation.** Segregation is the separation of people based on race or religion. Though it is very unfair, segregation of the Jews spread across most of Europe. Sometimes it was the Jews themselves who chose to live apart from other Europeans in order to protect themselves from harm! Who could blame them?

In England, things got really bad. Remember **King John,** the son of Eleanor of Aquitaine? He was especially cruel to the Jewish people. In 1210 he ordered all Jews to go to prison *and* he took their money! Some were tortured. The Jews begged to leave England but were denied—at least until all their money was taken. By 1290 **King Edward I** asked the Jews to leave because they no longer contributed to the economy (Of course, they couldn't if they were in jail! It was absurd.) In fleeing the country, many Jews drowned trying to cross the English Channel into France.

But worse than this, there was one German king who believed he had the right to "burn all the Jews, or show them mercy, and to save their lives, take the third penny of their property."[8] That means he could kill them or tax them! For those of you who know what the **Holocaust** was, this mentality may sound familiar. Adolf Hitler, whom I mentioned earlier, was a **German Nazi** in the 1940s who had some of these same ideas. He was the man responsible for killing millions of Jews! But I'm getting way ahead in history here. That's all part of **World War II.**

This crowded Jewish cemetery in Europe is the final resting place for thousands who died in the Holocaust.

Of course, another problem for the Jews was the crusaders. Though many crusaders were sincerely trying to recapture Jerusalem to honor God, many of them were completely out of control. Some went through the Holy Land killing anyone who breathed, including the Jews. There are numerous stories of a few good Christians who hid Jewish people to protect them from the slaughter. Some of these Christians risked their own lives to spare their Jewish friends!

Despite the good intentions of some, Jews were most often treated very harshly in Europe and Arab nations during the Middle Ages. To make matters more painful, the Jews didn't always agree with each other over doctrines and practices. Much like members of the Medieval Church fighting with one another over icons and investitures, the Jews bickered among themselves over the meaning of the scriptures. Some Jews believed every word of the Old Testament was to be interpreted literally. Others, like the Jewish philosopher **Moses ben Maimon,** taught that some Old Testament stories were only symbolic in nature. The violent disagreements led to Jews "excommunicating" each other, and persecuting each other, just like the members of the church did.

---

8. Will Durant, *The Age of Faith.* Vol. IV of *The Story of Civilization.* New York: Simon and Schuster, 1950; p. 375.

My lesson on the Jews of the Middle Ages wouldn't be complete without telling you more about Moses ben Maimon, the philosopher mentioned in the last paragraph (sometimes written as **Maimonides**). Born in Spain, he is one of the most famous Jewish scholars of all time. So revered was this man by most Jews that they said of him, "From Moses to Moses there arose none like Moses."[9]

What made Moses so popular? Most would say it was his brilliant writings. Maimonides took the books of the Law and the Talmud[10] (a collection of Jewish laws from oral tradition) and organized them into one volume. His work was called *Mishneh Torah*, meaning "Repetition of the Law."

Can you imagine why this book might be important to the Jews of the Middle Ages? At this point in history, the Law is all they had left. They did not yet believe the Messiah had come; they had no Temple to worship in; and they had no homeland. Therefore, the Law, as they interpreted it through the Talmud and the Mishneh Torah, was the one thing they had in common with one another. Of course, there were great disputes over the books and some who disagreed with them completely. But these teachings held most of the Jews together.

Moses Maimonides, a brilliant Jewish philosopher, organized the Law and the Talmud into the Mishneh Torah. It means "Repetition of the Law."

Survival

And "holding together" was important for the survival of the Jews. Besides the traditional teachings of the Law, I think their strength came in part from within. Because of their fear of others (never knowing whom they could trust), the Jews became very close within their own **families.** Men were faithful to their wives and committed to their children. In fact, a Jewish man's greatest pride was his children. Jewish women were valued, too, for their hard work, modesty, and devotion to the family. Jewish boys also worked hard. They went to school from sunup to sundown, with only a few breaks for meals.

There was very little divorce, crime, or heavy drinking among the Jews. It's been said that every father was a priest and every home a place of worship. According to one author, "warmth and dignity ... thoughtfulness, consideration, parental and fraternal affection," all marked the Jewish family.[11]

Besides home, a central place for the Jew was the **synagogue.** It was there that families celebrated births and weddings, and worshiped. It was also a place for business and religious training.

So, despite the great persecution the Jews faced, there were cords to hold them together—cords of faith, family, and tradition. But undoubtedly one question haunted them. What about the promised **Messiah**? Where was their deliverer? Well, there were a few men who tried to fit the bill. In 720 a Jew named **Serene** claimed to be the Messiah and tried to lead his own crusade to the Holy Land. He thought the Jews should be the ones to recapture the Holy Land, not the Christians! He failed and was put to death by a caliph. Years later, another Jew arose claiming to be the Messiah. His name was **Obadiah.** He

---

9. Ibid., p. 408.

10. For centuries, the Talmud (a collection of interpretations, extensions, and adaptations of the laws of Moses) was memorized and passed down by word of mouth from teacher to student—thus called "the oral laws." It was believed that this oral training in the laws would strengthen the bond between teachers and students. However, after the loss of many Jewish teachers under persecution, the oral law was put into writing in the 200s. Over the next 300 years, more scholarly comments—called the Gemara—were added to it.

11. Will Durant, *The Age of Faith*. Vol. IV of The Story of Civilization. New York: Simon and Schuster, 1950; p. 380.

led a revolt of 10,000 Jews. They failed as well. In 1160 yet another "messiah" arose. His name was **David Alrui.** His own father killed him in his sleep for fear of the disaster he was creating!

As you can conclude for yourself, the Jews of the Middle Ages suffered greatly. Their pain was real. Pray for Jews today who continue to suffer. Jesus can deliver them still!

ACTIVITIES FOR LESSON 60

ALL STUDENTS

1. **Make your Memory Cards for Lessons 58–60.**

2. Though the setting is a later time in history, I can think of no better musical to depict the love of a Jewish family than *Fiddler on the Roof.* Enjoy this classic play or 1971 movie together as a family appreciating the love shown by a Jewish father for his children.

3. Pray for the Jewish people of today.

Field Trip Possibility

Consider making arrangements to tour a local Jewish synagogue. (Use discretion based on the spiritual maturity of your students.)

60A—Younger and Middle Students

Make a scroll.

Materials: Two empty paper-towel rolls, three sheets of tan parchment-looking paper, tape, marker, foot-long cord

1. Lay the sheets of paper end to end on a flat working space.

2. Tape the sheets together to form one long sheet.

3. Lay the long sheet horizontally on your working space.

4. Lay an empty paper-towel roll vertically on either end of the long sheet.

5. In the fashion of a scroll, tape the rolls securely to the ends of the paper.

6. Use a marker to write out one or more of your favorite verses from the first five books of the Old Testament. I recommend Deuteronomy. 6:5–7.

7. Roll your scroll closed and secure it with a cord.

8. Take a photo of your scroll and file it in your Student Notebook under "Africa: Egypt" (because Moses ben Maimon lived there in the city of Cairo).

60B—Middle Students

Are you familiar with the first five books of the Old Testament? These are considered the books of the Law, or the Pentateuch. Read parts of them today. In places, they are very specific. Consider the purpose of the Law for the Israelites. What was the purpose of the dietary laws, the agricultural laws, the ceremonial laws of sacrifice? Discuss this with your teacher or class.

60C—Older Students

1. To view images of the Mishneh Torah and read the history of the writings *from a Jewish perspective,* visit the following Web site on the Internet:

    www.ucalgary.ca/~elsegal/TalmudMap/Maimonides.html

2. Read and discuss Romans 7. What does the New Testament teach in regard to the law?

3. The most well known Arab philosopher of the same time period was named **Averroës.** For a real stretching of the mind, research and compare the quest of both Maimonides and Averroës to reconcile the philosophies of Aristotle to their own faiths.

Wall of Fame

1. **The Petrobrusians and the Waldensians (1100s)**—Draw a Bible. Underneath write the names "Petrobrusians" and "Waldensians." [From *History Through the Ages*, use *Peter Waldo*.]

2. **Eleanor of Aquitaine, the Queen of Two Nations (1154)**—Sketch a small figure of Queen Eleanor and cut it out. Sketch a small figure of a castle and cut it out. Place Eleanor on the timeline first. Then, lay the figure of the castle on top as if she were enclosed. Title it "Eleanor Captive at Salisbury Castle." [Use *Eleanor of Aquitaine, Henry II (Henry of Anjou)*, and *Thomas Becket*.]

3. **The Jews of the Middle Ages (c. 12th century)**—Draw a circle. Inside the circle, create a three-piece "pie." In one piece, write the name "Muslim." In another, "Christian." In the other, "Jew." Underneath write "Jews Face Segregation." [Use *Moses Maimonides*]

SomeWHERE in Time

Let's take a closer look at France since Peter Bruis, Peter Waldo, and Eleanor of Aquitaine were all from there. Follow the directions below. This is a multistep mapping activity that graduates from easy to more difficult. Complete as is suitable for each student. All will use the same map.

Background Information: France is the largest country in Western Europe. It is surrounded by many natural boundaries. Its capital and most famous city is Paris, where one can find the Eiffel Tower and the beautiful Cathedral of Notre Dame. According to the authors of *Operation World*, although France has historically been Catholic, Islam is now the second religion in France. At the same time, there are more Jews living in France than in any other country in Europe.[12]

1. Using an atlas as a resource, on Outline Map 23, "England and France," find and label France and these surrounding countries: Spain, United Kingdom, Belgium, Germany, Luxembourg (a small country between Belgium and Germany), Switzerland, and Italy. Color as you desire.
   Middle and Older Students: Label the tiny countries of Andorra (only 181 square miles) and Monaco (which is less than a mile wide and only 2 1/2 miles long) as well. They too border France.

2. Find and label these bodies of water: Mediterranean Sea, Atlantic Ocean, Bay of Biscay, and English Channel. Color them all blue.

3. Find and label these cities: Paris, Lyon, Orleans, Bordeaux (bore DOH), and Nice (NEECE).

4. Find and label these main rivers: Rhine; Seine (SANE); Rhone; and Loire (luh WAHR), the longest river in France.

5. Find and label these mountains: Pyrenees and Alps.

6. File this map in your Student Notebook under "Europe: France."

---

12. Patrick Johnstone and Jason Mandryk, *Operation World*. Waynesboro, GA: Paternoster Publishing, 2001.

WHAT DID YOU LEARN?

WEEK 20: QUIZ

I. Fill in the Blanks.

1. The Apostles' _____ was written about one hundred years after Christ lived by the early Christians as a statement of their beliefs.

2. Jerome translated the Bible into _____, the common language of the Romans at that time. It was called the Vulgate.

3. Gregory the Great maintained the humble vows of a _____ although he became a powerful pope in the Middle Ages.

4. The _____ is considered by Muslims to be a holy book containing the revelations Mohammed claimed to receive.

5. _____ is the name of an epic poem and the name of the Swedish hero who wrangled the monster Grendel to death.

6. During the _____ Movement, church members disagreed over the use and practice of idols in the church.

II. Matching. Match the items by placing a letter from the right in the blanks on the left.

_____7. Treaty of Verdun   a. Another name for the Vikings

_____8. Baghdad   b. Created for the Slavic people

_____9. Norsemen   c. Capital of the Abbasid dynasty

_____10. Cyrillic alphabet   d. New Zealand

_____11. "Land of Fire and Ice"   e. Divided Charlemagne's empire among grandsons

_____12. Largest of the Polynesian Islands   f. Iceland

III. Staying in Shape. Use colored pencils to connect each name in the oval shapes to its description in one of the boxes.

A. Started Song dynasty, made Kaifeng his capital, followed teachings of Confucius

13. Wenceslas

B. Benedictine monk who became Pope Gregory VII; struggled against Henry IV over investitures

14. Vladimir

C. Wife to Louis VII and later Henry II, elevated the status of women, mother of Richard and John

15. General Zhao Kuang Yin

D. Great Jewish philosopher born in Spain; compiled the *Mishneh Torah* for the Jews

16. William the Conqueror

E. Kind, godly duke of Bohemia; forgave his mother for the murder of Ludmilla; was killed at church

17. Hildebrand

F. French Norman who invaded the English at Hastings; brought with him the feudal system

18. Peter Bruis & Peter Waldo

G. Grand Duke of Kiev; descendant of Vikings; chose Eastern Orthodox church for his country

19. Eleanor of Aquitaine

20. Moses ben Maimon

H. Frenchmen who read and taught the Bible in the twelfth century; one died at the stake for heresy

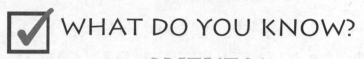

WHAT DO YOU KNOW?

PRETEST 21

Fill in the Blanks. Using a word from the bottom of the page, fill in the blanks.

1. Saladin was the _____ of Egypt. He captured Jerusalem.

2. The _____ Crusade was based on the effort of Richard the Lionhearted to regain the Holy Land from Saladin.

3. Saladin gave Richard the Lionhearted the gift of a _____.

4. The character of Robin Hood is based on the real-life outlaw named _____ _____.

5. In 1280 a French romantic added _____ to the tales of Robin Hood to make it more "interesting."

6. In Japan in 1192, Minamoto Yoritomo declared himself the first _____, which means "conquering general."

7. A special class of Japanese soldiers known as samurai was created to _____ the shogun and other lords.

8. Samurai soldiers, known for their distinctive _____, were always ready to defend their lord.

WORD BANK

protect	Robert, Earl of Huntingdon	horse	shogun
sultan	Maid Marian	Third	swords

RICHARD THE LIONHEARTED, SALADIN, AND THE THIRD CRUSADE
LESSON 61

War can be strange sometimes. It can bring out the best in men or the worse in men, depending upon whose side you're on! Today I'm going to share with you a war story that seemed to bring out the best in two men—though they were on opposite sides. Their names were **Richard the Lionhearted** and **Saladin** (SAL uh din). Their war was the **Third Crusade.**

I've already introduced you to Richard the Lionhearted in Lesson 59. He was the tall, handsome king of England and the favorite son of **Eleanor of Aquitaine.** I hope you remember that Eleanor was an inspiring romantic. By that I mean she loved life, literature, and people. By her mere personality Eleanor is remembered for spreading a more refined **chivalry** to Europe. (Remember that chivalry was the high standard by which kings and knights lived.) All of this is important to this story because it was the *chivalrous*, or gentlemanly, behavior of Richard that brought out the most unusual relationship between him and Saladin.

Richard I, the favorite son of Eleanor of Aquitaine, was in many ways a gentle knight as well as a brave soldier.

Saladin Captures Jerusalem

So who was this Saladin? Saladin was a Muslim. He was born in Mesopotamia along the **Tigris River.** For years he served as a Muslim warrior but eventually worked his way up to being the **sultan of Egypt.** That's like being a king. But being the sultan of Egypt wasn't enough for this ambitious man. Saladin spread his power to the north and in 1187 he *captured* **Jerusalem,** the holy city that Christians took in the **First Crusade**! You can only imagine what this defeat meant to the Christians. To add to their defeat, a gold cross was removed from the **Dome of the Rock** (a mosque on the site where Solomon's Temple once stood), and the Dome was again made into a Muslim place of worship.

Knowing this brief history, you may be able to figure out why the Third Crusade came to be. The Third Crusade was basically the effort of Richard the Lionhearted to take *back* Jerusalem and other parts of the Holy Land from Saladin. That should be easy to understand. Both Jews and Christians especially wanted to have back the site of the holy Temple. Richard was so serious about his campaign that he once declared he would sell the city of London itself to pay for the venture.

Though a proud Muslim leader, Saladin proved to have uncommon compassion on his foes.

What Richard didn't know was just how difficult the venture to win back Jerusalem would be. Nor did he know just how much of a chivalrous gentleman Saladin himself would prove to be. Saladin had a reputation for being both fierce *and* merciful. He was fierce in his pride as a Muslim and in his drive to keep control of the Holy Land. But, he was unusually merciful to those he captured along the way. (at least some of the time).

For example, in Saladin's campaign against Jerusalem, he said to the Christians living there, "I believe that Jerusalem is the city of God, as you also believe; and I will not willingly lay siege to it, or put it to assault."[1] With that, Saladin offered the people a chance to leave in peace. They refused to surrender their beloved city, and so fighting took place. Still, Saladin felt mercy for his foes. Because of the tears of some Christian women, he released many husbands and fathers who had been captured.

Even with control of Jerusalem, Saladin gave freedom to Jews and Christians alike to enter the city on **pilgrimage.** (A pilgrimage is a visit to or tour of a holy site.) Had Christians been content with that arrangement, the Crusades might have ended there. But obviously, that is not what happened because, as you know, there was yet a *third* Crusade.

The Third Crusade

Three kings of Europe felt led to "crusade" again against the Muslims, creating the Third Crusade. One was the Holy Roman Emperor **Frederick Barbarossa** (bar buh RAHS uh). He was 67 years old. The nickname "Barbarossa" meant "red beard," and it described him well. Frederick Barbarossa was redheaded, brave, and ambitious—but he made some fatal military mistakes during the Third Crusade. His troops were cut off by the Muslim Turks and hundreds of his men starved. Frederick himself drowned.

Frederick I was also known as Frederick Barbarossa, meaning "red beard." He drowned in the Third Crusade.

That leads us to the two other kings—Richard the Lionhearted and **Philip Augustus of France.** They went out together on the Third Crusade assuming there would be strength in numbers. Richard was only 31 years old and Philip just 23. After their first successful attack on the city of **Acre** (a city near Jerusalem), Philip grew ill with fever and returned to France. This left Richard on his own quest against Saladin.

In an effort to avoid further bloodshed, one of Richard's first ideas for accomplishing his mission was to offer his own sister in marriage to Saladin's brother! Though the plan may have helped to bring Christians and Muslims together on something, we will never know. Leaders of the church hated the idea, and the wedding never took place.

Saladin, in his efforts to make peace, offered Richard a plan giving Christians all the cities they already occupied in the Holy Land and half of Jerusalem. Richard rejoiced at the plan at first—but after some thought, rejected it. He decided instead to attack the city of **Jaffa,** another Muslim stronghold. This happened in **1192.**

Things got interesting in Jaffa. As the story goes, Richard was so excited to lead his troops into battle there that he leapt from his ship into waist-high water, yelling and waving his Danish axe wildly in the air. Richard's troops were greatly outnumbered but were far more inspired by Richard's brassy outburst. They successfully marched forward. It was then that Saladin caught a glimpse of Richard's bravery with his own eyes. But he thought it unbecoming that a king would be racing around on foot! So Saladin summoned one of his own men to send Richard a horse on which to ride!

In response to Saladin's graciousness, Richard sent him a gift of falcons. Yes, these two men exchanged gifts though they were in battle against one another. But then, in complete arrogance, Richard rode his new horse right past the front line of the Muslim troops without so much as lifting his sword. In absolute awe, or maybe in disbelief at such an act of courage, no one touched him!

---

1. Will Durant, *The Age of Faith*. Vol. IV of The Story of Civilization. New York: Simon and Schuster, 1950; p. 597.

If this wasn't bizarre enough, as far as war goes, listen to what unfolded next. The following day Richard grew ill with fever. In his discomfort he cried out for fruit and something cool to drink. Do you want to guess who came to his aid? It was Saladin. He sent Richard fresh pears, peaches, and snow to revive him. He also sent over his own personal doctor to help restore Richard to good health! Clearly, this was unusual behavior for rivals.

After that, it was apparent that neither of the heroes wanted to win at the expense of the death of the other. Perhaps there was some mutual respect for one another. I don't know exactly what each man was thinking. But soon after the events at Jaffa, on September 2, 1192, the two men signed a **three-year peace treaty.** This time both agreed to the conditions. The Christians were allowed to occupy some cities along the coast and to freely visit the holy sites in Jerusalem although the city would be ruled by Muslims, meaning that the Dome of the Rock would remain a mosque.

Being still true to his warrior side, Richard signed the treaty with this last threat to Saladin—that he would be back in three years to take Jerusalem completely. Saladin replied that if ever he were to lose to anyone, he would only want to lose to Richard.

Well, Saladin never had the chance to lose to Richard. The sultan passed away the next year—long before the peace treaty expired. He was only 55 years old. Several years later, Richard was shot and killed by a crossbow. Richard never lived to see the city of Jerusalem with his own eyes, though twice he was close enough to do so. (He said he would not gaze at the city until it was his.) There never was a standoff between the two warrior gentlemen. As Saladin's empire grew weaker, the Christians

Though Richard was seen waving an axe in battle, most knights of the Crusades carried long swords and daggers as seen on this model.

crusaded again against the Muslims. But that's another story. I find it interesting enough to stop here at this most unusual scenario of war between Richard the Lionhearted and Saladin, the sultan of Egypt.

ACTIVITIES FOR LESSON 61

ALL STUDENTS

See the Activity Supplement in the Appendix for a project on creating a coat of arms.

61A—Younger Students

1. To remember Saladin's act of kindness to Richard, serve your family or class pears, peaches, and "snow." With the help of an adult, you can make "snow" by placing several ice cubes in a blender.

2. Have you ever gotten a souvenir from a special place you visited? It is a common practice to bring something home from somewhere else as a memory. Well, it was no different in the Middle Ages. People who went on pilgrimage to the Holy Land often brought palm branches home with them. For this reason the devoted pilgrims were nicknamed *Palmers.*

   a. Can you think of a Bible story that included palm branches? They were used by the crowds to wave Christ into Jerusalem on a donkey, one week before he was crucified. Christians call the occasion Palm Sunday.

   b. Make a palm leaf out of construction paper. Attach it to a long stick. Pretend it is a souvenir from the Holy Land. Explain its meaning to other friends and family.

61B—Middle Students

1. Research the legend of *Blondel*, Richard's faithful companion. Write a short story of what you discover. File your report in your Student Notebook under "Europe: England."

2. Find out about the evolution and invention of the crossbow, the deadly weapon that killed Richard. Photocopy or print pictures of the weapon and add them to your Student Notebook under, "Europe: England."

3. There is an interesting legend surrounding the death of Frederick I (Barbarossa). Some say he never died! Research it for yourself. I suggest the *World Book Encyclopedia* as a resource.

61C—Older Students

1. In our lesson, Richard sent Saladin a gift of falcons. Research the sport of falconry. It was extremely popular in the Middle Ages among European noblemen but was probably started by the Persians. Invite a trained falconer to your classroom for a demonstration.

2. Research the wife and queen of Richard the Lionhearted. Her name was **Berengaria.** Not much is known of her as they were married only a short time before his death. Learn of how she spent her remaining years. Information may be difficult to find!

3. Find current photos of the Dome of the Rock. Photocopy or print them and add to your Student Notebook under "Asia: Israel."

UNKNOWN

THE CLASSIC TALE OF ROBIN HOOD
LESSON 62

Before we get too far away from the lesson about Richard the Lionhearted, I want to write about **Robin Hood.** Why? Well, in most stories about Robin Hood, Richard the Lionhearted and his brother John are mentioned. So, even though no one knows *exactly* when Robin Hood lived, it was probably right about this time in history. Though there are many versions of this story, I will do my best to summarize both the truth *and* the legends that exist about Robin Hood. Consider this lesson a lighthearted break from all the "gory stuff" we've been learning about in the Middle Ages.

When you hear the name "Robin Hood," what comes to your mind? Do you think of bows and arrows, **Sherwood Forest**, and characters like **Maid Marian**, **Friar Tuck**, or the evil **Sheriff of Nottingham**? Well, I found it very interesting to learn that most of our images of Robin Hood have evolved from ***fiction*** rather than ***fact.*** Do you know the difference between fact and fiction? Facts are pieces of information based on actual, real things. Fiction is all "make-believe," or things imagined.

The Facts

When it comes to the story of Robin Hood, there appears to be only *one* hard fact that supports that he existed at all. And here is that fact—in a cemetery in Yorkshire, England, there lies a tombstone that reads[2]:

---

2. Zelma Kallay, Kings, Queens, Castles, and Crusades: Life in the Middle Ages. Torrance, CA: Good Apple, 1997; p. 76.

Here underneath this little stone
Lies Robert, Earl of Huntingdon
Ne'er [never] archer was as he so good
And people called him Robin Hood
Such outlaws as he and his men
Will England never see again.
  1247

(The word in brackets is mine for easier reading.)

From this tombstone (if indeed it is credible), we can conclude several things that support the modern image of Robin Hood. One: he lived and died in England. Two: his real name was Robert. Three: he was the Earl of Huntingdon. Four: he was a good archer. Five: he was nicknamed Robin Hood. Six: he had a following of men. Seven: Robin and his men were outlaws. And eight: he died in 1247. If you think about it, there really is a lot of information packed into the words on his tombstone!

Though it is unclear in history, tradition says that Robin Hood stole from the rich and gave to the poor.

But, what about the rest of the story? I don't know about you, but from my childhood I remember Robin Hood and his Merry Men as good guys who "stole from the rich to give to the poor." Supposedly they lived in a hideout in Sherwood Forest and had numerous escapades against the Sheriff of Nottingham. The ever-clever Robin Hood always wore green, married a beautiful girl named Marian, and had a best friend named Little John. Robin and his men were good guys defending their favorite king, Richard the Lionhearted, from his evil brother, King John. You probably have your own impression of him.

Now, if you were to review the paragraph on the tombstone, would you see anything there to match my version of the story? No, not at all. So you have to ask yourself, from where did I get my picture of Robin Hood? Or from where did you get yours? I think it is safe to say that storytellers have greatly influenced us all. For some reason, Robin Hood has appealed more to the imagination of storytellers, singers, and playwrights, than to the writing of historians. So what we are left with are stories, songs, and plays that—be they fact or fiction—burn images deep into our minds. And the way mankind works, it appears to me that every few generations, a storyteller adds a little something to the basic story to make it more interesting! Just for fun, let's examine a few of these known additions more closely and sift through the facts.

The Fiction

The first known written account of Robin Hood is by William Langland in 1377. In a work called ***Piers Plowman,*** Langland makes a fleeting statement regarding the "rhymes of Robyn hood." Historians believe the "rhymes" spoken of were the ballads, or songs, that were sung about Robin in his memory. You see, back then people learned and repeated things more by mouth than by writing them down. Putting poems to song made them easier to remember and made them more entertaining.

But it may interest you to know that none of the early ballads of Robin said anything about him taking money from the rich to give to the poor. Nor do they mention jolly Friar Tuck, Maid Marian, or Richard the Lionhearted!

The early ballads do, however, mention Little John. It seems that Robin and Little John became acquainted through a playful fight with one another. In the end, they became dear friends and joined up together as outlaws with many other men. (An outlaw is anyone who lives outside the law.) Though legend portrays Robin and his men as "good" outlaws, we can't really be sure of this. Early ballads suggest Robin was fairly bloodthirsty and cut off the heads of his enemies (including the head of the Sheriff of Nottingham)!

If that was so, then where might the *good* reputation of Robin come from? Well, you have to consider the times in which Robin lived. The feudal system was breaking down as the rich got richer and the poor were getting poorer. There was a lot of corruption in the upper class. It seems that Robin's "enemies" were only those who were unjust, unfair, and overtaxing the poor. In particular, King John (who became the king of England after Richard the Lionhearted died) was severely overtaxing the peasants in England. So when Robin was out cutting off heads, he was supposedly doing so to defend his fellow countrymen. Or so the legend goes.

Now, let me explain the part about the Sherwood Forest. You see, a *forest* in medieval England was the name of any land (not just an area with trees) that was designated by the king or wealthy nobles as their own private property. So why was Robin living there in a hideout? It could be that he was "hiding" there because he wasn't allowed there! And the reason he would want to be in the forest would be because the land was full of animals to hunt. Remember, the rich were selfish with their resources. They wanted to keep the common people away from their hunting grounds by making it illegal to be there. Robin, like his other outlaws, may have just been trying to survive. There is really nothing romantic about that.

Speaking of romance, as I mentioned earlier, the first ballads of Robin give no mention of a girlfriend in his unstable life. But in 1280, someone wrote a French romance that used the names of Robin and Marian. Once Marian showed up, she definitely stuck around, making the tale just a little more interesting and far more romantic.

Another character that has stuck around was Friar Tuck. (A friar, by the way, is a special kind of monk.) Friar Tuck was first introduced in a play in 1475. His character was probably based on a real-life priest named **Robert Stafford.** Originally, Friar Tuck was described as serious and devout. Over time, though, Friar Tuck became a jolly but irresponsible fellow. Sadly enough, his character may have rightly reflected the lazy way that some of the friars lived in the early Renaissance, just before the Reformation.

In the 1800s, the story of Robin Hood came to a real peak through the brilliant authorship of **Sir Walter Scott.** He wrote the historical fiction named **Ivanhoe.** In this masterpiece of literature, Robin Hood (called Robert of **Locksley** in the story) teams up with others to help Richard the Lionhearted defeat his rival brother, John. It is from Scott's description of Locksley that we have our more modern portrait of Robin Hood.

Personally, what I find more interesting is how the tales of Robin Hood spread to North America after the founding of the **United States.** For example, in recent years Americans have enjoyed making comedy of the plot of Robin Hood. Opera writers, cartoon makers, and full-scale film directors have all run with the story to make us laugh. Perhaps you have seen Disney's version of *Robin Hood* that uses a fox to portray Robin and has many other animated creatures. To my own delight, even Warner Brothers' Daffy Duck and Bugs Bunny have acted out Robin Hood.

And in just the last 15 years, someone added a whole new character to the story that seems to keep reappearing under slightly different names. The character is that of a Muslim friend to Robin. He is called **Nasir, Azeem,** or even **Asneeze** in a comedy. From this new character, we can see firsthand how stories change with time. And that's exactly what has happened with Robin Hood.

Above it all, I think the story of Robin Hood simply changes to meet the need we all seem to have for a hero. He seems to represent the good spirit in all of us that hopes to right that which is wrong. And that is what makes Robin Hood a classic tale.

ACTIVITIES FOR LESSON 62

ALL STUDENTS

Just for fun, host a jousting tournament. See the Activity Supplement for suggestions.

62A—Younger Students

1. Obtain a play bow-and-arrow set. Have fun!

2. In remembering Maid Marian, create a high, pointy princess hat and long gown. See the Activity Supplement for directions.

3. Make a money pouch filled with chocolate gold coins following the directions in the Activity Supplement.

4. Watch Disney's animated version of *Robin Hood*. Look for both facts and fiction in the story.

62B—Middle Students

1. Many cultures have their own heroes. In North America, for example, there are numerous tall tales based on the early pioneers like Buffalo Bill, Davy Crockett, and Johnny Appleseed. Research any of these, or someone in your own culture, to see what parts of the story are based on fact and what parts are pure fiction.

2. Read any version of Robin Hood that is appropriate for your level.

62C—Older Students

1. Discuss with your teacher or class the issue of breaking civil laws. Can one justify breaking a law if a law is unfair or corrupt? What did Jesus teach the Jews about paying taxes to the Romans? Find this biblical guideline in the New Testament to add to your discussion.

2. Read or watch any film version of *Ivanhoe* by Sir Walter Scott.

3. Watch the 1976 film, *Robert and Marian*, starring Sean Connery and Audrey Hepburn. Analyze the obvious fictional parts of the story in contrast to the few known facts that exist about Robin Hood.

1192

THE SHOGUNS AND SAMURAI OF JAPAN

LESSON 63

The **shoguns** (SHOW goonz) and **samurai** (SAM moo rye) were the lords and knights of medieval Japan. The mere sound of these names is intriguing to me! But more than the names, the lives of the shoguns and the samurai are of great fascination. (Note that the word *samurai* is both singular and plural.) Let me tell you about these colorful yet dutiful characters and the history that led to their long control of Japan. They ruled for about 700 years.

The last we looked at Japan (Lesson 26), we learned of its natural beauty as a mountainous chain of islands in the Pacific Ocean. We also learned of the strong pride and heritage of the Japanese whose folklore claims they are descendants of a sun goddess. Last, we looked at **Prince Shotoku** (the **"founder of Japanese civilization"**), who brought the warring clans of the nation together for the first time. He also helped to spread **Buddhism** to the islands.

356

The Mystery of History-Volume II

Japanese noblewomen wrote poems about the delicate beauty of the cherry blossom that decorates Japan in the spring.

Between the time of Prince Shotoku and our lesson today, the **Fujiwara family** held the greatest control over Japan. For the most part, this was a long time of peace and prosperity for Japan—almost 600 years! Some of Japan's richest literature comes from this era because of the great writings of Japanese noblewomen. They took the time to write about the "little" things around them, like the crying of babies and the beauty of cherry blossoms in the spring. As simplistic as that all sounds, the Fujiwara emperors and their wives were guilty of living such a rich and luxurious lifestyle that it left them distant and cut off from the needs of the common man. So, in time, there was a need for change.

The Shoguns

Today's lesson is about that change. But it was an unusual one. In **1192** a warrior by the name of **Minamoto Yoritomo** single-handedly moved the *authority* of the emperor to himself. He took the title of shogun, which means, "conquering general." But the unusual part of the arrangement is that Yoritomo didn't conquer the emperor, as is so often the case in history. Rather, the emperor of Japan kept his rightful position and was treated with great respect.

Yoritomo, however, really ruled the country as the shogun of Japan. He did so by taking control over finances, the laws of Japan, and the appointment of constables. Yoritomo also collected taxes in the form of rice. (Rice was the main staple in Japan.) And Yoritomo even appointed his own heir. (An heir is the person who will inherit a position.) This new relationship between the emperor and the shogun was so successful that it was continued over the next 700 years!

The Samurai

But of even greater interest to most of us is the warring class of soldiers that surrounded the shogun and his lords. These were the *samurai.* The samurai were more than just warriors. They were a class of people that included wives and children. Almost 5 out of every 100 Japanese were part of this group. This class grew out of a need for the shogun and his lords to be protected and for laws to be enforced. In the same way that knights served their kings under the feudal system in Europe, so the samurai served the lords and shogun of Japan. In doing so they developed some of their own unique customs. Let me describe some of the more interesting ones.

First, the samurai warriors were known for their distinctive dress. Have you ever seen pictures of them? If so, you might agree that they look intimidating. The most famous costume for samurai soldiers was the **kamishimo.** It was a two-piece garment worn over a kimono. (A kimono was an everyday outfit usually made of silk and wrapped around the body.) The top of the kamishimo was like a vest with greatly exaggerated shoulders, making the samurai look bigger than he was. (And a little scarier!) The bottom was a pair of very wide, flowing trousers. And of most importance to the soldier, two weapons were always carried with him. A large sword called a **katana** was thrust through a belt, or **obi**, against the left

Minamoto Yoritomo took the title of shogun, meaning "conquering general." His authority surpassed that of the emperor.

side of the body. It was ready to be drawn in a split second. His other weapon was a short sword called a **_wakizashi._** It was also worn at the waist to show the samurai's readiness for a fight. Samurai are known in history for making some of the best swords in the world!

A samurai soldier wore special clothing over a garment like this to make him look bigger and scarier.

Samurai armor was equally impressive. The warrior wore beautifully decorated panels of armor that were bound together by leather or silk into one large boxlike piece that fastened at the waist. Horses were often adorned with matching pieces. Though lighter than the knights' armor in Europe, the samurai's armor was just as strong and probably easier to move around in. Metal helmets were highly decorated too, with special flaps that protected the warrior's neck. On his back, a warrior carried a small personal flag that identified him. A poem was usually included that told the samurai warrior's story or wishes if he were to die.

It may sound out of character for a tough-looking warrior to carry a poem around. But the samurai were well known for their poetic side. Like the romantic troubadours of Europe, it was considered part of a samurai soldier's training to be able to write and recite poetry as well as to appreciate other fine arts like dance and theater. Samurai warriors also learned the finer side of drinking tea at fancy teahouses. Furthermore, these special Japanese soldiers cared for their neat and clean appearance. For that reason they always bathed before a battle!

Like most male Japanese of this time period, the samurai warriors most often wore their hair in a topknot, which looked something like a high ponytail. But for the samurai, it was particularly important that his hair be neatly slicked back with oil. The pulled-back hair was sometimes folded and decorated. Other times, the hair was shaved at the forehead. The shaving started as a way to make wearing a helmet more comfortable. But it grew to be a fashion statement and something that was done ceremonially when a boy turned 14.

But even more distinctive than the samurai warrior's dress was the code of honor in which he lived. This code of honor was called **_bushido._** It meant "way of the warrior." Under bushido, the samurai were expected to be honest, respectful, and considerate. And above all, a samurai warrior was expected to be loyal to his master—even unto death! Nothing could be worse for a samurai soldier than to bring dishonor

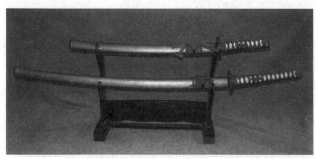

A larger samurai sword is called a katana. The shorter sword is a wakizashi. Both were regularly worn around the waist of a samurai soldier.

to his lord or master through disobedience or capture by an enemy. Even the samurai women were known to fight for their lords out of devotion and respect.

But this loyalty was probably best expressed by the ritual of **_seppuku._** It is sometimes called **_hara-kiri,_** or "belly slitting." In this ritual, if a soldier were to dishonor his lord, or be ordered to die, he was to stab himself to death in the stomach. He was basically committing suicide as an expression of honor. (An important side note here: Although it is admirable that Japanese soldiers were willing to die for their cause, most Christians would agree that suicide is a violation of the Sixth Commandment.)

Though for centuries the class of samurai warriors and their families held a place of high honor in Japan through their devotion and bravery, they were forced out in the late 1800s. But that is a whole other story for a future volume. I hope in this lesson you can simply appreciate the loyalty and manners of the samurai and understand the history that helped to create them.

ACTIVITIES FOR LESSON 63

ALL STUDENTS

Make your Memory Cards for Lessons 61–63.

63A—Younger Students

1. Dress like a samurai warrior using suggestions you'll find in the Activity Supplement.

2. Research the Internet for samples of samurai crests. They are typically well balanced and simple. Create a crest of your own to represent your family name. Perhaps work around the initial of your last name or a symbol of a family hobby. Make your design on a stiff piece of paper. Attach it to a straw. Use duct tape to secure it to your back. (The samurai carried their banners in this fashion.)

3. If you enjoy writing, add a short poem to the family banner or crest you made above.

4. Play "store" using *rice* to pay taxes on all items you purchase.

63B—Middle Students

1. Host a formal Japanese tea ceremony. Research the facts to make it more credible.

2. Write a "Noh" play. That is what the Japanese called their plays. They used very few actors. To differentiate between the characters, the actors wore different masks. There were no actresses involved. Make masks using paper plates, crayons, and elastic.

Centuries of tradition are behind the ritual of a Japanese tea ceremony.

63C—Older Students

1. Research the famous Forty-Seven Ronin. A ronin was a samurai without a master or lord.

2. Compare the countries of Japan and England. Write "Japan and England" at the top of a piece of notebook paper. Fold the piece of notebook paper in half. Subtitle the columns, "Similarities" and "Differences." Copy my ideas below and add some of your own. File this paper under "Asia: Japan" in your Student Notebook.

Japan and England

Similarities	Differences
Islands	Religion
Feudal system	Style of dress
Tea	Traditions
Knights and samurai	Role of women
[Others?]	

3. Read the sample death poems of the samurai given in the Activity Supplement. Write your own poem as if it were your last. Before doing so, please let me clarify again that although it is admirable that Japanese soldiers were loyal to death, most Christians would agree that it is against the Sixth Commandment to commit suicide. Consider this activity along the lines of writing a will in anticipation of death—rather than as a suicide note.

Wall of Fame

1. *Richard the Lionhearted, Saladin, and the Third Crusade (1192)*—Make a small banner with the title "The Third Crusade." Decorate it with symbols representing the lesson, such as snow, peaches, pears, falcons, horses, etc. [From *History Through the Ages, use Richard I, Saladin, Frederick I (Frederick Barbarossa.), Philip II (Philip Augustus).*]

2. *The Classic Tale of Robin Hood (Unknown)*—Draw a bow. Underneath it, write "Robin Hood." [Use *Robin Hood*.]

3. *The Shoguns and Samurai of Japan (1192)*—Draw a sword. Underneath it, write "Samurai Protect Shoguns." [Use *The Shoguns of Japan*.]

SomeWHERE in Time

Highlight the routes of the Third Crusade kings.

Materials: Map 24, "The Crusades"; three shades of highlighters (or crayons); pencil or pen. Older students also need an atlas.

1. There are three routes already drawn for you on Map 24, "The Crusades." Find the route that originates in London, England, travels around the west coast of Spain, through the Strait of Gibraltar, and across the Mediterranean Sea. Based on Lesson 61, which crusader king was from England and would have traveled this route to the Holy Land? (Answers are provided at the end of this Review.) Use a highlighter to trace this route. Make a key at the bottom of the map to indicate the name of the king who took this route. (For those who need it, I have provided a sample map key below.)

2. Find the route that originates in Vezelay, France, and also cuts across the Mediterranean Sea. Based on the lesson, which crusader king was from France? Use a different shade of highlighter to trace this route. Add this to your map key to identify it.

3. Find the route that originates in Regensburg, Germany, and crosses the continent of Europe. Based on the lesson, which crusader king was from Germany (the Holy Roman Empire)? Highlight this route in another color and label it as well on your map key.

Sample Map Key

[Draw a squiggle with a highlighter here.]	Frederick Barbarossa
[Draw a squiggle with a second highlighter here.]	Philip Augustus
[Draw a squiggle with a third highlighter here.]	Richard the Lionhearted

---

PUT IT ALL TOGETHER
WORKSHEET 3: LESSONS 43-63

We have covered 21 lessons in the third quarter of this history course. It's time again to "Put It All Together." Using your textbook, Memory Cards, maps, and timeline, go through this worksheet and answer the questions from Quarter 3. Remember, this is just an exercise to review what you've learned—it is not a test!

I—Dates to Memorize

Write out the names and dates that I have asked you to memorize four times each on the lines below.

Leif Ericsson Discovers America   **1003**

1. _____

2. _____

3. _____

4. _____

Battle of Hastings   **1066**

1. _____

2. _____

3. _____

4. _____

The Early Crusades   **1096**

1. _____

2. _____

3. _____

4. _____

II—Where in the World?   In the course of our studies this quarter, we have spanned several of the world's continents. Place the names of the following countries under the continent where they belong. I have provided one example.

Greenland   Spain   Israel   Scotland   Japan

Canada   Russia   Bohemia   Egypt   China

Holy Roman Empire   Iceland   England   Zimbabwe   France

NORTH AMERICA

1.

2.

EUROPE

1. *Spain*

2.

3.

4.

5.

6.

7

ASIA

1.

2.

3.

4.

AFRICA

1.

2.

III—People and Places.   Match people to these places by placing a letter to the left of each number.

_____1.   Iceland

_____2.   Bohemia

_____3.   Holy Roman Empire

_____4.   Russia

_____5.   China

a. Otto I

b. Macbeth

c. Wenceslas

d. St. Simon

e. El Cid

_____6. Egypt   f. Peter Bruis and Peter Waldo

_____7. Greenland   g. Minamoto Yoritomo

_____8. Canada   h. Leif Ericsson

_____9. Scotland   i. Zhao Kuang Yin

_____10. Spain   j. Robin Hood

_____11. England   k. Floki Vilgerdarson

_____12. France   l. Vladimir

_____13. Japan   m. Eric the Red

IV—Which Island? Circle the name of one of the three islands we studied that fits each fact below. Answers can be found using Lessons 43, 44, and 51. The first one has been done for you.

1. Nicknamed the "Land of Fire and Ice"

    (Iceland)   Greenland   New Zealand

2. Home of the kiwi bird

    Iceland   Greenland   New Zealand

3. Settled permanently by the Viking cousins, Ingolf Arnarson and Hjorleif

    Iceland   Greenland   New Zealand

4. Has an abundance of pounamu, or jade

    Iceland   Greenland   New Zealand

5. First called "Skerries" by Viking explorers

    Iceland   Greenland   New Zealand

6. Named by Abel Tasman after a province in the Netherlands

    Iceland   Greenland   New Zealand

7. Divided into chieftain-led "things"

    Iceland   Greenland   New Zealand

8. Home to the Sarqaq, the Independence people, and the Thulte

       Iceland   Greenland   New Zealand

9. Called Kallaallit Nunaat, meaning "Land of the People"

       Iceland   Greenland   New Zealand

10. Gives view of the Southern Cross

       Iceland   Greenland   New Zealand

11. Once home to Irish monks

       Iceland   Greenland   New Zealand

12. Part of Oceania and one of the Polynesian Islands

       Iceland   Greenland   New Zealand

V—Remember When. Use the Contents in the front of the book and various lessons to fill in the blanks below.

1. At the same time the Maori were settling in New _____, the people of _____ _____ were building magnificent stone homes and establishing a gold trade in Africa.

2. _____ was crowned Holy Roman Emperor by the pope just a few years after Good King _____ was murdered.

3. About a decade after St. Simon prayed to move a _____, Eric the _____ was settling Greenland.

4. At the same time that _____ served as king of Scotland, _____ _____ was involved in the Reconquista of Spain.

5. Not long after William the _____ invaded England at Hastings, Pope _____ VII and Henry IV struggled through the _____ Controversy.

6. While the Petrobrusians and the _____ suffered persecution for teaching the Bible, _____ of _____ helped raise the status of women in England.

7. During the reigns of Richard the Lionhearted and King _____, a man

nicknamed _____ _____ lived as an outlaw in the forests of

England.

8. About the same time that Richard the Lionhearted accepted a horse from _____,

Minamoto Yoritomo declared himself the first _____ of Japan.

VI—Word Association. What people group comes to your mind at the mention of the following items? Use colored pencils to connect them.

1. Greenstone (jade)   a. Waldensians

2. Stone houses   b. Thulte (Inuit)

3. Lily feet   c. Crusaders

4. Kayaks   d. Maori

5. Crosses of red cloth   e. Chinese women

6. Bibles   f. Samurai warriors

7. The Talmud   g. Jews

8. Two swords   h. Zimbabweans

VII—Timeline. Number from 1 to 10 the order of the events surrounding the life of Eleanor of Aquitaine. Use Lesson 59 as your guide. The first event has been numbered for you.

1. _____Eleanor married Henry II and became the queen of England.

2. _____Eleanor went on the Second Crusade.

3. _____Thomas Becket was murdered by the knights of Henry II.

4. _____Eleanor was captured by her grandson Arthur and rescued by her son John.

5. _____Eleanor retired to live with the nuns.

6. ___1___Eleanor married Louis VII and became the queen of France.

7. _____Eleanor unofficially ruled over England while her son Richard went on a Crusade.

8. _____Eleanor raised a large ransom for the release of Richard.

9. _____Eleanor was locked up in Salisbury Castle for 15 years.

10. _____Treacherous sea conditions almost killed Eleanor.

VIII—Make True. All the statements below are false. Cross out the word or words that make each statement false and insert the new word or words that make the statement true. The answers can be found in Lessons 61–63. The first one has been done for you.

1. When Jerusalem was captured in 1187, a cross was removed from ~~St. Peter's Cathedral,~~ the Dome of the Rock, and it again became a mosque.

2. Frederick Barbarossa, one of the three kings who began the Third Crusade, suffered military defeat and died of starvation.

3. Philip Augustus, also one of the three kings who began the Third Crusade, abandoned the mission upon getting shot by an arrow.

4. After receiving a horse from Saladin, Richard the Lionhearted offered a gift of figs to his rival.

5. The best source of facts that exist regarding Robin Hood can be found in an epic poem in England.

6. Many of our present images of Robin Hood come from the book titled *Ivanhoe* written by Josephus.

7. Before Yoritomo took control as a shogun, the Gupta family ruled Japan for almost 600 years.

8. A moko, which is the distinctive dress of a samurai, has large shoulders to make a warrior look big and scary.

IX—Bonus Essay. Writing in complete sentences, give some reasons why people went on the Crusades to the Holy Land. Earn half a point for each reason given. Use a separate sheet of paper if necessary.

THE FIRE SHINES:
1210 TO 1456

Here we are at the last quarter of the book. I hope you feel that you've already learned a lot, but we're not quite done. If you can imagine your school year looking like a baseball diamond, we're now at third base and finally heading home. This is our final stretch. I've titled this last quarter "The Fire Shines" because there were many bold believers who shone brightly for Christ during this time period. There were also many brilliant men and women who shone in their fields of expertise. Let me explain.

It was during the later Middle Ages that some men and women tried to be better examples of Christ by being less attached to money and other things of this world. At least that is how I would describe the mind-set of *St. Francis of Assisi*, *St. Clara*, and *St. Dominic*. Each of these saints gave up all luxury for the benefit of the kingdom of God. As a result, they started religious orders that were separate from the church, which had become very wealthy and at times cold. Like fire on a cold, dark night, these saints gave new warmth and meaning to Christianity through their dedicated service.

And, in the name of Christ, there were at least two other men of this time period who shone like fire. They were *John Wycliffe* and *John Huss* (pronounced *Hoose* and rhymes with *goose*). One of them was even burned at the stake for his beliefs. You see, these men so believed in the power of the Word of God that they taught it to others despite the persecution it brought on them. Some would call them "pre-reformers" because they were some of the first men to try to *reform* the church, which had drifted from teaching the Word of God.

"The Fire Shines."

Apart from spiritual matters, there were some brilliant men who did much to shine brightly in the late Middle Ages. There was *St. Thomas Aquinas* (uh QUINE nus)—an astounding philosopher; *Roger Bacon*—an amazing scientist; and master poets *Dante* (DAHN tay) and *Chaucer* (CHOW sir). Each of these men wrote down things that are still being studied and appreciated more than 800 years later.

Other "greats" of this time period would have to include the *Aztecs* and the *Inkas*. These were two fascinating cultures in Central and South America that rose to their greatest heights in the Middle Ages. Besides that, they are just plain interesting because of what they accomplished and the beliefs they held. Though some of their customs were gruesome, I think you will still enjoy learning about them.

Also of great fascination are the travels of *Marco Polo*. You may know his name best from yelling it in a pool game. At least that is a custom I grew up with in the United States. If you know the game or not, you will learn the true story of Marco Polo and his adventures in China under the great *Kublai Khan*.

These little girls live in Peru. They are descended from the great Inka civilization of the Middle Ages.

When considering China, we will also look at the building of the *Forbidden City* during the *Ming dynasty*. You will learn, for example, that the Forbidden City was not really a city but rather the name of an enormous palace. However, as the name implies, it was most certainly *forbidden!* Only the emperor of China and a few others were ever allowed to enter this magnificent place. (And it was magnificent!)

On the sad side of things, the *Crusades* were still going on in the 1200s. But these were nothing like the Crusades of earlier times. These Crusades were led by *children*. You read that correctly—children! Thousands of young boys and girls felt led to try to recapture the Holy Land on their own. It was tragic, however, because a good number of them died trying to be so heroic.

As awful as that was, the *Black Death* that hit Europe during the 1300s was maybe even worse. Millions of people died from it! The Black Death was a type of plague that wiped out nearly a third of the population of Europe without any warning. (The cause of it may surprise you.) Those who somehow survived the plague might have died instead in one of the longest wars in history. That would be the *Hundred Years' War* between France and England. It finally ended but not without the tragic death of *Joan of Arc*, a young peasant girl who tried her best to help the French win the war. Her story is world famous. You have probably heard of her before.

Though daunting from the outside, the Forbidden City was intricately decorated on the inside.

There were two Scotsmen who also risked their lives for their country. They were *William Wallace* and *Robert Bruce*. A popular movie titled *Braveheart* helped to make one of these heroes better known.

The last "bad guys" we will look at include *King John* (the villain in the tales of Robin Hood), *Frederick II* (whom some people loved), and the *Ottoman Turks*. Of course, if you were Islamic, you might not view the Ottoman Turks as "bad guys." You would see them as the great Muslim conquerors who took over Constantinople and brought down the Byzantine Empire at the same time. To the Arab world it was pure victory and has remained so for centuries.

In fact, the fall of the Byzantine Empire is so significant that many historians would consider it the closing point of the Middle Ages. But I prefer not to. I chose instead to focus on a common invention for the end of our study of the Middle Ages. I could tell you now what that invention was, but then there would be no suspense at all in what's left in this book. I'll let you just wonder about it instead—just wonder what I would find so important as to leave until the very last lesson of the book. I think you'll understand when we get there.

In closing, I like to look at history this way. Just as a person grows and develops through the phases of birth, babyhood, childhood, teen years, adulthood, and old age, so history grows and develops through phases. I would say that Creation is like birth. It's the beginning of all things. Ancient history (Volume I) is like babyhood. Events from this time period laid the foundation for the rest of time. The Early Church and the Middle Ages (Volume II) could be compared to childhood. It too lays the groundwork for centuries to come. Naturally, a person would never make it to their teen years, adulthood, or old age without having gone through childhood first. In the same way,

I broke my arm twice when I was a child! Growing up oftentimes includes mishaps like this.

the world would never have made it to the Renaissance, modern times, or the future without having gone through the Middle Ages. Though this time period had its bumps and bruises (as all children do), it was growing up to look like the world we know today. That is just one way to look at history.

And no matter the phase of life you are in, remember the purpose of life. Remember that we are created to know God and to make Him known. Remember that the study of history is just one way to better know the stories of God revealing Himself to mankind and to better appreciate His glorious plan for us. If you are in your childhood, teen years, adulthood, or old age, remember the mystery of history. The Bible, in Ephesians 3:8–12, says so clearly what my heart feels:

*"To me, who am less than the least of all the saints, this grace was given, that I should preach among the Gentiles the unsearchable riches of Christ, and to make all see what is the fellowship of the **mystery**, which from the beginning of the ages has been hidden in God who created all things through Jesus Christ; to the intent that now the manifold wisdom of God might be made known by the church to the principalities and powers in the heavenly places, according to the eternal purpose which He accomplished in Christ Jesus our Lord, in whom we have boldness and access with confidence through faith in Him."* (Bolded word is mine for emphasis.)

☑ WHAT DO YOU KNOW?

PRETEST 22

Who/What Am I? Choose the best answer from the list below.

1. I am in such awe over God the Creator that I've even encouraged the birds to praise Him. Who am I?

2. I opened a convent for women and influenced nuns to perform works of charity. Who am I?

3. Though I vowed myself to a life of poverty, I love to learn and encouraged priests to higher education. Who am I?

4. I am a 12-year-old German boy who tried to lead children on a Crusade. Who am I?

5. I am another 12-year-old boy who tried to lead children on a Crusade. But I am from France. Who am I?

6. I am one of the most important documents in history. What am I?

7. I was forced to place my seal of approval on the Magna Carta? Who am I?

8. I married King John of England but was neglected and mistreated. Who am I?

WORD BANK

Stephen of Cloyes	St. Dominic	Isabella	King John
St. Francis of Assisi	Magna Carta	Nicholas	St. Clara

ST. FRANCIS OF ASSISI, ST. CLARA, AND ST. DOMINIC

LESSON 64

We have learned about a lot of remarkable people in this book. But I think our main characters today are sure to stand out from the others. This lesson is about **St. Francis of Assisi, St. Clara,** and **St. Dominic.** You will learn that they lived their lives to the extreme in the name of Christ. Their stories are refreshing ones. I'll begin with Francis . . .

St. Francis

Like any of the rest of us, Francis wasn't born a saint. On the contrary, he was rather an ordinary youth. He had handsome black hair and eyes, a kind face, and the voice of a troubadour. Though he was very wealthy, he struggled with being responsible with his father's business and enjoyed partying with his friends instead. Like many young men, he entered the army in Italy looking for adventure rather than for war. Francis may have remained a typical rich kid working his way up in society. But special things began to happen to him.

First, Francis believed he heard the voice of the Lord telling him to leave the army and go home to **Assisi.** (Assisi is a city in Italy.) Francis obeyed. In returning home, he paid less and less attention to his father's business and spent more and more time in church. In February of 1207, Francis had another spiritual encounter. He felt that Christ Himself spoke to him from the altar of a small chapel named **St. Damian.** In response, Francis dedicated his life to Christ right then and there. Before he left he gave the money he had to the priest of St. Damian's.

Shortly after that, Francis passed by a leper in the streets and turned his face away from him in disgust. Then it bothered Francis that he had been so cruel. So he went back to the leper, gave him the money he had and kissed him on the hand! (It was unheard of to touch a leper, much less to kiss one.) Showing this kind of strong compassion for the poor and needy was just one way that Francis chose to live the rest of his life.

Two years later, Francis had yet another spiritual experience that shaped his life even more. While in church he was absolutely gripped by the reading of the following passage:

"And as you go, preach, saying, 'The kingdom of heaven is at hand.' Heal the sick, cleanse the lepers, raise the dead, cast out demons. Freely you have received, freely give. Provide neither gold nor silver nor copper in your money belts, nor bag for your journey, nor two tunics, nor sandals, nor staffs." (Matt. 10:7–10)

Francis took this Scripture literally. (That means word for word.) He felt that Christ Himself commissioned him to do two important things: to preach the kingdom of heaven, and to own nothing. And so, to the best of his ability, he obeyed. Francis preached freely in the city squares and on the road to all who would listen. And he owned absolutely nothing! Much against his father's wishes, he gave all his wealth away. It's been said Francis so often gave the clothes off his back to someone in greater need than himself that his friends had a hard time keeping him clothed at all!

In a short time, the humble devotion of Francis attracted 12 men to follow his example. They agreed to live a life of poverty, to preach Christ, and not to marry. They made themselves plain robes and built huts for sleeping when they couldn't find shelter otherwise. Each day they went out with Francis—penniless and barefoot—to preach to crowds of people. Each night they returned to have their feet washed by Francis and to share together a meal that had been collected that day (or begged for).

This dedicated group of men called themselves ***Fratres minores,*** which is Latin for "minor brothers." (We translate *fratre* as the word ***friar.***) They considered themselves brothers instead of priests and always the least, or most minor, of Christ's servants. They were later named **Franciscans** after St. Francis and are still known for cheerfully greeting others with the words: *"The Lord give thee peace."* (Even their modern Web sites use these words of introduction!)

Do you think these poor friars made a difference in the society around them? Of course they did. Their impact was huge. Not because they were perfect men, but because they modeled the life of a perfect Savior. You see, up until this time, the monks and nuns of the Middle Ages had kept mainly to themselves. Most had withdrawn to secluded lives in order to study and preserve the Scriptures. (For which we are grateful.) But, through their bold preaching, Francis and his friars changed the priorities of the monks. By mingling with the masses, they lived more like Christ Himself. And by their humility and simplicity, they lived more like true servants to mankind.

Keep in mind, too, that by this time in history the Medieval Church had grown to be more wealthy. Ornate churches were being constructed while poor people struggled for housing. Some priests and bishops dressed lavishly while the peasants struggled for clothing. So when Francis and the other friars set their wealth aside to bring people back to God and the church, it was very powerful. By expecting nothing in material gain, the friars demonstrated true care for the welfare of others.

Though successful in reaching souls, Francis didn't want to compete with the church. So, in **1210** he asked **Pope Innocent III** in Rome for permission to start a *religious order*. The pope personally felt that the friars lived too harshly for people to want to follow their lifestyle. He said:

"My dear children, your life appears to me too severe. I see indeed that your fervor is great . . . but I ought to consider those who will come after you, lest your mode of life be beyond their strength." [1]

Pope Innocent had a good point—that is, that most people would *not* want to live as poorly as the friars did. But in reality, the friars didn't ask everyone to live as they did. Rather they preached:

"Fear and honor God, praise and bless Him. . . . Repent. . . for you know that we shall soon die . . . Abstain from evil, persevere in the good." [2]

Those were words that thousands needed to hear. And they did when the pope granted Francis the religious order he desired. That same year, the friars were given a small chapel to work out of that was so tiny (10 feet across) it was nicknamed **Porziuncola**, or "little portion." It served as the first monastery of St. Francis.

And so that you might appreciate even more the kind soul that Francis was, I want to share with you his love for God's creation. Francis was supposedly so in awe over the perfect design of nature that he hated to even snuff out a candle for fear he might offend it. He once wrote of light:

---

1. Will Durant, *The Age of Faith.* Vol. IV of *The Story of Civilization.* New York: Simon and Schuster, 1950; p. 798.
2. Ibid.

"In the morning, when the sun rises, every man ought to praise God, who created it for our use . . . When it becomes night, every man ought to give praise on account of Brother Fire, by which our eyes are then enlightened; for we be all, as it were, blind; and the Lord by these two, our brothers, doth enlighten our eyes." [3]

St. Francis of Assisi was known for his love of God's Creation. He especially loved the little birds.

And of God's creatures, Francis had even more appreciation. Legend claims he preached a sermon to a flock of birds calling them "My little sisters the birds . . ." and pleading with them to praise their Maker who gave them so much! Whether or not the birds complied, I do not know. But Francis helped to protect them by asking the emperor to make it against the law to kill the larks. He asked, too, that it be required of every man on Christmas Day to throw out grain to feed the poor birds of the field.

Now lest you think that Francis was too gentle of a man, please know that he was also bold enough to cross the continent of Europe in order to share Christ with the Muslims. He was appalled at the massacres taking place through the Crusades and he hoped to intervene. He attempted visits to Syria, Egypt, and Spain, though none proved to be very successful.

St. Clara

One particular woman influenced by the gentleness, humility, and boldness of Francis was **Clara dei Sciffi.** Though only 18 years old and very wealthy, Clara yearned to make the same difference in the world as Francis and the friars. With the support of Francis, she vowed herself to poverty, chastity (not marrying), and a life of obedience to Christ. In **1212** she formed the **Second Order of St. Francis** and opened a convent for women. As Francis influenced the monks to leave seclusion, so Clara transformed the nuns to do the same.

Though the nuns in their humanity were certain to break some of their own strict rules, they did much to be admired. The nuns took in orphans, worked in hospitals, provided education to young girls, sewed and embroidered, copied Scriptures, and rose at midnight to pray. The nuns have historically been a hardworking, devout group of women living not at all for themselves but rather to please the Lord and serve mankind. Though Clara died in 1253, by the year 1300 there were probably as many nuns as there were monks due in part to the influence of Clara. The "Poor Clares," as they were often called, still exist today as a religious order devoted to service for the Lord.

Because the first convent for nuns was established in Egypt, the term nun comes from a Coptic (Egyptian Christian) word that means "pure."

---

3. Ibid., p. 797.

Another person who undoubtedly lived to please God was **Dominic.** Born in Spain and raised by his uncle priest, Dominic was influenced by the church at a young age. Unlike Francis, who turned from the ways of the world to serve Christ, Dominic was immersed in the teachings of the church from boyhood and appears to have followed them all his life.

Even as a young man, Dominic was impressed to give what little he had to help others. One time during a famine, Dominic sold the few possessions he owned—including his beloved books—to help feed the poor. He vowed to stay in poverty after that and for the next 10 years went about barefoot to teach and preach Christ. With much compassion and zeal, Dominic's primary mission was to put down **heresy.** That is a big word meaning false teachings. But rather than burn heretics at the stake (as was becoming all too common in the late Middle Ages), Dominic saved them from the flames to teach them truth! For this he was nicknamed "the pursuer of heretics."

Like the Franciscans, Dominic and his followers were recognized by the pope in **1216** for starting a new religious order. The **Dominicans**, as they were called, were headquartered in **Rome** but went as far as **Kiev, Russia,** and into other faraway lands to share the Gospel. They were recognizable because they wore robes of plain white cloth of the least expensive fabric of the time period. In 1240 they were described this way by someone in England:

Though Dominic was from Spain, his followers were headquartered in Rome and traveled as far away as Russia in the name of the Gospel.

"Very sparing in food and raiment, possessing neither gold nor silver nor anything of their own, they went through cities, towns, and villages, preaching the Gospel . . . living together by tens or sevens . . . thinking not of the morrow, nor keeping anything for the next morning . . . Whatsoever was left over from their table of the alms given them, this they gave forthwith to the poor. They went shod only with the Gospel, they slept in their clothes on mats, and laid stones for pillows under their heads." [4]

You may think that the Dominicans and the Franciscans sound just alike. And as barefoot, penniless, preachers, they were very similar. But there was at least one difference. Dominic was in favor of **higher education** but Francis was not. Francis saw no benefit in worldly knowledge except to gain wealth or power, neither of which interested him. Dominic, on the other hand, was saddened by the lack of education among the priests. He encouraged his followers to join the universities around them and shed the light of Christ there. And that they did. You will learn later that the Dominicans produced some of the greatest scholars and scientists of the Middle Ages. The Franciscans produced many famous scholars, too, as their view toward higher education relaxed over time.

You may be wondering what became of these two great saints—Francis and Dominic—and their devoted disciples. Francis lived only to age 45. He was in poor health but died singing a psalm while visiting back at Porziuncola, his first tiny monastery. At the time of his death, over 5,000 men were members of the Franciscan order that had spread into five other countries. By 1280 the Franciscans grew to include 200,000 monks and 8,000 monasteries.

---

4. Ibid., p. 803.

Dominic died on the younger side as well, only one year after establishing his new order. This fact makes it all the more amazing that the Dominicans are still an active group today as are the Franciscans and the Poor Clares. All three groups have members around the world. The Franciscans draw members from both Roman Catholic and Protestant churches alike. Though rules for living have been relaxed and modified, the orders are still committed to serving mankind under the name of Christ. Men, women, singles, couples, clergy, or laypersons—people from many walks of life—are involved.

Grace

I believe it is safe to say that these three people, Saints Francis, Clara, and Dominic, were truly extraordinary. Their personal sacrifice and devotion to Christ are to be much admired. At the same time, I do want to mention one thing. The works of these individuals and their followers were *so* extraordinary that they could be misleading. Some would argue that these people (or their followers) promoted *good works*

Neither Francis nor Dominic lived to be very old, but both men influenced thousands through their dedication and devotion to God.

as a means of salvation. Some of you might be too young to understand this concept. I suggest you discuss it with your teacher. But I will try to summarize the issue at hand.

The Bible teaches that we are saved by grace, not by our good works, because none of our good works are "good enough" to make up for our sinfulness. (Eph. 2:8–9; Rom. 3:10) Christ, though, who was fully God and fully man, lived a perfect life. In doing so, He chose not only to die for our sins but to stand in our place before God with *His* perfect record of obedience. In other words, it is *His* good works, not ours, that make us right before God. (Matt. 20:28; Rom. 5:6–8, 18; 8:3–4; Heb. 5:8–9;12:14) We call that being *justified*. Christ willingly lived a perfect life and died on the cross that we might be "justified" before God. (Rom. 5:1–2)

Once we are justified (by *accepting* the gift of God's grace through the faith He gives us) it is certainly God's desire that we live good lives! (Rom. 6:11–14; 1 Cor. 15:58) The Bible says, *"For we are His workmanship, created in Christ Jesus for good works."* (Eph. 2:10) We call that *sanctification*. It is a process of growing through the work of the Holy Spirit that takes place throughout our lives. In growing, we become more like Christ, and the Spirit produces in us the fruits of love, joy, peace, patience, kindness, goodness, faithfulness, gentleness, and self-control. (Gal. 5:22–23)

Though the Bible clearly teaches that we are saved by faith (Rom. 10:910), there are those who confuse *justification* (grace) with *sanctification* (good works). In other words, some may try to *earn* God's grace and favor through *their* good works for Him. Can we? No, not according to the Bible. (2 Tim. 1:8–12; Titus 3:4–7)

In the case of St. Francis, St. Clara, and St. Dominic, the historical record isn't clear as to whether or not they understood this important part of the Gospel. The good news is that it is not man's responsibility to judge the heart. Only God can do that. (2 Cor. 5:10) But it is the responsibility of believers to teach the Gospel according to God's Word—the Bible—which includes the message of grace and Christ's substitutionary death for us. (2 Tim. 2:1–2)

ACTIVITIES FOR LESSON 64

ALL STUDENTS

Sing the hymn, "All Creatures of Our God and King," written by Francis of Assisi. The beautiful words are a testimony of his love for God's Creation. You can find the words and hear the music at this Web site: www.cyberhymnal.org.

64A—Younger Students

1. With your teacher, light a simple candle to admire the perfect design of one of God's created elements.

2. It is written in today's lesson that the followers of St. Dominic slept with their clothes on using a rock for a pillow. Try sleeping in the same way for just one night to appreciate comfort.

3. In honor of St. Francis, make a pinecone birdfeeder. Simply spread peanut butter on the outside of a pinecone. Sprinkle birdseed over it. Hang in a tree or bush outdoors and enjoy the birds. Take a photo of the feeder (and hopefully some birds who have found it) and file it in your Student Notebook under "Europe: Italy."

64B—Middle Students

1. Take a "virtual tour" through the town of Assisi (the home of St. Francis) via the Internet site below. Print photos of the locations and file them in your Student Notebook under "Europe: Italy."

    www.wtu.edu/franciscan/packs/tour/index.html

2. Creative Writing: Pretend you are a bird and write a thank-you note to your Creator. For what things should a bird be thankful? How about you?

64C—Older Students

1. On the Internet, research the Franciscans, the Dominicans, or the Poor Clares. Record the mission statement of the group you choose. File it under the country and continent where the order appears to be strongest in number.

2. The following is a quote by St. Dominic regarding his disgust with the wealth of many clergy. Take his words and rewrite them in your own modern-day language. Discuss the meaning of unfamiliar terms.

    "It is not by the display of power and pomp, nor by cavalcades of retainers and richly houseled palfreys, nor by gorgeous apparel, that the heretics win proselytes; it is by zealous preaching, by apostolic humility, by austerity, by holiness." [5]

3. Art History Project: Use the Internet or library resources to search for a portrait of St. Francis by Francisco De Zurbaran (1598–1664). Print or photocopy the image and add it to your Student Notebook under "Europe: Italy."

---

5. Ibid., p. 803.

THE CHILDREN'S CRUSADE
LESSON 65

As the title suggests, this lesson is about children. But it is not the least bit fun, as writing about children ought to be. This lesson is but another *tragic* story from the Middle Ages. It is tragic because it involves the loss of thousands of children on one of the Crusades.

You probably remember the results of the **Third Crusade** (Lesson 61). The Third Crusade involved an unusual relationship between **Richard the Lionhearted** and **Saladin.** At the end, the two gentlemen settled on a peace treaty. But the Muslims were the real victors. They kept power over the holy city of Jerusalem and maintained Islamic worship at the Dome of the Rock (where the Temple once stood).

Well, many Christian hearts were broken over the inability to regain Jerusalem. Though Christians were given the right to pilgrimage through the Holy Land, it was not enough for many. Several more Crusades were initiated, but none had lasting effect.

Strangely enough, in the same year—1212—there were two different boys from two different countries who believed the Lord was speaking to them. Their mission was the same—to lead a crusade of children to take back Jerusalem. I will describe the boys and their stories separately because the two might not have met or even known that the other existed.

Nicholas

At the time of the **Children's Crusade, Nicholas** was a boy about 12 years old. He lived in **Germany.** Nicholas believed he heard the Lord instruct him to march on the Holy City. Now I don't know exactly what this boy was thinking, but in my imagination, I believe he may have thought "How? How can I, just a boy, lead a crusade?" That would have been a great question. But I suspect he never asked himself, "Why?" Nicholas probably grew up knowing *exactly why* the Crusades were being fought. He probably had heard all kinds of heroic and gruesome stories from his parents, grandparents, uncles, and friends. He probably understood why thousands and thousands of Europeans had risked their lives over the city of Jerusalem. And for reasons we can't fully understand, he was willing to do the same.

Somehow Nicholas managed to recruit thousands of other children to go with him. Most were boys around the age of 12, but some were girls dressed up like boys. Nicholas appealed to other children by proclaiming that God needed their pure and innocent spirits to fight this holy war. Priests of the church, and of course the parents of these children, begged them not to go. But they went anyway. In fact, nearly 30,000 children slipped away to follow Nicholas on his crusade!

Legend suggests it may be this mass exodus of children that led to the story of the **Pied Piper of Hamelin.** In that tale, hundreds of German children were lured from their homes by the piper and were never seen again. There are other theories about the story behind the Pied Piper, but the Children's Crusade is certainly one possibility.

Nicholas and his thousands of young followers left mainly from the city of **Cologne** in Germany. They traveled along the Rhine River and over the Alps. The Alps, by the way, is a large mountain system across Europe. You can only imagine the disaster this trip came to be.

The children were terribly unprepared for their journey. Many of them starved on the way. Some were attacked by wolves. Some were robbed by thieves who apparently had not a trace of conscience in them about stealing from children.

The children who did survive the dangerous hike over the Alps made it as far as **Genoa, Italy.** There the children were laughed at and scorned for their efforts to lead a crusade. Ship captains refused to sail them to the Holy Land. They were told to go home. Most of the children did just that, though home was a long way away. Some stayed to live in Genoa and learn the trading business.

The Alps form a natural barrier between Germany and Italy. Peaks range from 6,000 to 15,000 feet above sea level!

If our story could end here, it wouldn't be so bad. Not that climbing over the Alps and back again was easy. But at least many of these children lived through the journey. However, there's more to the story of the Children's Crusade. There is still the other boy.

Stephen of Cloyes

Stephen of Cloyes was also a boy about 12 years old. He was a shepherd living in **France.** He believed that the Lord spoke to him while tending his flocks. Stephen, like Nicholas, felt he was to lead a group of children to the Holy Land. He told this news to the king of France who promptly ordered him to return to his sheep!

However, much like Nicholas, Stephen didn't listen to the wisdom of adults. He recruited about 20,000 children to join him! Touched by the devotion of these children, **Pope Innocent III** gave his support to the young crusaders. "The very children put us to shame," he said.[6] And he watched them bravely begin their fatal march.

These youngsters traveled by foot across France to **Marseille** (mar SAY), a French city on the coast of the Mediterranean Sea. Trusting in the Lord, the children packed no provisions. Many of them starved before they reached the coast. Once there, they were instructed by Stephen to wait for the Lord to part the sea just as the Red Sea had been parted for Moses and the Israelites.

Unfortunately, this miracle never happened. In response, two ruthless shipowners named **Hugh the Iron** and **William the Pig** offered to sail the boys and girls to Palestine. Thousands of children crowded into seven different ships thinking this must be God's answer to crossing the sea. However, two of the ships sank, killing everyone onboard. But worse than that, the captains of the other ships veered in another direction. They sailed to the northern coast of Africa where the children were bought and sold by Arabs into slavery! Supposedly, only one child was ever heard from again and that was after spending 18 years in captivity. As for Hugh the Iron and William the Pig, they were hanged for their horrid crime by order of the king!

Impressed by their devotion, Pope Innocent III gave his blessings to the children crusaders.

---

6. Christopher Gibb, *Richard the Lionheart and the Crusades.* New York: The Bookwright Press, 1986; p. 51.

Because of the terrible outcome of the Children's Crusade, I can't help but wonder if these bold young boys really heard from the Lord. I imagine others wonder the same thing too. I will conclude with some personal thoughts. In both instances, the boys appeared to work *against* the authority of their parents and other adults in deciding to launch the crusades. Furthermore, neither boy reported the use of Scripture to back up his supposed visions. From these things alone, I am inclined to believe that the boys, and the thousands that followed them, were misguided by their own zealous passion. What do you think? Better yet, what does the Bible teach about these matters? I'll leave that discussion to you.

ACTIVITIES FOR LESSON 65

65A—Younger Students

1. Obtain a copy of the *Pied Piper of Hamelin*. Read it together with your teacher. Using a recorder or flute, act out the piper leading the children out of their homes.

2. The children who followed Stephen were unwise to board the ships for several reasons. But, primarily, because the ship captains were strangers who could not be trusted. Discuss safety tips with your teacher in regard to strangers. What are some commonsense rules about talking to strangers?

3. When police are searching for a missing child, it is helpful if they have the child's fingerprints. Check with your local police department; they may have a kit or instructions on how to take fingerprints. Have your teacher fingerprint you and your classmates as  a safety measure. File your fingerprints in your Student Notebook under the continent and country where you live. While you have the supplies out, you can make cute pictures out of your fingerprints like the ones shown here.

65B—Middle Students

1. The majority of children who followed Nicholas did so despite their parents' wishes. Use a Bible to find Scripture that warns against disobedience, especially to one's parents. Write down your verses and file them under "Europe: Germany." What things can be learned from this tragic story of the Children's Crusade?

2. One of the activities for younger students is to have their fingerprints taken as a safety measure. Do the same, but also research the uniqueness of fingerprints. Compare yours to those of other family members. Make a game of matching fingerprints to family members.

65C—Older Students

In my opinion, the implications of this lesson run deep in regard to knowing the will of God. Consider studying the book *Experiencing God* by Henry Blackaby. This well-done study will guide you through biblical decision making. It will help you understand how someone can know if God is leading him or her in a particular direction.

KING JOHN AND THE MAGNA CARTA
LESSON 66

I typically write about famous people in this book. But today I'm going to write about a famous English document. It's called the **Magna Carta,** which is Latin for **"Great Charter."** Although it is really just a piece of paper, it contains important ideas that have influenced the world. Let me tell you the story of how this Great Charter became so "great."

In order to understand the writing of the Magna Carta, you will need to know who **King John** was. He has already been mentioned in several lessons. Do you remember him? John was the favorite son of **Henry II**, the disappointing son of **Eleanor of Aquitaine,** and the embarrassing brother of **Richard the Lionhearted.** Like a spoiled child, John fought with Richard for years over the throne of England. As the older son, Richard had rightfully become the king of England after Henry II died. But, as you may remember from a previous lesson, Richard was unexpectedly killed by a crossbow at age 42. His death opened the door for John to become the king of England in 1199.

Unfortunately, John has been recorded as one of the worst kings that England ever had! That is why he is always portrayed as the "bad guy" in the stories of Robin Hood. It is important that I explain what gave John such a bad reputation because it was his awful reign that led to the writing of the Magna Carta.

King John

King John had numerous flaws. But mainly, he was ruthless. For example, though he first demonstrated tolerance toward the Jewish people in his kingdom, he in time turned against them by imposing high taxes. At least one Jewish man who refused to pay was tortured by the extraction of one tooth a day until payment was made!

Because of his bad reputation as king of England, King John is typically portrayed as the villain in the tales of Robin Hood.

But King John's cruelty didn't stop there. He was harsh to his own countrymen when it came to keeping strict laws about the forests. If you remember, an English forest was a special hunting ground for nobility. John hoarded these properties and severely punished intruders. This was the basis for his evil side in the tales of Robin Hood.

And closer to home, King John was even cruel to his wives. He divorced his first wife in order to steal another man's fiancée. Her name was **Isabella.** But after marrying her, John neglected Isabella and had children from other mistresses.

As might be obvious, King John was not a godly man of strong faith. On the contrary, the monks who knew him best thought he was an atheist. An atheist believes there is no god. Apparently, John lived much of his life acting as if there were no god. He once had such a spat with **Pope Innocent III** that he threatened to banish all the church leaders from England and "put out the eyes and cut off the nose of some of them for good measure." [7] As a result, the pope closed the churches in England except to perform baptisms. The church bells stopped ringing, and the dead were buried without any religious ceremony. It was a dark time for England.

---

7. Will Durant, *The Age of Faith.* Vol. IV of *The Story of Civilization.* New York: Simon and Schuster, 1950; p. 675.

Eventually Pope Innocent excommunicated King John from the church. Of course, spiritually, John didn't really care and ignored it. But in time, he needed the support of the pope for political reasons. In order to get back in good standing with him, King John surrendered his crown and the entire kingdom of England to Pope Innocent III! In the arrangement, the pope gave England back to John within five days—but only for a certain amount of money.

King John had really made a mess of things. His nobles were furious with him. But probably nothing made the nobles and barons more upset with John than his ridiculous taxes. England had already been heavily taxed under Richard the Lionhearted to help pay for the Crusades. With the Crusades over for awhile, people expected taxes to be lightened. But instead, John raised them even more for his own personal gain! England had had it with King John. It was said of him, "We search in vain for any good deed, one kindly act to set against his countless offendings." [8]

The Writing of the Magna Carta

For two years, the nobles and barons of King John tried to force him to follow the laws of the land. In those laws, the power of the king was limited. But John refused to comply. So finally, there rose up an army against King John. Their aim was not to fight or kill the king. They just wanted to make him behave.

This army of nobles and barons met King John at a place called **Runnymede.** It was a meadow near the **Thames** (TEMZ) **River**. John had run out of excuses with the barons for his bad behavior, and he didn't have enough supporters to fight for him. So, at Runnymede, on June 15, **1215,** the barons forced John to put his seal of approval on the Magna Carta. He couldn't actually "sign" the document because John didn't know how to write. But his kingly seal was enough to put the Magna Carta into effect.

What exactly was this document? It basically was a list of rights. In 63 articles written in Latin, the Magna Carta gave rights to the barons as well as to the free people under them. Most importantly, the Magna Carta put limits on the power of the king. For example, should the king not follow the law, the Magna Carta allowed 25 nobles to fight against the king without being guilty of treason. This meant that the king's authority did not go above the law of the land. Rather, the *law* was above the king! I hope you can picture just how important that concept is.

To prevent dictatorship, the Magna Carta put limits on the power of the king of England.

The amazing thing about the Magna Carta is how it has been continually used in history. It was used later to coin the famous phrase "No taxation without representation." This means that no one should pay taxes to a government without having some say in how that government is run. This is still considered a fundamental right in free countries. The Magna Carta was also used to guarantee people a trial by jury in the event they were accused of a crime. That is also considered a fundamental right in free countries. To some degree, the Magna Carta helped to shape the **Bill of Rights** of many nations including the **United States, Canada**, and **France.**

As you can imagine, the Magna Carta was used to keep kings from becoming dictators. Two later kings in England, Edward II and Richard II, were both *deposed* by the English people using the Magna Carta. *Deposed* means they were removed from the throne—legally! You can see where the charter placed power in the hands of the people. For that reason the Magna Carta has been called the "cornerstone of liberty" and the "basis for democracy." Some would say it is the most famous document in history.

---

8. T. Walter Wallbank and Alastair M. Taylor, *Civilization Past and Present*. Chicago: Scott, Foresman and Co., 1949; p. 444.

As for King John, he didn't appear to learn any lessons from the Great Charter. He immediately went against the document and tried to fight the barons who forced him to approve it. Not much later, in 1216, King John died suddenly of disease. He was only 49. His son **Henry III** became the next king at just age 6. He proved to be almost as bad a king as was his father (except that he inspired the beautiful expansion of Westminster Abbey). But well into Henry III's reign, the Magna Carta was in effect, giving the people of England some protection from his high taxes.

I hope you can appreciate the significance of the Magna Carta. Without it, England, and many free countries of the world, might look a little different today.

ACTIVITIES FOR LESSON 66

ALL STUDENTS

Make your Memory Cards for Lessons 64–66.

66A—Younger and Middle Students

Listed below are two activities. You could do either one separately, or incorporate them together, depending on how much time you have to spend on this project.

1. Create aged document paper.

   Materials: Paper, coffee, paper towel

   a. Have your teacher buy or make a cup of coffee. Allow it to cool.

   b. Dip a paper towel into the coffee.

   c. Smear the coffee onto your paper to give it an aged appearance.

   d. Allow it to dry.

2. For this next activity, you may use the aged-looking document you made above OR photocopy on parchment-colored paper a segment of the Magna Carta from the Activity Supplement in the Appendix. Obtain supplies for making a seal on a document. Use a rubber stamp, sealing wax, candle wax, a gold-foil sticker, or simple markers to create an official-looking seal on the bottom of the document. Punch three holes in the paper or slide it into a clear sheet protector and file it in your Student Notebook under "Europe: England."

66B—Middle Students

1. Research the famous Westminster Abbey in England. Who first built the cathedral? What did Henry III do to improve it? What is special about "French Gothic" architecture? Who is buried at Westminster Abbey? Find pictures of the abbey for your Student Notebook. File them under "Europe: England."

2. Discuss the expression "No taxation without representation." What does it mean? Is this true of the government where you live? If so, how are *you* represented? How can you make your opinion known to your local and/or national government? As a family or class, write a letter to authorities regarding any issue that concerns you.

66C—Older Students

1. Obtain and read a copy of the United States Bill of Rights. If you are a United States citizen, write a paragraph about what it means to you. If you live elsewhere, research whether your country has a Bill of Rights or something comparable.

2. Create a courtroom drama. Choose a jury for a trial and act out the freedom of trial by jury.

TAKE ANOTHER LOOK!
REVIEW 22: LESSONS 64–66

Wall of Fame

1. *St. Francis of Assisi, St. Clara, and St. Dominic (1210, 1212, 1216)*—On a small, square piece of paper, draw a little bird. Use a clear piece of tape to adhere some birdseed below the bird. Label it "St. Francis." Make a separate figure for St. Clara and one for St. Dominic. Place them in robes (make Dominic's white). [From *History Through the Ages*, use *Francis of Assisi* and *Saint Dominic*.]

2. *The Children's Crusade (1212)*—Draw two boys with crosses on their shirts and tears falling from their eyes. Name them "Nicholas" and "Stephen." [Use *Children's Crusade* and *Pope Innocent III*.]

3. *King John and the Magna Carta (1215)*—Depict a document with King John's seal of approval on it. [Use *King John* and *Magna Carta*.]

SomeWHERE in Time

Highlight the journeys of the Children's Crusades.

Materials: Outline Map 24, "The Crusades"; two highlighters or crayons

1. Find the city of Cologne, Germany. Find also the city of Genoa, Italy. Use a highlighter to connect these two cities but be sure to follow the Rhine River and cross over the Alps with your highlighter. This will mark the route of the children who tried to follow Nicholas to the Holy Land. Make a key at the bottom of your map to identify this route.

2. Find the city of Paris in France. Though we don't know if Paris was the exact origin of the French children who followed Stephen of Cloyes, we do know where they were headed. That was to the city of Marseille on the coast of the Mediterranean. Use a highlighter to connect Paris to Marseille. Draw also a line from Marseille to the northern coast of Africa where, unfortunately, many were taken into slavery. Label this route on a key at the bottom of your map.

3. File this map in your Student Notebook under "Europe: France *or* Germany."

WHAT DID YOU MISS?

WEEK 22: EXERCISE

Colorful Word Search. Today's exercise is a word search. But it is not the ordinary kind. Using colored pencils or markers, circle the words in the color suggested for each group. I think you'll find this word search to be a real challenge, but I'm confident you can do it! (Younger students may require assistance or choose to pass on this.) Note that there are backward and diagonal words and that the word search ignores spaces, periods, and hyphens in names. Good luck!

1. Find and circle in green the names of these three missionary companions to Paul.
   > Barnabas
   >
   > Silas
   >
   > Timothy

2. Find and circle in blue these three sects of Judaism.
   > Pharisees
   >
   > Sadducees
   >
   > Essenes

3. Find and circle in black these three Christian martyrs.
   > Ignatius
   >
   > Polycarp
   >
   > Justin

4. Find and circle in gold these three kings of England.
   > Arthur
   >
   > Alfred
   >
   > William

5. Find and circle in orange these three Christian missionaries.
   > Patrick
   >
   > Columba
   >
   > Boniface

6. Find and circle in red these three Chinese dynasties.
   > Sui
   >
   > Tang
   >
   > Song

7. Find and circle in brown these three Islamic leaders.

    Mohammed

    Harun al-Rashid

    Saladin

8. Find and circle in purple these three Holy Roman emperors.

    Otto

    Henry IV

    Frederick Barbarossa

9. Find and circle in pink these three women of the Middle Ages.

    Wu Zetian

    Eleanor

    St. Clara

10. Find and circle in gray this family of kings.

    Henry II

    Richard the Lionhearted

    King John

WEEK 22 WORD SEARCH

```
C Z P H A R I S E E S J I D E A M V Z R A Z E V A
V H Q C H D Y C A G Q G A E S W U H A R P A X Q N
G M I H A E J Y N L N S J M S X I S T U L M L J L
K A X J S M N A Q A I U T M E O B H W V L D O I Q
V A K D S I T R T Y Z S V A N H U S D E V R X E F
P C E D O A I I Y W U O I H E R V U F T V K Q O N
O M K C R V U L I I N P R O S K C I R T A P S M I
M T W B A S Y L U B I I Z M P F K I N G J O H N D
L F T I B F L C W A D F W Y R W N M U K O Z W U A
R U C O R I I S O N G P E U B A Z L C V V W B I L
D E T R A E H N O I L E H T D R A H C I R D A Y A
J Y U M B T D A O A T P E S G A M S Y B I V R I S
U S L K K I K B B C W A L F L U R U H C Y N C T
S V D L C S C M X M S L N Z T C N A S L O R A O G
T I A V I L A R O J U A V Q U E A A D F R T B Y D
I M S R R C D D S T I L O Z H S R D E R F L A O V
N M T X E K W Z D T H M O A H L T E K E N V S N R
U Z C T D U S N E U F Y B C A C Z E J Q Z Q V Z A
K A L Y E G U Z H F C G X N E L E A N O R Z E K H
H A A G R E U M B A P E U H U S B K G I L U T C X
M P R G F W Q P P L C R E S J G X V O J O Y E S Z
Q R A Z P Z U D O V A Z O S O L R E B G H C W C J
P V J I P C S A K H L Y A R X W N M W I B M I Z D
L N O E E R D L Q I B Q W U Z Z A D P J M F C F Z
P R A C Y L O P X Y Y Q V T Y L B G F W H E W T C
```

ALFRED
ARTHUR
BARNABAS
BONIFACE
COLUMBA
ELEANOR
ESSENES
FREDERICK BARBAROSSA
HARUN AL-RASHID
HENRY II
HENRY IV
IGNATIUS
JUSTIN
KING JOHN
MOHAMMED

OTTO
PATRICK
PHARISEES
POLYCARP
RICHARD THE LIONHEARTED
SADDUCEES
SALADIN
SILAS
SONG
ST. CLARA
SUI
TANG
TIMOTHY
WILLIAM
WU ZETIAN

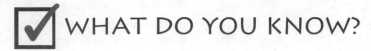 WHAT DO YOU KNOW?

PRETEST 23

Scramble! Unscramble the words to fill in the blanks. Use the word bank below.

1. Frederick II, the redheaded grandson of Frederick Barbarossa, became the king of (licyiS) _____ when he was just 4 years old.

2. "Stupor Mundi," the nickname of Frederick II, means "The Amazement of the (dorWl) _____.

3. Despite the disapproval of the (pepo) _____, Frederick II crowned himself the king of Jerusalem.

4. Thomas Aquinas felt a calling to join the (snacinimoD) _____ in service to God rather than work for the Holy Roman Emperor, Frederick II.

5. Thomas Aquinas's greatest work, *Summa Theologica*, included excerpts on (golic) _____, metaphysics, theology, psychology, ethics, politics, and religion.

6. Thomas Aquinas wrote extensively using ideas of Aristotle, the famous (kerGe) _____ philospher.

7. Roger Bacon, a member of the Franciscans and a brilliant scientist, predicted the invention of (scar) _____, airplanes, motorboats, and possibly even submarines.

8. Because the Franciscans did not encourage higher education, Roger Bacon wrote many of his works in (treecs) _____.

WORD BANK

Greek	cars	logic	Sicily
secret	Dominicans	pope	World

FREDERICK II,
"THE AMAZEMENT OF THE WORLD"
LESSON 67

Some figures in history are easy to label as good or bad. With **Frederick II**, however, it is difficult to say. As the king of three regions, it seems he was loved *and* hated, admired *and* despised, respected *and* condemned. How confusing is that to a history student? It's *very* confusing in my opinion. But I'll try to explain some reasons for Frederick's various reputations. I think he may have earned them all, including the title ***Stupor Mundi*** meaning "***The Amazement of the World.***"

As background to this story, Frederick II was the son of a Holy Roman Emperor. He was the grandson of **Frederick Barbarossa** (the emperor who drowned on the Third Crusade, Lesson 61). Frederick came from a strong family of rulers.

However, Frederick became the Holy Roman Emperor when he was only 2 years old! At age 4 he was declared the **king of Sicily**. (Sicily is the large Mediterranean island that looks like it is being "kicked" by Italy.) Obviously, at this young age, he wasn't out fighting for his crown. He inherited it. That means he was handed the throne when his father died.

Sadly, the very next year, when Frederick was just 5, his mother died. In her will, she asked **Pope Innocent III** to be the guardian, educator, and protector for her son. I suppose she thought he was a trustworthy man, being the pope and all. Well, he might have been trustworthy, but unfortunately, he was also very busy. As a result, Frederick was fairly neglected as a youngster and allowed to run the streets. He was at times living in poverty and had to beg for food to eat.

Being a child king and a neglected foster son of the pope makes for a rather unusual childhood. But Frederick made the most of it and learned from the experiences around him. Though he didn't go to school on any regular basis, he proved to be quite smart. In fact, he was brilliant. He grew up learning to speak at least nine different languages. Seven of those he could write. Besides that, he read volumes of history on his own ("Good for him!" the author is thinking), and he became a skilled horseman. Frederick was short in stature but strong, with "long, red, curly hair; clever, positive, and proud." [1]

Frederick's dying mother requested in her will that Pope Innocent III be the guardian and protector of her young son.

By the time he was 12, Frederick fired the regent who ruled above him and began to reign over his inherited kingdom. By 15, he was married. So much for childhood! Frederick II was ready and willing to live the life of a king. Pope Innocent didn't do anything to try to stop Frederick, but he did use their relationship for his own good. He constantly made deals with Frederick to keep Sicily and the Holy Roman Empire (Germany) where he wanted them. You see, like the middle of a sandwich, the pope lived in Italy just *between* the Holy Roman Empire and Sicily. It was to his advantage to try to keep peace

---

1. Will Durant, *The Age of Faith*. Vol. IV of *The Story of Civilization*. New York: Simon and Schuster, 1950; p. 715.

with these neighboring regions. As Frederick became more and more powerful, the pope probably wished he had treated this rising king much better when he had been just a boy under his care.

Frederick's quest for knowledge grew with his age. He was curious about everything. Frederick became good at mathematics; he loved science; and he was an expert in falcony. He wrote a book about falcons that is still considered outstanding today. When he was older, Frederick II started the **University of Naples** and helped to make the **University of Salerno** one of the best medical schools in Europe.

Outside of academics, Frederick II proved to be gifted in administration, an able soldier, and a lover of the arts. He particularly admired poetry and sculpture. In a way, he was the first of many gifted men who brought Europe into a time called the **Renaissance,** a time when great art flourished unlike any other time in the history of that continent.

Frederick Versus the Pope

Well—you may be wondering—if brilliance and talent led to so much admiration of Frederick, then what made some people despise him so? I wish that were easier to answer. The problem with Frederick II goes way back to the first time the pope crowned a king (Pepin the Short and later Charlemagne). If you remember, we have talked several times about that issue. That is the problem of who was really in charge of the land—the pope or the emperor. (Remember the lesson about Pope Gregory VII and Henry IV?) During Frederick II's reign, this power struggle was again quite serious.

Though not always admired for it, Frederick II was gifted in administration, military matters, and the arts.

It seems that in **1215**, when Frederick was just a boy, Pope Innocent III held a meeting called the **Fourth Lateran Council.** In this meeting, he made himself (and the popes that followed him) the *highest* authority in the land—higher than the Holy Roman Emperor! At the time Pope Innocent made this ruling, I think he was genuinely concerned for the well-being of the church and the government. Because *he* was an excellent politician and ruler, I think he felt comfortable with granting himself so much power. But unfortunately, not everyone else did—especially Frederick when he came of age to understand it.

While Pope Innocent was alive, he and Frederick kept a decent amount of peace between them, even though Frederick wanted equal power. The two men certainly had a long history together since the pope had been Frederick's guardian. But the popes that *followed* Innocent after his death were not the least bit tolerant of Frederick. They had no attachment to him. And so the tension began. It was especially bad between Frederick and **Pope Gregory IX.**

If the tension between Frederick and the pope wasn't bad enough at *home*, the problems between them were carried all the way to the Holy Land. You see, Frederick II led another crusade to Jerusalem. It is called the "Fifth" or sometimes the "Sixth" Crusade, depending on who is counting. Regardless, it was very different from the rest. Instead of lots of fighting, it involved a truce and a marriage. You see, before Frederick ever got to Palestine, he had been named the **king of Jerusalem.** He didn't earn the right to be the king of Jerusalem, but he married a girl who was considered a princess of the region. Frederick didn't particularly care about reclaiming the Holy City for spiritual reasons. He just wanted to claim his title.

Besides that, Frederick had become a great friend with the **Egyptian sultan** who oversaw Jerusalem. Without a single drop of blood being spilled, the two men made a truce (or a peaceful agreement) to allow Frederick to have Jerusalem for awhile!

Now, you would think that Pope Gregory would be thrilled with this. The Holy City was back in Christian hands! Well, according to the pope, the "hands" of Frederick were not really Christian at all. So, instead of being happy, Pope Gregory was furious. He was so furious that his anger echoed all the way to Jerusalem.

It seems that before Frederick ever made it to the Holy City, the pope had excommunicated him *twice* from the church! Why? Several reasons. Mainly, Frederick was not a strong Christian, if he was even a Christian at all. In his love of science and the arts, he had become enamored (that means he fell in love) with the Muslim world and its sophistication in these areas. That is one reason why he and the sultan of Egypt were such close friends. It made the pope extremely nervous that freethinking Frederick was in Jerusalem. He had no confidence in his properly establishing the church there. The pope said of Frederick that he was like a "scorpion spewing poison from the sting of his tail." [2]

Before Frederick arrived in the Holy Land, the pope spread word to the people that he was a "blasphemer" (one who speaks wrongly of God) and had been excommunicated. So rather than being welcomed, Frederick was shunned. The people in Acre snarled at his entrance to the city and threw trash at him! By the time he reached Jerusalem, there was not a bishop around who would dare crown him as king. So, in **1229**, Frederick II defiantly placed a crown on his head with his *own* hands and declared himself the king of Jerusalem!

In defense of Pope Gregory IX, he was probably right to be concerned about Frederick. He was not the least bit strong in Christian doctrine. Nor was he strong in his morals. Frederick was unfaithful to his wives and was accused of lewd practices forbidden in the Bible. He failed miserably in representing Christianity and might have even been an atheist. The pope claimed that Frederick called Moses, Jesus, and Mohammed *all* liars. That is why Frederick was despised, condemned, and actually hated.

The tension between Gregory and Frederick let up for a time when they signed a peace treaty with one another. This gave Frederick a chance to take care of things back in Germany and Sicily. Over the course of his reign, he had spent most of his time in Sicily because he loved the warm climate, the beautiful cities, and the Mediterranean coast. He worked on improving laws; he wrote books; he performed science experiments; and he held debates in his court. All the while, he claimed to be as important as the Son of God and that his rule was divine. Like one of the old Roman emperors, Frederick II lorded over the society much to the displeasure of the pope.

The only common ground between the pope and Frederick was the punishment of heretics (those who disagree with Scripture and the teachings of the church). Though Frederick didn't hide his own freethinking about religion, he wouldn't tolerate it from his other countrymen. He was quick to put away Germans or Sicilians who questioned the church—though he entertained and befriended Muslims and Jews in his own court. It's no wonder his legacy is a confusing one! When it came to religion, his life was a mixed message.

As you can imagine, Gregory and Frederick remained at odds with each other until the pope died in 1241. The next pope was less harsh toward Frederick. Frederick II died in 1250. With his death, it seems that the struggle between pope and emperor finally died as well. The next few Holy Roman emperors were not quite as brilliant or power hungry as Frederick. At the same time, the power of the pope grew less strong as individual countries began to form across Europe. And so the intense struggle faded over the following ages. What a relief.

Isn't it interesting, though, that if you look up Frederick II in most history books, he is remembered as one of the greatest kings of the Middle Ages? *"Stupor mundi,"* he is called, "The amazement of the world." What do you think about him?

---

2. Ibid., p. 384.

ACTIVITIES FOR LESSON 67

67A—Younger and Middle Students

Make a 3-D picture of Frederick II crowning himself the king of Jerusalem.

Materials: Photocopy of Frederick II (as found in the Activity Supplement in the Appendix); glue; crayons, markers, or colored pencils; gold glitter; red yarn; any other color yarn; toothpicks or uncooked spaghetti; loose sequins or small buttons; small feathers; other household items

1. On sturdy paper, photocopy the drawing of Frederick II from the Activity Supplement in the Appendix.

2. Collect the suggested materials or similar items from around your house or classroom.

3. Color the figure first with crayons, markers, or colored pencils.

4. Now begin to glue onto the figure your household items to give him a three-dimensional look as suggested here (but feel free to use your imagination): gold glitter on the crown, red yarn for hair, other yarn for the edge of his robe, spaghetti pieces for the straight lines of his throne and frontal piece, sequins or buttons for jewels on the throne and frontal piece, feathers on the falcon, etc.

5. Allow your 3-D figure to dry; store it in a plastic sheet protector. File it in your Student Notebook under "Europe: Germany."

67B—Middle and Older Students

In this book we have studied so many people whose actions and behavior are clearly good as well as those who are clearly bad. But many fall into the "either/or" category! In order to sort out who is who in the Middle Ages according to their character, formulate a list. Title a piece of notebook paper "Characters of the Middle Ages." Fold it in thirds lengthwise to create three columns. On one column, write "Good Guys." On another column, "Bad Guys." On the third, write "Both." Use the Contents section to refresh your memory (and to find only main characters from the lessons) and begin to write down who you think belongs where. I will provide a short sample and allow you to do the rest. I think what you will quickly learn is that it is hard to categorize everyone. (Bear in mind that no one is perfectly "good" or "bad"— we are generalizing here.) You may also observe that many of the true "good guys" in history are those who have followed the Lord!

Characters of the Middle Ages

"Good Guys"	"Bad Guys"	"Both"
St. Valentine	Nero	Paul (Saul)
St. Francis of Assisi	King John of England	Robin Hood

(For your interest, when I did this exercise, I found approximately 23 good guys, 5 bad guys, and 18 both good and bad. Your numbers may be different than mine. I will give away one of my answers, which is the answer to where I placed the Vikings. I ranked them as "Both" good and bad.)

1. I briefly mentioned the Fourth Lateran Council in this lesson. Because of the great significance of this meeting, I would like to see you research it in more depth, particularly the term *transubstantiation*. Depending on whether you are Protestant or Catholic, you may have a different opinion on the outcome of the meeting. The ramifications of it had a lot to do with the later Reformation. One suggested resource would be pages 80–81 in The 100 *Most Important Events in Christian History* by Curtis, Lang, and Petersen.

2. Had I more room in this book, I might have made a separate lesson on Pope Innocent III. Consider the lessons he has been a part of. Write your own short biography of this man, summarizing what you have already learned of him. (See Lessons 64–67.) It would be important to research and include his creation of the *Holy Office of the Inquisition*. File your lesson under "Europe: Italy" in your Student Notebook.

1252

ST. THOMAS AQUINAS, PHILOSOPHER OF THE MIDDLE AGES
LESSON 68

Philosophy is a complicated subject. It is basically man's attempt to explain both the visible and the invisible world around him. Webster's dictionary defines philosophy as "a pursuit of wisdom, and a search for truth through logic." No wonder it is complicated! I don't believe that anyone can adequately explain the things that God alone knows. But I give credit to men who have tried. One man who particularly impresses me is **St. Thomas Aquinas** (uh QUINE nus). He was one of the greatest philosophers of the Middle Ages. Or at least some people think so.

Thomas was born in a castle in Italy near the city of **Aquino.** That is where his last name comes from. His father was the nephew of **Frederick Barbarossa**; his mother was from **Sicily.** Thomas went to school at a nearby abbey and later attended the **University of Naples,** the school started by **Frederick II.** At the same time, one of Thomas's brothers worked for Frederick II taking care of his falcons. Thomas's brother begged him to join him at Frederick's palace. Thomas received an invitation from the king as well.

But Thomas heard a louder invitation in his heart. He decided to join the **Dominican friars** and abandon his wealth and worldly pursuits. Though most would think it was an honorable thing to do, Thomas's family was insulted instead. They just didn't understand his heart. On his way to **Paris** to study under the Dominicans, Thomas was kidnapped by his own brothers! Can you imagine that? With the approval of their mother, they forced him to live at his castle home for one to two years. Like a prisoner, he was kept under constant watch—all the while being persuaded to give up his "calling" to follow the Dominicans. But not even the charms of a beautiful girl lured him from his desire to serve the Lord. Legend says that while Thomas was sleeping, a pretty girl came into his bedroom to seduce him. He leapt from his bed, tossed her out, and made the sign of the cross on the door with a burning stick!

In time, Thomas's mother was impressed with his purity, felt pity for him, and helped him escape from his castle. She finally seemed to understand his unusual desires. Furthermore, Thomas's sister, who had tried to talk him out of joining the friars, became a Benedictine nun. It would seem that the philosopher-to-be was beginning to make an influence on others.

After being held captive by his family, Thomas Aquinas abandoned his wealth and joined the Dominicans.

When Thomas finally reached Paris to study in about **1252,** he met one of the most outstanding scholars of the time. His name was **Albert Magnus.** Some would say that had it not been for Albert, we might never have heard of St. Thomas. Albert, through his great wisdom, tutored Thomas and paved the way for him to become the great philosopher that he was. Albert once said of his upcoming student, "He will make such a roaring in theology that he will be heard through all the earth." [3]

Summa Theologica

Thomas was heard through all the earth though unfortunately he didn't live very long. Thomas Aquinas died when he was just 49 after enduring a long mule ride across Italy. His health had not been good for years. Some speculate that he was poisoned. But in the short time he was here on earth, he gave far more than most through his writings. Thomas authored countless numbers of books on lots of different subjects. His most famous work is called *Summa Theologica.* In it he addressed logic, metaphysics, theology, psychology, ethics, politics, and religion. Though many of his ideas were borrowed from other great thinkers, he was skilled in pulling them together like a great masterpiece.

Thomas's greatest challenge in *Summa Theologica* was to tackle the ideas of **Aristotle.** Aristotle was a Greek philosopher who lived 300 years before Christ. Though not a religious man, Aristotle had some profound ideas on the nature of mankind. Though controversial, these ideas were still being circulated in Europe and in Arab nations hundreds of years later.

Maimonides, the great *Jewish* philosopher, tried to fit Aristotle into his framework of thought. Some Jews embraced these teachings; others burned them. **Averroës,** a Muslim philosopher, tried to make Aristotle fit into *Islamic* thought. Some Muslims admired the work; others banished it. Then came Thomas Aquinas. He attempted to take the ideas of Aristotle and blend them with *Christian* principles. Some men praised him for his efforts; others condemned him, thinking it futile (or impossible) to try to explain God through human understanding.

Interestingly, Aquinas didn't write for Christians alone. He also wrote for Jews and Muslims. In a famous work titled *Summa Contra Gentiles,* Aquinas defended the Christian faith to non-Christian scholars and thinkers in a way they might understand—using the Christians' shared acceptance of the Old Testament when addressing Jewish scholars and the teachings of Aristotle when addressing Islamic scholars.

Though Aristotle lived hundreds of years before Christ, his philosophies were still being discussed and debated well into the Middle Ages.

3. David S. Schaff, *History of the Christian Church (Vol. 5: The Middle Ages, 1049–1294).* Peabody, MA: Hendrickson Publishers, Inc., 1966; p. 663.

There are some fancy terms to describe the process of mixing worldly ideas (like those of Aristotle) and spiritual ones (like those of St. Thomas). Some would call it **Scholasticism.** Others would call it the coming together of **reason** and **faith.** And that was a big deal in the Middle Ages when European men were coming together for the first time in large universities. It was there, in the universities, that great minds were discussing the Greek thinkers, the Muslim classics, the Jewish philosophers, and Christian principles.

St. Thomas had his work cut out for him in taking the differing ideas of mankind and presenting them from a Christian worldview. It wasn't easy then—and it isn't easy now—to explain the ways of God and man. Thomas at least tried. His ideas became so popular that they were nicknamed as the principles of **"Thomism"** (TOE miz'm). Later in history, the Roman Catholic Church adopted some of these ideas.

Strangely enough, Thomas was never impressed with his elaborate work. Three months before his death, he claimed he saw in a heavenly vision that his theology was only "so much straw." [4] I suppose he was being humble. And so he quit writing about theology and never completed the *Summa Theologica*.

Complete or not, I wish I could summarize the *Summa Theologica* for you. But the writings are so vast, it would take me the rest of this book to explain them all. Let me conclude instead with a few of his quotes for you to think about.

- "The highest knowledge we can have of God in this life is to know that He is above all that we can think concerning Him." [5]

- "Perfect and true happiness cannot be had in this life." [6]

- "The prince holds the power of legislating only so far as he represents the will of the people." [7]

- "Man ought to possess external things not as his own but as common, so that he is ready to communicate [give] them to others in need." [8] (Word in brackets is mine for better understanding.)

- "Nobody has been so insane as to say that merit is the cause of divine predestination." [9]

- From a hymn:
  "Sing, O tongue, the mystery
      Of the body glorious,
      And of blood beyond all price,
      Which, in ransom of the world,
      Fruit of womb most bountiful,
      All the people's King poured forth." [10]

---

4. A. Kenneth Curtis, J. Stephen Lang, and Randy Petersen, *The 100 Most Important Events in Christian History.* Grand Rapids, MI: Fleming H. Revell, 1991; p. 83.
5. Will Durant, *The Age of Faith.* Vol. IV of *The Story of Civilization.* New York: Simon and Schuster, 1950; p. 969.
6. Ibid., p. 973.
7. Ibid., p. 975.
8. Ibid., p. 975.
9. Ibid., p. 976.
10. Ibid., p. 965.

ACTIVITIES FOR LESSON 68

68A—Younger Students

Discuss with your teacher what it means to have a "philosophy of life." It's like having a motto. Use a Bible to find verses that would make a great philosophy for you and your family to live by. For example, consider Jesus' saying, *"Love the Lord your God with all your heart, with all your soul, and with all your mind. . .You shall love your neighbor as yourself."* (Matt. 22:37, 39) Discuss how the world might be influenced by someone's *philosophy of life.*

68B—Middle Students

1. ***Adult Supervision Needed.*** As a reminder of the purity of St. Thomas, burn a cross onto paper or wood. If available, use a woodburning kit. File your paper, or a photo of your work, in your Student Notebook under "Europe: Italy."

2. Using a dictionary, define the following terms: *logic, metaphysics, theology, psychology, ethics, politics,* and *religion.* File these definitions in your Student Notebook under "Europe: Italy." Title your page "Thomas Aquinas—Master of Philosophy."

68C—Older Students

1. St. Thomas Aquinas had many critics. Research what John Duns Scotus had to say about his works. I found it interesting to learn that the term *dunce* is a derivation of Duns Scotus. Not that he wasn't a smart man, but his name was associated with Dunsmen who were known for being "hairsplitting fools, dull sophists, dunces." [11]

Plato studied under the Greek philosopher Socrates and helped teach Aristotle.

2. There are more interesting people to write about than there is room in this book. Consider researching Raymond Lully (also called Raymon Lull), 1232?–1315. He was a missionary/martyr to the Arabs during the Crusades.

3. Search the Internet for original sources of St. Thomas Aquinas and/or Aristotle. Thomas's *Summa Theologica* is very difficult to interpret because of its question-and-answer format, but it is worthwhile to become familiar with it.

4. In considering the works of Thomas Aquinas, we are treading through some very deep philosophy. To help sort through it, I suggest you research and write a brief summary of the following schools of thought. (This is not an easy assignment!)

   · Platonism

   · Aristotelianism

   · Augustinianism

   · Thomism

5. Early attempts to coordinate Plato's works with Christianity were condemned by Tertullian in his work *What Has Jerusalem to Do with Athens?* Though debate still exists between philosophers and theologians, check it out!

---

11. Ibid., p. 982.

ROGER BACON, SCIENTIST OF THE MIDDLE AGES
LESSON 69

Do you think that during the Middle Ages people could imagine driving a car, flying a plane, or steering a motorboat? I doubt that most could conceive of these things, which in modern times we take for granted. But there was one man in the Middle Ages who did imagine these things. He actually predicted the invention of the car, the plane, *and* the motorboat. His name was **Roger Bacon.** As far as mechanics went, he was way ahead of his time!

Roger Bacon was an Englishman. He went to school at **Oxford** in England. Roger was extremely bright. He taught for a time at a university in Paris, France, but found it not nearly as stimulating as Oxford. So back to England he went in search of higher academics.

But upon returning to England, Roger came across a group of people who challenged him on another level. He met the **Franciscans.** Remember them? They are the religious order started by St. Francis of Assisi. Roger was so challenged by their level of *spiritual* devotion that he joined them in **1253.**

Now, you may remember that the Franciscans were the ones who didn't place much value on higher learning. Well, fortunately for Roger Bacon, by this time in history the friars had relaxed a bit on this viewpoint. Roger was still allowed to study and do research although he probably did most of his work secretly so as not to offend his brothers. Of course, eventually he was found out and got into all sorts of trouble with the Franciscans, but I will get to that later. For now, let me share just a few of his brilliant ideas.

Though dedicated to academics, Roger Bacon was inspired by the spirituality of the Franciscans and joined them in 1253.

Brilliant Ideas of Roger Bacon

First, Roger had a great understanding for the amazing properties of light. He developed the ideas of **reflection** and **refraction.** Reflection is easier to understand. It is when light bounces off an object like an image in a mirror or headlights off a bike reflector. Refraction, however, is a bit more difficult to explain. Refraction is what happens when light rays bend and divide into the colors of the rainbow. You've probably seen this many times in the sky as well as on a small scale when light hits a crystal object. It's a beautiful phenomenon.

The great thing about these ideas was that Roger used them to invent something extremely practical in 1266. That is the **magnifying glass.** And from that concept came the invention of the first **eyeglasses**, or spectacles as they were called. At least at this point in history, farsighted people were helped by this new understanding of magnification. It was a few hundred years, though, before nearsighted people were helped. It was also a few hundred years before the **telescope** was invented (1571), but that invention can be traced back to research done by Roger Bacon.

Roger Bacon also used his sharp mind to learn the **languages** of the Bible. He spent years studying Hebrew, Greek, and Aramaic, believing that the Scriptures could only be rightly understood in their original languages. Roger also loved **mathematics.** He thought that almost everything could be explained with numbers, believing that God was the source of this system. He used his mind to appreciate God rather than question Him. He once wrote, "I wish to show that there is one wisdom which is perfect, and that this is contained in the Scriptures." [12]

And it might be of great interest to North Americans to know that Roger Bacon was one of the first to think someone could sail west from Europe to reach China and India. He wrote, "the sea between the end of Spain on the west and the beginning of India on the east is navigable in a very few days if the wind is favorable." [13] Of course, **Christopher Columbus** has been given credit for the famous voyage west that led to the discovery of the North American continent. But isn't it interesting that Columbus used this passage by Roger Bacon in a letter in 1498 to help explain his inspiration to explore?[14] I love it when we see history connect like this.

Besides geography, Roger had an understanding of **astronomy** and the **calendar.** He noted that the calendar was off by several days. He also had a grasp of what **gunpowder** could do should it be contained in a solid material (in other words, a gun!). Though Roger didn't invent gunpowder or guns, he foresaw the possibilities of how to use them together.

Probably most amazing were the possibilities he saw in mechanics. As I stated earlier, Roger Bacon predicted the use of cars, airplanes, motorized boats, and possibly even submarines. He wrote:

"Science concerns the fabrication [making] of . . . machines for flying, or for moving in vehicles without animals and yet with incomparable speed, or of navigating without oarsmen more swiftly than would be thought possible through the hands of men. . . Flying machines can be made, and a man sitting in the middle of the machine may revolve some ingenious device by which artificial wings may beat the air in the manner of a flying bird. . . Also machines can be made for walking in the sea and the rivers, even to the bottom, without danger." [15] (Word in brackets is mine for clarity.)

As amazing as that was, scientists today are probably most grateful for Roger Bacon's thoughts on **experimentation**. Roger's teacher, a bishop named **Robert Grosseteste**, believed it necessary to prove ideas through observation and experimentation rather than trust someone's opinion or personal experience. We call this kind of reasoning and testing the **scientific,** or **inductive, method.** Though Grosseteste first came up with the scientific method, his pupil Roger Bacon became more famous for it.

Because he foresaw the possibilities of it, I imagine that Roger Bacon would love to have taken a ride in a speedboat like this!

---

12. Ibid., 1008.
13. Ibid., 1010
14. Ibid.
15. Ibid.

Oddly enough, Roger Bacon didn't perform that many experiments himself. You could say he was a better *philosopher* of science than he was a practicing scientist. Regardless, his ideas were noticed by the pope himself. **Pope Clement IV** asked Roger to secretly send him samples of the many books he was writing. These books were the beginning of a set of encyclopedias. Without the invention of a copy machine, it was going to take years for Roger to rewrite his works. So, he began to condense his materials into his famous **Opus Maius,** meaning *Larger Works.* It is still recognized today as a scientific masterpiece.

Did you notice in that last paragraph that the pope asked Roger to "secretly" copy his works? Why would Roger's great works need to be a secret? Well, it goes back to the mind-set of the early Franciscans. They were concerned that *too* much education would lead to unnecessary money or power. So Roger's academic pursuits were discouraged. I mean really discouraged. So much so that the Franciscans sent Roger into exile for 15 years! It may have been more like prison. No one really knows what the friars found to be Roger's crime. Nor does anyone really know the conditions that he lived in during those years in exile.

We do know that Roger was released some time before his death and that he spent his last years writing. We also know that he died in 1292 without much publicity. Though his contemporaries didn't give him much credit, others have. He has been remembered all over the world for his brilliance. But besides predicting cars and planes, Roger Bacon displayed wisdom—for he also predicted that science would never be able to save man from his sins. I think that despite all the technology of our times, I would agree!

ACTIVITIES FOR LESSON 69

ALL STUDENTS

Make your Memory Cards for Lessons 67–69.

69A—Younger Students

1. To have fun with the concept of reflection, I want you to try this out.

    a. Write your name on a piece of paper. Next, write your name backward. Now, hold your paper up to a mirror. The name you wrote backward should appear perfect in the mirror. Send a secret message to someone using this method, or

    b. Experiment with a flashlight and a mirror trying to predict where the rays of light will go.

2. To appreciate Roger Bacon's understanding of refraction, obtain a prism or crystal. Experiment with bending light rays through the glass and creating tiny rainbows with it. It's fun and beautiful!

3. Obtain a large magnifying glass. Experiment with magnifying everyday objects such as a coin, an insect's wing, a leaf, your skin, and more. Have fun with it.

4. Conduct a family eye test. Create a chart of single letters of all different sizes. Mount it on the wall and see who in your class or family can read the letters from the farthest distance. This will check "farsightedness." Now, reverse the experiment. Determine who can read letters at the closest distance. This will check "nearsightedness."

69B—Younger and Middle Students

1. Buy or borrow a remote-control airplane. Enjoy the marvel of man's invention as predicted by Roger Bacon.

2. One of Roger Bacon's greatest contributions to science was his push for experimentation. Perform your own experiment today using several food colors. Predict the colors you will create by mixing them. Then prove your predictions true or false by experimentation.

69C—Older Students

1. ***Adult Supervision Needed.*** Have fun today with a magnifying glass, a piece of paper, and the sun. Attempt to magnify the sun's rays to the point of being able to burn small holes into a piece of paper. Burn the name of Roger Bacon into the paper and place it in your Student Notebook under "Europe: England."

2. Research elements of the scientific method. What are they? How important are they to the standardization of science? Discuss this with your teacher or class.

TAKE ANOTHER LOOK!

REVIEW 23: LESSONS 67–69

Wall of Fame

1. *Frederick II, "The Amazement of the World" (1229)*—Using red yarn or crayons, create the figure of a short man with red hair. Draw a line down the figure and depict his popular side and his despised side by making one eye look kind and the other eye look evil. [From *History Through the Ages*, use *Frederick II*.]

2. *St. Thomas Aquinas, Philosopher of the Middle Ages (1252)*—Create what looks like a thick book titled *Summa Theologica*. In fine print, add "Written by Thomas Aquinas." [Use *Thomas Aquinas*.]

3. *Roger Bacon, Scientist of the Middle Ages (1253)*—Depict the face of a man with a "cloud of thought" over his head. In the cloud, draw a tiny airplane, car, or submarine. Write the name "Roger Bacon" at the bottom. [Use *Roger Bacon*.]

SomeWHERE in Time

1. Make a sandwich map.

   Materials: Two slices of bread, one piece of salami (or other deli meat), mustard in a squeeze bottle

   In Lesson 67, I refer to Italy as being like the middle of a sandwich between the Holy Roman Empire and Sicily. Bring this word picture to life by making a real sandwich. Consider the top piece of bread to represent the Holy Roman Empire (Germany). Drizzle the letters "HRE" with mustard on the inside of it. Consider a piece of salami (or other deli meat) to represent Rome, Italy. Drizzle the letter "R" with mustard on the meat. Consider the bottom piece of bread to be Sicily. Drizzle the letter "S" on it. Use an atlas or a globe to find each of these places while you enjoy your sandwich. While you eat, answer these questions according to the lesson (you'll find answers at the end of this Review):

   a. What place did Frederick inherit at age 2?

   b. What place did Frederick inherit at age 4?

   c. Where did the pope live?

   d. Where did Frederick spend most of his time?

2. Map the Mediterranean.

   Materials: Outline Map 1, "Mediterranean"; an atlas; colored pencils. This mapping project varies in difficulty. Younger Students: Map only the items listed below that are in capital letters. Middle Students: Map the items that are in capital letters and those in bold letters. Older Students: Map the items in capital letters, bold letters, and those in italics. (In other words, everything!)

   a. Label the continents of EUROPE and AFRICA.

   b. Label and color these islands: SICILY, **Sardinia, Corsica**, *Balearic Islands, Crete, Cyprus.*

c. Label and color these bodies of water: MEDITERRANEAN SEA, **Black Sea**, *Tyrrhenian Sea, Adriatic Sea, Ionian Sea, Aegean Sea, Sea of Azov (part of the Black Sea), Red Sea, Khalij Surt (an inlet of northern Africa).*

d. Label and color these channels of water: STRAIT OF GIBRALTAR, **Bosporus,** *Dardanelles.*

e. File this map in your Student Notebook behind the divider for "Europe."

3. Consider your "extent of influence."

a. In an atlas, find the city of Aquino, Italy, the birthplace of Thomas Aquinas. Use your finger to trace a path to two cities where Thomas attended university—Naples (Italy) and Paris (France). According to the lesson, was Thomas kidnapped by his own brothers on the way to Naples or on his way to Paris? Where was he planning to study under the Dominicans?

b. In an atlas, find Oxford, England. This is where Roger Bacon attended university. Trace with your finger a path to Paris, France, where he also attended university for a time. According to the lesson, in which country did he encounter the Franciscans?

c. From *a.* and *b.* above, consider the "extent of influence" that St. Francis and St. Dominic had. Where was St. Francis born? Where was St. Dominic born? Though neither was born in France or England, these men certainly had a widespread influence. Consider *your* possible "extent of influence." Will your life one day shape the lives of people in other countries? Discuss the possibilities!

Answers: (a) the Holy Roman Empire (b) Sicily (c) Rome, Italy (d) Sicily

WHAT DID YOU LEARN?

WEEK 23: QUIZ

I.   People and Places. Match the following people and places by placing a letter to the left of each number.

_____1. Essenes

_____2. Samudragupta

_____3. Maya

_____4. St. Augustine

_____5. Justinian and Theodora

_____6. Prince Shotoku

_____7. Li Shi Min

_____8. Mohammed

a. Hippo, North Africa

b. Byzantine Empire

c. China

d. India

e. Japan

f. Dead Sea

g. Arabia

h. Mexico and Central America

II.   Circle Sense. In the sentences below, *circle* the word that makes the most sense.

9.   Long before Mohammed lived, the Arab people worshiped hundreds of gods at the (Koran, Kaaba).

10. In the poem *Beowulf*, the hero by the same name wrestles the monster (Grendel, Gibraltar).

11. A nun in the Middle Ages nicknamed Southern Spain, "The (Ornament, Headlight) of the World" for its amazing splendor.

12. Charlemagne was crowned the Emperor of Rome on (Valentine's, Christmas) Day in 800.

13. The first documented attack by the (Vikings, Maoris) was in 793 against a poorly guarded monastery on Lindisfarne, a small island near England.

14. Alfred the Great, the king of England, based English common law on the Ten (Chronicles, Commandments).

15. Great Zimbabwe at its height was part of a significant trade route for (salt, gold).

16. Vladimir, the fifth (Duck, Duke) of Kiev, was instrumental in bringing the (Eastern, Coptic) Orthodox Church into Russia.

III. Multiple Choice. Circle the correct answer for each question.

17. When General Zhao Kuang Yin started the Song dynasty in China, he reinstituted the teachings of _____.

a. Buddha

b. Confucius

c. Mohammed

d. Christ

18. Christians living in Egypt under Arab rule were called the _____.
    a. Jomsvikings
    b. Inuits
    c. Copts
    d. Kiwis

19. _____ explored parts of North America, including Baffin Island, Labrador, Newfoundland, and possibly Nova Scotia.
    a. Floki Vildgerdarson
    b. Abel Tasman
    c. King Wenceslas
    d. Leif Ericsson

20. During the _____, Henry IV begged in the snow for three days for the forgiveness of Pope Gregory VII.
    a. Investiture Controversy
    b. Battle of Hastings
    c. Iconoclast Movement
    d. Children's Crusade

21. The _____, who called themselves the "minor brothers," were given a small chapel to work out of named Porziuncola, or "little portion."
    a. Poor Clares
    b. Dominicans
    c. Franciscans
    d. Augustinians

22. Though he fought against it, _____ gave the Magna Carta his seal of approval.
    a. Thomas Aquinas
    b. Richard the Lionhearted
    c. Frederick Barbarossa
    d. King John

23. At very young ages, Frederick II became the Holy Roman Emperor and the king of _____, an island in the Mediterranean.
    a. Sicily
    b. Lydveldid Island
    c. Corsica
    d. Crete

24. Though he had many brilliant ideas and wrote *Opus Maius* for the pope, Roger Bacon was exiled for 15 years by the _____.

    a. Vikings

    b. Holy Roman Emperor

    c. Franciscans

    d. Poor Clares

IV. **Bonus Essay.** Answer the following questions using complete sentences. Use a separate sheet of paper if necessary.

1. What are examples of the *culture* found only in New Zealand? (Remember, *culture* can be defined as "the unique characteristics of a group or class of people.")

2. What were some of the amazing ideas of Roger Bacon?

WEEK 24

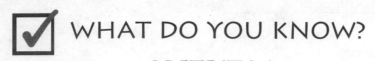

☑ WHAT DO YOU KNOW?

PRETEST 24

True or False? Circle your answers.

1. Mongolia is a vast region in southern China.   T   F

2. Genghis Khan was referred to as "lord of all the peoples dwelling
   in felt tents."   T   F

3. Kublai Khan, the grandson of Genghis Khan, allowed the Franciscans
   to build a church in China.   T   F

4. "Marco Polo," the name of an Italian merchant, is also the name of a
   game commonly played in the sand.   T   F

5. *Cathay* is the name that Marco Polo and his family used to refer to China.   T   F

6. Marco Polo became a prisoner of war in a battle between Venice
   and Genoa.   T   F

7. A well-known movie titled *Braveheart* portrays the true life story of
   William Wallace and his fight for the freedom of Scotland.   T   F

8. Robert Bruce was inspired to keep fighting for Scotland by observing
   the diligence of ants rebuilding an anthill.   T   F

THE GREAT KHANS AND THE MONGOL INVASION OF CHINA

LESSON 70

I don't know if you have ever heard of the Great Khans of the **Mongolian** (mon GOAL yan) **empire,** but they were something to be feared in the late Middle Ages. Especially **Genghis** (JING gis) **Khan!** With notable ruthlessness, he and his descendants conquered the largest part of the world ever conquered in history! It was larger than the Roman Empire, larger than the lands of Alexander the Great, and larger than the empire of Charlemagne! First, let me tell you about the spread of the Mongols under the terrible Genghis Khan. Then we'll look at his grandson **Kublai Khan.** He was a much nicer guy.

The Terrible Genghis Khan

In the late 1100s, when Genghis Khan was just 13 years old, he became the chief of his tribe in **Mongolia** (mon GOAL ya). Mongolia is a region located north of China and is made up of rolling plains and desert. The people of Mongolia are especially known for living in felt tents called **yurts.** A yurt is easy to pack up and travel with. These traveling homes were needed because the Mongolian people would typically follow their herds across the plains and the great **Gobi Desert.** Their herds included camels, sheep, ponies, goats, and oxen. The Mongolian diet consisted mainly of meat and milk products from these animals.

In a short time, Genghis Khan's rule spread to other tribes in Mongolia. He was called "lord of all the peoples dwelling in felt tents." [1] What seemed to make Genghis the "lord" of the Mongols was the way he pulled the wandering people together to form an army. He was a gifted military leader and trained his army in the skill of **siege attacks.** Much like the Vikings we studied earlier, the Mongols mastered the

Though the cities of Mongolia are modern now, it is not uncommon to still see a yurt out in the rural regions.

use of the surprise attack against their enemies. This unfair method of warfare is one reason why the Mongols were so feared. They learned how to use storm ladders, fill moats with sandbags to cross them, and protect themselves with giant shields. And when the great Khan's army took to crossing the deserts, each rider took two horses—one to ride and one as a spare. Imagine the sound of all those horses' hooves thundering across the plains!

As far as Genghis Khan was concerned, all methods of war were fair, as long as he won. He had the ambition of conquering the entire world, claiming he was led by the "eternal blue sky." [2] The sky was thought to be the highest supernatural power according to an old Mongolian religion. Genghis Khan had no problem ordering his men to slaughter the inhabitants of whole cities if they resisted his rule! And

---

1. *World Book Encyclopedia*, 50th Anniversary ed., s.v. "Mongol Empire." Chicago: Field Educational Corp., 1966.
2. Ibid., s.v. "Genghis Khan."

Genghis Khan used both terror and brilliance to conquer two-thirds of the known world in the Middle Ages.

that is what happened under the horrific reign of Genghis Khan. He laid waste to town after town, destroying anyone and everything in his path.

As harsh as this sounds, Genghis Khan was amazing in what he accomplished. He may have been tough, but he was equally brilliant. First, to stabilize his own people, he established the first Mongol code of laws called the **Yassa**. Then he went on a conquering spree that led to one of the largest empires in history. Genghis started in China by capturing the **Hsi Hsia empire**. From there he gained the **Chin empire** in northern China. He had the city of **Peking** by 1215, **Kara Kitai empire** by 1218, and parts of the **Muslim Persian world** by 1220. If that wasn't enough, Genghis Khan sent some of his generals to capture armies in the south of Russia. They also overthrew the army of a Russian princess in 1223.

Considering the amount of land he gained, which was eventually two-thirds of the known world, it appeared that Genghis Khan and the Mongols were unstoppable. For many years, they practically were.

Of course, in time, the great Genghis Khan died. He willed his empire to his four sons. But as we often see in history, they weren't made of the exact same stuff as Genghis. The empire was shaky for awhile. The wide expanse of the empire made it difficult to rule. But then entered the grandson of Genghis. His name was Kublai Khan.

Kublai Khan

Kublai Khan was also a conqueror. With the wrath of Genghis in his blood, Kublai Khan leveled a few cities of his own, taking the rule of the Mongols farther than ever before. By 1264 he made **Peking, China,** his capital. By 1276 Kublai's forces took the capital of the **Song dynasty.** By 1279 *all* of China was under Kublai Khan's rule. Keep in mind, the Mongols were the first outsiders to ever take China from the Chinese! Can you imagine how the Chinese felt about this? With the Song dynasty destroyed and humiliated, Kublai started the **Yuan dynasty.** It remained in place from **1260** to 1358.

In addition to China, Kublai Khan spread his rule to **Burma** and **Cambodia.** He tried to get **Japan** in 1274 but was defeated by the samurai. I'm sure you remember them. Kublai tried to attack Japan again in 1281. However, the Japanese believe that a "divine wind," or **kamikaze**, spared them when a typhoon hit Kublai Khan's men and destroyed their fleet. What Kublai Khan learned was that his large army of men and horses weren't very effective on the sea! (Horses don't swim very well.)

In the end, what Kublai Khan did have was land stretching from the Yellow Sea in eastern Asia to the borders of Europe in the West. This vast territory included China, Korea, Mongolia, Persia

Because of China's mountainous western borders, it was easier for Kublai Khan to spread his rule to southern and eastern parts of Asia.

(Iran), Turkistan, Armenia, and parts of Burma, Vietnam, Thailand, and Russia. Knowing this, think with me what it might mean for one man to have exposure to all these different cultures. Do you think it might broaden his perspective just a little? Well, in the case of Kublai Khan, that is exactly what happened.

It seems that Kublai Khan found he was intrigued by all the different religions and peoples he came across. And so, unlike his grandfather, Kublai Khan became a much more thoughtful Mongol. This is probably best demonstrated by the way he invited outsiders into his court. He employed Muslims, Christians, Buddhists, and followers of Confucius. He brought in thinkers, doctors, and writers. As a result, art and science flourished. Though Kublai Khan did not outwardly confess Christianity, he wanted more Christian missionaries in his empire. So he invited the Franciscans and Dominicans to his capital. (I imagine that St. Francis and St. Dominic would have been thrilled to know how far their followers took the message of the Gospel.) **John of Montecorvino** was just one Franciscan we know by name who built a church in Kublai Khan's city. He had many converts.

Kublai Khan, intrigued by the wide range of cultures under his rule, openly invited missionaries of other faiths into his empire.

As significant as that was, probably the most famous foreigner to be entertained by Kublai Khan was **Marco Polo,** an Italian merchant. Personally, I find Marco Polo so interesting that I'm saving the next lesson just for him.

Although the Mongols were savage in their approach to gaining land, they probably did more to bridge the gap between the East and the West than any others before them. With the Mongolian empire being so broad and so diverse, it exposed people to unknown customs. The West learned of paper money, gunpowder, and the compass. The East learned of Christ and the church.

To some degree, this cultural diversity also proved to weaken the Mongolian empire. The cultures under the great khans were so different that there was little unity or bonding between them. A few notable Mongol leaders rose from time to time—like **Tamerlane,** who was one of the cruelest leaders that ever lived, and **Shah Jahan,** the man who built the famous **Taj Mahal** in India. But slowly, the Mongols weakened, and eventually the Chinese completely took back their homeland. But that is another lesson. I think it's enough to absorb the strength of the Mongolian empire that all started with the incredible personality and vision of the great and terrible Genghis Khan.

ACTIVITIES FOR LESSON 70

ALL STUDENTS

The *Book of Virtues* by William J. Bennett contains a tale about Genghis Khan (see pages 37–39). The tale involves controlling one's anger. Read and discuss it together.

70A—Younger Students

1. Build a yurt.

Materials: Scraps of felt, fabric, or old cloth; cord; goat's milk

Create a "felt tent" using your scraps of felt, fabric, or old sheets. Wrap up your yurt, tie it with cord, and travel with it to another location. To add to your experience, try drinking goat's milk in your yurt. It's a common product in many countries besides Mongolia. Take a photo of your yurt and file it in your Student Notebook under "Asia: Mongolia."

2. Research the differences between a pony and a horse. Photocopy or print images of both from the Internet. File these in your Student Notebook under "Asia: Mongolia."

3. Play with army men and horses in a sandbox. Fill little bags with sand to create a way to cross over the moat of a castle!

70B—Middle Students

Research the famous Taj Mahal following the Who, What, Where, When, and Why approach. Make a creative presentation on paper answering these various questions. File your report in your Student Notebook under "Asia: India."

70C—Older Students

1. Research present-day Mongolia. Specifically, find out the difference between Outer Mongolia and Inner Mongolia. Make a creative presentation using the "outside" of a booklet to describe/represent/ illustrate Outer Mongolia, and the inside of a booklet to describe/represent/illustrate Inner Mongolia. File this information in your Student Notebook under "Asia: Mongolia."

2. Investigate the poem by Samuel Taylor Coleridge about Kublai Khan. It can be found at the following Web site on the Internet:

    www.zyra.org.uk/kublai.htm

3. Research the Mongol warrior named Tamerlane (1336–1405). Though his empire was short-lived, he too is famous for conquering a vast part of Asia.

4. Add the Yuan dynasty to the list of dynasties in your Student Notebook, as started in Volume I or with Lesson 28 of Volume II.

The Dynasties of China (cont'd)

Date of Power	Years Ruling	Name of Dynasty	Special Notes
1279–1368	89 yrs.	Yuan	Add your own summary statements here.

1271

MARCO POLO TRAVELS EAST
LESSON 71

"Marrrrr - co!" "Pohhh - lo!" I imagine I yelled this name hundreds of times when I was a kid as part of a simple game in a swimming pool. In our version of the game, the person in the pool yelling "Marco!" was supposed to keep his or her eyes shut. (Though we suspected occasional cheaters!) The other players yelled in return, "Polo!" But they kept their eyes open. The object of the game of chase was for the one yelling "Marco" to find the ones yelling "Polo"—without looking! As often as I played that game and loved it, I never stopped to think about who **Marco Polo** really was. I had some idea that he was Italian. But that was about it. Maybe you're guilty of the same thing. Today we'll learn about the man behind the name and behind all that splashing in the pool!

Marco Polo was born in **Venice**—the famous Italian city surrounded by waterways. Though parts of the city are on solid ground, many people in Venice travel from home to home and store to store by boats called **gondolas.** These charming boats make Venice a beautiful city (and very romantic, too). More importantly, because the city is on the edge of the Mediterranean Sea, it attracts many merchants and traders.

As you can see, Venice is a very romantic city. (That 's my husband and me riding in a gondola!)

Marco Polo's father and uncle were traders. They were not the wealthiest of men, so they had to rely on their own means to trade some of their goods. That is what led them into becoming traveling merchants. Before Marco was born, his father and uncle sailed to faraway cities like **Constantinople** to do business. It led them to venture all the way to **Cathay,** which is what they called **China.** They liked it so much that they decided to return there. But the next time they went, they took young Marco along with them. He was about 17.

It was **1271** when the three Polos ventured East together. I doubt then if they could have realized the significance of their journey. (I'm sure they never dreamed of starting a swimming-pool game either!) They traveled first by boat to reach **Palestine.** From there they crossed Asia by caravan. Their goal was to reach the city of **Peking** (now Beijing)— the capital of the great **Kublai Khan.**

It took the Polos about three years to make the trip. It was one of the longest journeys ever recorded in the Middle Ages. From what you have already learned about the culture of the Chinese, can you imagine the sights, smells, and sounds they encountered? Think about seeing fireworks for the first time, the wrapped-up lily feet of Chinese women, or a kite-flying demonstration? How about observing the spin of a magnetic needle on a compass, eating sushi, or writing on paper vertically? There would also have been new spices such as ginger and saffron, Chinese music on a shorter scale, ornate pagodas, and the adorable black-and-white panda bear. All these things were completely new to Marco Polo and his family.

Marco must have shown great delight in the Chinese culture because Kublai Khan enjoyed showing it off to him and eventually made Marco a governor. The great khan sent Marco on numerous "errands" all over his vast empire, showing Marco more than he could ever imagine. Kublai Khan didn't seem to mind either the chance to absorb the trade secrets of the Polos. After all, the Polos were from Venice—one of the greatest trading cities in the world.

"Marco Millions" Returns Home

Finally, in 1292, after spending more than *20 years* in the company of Kublai Khan, Marco Polo and his family headed for home. Rather than caravan across Asia, this time they traveled by boat wrapping around Southeast Asia and India, and entering the mainland of Turkey. Since the trip back to Venice took them

Kublai Khan made Marco Polo one of China's governors. It may have been in exchange for trade secrets of the Venetians.

Distinctive Chinese architecture like this was one of many intriguing things for Marco Polo to share with the Western world.

another 3 years, it was a total of 24 years that they were away! When they finally entered their watery Italian home, laden with bundles and covered in desert sand, hardly anyone recognized them.

But what was worse, hardly anyone believed what the Polos had seen! Their stories about the treasures and lifestyles of the Chinese were so exotic that they seemed made up. The Venetians taunted Marco and called him "Marco Millions" because it appeared he told a million lies. Well, to help solve that problem, the Polos held a great party. As the party went on through the night, the Polos brought out great treasures from China—one by one—to prove their stories to be true. Silk robes, rubies, emeralds, and the like were displayed, much to the "oohs" and "ahs" of the crowd.

As for Marco, a few years later he somehow got caught in a local sea battle between the cities of Venice and **Genoa.** In the process, he was captured and made a prisoner of war! To help survive his captivity, Marco shared the fantastic tales of his travels with another prisoner. He was a Frenchman named **Rustichello.**

Marco explained in great detail to his prison mate, Rustichello, the unusual things of China such as paper money, the burning of coal briquettes for heating, and the extravagant use of silk. Marco Polo described Kublai Khan's battles against the Japanese, whom the Europeans were largely unacquainted with. He told of cities far more glamorous than those of Europe, with distinctive Chinese buildings, highly arched bridges, immaculately clean hospitals, and oriental charm. This Frenchman couldn't contain Marco's stories to himself. Once released from prison, Rustichello wrote them down and had them published in **The Book of Marco Polo.** It became very popular and was translated into several languages.

Though there were many skeptics who thought the stories too amazing to be true, in time, all of Marco's descriptions of China proved to be accurate. He proved, too, that the extraordinary sights and sounds of China had made a lasting impression on Marco Polo's memory. And evidently, Marco Polo has made a lasting impression on many of us, although I'm still not sure exactly why the swimming-pool game bears his name! It might have something to do with his being a merchant from the watery city of Venice. Can you figure it out?

The watery city of Venice remains a busy and bustling port for traders and tourists alike.

ACTIVITIES FOR LESSON 71

ALL STUDENTS

Marco Polo Travels East (1271) is a date to memorize.

71A—Younger and Middle Students

1. Play the game of Marco Polo. If a pool is not available, play without one by spreading around your home or classroom. Caution to the one with his or her eyes closed—it could be dangerous!

2. When visiting China, Marco Polo experienced new *spices*. What is a spice and how are spices used? According to *World Book Encyclopedia*, "spice is the name given to food seasonings from plants. Spices have a sharp taste and odor. Some spices are valued for their taste, and others for their smell. Common spices include pepper, nutmeg, cloves, ginger, allspice, mace, mustard, and cinnamon."[3]

Create a guessing game of spices from around your home. Collect your spices. Sniff or taste each one. Now, have someone blindfold you. Take another sniff or taste of the spices and try to identify them. Spices are one of God's delicious creations!

71B—Middle and Older Students

1. Create a travel brochure for a trip to the beautiful city of Venice. Use the Internet or a library resource to learn of common tourist sites. Cut, paste, or color your brochure with photos of Venice to make it attractive. Include the climate, the names of a few hotels, and the approximate price of an airline ticket from your home. (This will require some information from a travel agency or airline.) File your brochure in your Student Notebook under "Europe: Italy."

2. The musical scale in China is different from the musical scale elsewhere. It is based on a scale of five notes rather than eight. Find samples of Chinese music to hear the unique sounds and tones. (Lunch or dinner at an upscale Chinese restaurant might make for more entertaining research!) There exists a debate over these musical differences. According to the Needham-Robinson theory, Chinese music lacks a true octave based on mathematics. The Chinese would argue differently. What do you think? What do you think mathematics has to do with music?

71C—Older Students

1. Research **Ibn Battuta** (1304–1368). He was an Arab explorer who, like Marco Polo, saw more of the world than most in the Middle Ages.

2. Research **Cheng Ho.** He was a Chinese explorer who traveled west. Compare or contrast his experiences to those of Marco Polo.

3. In 1420 the Chinese successfully rounded the **Cape of Good Hope.** Where is the Cape of Good Hope? From what direction do you imagine they sailed? Who else has been recorded in history as having rounded the Cape of Good Hope? How was that different?

---

3. Ibid., s.v. "Spice."

SIR WILLIAM WALLACE AND ROBERT BRUCE, "BRAVEHEARTS" OF SCOTLAND
LESSON 72

A few years ago, Hollywood made a motion picture about the real-life character of **Sir William Wallace.** The title of the movie is *Braveheart.* Though I don't find the movie appropriate for young people, it realistically portrays the story of a man's passion to protect his homeland. His home was **Scotland.** His passion was to stop the **English** from taking control of it. Today we will look at the "brave hearts" of both William Wallace and one of his successors, **Robert Bruce.** Both men were extraordinary patriots.

William Wallace

In 1292 **Edward I** of England made himself the overlord of Scotland, meaning that although there was a king over Scotland, that king was supposed to be under the rule and authority of England. Do you think the Scottish were very happy about this arrangement? Obviously not. They wanted control over their own land. It led to years of battles between the Scots and the English who inhabit the same small island.

As the result of one of the battles between Scotland and England, the **Battle of Dunbar** to be exact, Edward I appointed three Englishmen to rule over Scotland in place of the Scottish king. This really upset the Scottish. But probably no one was more upset than Sir William Wallace. And rather than just complain about the injustice, Wallace raised an army of commoners to fight for the freedom of Scotland.

When Edward I first heard about Sir William Wallace, he underestimated Wallace's abilities. "Why be afraid of a local patriot and his civilian army?" he may have asked. "What harm could they be to the royal army of England?" Edward was so confident in his own forces that he wasn't even in the country when he first sent out troops to fight Wallace.

Well, much to Edward's surprise, Wallace and his band of Scotsmen beat the English at the **Battle of Stirling Bridge.** With news of that, Edward hurried back to Scotland to pay more attention to the situation. This time the English rallied alongside their king and crushed the Scots at a place called **Falkirk** in **1298.** Though successful at Falkirk, they failed to get the one they really wanted—and that was William Wallace.

Wallace escaped to the mountains of Scotland and continued his fight from there. Details of his life on the run are unclear. I suppose he worked on recruiting his fellow Scotsmen to keep up their fight against the English. To this day, Sir William Wallace stirs the hearts of the Scottish for his bravery, his persistence, and his patriotism.

At the Battle of Stirling Bridge, William Wallace and his fellow patriots proved to be a greater challenge than Edward I imagined.

Unfortunately, after seven years of life on the run, William Wallace was captured. The English had quite a case against him. He was tortured and executed on the grounds of **treason** against the king of England. This happened in 1305.

Robert Bruce

Fortunately for the Scottish, the battle for Scotland didn't end with the death of William Wallace. There were other patriots to pick up where he left off. The most famous of these was Robert Bruce. Though Bruce first signed allegiance to Edward I of England, he eventually sided with Wallace in the fight for Scotland.

At one point, Robert Bruce was so bold as to crown himself the king of Scotland, though he risked his life in doing so. Like Wallace, Bruce would have been executed for treason had he been caught. But he wasn't caught. In fact, after losing a battle against the English, Robert Bruce faked his death and fled to **Ireland.** I don't think he was being a coward when he fled. I think he was making a better plan of attack.

Before his execution, William Wallace was tortured for treason. One common method of medieval torture was locking a person's head and hands in the "stocks."

Legend says there was an inspiration for his new plan of attack. That inspiration came from a little **spider.** Apparently, at some point in the battles between Robert Bruce and the English, Bruce was in hiding. From his secret place, he was able to observe a spider spinning its web. Six times he saw the spider fail to attach new strands to its web. Bruce realized that he had failed *six times* to defeat his enemies. As he studied the persistence of the spider, he thought to himself something like this, "If this simple spider tries a seventh time to spin its web, *and is successful,* then surely I can be, too!"

Well, three cheers for the spider. He was successful! And Robert Bruce was too. He left Ireland and first attacked the English at the city of **Carrick.** Within two years, all of Scotland was his! In order to firm up his Scottish kingdom, Bruce attacked English forces at the **Battle of Bannockburn** in **1314.**

By this time, Edward I was already dead. It was **Edward II** that Robert Bruce had to face. At Bannockburn, there were 60,000 Englishmen lined up and ready for battle. The Scots had only 40,000 men. But under the ingenious leadership of Robert Bruce, the Scots prevailed even though they were so outnumbered. They did so by digging massive pits alongside their front line of soldiers. It seems that at least 10,000 foot soldiers and 200 knights fell down in the trenches where they were easily killed. The Scots lost only 4,000 men in the same battle. Victory belonged to Scotland.

By the time **Edward III** was king of England, he was ready and willing to recognize Robert Bruce as the sole king of Scotland, without any English interference. Bruce was proudly crowned **King Robert I** in 1328.

The sad ending to this story is that Robert Bruce lived only a year longer to enjoy his hard-earned title as king. He died in 1329. His death, however, was not in vain. He accomplished for Scotland what William Wallace and thousands of other Scottish patriots wanted—and that was freedom from England.

ACTIVITIES FOR LESSON 72

ALL STUDENTS

Make your Memory Cards for Lessons 70–72. Remember to highlight Marco Polo Travels East (1271) as a date to memorize.

72A—Younger Students

Research how a spider spins a web. Use a can of Silly String plastic stream material to pretend to be a spider. Try to connect a piece of your web seven times just like the spider that inspired Robert Bruce. Take a picture of your "web" and place it in your Student Notebook under "Europe: Scotland."

72B—Middle Students

Who am I? Play a guessing game with your family or classroom. On small slips of paper, write the names of the following national heroes, saints, legends, or "prophets" that we have studied so far in Volume II. Without peeking at the names, attach these slips of paper with tape to the forehead of each participant. You may only ask yes or no questions of other participants to try to guess who you are. (If you have a very small group, you can repeat the game several times to use up the names. Even two people can play if they each make a slip for the other person! To accommodate a larger group, add other names from Volume II to this list—your choice.)

Paul	Wenceslas
Bar-Kokhba	Confucius
St. Patrick	El Cid
King Arthur	Robin Hood
Mohammed	A samurai warrior
Buddha	William Wallace
Aladdin	Robert Bruce
Odin	

72C—Older Students

1. Though we may typically think of patriotism as an admirable quality, can you think of examples in history when strong patriotism and/or nationalism became negative? For example, consider the mentality of the Nazis under Adolf Hitler. What were the results of their thinking? What other instances can we find in history where unchecked patriotism led to war or bloodshed? Discuss this as a class or family.

2. Turn to the Activity Supplement in the Appendix for a poem by Robert Burns titled *Bannockburn*. Read and discuss the content, the dialect, and the perspective from which it was written. How much patriotism is stirred by this passionate poem? Photocopy the poem for your Student Notebook and file it under "Europe: Scotland."

TAKE ANOTHER LOOK!

REVIEW 24: LESSONS 70–72

Wall of Fame

1. *The Great Khans and the Mongol Invasion of China (1260)*—Depict two men. Make one look terrifying to represent Genghis Khan. Make one look nice to represent Kublai Khan. [From *History Through the Ages*, use *Genghis Khan, Kublai Khan,* and *Mongol Invasions*.]

2. **MARCO POLO TRAVELS EAST (1271)**—Depict a man. Drizzle a little bit of glue on him and sprinkle him with spices. **Remember, this is a date to memorize.** [Use *Marco Polo*.]

3. *Sir William Wallace and Robert Bruce, "Bravehearts" of Scotland (1298, 1314)*—Depict two men. Glue plaid skirts on them. Place a sword in the hands of William Wallace and place a crown on the head of Robert Bruce. [Use *William Wallace* and *Edward I*.]

SomeWHERE in Time

1. Younger and Middle Students: Highlight the journeys of Marco Polo.

   Materials: Outline Map 25, "The Mongol Empire"; three different shades of highlighters; colored map pencils

   a. On a copy of Map 25, "The Mongol Empire," use a highlighter to trace over the dashed line titled "Depart" in the map key box. Find the starting point of this broken line on the map. (It's in Italy.) Trace and follow the journey to eastern China with the same highlighter, showing how far the Polos traveled from home!

   b. With a second highlighter (of another color), trace the dotted line in the map key box titled "Back and Forth." Find this short dotted line on your map. Trace and follow with the same highlighter. This line represents some of the trips Marco Polo made around the Mongol Empire.

   c. With a third highlighter (of another color), trace the line of dashes and dots in the map key box titled "Return." Find this long line on your map. Trace and follow with the same highlighter. Obviously, most of this trip was on the sea.

   d. Color the rest of your map with colored pencils as desired. Title the map in the top left corner, "The Journeys of Marco Polo." File it in your Student Notebook under "Asia: China."

2. Older Students: Map out the Mongol Empire.

   Materials: Same as above; in addition, Outline Map 3, "World"

   a. Following the directions above, highlight the journeys of Marco Polo on Map 25, "The Mongol Empire."

   b. Now, to appreciate the size of the Mongol Empire, I want you also to transfer the boundaries of the Mongol Empire from Map 25 (which you just created) to a fresh, blank copy of Map 3, the "World." I suggest you do this with pencil and eraser, getting the borders as accurate as possible with Map 25 as your guide.

   c. Once you have successfully transferred the boundaries, trace the borders with a dark-colored map pencil; shade the entire Mongol Empire in one color, and the rest of the world in another. File your map in your Student Notebook under "Asia: China."

WHAT DID YOU MISS?

WEEK 24: EXERCISE

Play "Smart Bucks." This game is fun but simple—you earn "bucks" for being "smart"! Select a "host" to read out loud the following multiple-choice questions and answers. Students take turns as "contestants," giving your answers out loud. You have one minute to answer correctly. Because this is an exercise, you may *within your one minute* use your textbook, timeline, worksheets, or Memory Cards to help you with an answer. (Lesson numbers are given at the start of each question.) The questions will start easy and get increasingly more difficult! As a fun incentive, earn money for all *correct* answers on the basis suggested below. (If you live outside the United States, use comparable currency to make your game exciting but affordable!)

- Questions 1–5 receive a penny each.
- Questions 6–10 receive a nickel each.
- Questions 11–15 receive a dime each.
- Questions 16–20 receive a quarter each.
- Questions 21–25 receive one dollar each!

Penny Questions

1. (Lesson 1) According to Acts 2:1–4, the Holy Spirit came upon the disciples on the day of _____.

   a. Easter

   b. Pentecost

   c. Atonement

   d. Valentine's

2. (Lesson 9) On August 24, A.D. 79, the city of Pompeii was completely smothered from the volcanic ashes of Mt. _____.

   a. Rushmore

   b. Fuji

   c. Saint Helens

   d. Vesuvius

3. (Lesson 14) In 313, to give Christians in Rome freedom from persecution, Constantine signed the Edict of _____.

   a. Milan

   b. Hippo

   c. Hastings

   d. Verdun

4.   (Lesson 18) As a great benefit to believers in the Roman Empire, Jerome translated the Bible into _____.

   a. Chinese

   b. Latin

   c. Roman

   d. Greek

5.   (Lesson 21) The fall of the Western Roman Empire is said to have ushered in the _____.

   a. Dark Ages

   b. Renaissance

   c. Civil War

   d. World War I

Nickel Questions

6.   (Lesson 22) During the Dark Ages in Europe, which professional was most often responsible for performing "bloodletting"?

   a. The baker

   b. The butcher

   c. The barber

   d. The butler

7.   (Lesson 24) During the reign of Justinian and Theodora, a rowdy mob ran through the streets of Constantinople yelling _____.

   a. "Fire!"

   b. "Puma!"

   c. "Nika!"

   d. "Revolution!"

8.   (Lesson 27) Always concerned for the lost, Gregory the Great sent Augustine to convert the "Angles" whom he thought looked like " _____."

   a. animals

   b. angels

   c. demons

   d. children

9.   (Lesson 30) After the death of Mohammed, who became the first caliph of Islam despite great controversy?

   a. Saladin

   b. Abd al-Rahman

   c. Tariq

   d. Abu Bekr

10. (Lesson 40) A "lazy" child in Viking times was referred to as a "_____."

    a. fire spitter

    b. couch potato

    c. charcoal chewer

    d. bottom dweller

Dime Questions (Getting Harder!)

11. (Lesson 43) The FIRST Viking to sight Iceland while on his way to claim Hebrides was

    _____.

    a. Gardar

    b. Naddod

    c. Vilgerdarson

    d. Arnarson

12. (Lesson 44) The three islands that comprise New Zealand are the North Island, the South Island, and _____ Island.

    a. Lydveldid

    b. Stewart

    c. Meroe

    d. Fiji

13. (Lesson 50) According to Coptic tradition, which of these apostles started the Coptic Orthodox Church in Egypt?

    a. Matthew

    b. Mark

    c. Luke

    d. John

14. (Lesson 53) Who killed Macbeth to gain the throne of Scotland and revenge his father's death?

    a. Duncan I

    b. Shakespeare

    c. Columba

    d. Malcolm III

15. (Lesson 55) Which queen embroidered the Bayeux Tapestry in honor of the Battle of Hastings?

    a. Queen Guinevere

    b. Queen Matilda

    c. Queen Eleanor

    d. Queen Isabella

Quarter Questions

16. (Lesson 57) Which of these popes first rallied crusaders to storm the Holy Land?

    a. Urban II

    b. Gregory VII

    c. Innocent III

    d. Lucius III

17. (Lesson 59) What was the name of the archbishop of Canterbury who was ruthlessly murdered by knights of Henry II?

    a. Stephen of Cloyes

    b. Henry Plantagenet

    c. Roger Bacon

    d. Thomas à Becket

18. (Lesson 60) Which of these Jewish men wrote the *Mishneh Torah* to better organize the books of the Law and the Talmud?

    a. Josephus

    b. Eleazar Ben Yair

    c. Bar-Kokhba

    d. Moses ben Maimon

19. (Lesson 61) Which of these Crusades involved the unusual relationship between Richard the Lionhearted and Saladin?

    a. First Crusade

    b. Second Crusade

    c. Third Crusade

    d. Fourth Crusade

20. (Lesson 63) Which of these Japanese words refers to the ritual of "belly splitting" practiced by the samurai as an extreme measure of devotion?

    a. hara-kiri

    b. sushi

    c. kimono

    d. wakizashi

One-Dollar Questions! (The Hardest Yet!)

21. (Lesson 66) What was the name of the son of King John who was nearly as dreadful a king as his father?

    a. Arthur IV

    b. William III

    c. Henry III

    d. Edward the Cruel

22. (Lessons 67 and 68) What university was started by Frederick II and attended by Thomas Aquinas?

    a. University of Prague

    b. University of Naples

    c. University of Salerno

    d. University of Paris

23. (Lesson 68) What was the name of the Arab philosopher who, like Thomas Aquinas, attempted to integrate the teachings of Aristotle with his faith?

a. Averroës

b. Maimonides

c. Tariq

d. Saladin

24. (Lesson 71) What is the MODERN name of the city that was the capital of the Mongol Empire under Kublai Khan?

a. Xi'an

b. Hong Kong

c. Peking

d. Beijing

25. (Lesson 72) What battle was successfully won by Robert Bruce, which ensured the independence of Scotland from England?

a. Battle of Dunbar

b. Battle of Bannockburn

c. Battle of Stirling Bridge

d. Battle of Carrick

WEEK 25

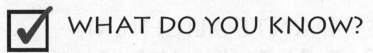

WHAT DO YOU KNOW?

PRETEST 25

Circle Sense. In the sentences below, *circle* the word (or number) that makes the most *sense*.

1. Dante Alighieri was a famous (poet, astronaut) of the Middle Ages.

2. Dante wrote *The Divine Comedy*, based on the number (three, five), to represent the perfect Trinity.

3. As an interesting twist, Dante incorporated his childhood love of a (mouse, girl) into the story line of *The Divine Comedy*.

4. The Aztecs believed in a (hummingbird, snake) god named Huitzilopochtli [wet-se-lo-pocht-le].

5. To regulate activities through the day and through the night, the Aztecs blew a (trombone, conch shell) up to nine times every 24 hours.

6. In the Aztec culture, only the king was allowed to wear a (turquoise, diamond) stone in his nose.

7. The invention of the steel-tipped (rifle, crossbow) had much to do with the English domination of the Hundred Years' War.

8. In an attempt to bring peace to the Hundred Years' War, Richard II of England offered to marry the (7, 70)-year-old Isabelle of France.

DANTE ALIGHIERI,
POET OF THE MIDDLE AGES
LESSON 73

We have recently studied a famous *philosopher*, a famous *scientist*, and a famous *merchant* of the Middle Ages. (Can you name them?) It seems only fair to add a famous *poet* to this collection of extraordinary biographies. Probably none is more magnificent for this time period than **Dante Alighieri** (DAN tee, or DAHN tay, AH lee GYAY ree). His most well known work, ***The Divine Comedy***, is completely out of this world! Literally. It's a story about heaven and hell.

Dante was born in **Florence, Italy.** He did not have a particularly easy childhood because his mother died when he was quite young and his father died by the time he was 18. But something else happened to him when he was just 9 years old that affected him the rest of his life. He met a pretty little girl!

This little girl was obviously very special to Dante, because even as a child, he was completely taken by her. In his later life, he fondly wrote this about their first meeting:

"At that moment I say most truly that the spirit of life, which hath its dwelling in the secretest chamber of the heart, began to tremble so violently that the least pulses of my body shook therewith; and in trembling it said these words: 'Ecce deus fortior me, qui veniens dominabitur mihi.' ['Behold a deity stronger than I, who, coming, will rule me.'] . . From that time forward Love quite governed my soul." [1]

Dante and this girl met again when he was 18. His feelings were as strong as before! With more maturity than he had at age 9, he was able to put his deep thoughts into beautifully profound words. And that he did. For years to come, Dante wrote of his love for this girl.

The young woman of whom Dante was so fond was named **Beatrice.** We are unsure if she had the same feelings for him, if any at all. It would appear not because Beatrice married someone else. But, in the most odd and romantic way, this obstacle didn't stop Dante from writing of his love for her. (He just didn't use her name to protect her honor.)

But, like a scene from a terribly sad movie, Beatrice, the enchanting beauty, died suddenly. She was only 24 years old. It moved Dante in his deep grief to write the tender words found in ***La Vita Nuova,*** which is Italian for **"The New Life."** He gently wrote of her as being possibly just too special for this mortal world. And this time, he was bold enough to use her name. Dante wrote[2]

> *"Beatrice is gone up into high heaven,*
> *The Kingdom where the angels are at peace . . .*
> *Such an exceeding glory went up hence*
> *That it woke wonder in the Eternal Sire,*
> *Until a sweet desire*
> *Entered Him for that lovely excellence,*
> *So that He bade her to Himself aspire,*
> *Counting this weary and most evil place*
> *Unworthy of a thing so full of grace."*

---

1. Will Durant, *The Age of Faith*. Vol. IV of *The Story of Civilization*. New York: Simon and Schuster, 1950; p. 1059.
2. Ibid., pp. 1060–1061.

I share all of this with you because the love and death of Beatrice had something to do with Dante's greatest work, *The Divine Comedy*. But we're not there yet. Let me fill in the parts of the poet's life before he began to write his most famous work.

Though it took a long time, Dante found that his heart could mend. He met and married **Gemma Donati,** and they had several children together. Dante also found great fulfillment in studying philosophy and theology. He was especially fond of the works of **Albertus Magnus** and **St. Thomas Aquinas.** (We studied Aquinas in Lesson 68.)

While philosophy was stimulating to Dante's mind, politics proved to be more challenging. Dante found that he was caught in the old debate between the emperor and the pope—the debate about who should have the final authority in the Holy Roman Empire. (Though the debate had dwindled after Gregory VII and Henry IV, it still simmered and sizzled from time to time.) When the debate was in question, Dante felt the emperor should be more powerful than the pope. He was a great advocate (or strong believer) of "the separation of church and state" and supported the emperor, **Henry VII,** in every way possible. This included writing a piece in 1312 called *de Monarchia,* which boldly explains Dante's viewpoint.

But, like Beatrice, Henry VII died suddenly, leaving Dante again with unfulfilled ambitions. The man he supported and poured so much energy into was gone. Furthermore, his strong support of the emperor cost him his position in government matters. He was exiled from his homeland of Italy for many years!

Knowing now the background of Dante—his losses in childhood, his infatuation for Beatrice, his love of philosophy and religion, his struggles with politics, *and* his unfortunate exile—you will better understand his final years. In particular, you will better understand **1318,** the year he wrote *The Divine Comedy*. He seemed to write with the hope of bringing understanding to the meaning of his life and of trying to make sense of all he believed about God. Let me describe his great masterpiece.

Through death and exile, Dante experienced much grief before writing his masterpiece, The Divine Comedy.

The Divine Comedy

One of the things that make *The Divine Comedy* so unique (and so amazing) is its structure. Like a genius architect, Dante built the entire poem on the number three to represent the perfect Trinity (Father, Son, and Holy Spirit). There are three main parts or canticles to the poem. Each of these contains 33 cantos. (Dante used 33 to represent the number of years of Christ's life on earth.) Each canto was written in groups of three lines with the appearance that every other line rhymes. Unfortunately, when we translate the poem from Italian to English, we lose the graceful flow of these rhymes! That is truly our loss.

As for content, *The Divine Comedy* reads like a supernatural journey. As an expression of Dante's faith in God, he leads the reader through a tour of the afterlife, or what he believes the afterlife to be like. The first part of the poem is titled *Inferno*. It describes in gory detail Dante's idea of a visit to **hell.** In his imagination, Dante is guided through nine levels of a deep, dark pit with the help of an old Roman poet named **Virgil** as his guide. Written like historical fiction, Dante uses the names of real people from history throughout the entire poem. Without apology, he lets the reader know who he thinks will suffer eternally in hell! He places the lesser of the evil people on the higher levels of hell and the worst of them at the bottom. (To the alarm of the church, Dante wrote of seeing a few of the popes in this dark place!)

The second part of the poem is called *Purgatorio*, or **purgatory** (a supposed waiting place between heaven and hell). In this section, Dante is surrounded by people on nine different levels who are "working" toward heaven, carrying out various tasks. Of course, the Bible does not describe this kind of "in-between" place. Nor does the Bible teach that we are saved as a result of our own "works." (See Eph. 2:8–9) Dante was again using his imagination here. But he did such a good job of it that many people today *still* talk about Purgatory as if it really exists.

The third part of the poem is titled *Paradiso*. It is Dante's idea of paradise, or **heaven.** Do you want to guess who Dante uses as his guide in heaven? It is Beatrice. (I told you she had something to do with his greatest work.) Because she was the closest thing he knew to heaven on earth, he imagined her being the celestial one in paradise to greet him. In the poem, Beatrice takes Dante to what he describes as nine levels of heaven, each with its own increasing beauty, peace, and joy. In this fiction, Dante is also led about by **Bernard of Clairvaux,** the monk who inspired the masses to carry out the Second Crusade.

But in a sweet and reverent way, Dante's relationship with Beatrice in the poem pales in comparison to being in the glorious presence of God. In what he imagines as complete awe of the Lord, Dante chooses not to use any words to describe Him. He speaks of the Lord only in terms of an incredible luminous light that is completely beyond man's comprehension. Like petals of a rose, Dante descriptively arranges the throngs of heaven around God and ends with paying tribute to "That Love that moves the sun and other stars." [3]

A guide in The Divine Comedy, Virgil was a real Roman poet who lived just before the birth of Christ. Much like Dante's, his works were exceptional.

I could try to summarize this poem more for you, but it's like trying to describe music written by Mozart, a painting by Renoir, or a sculpture carved by Michelangelo. I'm afraid my words are inadequate. We call great works like these "classics" because they stand out as exceptional works throughout time. You may be too young now to appreciate all the classics, but my hope is that as I expose you to them, you will begin to absorb them one by one. And that, as you grow, you will take time to know the classics better—especially Dante's *The Divine Comedy*. Of course, to really appreciate it you might want to learn some Italian first!

ACTIVITIES FOR LESSON 73

73A—Younger Students

Be a poet. Practice writing poetry today about someone you love. It could be a special pet, friend, relative, parent, or God. Though a lot of poetry rhymes, your poem doesn't have to. It is your choice.

73B—Middle Students

1. Just for fun, obtain an Italian/English dictionary. Learn a few phrases of this beautiful language.
2. What does the Bible say about heaven? How is it described? List on a piece of paper as many Bible verses as you can find that tell us what heaven will be like. File your paper under "Europe: Italy" in your Student Notebook.

---

3. A. Kenneth Curtis, J. Stephen Lang, and Randy Petersen, *The 100 Most Important Events in Christian History*. Grand Rapids, MI: Fleming H. Revell, 1991; p. 84.

73C—Older Students

1. Read a copy of *The Divine Comedy*. Analyze, discuss, and contrast Dante's description of heaven and/or hell with what the Bible says. This will require some in-depth work. A Bible concordance may be needed to find Scripture regarding heaven and hell.

2. Research Virgil, the Roman whom Dante portrayed as his guide through hell. Some would suggest that he depicts man's best effort of virtue, though still cursed to spend eternity in hell. Learn about the life of Virgil. Discuss what the Bible says regarding our efforts to satisfy God with our good works.

3. Research **Francesco Petrarch.** He was a famous Italian poet and scholar who did much to keep Latin alive. Like Dante, he loved a woman whom he never married. He loved her from afar and wrote beautiful poems of her. In response to her death, which was probably from the plague, Petrarch wrote what has been called one of the world's most beautiful poems, titled *Triumphs*. Search for this masterpiece. (In electronic form, I could only find it in Italian.)

1325

THE AZTECS (THE MEXICA)
LESSON 74

Have you ever heard of **Mexico City**? Maybe you've been there. It's the beautiful capital city of **Mexico.** (Mexico, if you don't already know, is a country just south of the United States on the North American continent.) But long before Mexico City became the capital of Mexico, it was inhabited by an unusually strict and savage people. These short, bronze-skinned people were the **Aztecs.** They called themselves the *Mexica.* (I'll call them by both names throughout this lesson.) Unfortunately, the Aztecs are probably best remembered for sacrificing thousands and thousands of people to one of their most feared gods! Let me explain this gruesome part of their story as well as their remarkable society.

Before the Mexica settled in the area that is present-day Mexico City, they were wanderers. Like many tribes in the region, they traveled and fought for land, for wives, and for prisoners. But unlike other tribes, the Aztecs believed they were "led" by **Huitzilopochtli** (wet-se-lo-pocht-le), the hummingbird god, to settle a new place. Huitzilopochtli was the supposed god of war and the sun. The Aztecs believed they would know they had found their new place when they spotted an eagle eating a snake on top of a blooming cactus. (Not exactly an everyday sight!)

The Aztecs, who called themselves the Mexica, have been remembered for their gruesome practice of human sacrifice.

The Mexica supposedly left an island home called **Aztlan** to follow their hummingbird god. It is from this legendary home of Aztlan that they received the name of the Aztecs. (As a mysterious side note, this original island home has never been found.)

In searching and wandering for their new home, the Aztecs encountered many obstacles. For a period of time, they came under the rule of the **Culhuan tribe.** As a reward for their loyalty, the Culhuan chief offered his daughter in marriage to the Aztec chief. He probably thought he had made a nice gesture. But when he arrived for the wedding, he discovered that the Aztecs had removed his daughter's heart and offered it in sacrifice to one of their gods! Why on earth would they do such a horrible thing? Well, according to the Aztecs, it was neither cruel nor terrible, but rather, necessary. I'll explain more about that later. But for now, realize that for centuries the Aztecs were the fear and dread of Mexico for their bizarre acts of sacrifice. Few ever dared to cross them or ever offer their daughters as gifts in marriage!

Tradition says that in **1325** the wandering Aztecs finally found the home they were looking for. Supposedly they spotted an eagle eating a snake on a cactus! They found it on a watery island in the middle of **Lake Texcoco** (Tesh-ko-ko). It is where Mexico City stands today. The Aztecs named their new homeland **Tenochtitlan** (tay-nosh-teet-LAHN). Within 200 years it became one of the largest cities in the world and spanned a great deal of Mexico.

The Aztecs built a well-structured society on their new island. They lived by strict customs affecting everything from how they farmed to what they wore, when they went to bed, and what they learned in school. Let me describe just some of the interesting customs of the Aztecs.

Customs of the Aztecs

The morning would begin with the blowing of a conch shell and the beating of drums. The sounds indicated to all in ear range that the day had begun. Women would set themselves to the task of grinding corn or maize for making the day's tortillas. Men would take steam baths and tend their allotted fields. To make the most of the swampy spaces around them, farmers set up *chinampas.* These were plots of land created from rich piles of mud from around Lake Texcoco. Fast-growing willow trees were planted on all sides to give strength to the "floating" plot. Canal boats were used to cross from one to another. A chinampa was large enough for a small hut and family garden. (Some have been preserved to this day just south of Mexico City at the **Floating Gardens of Xochimilco.**)

By 10 A.M. the conch shells were blown again to indicate that it was time for a midmorning meal for the farmers. Later in the day, after the blaring of the conch shells again, men would gather for their largest meal of the day while sitting on mats around the hearth. Women were respected but ate separately. Children played with pull toys on wheels although the wheel was *not* used for carting things or grinding grain. Heavy loads were carried on a person's back.

Besides fresh fruits, vegetables, and lots of hot chilies, the diet of the Aztecs revolved around the items that are commonly found in a lake, such as fish, frogs, snails, worms, turtles, and snakes. (Not very appetizing to me!) Food was strictly portioned out to children according to their age. For example, a 3-year-old child received one-half of a maize cake, or tortilla, a day. A 4- to 5-year-old received one whole tortilla. A child between 6 and 12 years of age got one and one-half maize cakes, and those 13 years and up received two cakes a day. There was no asking for seconds if you were a child!

Speaking of children, Aztec kids were expected to work hard at home and school. By age 3 they were given small chores. If the chores weren't done, a child might be pricked with cactus needles, held over a fire of hot chili peppers, or left tied up in a mud puddle overnight! Laziness just wasn't tolerated. Poor boys went to school to learn to fight and farm; rich boys went to school to learn history, astrology, and how to interpret dreams as well as how to become strong warriors. Though the rich had more opportunity, they were

This Aztec calendar is a reminder of the Aztecs' advanced understanding of astronomy, which is the science of the sun, the stars, and the planets.

also expected to be more disciplined. Rich boys were expected to give blood offerings in school, ritually bathe in frigid waters, and fast on a regular basis.

Bravery was seriously valued by both the rich and the poor. When a young man captured his first prisoner in war, he was allowed to cut off a long lock of his own hair from the back of his head. He was then free to quit school and advance in society. The boy who failed to ever capture anyone in war was left to wear his embarrassing long strand of hair! He was never allowed to hold an office and was forbidden to wear finer clothes. There was little tolerance for cowards.

At the end of a school day, young men had the freedom to take special baths, paint their bodies, and sing and dance into the night—even as late as midnight. Noblemen played a difficult game of basketball—*tlachtli*—much like the sport created by the Maya. Without being able to use their hands, it was *so* hard to make a basket that the game was over after just one point was scored! A board game named *patolli* was similar to "checkers" and enjoyed by all.

Men were usually married by age 20 to girls about 16 years old. Marriages were arranged by a local "matchmaker" and sealed by a ceremony that included tying the young groom's cape to his bride's blouse. Oddly enough, the bride's arms and legs were often adorned in red feathers!

To the sound of the conch shell in the evenings, women kept busy sweeping, weaving, and embroidering. A woman's favorite pastime was shopping at the large markets. It's no wonder—Aztec markets held up to 60,000 people! That's more than a day at the mall. Before nightfall, men sharpened their farm tools and worked on their homes. A commoner's house was made of mud with a dirt floor and no windows. Wealthier families had adobe-style homes made from sun-dried clay bricks or stones. The homes were painted white. They had several rooms neatly arranged around an inner garden.

As you can see, this wide-open Aztec plaza could hold thousands of people on market day.

The Aztec day ended with the blowing of the conch shell again and the beating of drums. The sounds summoned the priests to prayer and everyone else to bed. By the time the day was over, the conch shell was blown up to *nine* times to dictate exactly what a person ought to be doing. That's just the way life was for the Aztecs.

These ruins indicate that Aztec homes of both the rich and the poor were carefully laid out around the city.

Besides following a strict regimen of time, the Mexica followed a strict dress code. Each of the three classes of the society had its own style. The *nobility*, or *pipiltin*, wore long, soft capes made of cotton that fastened in a knot at the neck. Their capes were embroidered with their military achievements. Sandals, which were worn only by nobility, were decorated with turquoise and gems. Jewels and gold bands were worn on arms and anklets. Men pierced themselves just below the lower lip. Everyone seemed to pierce his or her ears, but only a king could pierce a turquoise stone in his nose! Elaborate feather headdresses were a sign of great accomplishment—especially if they came from the rare **quetzal,** a beautiful bird that was sacred to the Aztecs and Maya and that is considered endangered today.

Commoners, or the *macehualtin*, wore shorter coarse clothing made from the fibers of a cactus. (Not the prickly part, of course!) It was forbidden for their tunics to hang longer than their ankles. The penalty for violating that rule was death! *Slaves*, or the *tlacotin*, who made up the third class, wore the shortest and most uncomfortable clothes of all. All men wore a loincloth called a *maxtli* (MASH-tlee) that wrapped around their waist, came up between their legs, and tied in front.

Women's hairstyles varied according to their status. A single woman wore her hair long and hanging down; a married woman wore her hair up—usually in two wrapped braids that ended at the sides of her head.

Human Sacrifice

In case you are wondering how historians know all these details about the lives of the Mexica, it has to do with the detailed records they kept. As strict as they were about everything else, you should have expected it. The Aztecs used hundreds of symbols and drawings to capture great details of their history in books called **codices.** Scribes used brightly colored paints on deerskin or tree-bark paper that folded like an accordion. These books contained prayers, speeches, tax codes, and how children ought to be disciplined. More of these would exist except that some Aztec kings burned their early history books to hide their brutal customs from others. Even so, as outsiders like the Spanish moved into Mexico, they discovered the unbelievable atrocities of human sacrifice done by the Aztecs. In turn, the Spanish also destroyed many of the codices as if to erase what had happened there.

I suppose you can hardly blame the Spanish explorers for being appalled at the Aztecs. As they grew in number, the Aztecs seemed to create war just for the sake of taking prisoners whom they would sacrifice to their sun god. In all likelihood, there were times when 10,000 to 80,000 people were sacrificed in a single ceremony by Aztec priests! It was recorded that at one religious festival, it took four straight days of killing for the priests to finish their task.

(Teacher: Please edit the next two italicized paragraphs as needed for sensitive students.)

Though food and marigolds were sometimes offered to the gods, in most cases priests offered the heart of their victim to the sun god Huitzilopochtli at the highest point of their steep temples. They then collected the skulls of the dead on racks. Sometimes cannibalism was part of the ceremony. (Cannibalism is the act of eating one's own species.)

The belief behind the sacrifices was that, without them, the sun would cease to shine and bring death to all. Obsessed with the gruesome ritual, the dark-robed priests who performed sacrifices were known for living with the blood of their victims matted into their long black hair. (The stench of their jobs is probably why the priests burned incense four times during the day and five times at night!)

As if to reach the gods they feared, the Aztecs built their temples to enormous heights. Pictured here is the Pyramid of the Sun in Teotihuacan.

(Resume reading here.)

From this distorted practice of killing, the Mexica grew in power. For two hundred years they dominated surrounding tribes and most of Mexico through absolute fear. To stay alive, the tribes around them eagerly paid tribute, making the Aztecs one of the richest empires of that era. That is, until the Spanish invaded. But that is a lesson I'll save for the next volume. It involves a standoff between **Montezuma,** one of the last of the Aztec kings, and **Cortes**, a Spanish explorer.

If you think about it, the Aztecs were, in a way, familiar with the biblical concept that *"the wages of sin is death."* (Rom. 6:23) They seemed to understand that sacrifice was needed for their redemption. Imagine their joy and relief when they later learned from the Spanish that Jesus Christ paid the penalty for their sins with *His* divine blood and substituted *His* perfect life for theirs. Had they grasped the Gospel earlier in history, they would not have needed to spill the blood of so many thousands of humans on an altar. Pray and thank God for His gift of salvation through the perfect life and death of just one—Jesus Christ. Consider these verses from the Bible:

"While we were still sinners, Christ died for us . . . having now been justified by His blood, we shall be saved from wrath through Him . . . so also by one Man's obedience many will be made righteous." (Rom. 5:8, 9, 19)

ACTIVITIES FOR LESSON 74

ALL STUDENTS

Try an Aztec meal of frog legs, fish, or turtle soup. At the same meal, ration out corn tortillas according to the age of family members as given in the lesson.

"For example, a 3-year-old child received one-half of a maize cake, or tortilla, a day. A 4- to 5-year-old received one whole tortilla. A child between 6 and 12 years of age got one and one-half maize cakes, and those 13 years and up received two cakes a day. There was no asking for seconds if you were a child!"

74A—Younger Students

1. The Aztecs believed they would know their land when they saw an eagle eating a snake while perched on a blooming cactus. Use red construction paper to make heart-shaped cactus blooms. Cut and glue these to the cactus on a coloring page provided for you in the Activity Supplement in the Appendix. Color the entire picture and file it in your Student Notebook under "North America: Mexico."

2. GIRLS: Make a pair of noble's sandals.

   Materials: Plain pair of inexpensive thong sandals, glue (hot glue will be the most effective but requires adult assistance), fake jewels, gems, turquoise stones

   Glue a pretty arrangement of stones on the "V" strap of a pair of thong sandals. Have someone take a photo of you in your sandals; file it in your Student Notebook under "North America: Mexico."

3. Live the rest of the day today (or begin tomorrow) on the strict schedule of the Aztecs. Blow a small horn announcing these nine daily events: (1) Sunrise, 2) Midmorning meal at 10 A.M., (3) Noon meal, (4) Sunset, (5) Beginning of night, (6) Bedtime for young ones and prayer time for adults, (7) Midnight, (8) Rising time, and (9) Just before dawn. You will quickly see that this is difficult to do. I suggest that the horn-blowing be rotated among family members as each serves his or her "duty." Afterward, discuss how it made you feel to hear the horns. In a culture that didn't have watches, would this have been a helpful custom? Why or why not?

4. If it is difficult to imagine a shell functioning as a horn, go to www.google.com and click on "Images." Type in the words "conch shell" with or without the quotes. You will see examples of them being used as horns.

74B—Middle Students

1. Research the present-day flag of Mexico. What emblem does it bear that is related to our lesson? Make a copy of the flag and place it in your Student Notebook under "North America: Mexico."

2. *Adult Supervision Needed.* If the trees in your area are suitable, use an appropriate tool to gently shave the bark off a tree trunk. Use crayons or markers to draw pictures of your life. As the Aztecs did, depict people of great significance as larger than others (i.e., the father of the household). Place your bark pieces in a large zipper plastic bag. Punch three-holes in the bag and place it in your Student Notebook under "North America: Mexico."

Note to Teacher: For this activity, select only trees with a large trunk. Shave only a few patches off any one tree and do not completely remove the bark in a circle around the tree. Doing so could seriously damage the tree.

3. Research *cochineal* (kahgh uh NEEL). It is the name of a bright red dye made in Mexico. Where does it come from? How is it made? Write a paragraph about cochineal and file it in your Student Notebook under "North America: Mexico."

74C—Middle and Older Students

1. Create a diorama of a wealthy Aztec home and/or a commoner's home using information from the lesson. Use small boxes, spray paint, clay, etc. Take a photo of your home. File it in your Student Notebook under "North America: Mexico."

2. Make a turquoise jewelry necklace with supplies from a craft store or bead shop.

3. Consider the Aztec belief system. It included the idea that the gods had two natures—both good and bad. Contrast this idea to the Christian/Judeo belief that God is only good, holy, and unchanging. Find Scripture to defend this belief. Make a list and file it in your Student Notebook under "North America: Mexico."

1337–1453

THE HUNDRED YEARS' WAR
LESSON 75

First of all, the **Hundred Years' War** didn't last a hundred years. It lasted off and on for 116 years. But the word "hundred" rolls off the tongue a little easier than "one hundred and sixteen." And so, the name has stuck. The Hundred Years' War was between **France** and **England.** It had something to do with revenge against the French for taking over England in 1066. Do you remember who did that? It was **William the Conqueror** at the **Battle of Hastings.** Here's the "rest of the story" of the great conflict between the French and the English.

In 1328, the king of France died. Unfortunately, he had no son in place to rule after him. I don't like it when that happens in history because it always seems to lead to war! It definitely did in this situation. The king's cousin in France (**Philip VI**) and the king's nephew in England (**Edward III**) were left behind to battle over who would rule France. Besides that, there were plenty of Englishmen who still held a grudge against the French Normans for invading under William the Conqueror. They were more than eager to make things even!

It was Edward III who really stirred up the trouble. This is the same Edward III from Lesson 72 who finally made peace with the Scottish by crowning Robert Bruce a king. Though Edward may have made peace with the Scots, he was looking for war with the French! Edward III crossed the English Channel to fight Philip VI over the crown of France. He did a good job, too. On the sea, he defeated the French near **Sluys.** Once on French soil, he won battles at **Crecy** (KRAY-see) and **Calais** (ke-LAY).

A good deal of Edward III's victory had to do with the kind of weapons the English had come up with. It seems they had crafted a powerful version of the **crossbow** that allowed them to fire steel-tipped arrows sharp enough to pierce through any armor. They also introduced gunpowder onto the battlefield. So, even though the English usually fought with fewer soldiers (thousands less, in fact) they managed to defeat the French time and time again with showers of deadly arrows and powerful blasts. However, both the French and the English ran low on money, and the two countries declared a truce from 1347 to 1355. A **truce** is an agreement to stop war without either side winning or losing.

After Edward III, another Edward ruled England. He was the **prince of Wales** and nicknamed "**Edward the Black Prince**" because of the dark armor he wore. The Black Prince started up the war again between the English and the French. In 1355 he managed to *capture* the king of France and his son in the **Battle of Poitiers** (pwah-TYAY). With this humiliating defeat, the French agreed to sign the **Treaty of Bretigny** in 1360. It gave the English a great deal of land in France and helped stop the Hundred Years' War—at least for awhile.

Edward the Black Prince was so named for the dark armor he wore. He captured the king of France and his son at the Battle of Poitiers.

Richard II Marries Princess Isabelle

The next men to inherit the thrones of England and France were just young children. This kept things peaceful for a little more time as these children couldn't begin to understand the problems they inherited. But eventually these little boys grew up to be greedy kings. Each man wanted both England and France for his own. One of the more interesting solutions to bring the nations together was a royal marriage between the two families. It seems that in 1396 the king of England—**Richard II**—asked to marry the daughter of **Charles VI** of France. The bride-to-be was named **Princess Isabelle.** Considering that Isabelle was only a little 7-year-old girl, she managed her role quite well and helped keep peace between the nations. For 20 years all was calm in the Hundred Years' War through this marriage.

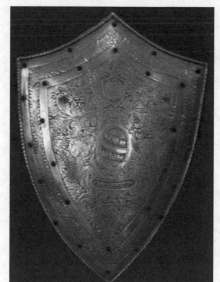

Strong medieval shields like this were not enough to stop the streams of deadly arrows that led the English to victory at the Battle of Agincourt.

Keep in mind, though, that even when the fighting stops in a war, there are still terrible results from it. It was not uncommon during this time in England or France to find abandoned farms, burned villages, or hungry wanderers. Supposedly, one group of starving villagers ate common grass just to stay alive. With chaos of this sort, it was not unusual for robbers to take advantage of wrecked homes and steal things. We call that "looting." It still happens today all over the world when there is chaos from war or other national disasters. Plus, it was during the Hundred Years' War that the Black Death plague broke out and peasants revolted against their landowners. (As a side note, the Black Death had such an impact on Europe that I am devoting a whole lesson to it.) All this to say that the Hundred Years' War was a difficult time to live through—whether fighting was happening or not!

Battle of Agincourt

Despite the terrible results of war, the English started it up again under **Henry V** at the **Battle of Agincourt** (AJ-in-kort) in 1415. Henry's goal was to make the throne of France his own. In other words, he insisted on being the king over France as well as England. Though he had less than half the number of troops the French had, in half an hour the English won the Battle of Agincourt using streams of deadly arrows. Five years later, Henry married Catherine of Valois, a French princess, to try to secure the throne for good. Finally, in 1420, the French were forced to sign another treaty. This one, the **Treaty of Troyes**, actually gave the French crown to the English. This was such a significant event in history that **William Shakespeare** wrote a play about it called *Henry V*. But this big victory for the English was *not* the end of the Hundred Years' War!

For one thing, Henry V lived only two more years as king of France before he died. His death set off a wave of retaliation from the French for their nation. And then, someone young and unsuspecting stepped forward to turn history around. It was a teenage French girl named Joan of Arc. Her story is so dramatic that I must make a whole lesson of it. So, I will end here, without telling you yet who won the Hundred Years' War. You will just have to wait and see!

ACTIVITIES FOR LESSON 75

ALL STUDENTS

Make your Memory Cards for Lessons 73–75.

75A—Younger Students

1. GIRLS: Dress up like a young princess bride. Imagine being Princess Isabelle and marrying a king when you are only 7 years old! Though it is fun to pretend to be a bride at your young age, most countries would never allow that to happen today.

2. BOYS: Dress like the Black Prince from the lesson. Though you may not own black armor, I think that all-black clothing and a black cape might do the job.

75B—Middle Students

1. Write a creative report about medieval weaponry—including the steel-tipped crossbow. Include reprints or photos of weapons that could actually have been used in the Hundred Years' War. File your report under "Europe: France *or* England."

2. Write a creative report on the evolution of armor through the Middle Ages. Include reprints or photos to depict the changes in armor over the centuries. File your report under "Europe: [Country of your choice.]"

75C—Older Students

1. Read or view *Henry V* by William Shakespeare.

2. Research the chronicles of the Hundred Years' War written by **Jean Froissart** (c. 1337–c. 1410). He was a French poet and historian. His writings give us much detail about the long war that spanned generations.

3. Research **Sir Thomas Malory.** He was a knight who fought in the Hundred Years' War. What famous king did he write about? (Hint: It is a king from this volume.) Who was the first to print the works of Sir Thomas Malory, and what was the significance of that printing?

4. Try to find an old poem titled the *Ballad of Agincourt* by Michael Drayton. From whose perspective do you believe it was written—the French or the English?

TAKE ANOTHER LOOK!
REVIEW 25: LESSONS 73–75

Wall of Fame

1. *Dante Alighieri, Poet of the Middle Ages (1318)*—Draw the cover of a book with stars on it to represent heaven. Write on it "*The Divine Comedy* by Dante." [From *History Through the Ages*, use *Dante Alighieri*.]

2. *The Aztecs (The Mexica) (1325)*—Sketch a man wearing a headdress. Glue feathers around it. Title it "The Aztecs." [Use *Tenochtitlan*.]

3. *The Hundred Years' War (1337-1453)*—On a small square piece of paper, write "France vs. England: Hundred Years' War" [Use *Hundred Years War* and *Edward the Black Prince*.]

SomeWHERE in Time

Map modern Mexico.

Materials: Outline Map 8, "Mexico and Central America"; Outline Map 26, "Review 25 Answer Key"; colored pencils; modern atlas

As we've done before, this mapping project varies in difficulty. Younger Students: Map the items that are listed in all-capital letters. Middle Students: Map the items that are listed in all-capital letters and bold letters. Older Students: Map the items that are listed in all-capital letters, bold letters, and italics. All Students: File your completed map in your Student Notebook under "North America: Mexico."

1. MEXICO.

2. Cities: MEXICO CITY, **Guadalajara, Monterrey**, *Mazatlan, Acapulco de Juarez, Tampico, Veracruz.*

3. Borders of Mexico: UNITED STATES (**California, Arizona, New Mexico, Texas**), GUATEMALA.

4. Rivers: RIO GRANDE, **Conchos, Balsas**, *Fuerte, Rio Grande de Santiago, Sonora.*

5. Peninsulas: **Yucatan, Baja California** (*Baja* means "lower.").

6. Bodies of Water: PACIFIC OCEAN, GULF OF MEXICO, **Gulf of California, Caribbean Sea,** *Bay of Campeche, Gulf of Tehuantepec.*

7. Mountain Ranges: **Sierra Madre Occidental** (Western Sierra Madre), **Sierra Madre Oriental** (Eastern Sierra Madre), *Orizaba* (the highest peak in Mexico and Central America at 18,410 feet; called Citlaltepetl by the Aztecs).

8. Deserts: **Sonoran,** *Chihuahuan* (che WA wan).

9. *Isthmus of Tehuantepec.*

WHAT DID YOU LEARN?

WEEK 25: QUIZ

I. Who/What Am I? Choose the best answer from the list below.

1. I was commissioned with Paul as one of the first missionaries. Who am I?

2. I am the Roman emperor who falsely blamed the burning of Rome on the Christians. Who am I?

3. I claimed to be the Messiah and led the Second Jewish Revolt. Who am I?

4. I am one of the most beloved pieces of sacred literature in India. I am still quoted at some Indian weddings today. What am I?

5. I grew up in Great Britain, was captured by Irish pirates, and returned to Ireland as a missionary of the Gospel. Who am I?

6. I became a legend in England for fighting the Saxons at the fall of the Western Roman Empire. I had a round table for my knights. Who am I?

7. I was a compassionate pope and chose the simple lifestyle of a monk. I called myself the "servant of the servants of God." Who am I?

8. I am from Arabia. I believed I heard revelations from Gabriel and founded the Islamic faith. Who am I?

9. After my family was murdered, I escaped from Damascus and led an Arab nation in southern Spain. Who am I?

WORD BANK

Bar-Kokhba	St. Patrick	Gregory the Great	Nero
King Arthur	Mohammed	Barnabas	*Ramayana*	Abd al-Rahman

II. True or False? Circle your answers.

10. Iconoclast means "image breakers."   T   F

11. "Charlemagne" translated in English means "Charles the Mad."   T   F

12. In the 700s, the Vikings invaded England and Europe from their icy home in Greenland.   T   F

13. Methodius and Cyril responded to King Rostislav's calls to evangelize the Slavic people.   T   F

14. New Zealand was discovered by the Inuit people.   T   F

15. Despite some inconsistencies, El Cid has been best remembered as a hero for leading the Reconquista in Spain.   T   F

16. During the Investiture Controversy, Henry IV stood for three weeks in the snow, begging forgiveness from Gregory VII.   T   F

17. As a lover of God's Word, Peter Waldo funded the translation of the Bible into everyday French.   T   F

18. Eleanor of Aquitaine became the queen of France, England, and Spain.   T   F

III. Fill in the Blanks. See if you can fill in the blanks without the help of a word bank!

19. Moses ben Maimon, one of the greatest Jewish philosophers of the Middle Ages, put the books of the _____ and the Talmud into the Mishneh Torah.

20. During the Third Crusade, _____ the Lionhearted and Saladin proved to be gentlemen as well as enemies.

21. According to a tombstone in England, Robert, Earl of Huntingdon, was a good archer, an outlaw, and nicknamed _____.

22. Minamoto Yoritomo declared himself the first _____ of Japan when he transferred power from the emperor to himself.

23. Roger _____, a brilliant Franciscan, was far ahead of his time in thinking about cars, airplanes, and submarines.

24. _____, a merchant from Venice, was well liked by Kublai Khan and given the opportunity to travel extensively across the Mongolian empire.

25. Robert Bruce was inspired by a _____ to persevere in trying to take the throne of Scotland away from England.

26. In The _____ Comedy, Dante Alighieri imagined Beatrice and Bernard of Clairvaux as his guides through Paradise.

27. The Aztecs offered thousands of human _____ in sacrifice to their gods.

IV. Bonus: Guided Essay. Use the groups of words on the next page to make complete sentences about the Hundred Years' War. Earn a point for each completed sentence that contains all the words in a group. One example is provided. Use a separate sheet of paper if necessary.

Example: war   France   England

"The Hundred Years' **War** was between **France** and **England**."

1. armies   Edward III   Philip VI   crossbow

2. children   Charles VI   Richard II

3. Richard II   Isabelle   7

4. Battle of Agincourt   Henry V   married   Catherine

5. William Shakespeare   play   Henry V

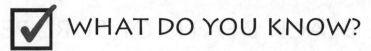

☑ WHAT DO YOU KNOW?

PRETEST 26

Match Me! Connect the words on the left to the definitions on the right. (Using different-colored pencils may make it more fun to work and easier to grade.)

1. Black

    a. A trade city on the coast of the Black Sea

2. "Flagellants"

    b. A Chinese palace-city restricted for the emperor

3. Caffa

    c. Means "brilliant" in Chinese

4. Ming

    d. "Whips" used for self-punishment during the plague

5. Forbidden City

    e. Followers of John Wycliffe

6. Nine

    f. The color used to describe death from the bubonic plague

7. A "morning star"

    g. A bright planet seen just before or at sunrise

8. The Lollards

    h. A mystical Chinese number

THE BLACK DEATH OF EUROPE
LESSON 76

Death doesn't really come in colors. But if there were one color to best describe the medieval plague, it would be "black." The **Black Death** of the fourteenth century killed about 25 million people in Europe. That was about one-third of the total population! For that reason, the Black Death has been labeled by some as *the* worst disaster in history.

The Black Death was a form of **bubonic plague.** The bubonic plague gets its name from the *buboes,* or glands, that swell on a person with the illness. These buboes were known to swell as large as an egg under the armpit and in the groin. Oftentimes, the blood under the skin turned dark purple in patches, giving the appearance of "black" spots. So, the medieval plague has been labeled the *Black Death.* Its other symptoms included fever and the vomiting of blood.

For centuries, the cause of the Black Death was a mystery. That is one reason why it killed so many people. No one understood it well enough to prevent it! This plague wasn't particular about whom it killed either. It took the lives of the young, the old, the rich, and the poor. It killed kings, peasants, priests, and even doctors. The death toll was beyond our imagination. So many died that there wasn't time or place for proper burial. Some were not buried at all, which added gross images of death and stench to the already horrible situation.

The Real Culprit

Though no one understood the plague *then,* it is known *now* for being spread by rats and fleas. That's right—rats and tiny fleas! Actually, the real culprit is a germ called *Pasteurella pestis.* It invades the bodies of rats and eventually kills them. But before the rat dies, the germ is picked up by fleas that live on its body. (The germ doesn't kill the flea; rather, it multiplies in the flea's little stomach!) It is really the flea that carries the plague to other rats or humans by biting them and injecting the bad germs. Of course, fleas always bite because they survive by sucking blood from other creatures. It's just the way God designed them to live.

But few survived the spread of the plague. Depending on which strain was passed on, a person could die from within one to five days of being infected. Most died in three days! You can only imagine the confusion in people's minds when they saw others dying so quickly. Some believed it was the wrath of God against the crusaders. Others thought it the fault of the Jews. A group of fanatics known as the **Flagellant Brothers** walked through the towns whipping themselves as punishment for the plague. (They were named for the *flagellants,* or whips, that they carried to beat themselves with.)

Most people assumed that the plague was contagious when in fact not all strains were. Only those with infected lungs could pass it to others by coughing and spewing their germs through the air. It was the fleas that were the primary carriers of the plague—not infected victims.

So despite all the efforts made by people to avoid the disease, people died from it anyway. Kings and queens hid

Though not understood in medieval times, the Black Death was primarily spread through infected fleas and rats.

in their castles, monks hid in their monasteries, and priests hid in their churches. Still, many of them died from the Black Death. Townsmen tried to burn the plague away by torching homes and clothes of the deceased. Still, many died. Often when the plague would strike a village, people would panic and run to the next village to escape it. What they did instead was take the germ with them through their flea-infested belongings or the germs in their lungs.

And so the plague was spread from town to town like a wildfire out of control. It didn't help that cleanliness was not a priority in the cities. Europeans were notorious for dumping their sewage, which is human waste, right out of their windows and onto the streets! They were at least courteous enough in some places to first yell *"gardez-lo!"*—which we would interpret as "look out below!"

The Spread of Death

You may be wondering what started the Black Death in the first place. Well, like all disease, it is difficult to pin down exactly what started it. Only God knows the answer to that. But it seems that the medieval plague first flared up somewhere in **Asia.** It killed about 13 million people there! After that, the plague seemed to spread easily to Europe through trading ships on the **Black Sea.** For where there are traders, there are usually ships, and where there are ships, there are plenty of rats, and where there are rats, there are fleas. I think you get the point. It was the world-traveling flea that was most responsible for spreading the deadly disease. But no one figured that out until 1904—nearly 600 years later!

Historians believe that the first traders to pick up the plague from Asia were Italians who lived on the coast of the Black Sea. It was there, in the trade city of **Caffa**, that the Italians were exposed to the plague. How? Well, it's rather gruesome, but it seems that a group of raiding Mongols *purposefully* spread the disease as part of a war tactic. **(Teacher: Edit the following italicized sentences as needed.)** *They did this by catapulting infected dead bodies (fleas and all) over the wall of the city! In modern times, we would call that biological warfare! It's been around a long time.*

(Resume reading here.)

Anyway, when the Italians fled from Caffa by ship, they naturally carried the Black Death with them to the port city of **Genoa** in Italy. From there, it spread all over Europe. The plague reached **Paris** and **London** by **1348** and spread to **Scandinavia** and **Russia** by 1349. Two-thirds of the students at **Oxford University** died in England. Fifty thousand were buried in London. Towns in Germany, Persia, France, and Italy were all hit. Few places if any were left untouched, although practicing **Jews** were less affected by the plague. This was probably due to their strict sanitation laws as laid out by the Lord in Deuteronomy. (Hmm! That's an interesting reminder of the wisdom found in God's Word.)

Results of the Black Death

The results of the Black Death were, of course, devastating because it killed millions of people in a few years. But it was actually 50 years before it left Europe for good. And even those who didn't die from the plague suffered. It took away "the butchers, the bakers, and the candlestick makers." It especially robbed Europe of its farmers. The few who were left to work had to work harder! Peasants across Europe revolted against these unfair conditions by demanding higher pay or refusing to work at all. The system of feudalism (where people worked for the lord nearest them in exchange for land) began to fall apart. It was growing weaker anyway as the countries of Europe began to take more shape and have stronger governments.

On the positive side, the Black Death may have caused many to seek God. It is clear from the heavenly artwork of the early Renaissance that spiritual matters were heavy on people's minds. (Coming close to death and dying has a way of doing that to people.) We see this clearly in the **Book of Job**—a story in the Bible of a man who suffered many horrible things (including disease) but never blamed God for it. Instead, he sought God for understanding and comfort.

Now, before I leave this lesson, I want to clear up something that you might be feeling—and that is fear. You might be afraid that the plague could come back! Well, although anything is possible, it is highly unlikely that the Black Death could *ever* spread like it did in medieval times. For one, modern man has many powerful antibiotics to help treat people with plague symptoms. Rare cases of it that *have* popped up in the last century have been stopped from spreading. Second, the cause of bubonic plague is now understood. Health officials go to great lengths to control rat populations, especially at ports around the world. Third, most countries today have elaborate methods to handle human waste and sewage, which greatly helps to control any disease.

In times of great suffering, many people are drawn to the church in search of spiritual guidance and understanding.

I hope that knowing these things will help you not to worry about the return of the plague. Our generation has its own diseases to take care of, such as cancer and AIDS. These are serious problems now that may be solved one day in the future! But until then, rather than worry, I prefer to look at diseases as an ever-present reminder that life is very precious and every day is a gift. That we can thank God for!

ACTIVITIES FOR LESSON 76

76A—Younger Students

1. Health officials claim that frequent handwashing is a great way to help prevent the spread of germs and sickness. Prepare a chart for the family bathroom or your classroom bathroom in which students and teachers can record the number of times they wash their hands in a day. Discuss as a family or class when are the times the hands should be washed. For example, it is always wise to wash hands before eating a meal. Have a prize for the student (or teacher) who most faithfully remembers to wash his or her hands before meals in a one-week time period.

2. A healthy diet rich in natural vitamins and minerals can help prevent sickness. Use raw and/or dried fruits and vegetables as building blocks to make "people." (You will need toothpicks to hold them together.) For example, make a carrot man out of one carrot, two raisins, and a green onion for a smile. Be creative. Before you eat them, discuss the benefits of these natural foods. Take pictures of your fruit and vegetable people and place them in your Student Notebook under "Miscellaneous."

76B—Middle Students

1. Research the number-one killing disease in your country. What practical measures can your family or class take in helping to prevent this disease?

2. Pray for family, friends, loved ones, or church members suffering from terminal disease. Send a special card of encouragement.

3. Research the flea. Write a few paragraphs on the life cycle of a flea and its unique habits. Include

photos in your report. File it in your Student Notebook under "Europe: Italy."

76C—Older Students

1. Research other historic plagues. Consider the plague in Athens that killed Pericles (*The Mystery of History*, Volume I); the plague in Rome in A.D. 262 that killed 5,000 a day; the plague in Hong Kong in the 1800s that killed 10,000,000. In more recent times, plague has hit the United States ports of New York, San Francisco, New Orleans, and Seattle. What measures were taken to keep these outbreaks successfully confined?

2. Research **St. Catherine of Siena.** She bravely devoted herself to helping the dying during the Black Death.

3. Theologically speaking, in what manner did the Flagellants distort the Gospel of Christ? Research more on this curious group. Provide Scripture in your report.

4. Read the ***Decameron,*** by **Giovanni Boccaccio.** It is a classic collection of 100 tales from the perspective of a group of young people who fled the plague-ridden city of Florence for the country.

5. As part of the *Decameron,* Boccaccio gives an excellent description of the plague. Research his account of it on the Internet at the following site:

www.nmsu.edu/~honors/decameron.html

THE MING DYNASTY OF CHINA AND THE FORBIDDEN CITY
LESSON 77

The word *forbidden* is a strong word. It means *restricted, excluded, or prohibited from use.* The Chinese use this intimidating word (as translated in English) to describe a large, beautiful palace in **Beijing.** They call it the **Forbidden City.** But why would a large, beautiful palace be forbidden? Well, it isn't anymore. But for 500 years, it was restricted to anyone except the emperor of China, his household, and a few top advisers. The palace was designed to keep the emperor in, and the rest of the world out! This amazing structure was built during the **Ming dynasty.** Let me first explain where the Ming dynasty came from.

In our last lesson on China, we learned that the **Mongols** had taken over. Do you remember the names of the two most famous Mongol kings? They were **Genghis Khan** and **Kublai Khan.** It was Kublai Khan who entertained **Marco Polo** in his court.

Well, the Chinese grew weary of foreign rule. (The Mongols were "foreigners" because they came from **Mongolia.**) The Mongol kings after Kublai Khan proved to be weak. So, the Chinese made themselves a new ruler. He was **Zhu Yuanzhang.** Zhu Yuanzhang was not a likely candidate for emperor. He was a Buddhist monk, a beggar, and a bandit chief. Nevertheless, after a 13-year struggle, Zhu Yuanzhang drove the Mongols out of **Beijing** (the capital of China). The name of

In China, Genghis Khan and his grandson Kublai Khan were considered foreign rulers because they were from Mongolia, a country north of China.

his imperial reign was **Hungwu**, which means "warlike." It described him well and became his accepted title as an emperor.

Emperor Hungwu ruled China like a dictator. He considered himself *"the son of heaven"* and the mediator between earth and heaven. He killed anyone who opposed him. But he gave the Chinese back a strong government. He named his dynasty the *Ming*. It means *"bright"* or *"brilliant"* and describes the Ming dynasty well. This dynasty lasted from **1368 to 1644.**

The brightness of the Ming dynasty came from quite a few things. For one, Emperor Hungwu reinstated the old Chinese tradition of **state exams** for anyone who worked for the government. Now, I don't mean that these people just had to take a quiz or pass a driver's test. No, they had to take tests that lasted for days and nights and covered the ancient history of China, numerous customs, and all the Chinese classics in art and literature. These tests were so grueling that some went mad or committed suicide from the pressure! The tests were administered in great halls that contained over 8,000, 6-foot-wide cubicles for the test-takers. The state exams proved to make those who passed them much more "brilliant."

Otherwise, the Ming dynasty shone brightly for creating some of the most beautiful art in China's history. The Ming era is especially known for its **blue-and-white porcelain, bronze pieces,** and **enamelware.** You've probably seen some of the elegant porcelain (or copies of it) because it is still popular today. During the Ming period, the Chinese also designed elaborate gardens and made richly illustrated books.

Emperor Hungwu, who was once a Buddhist monk, ruled China like a strict dictator and started the Ming dynasty. Ming means "bright" or "brilliant."

But more amazing than any of this was the **architecture** of the Ming. This leads us back to the beautiful Forbidden City that I mentioned earlier. Let me explain it in more detail. It is quite possibly the greatest achievement of Chinese builders and artists.

The Forbidden City

It was the third emperor of the Ming dynasty (Emperor **Yongle**) who built the Forbidden City. He placed it in Beijing for two reasons. First, having a palace and capital in the north would help him keep a better eye on his Mongol enemies. Second, to remind the Mongols of their defeat, he built the Forbidden City on the old site of Kublai Khan's court. Interestingly, every doorway in the Forbidden City opens to the south, the farthest direction away from Mongolia!

The Forbidden City is really a city within a city within a city! You see, like the middle of an onion, the Forbidden City lies in the center of two other cities for privacy. The **Outer City** is just what it says it is. Like the outer layer of an onion, it serves to protect the center and is surrounded by a massive wall that still stands today. In the 1400s, nearly one million commoners lived and worked in the Outer City.

Within the Outer City, and surrounding the Forbidden City, is the **Imperial City.** The Imperial City contained large

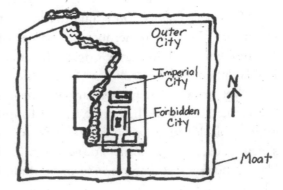

offices for government advisers, ornate temples, and many beautiful lakes and parks. It was the perfect meeting place for the emperor and his staff and a great location for special ceremonies and marches. The emperor often rode through on an elephant!

One famous wide-open court within the Imperial City is **Tiananmen** (tee AN an man) **Square.** At one hundred acres, it is the largest square in the world and can hold up to a million people! Tiananmen Square became best known to the modern world when a huge student protest took place there in 1989. Nearly 10,000 rioters were tragically shot down for protesting against the Communist Chinese government! (That's a lesson for a future volume.)

And finally, within the great walls of the Imperial City is the elaborate Forbidden City. It was a palace home to 24 emperors and their families over the course of 500 years. Besides the emperor and his household, only a few top advisors were allowed in. For security, it is completely surrounded by a deep moat and high walls. Though the Forbidden City is one of the largest palace complexes in the world (covering 720,000 square meters), it is not bold like the great Roman and Greek buildings. Rather it is delicate, ornate, and well balanced. Over 100,000 artists decorated it using every art form imaginable. Every pillar, floor, ceiling, wall, and door is embellished with beautiful detail.

If you were to wander around the Forbidden City today, you would find intricate images of turtles,

Indescribable balance and beauty are well defined in the Forbidden City, with great meaning and significance found in every aspect of its design.

cranes, and lions, which were considered symbols of long life. You would also find bold statues of five-clawed dragons to represent the power of the emperor. (Dragons were otherwise depicted with only four claws.) You would find unusual things like a room with 85 clocks, pots of twisted bonsai, trees made of coral, and carved ivory dragons. At its height, the Forbidden City was home to 70,000 rare treasures and trinkets like lapis elephants inlaid with pearls, glass bottles painted on the inside (not an easy thing to do!), and lacquer boxes decorated with rare gems.

But these are just the outward beauties of the Forbidden City that are *visible* to the eye. Much of the beauty and enchantment of the palace is found in the *invisible* structure and hidden design. For example, before the city was ever built, the designers planned it to match the four directions of the compass. Every line of every structure was built in balance. As if the palace were a living creature, each gate and space was laid out to represent a vital organ of the body. It was designed with a mouth, lungs, heart, liver, kidneys, and stomach. Beyond that, the important five elements of wood, metal, water, fire, and earth were all woven into the making.

Furthermore, the numbers nine and five are considered mystical numbers in China. So these numbers were creatively used inside and out. The palace was built with 9,999 rooms; its doors are fastened with nine nails (or multiples of the number nine); and nine guardian statuettes line the eaves of the roofs. Five bridges span the Golden Stream; five styles of roofing were used;

Even the rooftops of the palace were meticulously designed to have great meaning. Notice also the high walls that served to protect the Forbidden City.

and five ridges appear on the roof of the Hall of Supreme Harmony. To say the least, much thought and detail went into the building of the Forbidden City!

In the past, the Chinese would refer to their great palace as the "Purple Forbidden City." It wasn't painted purple, but purple is believed to be a sign of heaven. And so, the home of the emperor was symbolically called "purple." In reality, the buildings and roofs of the Forbidden City are red and yellow. Today, the Chinese call the palace complex **Gu Gong,** meaning **"Palace Museum."** It is open to tourists. Millions visit every year as a chance to finally see that which was forbidden for so long.

Despite how luxurious, spacious, and private the Forbidden City was, it wasn't able to protect the emperors from everything. They still had problems to deal with and enemies to fight. Their greatest enemy was death itself. Only 6 of the 14 Ming emperors who lived in the Forbidden City ever lived past the age of 40! Their lives may have been rich and powerful, but they were also short.

Forbidden China

Before I leave this lesson, I need to explain something very important to understanding China. It has to do with the idea of being "forbidden." You see, it was not only the emperor's palace that was off-limits to outsiders. The entire nation of China took on this mentality and was isolated from the rest of the world for hundreds of years. Why? There are several reasons, but unfortunately at least one reason had to do with the poor behavior of some Europeans. It seems that several times in the Middle Ages, **Portuguese traders** sailed to the coast of China to settle and do business. No crime in that. But their trading turned into barbaric treatment of the Chinese. The Portuguese began to pillage the local villages and take over the towns. Some outsiders even kidnapped Chinese children for slavery! Westerners were called **"ocean devils"** for their cruelty.

As a result, the Chinese put a stop to all trading with outsiders. Emperors quit sending out explorers although they had been making great progress. They simply wouldn't trust Westerners anymore. Even the famous **Silk Road** that once created a bridge from the East to the West was shut down by 1453. And so, China learned to be self-sufficient for a long period of time. This means that as a nation, they looked only to themselves for what they needed. They took nothing from the West and gave nothing in return. Though things have changed since then, knowing this story from the Middle Ages may give you a better understanding of why there are such vast differences between the East and the West that still exist today.

ACTIVITIES FOR LESSON 77

ALL STUDENTS

Take a "virtual tour" of the Forbidden City online by searching the Internet for photos. Print them for your Student Notebook under "Asia: China." (Better yet, consider a real visit to the Forbidden City if circumstances would allow!)

Field Trip Possibility

Though most cities don't have something as ornate as the Forbidden City, discover the workplace of your nearest government officials. Consider touring the office of your mayor, your governor, or your local legislator. If you are in the United States, consider visiting the White House—which is both the home *and* the workplace of the president!

77A—Younger and Middle Students

Out of respect for the emperor of China, those who were allowed to see him were forbidden to sit in his presence. Select a class or family member as the emperor for the day. Practice this gesture of respect by not sitting in his or her presence! How does it make you feel if you are one of the subjects of the emperor? How about if you are the emperor?

77B—Middle Students

1. Nine is a lucky number in China. The Forbidden City was built in some places using multiples of nine. How high can you name multiples of nine? Have a contest to see who can go the highest and the fastest with these numbers.

2. Research "dragons" as they appear in Chinese art. What seems to be their origin, their purpose, or their significance? Use charcoal to sketch your own image of a dragon using images from the Internet.

77C—Older Students

1. Research the tragic details of the 1989 riot in Tiananmen Square. File your information under "Asia: China" in your Student Notebook.

2. Thousands of people crowd the Forbidden City every year on October 1 to celebrate the founding of the People's Republic of China. Research this annual event that involves fireworks and parades. What year was the People's Republic of China founded? What form of government is it? Is there religious freedom under this form of government? File your information under "Asia: China" in your Student Notebook.

3. Update your chart on the dynasties of China.

Dynasties of China (cont'd)

Date of Power Years Ruling	Name of Dynasty	Special Notes
1368–1644 276 yrs.	Ming	Add your own summary statements here. Don't forget the Forbidden City!

JOHN WYCLIFFE, "MORNING STAR OF THE REFORMATION"

LESSON 78

John Wycliffe (WICK liff) has been called the *"morning star of the Reformation."* That's a beautiful expression, but you may be wondering what exactly it means. What is a "morning star"? Well according to Webster's dictionary, a morning star is *"a bright planet (as Venus) seen in the eastern sky before or at sunrise."* Though we're closer, that might not be of much help. I think I have a lot of explaining to do to help you understand John Wycliffe's nickname. To do so, I will also need to explain the **Reformation.** That won't be easy either, but I'll try!

John Wycliffe grew up in England. He attended **Oxford University.** He probably helped give the school the fine reputation it has today. He was very intelligent. But John had one flaw—although some would consider it a strength—he didn't know when to keep quiet! Most of what John Wycliffe said was controversial. That means that some people loved him for the things he spoke and some despised him.

The people who despised John Wycliffe were members of the Medieval (or Roman) Church. They didn't like the things he said about the practices of the church. For example, John complained of the fact that the pope lived a life of luxury. It bothered him that the church had become wealthy, powerful, and at times less caring of the needs of the people. (In England, the church owned about one-third of all the property but

A "morning star" is a bright planet that shows just before or at sunrise.

was exempt from paying taxes.) John went on to claim that the pope and the priests should not have the authority they had, especially to forgive sins! He hoped people would turn to God to confess their sins rather than to a priest.

Furthermore, Wycliffe openly questioned the church's selling of **indulgences.** These were letters sold to pardon sins! Besides that, John thought that the worship of Mary, Jesus' mother, had become too serious and that priests were wrong in how they practiced **communion.** Communion is an ordinance where Christians eat bread and sip wine to remember the body and blood of Christ. Jesus said to do this "in remembrance" of Him in 1 Corinthians 11:24–28. But, when the priests gave communion, they were claiming the bread and wine were *literally* the body and blood of Christ and that apart from the blessed bread and wine, a person could not be saved. (These are serious doctrines that Protestants and Roman Catholics still disagree over.)

But what bothered John Wycliffe the most about the Medieval Church was the handling of the Word of God. Church scholars were not looking to God's word alone as the final source of authority. They were considering also the books of other men and the words of the pope as having the *same* authority as the Bible. They believed in fact that some of man's writings were *necessary* for understanding the Bible. Wycliffe believed the Bible *alone* contained the truths needed for men to understand salvation. He once said, "This lore [teaching] that Christ taught us is enough for this life." [1]

John Wycliffe proclaimed, "This lore that Christ taught us is enough for this life."

To complicate matters more, very few Bibles were available to the common man. The Bibles that were around were written in Latin. But Latin wasn't being read or spoken in England anymore—English was. This meant that the only people who could read the Bible were the priests of the church who were trained in Latin. To this imbalance Wycliffe said, "Forasmuch as the Bible contains Christ, that is all that is necessary for salvation, it is necessary for all men, not for priests alone." [2]

Fortunately for John Wycliffe, the king of England (Edward III) liked him. Edward encouraged John to visit Pope Gregory XI and debate these matters of controversy. It was a good idea, but it didn't help John any. Instead he was fired from teaching at Oxford. And in **1377,** Pope Gregory ordered that all Wycliffe's teachings be banned and his writings burned! In 1382 another council condemned his writings. Ironically, an earthquake broke out during the council. Wycliffe believed that it was a sign of God's displeasure with the church, but his

1. Roger L. Berry, *God's World: His Story.* Harrisonburg, VA: Christian Light Publications, Inc., 1976; p. 333.
2. A. Kenneth Curtis, J. Stephen Lang, and Randy Petersen, *The 100 Most Important Events in Christian History.* Grand Rapids, MI: Fleming H. Revell, 1991; p. 87.

opponents interpreted the event as a sign of God's favor for putting down Wycliffe! These were tough times for sure.

The Wycliffe Bible and the Lollards

Though it was tragic for John to be outcast in this way, it may be the very thing that spurred him into his life's greatest work. Wycliffe turned his energies toward overseeing the translation of the Bible from Latin to English. It is unclear whether Wycliffe actually translated the Bible or just supervised the work. But whoever was involved had to use handwritten copies of the Latin Vulgate as translated by Jerome centuries before. (Remember Jerome from Lesson 18? He translated the Bible into Latin from Greek and Hebrew.)

Unfortunately, John Wycliffe never saw the entire Bible in English in his lifetime nor was he able to see the great effect he had on England. He died of a stroke in 1384. But, before his death, Wycliffe did see the entire New Testament translated into English and a good deal of the Old Testament as well. Another man finished the work in 1388, but it has been called the **Wycliffe Bible** ever since.

Jerome dedicated most of his life to translating the Bible into Latin. His tedious work laid the foundation for Wycliffe.

Besides that, John Wycliffe had many dedicated followers who helped to get out the Word of God. They were called the **Lollards,** which means "*the mumblers*." Like Wycliffe, the Lollards *mumbled* about problems and wealth within the church. They refused to wear the long ruffled clothes that were stylish at that time or the long pointed shoes that might prevent them from kneeling in prayer. The Lollards wore plain robes and chose to live in poverty. The Lollards were not a religious order like the monks or friars—just poor preachers who believed in spreading the Scriptures. Keep in mind, too, that the printing press had still not been invented (though we are getting to that lesson soon). And so every copy of the Bible that the Lollards gave out was handwritten!

Of course, as you might understand by now, God does have an enemy. And so, where the Word of God flourishes, there usually is conflict. We see it again when, in time, the Lollards were persecuted for their bold practices. Because they would not work with the church as it existed, they were considered heretics. Many were burned at the stake. Even John Wycliffe, after his death, suffered persecution—or rather his body did. Thirty-one years after Wycliffe died, Pope Martin V had his body dug up from its grave, his bones burned, and his ashes scattered on the River Swift. Wycliffe was accused of over 200 crimes against the church.

The Protestant Reformation

Now, what about Wycliffe being called the "morning star of the Reformation"? I've still not explained that. Well, the problems that Wycliffe found in the Roman Church were serious problems. Many had evolved from the **Fourth Lateran Council** in which the pope gave himself *more* power in order to *keep* power away from the Holy Roman Emperor. We've discussed that issue many times before. But in doing this, the church began to lose its focus.

In time, more and more people saw these problems in the church. By openly discussing them, they hoped to *reform* the church. To *reform* means to make changes for the better. From this word we get the term for the *Reformation.* The people demanding reform in the church became known as *Protestants* for "protesting" against the church. If you put the two words together you get the *Protestant Reformation.*

What you will learn in Volume III of *The Mystery of History* is that the Protestant Reformation became a huge movement in the 1500s. Men like **Martin Luther** finished the work started by John Wycliffe by breaking away from the Roman Church altogether. This started the Protestant line of churches that exists today. You see, like a star that shines early in the morning, John Wycliffe, with all his outspoken beliefs, was one of the earliest to seek reform in the church. And so he has been given the poetic nickname, "morning star of the Reformation." I believe it is very fitting.

ACTIVITIES FOR LESSON 78

ALL STUDENTS

1. **Make your Memory Cards for Lessons 76–78. John Wycliffe, "Morning Star of the Reformation," (1377) is a date to memorize. Highlight the card accordingly.**

2. Host a Bible drive. Find a new church or missionary group in need of Bibles. Collect new or used Bibles through your class, church, or family to donate. Consider making it an ongoing ministry by providing receptacles for old Bibles at a convenient location at your church or school.

3. Play a simple Bible trivia game. Create two teams. Take turns having one person draw on paper, chalkboard, or erasable white board a scene or character from the Bible without using any words or gestures. If the other team can guess what it is in less than one minute, that team receives a point. Continue in this manner until one team reaches an agreed-upon winning score (e.g., the first team to reach 10 wins).

78A—Younger Students

In medieval times, some people wore shoes with extremely long points on the toe. Visit the following site for a great example:

www.costumes.org/history/kohler/225Medieval.JPG

Borrow a pair of pointy dress shoes. (Perhaps a pair of your mother's?) Attempt to kneel in them as if you were in prayer. Is it hard? The Lollards chose not to wear these elaborate slippers because they were showy, impractical, and difficult to kneel and pray in. Discuss as a family or class popular items of clothing today that might be considered showy or impractical.

78B—Middle and Older Students

1. View a video on the life of John Wycliffe by Gateway Films titled *Wycliffe; The Morning Star.*

2. Research an organization that bears the name of John Wycliffe called Wycliffe Bible Translators. What is their mission statement? In how many languages have they translated the Bible? Find the answers to these questions and more. File your report under "Europe: England" in your Student Notebook.

78C—Older Students

1. To better understand the matter of selling indulgences, read the two paragraphs below.

"The position of the Church in regard to indulgences has been much misunderstood. An indulgence never permitted a person to sin. Rather, it was a promise of remission of part or the whole of the penalty which a person must receive after death on account of his sins. The indulgence demanded that the sinner repent of his deeds and do some form of penance. The penitent had to perform good works by saying prayers, visiting shrines, or donating money for worthy ecclesiastical purposes.

"The common people held a wrong view of the practice. Most of them could not read the language of the indulgence, and they thought that a payment of money was all that was required to escape both the temporal and eternal penalties of sin. Because Tetzel [an Italian leader] did nothing to enlighten the populace as to the true nature of indulgences but rather exhorted them to give liberally for themselves and for their dead relatives in purgatory who were 'crying to them for help,' [Martin] Luther angrily questioned the validity of the whole system of indulgences."[3] (Words in brackets are mine for clarity.)

Discuss the issue of selling "indulgences." Why would Wycliffe condemn this practice? What does the Bible say about the washing away of sins?

2. If you have Dutch roots, consider researching a Dutch contemporary of Wycliffe. His name is **Gerhard Groote** (GROW te). He organized the Brethren of Common Life in 1380.

3. T. Walter Wallbank and Alastair M. Taylor, *Civilization Past and Present*. Chicago: Scott, Foresman and Co., 1949; p. 505.

TAKE ANOTHER LOOK!

Wall of Fame

1. ***The Black Death of Europe (1348)***—Use white chalk on a small square of black construction paper to write "Black Death Hits Europe." [From *History Through the Ages*, use *The Black Death*.]

2. ***The Ming Dynasty of China and the Forbidden City (1368–1644)***—Depict a large locked gate. Write the name of the lesson underneath. [Use *Ming Dynasty*.]

3. ***JOHN WYCLIFFE, "MORNING STAR OF THE REFORMATION" (1377)***—Use a glitter glue stick to draw a pretty five-pointed star. (Or draw a star in pencil and drizzle it with glue and glitter.) Write the name of the lesson underneath. **Remember, this is a date to memorize.** [Use *John Wycliffe*.]

SomeWHERE in Time

1. Make a population map. To grasp the concept of the severity of the Black Death in Europe, follow the directions below.

   Materials: Outline Map 1, "Mediterranean"; green and black markers

   a. Title a blank copy of Outline Map 1, "Mediterranean," with the words "The Black Death."

   b. Randomly place 40 green dots across the whole of Europe to represent two-thirds of the population that did not have the plague.

   c. Randomly place 20 black dots across Europe to represent a third of the population that DID have the plague.

   d. Recognize that, as your dots indicate, one out of every three persons was likely to die from the Black Death in Europe during the later Middle Ages.

   e. File your map in your Student Notebook behind the divider labeled "Europe."

2. Use a globe or an atlas to locate the city of Beijing. How close is it to Mongolia? Remember that every doorway of the Forbidden City was built to face south, away from the Mongol enemies of the Chinese!

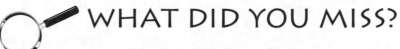

The Chocolate Chip Game. You will need one bag of chocolate chips and a sharp mind to play this simple game. I have provided questions below in a basic "Who was _____?" format. If you can give a reasonable answer to your teacher in less than 10 seconds, you get a chocolate chip. If not, you have to pass.

(*Note to Teacher:* Modify the time limit as is appropriate for the age group. And, if sugar is off-limits, consider a healthy brand of carob chips instead. For your convenience, you will find one-third of the questions marked "(E)" for "Easy," one-third marked "(M)" for "Moderate," and one-third marked "(H)" for "Hard." Choose all the questions or pick and choose among them to accommodate your class size or age group. Brief answers can be found in the Answer Key.)

1. (E) Who was Paul?
2. (M) Who was Nero?
3. (H) Who was Polycarp?
4. (E) Who was St. Valentine?
5. (M) Who was Constantine?
6. (H) Who was Samudragupta?
7. (E) Who was St. Patrick?
8. (M) Who was Attila the Hun?
9. (H) Who was Romulus Augustus?
10. (E) Who was King Arthur?
11. (M) Who was Justinian?
12. (H) Who was Belisarius?
13. (E) Who was Columba?
14. (M) Who was Prince Shotoku?
15. (H) Who was Li Shi Min?
16. (E) Who was Mohammed?
17. (M) Who was Wu Zetian?
18. (H) Who was Wiglaf?
19. (E) Who was St. Boniface?
20. (M) Who was Charles Martel?
21. (H) Who was Pepin?
22. (E) Who was Aladdin?
23. (M) Who was Thor?
24. (H) Who was Rostislav?
25. (E) Who was Good King Wenceslas?
26. (M) Who was Vladimir?
27. (H) Who was General Zhao Kuang Yin?
28. (E) Who was St. Simon?
29. (M) Who was Eric the Red?
30. (H) Who was Malcolm III?
31. (E) Who was El Cid?
32. (M) Who was William the Conqueror?
33. (H) Who was Hildebrand?
34. (E) Who was Eleanor of Aquitaine?
35. (M) Who was Maimonides?
36. (H) Who was Frederick Barbarossa?
37. (E) Who was Robin Hood?
38. (M) Who was Minamoto Yoritomo?
39. (H) Who was Stephen of Cloyes?
40. (E) Who was King John?
41. (M) Who was Frederick II?
42. (H) Who was Albertus Magnus?
43. (E) Who was Roger Bacon?
44. (M) Who was Genghis Khan?
45. (H) Who was Rustichello?
46. (E) Who was Beatrice?
47. (M) Who was Montezuma?
48. (H) Who was Henry V?
49. (E) Who was the carrier of the bubonic plague? (Hint: It's a bug.)
50. (M) Who was John Wycliffe?
51. (H) Who was Edward III?

✓ WHAT DO YOU KNOW?

PRETEST 27

Jeopardy. Just as they do on the *Jeopardy* television game show, I have provided the "answers." You find the right question for each answer from the bottom of the page.

1. The shrine of Thomas à Becket.

2. Geoffrey Chaucer.

3. A fanciful rooster who outsmarts a fox.

4. A 40-year dispute over who was the pope.

5. The Hussites.

6. The oldest son of a French king.

7. Maiden of Orleans.

8. The Burgundians of France.

    Who is called the "father of the English language"?

    What was the Great Schism?

    Who captured Joan of Arc?

    What was the destination of the pilgrims in *The Canterbury Tales*?

    What is a *dauphin?*

    Who is Chanticleer?

    What was the nickname of Joan of Arc?

    Who were the followers of John Huss?

GEOFFREY CHAUCER AND THE CANTERBURY TALES
LESSON 79

Do you know what historical fiction is? It is when an author writes a story mingling historical facts with fiction. It is usually the fiction (or the made-up part of the story) that makes the facts a bit more interesting. During the Middle Ages, there couldn't have been a better writer of historical fiction than **Geoffrey Chaucer.** He was a fascinating storyteller. Now, in writing his famous work, ***The Canterbury Tales,*** Chaucer not only entertains his readers with delightful fiction, but he also teaches them something about "real" life in the Middle Ages.

The Canterbury Tales opens with a scene from **1387.** The month is April. The place is **Tabard Inn** in **London, England.** This is a real place, making that part of the story *fact*. But what isn't fact are the 29 characters that Chaucer proceeds to introduce. Though they are not real, the characters are *based* on the real lives of ordinary people—the kind who usually don't make it into history books. It is these 29 "everyday" people who make *The Canterbury Tales* unique, informative, and a bit amusing. Let me include descriptions of a few of them for you.[1] Chaucer writes so well and with such wit that they're easy to imagine. (Note, the bolded words are my key terms. They are not bold in the original work.)

First, there is the "gentle knight." Chaucer writes of him:

> "A **Knight** there was, and that a worthy man,
>
> That from the very time he first began
>
> To ride abroad, had loved high chivalry,
>
> Truth, and all honor, freedom, and courtesy;
>
> . . . And in his bearing meek as is a maid.
>
> He never had in all his lifetime said
>
> An ill-bred word to serf or man of might:
>
> He was a very perfect gentle knight."

As you might have noticed, Chaucer used rhyming words to tell his tales. That is part of what makes *The Canterbury Tales* so lively. Of the 17,000 lines in the poem, every two of them rhyme (or come close to it with a little help from the reader). Here is how he describes four more of his characters. Listen carefully for the words that rhyme and try to picture these people in your mind.

> There was a **Nun,** a pleasant *Prioress.*
>
> This lady's smile was coy, I must confess.
>
> . . . Her table manners were indeed a treat.

According to Chaucer, the perfect gentle knight would love "high chivalry, truth, and all honor, freedom, and courtesy."

---

1. Excerpts from Rewey Belle Inglis, Donald A. Stauffer, and Cecil Evva Larsen, *Adventures in English Literature* (Mercury ed.). New York: Harcourt, Brace and Co., 1949; pp. 80-100.

With dainty grace she reached to take her meat;
    Her upper lip she wiped so very clean
    That never was the slightest fraction seen
    Of grease within the rim upon her cup;
        She never let a morsel she took up
Drop down upon her breast; nor did she wet
Her fingers in her sauce too deep. And yet,
    In spite of all her social poise an art,
        She had a very, very tender heart.
    Upon my word, this Prioress would cry
    To see a mouse caught in a trap and die!

    A **Wife of Bath** did much to keep us gay
With tales of love and love charms, on the way –
    A lively soul, who knew the inmost art
    Of how to win a spouse and hold his heart;
    For she had had five husbands in her time
    Not counting scores of lovers in her prime!
She'd grown a little deaf, but nought she cared:
    Now forth to foreign lands each year she fared,
        Since fate decreed she seek out every shrine.
        (Her teeth grew far apart – a certain sign
That she should travel far!) She'd seen Boulogne
    And Rome, and Palestine, Spain, and Cologne.
    . . . The towering headdress worn upon her hair
On Sunday weighed a full ten pounds I'd swear!
    . . . The mantel round her waist did not conceal
        Red stockings, and a spur upon each heel.
        She kept the other pilgrims all in gales
        Of laughter, listening to her merry tales.

    A kindly **Parson** took the journey too.
    He was a scholar, learned, wise, and true
    And rich in holiness though poor in gold.
    A gentle priest: whenever he was told
That poor folks could not meet their tithes that year,
    He paid them up himself; for priests, it's clear,
        Could be content with little, in God's way.
        He lived Christ's gospel truly every day,
    . . . He was a Christian both in deed and thought;

He lived himself the Golden Rule he taught.

The **Miller**, Robin, was a thickset lout,

So big of bone and brawn, so broad and stout

That he was champion wrestler at the matches.

He'd even break a door right off its latches

By running at it with his burly head!

His beard, broad as a spade, was fiery red;

His mouth, a yawning furnace you'd suppose!

A wart with bristly hairs stood on his nose.

. . . His share of grain, he sneaked the payment thrice!

The jokes and tales he told were not so nice.

A drunk and vulgar rogue he proved to be.

But yet he played the bagpipe cleverly,

And to its tune he led us out of town.

A blue hood wore he, and a short white gown.

Now, I've given you a glimpse of five of Chaucer's characters. Don't they sound believable? There is the gentle Knight, the well-mannered Nun, the lively Wife of Bath, the godly Parson, and the crude Miller with red hair growing from a wart on his nose! I find them easy to picture. But let me tell you what they are up to, for their adventure is what makes up the rest of *The Canterbury Tales.*

These 29 people are meeting together to begin a pilgrimage. (There are really 30 because Chaucer includes himself in the group.) If you remember, a pilgrimage is a trip to a holy place. This particular group of pilgrims is going to visit the shrine, or burial site, of **Thomas à Becket.** This is where Chaucer uses history to build his story, for in real life, thousands of people every year went to visit the tomb of Becket in the town of Canterbury, England. Thomas à Becket was a godly man who had been murdered in 1170 by friends of Henry II. (Lesson 59) An elaborate burial site of gold, gems, and ornate carvings had been built in his honor. It was a sight worth seeing then and still is now!

Knowing this historical background, you might better understand a few of the lines describing the Wife of Bath. It mentions that "She'd seen Boulogne, and Rome, and Palestine" etc. to "seek out every shrine." That means she was a regular tourist of holy sites as were many during the Middle Ages.

As the story goes, the 30 pilgrims are stopping at Tabard Inn for a rest from their journey. There they meet a kindly innkeeper. He notices their weariness and comes up with an idea to boost their morale. He suggests that each traveler tell four stories while on the road—two on the way to Becket's shrine and two on the way home. To make it more interesting, the innkeeper suggests that at the end of their journey, all pitch in to give a free meal to the best storyteller of the group.

The rest of *The Canterbury Tales* is a collection of these stories as supposedly told by the pilgrims. Unfortunately, Chaucer only completed one-fifth of

The 30 colorful pilgrims in The Canterbury Tales are on their way to visit the elaborate shrine of Thomas à Becket.

the tales. He died before he could finish. But those he completed are a masterpiece. And unlike Dante's great work (which is in Italian), we can read Chaucer's work in its original English language catching all the rhymes and rhythms as they exist.

I only have room to retell one of these fabulous tales. I will choose the story of **Chanticleer and the Fox,** as told by the Nun's Priest. (Of course, the priest was fictitious! Chaucer really wrote all the tales.) In this fanciful fable, Chanticleer is a proud rooster who is tormented over a bad dream. His wife, a pretty little hen, scolds him in a nagging tone for being afraid. She says,

> "Have you a beard and call yourself a man?
>
> I cannot love a coward; no woman can.
>
> We want our husbands hardy, wise, and free.
>
> What is a dream? Nothing but vanity.
>
> It may arise from eating too rich food."

With this, Chanticleer struts about the yard deciding not to be afraid. Full of new pride and confidence, he speaks with a fox. The fox flatters Chanticleer by begging him to sing a pretty song. But it turns out to be a trick. As soon as Chanticleer stretches out his neck to project his great voice, the fox grabs him by the throat and carries him off!

Well, not to be outdone by the fox, Chanticleer (still in the clutches of the fox) utters to the fox that he ought to shout to the rest of the barnyard how he cleverly caught the rooster. The fox falls for the very trick of flattery that he played on Chanticleer! As soon as the fox opens his jaws to brag, the rooster flies away free. The moral of the story is summed up well by the fox. (Note that the italics in the last line are mine for emphasis.) He says:

> "Nay," quoth the fox, "and God shall never cease
>
> To plague the chattering tongue that should keep peace."
>
> Lo, thus it goes with carelessness, you see,
>
> And with *too great a trust in flattery.*

As you can tell, Chaucer used his tales to poke fun at the flaws of mankind. That is what makes *The Canterbury Tales* a classic. For though customs have changed since the Middle Ages, the nature of mankind has remained much the same.

As for Geoffrey Chaucer himself, he has been remembered as the **"father of the English language."** You see, in writing *The Canterbury Tales,* he blended Saxon words, French words, Latin words—and some words he just made up. In doing so, he created a language that is the basis for English today. He had gathered words from his own life experiences growing up in London and traveling around Europe. I doubt he realized when he wrote what an influence he would have on the world, which speaks a great deal of English!

ACTIVITIES FOR LESSON 79

Field Trip Possibility

Like the pilgrims in *The Canterbury Tales,* visit a public historical cemetery. (Be sure to obtain permission if necessary.) Before you go, discuss proper manners that demonstrate respect for the deceased. Observe similarities and differences in tombstones. Note the common sights and sounds of a cemetery. Discuss the benefits of reflecting on life and death. How does it help us keep perspective on temporal things? How does it help us with our faith? How can it motivate us to share the Gospel with others?

(*Note to Teacher:* I suggest visiting a *historical* cemetery rather than a modern cemetery simply to be sensitive to those who may have recently lost loved ones. Please use your own discretion and judgment as to the benefit of such a field trip. At the right time and place, this could be a meaningful experience for students and adults alike.)

79A—Younger Students

1. Act out one of the five characters of *The Canterbury Tales* as described in the lesson and allow others to guess who it is.

2. Play the "Canterbury Tales Car Game." The next long trip you make in a car, have each family member tell two stories on the way there and two on the way home. Choose a fun prize for those with the best stories (or all who participate).

3. Print or copy a short poem with rhyming words. Circle the rhyming words. Just for fun, try to replace the words with rhyming words of your own.

4. Read a children's version of *The Canterbury Tales.*

79B—Middle Students

1. Picture in your mind these five real-life characters from your own experience: a librarian, a postman, a grocery store worker, a banker, and a pastor. Using metaphors and similes, write a descriptive paragraph or poem on each person. Imagine Chaucer doing much the same thing when he wrote his tales. File your writings under "Europe: England" in your Student Notebook.

2. As a young boy growing up in England, Chaucer served as a page. Research the duties of a page. Knowing this information, do you think Chaucer's description of a knight was possibly born from his own experience?

3. Research the burial site of Geoffrey Chaucer. Like Becket's tomb, it too became a popular tourist site. Where is he buried? Why is the area called the Poet's Corner?

79C—Older Students

1. There are many versions of *The Canterbury Tales.* One suggested version would be Geoffrey Chaucer, *Selected Canterbury Tales,* Unabridged. (Dover Thrift Editions. ISBN # 0-486-28241-4) This particular version contains only selected portions of the book in 135 pages. (In other words, this small paperback is not as long as the original and will more likely be read and appreciated by students!)

2. Research and write the biography of Geoffrey Chaucer. It is more interesting than you would think as he was captured during the Hundred Years' War and ransomed by the king! (Lesson 81) File your biography under "Europe: England."

3. Read other works by Chaucer such as *Troilus and Criseyde* and *Legend of Good Women.*

4. In *Troilus and Criseyde,* Book IV, line 435, Chaucer wrote this famous line, "One eare it heard, at the other out it went." Put this line in modern terms. Americans use this phrase all the time—now you know where it came from.

5. Make a list of the characters in the full tales. Where possible, reclassify the characters on the list into their modern-day counterparts. For example, a knight might best be represented by a marine, a miller by a grocery store manager, etc. File your list under "Europe: England."

6. Discuss Chaucer's description of a monk, a friar, and "the Pardoner." (The Pardoner sold religious relics.) Why was Chaucer's description of the Pardoner so negative? Why did he poke fun at him? What negative stereotypes exist today of "religious" people? Why? What can Christians do today to counter negative stereotypes?

JOHN HUSS

LESSON 80

The study of persecution wearies me. No matter how much I read about it, it still makes my heart heavy. Today is no different. We will look at yet another brave soul who died for the sake of the Gospel. His name was **John Huss,** also written as Jan Hus. (His name rhymes with "goose" and in fact means "goose" in the Slavic language.)

John Huss grew up in **Bohemia,** which is present-day **Czech Republic.** He was just 10 years old when **John Wycliffe** died. To understand today's lesson, it is important that you remember exactly who John Wycliffe was. (Wycliffe had spoken openly about problems he saw in the Medieval Church, was kicked out of Oxford University, and eventually helped translate the Bible into English.)

Though the two never met, there is an interesting connection between John Huss and John Wycliffe. It seems that the king of *England* (the home of Wycliffe) married a princess from *Bohemia* (the home of Huss). This royal marriage opened the door for students in Bohemia to more easily enter Oxford University in England. Aha! There is the connection. Oxford is where Wycliffe had become famous! No one could attend Oxford without hearing about John Wycliffe. And so, as Bohemian students made their way to Oxford, they heard about Wycliffe and his teachings of reform. Naturally, they took these ideas of reform back to Bohemia. That is where John Huss and many others first began to hear of Wycliffe and his concerns for the church.

John Huss was an ordained priest and a scholar. He taught at **Charles University** in Prague. By the time Huss began teaching, Wycliffe had already died in England. But, with open ears and an open heart, John Huss carefully studied the things that John Wycliffe believed were errors in the Medieval Church. He was so impressed that he translated Wycliffe's writings for the Bohemians and distributed them at his school. What he did eventually cost him his life!

By 1408 Huss was forbidden by an archbishop to discuss Wycliffe's ideas of reform anymore. He did so anyway. In fact, Huss's teachings became very popular with the masses and with the queen. The main point he preached was that Christ alone is the head of the church and that only God could forgive sin. He saw the pope as any other man. This greatly threatened the leaders of the church who thought differently and exalted the position of the pope. The archbishop ordered that Huss's teachings be burned! The pope ordered the entire city of Prague under ***interdict***, or punishment, because of Huss. For his safety, John Huss was forced to flee from the city of Prague.

Though he was from Bohemia, John Huss was greatly influenced by John Wycliffe who was from England.

The Great Schism

To complicate matters, let me tell you a little bit about what was going on with the church during this time. It was having some serious problems. It seems that there was a 40-year dispute over who was the rightful pope. One man claiming to be the pope lived in France. The other man claiming to be the pope lived in Rome. Later on, a man in Germany claimed to be the rightful pope. That meant that at one point, there were three men each claiming to be the real pope! This unfortunate event has been called the **Great Schism** ever since. (A *schism* is a division. With three men acting as pope in three different countries, no wonder it was called the great division!)

The reason I bring up the Great Schism is that it demonstrates the difficult times the church was in during the lifetime of John Huss. It would appear that he had legitimate reasons to be concerned.

The Great Schism was a power struggle lasting for decades over who was the rightful pope.

The Council of Constance

Well, with this problem going on and with the teachings of Huss and Wycliffe going around, the Holy Roman Emperor decided it was a good time to call a meeting. In **1415** he called a really big meeting called the **Council of Constance.** (Constance is a town on the border of Germany and Switzerland.) This was the first time that members of four nations in Europe met together for business. Representatives from France, England, Italy, and the Holy Roman Empire (Germany) gathered to try to solve the Great Schism and to stomp out all supposed heresy against the church. Thousands of curious onlookers and peasants crowded the streets and squares where the council was held. So many were there that one of the walls crumbled underneath from the crush of the crowd. Innocent bystanders were killed in the tragedy. As you can imagine, this was the biggest event of the decade. Were it in modern times, all the large news stations would have been there with live reporters.

Imagine the damage that would be done if old European walls and towers like these crumbled from the presence of too many onlookers—or tourists—today.

The good thing about the Council of Constance was that it ended the Great Schism. All nations agreed to oust the three existing popes and install a new one (**Martin V**). The bad news about the council meeting was that it was a trap for John Huss. He was ordered to attend and promised by the Holy Roman Emperor that he would be safely guarded to and from the meeting. But that didn't exactly happen. Though Huss may have been suspicious of the council's intentions, he gladly accepted the opportunity to go there and hoped it would become an opportunity to preach his strong beliefs.

Just for the record, there was an eyewitness of the Council of Constance named **Fra Poggius** who was able to write down exactly what happened there. His report is a shocking one. According to Poggius, before Huss ever got to the council his fate had been sealed. It was already decided that he would be put on trial. But in one harsh session with the delegates, Huss was hardly given the chance to speak in his own defense. He was immediately arrested for speaking out of line and imprisoned for months on end in a dark, damp cell that wasn't much larger than a hole in the ground. The conditions were so poor that his teeth grew rotten and fell out. His clothes deteriorated, and he was practically starved to death.

What most amazes me about this story is that there were several ways in which John Huss could have escaped from his horrible prison cell. For one, townspeople were rioting on his behalf about the unjust treatment he was receiving. They would have gladly broken him out of prison. Second, friends begged to sneak him out in the dark of the night. Third, Huss could have recanted or denied the things he was preaching about the church and been immediately released! But he refused to be swayed by any of these options. Why? Huss firmly believed his teachings were the truth. Here is how he put it, according to Poggius, the eyewitness:

"What else is it, that you cardinals, bishops, and judges ask of me than to sin, by untruth and deceit, against the Holy Spirit? . . . how much more would my soul deserve a terrible end, if I would bury the heritage that you and I have received. . . . You offer me gold and want thereby to hand a lock upon my lips; you want to give me rich revenues, clothe me in soft garments and give me well cooked food, so that I may be lost in everything that is called folly and worldly desire, leading to disaster and damnation. I tell you, that I will not finish in the flesh, . . . what I have begun in spirit. Your law is a spoiled structure of sentences, just to no one, resembling stinking, foul water, from which truly no thirsty man can drink, in the midst of which all sorts of terrible beasts, worse than snakes, newts and salamander, creep and wade about clumsily, at home in the slime, fearing the light and devouring all flesh which strays into their filth. And all this uncleanliness is to a great extent your, my present preachers, fault. For that , because I have the courage to shed light into this desert, you confine me behind dark walls, gruesome bars and iron-bound doors with heavy bars and locks, grant for my body less foul straw than to a murderer and killer. For the last three months and more I have not breathed clean air, as if I were carrion and already decomposing. And these misdeeds against me are committed by you, who have not as yet lent me a kind ear, who have not heard my evangelical teachings undistorted, neither from myself nor from others, only for that reason because you believe that it might bring you damage and dishonor." [2]

You can imagine how stinging these words were to those in charge. Huss's trial dragged on and on, and his days of imprisonment lengthened. Huss was asked over and over to take back his words. He refused, saying:

"As long as I cannot be shown, out of the Holy Bible, that I am in error, I shall insist upon my argument. . . Pope and laymen, Emperor and soldier, I cannot keep silent because of fear, but I shall obey God. . . If I have sinned against my oath,. . . show where my tongue has spoken falsely." [3]

Huss requested only to be given a cell with a view of the blue sky. Perhaps it was to help him keep a view of the heavens.

Time passed. Eventually members of the council were given a chance to vote for the life or death of John Huss. Though many godly council members spoke well of Huss and voted for him to live, the majority found him guilty as charged for heresy against the church. One of his accusers sneered, "It is nothing for a goose to be cleaned and roasted. We have started to clean her, let her be roasted—today."[4] Huss was condemned to burn at the stake. While they were at it, the council condemned John Wycliffe even though he was already dead. (This was when they dug up his bones and had them burned, as I described in Lesson 78.)

---

2. Fra Poggius, *The Trial and Burning of John Huss! An Eyewitness Account By a Member of the Council of Constance*. Toronto: Wittenburg Publications; pp. 21-22.
3. Ibid., pp. 36, 42-43.
4. Ibid., p. 61.

When word of the final sentence broke out, chairs were broken and thrown about. Many council members were outraged. The emperor was forced to sneak out, and Huss could probably have escaped in the turmoil and confusion. But he was found back in his cell, on his knees, praying. His cell was never locked again. He remained inside—content and prepared to die for his Lord. He spent his last days writing letters of encouragement to his followers. In one such letter, he wrote this:

"The only thing which hurts me is that I cannot see you once more in this world and that I must cease to preach the honor of God and the gospel of His Son. Do not grieve, dear friend, God's providence has willed another road for me and even if it is full of thorns and stones, I still hope that it will lead to a victorious goal, from doubt to faith, from wavering to steadfastness. . . Let the remembrance of me rest in a pure heart and teach your children what I have taught you: to love your neighbor, to be peaceful and modest and then you will fare well, now and in eternity. Farewell and do not mourn too much for me, for soon my cup will be full. . . Written at Constance, during my last night, on the 5th day of July 1415 on which day I was just 42 years old. John of Hussinecz." [5]

So that his heroic death might not be forgotten, there stands a statue of John Huss in the city of Prague today.

One thousand bodyguards escorted John Huss to the stake for his execution. (It was customary to burn heretics at the stake because it appeared to keep the church from "spilling blood.") A paper crown was placed mockingly on his head. Upon the crown three demons were drawn with the words "this is an archheretic," meaning a chief heretic. While being prepared for death, Huss appeared to be at peace and sang hymns of his faith.

Once tied up, Huss was again given the chance to take back the words that were costing him his life. To this he replied, "God is my witness that the evidence against me is false. I have never thought nor preached except with the one intention of winning men, if possible, from their sins. Today I will gladly die." [6] Above the crackle of the flames, he sang hymns until at last his voice became silent through the billowing smoke.

Though John Huss died that day in 1415, his ideas didn't. Like Wycliffe, who had the Lollards pick up his cause, John Huss had faithful followers to further his work. They called themselves the **Hussites.** They were such a large group that their presence in Bohemia started a civil war there. Because of the war, some broke away from the Hussites and called themselves the **Unity of the Brethren.** They were known for wearing plain clothes.

Though sad to imagine a good man having to die, I think we can be inspired by men like John Huss. He was intelligent, brave, and unwavering. Had his death not counted, it would be even sadder. But that is not at all the case. Huss stirred the hearts of many men and women to seek the truths of the Bible and bring about reform in the church. We call it the **Reformation.** We will look much more closely at it in Volume III.

5. Ibid., pp. 77-78.
6. A. Kenneth Curtis, J. Stephen Lang, and Randy Petersen, *The 100 Most Important Events in Christian History*. Grand Rapids, MI: Fleming H. Revell, 1991; p. 89.

ACTIVITIES FOR LESSON 80

80A—Younger Students

John Huss sang hymns before he died. What are some of your favorite hymns? What would you sing in a time of great trouble? Survey class members or family members for their favorite hymns. Sing them or write down the words of one verse. File it in your Student Notebook under "Europe: Czech Republic."

80B—Middle and Older Students

1. A must-read would be *The Trial and Burning of John Huss! An Eyewitness Account By a Member of the Council of Constance.* (ISBN # 0-921716-10-9) This small paperback of only 125 pages can be found through Inheritance Publications (1-800-563-3594) or on the Internet at:

   www.telusplanet.net/public/inhpubl/webip/ip.htm)

   Another choice would be *Crushed Yet Conquering* by Deborah Alcock. (ISBN # 1-894666-01-1) This can also be found through Inheritance Publications.

2. Research the famous Charles Bridge in Prague, Czech Republic. Who built it? When? What river does it span? File your answers with a picture of the bridge under "Europe: Czech Republic."

3. Research more on the lives of the Hussites. Find out what they printed in 1501.

80C—Older Students

1. Who were the three popes of the Great Schism? One of the three popes placed Prague under interdict. Who was it? What country did he represent?

2. If you did not do so in Activity 76C, research the life of **St. Catherine of Siena.** She not only ministered to those dying from the Black Death, but she also made efforts to heal the breach of the Great Schism. She was known for ministering to others through letter writing. Pretend to step into her shoes and write a letter to the pope in France requesting that he move back to Rome to make peace. File it under "Europe: Rome" in your Student Notebook.

3. Don't miss the reading selections recommended under Middle and Older Students above!

1431

THE LIFE AND DEATH OF JOAN OF ARC
LESSON 81

It was May 30, **1431.** The sky was blue and clear, but the air was heavy. A great crowd gathered in the market place in **Rouen, France.** Most in the crowd were English. They weren't there to shop, or visit, or do business, as normally would be the case. They were there to watch an execution. Some were excited. Some were curious. And some were already weeping at the tragedy that was about to occur.

Joan of Arc, a black-haired peasant girl, was quiet as a priest read her a last sermon. Then, when given a last chance to speak, this 19-year-old broke down crying. Through tears and sobbing, Joan spoke words of tenderness. She forgave those who were about to burn her at the stake! She asked only that they pray for her.

The stern-faced judges began to weep, as did Joan's accusers. English soldiers and officials were openly sobbing. Joan had offered them forgiveness, but would they ever be able to forgive themselves? Few there believed this young woman was guilty of *any* crime. Yet, she was tied to a stake that stood high above the crowd for all to see. Bundles of straw were piled at her feet. A torch was lit and the executioner commanded to do his "duty."

Joan had only one more request. It was for a cross. A sympathetic soldier tried quickly to make her one out of broken pieces of wood. Before he could finish, a kindly friar brought a crucifix from a nearby church. He extended it out to the young maiden as the flames rose around her. Joan screamed from the pain and shouted only the name of Jesus and the saints while looking up into heaven. Her head dropped and she died.

How and Why?

The death of Joan of Arc is one of the most well known in history. Personally, it moves me to tears. I find myself wondering how and why this horrible thing happened. I wish it were easier to understand. Some tragedies just aren't. I will try to make sense of it for you.

The story of Joan of Arc goes back to the **Hundred Years' War** between France and England. If you remember, England had invaded France over and over again. (Geoffrey Chaucer himself was caught up in the politics of this war before he wrote *The Canterbury Tales*.) It took two royal marriages, two treaties, a truce, and 83 years of battles for the English to finally get what they wanted. What they wanted was the crown of France. It was **Henry V** (the king of England) who finally got to wear the French crown after his stunning victory at **Agincourt.** However, as I told you at the end of Lesson 75, that was not the end of the Hundred Years' War!

Charles needed to reach the stained-glass cathedral of Reims to be properly crowned king. Large stained-glass windows were characteristic of Gothic cathedrals with high, vaulted ceilings.

After all that hard work to obtain the throne and crown of France, Henry V died just two years later. When he did, France was left in chaos. Parts of it were still ruled by the English—parts of it were free. War waged on between the two countries. It is here that Joan enters our story.

Joan of Arc, named Jeanne d'Arc in her language, was born in **Domremy, France.** She grew up in a peasant home. Her parents were devout in their faith and took her and her brothers to church. Like most peasant girls, Joan never learned to read or write.

But unlike most peasant girls, Joan believed she heard voices. She believed them to be the voices of **St. Catherine of Alexandria, St. Margaret,** and **Michael the Archangel.** As young as 12, Joan claims these voices told her to be good, obey her parents, and pray. With great faith, she did.

But by age 17, Joan believed she heard more serious commands. She claimed that voices told her she was to lead the prince of France to take his throne and become the next king! Let me explain who this prince was. The French called him a **"dauphin"** (daw FAN). The term referred to whomever was the oldest son of the king of France.

The dauphin in this real-life story was named **Charles VII.** As the son of King Charles VI, he was the rightful heir to the French throne. But Charles was not in any position to claim his title as king. You see, for one, he had no money. The Hundred Years' War had cost the royal family a great deal. Second, the traditional location for crowning a prince to be king was in the hands of the enemy on the other side of France! That place was a stain-glassed cathedral in the city of **Reims** (reemz). Charles was living, or practically hiding, in a castle in **Chinon** near **Tours.** Charles would have to fight the English to get all the way to Reims and fight them again to keep his crown. He had neither the courage nor the manpower.

What Charles did have was the faith to pray. Supposedly he prayed a private prayer that the Lord would give him the strength and ability to rule France. His answer came in the form of Joan of Arc—at least as some would say.

Joan claimed that at first she shunned the heavenly voices she heard. But after some time, she felt she could only obey them. With great faith, she sent word to Charles that *she* was coming to help *him* become the next king. She cut her long hair and showed up in men's clothing with the hope of being taken seriously. Her disguise as a man was also to protect her from harm.

As you can imagine, Charles was stunned at first. Who was this peasant girl? Was she insane to make such claims? Charles put her through several tests to "prove" her calling. For example, upon Joan's arrival at his castle, Charles placed someone else in his chair to pretend to be him. Then he stood in a line of soldiers to watch Joan enter the room. (She had never seen Charles before.) Much to his amazement, and everyone else's, Joan only glanced at the man in his chair. She then walked straight up to Charles in the line of soldiers and curtsied before him! Her words were these: "Most Illustrious lord Dauphin, I have come and am sent in the name of God to bring aid to yourself and to the kingdom." [7] Needless to say, Joan passed her first test in proving she was for real.

Charles's second test was more challenging. He asked Joan what the words were to his private prayer. Much to his astonishment, she answered him correctly! With that, Charles sent Joan to church officials for three more weeks of questioning. They sent her back to Charles with their approval and suggested he give her charge over the French royal army! Can you imagine that?

Joan in Battle

The rest of the story is amazing. Joan *was* placed in charge of the army. (Remember that she was only a 17-year-old peasant girl!) She was given six servants, a horse, and outfitted with white armor made to fit her small-framed body. Interestingly, the first "battle" Joan fought was a spiritual one. She battled against the immorality of her own troops! Like a prophet out of the Old Testament, Joan dismissed any prostitutes (immoral women) found hiding among the French army and required the soldiers to repent of their sins. They were instructed to pray and forbidden from swearing or looting.

Though some of the troops were skeptical of the fair, young leader (*skeptical* means they were doubtful of her), Joan soon proved her worth. When they followed her lead, they were successful; when they didn't, they failed. In most battles, Joan of Arc carried a large white banner bearing an image of Christ, two angels, and the ***fleur-de-lis*** of France. She carried no weapon (according to some historians) though she placed herself in harm's way. As long as the banner waved, the troops were inspired to move forward. And they did.

At 17, Joan was outfitted with six servants, a horse, and her own white armor to help her lead the French army.

---

7. Allen Williamson, "Joan of Arc, Brief Biography" (p. 3). Accessed on the Joan of Arc Online Archive Web site: www.joan-of-arc.org/joanofarc_short_biography.html

Was Joan ever frightened in battle? By her own admission, she was. Her greatest fear was being captured. At least three times she was wounded. Eyewitnesses say she cried when soldiers were killed around her—French or English! But her mission was to see Charles the Dauphin placed on the throne. And so, with great courage, she pressed on.

Joan's first official victory was at the city of **Orleans** in 1429. From there she was nicknamed the **Maiden of Orleans**—a name she liked to call herself. She believed the term "maiden" (sometimes translated "virgin") would remind young men that she was pure and not to be touched! Also, to be modest around the soldiers, Joan wore articles of men's clothing that tied her shirt tightly to her pants. (Remember this detail because it was later used against her!)

Four more battles were fought under Joan before the city of Reims was at last conquered. In each instance, Joan proved to be a military genius according to other soldiers. Her "mission" was finally complete. On July 16, 1429, Charles VII was crowned the king of France in Reims with Joan of Arc standing triumphantly by his side. Those who watched her stand with her banner in hand claim she "wept many tears and said, 'Noble king, now is accomplished the pleasure of God, who wished me to lift the siege of Orleans, and to bring you to this city of Reims to receive your holy anointing, to show that you are the true king, and the one to whom the kingdom of France should belong.' "[8] It would be so nice if I could write that the story ended here. But as you already know, things were going to turn for the worst, at least for the Maiden of Orleans.

The Capture of Joan of Arc

At first, Joan wished to go home after Charles VII was crowned king. She felt her job was done according to the voices she had claimed to hear. But there was still much to be done to take back the rest of France. Perhaps this is where Joan went wrong. Despite the completion of her mission, she stayed on with the troops for some time, involving herself more and more with the politics behind the war. She even went so far as to send a letter to the **Hussites** (the followers of John Huss) to plead with them to stay with the church. (This was later used against her!)

As you can only imagine, the English were quite upset over their losses. They had invested almost one hundred years in this war that they were slowly losing to a teenage girl! I suppose they felt no other option but to try to do away with her. They collaborated with the **Burgundians,** a group of French who were not loyal to the king. Outside the city of **Compiegne,** Joan and a small troop of men were ambushed by Burgundian soldiers. Though Joan initially refused to surrender, she was pulled off her horse by an archer and taken away.

Though put in captivity, Joan never left her beloved country. She spent the next four months in a Burgundian prison on French soil. She tried to escape, and three attempts were made to rescue her. King Charles VII himself offered to pay her captors a large ransom for her safe return. (Though some historians would argue that Charles completely turned his back on Joan.) The Burgundians refused to accept Charles's payment and sold her instead to the English! Yes, she was sold to the English, her real enemy, for the price of about $3,000. They moved her to a prison in Rouen (a town northwest of Paris in English territory) and put her on trial for heresy.

Now, you may be wondering why the English tried her for *heresy* when she wasn't the least bit opposed to the teachings of the church. Well, for one, many church leaders had become corrupt at this point in history—meaning that they abused the power that they had. Second, it seemed that the charge of heresy was the only way the English could "legally" kill Joan without having it look like complete murder. Unfortunately, burning supposed heretics at the stake had become all too common a practice in

---

8. Ibid., p. 6.

Europe, as we saw with the death of John Huss and others. It was the perfect cover-up for revenge against young Joan who had dared to lead the French against them.

And so the English proceeded to put Joan on trial as a heretic. She had no one to speak on her behalf. She had only herself for a witness. As for her crimes, Joan of Arc was first condemned for wearing men's clothes (which she did for practical reasons). Second, her accusers claimed she was a liar because only church leaders could hear heavenly voices. Third, she was accused of witchcraft because there appeared to be magical powers in her banner. Last, she was condemned for planning to lead a crusade against the Hussites—something that only the pope could do.

At any time, Joan could have admitted to her supposed crimes and received lifetime imprisonment rather than death. But she wouldn't do it. At least for 10 weeks she wouldn't. But after being worn down by little food and sleep, Joan signed a paper that she was guilty. The tragedy might have ended there.

However, the next day Joan took back her statement with a clear mind. It cost her her life. She was immediately given the death penalty. Joan's black hair was shaved, and she was given a dress and a dunce's hat to wear. The hat labeled her a heretic and a witch.

I've already described to you the day she died. Few at the scene of her execution believed she was really a heretic—much less a witch. Few thought she deserved to die. Even the executioner was afraid he was burning a "saint." But the death sentence was upheld anyway to put an end to Joan's success. To add insult to the tragedy, the English refused to bury her ashes, but rather threw them into the Seine River.

But the success of the French didn't die with Joan. With even greater passion, and in memory of the Maiden of Orleans, the French drove the English out of their land for good. By 1453 they had won the Hundred Years' War! Only one city in France remained under English rule until later in history.

Twenty-four years after her death, Joan of Arc was again put on trial. Though she was dead,

As a final act of disrespect, it was not uncommon for the ashes of a supposed heretic to be thrown into a rushing river, never to be seen again.

her case was heard to clear her name. Joan's mother and King Charles, the very prince she helped place on the throne, both fought the courts to overturn Joan's earlier sentence. Of course, she was found innocent this time. Her previous trial was determined to be illegal for having been unfair.

Much later, in 1920, Joan of Arc was declared a "saint" by the Roman Catholic Church. Had the church made that decision or not, I believe her name would have gone down in history in the same category as the saints of old. Though some believe Joan of Arc was misguided by her visions, she nonetheless proved to be a young woman of great courage and faith.

ACTIVITIES FOR LESSON 81

ALL STUDENTS

Make your Memory Cards for Lessons 79–81. The Death of Joan of Arc (1431) is a date to memorize. Remember to highlight the card accordingly.

81A—Younger and Middle Students

1. Do you know what a fleur-de-lis is? Turn to the Activity Supplement in the Appendix to find more information on the fleur-de-lis as well as a coloring page and directions for making a stained-glass

puzzle. You have the option to choose which of these two projects you'd like to complete for this activity—or complete both if you prefer!

2. A sympathetic soldier tried to make a cross for Joan out of wood. Collect sticks and try to fashion a cross out of them. Use twine to tie them together.

3. Can you think of a city in Louisiana named after a main city in our lesson? Hint: Joan was called the "Maiden" of this city.

81B—Middle and Older Students

1. A great amount of information can be found about Joan of Arc on the Internet. I suggest reading copies of her letters as found at the following site:

   http://archive.joan-of-arc.org/joanofarc_letters.html

   Copy any one of these letters, trim it, and tea-stain it to look aged. File the letter in your Student Notebook under "Europe: France."

2. Many books and plays have been written to commemorate Joan of Arc, including *Saint Joan*, written in 1923 by George Bernard Shaw, and a historical novel titled *Joan of Arc* by Mark Twain. Choose one of these to read or a book by any other author about the life and death of Joan of Arc.

3. With parental discretion, search for and view a modern film on Joan of Arc. If at all possible, try to obtain an older film titled *The Passion of Joan of Arc* (1928), no rating. This film is said to be very historically accurate because it is based on actual trial transcripts.

4. Research what the Bible says about Michael the Archangel. What are examples of his appearance, his role, his duty, and his message?

TAKE ANOTHER LOOK!

REVIEW 27: LESSONS 79–81

Wall of Fame

1. **Geoffrey Chaucer and The Canterbury Tales (1387)**—Draw the shape of a book and title it "The Canterbury Tales by Chaucer." [From *History Through the Ages*, use *Geoffrey Chaucer.*]

2. **John Huss (1415)**—Depict a man with a paper crown on his head but a smile on his face. Draw fire at his feet. [Use *Jan Hus, The Great Schism,* and *Martin V.*]

3. **The Life and DEATH OF JOAN OF ARC (1431)**—Create a small banner with a fleur-de-lis on it. Write on the banner the name of Joan of Arc. **Remember, this is a date to memorize.** [Use *Joan of Arc.*]

SomeWHERE in Time

1. Younger Students: Use an atlas to find the city of Constance, the place where John Huss was tried and burned at the stake. You will find it on the border between Germany and Switzerland. Find present-day Czech Republic. Trace with your finger the journey that John Huss made to his trial in Constance. Remember, without cars or trains in the Middle Ages, travel wasn't very easy!

2. Middle and Older Students: Retrace the steps of Joan of Arc.

   Materials: Outline Map 27, "France"; atlas; colored pencils

   a. Label **France.**

   b. Find and label **Domremy.** (It is hard to find in an atlas. It lies southwest of Nancy, a larger city that is easier to find.)

   c. Find and label **Chinon,** a town southwest of Tours where Joan of Arc first met Charles VII. (This town may be difficult to find as well. If so, locate Tours and estimate its southwest location.)

   d. Find and label the city of **Orleans,** the place of Joan's first victory.

   e. Find and label the city of **Reims,** the location of the crowning of Charles VII.

   f. Find and label the city of **Compiegne,** the site where Joan was captured by the Burgundians.

   g. Find and label the city of **Rouen,** the place where Joan was put on trial and executed. Now that the cities are labeled, connect them as follows.

   h. Use a colored pencil to draw a line from Domremy to Chinon. Label the line "#1."

   i. Use another colored pencil to draw a line from Chinon to Orleans. Label it line #2.

   j. Use a different-colored pencil to draw a line from Orleans to Reims. Label it line #3.

   k. Use another colored pencil to draw a line from Reims to Compiegne. Label it line #4.

   l. Use yet another colored pencil to draw a line from Compiegne to Rouen. Label it line #5.

   m. Make a key on a separate piece of paper to explain the major events that each line depicts. I will start you with two examples. You complete the rest.

Line #1: Joan was born in Domremy and traveled to Chinon to meet Charles VII.

Line #2: After confronting Charles at the castle in Chinon, Joan led troops to a French victory in Orleans.

Line #3: [You fill in the rest!]

Line #4:

Line #5:

n. File your map in your Student Notebook under "Europe: France."

WHAT DID YOU LEARN?

WEEK 27: QUIZ

I. Matching. Match the items by placing a letter from the right in the blanks on the left.

_____1. St. Valentine   a Female empress of China

_____2. Diocletian   b. Missionary to Ireland; used symbol of clover

_____3. Constantine   c. Leader of the Huns

_____4. St. Patrick   d. Creator of the Cyrillic alphabet for the Slavs

_____5. Attila   e. Godly English king who conquered the Danes

_____6. Gregory the Great   f. Humble monk who became a pope

_____7. Wu Zetian   g. "Sealed" the Edict of Milan to give religious freedom

_____8. St. Boniface   h. Was martyred on February 14

_____9. Cyril   i. Emperor who divided Rome; persecuted Christians

_____10. Alfred the Great   j. Missionary to Germany; used symbol of evergreen

II. Who Did It? Circle the correct answer.

11. In despair and haste, I named the island of Iceland during a difficult winter there.

      Gardar   Floki Vilgerdarson   Macbeth

12. We built a magnificent city with stone houses in Africa.

      The Maori   The Inuit   The Zimbabweans

13. As the duke of Bohemia, I freed my mother from banishment even though she had murdered my godly grandmother.

      Roger Bacon   Wenceslas   Vladimir

14. I started the Song dynasty and made my capital in Kaifeng.

      St. Simon   Prince Shotoku   General Zhao Kuang Yin

15. I named Greenland and took many settlers there.

      Eric the Red   Beowulf   Leif Ericsson

16. I discovered parts of Canada in North America in A.D. 1000.

      El Cid   Leif Ericsson   Columbus

17. I murdered another king to become the king of Scotland.

      Macbeth   Columba   Eric the Red

18. I invaded England at the Battle of Hastings and started the Norman line of rulers.

      Edward III   William the Conqueror   King Arthur

19. I preached to recruit men and women to take part in the First Crusade.

      Pope Urban II   Eleanor of Aquitaine   King John

20. I was a noble Arab who faced Richard the Lionhearted in the Third Crusade.

        Robin Hood   Maimonides   Saladin

III. People and Places. Use colored pencils to connect the people and places.

21. St. Francis   a. The Forbidden City

22. King John   b. The Holy Roman Empire

23. Frederick II   c. Bohemia (Czech Republic)

24. Genghis Khan (his original homeland)   d. Mexico

25. Marco Polo (his original home city)   e. Assisi, Italy

26. William Wallace   f. Mongolia

27. Aztecs   g. England

28. Ming dynasty   h. Venice, Italy

29. John Huss   i. France

30. Joan of Arc   j. Scotland

IV. Bonus Essay. Write in complete sentences to answer each of the following questions. (Earn half a point per correct answer.) Use a separate sheet of paper if necessary.

1. What is one reason why it was not wise for Nicholas and Stephen to lead other children on crusades to the Holy Land?

2. How was the Black Death most commonly spread in the Middle Ages?

3. Why was the Forbidden City "forbidden"?

4. What was one of the crimes that Joan of Arc was accused of at her trial?

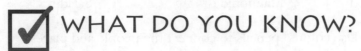

☑ WHAT DO YOU KNOW?

PRETEST 28

Fill in the Blanks. Using a word from the bottom of the page, fill in the blanks.

1. The Inkas lived on the continent of _____ _____.

2. The largest rain forest in the world is the _____.

3. The magnificent city of Cuzco was built in the shape of a _____, a leopard-like animal.

4. The _____ are a group of countries between Italy and Asia Minor. They are nicknamed the "Powder Keg of Europe" for all the fighting that occurs there.

5. The city of Constantinople was conquered and renamed _____ under the Ottoman Turks.

6. Johannes Gutenberg fashioned the first printing press after a _____ press.

7. The first book printed by Gutenberg was the _____.

8. The printing press helped spread the _____ of God to Europe and bring about the close of the Middle Ages.

WORD BANK

puma	Istanbul	South America	cheese
Amazon	Bible	Balkans	Word

THE INKAS OF SOUTH AMERICA
LESSON 82

We have covered a lot of territory in this book. Just to name a few places—we have studied faraway China, Japan, and India. We have learned the history of England, France, and Spain. We have looked at remote cultures in Zimbabwe, Iceland, and New Zealand. But we haven't yet had a lesson on **South America**! Let me explain why I've waited until now to introduce this continent to you. (It's not because people weren't living there!)

Some of you will remember learning in Volume I that a few thousand years ago the continents of North America and Asia were connected by a natural land bridge. It formed during the Ice Age as a result of the Great Flood that Noah was in. This land bridge allowed people to travel from Asia all the way to the Americas by foot. So, South America *has* had people living there for a long, long time.

But unlike the other places we've studied, early South Americans didn't have a *written* language that we know of. That means we don't have documents, diaries, or literature of these people from long ago. We don't have the names of ancient heroes, kings, or battles—though I'm sure there were some. We just have sketchy clues of people groups who lived across the continent in isolated communities. That is, until the 1400s. In **1438** there emerged in South America an empire that was so well organized and so rich that it made a lasting mark in history. This impressive empire was that of the **Inkas** (sometimes spelled Incas).

Though ancient civilizations inhabited South America, little is known of them.

The Inkas lived along the west coast of South America. That wasn't easy though. The west coast of South America has the world's driest desert—the **Atacama Desert.** It is so dry that cactus doesn't even grow there! Just beyond that lies the world's longest mountain range—or more precisely, mountain system— called the **Andes.** It contains some of the tallest, most treacherous mountains ever created. And just beyond them is the largest rain forest in the world—better known as the **Amazon**! It was quite an accomplishment to settle this hostile landscape. The Inkas called their homeland **Tawantinsuyo.** It meant **"Land of the Four Quarters"** because the empire was neatly organized into four regions.

The Andes mountain range stretches across South America for 4,500 miles! Its name comes from the word anti, which means "copper" in a native language.

The man who has been given the most credit for making the Inkas great was named **Pachacuti** (Pat-char-coo-tee). He wasn't the first emperor. In fact he shouldn't have been emperor at all. His father had given the title to one of his other sons. But Pachacuti was very ambitious. As a warrior prince, he conquered small tribes around the Inkas, expanding his father's kingdom. In doing so, he became a great hero. To celebrate his victories, Pachacuti drank corn beer from the skulls of his enemies! He took the throne from his brother and gave himself a name meaning "earth shaker," or "one who turns the world upside down." From the Inkas' perspective, he did just that.

Pachacuti spent 10 years battling scattered tribes around him to further his empire. Sometimes he was ruthless. But militarily, he was a genius. Rather than make enemies of those he conquered, he lured them into his empire to serve and teach. In doing this, the Inkas learned valuable skills from other tribes. They learned how to mine gold, build roads, make perfect bricks, hunt, and more. All these trades made the Inkas a rich empire in a short amount of time.

Cuzco

After 10 years on the battlefront, Pachacuti gave his military job over to his son. He then poured his ambition into building a great capital city. It was named **Cuzco.** That means "naval" in the Inka language because it sat right in the middle of the empire (like a belly button) and marked where the four quarters met. Today it is in the middle of the country of **Peru.** The empire stretched from present-day **Ecuador** down to **Chile** and included parts of **Bolivia** and **Argentina.**

Cuzco was spectacular. Looking down on the ancient city from above, you'd have seen that Cuzco was laid out in the shape of a **puma,** which is a leopard-like animal. At the head of the puma, three large, zigzag walls called **Sacsahuaman** had been built. The jagged shape of the walls made up the teeth of the puma and served as an intimidating barrier to outsiders. The stones in this wall were so well laid that a knife could not pass between them even though no mortar was used in setting them. Sacsahuaman still stands today as if to guard the Inka ruins with the snarling teeth of a puma.

Within the body of the puma were clean, well-planned streets where 40,000 nobles and delegates lived. In the center was a holy place. The tail contained a sacred temple to the sun (**Intihuatana**) and an inner palace where only the emperor was allowed. Much like the Forbidden City of China, this site was restricted! To enter without permission was sure death.

One reason for the high palace security was that Pachacuti made himself out to be a representation of the Inka sun god. No one was allowed to look him in the eye. His spit was collected as a treasure, and his fallen hair eaten by attendants! Every day that he was king, Pachacuti was adorned with an elaborate new outfit. Many of these would have been delicately woven from the fine wool of the alpaca. For further distinction, the king wore the largest gold earplugs in the society. (An earplug was like an earring, but it was made bigger and bigger to stretch out the earlobe.) Out of reverence, Pachacuti's old clothes and leftover food were burned.

The bloodline of the Inkas has remained strong with over six million people today speaking Quechua, the language of the early Inkas.

The self-made emperor married his sister to keep his bloodline pure but allowed himself hundreds of other wives in order to create a class of noble offspring.

Pachacuti's palace was also restricted because of the great wealth it contained. Much of it was made of pure gold! His throne was gold; walls were lined with sheets of gold; and the royal garden was crafted of gold and silver plants and animals to glisten in the sun and delight the emperor.

The sun was very important to the Inkas. They named it **Inti** and believed it to be one of their greatest gods. They also revered the moon, the earth, and thunder. It was Pachacuti who made the worship of the sun an official religion. He believed the Intihuatana, or sacred sun temple, to be the center of Inka worship. When the sun was straight up overhead, it of course cast no shadow on the temple stone. It was then, the Inkas believed, that Inti, the sun god, was sitting in their midst. And, like rays of the sun, all other holy sites radiated out from there.

One of the most important of these holy sites was **Lake Titicaca.** Nestled in the tops of the Andes, Titicaca is the highest lake in the world. The air is so thin that it is hard for outsiders to breathe there. This 120-mile-long lake contains 25 islands. One of them was called **Island of the Sun** and held a great palace where, it is believed, the first Inkas sprang forth after a great flood. (The Inka flood myth is similar to the biblical flood. It probably was passed down by word of mouth!) This island palace held tremendous amounts of wealth. The emperor visited at least once a year to pay tribute to his ancestors.

Lake Titicaca also contained the **Island of the Moon** where thousands of special Inka women lived. These **Acllas** (Ak-lyaz), or "Chosen Women," were picked for their beauty as young as 10 years of age. Some Chosen Women were trained to be priestesses and work in the temples. Others were sent to be servants to the emperor. The loveliest of the Acllas were selected to be wives to the emperor or gifts to other tribes. It was considered a great honor to have any of these roles. Girls "not chosen" were destined for a peasant's life.

Though this social system was unfair, the emperor ran an efficient empire. Like Julius Caesar of the Roman Republic, Pachucuti improved the calendar, the legal system, the government, and the roads. Tawantinsuyo, the "Land of the Four Quarters," was connected by 15,000 miles of highway covering deserts, mountains, and valleys. The highways had stone markers every six miles, rest houses, stores, and water. A messenger service could cover the entire empire in two days. Long, dangerous rope bridges were not uncommon sights as they were

Well-constructed Inka bridges made of stone and rope still span the rushing rivers of South America.

used to span the wide South American rivers and rocky gorges. According to Spanish invaders, these bridges were strong enough for a horse to gallop across! (I wouldn't want to try it, though.)

Machu Picchu

This message system was especially helpful to the emperor when he was visiting his favorite getaway. It seems he built a religious sanctuary even more magnificent than Cuzco as a special place for spiritual ceremonies and rest. This mountain resort was named **Machu Picchu** (MAH choo PEEK choo). Nestled among some of the most beautiful rock formations in the world, Machu Picchu is still a breathtaking sight. A thousand of the most elite nobility lived and worked there. They were very well taken care of by the emperor, who saw to it that exotic foods were regularly delivered to them. One of these was the **coca leaf** from which cocaine is derived. Inkas chewed the leaves to soothe their ailments and relieve exhaustion.

Machu Picchu stands unique from other Inka settlements in many ways. I can't begin to do it justice here. Its observatories (special buildings to study the stars) were more elaborate than those in Europe. Even the stones used to build the city were special. Windows and openings were crafted in polygonal (many-sided) shapes unlike any other in the world. One temple stone was cut to have 33 corners! Fortunately for historians, this treasure trove was undiscovered by Spanish settlers and left untouched and abandoned for centuries. Machu Picchu was only discovered in 1911!

As skilled as the Inkas were, however, they were not so advanced as to make use of the wheel, horses, or money. Every traveler on the road was on foot or carried on special pallets called **litters.** Llamas and alpacas were used for heavy cargo although a llama can't carry more than 100 pounds. Crops plowed by hand and foot were accepted for trade and taxes instead of money. Counting was done through an unusual system of knots on colored string. This counter was called a **khipu** (key-poo).

Speaking of taxes, if you were lucky enough to be "just married" in the Inka empire, you were exempt from paying taxes for a whole year. Marriages were arranged for men when they turned 25 to girls usually much younger than themselves. As part of the wedding ceremony, a bride gave her sandal to her new husband. Marriage was taken seriously and divorce was forbidden. Adultery was punished by death.

Like silent statues, the breathtaking peaks of Machu Picchu rise high into the clouds to enclose the mountainous resort.

The death penalty was used for other crimes, too, such as murder or theft. This was especially true if you were of the nobility. More was expected from these upper-class citizens. For them, even laziness was punishable by death! The most common method of execution was pushing a criminal off a cliff! (I think that would be a powerful deterrent to crime.)

From time to time, human sacrifice was performed to honor the Inka gods. Fortunately, this

Similar to their ancestors, Inka farmers continue to live in simple homes across Peru, Bolivia, and Ecuador.

practice was much rarer than it was among the Aztecs whom we studied earlier. But the Inkas did have their own peculiar ritual with the dead. Mummified bodies of important rulers were brought out on special occasions to be paraded through the cities. And so that these mummies could "sit up" at banquet tables, they were preserved (or mummified) in a sitting position. At least we think that is why they were buried upright. There may be other reasons.

If you remember, there wasn't a written language of the Inkas to explain their beliefs and customs. Much of what I've shared with you was written down and documented by Spanish explorers in the 1500s. We are grateful for these rare records of the past. However, the Spanish unfortunately did much to destroy the Inka culture they discovered. They found unbelievable amounts of gold that I described earlier and practically annihilated the Inkas to steal it! But that is really a lesson for the next volume.

The Inka empire at its height encompassed 10 to 12 million people. Though the Spanish crushed them down to a million, there are Inkas that have survived until today. Like their ancestors, they still use the magnificent highways once laid down for Pachacuti; they farm the same valleys; and they weave the same textiles from the delicate coat of the alpaca. Though times have changed much in South America since Pachacuti, some history keeps itself alive!

ACTIVITIES FOR LESSON 82

ALL STUDENTS

Eat popcorn as you complete your work today. The Inkas believed it was a delicacy!

82A—Younger Students

1. A clan in the Inka culture was called an *ayllu*. It describes a group of people who shared the same ancestor. Create a diagram or list of your family clan. For example, write down the name of one set of your grandparents, their children (which should include one of your parents), and you with your siblings. Do you have any nephews or nieces? Be sure to include them. What members of your clan are still living? Does your clan live near one another? Does your clan celebrate special things together? Discuss the importance of these close family ties. File your clan information under "South America: Peru."

2. The Inkas had an interesting way of keeping track of numbers. They tied knots on a rope to represent the things they were counting. Make a fun game of this. Take a count of something in your home such as the number of shoes in the house or windows or doors. For every item you count, tie a knot in a small piece of rope. Don't tell others what you are counting. When you're done, see if they can guess by counting the number of knots in your rope and examining things around your home or classroom.

3. The Inkas used a tumpline, or a wide headband, to carry loads on top of their heads. Practice carrying something on your head! (Nothing too fragile, of course.) Take a picture and file it in your Student Notebook under "South America: Peru."

4. The Inkas were fascinated with the sun and believed their sun god was sitting in their midst at high noon when shadows typically disappear. Observe your shadow on the next sunny day. Stand in the same place outside sometime in the morning, again at noon, and sometime in the late afternoon. Observe how your shadow changes and why it moves. You can "keep" your shadow by laying a piece of paper or poster board near you on the ground and allowing someone else to trace your shadow. File a small sample of your "shadow" in your Student Notebook under "South America: Peru."

82B—Middle Students

1. The Inkas used dry, hollowed-out gourds as containers and pots. Purchase a gourd at the grocery store. (If not in season, consider a melon or squash as a *temporary* substitute although it will not become as dry and hard as a gourd will.) Remove the top of the gourd and hollow it out. Bake in the oven on a low temperature until hard. Use permanent markers of various colors to decorate your gourd with beautiful, geometric patterns. Take a picture of your creation and file it in your Student Notebook under "South America: Peru."

2. The Inkas ate spicy hot peppers. Have a pepper-eating contest to see who in your class or family can eat the hottest pepper! (Provide plenty of water and crackers.)

3. What makes a rain forest a rain forest? Research the things that distinguish a rain forest from an ordinary forest. Write a short report on rain forests including where they are found, what animals are unique to them, and what makes them so dangerous. File your report in your Student Notebook under "South America: Brazil."

82C—Older Students

1. Design a miniature rope bridge out of rope and craft sticks. Create an entire three-dimensional scene including a river, rocks, and greenery. Take a photo and file it in your Student Notebook under "South America: Peru."

2. Read and discuss Romans 2:14–16 in relation to the strict society of laws that the Inkas created. Without Scripture to guide them, from what source or inspiration did the Inkas formulate their moral laws? It is thought-provoking.

1453

THE OTTOMAN TURKS TAKE CONSTANTINOPLE

LESSON 83

History isn't just the story of one person here and another person there. History is more so the story of how one person here *connects* to another person there. Like long, delicate threads of a tapestry, the events in history are tightly woven together to create a picture of our present world. Today's lesson is a perfect example of that. To understand this lesson about the **Ottoman Turks** and their takeover of **Constantinople,** you will need to think back with me on several previous lessons. (Remember, we are connecting threads of history here.) We will consider the cities visited by **Paul** on his missionary journeys, **Constantine** renaming Byzantium, the fall of the **Western Roman Empire,** the style of **Justinian and Theodora,** and the terrifying reign of **Genghis Khan.** Believe it or not, they all relate to one another to explain the fall of one great empire and the rise of another. Since we are so near the end of this book, think of this lesson as a review connecting several people and places you've already learned about.

Let's take **Paul** first. I'm sure you will remember that he traveled to city after city in Europe and Asia Minor telling his story of coming to know Jesus Christ. As a result, we have seven New Testament books bearing the names of these cities. Six of them were located in what *became* the Ottoman Empire. The Ottoman Empire, however, was Islamic. You may be wondering how these Christian cities fared under Islamic rule. I will get to that.

Think next about **Constantine.** You should remember him for the Edict of Milan that freed Christians from horrible persecution. But, relevant to our lesson today, he also made the city of **Byzantium** his capital. It was renamed **Constantinople** in his honor. In creating this capital, Constantine influenced the future Byzantine Empire to be strongly Christian.

I'm sure you will remember, too, the fall of the **Western Roman Empire.** The fall influenced all of Europe. It particularly affected the flow of great thinkers, artists, and scientists who fled from the

West to the Eastern Roman Empire. The main city of attraction was Constantinople. (We're getting close to the lesson at hand now.)

Think for a minute about **Justinian and Theodora.** They were the rags-to-riches couple that transformed Constantinople into a truly beautiful and spectacular city. Justinian was inspired to build one of the most magnificent churches in the world. It was **Saint Sophia,** or Hagia Sophia. (Remember that.) The wealth of the city drew even more great thinkers, artists, and scientists to the area, making Constantinople a world center of learning. (Remember that, too.)

Last in our review is **Genghis Khan.** His terrifying reign chased people out of their homelands in search of new ones. That finally leads us to the Ottoman Turks, the main subject of our lesson. The Ottoman Turks were originally a band of fugitives led by a man named **Osman.** (A fugitive is someone on the run.) Osman and his followers, the Ottomans, were *on the run* from somewhere in Asia to escape the wrath of Genghis

Unlike any other city in the world, Constantinople (Istanbul) lies on the two continents of Europe and Asia. The Black Sea, pictured here, separates the two.

Khan! Their place of refuge? The Ottomans found shelter among the **Seljuk Turks** living around the **Black Sea.** The Black Sea, if you don't remember, is the large body of water that guards the city of Constantinople from the Mediterranean. Now, let's put all these review pieces together.

The Ottomans Take the Balkans

Osman wasn't content to simply live among the Seljuk Turks around the Black Sea. With the help of his army, he quickly began to conquer them and declared himself **Sultan** (or king) of the Turks. Now, the Black Sea stretches across both Europe and Asia. Had Osman stayed on the Asian side of the Black Sea, we might not have heard more about him. But the sultan soon crossed the sea to the European side. With that move, he made his mark in history. In 1326 the Ottoman Turks took control of a region called the **Balkans.** Before we go any further, let me introduce the Balkans to you more specifically because they are a hotbed of conflict even in modern times. (This region has been nicknamed **"The Powder Keg of Europe"** for being so quick to erupt into war!)

The Balkan countries are named for the Balkan Mountains that run through Bulgaria and Yugoslavia. *Balkan* in the Turkish language means "mountain." The Balkan Peninsula is squeezed between the peninsula of Italy and the coast of Asia Minor. Look at a globe or atlas now to follow along with me. The Balkans include **Greece, Albania, Bulgaria,** the **European part of Turkey,** and **most of Yugoslavia.** Some would also include **Romania** in this list. The fighting that still goes on there has some connection to what happened in the Middle Ages. Now back to our story of the Ottomans.

When the Ottomans crossed into Europe and conquered the Balkans, they found the **Bulgarians** and the **Serbs (Yugoslavians)** to be much like themselves. They were a similar race with a similar culture. That is, except for one important thing. The Bulgarians and the Serbs were Christian. The Ottomans were Islamic. Hmm! This was sure to bring problems. And it did. As the Ottomans invaded the European Balkans, they brought their belief system with them. If people were unwilling to convert to the Islamic faith, they were heavily taxed. We've seen this before in history. And so, from economic and political pressure, the Christian cities of the New Testament fell one by one to Islam.

However, there was one Christian city that up to this point in history had survived—one city that was yet to be captured by the Ottoman Turks. From all our previous review, can you guess which one it was? It was Constantinople. This magnificent city had been a world center for over 1,000 years. It was the capital of Constantine, the home of Justinian, and the heart of the Byzantine Empire. To take it was no small task. But in the late 1400s, a new sultan rose to the challenge. His name was **Mohammed II** (not to be confused with Mohammed, the founder of the Islamic faith who lived hundreds of years earlier).

The Capture of Constantinople

Mohammed II came to rule the Ottoman Turks in 1451. Like Pachacuti to the Inkas, Mohammed II was an "earth shaker." To attack Constantinople, he recruited 150,000 soldiers, knowing that his enemy had an army of only 8,000 to 10,000 men. In other words, to make sure he wouldn't lose, he created an army more than 10 times the size of his opponent! It proved to be a brilliant strategy.

Mohammed II intended to sail his warships through the **Golden Horn,** which is the great harbor of Constantinople. But a huge underwater iron chain prevented his large ships from sailing through. So, Mohammed improvised. He dragged 70 smaller warships over the land. How? His army placed them on beds of long logs and rolled them across dry land! The boats were then positioned to gain entry to the harbor. Mohammed surrounded the city on two other fronts, giving him three sides from which to attack.

Under the Byzantine emperor **Constantine XI,** the city of Constantinople fought back for 54 days. That is about seven weeks. Constantine XI pleaded with the West for help. But none came. The armies of Constantinople were no match for Mohammed's special forces. They were called **Janissaries.** The Janissaries were elite soldiers, most of whom were recent converts to Islam. Their name means "new

Mohammed II successfully stormed the city of Constantinople with 150,000 soldiers and warships that he cleverly maneuvered over dry land.

forces" since with each new Ottoman victory, Janissary soldiers were newly added to the army. On May 29, **1453**, the weakened city of Constantinople fell to the Ottoman Turks. Constantine XI was killed in battle. This tragic blow to the city marked the end of the once great Byzantine Empire.

One of many great losses was the church of Saint Sophia. Built by Justinian in 532, the church was looted and turned into a mosque. Though designed in the shape of a cross, it remained a mosque until 1933. (It is now a museum.) Among other things, the magnificent city even lost its name. The Ottoman Turks renamed it **Istanbul,** which is the name it goes by today.

But of most significance, it seems that the *greatness* of Constantinople was lost, too. You see, when the Ottomans took over, the brilliant thinkers, artists, and scientists that made the city so great, fled. They didn't go to Asia, or Russia, or Africa. They fled to Western Europe. And from them sprang forth a movement across Europe known as the **Renaissance**. In French, Renaissance means "rebirth."

As one result of the invasion of the Ottoman Turks, mosques rather than churches line the streets of Istanbul today.

It describes the transformation of Europe that soon took place. But that is one of the main themes of Volume III. So I'll say no more about it here.

As for the Ottoman Turks, they continued to grow under Mohammed II. He set his sights on Rome next (if you can imagine), but he died before any damage was done there. In future volumes we will look at the rise of other great sultans who led the Ottoman Empire through its golden age. The Ottomans kept a strong empire until as recently as 1918! They were actually part of World War I. But that is a long way off. When we get to them again, they will remind us of the tightly woven threads of history that make up the intricate picture of our world today.

ACTIVITIES FOR LESSON 83

83A—Younger Students

Make a paper chain of any five events in history. They can be events from this book or events out of your own life. Write the events on narrow strips of paper. Staple the ends of the first event together to form a loop. In the form of a chain, run the next piece of paper through the first loop and staple it. Continue in this fashion, interlocking all five events to form a chain. Discuss how one event in history affects other events in history. (A great example of interconnecting family events would be if your great-grandparents immigrated to the United States in the 1800s, your parents met and married in 1984, and you were born in the United States in the year 1997. The third event could not have taken place without the first two!)

83B—Middle Students

Create a model of a rolling bed of logs like the one described in the lesson. Lay about 20 pencils side by side on a table. Tie a piece of string around a brick. Lay the brick on top of the pencils. Gently pull the brick. As the brick moves forward and exposes the pencils, take one pencil from the back of the rolling bed and place it in the front. Continue this method of pulling the brick and moving the pencils one by one until the brick travels all the way across the table. Imagine the brick being a small fleet of warships and the pencils being large rolling timbers! Mohammed's technique for transporting boats and troops across land was ingenious. Take a photo of your model and file it in your Student Notebook under "Asia: Turkey."

83C—Older Students

Write a report on the present city of Istanbul. What is the population? What is the primary religion? What form of government exists there? Is there religious freedom in Istanbul? What are the major imports and exports? Be creative in your presentation. Include photos. File your report under "Asia: Turkey."

JOHANNES GUTENBERG
INVENTS THE PRINTING PRESS
LESSON 84

Look around you. Wherever you are, indoors or out, name out loud the modern inventions that you see. From where I sit, I see a telephone, a fax machine, a lamp, and a computer. These are obvious inventions right in front of me. Some are less noticeable. In a drawer near me there are lots of little things like rubber bands, mechanical pencils, keys, and paper clips. These items are so common, I hardly think of them as inventions. But they are. The same is true with the very words you are reading. Did you realize that they are really an invention, too? I don't mean the alphabet, although somebody created it. I'm referring to the typed, printed page you're reading right now. It is so common for us to read *printed text* that we rarely think of it as having once been invented. But, it was! And the man who did it was **Johannes Gutenberg** (yo HANN us GOOT uhn burg). As I've mentioned before, I was saving this important invention for last. I think you'll understand why.

Johannes was born an aristocrat in the town of **Mainz** (MYNTZ), **Germany.** That means his family was wealthy and he probably received a good education. In doing so, he was one of a small group of people in Europe who could read. And like anyone who loves to read, Johannes appreciated books.

But books were hard to come by in Europe. The only books available at this time were handwritten ones. It took a monk or scribe an entire year to hand-copy one Bible! To help speed things up, sometimes one person would read out loud to a dozen people or more so they could all be writing at the same time. (By not having to actually *look* at the same copy, more could be writing at one time.) But the problem with this method was the possibility of the writers making spelling mistakes or missing a word here and there! (I imagine, too, that a few writers might also have drifted off to sleep from time to time!) So difficult was the process of bookmaking that only a few thousand were in existence. Their rarity made them very expensive, too. One Bible cost about the same as one year's wages! That might be comparable to 50,000 U.S. dollars today.

Then came along Johannes Gutenberg. He had the idea of forming one letter out of a piece of metal and turning it into a stamp. He then could line up several letters in a frame and create words. Of course, words make sentences, sentences make paragraphs, and paragraphs make pages. Why not create a whole page of metal letters, apply ink, and copy it? That is, copy it hundreds of times in the course of one day. It made great sense to Johannes. He dedicated his life to mastering this technique of printing.

It helped that Johannes's uncle was a metal coin maker. I imagine Johannes gained some skill from him to help in the crafting of his movable metal letters. It also helped that Mainz was a center for goldsmiths and jewelry makers. These craftsmen would have been helpful to him as well. It took Joahnnes years of experimenting to create his movable type pieces. But he did.

The marvel of Johannes's invention was the endless possibility of words that could be made with the rearranging of the letters of the alphabet. The Chinese and Koreans had thought of a similar idea of making stamps for printing using porcelain pieces for the raised stamp. But they chose to make wood-block stamps of whole *words* rather than individual letters. So they were very limited with the manuscripts they could create. Besides that, the thousands of Chinese characters that existed made duplication nearly impossible.

The heavy frame of Johannes Gutenberg's ingenious printing press somewhat resembled that of a cheese press.

Johannes borrowed the idea of a cheese press to build the frame for the first printing press. It worked something like this: He lined up letters in a small form called a **quoin** to create a word. Each letter was a raised mirror image of the alphabet letter. He inserted "blanks" where needed to create spaces between the words. Johannes then wedged together row upon row of words, or quoins, until he completed an entire page. It would take an entire day to lay down the letters for one page in this manner and secure them in an upright wooden frame. But it was worth it.

The following day, Johannes could begin to print. He would dab the stamps with ink, lay a piece of paper on top, and unscrew a heavy block on top of the paper to "press" the ink to the paper. It was the idea of a heavy block that came from the cheese press. It required a strong man to push and pull the wooden arm of the heavy press. The ink Johannes borrowed was from the best Flemish artists so it would be sure not to smear or fade. The paper he used was made of cotton. It had been invented by the Arabs and brought to Spain. It was much smoother than the standard papyrus or animal skin used up until then. (By the way, the word *paper* comes from *papyrus*.)

What Johannes quickly learned was that he could print 200 to 300 copies of one page of a book in a day. Did you catch that? Two to three hundred pages a day could be printed through the amazing press. The next day, Johannes could rearrange the letters again and start all over. The cost? It was one-eighth the cost of a handwritten page. Are you beginning to see the significance of this invention? I hope so. It meant that, for the first time in history, ordinary people might be able to afford books and there would be a whole lot more books around!

The Printing of the Word of God

Of course, as a believer in Jesus Christ, I can think of no greater book to have more of than the Bible. Fortunately, Gutenberg thought the same thing. In **1456** he and his associates completed printing 300 copies of the Bible. It had taken them a year to lay down the type that included 1,282 lines. The version selected was a copy of **Jerome's Latin Vulgate.** (Thank you Jerome for all those long hours of translating!) This Bible was nicknamed the *Forty-Two-Line Bible* because each column contained 42 lines. Gutenberg made the pages beautiful, too, with Gothic-style letters made larger and more decorative at the beginning of the paragraphs. It was the Italians who later created the Roman-style font similar to what you are reading now.

The town of Mainz tried to keep the skill of printing a trade secret at first. But within 20 years, every country in Europe had a printing press of its own. Within 50 years, more books and Bibles were produced than in all the centuries of hand-copying done before then. By 1500 there were as many as nine million books in print! It was in 1476 that **William Caxton** set up a printing press in England. Can you guess what was one of the famous English books he chose to print? It was *The Canterbury Tales* by Geoffrey Chaucer, of course. William Caxton also printed an encyclopedia.

But of all the books printed, the Bible was the most popular. Do you remember the **Lollards**? They were the followers of **John Wycliffe** who strongly believed in the power of God's Word. They set up the first printing press in England exclusively for the printing of the Bible in English. For the same reasons, **The Brethren** (the followers of **John Huss** in Bohemia) set up a printing press only 15 years after it was invented. They had three presses used for Bible printing alone and became the largest producers of the

Bible in Europe. Considering their strong convictions, I can only imagine their excitement at the possibility of getting the Word out to so many needy people.

There are many historians who would consider the fall of Constantinople to the Ottoman Turks as the close of the Middle Ages. It certainly was significant. But far more important to me are the implications of this lesson. I prefer to mark the invention of the printing press and the spread of the Word of God as the *end* of a dark era and the beginning of a brighter one.

As I mentioned in our last lesson, when Constantinople was overrun, many of the great thinkers and artists there moved to Western Europe and helped usher in the Renaissance. But imagine how much more influence on the world the spread of the Word of God was going to have! It certainly helped to bring about a surge of ideas, thought, and inspiration, while at the same time revealing truth.

As I've said over and over, I believe that history is God revealing Himself to mankind—that He might not be such a mystery. And He best revealed Himself through Jesus Christ, Who, the Bible says, *is* the Word. This emphasis on the Word is what I felt was so important as to leave until the very last lesson of the book. For it says in the Bible, in one of my favorite passages . . .

"In the beginning was the Word, and the Word was with God, and the Word was God. He was in the beginning with God. All things were made through Him, and without Him nothing was made that was made. In Him was life, and the life was the light of men . . . And the Word became flesh and dwelt among us, and we beheld His glory, the glory as of the only begotten of the Father, full of grace and truth." (John 1:1–4, 14)

ACTIVITIES FOR LESSON 84

ALL STUDENTS

1. **Make your Memory Cards for Lessons 82–84.** (And of course, if you have fallen behind on making cards, now is the time to catch up. These are the last ones!)

2. With this being the last set of activities in Volume II, take time to review your Student Notebook this week with a parent, teacher, or friend. Review the things you've learned.

Field Trip Possibility

Make a field trip to visit a print shop. Find out what it costs today to have a book printed. (If you could travel all the way to Mainz, Germany, you would find there a replica of Johannes's first printing press in his original workshop!)

84A—Younger Students

1. Just for fun, try to count the number of books in your home or classroom. Do you have 50 books? Hundreds of books? Thousands of books? How important are books to you?

2. ***Adult Supervision Needed.*** Make a potato stamp of your initials. Cut a potato in half. Use a dull pencil to lightly etch your backward initials into the meat of the potato. Now, gently carve away a layer of exposed potato around the initials. You should be left with a raised imprint of your initials.

Dip the stamp you've created into ink and practice printing! Include a sample of your initials in your Student Notebook under "Europe: Germany."

84B—Middle Students

If you have a computer at home, investigate the number of fonts available. Create a sample of these fonts to file in your Student Notebook under "Europe: Germany." Note the names of the fonts that remind you of the Middle Ages (i.e., Times New Roman, Gothic, etc.).

84C—Older Students

1. Create a questionnaire to give to adults asking them questions about their lives before computers were so widespread. For example, before computers, how did your parents write a research paper? When did they first own a computer? How fast was it? And so forth.

2. Have a discussion about the freedom of speech and censorship. With the invention of the printing press came the ability for man to communicate his ideas more easily—ideas that are both good and bad. The issue of censorship arose quickly in the late Middle Ages as a controversial issue. To some degree, censorship and freedom of speech remain controversial issues. Talk about examples of this in history.

TAKE ANOTHER LOOK!

REVIEW 28: LESSONS 82–84

Wall of Fame

1. *The Inkas of South America (1438)*—Roughly draw the continent of South America. Color it in bright colors with the name "Inkas" in gold. [From *History Through the Ages*, use *The Inca Civilization*.]

2. *The Ottoman Turks Take Constantinople (1453)*—Write the name "Constantinople" on a piece of paper. Cross it out and write "Istanbul" over it with the date of 1453. [Use *Fall of Constantinople*.]

3. *Johannes Gutenberg Invents the Printing Press (1456)*—Cut out a round piece of paper to represent the earth. Write "Gutenberg Invents the Printing Press" on it to signify the spread of the Word of God to the whole world! [*Use Johannes Gutenberg.*]

SomeWHERE in Time

Complete this map work of South America.

Materials: Outline Map 28, "South America"; colored pencils; modern atlas

For the sake of all students, this mapping project varies in difficulty. Younger Students: Map the items that are listed in capital letters. Middle Students: Map the items that are listed in capital letters and bold letters. Older Students: Map the items that are listed in capital letters, bold letters, and italics. All Students: File your completed map behind "South America" (no country) in your Student Notebook.

1. SOUTH AMERICA.

2. Countries (in order of size): BRAZIL, ARGENTINA, PERU, COLOMBIA, BOLIVIA, **Venezuela, Chile, Paraguay, Ecuador, Uruguay**, **Suriname.**

3. Colonies (the facts in parentheses are just for your information; not to be written out): **Guyana** (a colony of Great Britain), **French Guiana** (a colony of France).

4. Rivers: AMAZON, **Rio de la Plata** system, *Magdalena, Orinoco, Sao Francisco.*

5. Bodies of Water: ATLANTIC OCEAN, PACIFIC OCEAN, **Caribbean Sea, Lake Titicaca,** *Drake Passage.*

6. Mountain Range: ANDES (the longest mountain system in the world).

7. Famous Waterfall: **Angel Falls** (dropping 3,212 feet in southeastern Venezuela at the Caroni River).

8. Islands: **Galapagos Islands** (owned by Ecuador), *Falkland Islands* (a United Kingdom Overseas Territory).

PUT IT ALL TOGETHER
WORKSHEET 4: LESSONS 64-84

We have covered another 21 lessons in the fourth and last quarter of this history course. It's time again to "Put It All Together." Using your textbook, Memory Cards, maps, and timeline, go through this worksheet and answer the questions from Quarter 4. This worksheet, along with Worksheet 3, will help you prepare for the upcoming Semester II Test. So take your time. Use this review to your advantage.

I—Dates to Memorize

Write out the names and dates that I have asked you to memorize four times each on the lines below.

Marco Polo Travels East   **1271**

1. _____

2. _____

3. _____

4. _____

John Wycliffe, "Morning Star of the Reformation"   **1377**

1. _____

2. _____

3. _____

4. _____

Death of Joan of Arc   **1431**

1. _____

2. _____

3. _____

4. _____

II—Circle the Saint.   Circle the name of the "saint" that best matches each of the following descriptions.

1. The saint who was burned at the stake for supposed heresy.

    St. Francis   St. Clara   St. Dominic   St. Thomas Aquinas   St. Joan of Arc

2. The saint who was born in Spain, loved books, and started a religious order.

    St. Francis   St. Clara   St. Dominic   St. Thomas Aquinas   St. Joan of Arc

3. The saint who opened a convent for women patterned after the works of St. Francis.

    St. Francis   St. Clara   St. Dominic   St. Thomas Aquinas   St. Joan of Arc

4. The saint who was kidnapped by his brothers and later wrote *Summa Theologica*.

    St. Francis   St. Clara   St. Dominic   St. Thomas Aquinas   St. Joan of Arc

5. The saint who gave away food and clothing and was known for looking after the birds.

    St. Francis   St. Clara   St. Dominic   St. Thomas Aquinas   St. Joan of Arc

III—Unusual Boys.   Draw a line to match the names of these boys with their unusual circumstances.

1. Nicholas   a. Became Holy Roman Emperor at 2 and the king of Sicily at 4

2. Stephen of Cloyes   b. Met a girl at age 9 who influenced his writing career

3. Frederick II   c. Led 30,000 children from Germany to Italy on a crusade

4. Marco Polo   d. Left home around 17 to travel from Italy to China

5. Dante   e. Tried to lead 20,000 children from France to the Holy Land

IV—Object Lessons. Use different-colored pencils and a small ruler to draw a line from the object to the lesson that it matches. Correct answers should create a geometric design.

5. Yurt   6. Crossbow   7. Magna Carta   8. Spider

4. Rat   a. Gutenberg

3. Morning Star   b. Chaucer

2. Tales   c. Wycliffe

1. Cheese Press   d. Black Death

e. Genghis Khan   f. 100 Years' War   g. King John   h. Robert Bruce

V—Marvels of the Forbidden City. Follow Lesson 77 to fill in the blanks about the marvels of the Forbidden City.

1. It was the third emperor of the Ming dynasty, _____ _____ , who built the Forbidden City.

2. Interestingly, every doorway in the Forbidden City opens to the _____ , the farthest direction away from Mongolia!

3. One famous wide-open court within the Imperial City is _____ Square. At one hundred acres, it is the largest square in the world and can hold up to a million people!

4. Though the Forbidden City is one of the largest palace complexes in the world (covering _____ square meters), it is not bold like the great buildings of the Romans and Greeks. Rather, it is delicate, ornate, and well balanced.

5. If you were to wander around the Forbidden City today, you would find intricate images of turtles, cranes, and lions, which were considered symbols of _____ _____ .

6. You would find unusual things like a room with 85 _____ , pots of twisted _____ , trees made of coral, and carved ivory dragons.

7. Much of the beauty and enchantment of the palace is found in the _____ structure and hidden design. For example, before the city was ever built, the designers planned it to match the four directions of the _____ .

8. The palace was built with _____ rooms; its doors are fastened with _____ nails (or multiples of the number nine); and _____ guardian statuettes line the eaves of the roofs.

9. _____ bridges span the Golden Stream; _____ styles of roofing were used; and _____ ridges appear on the roof of the Hall of Supreme Harmony.

10. In the past, the Chinese would refer to their great palace as the "_____ Forbidden City." Today, the Chinese call the palace complex _____ _____, meaning "Palace Museum."

VI—Symbols of Courage.

Through their tragic deaths, William Wallace, John Huss, and Joan of Arc have become symbols of courage. Review Lessons 72, 80, and 81 to determine which symbol to circle to match each statement below. Circle the flag for William Wallace, the cross for John Huss, or the teardrop for Joan of Arc. (Some questions have more than one answer.)

1. I grew up in Bohemia and taught at Charles University in Prague.

    ⚑ William Wallace   ✝ John Huss   🔻 Joan of Arc

2. I lost the Battle of Falkirk to the English in 1298.

    ⚑ William Wallace   ✝ John Huss   🔻 Joan of Arc

3. I sang hymns at my execution.

    ⚑ William Wallace   ✝ John Huss   🔻 Joan of Arc

4. I wore men's clothing and specially made armor for battle.

    ⚑ William Wallace   ✝ John Huss   🔻 Joan of Arc

5. I led my fellow Scotsmen in winning the Battle of Stirling Bridge.

    ⚑ William Wallace   ✝ John Huss   🔻 Joan of Arc

6. We fought for our countries against the English.

    ⚑ William Wallace   ✝ John Huss   🔻 Joan of Arc

7. I was captured by the Burgundians.

    ⚑ William Wallace   ✝ John Huss   🔻 Joan of Arc

8. For seven years I was on the run to escape from the English.

    ⚑ William Wallace   ✝ John Huss   🔻 Joan of Arc

9. I died in Rouen, France, which was occupied by the English.

        ⚑ William Wallace   ✝ John Huss   ♦ Joan of Arc

10. Though I was captured and executed, I am considered a hero in Scotland.

        ⚑ William Wallace   ✝ John Huss   ♦ Joan of Arc

11. I was invited to attend the Council of Constance.

        ⚑ William Wallace   ✝ John Huss   ♦ Joan of Arc

12. We died at the stake for supposed heresy.

        ⚑ William Wallace   ✝ John Huss   ♦ Joan of Arc

13. I was forbidden to discuss the teachings of John Wycliffe.

        ⚑ William Wallace   ✝ John Huss   ♦ Joan of Arc

VII—Aztec or Inka? We studied two cultures living near the equator in the Western Hemisphere that might easily be confused. Follow Lessons 74 and 82 to sort through the following facts. Circle your answers.

1. We counted using a knotted string called a *khipu*.   Aztec or Inka

2. The name of our king, *Pachacuti*, means "earth shaker."   Aztec or Inka

3. Only our king wore a turquoise jewel in his nose.   Aztec or Inka

4. Our capital city was *Cuzco*, which means "naval."   Aztec or Inka

5. Lake Titicaca, the highest lake in the world, was one of our holy sites.   Aztec or Inka

6. After wandering for a time, we settled in the middle of Lake Texcoco.   Aztec or Inka

7. We called ourselves the *Mexica*.   Aztec or Inka

8. Our young brides adorned their arms with red feathers.   Aztec or Inka

9. Our "just-married" couples did not have to pay taxes for a year.   Aztec or Inka

10. Our farmers set up plots of land called *chinampas* on the watery grounds around us.   Aztec or Inka

11. *Machu Picchu* was one of our emperor's favorite resorts.   Aztec or Inka

12. We worshiped the sun (*Inti*) as one of the greatest gods.   Aztec or Inka

13. We followed Huitzilopochtli, the hummingbird god.   Aztec or Inka

14. We followed the blowing sound of the conch shell to
    structure our activities.   Aztec or Inka

VIII—Turkish Terms. Following Lesson 83, match each of the following terms (and names) to its description by placing the correct letter next to the number.

_____1. Osman   a. Group of countries named for the Balkan Mountains

_____2. Seljuk Turks   b. The great harbor of Constantinople

_____3. Sultan   c. First leader of the fugitive Ottomans

_____4. The Balkans   d. Elite soldiers in Mohammed II's army

_____5. Serbs   e. "King"

_____6. Mohammed II   f. Modern name of Constantinople

_____7. Golden Horn   g. People group living around the Black Sea

_____8. Janissaries   h. The Ottoman sultan who conquered Constantinople

_____9. Istanbul   i. Another name for Yugoslavians

IX—Brilliance in the Middle Ages. Connect the brilliant thoughts or published works to these men.

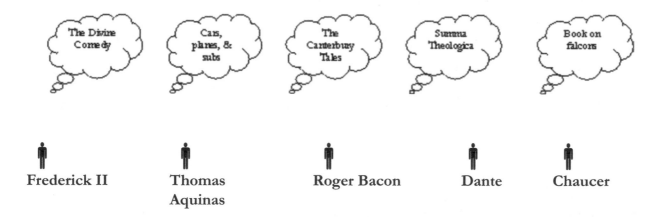

Frederick II   Thomas   Roger Bacon   Dante   Chaucer
                    Aquinas

X—Essay. Earn extra credit by answering the following in complete sentences. Use a separate sheet of paper if necessary.

1. What is the significance of the invention of the printing press?

2. In what ways have you observed God working in history in lessons from Quarter 4?

SEMESTER II TEST

LESSONS 43–84

Much like the biweekly quizzes you have been taking throughout Quarters 3 and 4, this semester test will challenge your ability to recall information learned in the second half of this book. I suggest you study beforehand using your textbook, Memory Cards, former quizzes, and worksheets. You can expect to find one question from every lesson in Semester II plus a bonus essay question worth 2 points. I will not test you on any dates other than those six that I specifically challenged you to memorize in this semester.

Note to Teacher: Younger students or those with special needs may require teacher assistance, may choose to do this as an open-book test, or may skip this test entirely and celebrate the completion of Volume II!

I—Memory Lane. Match the event on the left with one of the dates on the right.

_____1. Marco Polo Travels East   a. 1377

_____2. Death of Joan of Arc   b. 1271

_____3. Battle of Hastings   c. 1003

_____4. John Wycliffe, "Morning Star of the Reformation"   d. 1096

_____5. Leif Ericsson Discovers America   e. 1431

_____6. The Early Crusades   f. 1066

Note to Teacher: From this point on, the number of each question corresponds to the number of the lesson in the textbook.

II—True or False? Circle if the statement is true or false.

43. Floki Vilgerdarson gave Iceland its name because he loved the beautiful ice crystals he found there.   T   F

44. New Zealand, settled by the Maori, is the largest of the Polynesian Islands.   T   F

45. The name *Zimbabwe* means "house of gold" and refers to great golden houses built in Africa.   T   F

46. Wenceslas, the king of the Vikings, was known for his ruthless and violent behavior.   T   F

47. Though the Holy Roman Empire remained prosperous for centuries, it was neither very "holy" nor very "Roman."   T   F

48. Vladimir of Russia has been credited with establishing the Eastern Orthodox Church in his country.   T   F

Choose one answer for each question or statement.

49. The Song dynasty of China was known for

    a. being started by General Zhao Kuang Yin.

    b. the making of porcelain.

    c. the practice of shaping "lily feet."

    d. All of the above.

50. It is believed by the Coptic Orthodox Church that St. Simon

    a. removed a certain "sword from the stone."

    b. founded the city of Alexandria.

    c. prayed to move a mountain.

    d. led the Spanish Reconquista.

51. Eric the Red, who settled Greenland, was born in

    a. Turkey.

    b. Norway.

    c. Ireland.

    d. Nova Scotia.

52. Leif Ericsson, who sailed to North America in 1003, converted to _____ after meeting the king of Norway.

    a. Christianity

    b. Islam

    c. Buddhism

    d. Judaism

53. Though not particularly historical, _____ is a play written by William Shakespeare and based on the real-life murderous plot against the king of Scotland.

    a. *Julius Caesar*

    b. *Camelot*

    c. *Romeo and Juliet*

    d. *Macbeth*

54. Not always pure in his loyalties, El Cid is nonetheless remembered and even revered by many for leading the _____ of Spain against the Muslims.

    a. renegades

    b. Reconquista

    c. Reformation

    d. revolution

IV—Fill in the Blanks. Fill in the blanks using the most appropriate word from the word bank below.

55. At the famous Battle of _____, William the Conqueror invaded England from Normandy and became the king.

56. During the _____ Controversy, there was great conflict between Pope Gregory VII and Henry IV over authority in the Holy Roman Empire.

57. Peter the _____ and Walter the Penniless were responsible for leading thousands of unprepared crusaders in a failed attempt to take the Holy Land.

58. Peter Bruis, a priest who read the Bible and taught it to others for many years, was burned at the stake for _____.

59. Spreading chivalry and the poetry of the troubadours, Eleanor of Aquitaine was the queen of France and the queen of _____.

60. For the Jews of the Middle Ages, Moses ben Maimon compiled the books of the Law and the Talmud into the _____ _____.

WORD BANK

Investiture	heresy	Mishneh Torah
Hermit	Hastings	England

V—Who Am I? Using different-colored pencils for easier grading, connect the names on the left with clues about them on the right.

61. Richard the Lionhearted
62. Robin Hood
63. Minamoto Yoritomo
64. St. Francis of Assisi
65. Stephen of Cloyes
66. King John

a. A legendary English outlaw and archer
b. Started "Minor Brothers," or friars
c. Was forced to approve the Magna Carta
d. Gave a gift of falcons to Saladin
e. Led children in a crusade
f. First shogun of Japan

VI—Circle Sense. In the sentences below, *circle* the word that makes the most *sense*.

67. Though already the Holy Roman Emperor and the king of Sicily, at age 5, Frederick II was placed in the care of the (samurai, pope).

68. St. Thomas Aquinas, who attempted to incorporate the teachings of Aristotle with Christianity, was a member of the (Franciscans, Dominicans).

69. Roger Bacon, a brilliant scientist of the Middle Ages, was exiled for 15 years by fellow members of the (Franciscans, Dominicans).

70. (Genghis, Kublai) Khan found great pleasure in entertaining Marco Polo in his court.

71. Marco Polo was nicknamed "Marco (Millions, Maniac)" by those who could not believe the endless stories of sights he had seen in China.

72. After years of fighting, Edward III finally recognized (William Wallace, Robert Bruce) as the king of Scotland.

VII—People and Places. Match the places listed below with the people or events most likely to be associated with them.

_____73. Florence, Italy   a. Hundred Years' War

_____74. Tenochtitlan   b. Ming dynasty

_____75. France and England   c. Dante

_____76. Europe   d. John Wycliffe

_____77. Forbidden City   e. Aztecs

_____78. England   f. Black Death

VIII—Who Did It? From the word bank below, choose the correct answer for each question and write it in the blank provided.

79. Though never completed, I wrote *The Canterbury Tales*.

_____

80. Following the teachings of John Wycliffe, I was burned at the stake for heresy.

_____

81. For leading an army against the English, I was also burned at the stake for heresy.

_____

82. I built the beautiful capital city of Cuzco in the middle of my empire.

_____

83. With an army more than 10 times the size of my opponent, I conquered the city of Constantinople. It was later named Istanbul. _____

84. I invented the printing press, which helped to spread God's Word in Europe and beyond.

_____

WORD BANK

Pachacuti	John Huss	Johannes Gutenberg
Mohammed II	Joan of Arc	Geoffrey Chaucer

IX—Bonus Essay. Earn two extra points for using complete sentences to answer the following question: What factors contributed to the spread of the Black Death in Europe?

X. Older Students (Or those who dare!): If you completed Volume I of *The Mystery of History,* then give yourself the ultimate bonus by taking the "Semester II Test" from Volume I. I suggest that it be done as an open-book test for extra credit. Consider it a trip back in time to see what you remember of Nebuchadnezzar, Alexander the Great, Cleopatra, and more!

OUTLINE MAPS

CONTENTS

1	MEDITERRANEAN	(4)
2	EASTERN MEDITERRANEAN	(1)
3	WORLD	(4)
4	ISRAEL	(1)
5	REVIEW 4 ANSWER KEY	(1)
6	UNITED STATES	(1)
7	EAST ASIA	(3)
8	MEXICO AND CENTRAL AMERICA	(2)
9	NORTHERN AFRICA	(1)
10	BRITISH ISLES	(2)
11	BYZANTINE EMPIRE C. 568	(1)
12	JAPAN	(1)
13	HONSHU	(1)
14	HOKKAIDO, SHIKOKU AND KYUSHU	(1)
15	SAUDIA ARABIA	(1)
16	REVIEW 10 ANSWER KEY	(1)
17	SPAIN	(1)
18	FRANCE AND SPAIN	(1)
19	CHARLEMAGNE'S EMPIRE	(1)
20	VIKING VOYAGES	(1)
21	SLAVIC NATIONS AND THE BYZANTINE EMPIRE C. 888	(1)
22	CANADA	(1)
23	ENGLAND AND FRANCE	(1)
24	THE CRUSADES	(2)
25	THE MONGOL EMPIRE	(1)
26	REVIEW 25 ANSWER KEY	(1)
27	FRANCE	(1)
28	SOUTH AMERICA	(1)

(Note to Teacher: Number in parentheses is the number of copies of each map that you will need per student. A mapping answer key is available at https://www.brightideaspress.com/shop/mystery-of-history-vol2/.)

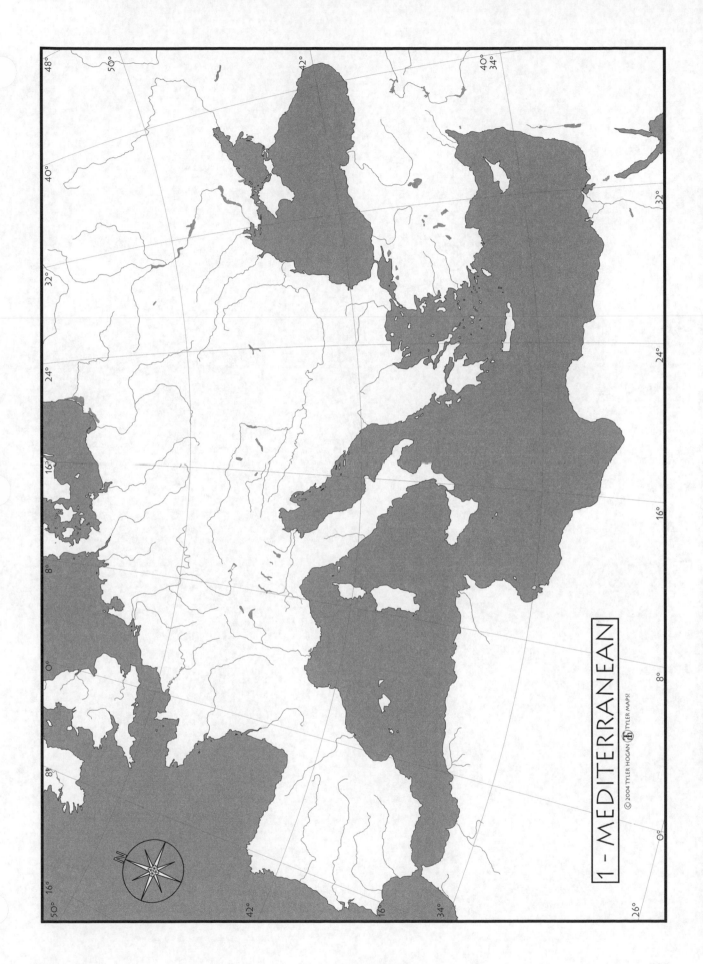

1 — MEDITERRANEAN

© 2004 TYLER HOGAN ℍ TYLER MAPS!

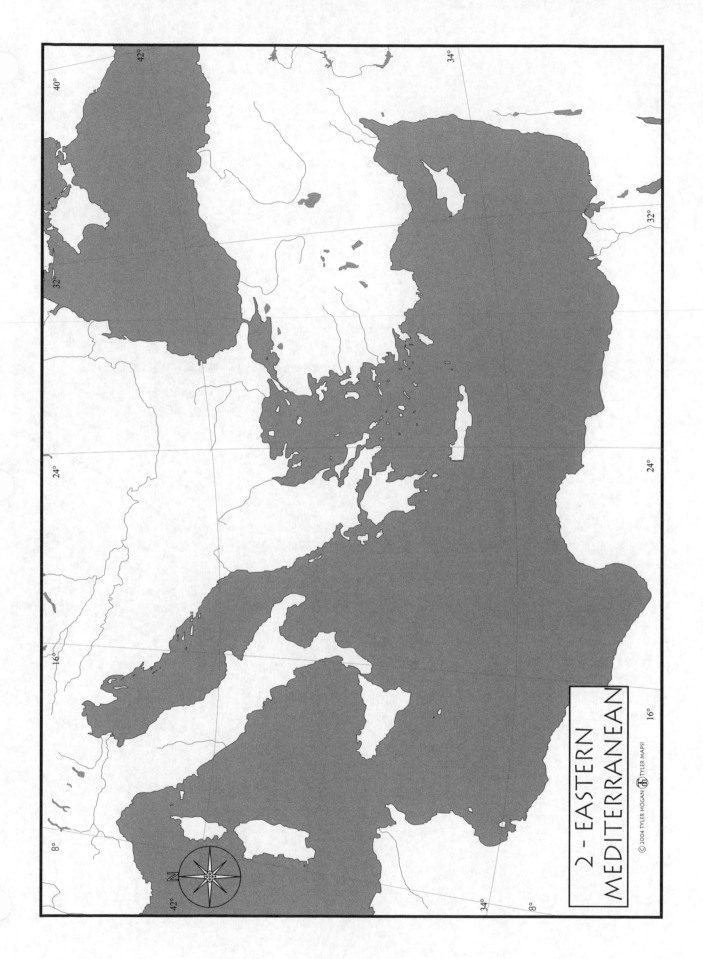

2 - EASTERN
MEDITERRANEAN

© 2004 TYLER HOGAN ⒽTYLER MAPS!

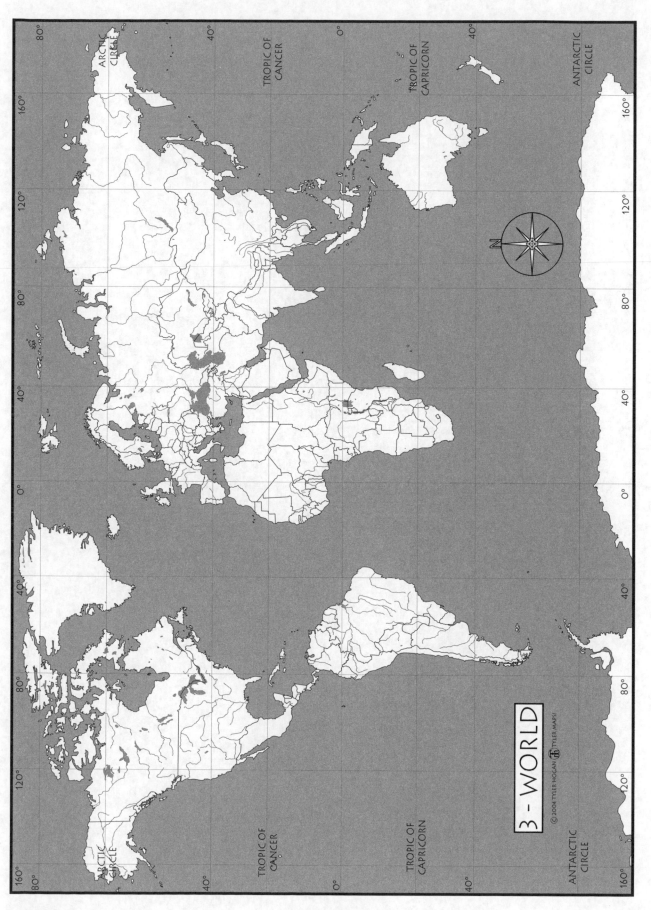

3 - WORLD

© 2004 TYLER HOGAN [T] TYLER MAPS

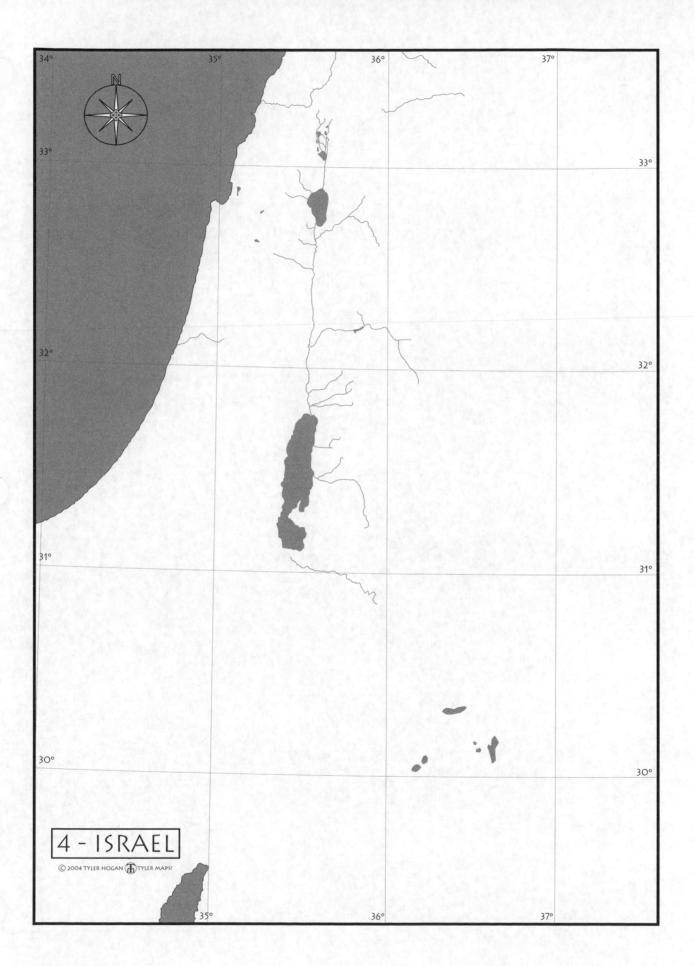

34°　　　　35°　　　　36°　　　　37°

N

33°　　　　　　　　　　　　　　　　33°

32°　　　　　　　　　　　　　　　　32°

31°　　　　　　　　　　　　　　　　31°

30°　　　　　　　　　　　　　　　　30°

4 - ISRAEL

© 2004 TYLER HOGAN TYLER MAPS!

35°　　　　36°　　　　37°

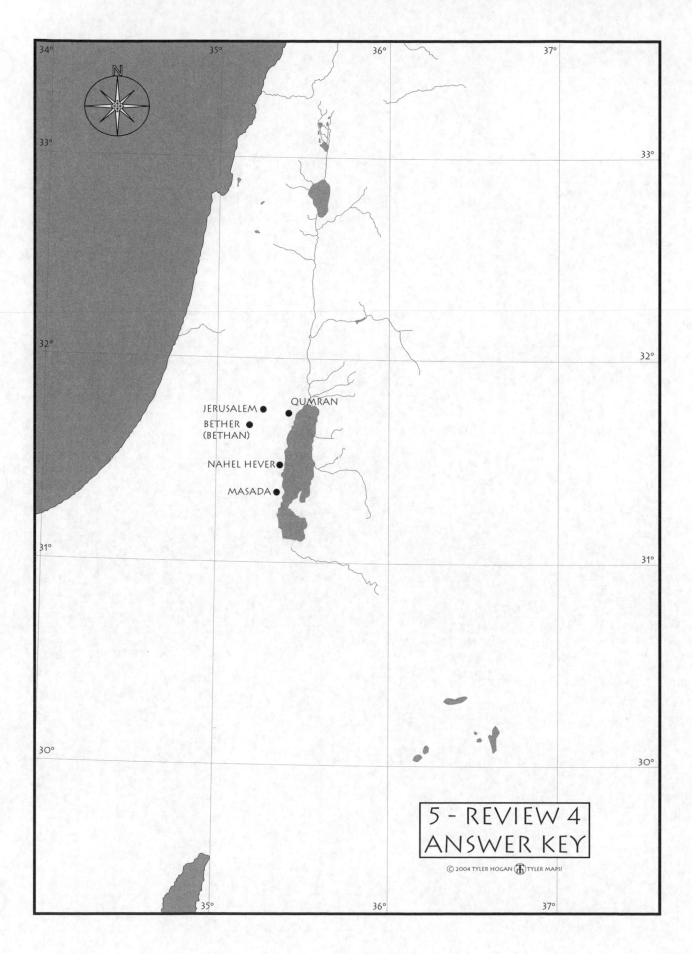

JERUSALEM ● ● QUMRAN

BETHER ●
(BETHAN)

NAHEL HEVER ●

MASADA ●

5 - REVIEW 4
ANSWER KEY

© 2004 TYLER HOGAN 🅗 TYLER MAPS!

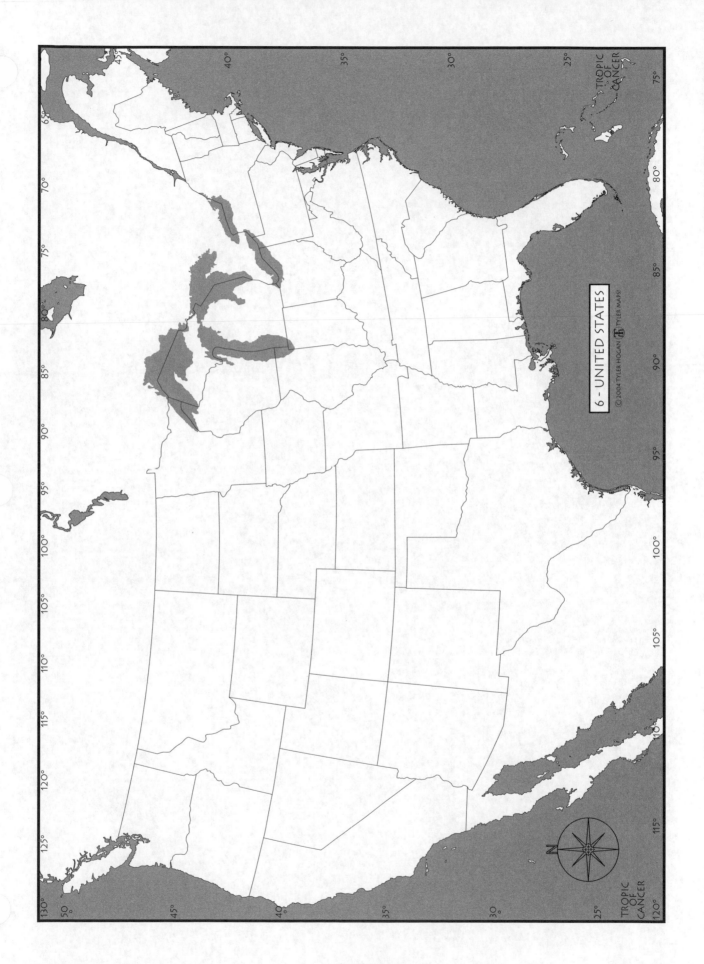

6 – UNITED STATES

© 2004 TYLER HOGAN (TYLER MAPS)

TROPIC OF CANCER

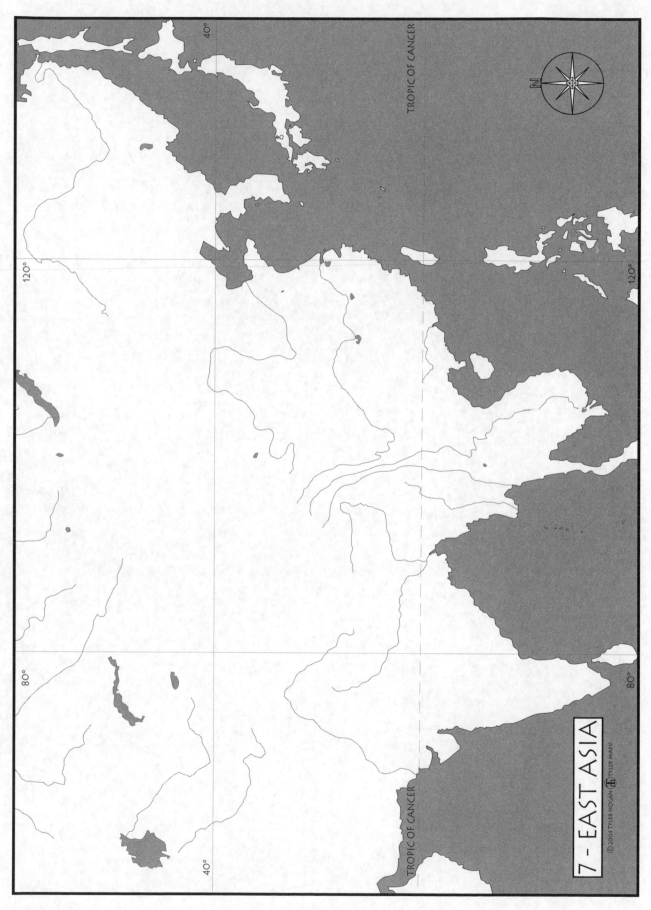

7 - EAST ASIA

© 2004 TYLER HOGAN ⒣ TYLER MAPS

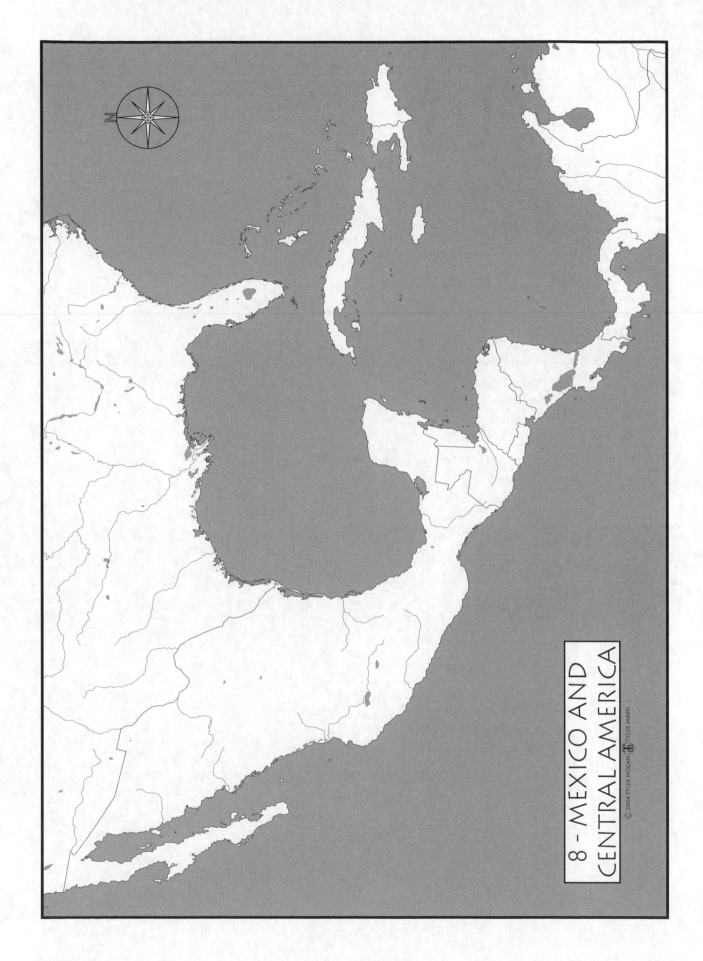

8 – MEXICO AND CENTRAL AMERICA

© 2004 TYLER HOGAN, TYLER MAPS

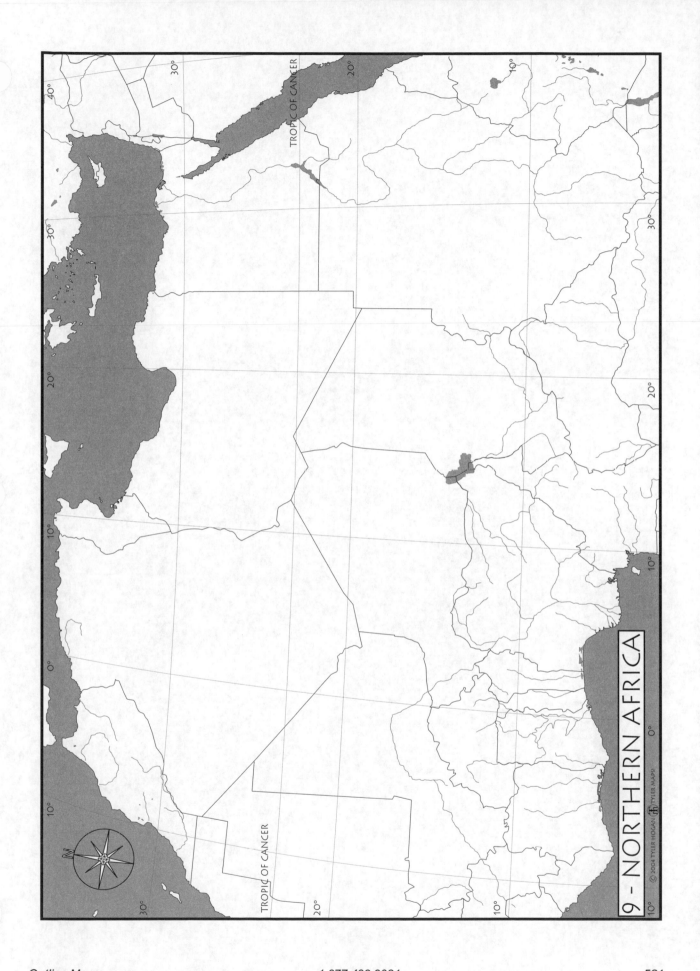

9 - NORTHERN AFRICA

TROPIC OF CANCER

TROPIC OF CANCER

© 2004 TYLER HOGAN & TYLER MAPS

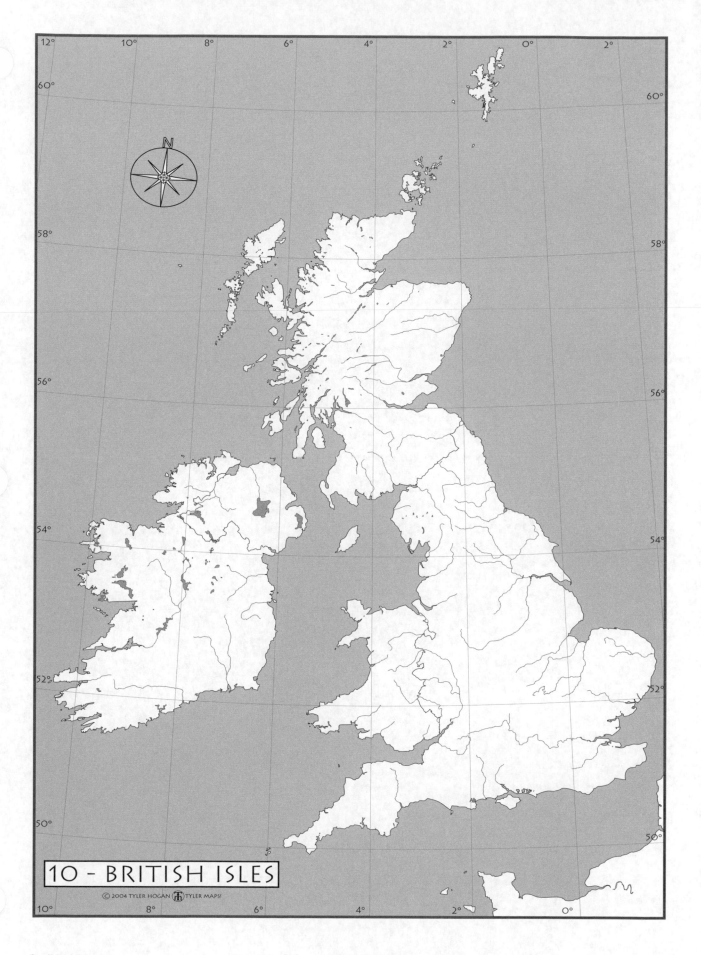

10 - BRITISH ISLES

©2004 TYLER HOGAN TYLER MAPS!

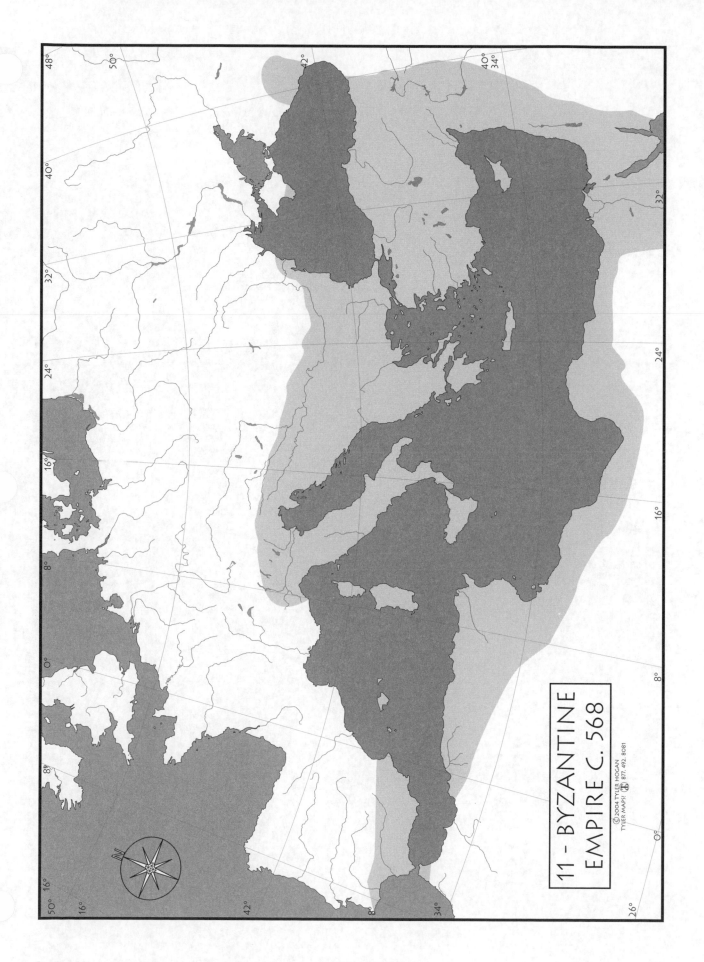

11 – BYZANTINE EMPIRE C. 568

© 2004 TYLER HOGAN
TYLER MAPS! 1.877.492.8081

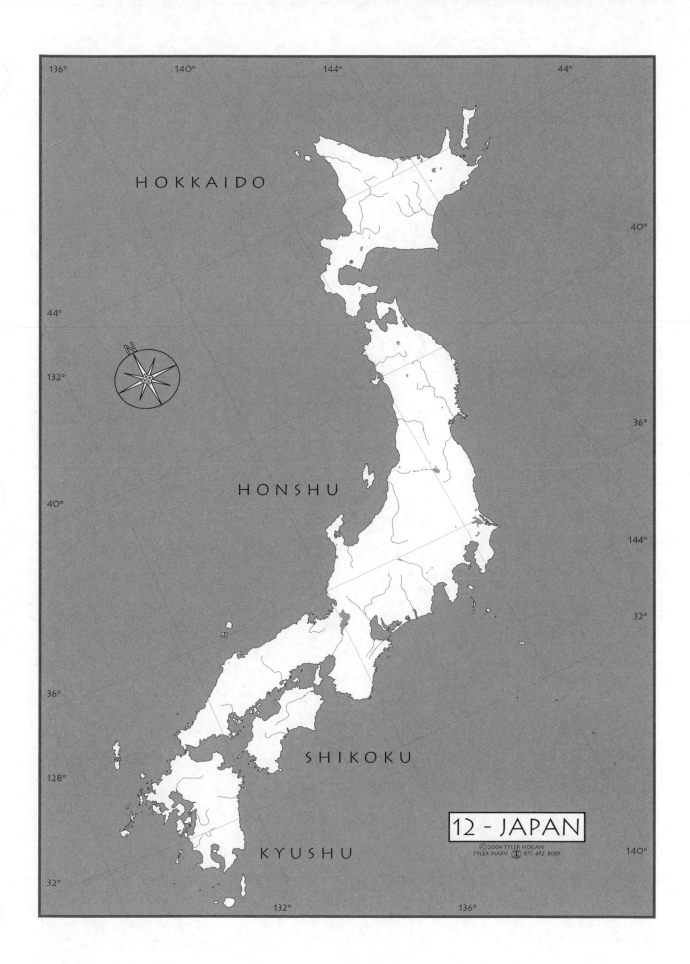

136°   140°   144°   44°

HOKKAIDO

44°   40°

N

132°

HONSHU   36°

40°   144°

32°

36°   SHIKOKU

128°

12 - JAPAN

KYUSHU   140°
© 2004 TYLER HOGAN
TYLER MAPS! (TB) 877. 492. 8081

32°

132°   136°

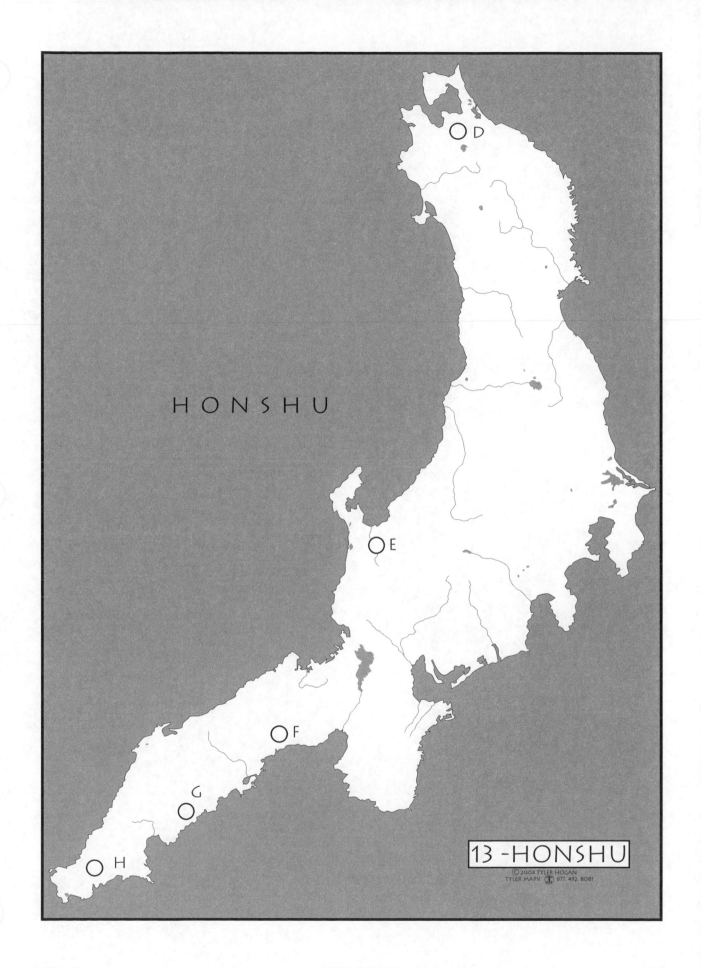

HONSHU

13 -HONSHU

© 2004 TYLER HOGAN
TYLER MAPS! 877. 492. 8081

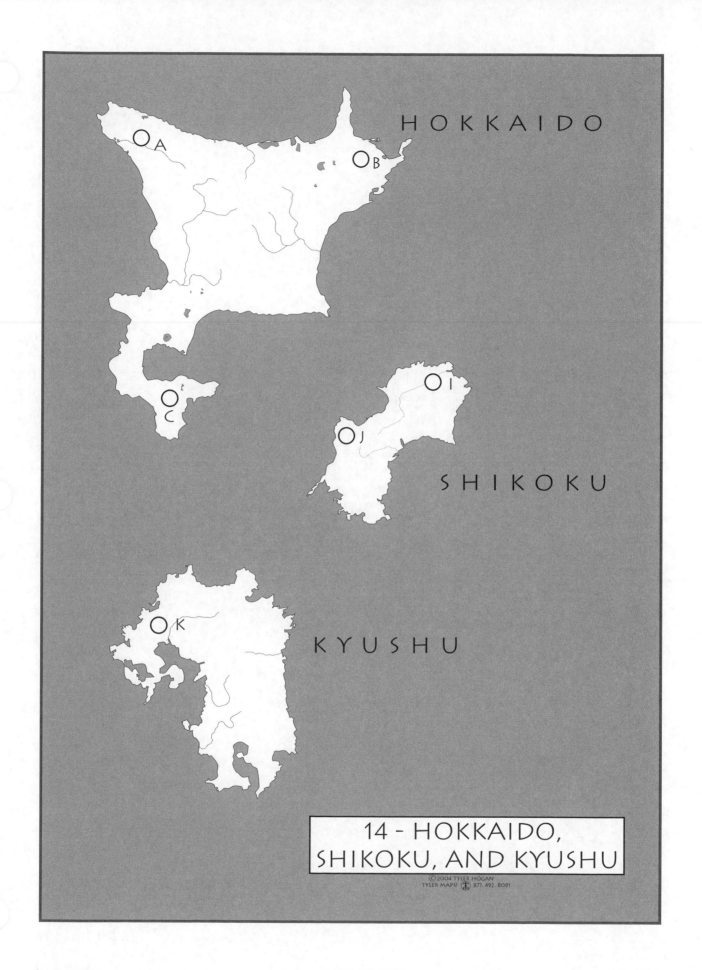

HOKKAIDO

SHIKOKU

KYUSHU

14 - HOKKAIDO,
SHIKOKU, AND KYUSHU

© 2004 TYLER HOGAN
TYLER MAPS! 877. 492. 8081

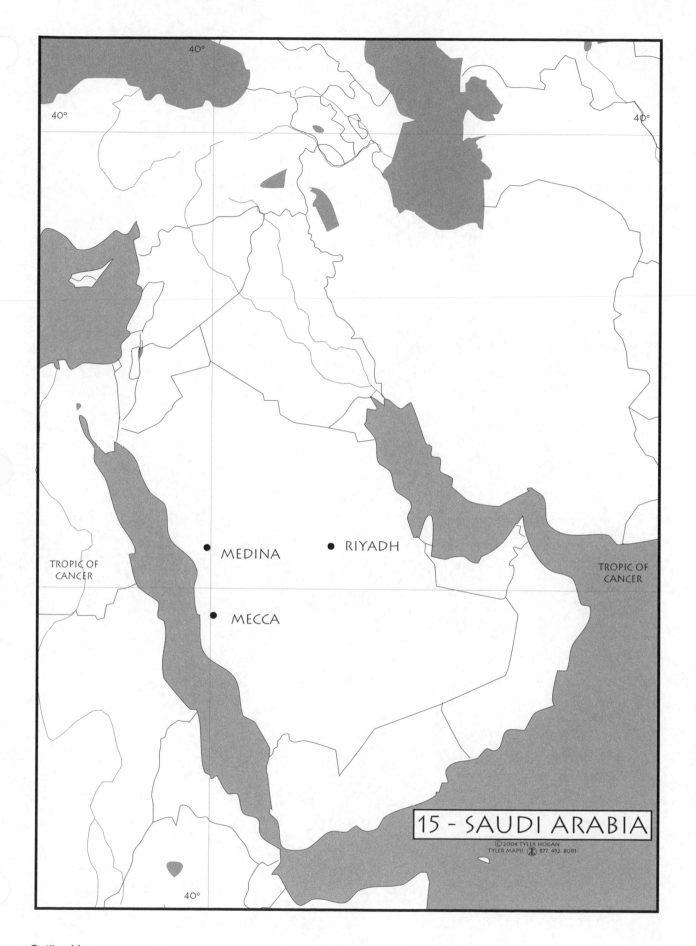

40°

40° 40°

TROPIC OF
CANCER

• MEDINA   • RIYADH

TROPIC OF
CANCER

• MECCA

15 - SAUDI ARABIA

© 2004 TYLER HOGAN
TYLER MAPS! 877. 492. 8081

40°

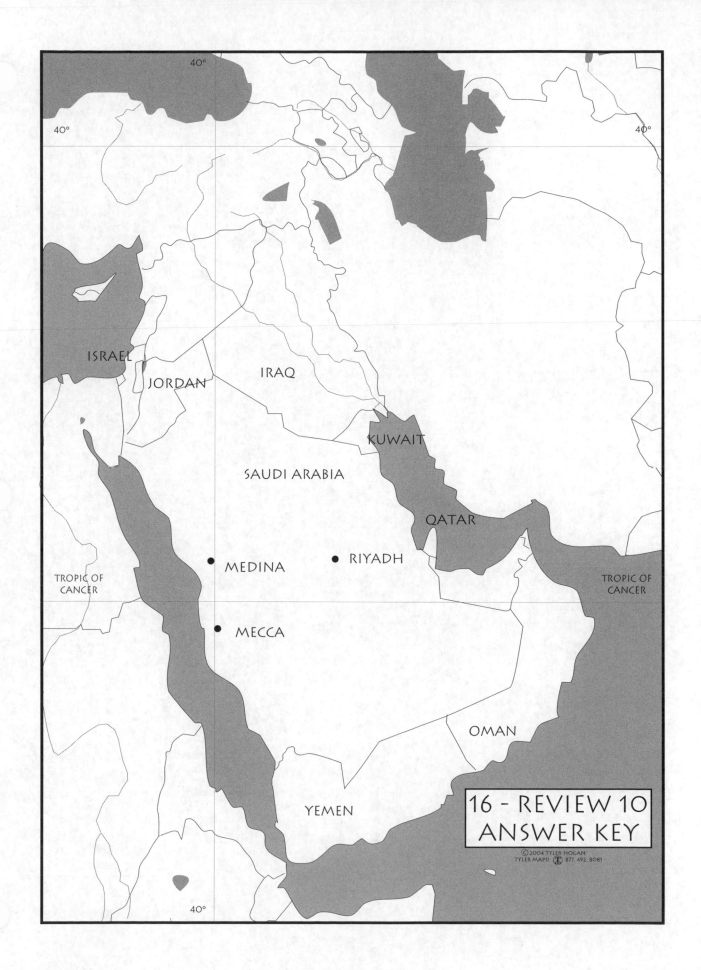

ISRAEL

JORDAN

IRAQ

KUWAIT

SAUDI ARABIA

QATAR

● MEDINA

● RIYADH

TROPIC OF
CANCER

TROPIC OF
CANCER

● MECCA

OMAN

YEMEN

**16 – REVIEW 10
ANSWER KEY**

© 2004 TYLER HOGAN
TYLER MAPS! ☏ 877. 492. 8081

40°

40°

40°

40°

40°

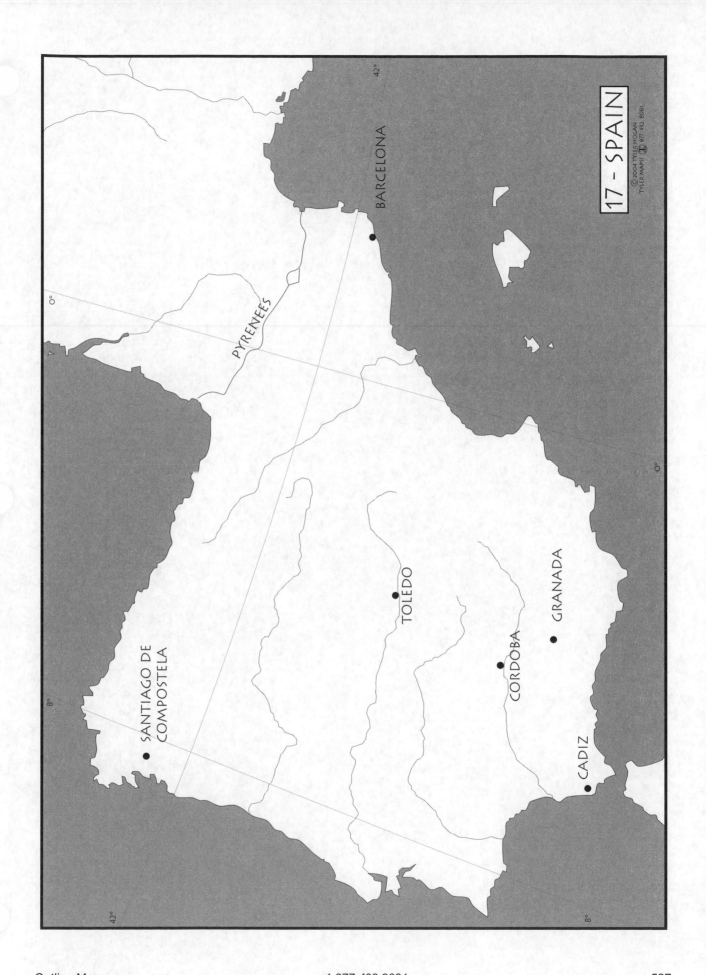

17 – SPAIN

© 2004 TYLER HOGAN
TYLER MAPS ☎ 877. 492. 8081

BARCELONA

PYRENEES

SANTIAGO DE
COMPOSTELA

TOLEDO

CORDOBA

GRANADA

CADIZ

42°

8°

0°

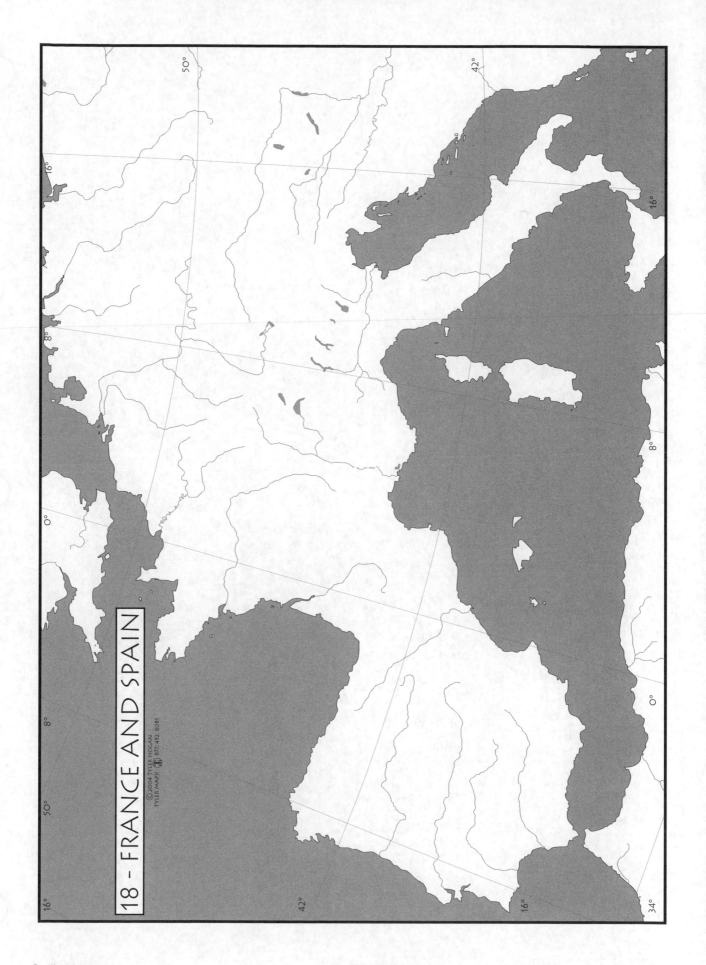

18 - FRANCE AND SPAIN

© 2004 TYLER HOGAN
TYLER MAPS ☏ 877.492.8081

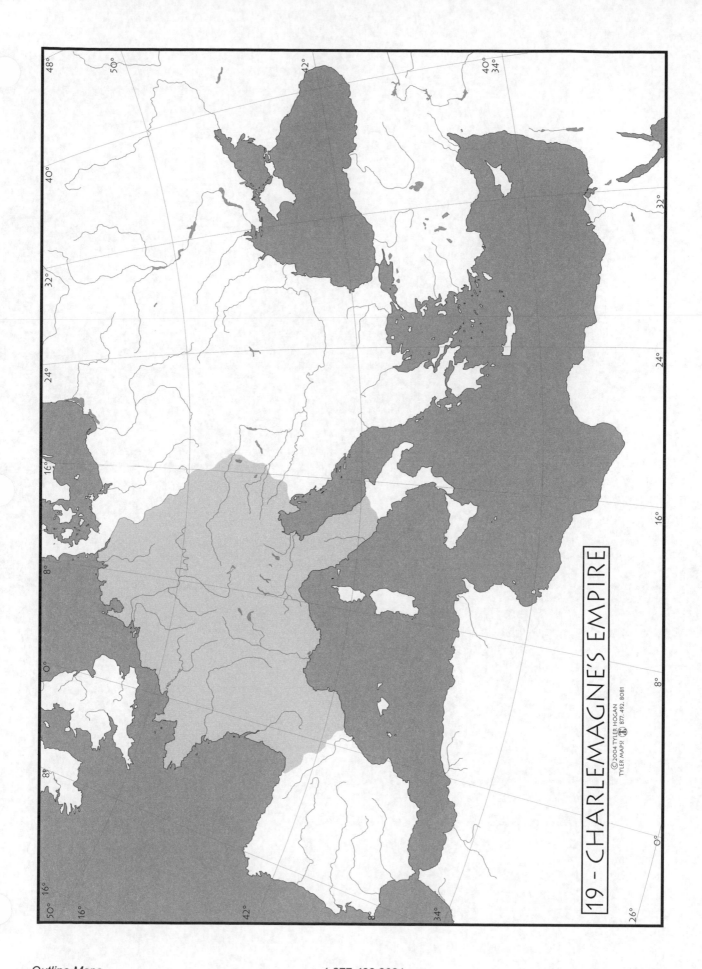

19 – CHARLEMAGNE'S EMPIRE

©2004 TYLER HOGAN
TYLER MAPS! ⓑ 877.492.8081

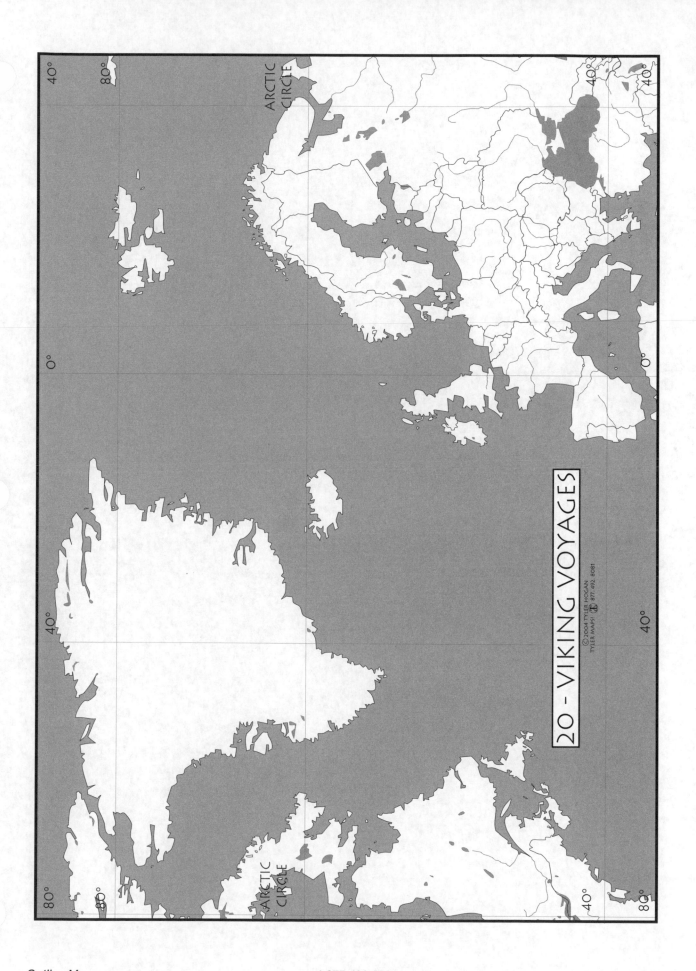

20 - VIKING VOYAGES

© 2004 TYLER HOGAN
TYLER MAPS ✆ 877.492.8081

ARCTIC CIRCLE

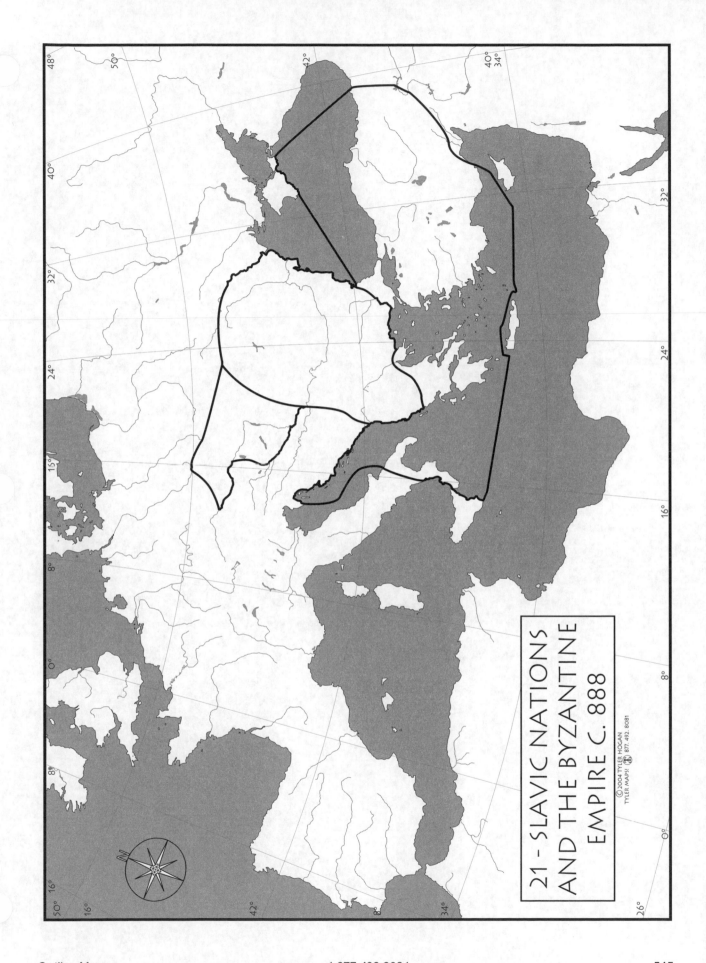

21 - SLAVIC NATIONS
AND THE BYZANTINE
EMPIRE C. 888

© 2004 TYLER HOGAN
TYLER MAPS! 877. 492. 8081

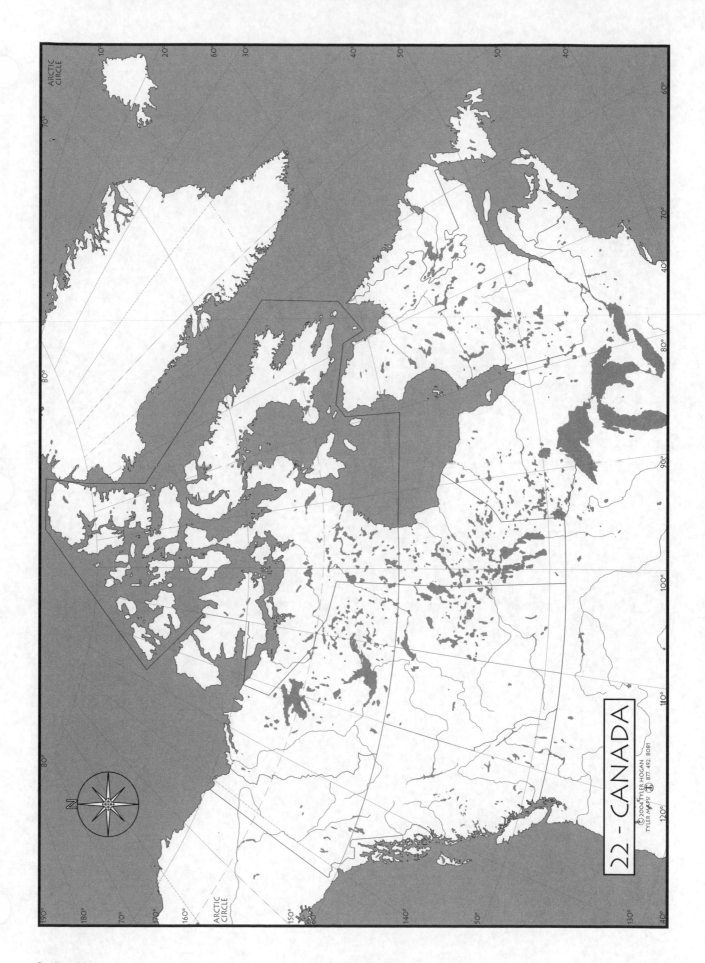

22 - CANADA

© 2004 TYLER HOGAN
TYLER MAPS! ☎ 877. 492. 8081

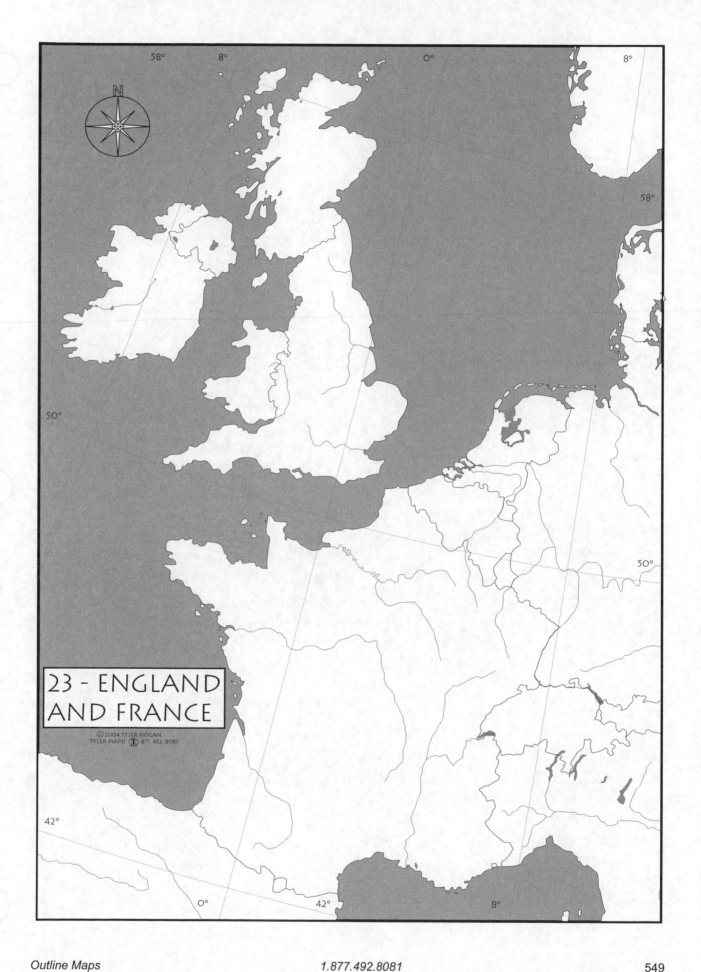

23 – ENGLAND
AND FRANCE

©2004 TYLER HOGAN
TYLER MAPS! 877. 492. 8081

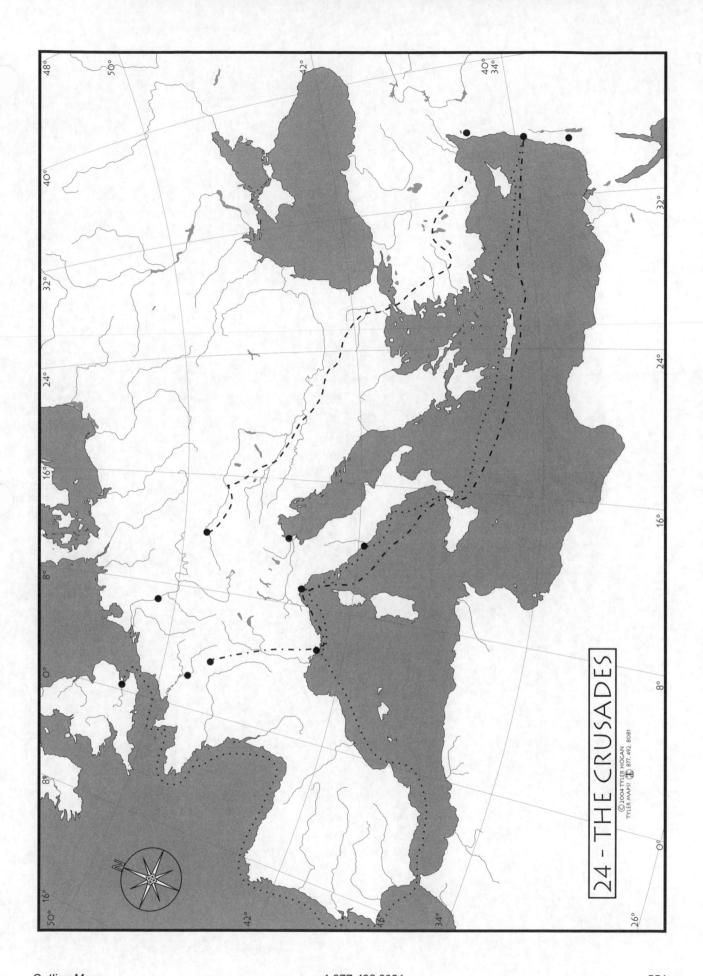

24 - THE CRUSADES

© 2004 TYLER HOGAN
TYLER MAPS! ☎ 877. 492. 8081

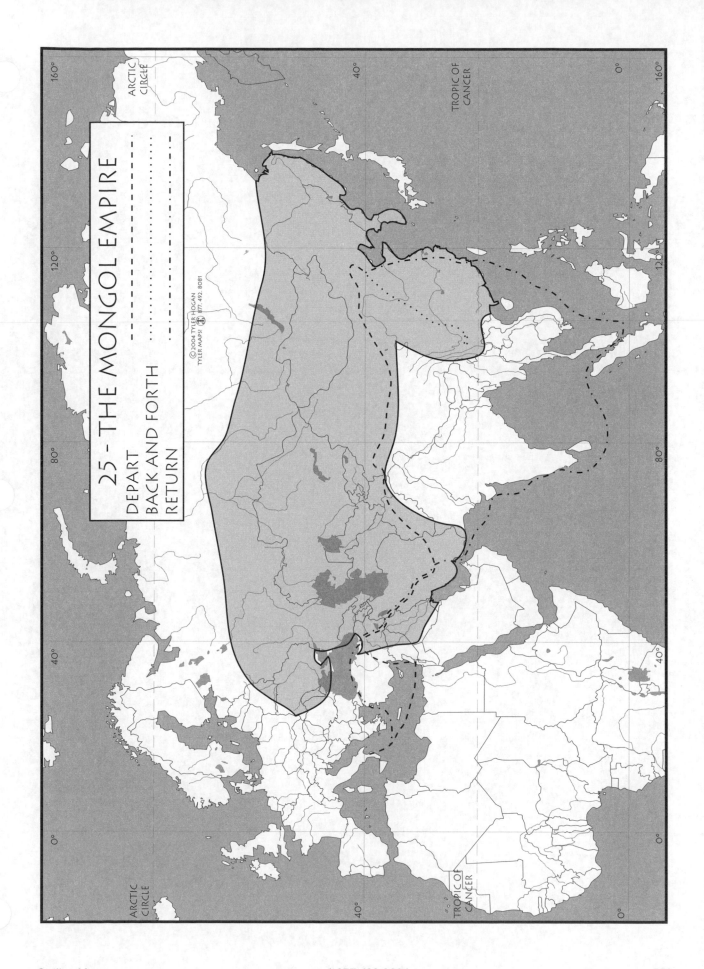

25 – THE MONGOL EMPIRE

DEPART
BACK AND FORTH
RETURN

© 2004 TYLER HOGAN
TYLER MAPS! 877.492.8081

ARCTIC CIRCLE

TROPIC OF CANCER

TROPIC OF CANCER

160° 120° 80° 40° 0° 160° 120° 80° 40° 0°

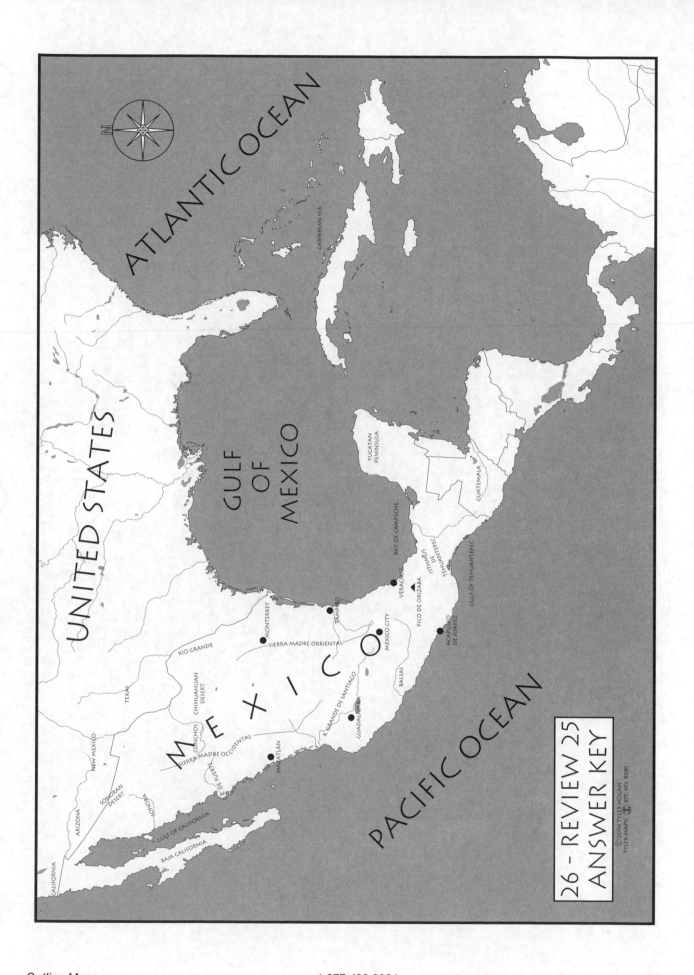

ATLANTIC OCEAN

CARIBBEAN SEA

UNITED STATES

GULF OF MEXICO

YUCATAN PENINSULA

GUATEMALA

BAY OF CAMPECHE

VERACRUZ

ISTHMUS DE TEHUANTEPEC

GULF OF TEHUANTEPEC

TAMPICO

MONTERREY

SIERRA MADRE ORRIENTAL

MEXICO CITY

PICO DE ORIZABA

ACAPULCO DE JUAREZ

RIO GRANDE

M E X I C O

CHIHUAHUAN DESERT

CONCHOS

BALSAS

R. GRANDE DE SANTIAGO

GUADALAJARA

SIERRA MADRE OCCIDENTAL

DE FUERTE

MAZATLAN

TEXAS

NEW MEXICO

SONORAN DESERT

ARIZONA

SONORA

GULF OF CALIFORNIA

BAJA CALIFORNIA

CALIFORNIA

PACIFIC OCEAN

©2004 TYLER HOGAN
TYLER MAPS 1.877.492.8081

26 – REVIEW 25
ANSWER KEY

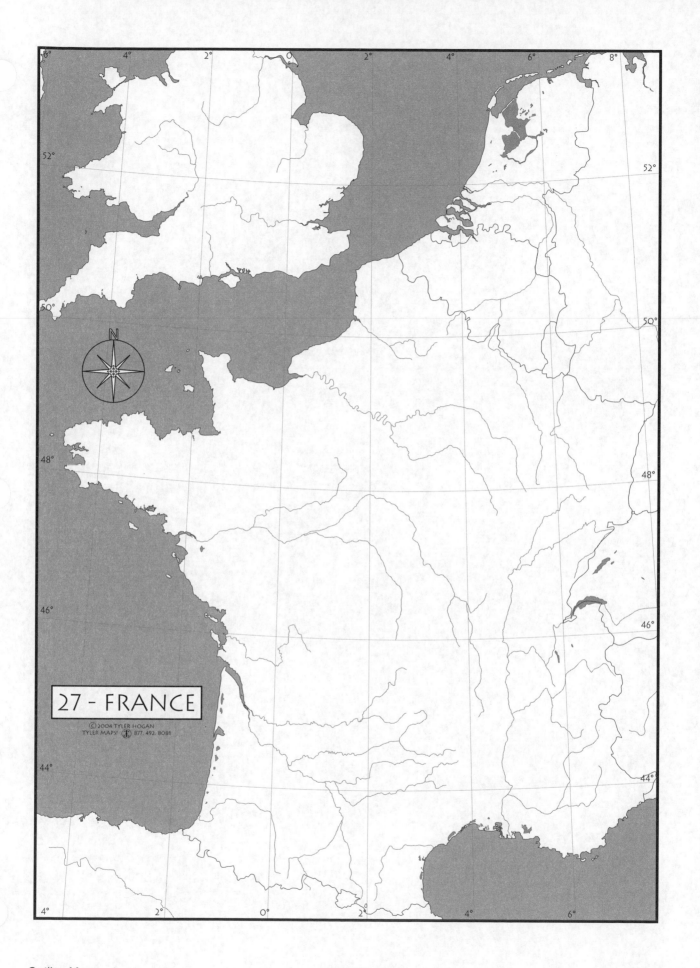

27 - FRANCE

© 2004 TYLER HOGAN
TYLER MAPS! 877. 492. 8081

28 - SOUTH AMERICA

© 2004 TYLER HOGAN
TYLER MAPS! 877. 492. 8081

APPENDIX

CONTENTS

SECTION A   Would You Like to Belong to God's Family?

SECTION B   Activity Supplement

SECTION C   Supplemental Books and Resources

SECTION D   Materials Lists

SECTION E   Bibliography

SECTION F   Pretest Answer Key

SECTION G   Answer Key

We all belong to a family, but did you know that God has His own family, too? If you are a member of His family, He will always be there for you. To belong to God's family, you have to know four facts:

FACT 1: God loves you and has a plan to make you part of His family.

God's Word, the Bible, says:

God loves you.

God loved the world so much that He gave His only Son [Jesus] . . . so that whoever believes in Him may not be lost, but have eternal life (John 3:16).

God has a wonderful life planned for you.

(Jesus speaking) *I came to give life—life in all its fullness* (John 10:10).

But why aren't we part of God's family already?

FACT 2: Your sins keep you from being part of God's family.

What is sin?

Sin is something we do or say or think that does not please God. The Bible says that *everyone* has sinned. What are some sins? (Fighting, bad thoughts, lying, stealing, disobeying parents, bad words)

All people have sinned and are not good enough for God's glory (Romans 3:23).

Even though God made us and loves us, sin causes us to be far away from God. Because of our sin, we deserve punishment for doing wrong things. But God doesn't want to see anyone punished. He wants to give us a gift instead. That gift is a new kind of life.

When someone sins, he earns what sin pays . . . But God gives us a free gift—life forever in Christ Jesus (Romans 6:23).

This picture shows how our sin keeps us from knowing and pleasing God. Many people try to please God by doing good things, such as going to church, praying more, and helping others. Doing these things makes you a nicer person, but they can't erase your sin or make you part of God's family.

FACT 3: Jesus is the only One who can take away your sin.

Jesus was punished in your place by dying on a cross.

[Jesus] died for us while we were still sinners. In this way God shows His great love for us (Romans 5:8).

And Jesus came back to life!

[Jesus] was buried and was raised to life on the third day (1 Corinthians 15:4).

Jesus is your way to God.

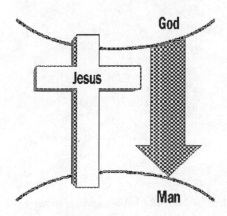

Jesus answered, "I am the way. And I am the truth and the life. The only way to the Father is through Me" (John 14:6).

Jesus made a way for us to come to God, our heavenly Father, and be a part of God's family. Jesus did this by paying for your sin when He died on the cross. But just knowing this is not enough ...

FACT 4: To become part of God's family, you must accept God's gift. Jesus is God's gift to you. When you accept Jesus, God's Son, you become God's child.

Some people did accept [Jesus]. They believed in Him. To them He gave the right to become children of God (John 1:12).

How do I accept God's gift?

You accept God's gift by asking Jesus to forgive you of your sins. Right now, Jesus is waiting to forgive your sins and come into your life.

(Jesus speaking) *Here I am! I stand at the door and knock. If anyone hears My voice and opens the door, I will come in* (Revelation 3:20).

God's book, the Bible, tells us that there are two kinds of people. Some people run their own lives. Others let Jesus control their lives.

You can accept God's gift right now by asking Jesus to forgive your sins. Talking to Jesus is called prayer. If you pray this prayer, you will belong to God's family!

Dear Jesus:

I need You. Thank You for dying on the cross for my sins. Thank You for forgiving my sins and making me part of God's family. Take control of my life and make me the kind of person You want me to be. Amen.

If you prayed this prayer—and really meant it—you are part of God's family **right now!**

But what happens if you sin again? Will you still be part of God's family?

Yes!

When you disobey your parents you make them unhappy. But you are still their child. To make things right, you tell them you are sorry for what you did. When you disobey God, He is not pleased, but you are still part of His family. He still loves you. But you need to tell Him you are sorry for what you did.

If we confess our sins, He will forgive our sins. We can trust God. He does what is right. He will make us clean from all the wrongs we have done (1 John 1:9).

As soon as you sin, tell God you are sorry. then God will forgive you and things will be right again between you and God.

Section A is from the booklet, "Would You Like to Belong to God's Family?" published by New Life Publications, a ministry of Campus Crusade for Christ. Used by permission of New Life Publications.

ACTIVITY 4A

MAKE A LYRE

Let's make a lyre! Lyres come in many different shapes and sizes, but each has strings running up and down to strum like a harp. The lyre depicted here is like one the ancient Greeks would have used. Because Nero enjoyed Greek art and music, he may have played one similar to this.

Materials: One photocopy of the lyre on the next page; medium-weight cardboard (8½" by 11"); pencil; scissors; tape; hole punch, 6 rubber bands; crayons, markers, or fabric paint

1. Photocopy the drawing of a lyre.
2. Cut out the lyre on the heavy lines. (Don't forget to cut out the inside of the lyre where the strings go. The "string" lines in the drawing are there only as guides.)
3. Lay the pattern of the lyre on a piece of medium-weight cardboard.
4. Lightly tape the pattern down and trace it with a pencil.
5. Remove the paper pattern of the lyre.
6. Cut out the cardboard lyre. (This may require your teacher's help if the cardboard is thick.)
7. Use a hole punch to create six holes in the cardboard. (Look at the pattern to determine placement of these holes.)
8. Cut the rubber bands once each and open them up.
9. Stretch the rubber bands lengthwise from one side of the lyre to the other. Tie them at the holes that you punched.
10. Using the paper pattern as a guide, decorate the lower portion of the lyre with crayons, markers, or fabric paint.
11. Strum the lyre as Nero might have. Take your photo and file it in your Student Notebook under "Europe: Rome."

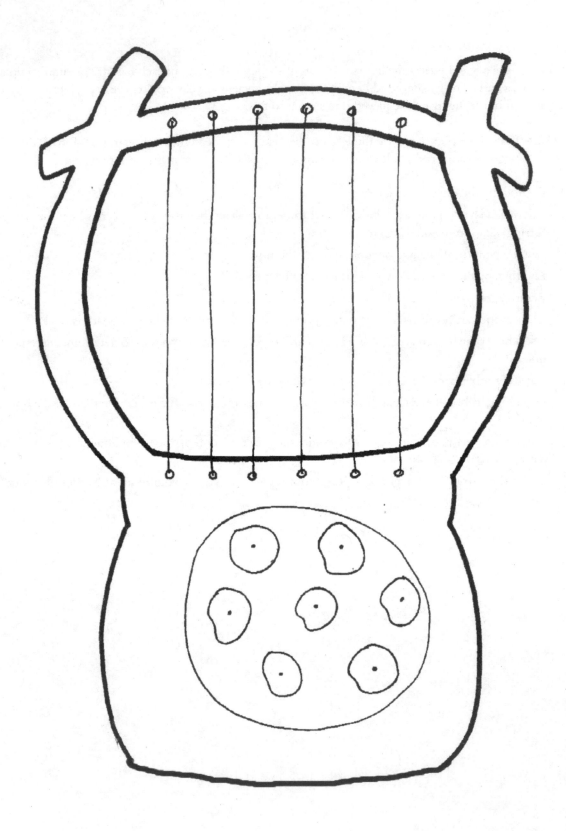

ACTIVITY 4C
LETTER FROM NERO'S MOTHER PLEADING FOR HER LIFE

"Don't you know, my son, that affection all mothers naturally bear their children? Our love is unbounded, incessantly fed by that tenderness unknown to all but ourselves. Nothing should be more dear to us than what we have bought with the risk of our lives; nothing more precious than what we have endured such grief and pain to procure. These are so acute and unbearable that if it were not for the mission of a successful birth, which makes us forget our agonies, generation would soon cease.

Do you forget that nine full months I carried you in my womb and nourished you with my blood? How likely is it, then, that I would destroy the dear child who cost me so much anguish to bring into the world? It may be that the just gods were angry at my excessive love of you, and used this way to punish me. . . .

Tell me, why should I plot against your life? To plunge myself into a worse fate? That's not likely. What hopes could induce me to build upon your downfall? I know that the lust for empire often corrupts the laws of nature; that justice has no sword to punish those who offend in this way; and that ambition disregards wrong so long as it succeeds in its aim . . . Nay, to what deity could I turn for absolution after I had committed so black a deed?"

Despite this moving plea for her life, Nero's mother, Agrippina, was strangled to death in A.D. 59 under the orders of Nero. In a rage, Nero kicked his mistress, who was with child, and killed her, too.

Excerpt from *The World's Great Letters*, edited by M. Lincoln Schuster. New York: Simon and Schuster, 1940; published by special arrangement by Konecky and Konecky, 2000; pp. 21–22.

ACTIVITY 9C
DESCRIPTION OF THE ERUPTION OF MT. VESUVIUS

The following letter was written by Pliny the Younger describing what his uncle, Pliny the Elder, encountered at the eruption of Mt. Vesuvius in A.D. 79. It is perhaps the only written account by someone so close to the event.

"My uncle was stationed at Misenum, in active command of the fleet. On 24 August, in the early afternoon, my mother drew his attention to a cloud of unusual size and appearance . . . like a pine . . . for it rose to a great height on a sort of trunk and then split off into branches. My uncle ordered a boat to be made ready. As he was leaving the house he was handed a message from Rectina . . . She implored him to rescue her from her fate. He gave orders for the warships to be launched and went on board with the intention of bringing help to many more people besides Rectina. Ashes were already falling, hotter and thicker as the ships drew near, followed by bits of pumice and blackened stones, charred and cracked by the flames: then suddenly they were in shallow water, and the shore was blocked by the debris from the mountain . . . [The] wind was full in my uncle's favour, and he was able to bring his ship in.

Meanwhile on Mount Vesuvius broad sheets of fire and leaping flames blazed at several points. My uncle tried to allay the fears of his companions by repeatedly declaring that these were nothing but bonfires left by peasants or empty houses on fire . . . Then he went to rest . . . By this time the courtyard giving access to his room was full of ashes mixed with pumice-stones, and if he had stayed in the room any longer he would never have got out. He was wakened and joined the rest of the household who had sat up all night. They debated whether to stay indoors or take their chance in the open, for the buildings were now shaking with violent shocks, and seemed to be swaying to and fro as if they were torn from their foundations. Outside there was the danger of falling pumice-stones, even though these were light and porous . . . [A]fter comparing the risks, they chose the latter."

Unfortunately, Pliny the Elder didn't make it. Like many others, he was overcome by the poisonous flames that engulfed the entire region. Pliny the Younger wrote this additional letter regarding his own escape.

"[D]arkness fell, not the dark of a moonless or cloudy night, but as if the lamp had been put out in a closed room. You could hear the shrieks of women, the wailing of infants, and the shouting of men. Many besought the aid of the gods, but still more imagined that there were no gods left . . . At last the darkness thinned . . . We were terrified to see everything changed, buried deep in ashes like snowdrifts."

Excerpt from Ron Goor and Nancy Goor, *Pompeii: Exploring a Roman Ghost Town*. New York: Thomas Y. Crowell, 1986; p. ix.

ACTIVITY 11B
THE APOSTLES' CREED

Presented below is one version of the simple but profound creed that was written by early Christians and became a cornerstone of the Early Church.

APOSTLES' CREED

I believe in God the Father Almighty, Maker of heaven and earth;

And in Jesus Christ his only Son, our Lord;

Who was conceived by the Holy Ghost,

Born of the Virgin Mary,

Suffered under Pontius Pilate,

Was crucified, dead, and buried:

He descended into hell;

The third day He rose again from the dead;

He ascended into heaven,

And sitteth on the right hand of God the Father Almighty;

From thence He shall come to judge the quick and the dead.

I believe in the Holy Ghost;

The holy catholic Church;

The communion of saints;

The forgiveness of sins;

The resurrection of the body;

And the life everlasting. Amen.

ACTIVITY 14A

BATTLESHIELD CROSS

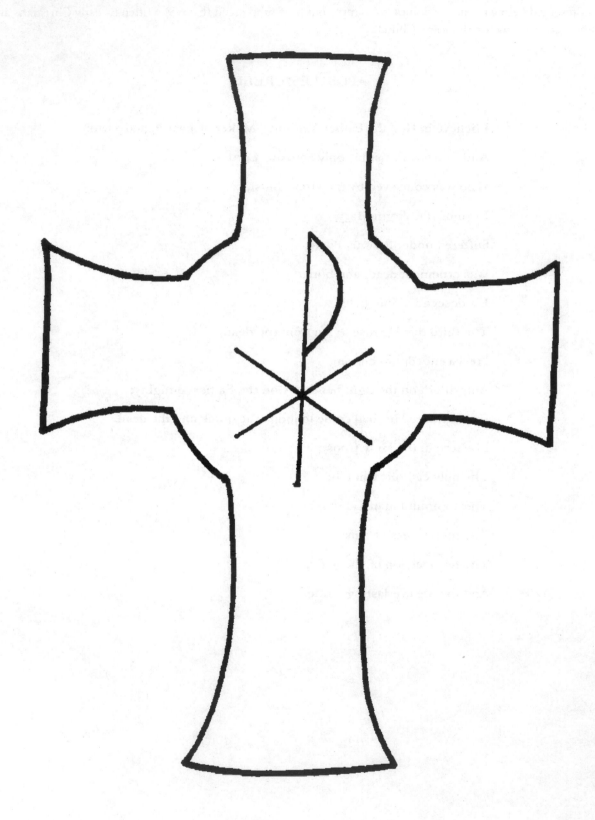

ACTIVITY 14B

THE NICENE CREED

Written as a result of the Council of Nicaea in 325, the Nicene Creed is of great significance to Christians even now. Similar to the Apostles' Creed, it states exactly what Christians believe to be the truth about Jesus Christ. In summary, it states that Jesus *is God*, not just similar to God.

NICENE CREED

We believe in one God, the Father Almighty, maker of all things,

Both visible and invisible;

And in one Lord, Jesus Christ, the Son of God,

Only begotten of the Father, that is to say, of the substance of the Father,

God of God and Light of Light, very God of very God,

Begotten, not made, being of one substance with the Father,

By whom all things were made,

Both things in heaven and things on earth;

Who, for us men and for our salvation,

Came down and was made flesh,

Was made man, suffered, and rose again on the third day,

Went up into the heavens,

And is to come again to judge both the quick and the dead;

And in the Holy Ghost.

ACTIVITY 17C

EXCERPT FROM
THE CONFESSIONS OF ST. AUGUSTINE

"Too late I came to love Thee, O Thou Beauty both so ancient and so fresh . . . Yea, also the heaven and the earth, and all that is in them, bid me on every side that I should love Thee . . . What now do I love when I love Thee? . . . I asked the earth, and it answered, I am not it . . . I asked the sea and the deeps and the creeping things, and they answered: We are not thy God; seek above us. I asked the fleeting winds, and the whole air with its inhabitants answered me: Anaximenes was deceived; I am not God, I asked the heavens the sun and moon and star; nor, said they, are we the God whom Thou seekest. And I replied unto all these: . . . Answer, me concerning Him. And they cried one with a loud voice: He made us . . . They are not well in their wits to whom anything which Thou hast created is displeasing . . . In Thy gift we rest . . . in Thy good pleasure lies our peace."

Excerpt from Will Durant, *The Age of Faith*. Vol. I of *The Story of Civilization*. New York: Simon and Schuster, 1950; pp. 71–72.

ACTIVITY 20C

DESCRIPTION OF ATTILA THE HUN

"He was born into the world to shake the nations, the scourge of all the lands, who in some way terrified all mankind by the rumors noised abroad concerning him. He was haughty in his walk, rolling his eyes hither and thither, so that the power of his proud spirit appeared in the movement of his body. He was indeed a lover of war, yet restrained in action; mighty in counsel, gracious to suppliants, and lenient to those who were once received under his protection. He was short of stature, with a broad chest and a large head; his eyes were small, his beard was thin and sprinkled with gray. He had a flat nose and a swarthy complexion, revealing his origin." (Jordanes, a Gothic historian)

From Will Durant, *The Age of Faith*. Vol. I of *The Story of Civilization*. New York: Simon and Schuster, 1950; p. 39.

ACTIVITY 21C

A LETTER FROM JEROME
ON THE FALL OF ROME

"I shudder when I think of the calamities of our time. For twenty years the blood of Romans has been shed daily between Constantinople and the Alps . . . How many noble and virtuous women have been made the sport of these beasts! Churches have been overthrown, horses stalled in the holy places, the bones of the saints dug up and scattered.

Indeed the Roman world is falling; yet we still hold up our heads instead of bowing them . . . Well may we be unhappy, for it is our sins that have made the barbarians strong; as in the days of Hezekiah, so today is God using the fury of the barbarian to execute His fierce anger. . . .

Who will hereafter believe that Rome has to fight now within her own borders, not for glory but for life? And as the poet Lucan says, "If Rome be weak, where shall strength be found?"

And now a dreadful rumor has come to hand. Rome has been besieged, and its citizens have been forced to buy off their lives with gold. My voice cleaves to my throat; sobs choke my utterance. The city which had taken the whole world captive is itself taken. Famine too has done its awful work.

The world sinks into ruin; all things are perishing save our sins; these alone flourish . . . Who could believe it? Who could believe that Rome, built up through the ages by the conquest of the world, had fallen; that the mother of nations had become their tomb? . . . We cannot indeed help them; all we can do is sympathize with them, and mingle our tears with theirs."

Excerpt from *The World's Great Letters*, edited by M. Lincoln Schuster. New York: Barnes & Noble Books, 2003.

ACTIVITY 22

TRADE AND BARTER DAY

This Trade and Barter Day will explore and develop the roles of **masters**, **journeymen**, and **apprentices** in the Dark Ages. Though about two weeks of preparation may be necessary, the actual trade event may require about two hours. In reading the following suggestions, consider adults to be "masters," teenagers to be "journeymen," and all other children to be "apprentices." This event will require cooperation between families because journeymen and young apprentices will be assigned to masters (or families) other than their own!

1. **About Two Weeks Before Trade and Barter Day:**

Most adults in your group will have some experience in one or more trades or crafts. I suggest that adults volunteer among themselves as "masters" of their trade or craft. They are responsible for their booth or stall on trade day in regard to supplies and activities. For example, the adult who knows how to bake bread may volunteer to be the master baker. This adult will provide bread or other baked treats for trading as well as provide a small project for a teenage journeyman and a small activity for a young apprentice (or apprentices) assigned to him or her.

Trade or craft suggestions would include but are not limited to the following: Stained-glass maker; baker; shoemaker; tailor; silversmith; rope maker; butcher (for safety, I do not suggest handling raw meat but rather, use precooked deli meats); candlemaker; illuminator (calligrapher); potter; weaver; tanner; butter maker; wool maker; barber; alchemist (for safety, I do not suggest using real medicine but rather, use home remedies such as aloe vera or first-aid supplies like bandages, etc.); goldsmith; jeweler; embroiderer; dish maker; fast-food cook; armor maker; carpenter; cartographer (mapmaker); cooper (barrel maker); fruit and vegetable seller; florist; soap maker.

Masters should use their two weeks prior to Trade and Barter Day to prepare simple items for trade. Suggestions might include pieces of rope, beads, stray dishes, nails, flowers, apples, vegetables, scraps of fabric, deli meats, candles, shoelaces, buttons, butter packets, hot corncobs on a stick, etc. (On Trade Day, the apprentices and journeymen will be given "wares," or goods, from their own stall to trade with other stalls. So, in determining the number of items to make, include giving some items to your journeymen and apprentices for trade and barter. No money will be used.)

Also during these two weeks, masters should prepare a mini-lesson or activity to be performed at their booth or stall just for their assigned journeymen and apprentices. In the first hour of Trade and Barter Day, the masters will teach, demonstrate, or do something related to their craft or trade. For example, the master jeweler may have his or her journeymen and apprentices string beads for trading that day. The bread baker may explain the role of yeast in baking and then allow students to dissolve yeast and watch it grow—or simply have them sprinkle cinnamon and sugar on treats to be traded that day. The rope maker may teach students fancy knot tying or discuss the natural fibers used to make rope. The butcher may teach about where particular cuts of meat come from. Use your imagination, but keep this teaching/activity time to one hour or less.

2. **About One Week Before Trade and Barter Day:**

For Apprentices: Explain to all participating apprentices that in the Dark Ages most young people had no choice of their trade or craft. They were subject to joining the trade that had the greatest need or that was made available to them through a family member. To recreate the feelings that a young apprentice might have had, each apprentice is to randomly draw the name of a trade or craft from a bowl. (Include only the trades that will be represented by volunteer adults or masters.) Depending on the number of masters available, it may be necessary to assign more than one apprentice to each master. They are now the unpaid help for their masters and will be subject to their masters on Trade Day. If the setting allows for it, I recommend that apprentices introduce themselves to their masters at this time. I also suggest that these new apprentices research their trade or craft during the week before Trade Day.

For *Journeymen:* Journeymen in your group can choose which trade they would like to join. In this way, they are able to join the trade of their parent to be of real help! During the week, journeymen are responsible for creating a sign for their booth or stall. (A poster board would be adequate.) Remember, the sign should contain no words, but rather a symbol or emblem to represent the craft or trade (symbols were used rather than words because so few could read). If the number of teenagers is small, this duty might fall back on the master. More than likely, not all masters will be fortunate enough to have journeymen.

3. Trade and Barter Day:

There are many factors to consider on Trade and Barter Day to help make it a success. I have provided some guidelines for you. Improvise as necessary depending on your facility, the number of participants, and the difficulty of activities. Dressing in period clothing will add to the fun.

- Set up tables as booths or stalls prior to your event.

- Secure permission to hang poster signs on the walls of your facility or hang them on the tables themselves.

- Provide adequate space (chairs, drop cloths, etc.) at each booth for each master to teach his or her activity.

- Allow setup time prior to the event. Masters will need to transport supplies to their booths. Journeymen will need to hang their signs. Apprentices will need to be available to masters to assist in setting up the booths.

- When all booths appear to be set up, allow approximately one hour for the teaching/activity time.

- I suggest that a traveling photographer capture a photo of each apprentice and journeymen that can be filed in the Student Notebook.

- Allow a few minutes for masters, journeymen, and apprentices to clean up their activities if necessary.

- Begin the public Trade and Barter Day. Allow about one hour for apprentices and journeymen to take their goods and visit other booths. They should trade and barter their items with others. To prevent chaos, you might want to send traders out in small groups (i.e., "Tables 1 to 3 are now allowed to trade," etc.) so that some apprentices are still available at their booths to help.

- Monitor that young apprentices are able to acquire the goods they are interested in. Bags might be helpful.

- When trading has ceased, direct all apprentices and journeymen back to their masters. Allow a few minutes for enthusiastic apprentices to "show and tell" their goods with their masters and others. Have them discuss with their masters the trades of others and what would interest them if they lived during the Dark Ages.

- Allow time for cleanup using the help of all masters, journeymen, and apprentices.
- Leave the facility as clean as you found it.
- If appropriate, send a thank-you note to the facility that accommodated your group.

ACTIVITY 24B

THEODORA'S SPEECH TO JUSTINIAN

"My [Theodora's] opinion is that now. . . is a bad time to flee, even if this should bring safety. . . . For a man who has been an Emperor to become a refugee is not to be borne. May I never be separated from the purple [the imperial color] and may I no longer live on that day when those who meet me shall not call me mistress. Now if you wish to save yourself, O Emperor, this is not hard. For we have much money; there is the sea, here are the boats. But think whether after you have been saved you may not come to feel that you would have preferred to die. As for me, I like a certain old proverb that says: royalty is a good shroud [burial garment]." (Words in brackets are mine for clarification.)

Excerpt from James A. Corrick, *World History Series: The Early Middle Ages.* San Diego: Lucent Books, 1995; p. 82.

ACTIVITY 26C
SHINTOISM

1. **The founder of the religion and date of origination.**
    There is no one founder of Shintoism and the date of origin is unknown. However, it is one of the oldest religions in the world.

2. **The source of authority (written works of the religion, visions, prophecy).**
    There are no sacred written works of the religion although there are historical books held with great reverence that give the history of early Japan, mixing fact, myths, and legends. The books are titled *Ko-ji-ki* (the "records of ancient matters") and *Nihongi* (the "chronicles of Japan"). Both works were composed around A.D. 720.

3. **The doctrine of God (believing there is one God or many gods).**
    Shinto is a polytheistic religion (belief in many gods).

4. **The doctrine of Jesus Christ (believing Jesus was God in the flesh or just a prophet).**
    Jesus is not acknowledged as Lord or prophet.

5. **Their belief in sin.**
    Shinto teaches the basic goodness of the Japanese people because they are considered to be descendants of the gods.

6. **The doctrine of salvation. (On what basis is sin forgiven or accounted for?)**
    Because sin is not an issue, salvation or forgiveness of sin is not a part of Shintoism.

7. **The doctrine of things to come. (Is there a belief in life after death or in a coming judgment of the world?)**
    Shintoism holds great respect for ancestry, nature, and the past. However, it does not address things to come or the afterlife.

8. **What draws people to this religion (lifestyle, ritual, heritage, etc.)?**
    Shintoism appeals solely to the heritage of the Japanese people. It is based on the traditions of respect for nature and a belief in the superiority of the Japanese.

Supplemental information from Josh McDowell and Don Stewart, *Handbook of Today's Religions*. San Bernardino, CA: Here's Life Publishers, Inc., 1983; pp. 349–355.

ACTIVITY 28B

A CHINESE WOMAN'S SONG

In the lesson, I mentioned that the average woman in China did not hold a high place in society. Read this song written about being a Chinese woman. Discuss it with your teacher. Then see if you can find the complete song on the Internet.

How sad it is to be a woman!
Nothing on earth is held so cheap.
Boys stand leaning at the door
Like gods fallen out of heaven.
Their hearts brave the Four Oceans,
The wind and dust of a thousand miles.
No one is glad when a girl is born:
By her the family sets no store.
When she grows up she hides in her room,
Afraid to look a man in the face.
No one cries when she leaves her home-
Sudden as clouds when the rain stops.
She bows her head and composes her face,
Her teeth are pressed on her red lips:
She bows and kneels countless times.

—Written by Fu Hsüan
Third Century A.D.

From Will Durant, *Our Oriental Heritage*. Vol. I of *The Story of Civilization*. New York: Simon and Schuster, 1954; pp. 793–794.

ACTIVITY 30B

ISLAM

1. **The founder of the religion and date of origination.**
   Mohammed founded Islam in A.D. 622, the year of the Hegira.

2. **The source of authority (written works of the religion, visions, prophecy).**
   Islam is based on the revelations "given" to Mohammed and written down in the Koran.

3. **The doctrine of God (believing there is one God or many gods).**
   Muslims believe in one god named Allah.

4. **The doctrine of Jesus Christ (believing Jesus was God in the flesh or just a prophet).**
   Muslims believe that Jesus was a prophet but not God in the flesh.

5. **Their belief in sin.**
   Muslims believe that man is sinful but that he attains righteousness by following the duties of a Muslim. They believe that disobedience to Allah is sin; therefore, sinfulness is brought about by action, not by the nature of man.

6. **The doctrine of salvation. (On what basis is sin forgiven or accounted for?)**
   One is granted a place in Paradise according to the keeping of the duties of Islam and as determined by Allah. Paradise is guaranteed to those who participate in a jihad, or holy war, to spread or defend Islam.

7. **The doctrine of things to come. (Is there a belief in life after death or in a coming judgment of the world?)**
   There is a belief in the afterlife as either a burning inferno or Paradise. Belief in a coming judgment is unclear.

8. **What draws people to this religion (lifestyle, ritual, heritage, etc.)?**
   One is most often born into the Islamic faith although there are many who convert to Islam based on its strong moral teachings. Because of the doctrine of salvation by works, Islam appeals to man's sense of "fairness." According to Islam, it would appear that one gets what one earns.

Supplemental information from Josh McDowell and Don Stewart, *Handbook of Today's Religions*. San Bernardino, CA: Here's Life Publishers, Inc., 1983; pp. 377–399.

ACTIVITY 31A
PAGODA BIRDFEEDER

Background Information: The pagoda is a decorative structure found not only in China but also in India, Thailand, Burma, and Japan. The pagodas of China are commonly built with eight sides and are not as ornate as those found in India. A Chinese pagoda is most often built as a memorial or shrine. Generally, the taller the pagoda, the more sacred the shrine. Some pagodas house Buddhist relics. Others are solid constructions.

Build a pagoda birdfeeder for your own yard.

Materials: Seven paper or plastic bowls (the size of a common cereal bowl), four paper or plastic dinner plates, one paper or plastic coffee cup, dull pencil, approximately 1 yard of yarn, clear tape, small piece of duct tape, glue, birdseed. (Photo 1)

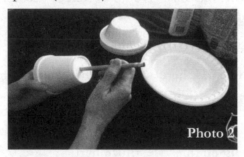
Photo 1

1. Use the point of a dull pencil to poke a *small* hole in the middle of the bottom of the coffee cup, each of the seven bowls, and the four dinner plates. (Photo 2)

Photo 2

2. Wrap a small piece of tape around one end of your piece of yarn to create a "stiff" end. (This stiff end will serve as a needle for threading your pieces together.)

3. Holding the coffee cup upside down, thread the yarn through the hole in the bottom. Pull the yarn through only a few inches. Do not pull it all the way through yet. (Photo 3)

Photo 3

4. Hold a bowl upside down. Thread the end of your yarn through the hole in the center. Pull the yarn just tight enough for the cup and the bowl to nestle together. (Photo 4)

Photo 4

5. Continue to thread your pieces together in the following order. (I'll start back at the beginning with the order.) You will soon see a pattern that will create a pagoda!

a. Upside-down cup

b. Upside-down bowl

c. Right-side-up plate (Photo 5)

d. Right-side-up bowl

e. Upside-down bowl

f. Right-side-up plate

g. Right-side-up bowl

h. Upside-down bowl

i. Right-side-up plate (Photo 6)

j. Right-side-up bowl

k. Upside-down bowl

l. UPSIDE-down plate

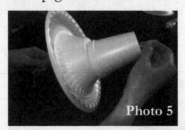

Photo 5

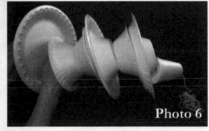

Photo 6

6. Before these items slip off your yarn, tie a large, sturdy knot on the stiff end. For additional sturdiness, apply a piece of duct tape to the knotted end of your yarn on the underside of the last plate. (Photo 7)

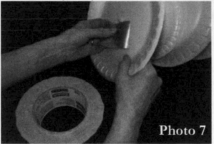

Photo 7

7. Firmly hold the loose end of your yarn and allow the pieces to nestle together with a gentle pull. (Photo 8)

Photo 8

8. Set the pagoda in a sturdy place where you can let it sit overnight.
9. Apply glue between your pieces to strengthen the structure. Allow to dry. (Photo 9)

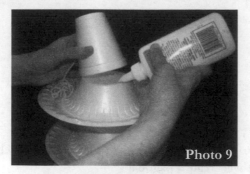

Photo 9

10. Using the free end of your yarn, tie the pagoda birdfeeder to a low place outdoors.
11. Once it is hanging, add birdseed around the exposed edges of the plates. (Photo 10)

Photo 10

12. Enjoy your pagoda birdfeeder. Take a photo of it and add it to your Student Notebook under "Asia: China."

ACTIVITY 32A

SHIELD AND SWORD PROJECT

Make a shield and sword. (This project may require a few hours or an extra day to complete.)

FOR SHIELD:

Materials: Cardboard from the side of a large box , hole punch, scissors, carbon paper, photocopy of dragon picture in this activity (see next page), stapler, tape, pencil, crayons or markers, two pieces of string or elastic about 2 feet long each

1. Have your teacher trace the outline of a shield onto your cardboard following the basic pattern provided here. (*Teacher:* Create the shield large enough to cover the student's chest.)

2. Cut out the shield.

3. Punch holes in each of the four corners of the shield as shown on the pattern.

4. Lay one piece of carbon paper underneath the photocopy of the dragon picture and staple them together. (Make sure the ink side of the carbon paper is facing down.)

5. Lay the stapled dragon and carbon paper over the center of your shield and lightly tape it to keep it from moving.

6. Using a pencil, trace the dragon onto your shield by pressing hard through the carbon paper.

7. Remove the papers to reveal your dragon. Color it in with crayons or markers.

8. Run string or elastic through the holes you punched at the shoulders. Tie these securely.

9. Place your shield on your body. With someone's help, crisscross the string or elastic across your back to the bottom holes you punched and tie these off loosely. To keep the shield secure, you will want to crisscross these straps each time you put on your shield. So don't tie the bottom knots too tightly!

FOR SWORD:

(Teacher: If the following instructions and materials are too difficult to master, you can always resort to empty cardboard tubes from paper towels or wrapping paper! These are great fun, too.)

Materials: From a lumber store, obtain a piece of wood 2½ feet long, 2½ inches wide, and ½ inch thick. Request that the board be trimmed to make a dull point on one end. Request that the other end be trimmed to create a narrow handle. Obtain two blocks of wood, each approximately 6 inches long, 1 inch wide, and ½ inch thick. Also, sandpaper, silver and gold paints, nails, hammer, permanent marker.

1. After receiving your trimmed wood, use sandpaper to smooth all edges and remove splinters.
2. Paint the small blocks of wood (which will be your handle) with gold paint and the sword itself with silver paint. Allow to dry.
3. Create the handle by nailing the two small blocks of wood to the end of your sword.
4. Use a permanent marker to create an "engraving" of your last name on the handle of your sword. Create decorative swirls on the body of the sword.
5. Don't forget to take a photo and insert it in your Student Notebook under "Europe: Denmark."

ACTIVITY 33B
THE ARABIC ALPHABET

The following is a very basic introduction:

1. The Arabic language connects the letters together, so that is why every letter is written twice here: the first to the right is how it would look when it is not part of a word while the second one is how it would look as part of a word.

2. The letters that are underlined have more of a deep, strong sound to them.

3. Some letters have a different pronunciation depending on their position in the word.

4. In writing or reading Arabic, you start from the right-hand side and go left.

a	b	t	th
أ ا	ب ب	ت ت	ث ش
g	***h***	**kh**	**d**
ج ج	ح ح	خ خ	د د
th	**r**	**z**	**s**
ذ ذ	ر ر	ز ز	س س
sh	***s***	***d***	***t***
ش ش	ص ص	ض ض	ط ط
z	***a***	**gh**	**f**
ظ ظ	ع ع	غ غ	ف ف
k	**k**	**l**	**m**
ق ق	ك ك	ل ل	م م
n	**h**	**wa**	**ye**
ن ن	ه ه	و و	ى ى

ACTIVITY 33C
ISLAMIC ART AND ARCHITECTURE

Create a visual mini-report of Islamic art and architecture.

Background Information: Islamic art and architecture is distinctive in its use of symmetry, geometric patterns, arches, domes, and minarets (tall, spindly towers used for calling Muslims to worship). Little is drawn of living things because it was forbidden by Mohammed to do so. He thought it might lead to idol worship. Great examples of both Islamic art and architecture can be found in Granada, Spain, at the ornate palace called the **Alhambra.** It is easy to find in an encyclopedia.

Materials: Prints or photocopies of Islamic art and architecture as suggested in Step 1. (This search may be the most time-consuming part of this activity.) Also, colored paper (any color or assortment), scissors, dictionary, heavy marker, pen or pencil, glue stick, three-hole punch. (Photo 1)

Photo 1

1. Research the Internet or reference books to find examples of each of the five distinctive styles listed above (symmetry, geometric patterns, arches, domes, and minarets). For each one you find, print or photocopy a small image that represents the feature.

2. Trim each individual image. Glue each one onto the outside of a piece of colored paper that is twice the length of the image. In this way, you can fold the paper in half and create a small "image book" with the image on the outside cover. (Photos 2 and 3)

Photo 2

Photo 3

3. On the upper inside flap of each image book, use a heavy marker to write the distinctive style depicted for that image, i.e., "Symmetry." (Photo 4)

Photo 4

4. On the lower inside flap of each image book, use a pen or pencil to write out a definition of that distinctive style from a dictionary. (Photo 5)

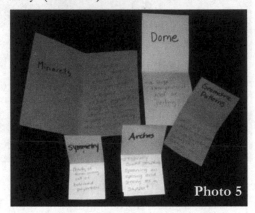

Photo 5

5. Leaving room at the top of the page for a title, take each image book and glue it to one 8½-by-11-inch piece of colored paper. Title the paper "Islamic Art and Architecture." (Photo 6)

Photo 6

6. Use a three-hole punch on one edge of the paper, then insert it in your Student Notebook under "Europe: Spain."

REVIEW 11

MAP SYMBOLS

Aqueducts

Arabian
Horses

Books

Copper

Coral

Flying
Machine

Fountains

Leather

Libraries

Mosques

Palaces

Paved,
Lit Streets

Pearls

Postal Service

Schools

Shields

Silver and Gold

Swords

Spectacles

Waterwheels

ACTIVITY 35B
DECORATIVE CROSS

I have created two versions of a decorative cross for you to make—you can choose the one you prefer or make both if you'd like! One is "elegant" and the other, "rugged."

THE ELEGANT CROSS:

Materials: Photocopy of cross pattern, small bunches of tiny dried herbs or flowers, decorative ribbon, beads, buttons, cardboard, glue, large paper clip

1. Photocopy the pattern.

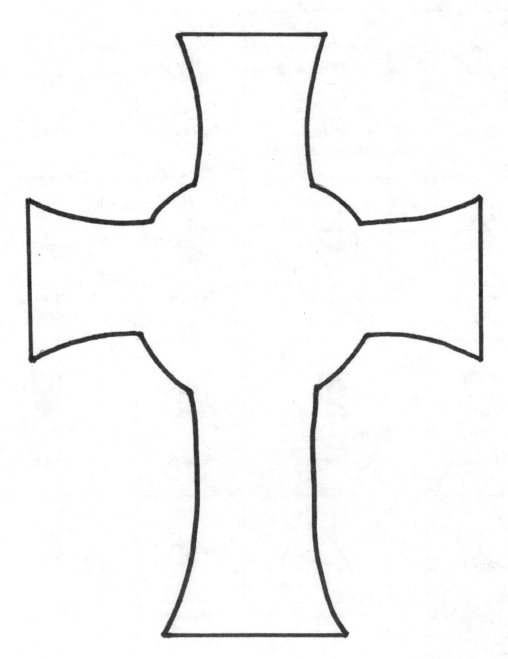

2. Cut out the pattern and lightly tape it over a piece of lightweight cardboard.

3. Using the pattern as a stencil, trace the cross onto your cardboard. Discard the pattern. (Photo 1)

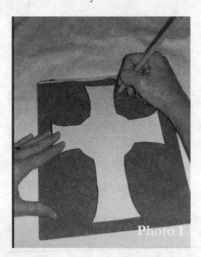

4. Cut out the cardboard cross. (Photo 2)

5. Use assorted items such as dried flowers, buttons, strips of ribbon, etc., to decorate your cross. Arrange all your items to your satisfaction before you begin to glue them down. (Photo 3)

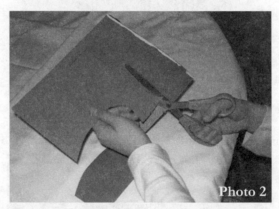

6. Glue the decorations in place and allow them to dry. (Photo 4)

7. Bend a large paper clip into an "S"-shaped curve. Tape or glue it to the back of the cross to serve as a hanger. (Photo 5)

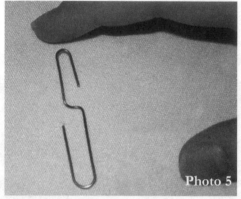

8. Write your name, the year, and the lesson title on the back of the cross. (Photo 6)

9. Give the cross as a gift or hang it in your own home as a reminder of our Lord's sacrifice. (See our completed cross in Photo 7.)

10. Take a photo and place it in your Student Notebook under "Asia: Turkey (Byzantine Empire)"

THE RUGGED CROSS:

Materials: Cardboard; ruler; pencil; scissors; one package of small, dried cinnamon sticks (approximately 4-inch-long sticks); two packages of black hemp cord (found at craft stores) *or* thick twine *or* leather lace (I found the hemp cord to be much less expensive than leather and much easier to work with); glue; large paper clip

1. Using a pencil and ruler, draw a cross on the cardboard following these exact dimensions: make the vertical bar 1¾ inches wide and 13½ inches long. Four inches from the top of the vertical bar, create a horizontal bar that is 1¾ inches wide and 8 inches long. (Photo 8)

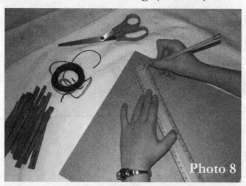

Photo 8

2. Cut out the cross. (Photo 9)

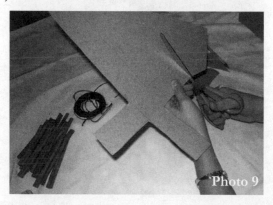

Photo 9

3. Lay four cinnamon sticks side by side vertically on the top portion of the vertical bar.

4. Lay four cinnamon sticks side by side horizontally on the left portion of the horizontal bar. Lay an additional four sticks on the right portion of the horizontal bar.

5. On the portion of the cross just under the horizontal bar, lay four cinnamon sticks side by side vertically. Do the same with four more sticks to cover the last portion of the cross. .

6. With all pieces properly arranged, begin to glue the cinnamon sticks in place. (Photo 10)

Photo 10

7. Divide the hemp cord (or twine or leather lace) into seven equal lengths.

8. At approximately ½ inch below the top of the vertical bar, wrap one length of hemp cord. Tie it off with a knot on the front side. Repeat this step on each of the other three ends of the bars.

9. Use two lengths of hemp cord to create a crisscross "X" where the two bars meet. (Photo 11)

Photo 11

10. Four inches from the bottom of the vertical bar (where the cinnamon sticks meet), wrap the remaining piece of hemp cord to hide the "seam." (Photo 12)

Photo 12

11. Bend a large paper clip into an "S"-shaped curve. Tape or glue it to the back of the cross to serve as a hanger.

12. Give the cross as a gift or hang it in your own home as a reminder of our Lord's sacrifice. (Photo 13)

Photo 13

13. Take a photo and place it in your Student Notebook under "Asia: Turkey (Byzantine Empire)"

ACTIVITY 35D

DEATH ON A CROSS

The Question: How does a person physically die from the act of crucifixion?

The Answer: When a person hangs from two hands, blood quickly sinks to the lower parts of the body. Within about 10 minutes, blood pressure drops 50 percent. At the same time, the pulse doubles. Fainting soon follows as the heart loses blood. Circulation ceases. Suffocation is one result of the havoc placed on the body. Ultimately, however, the heart fails. You could say that when Jesus was crucified, He died of a broken heart! It is a fitting statement as He died because of our SINS, which broke His heart.

One of the cruelties of crucifixion is the fact that a board is placed at the feet of the victim that will allow him to push his body up. When he does so, he is better able to breathe, but it would be excruciating to do so because of the nails driven through the feet. The person would constantly be battling between the two pains. This is the reason why some victims had their legs broken. It would speed up the death process because the person would be unable to catch his breath. *"But when they came to Jesus and saw that He was already dead, they did not break His legs."* (John 19:33)

To add to the pain would be the fact that most victims were scourged before being placed on the cross. A "scourging" was being whipped by a rope with bits of sharp metal or bone on the end. Sometimes a scourging alone could kill a man. As a person hung on a cross, pushing himself up and down to breathe would be worsened by the pain of the open wounds on the back.

Reflect on the passages found in Isaiah 53:5:

"But He was wounded for our transgressions, He was bruised for our iniquities; the chastisement for our peace was upon Him, and by His stripes we are healed."

In prayer, just thank Christ for what He did for us!

From *The Living Bible Encyclopedia in Story and Pictures*, Art Treasure ed., Vol. 4. New York: H. S. Stuttman Co., Inc., 1968; p. 461.

ACTIVITY 39A

VIKING HELMET MASK

Make a Viking helmet mask with a little glitter!

Materials: One photocopy of the mask pattern (see next page), crayons, scissors, paper or plastic plate, glue, glittery gold and silver fabric paints, hole punch, piece of elastic or a rubber band

1. Photocopy the mask pattern in this activity.

2. If desired, use gray, brown, or black crayons to color any or all parts of the mask. (The mask will later be decorated with gold and silver fabric paints.)

3. Cut out the mask on the bold outer lines. Carefully cut out the eye pieces from within the mask as indicated. (An adult may be needed for this tedious task.)

4. Center the paper mask onto the back of a paper or plastic plate and glue it in place. (Photo 1)

5. Cut away the lower portion of the plate that is not covered by the mask. (Photo 2)

6. Carefully cut the eyes out also. (Photo 3)

7. Now that the mask is in place on the plate, use gold and silver fabric paints to decorate it. When the paint dries, the glitter really shows. If the paint is too thick, it may not dry very easily.

8. When the paint has dried, use a hole punch to create a hole on either side of the mask. (Photo 4)

9. Tie an elastic band or cut rubber band through one of the holes. Hold the mask against your face and line your eyes up with the eye holes of the mask. Then tie the other end of the elastic or rubber band to the other hole, measuring how much length is needed for comfort and a firm fit. (Photo 5)

10. Take a photo in your Viking helmet mask and file it in your Student Notebook under "Europe: Sweden, Norway, *or* Denmark."

Photo 1

Photo 2

Photo 3

Photo 4

Photo 5

The Mystery of History-Volume II

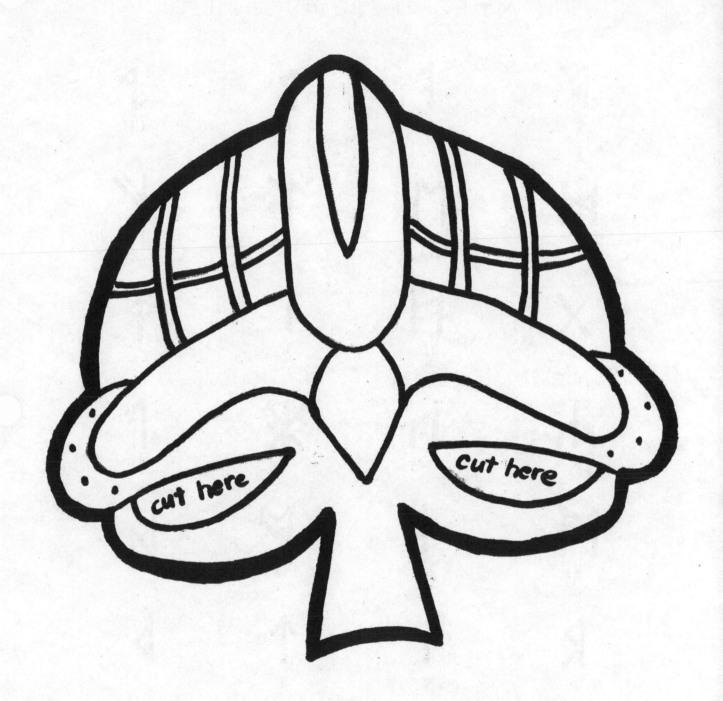

cut here

cut here

ACTIVITY 40B

SAMPLE OF THE RUNE ALPHABET

Rune	Letter
ᚠ	A
ᚱ	AE
ᛒ	B
ᛋ	CH
ᚼ	D
ᛗ	E
ᛏ	EA
ᚥ	F
ᚷ	G
ᚻ	H
ᛁ	I
ᛄ	J
ᛉ	K
ᚿ	K
ᛟ	K
ᚱ	L
ᛗ	M
ᛏ	N
ᛈ	O
ᚼ	P
ᚱ	R
ᛋ	S
ᛏ	T
ᚦ	TH
ᚢ	U
ᚹ	W
ᛘ	Y

Information derived from *World Book Encyclopedia*, 50th Anniversary ed., s.v. "Rune." Chicago: Field Enterprises Educational Corp., 1966.

ACTIVITY 41B
THE CYRILLIC ALPHABET

It is very difficult to give an exact representation of the Cyrillic alphabet in English. The following guide is a simplified version.

A	Аа	L	Лл	W	
B	Бб	M	Мм	X	
C		N	Нн	Y	Йй
D	Дд	O	Оо	Z	Зз
E	Ее or Ээ	P	Пп	CH	Чч
F	Фф	Q		KH	Хх
G	Гг	R	Рр	SH	Шш
H		S	Сс	ZH	Жж
I	Ии	T	Тт	YA	Яя
J		U	Уу	YO	Ёё
K	Кк	V	Вв	TS	Цц

ACTIVITY 46A

GOOD KING WENCESLAS

Good King Wenceslas looked out on the Feast of Stephen,
When the snow lay round about, deep and crisp and even.
Brightly shone the moon that night, though the frost was cruel,
When a poor man came in sight, gathering winter fuel.

"Hither, page, and stand by me, if you know it, telling,
Yonder peasant, who is he? Where and what his dwelling?"
"Sire, he lives a good league hence, underneath the mountain,
Right against the forest fence, by Saint Agnes' fountain."

"Bring me food and bring me wine, bring me pine logs hither,
You and I will see him dine, when we bear them thither."
Page and monarch, forth they went, forth they went together,
Through the cold wind's wild lament and the bitter weather.

"Sire, the night is darker now, and the wind blows stronger,
Fails my heart, I know not how; I can go no longer."
"Mark my footsteps, my good page, tread now in them boldly,
You shall find the winter's rage freeze your blood less coldly."

In his master's steps he trod, where the snow lay dinted;
Heat was in the very sod which the saint had printed.
Therefore, Christian men, be sure, wealth or rank possessing,
You who now will bless the poor shall yourselves find blessing.

From www.cyberhymnal.org. You can also hear the melody to this favorite Christmas carol at the same Web site.

ACTIVITY 53A
MEDIEVAL CROWN

Make a crown fit for a king or a queen.

Materials: Silver, gold, or blue poster board; one photocopy of the crown pattern; pencil; scissors; stapler; approximately 2 yards of shimmery cloth cut into 6- to 8-inch-wide strips (a king's crown will require only 1 yard or less of fabric, but a queen's crown will require about 2 yards); tape; one small package of flat-sided fake jewels (from the craft store); glue; markers or crayons

1. Photocopy and cut out the pattern provided on next page.
2. Lay your pattern on the bottom edge of a piece of poster board. Trace the pattern as many times as you need to fill up the length of the poster board. (Photo 1)

3. Cut out the crown. (Photo 2)

4. Measure the crown to your head, leaving a little extra room for the fabric that will be wrapped around the crown. Staple the ends of the crown together. (Photo 3)

5. Find the center of your fabric strip. Starting with the fabric's center point at the very front of your crown, weave the fabric over the top and around the bottom of the crown, leaving the tips of the crown exposed. (Photo 4)

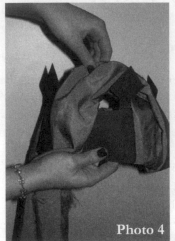

Photo 4

6. For a king, cut and trim excess fabric. Tuck and tape the ends of the fabric to the crown.
7. For a queen, leave the excess fabric as a "tail" to hang majestically from the back of the crown. Secure the fabric with a little tape, if needed, on the inside of the crown. (Photo 5)

Photo 5

8. Decorate the exposed tips and surfaces of the crown with jewels and glue, or use markers to color them in.
9. Take a photo of yourself in your king or queen crown. File it under "Europe: Scotland."

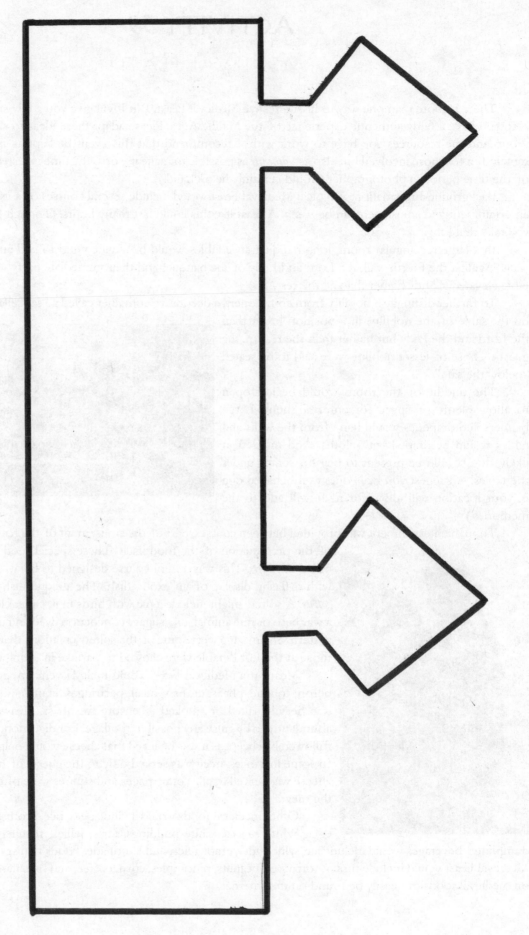

ACTIVITY 59
MEDIEVAL FEAST

There is more than one way to host a festive Medieval Feast. But I will give you a few suggestions that will help you have a fairly authentic experience of the Middle Ages. Please adapt these ideas to suit the size of your group and the resources you have to work with. I recommend that this event be kept as *simple* as possible to remain fun for those involved but also as *authentic* as possible to make it worth the time invested! (And though not of the time period, a photographer should certainly be on hand.)

Background Information: A typical Medieval Feast would include several courses of a variety of foods with entertainment and amusements in between. A feast like this could last many hours. (Though I don't recommend you take that long.)

In a large rectangular room, long banquet-style tables would be situated end to end and line three of the walls. Against the fourth wall, the Lord and Lady of the banquet and their immediate party would be seated at a table elevated slightly higher than all the rest.

To further distinguish nobility from commoners, a decorative container called a "saltcellar" would be placed on the table of the nobility, in a position lower than the Lord and the Lady but higher than the rest of the guests. Those of lesser nobility were said to be seated "below the salt."

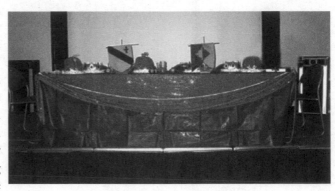

The middle of the room would be left open to allow plenty of space for entertainment. Large banners and draperies would hang from the walls and tables would be draped with cloths. And more than likely, dogs would be present to beg for scraps under the tables! (I suggest you have one, well-behaved dog if your location will allow for it! It will add to the memories.)

Though entertainment was provided between courses, part of the amusement of the feast was the creativity of the presentation of the food itself. These special food presentations were called *entremets*. This was a mini-course designed to break up the main course with a flashy display of an exotic dish. The unique dish itself was called a *soltety*. A soltety might include a pie with birds in it, a meat loaf in the shape of a war hero or rare animal, or a sugary concoction dyed and designed in a special pattern. So amazing were some of the soltety creations that in some cases only those at the Lord's table were allowed to partake in eating them.

Meats at a Medieval Feast would include venison, pork, chicken, swan, heron, tongue, pheasant, fish, quail, partridges, crane, and rabbit. Most meat was heavily salted or smoked to ensure freshness. Heavy sauces were used abundantly to disguise any possible spoilage. For digestion, meats were usually followed by cheese as it was believed that cheese would help break them down. In some instances, meat was served only to the guests of higher class, though cheese was served to all. Young pages and squires were often selected to carve the meat.

Other medieval foods would include peas, rice, broths, soups, dried fruits, eggs, white sauces, white puddings, tarts, jellies, fritters, pastries, and fruit dumplings. Beverages would include ale, wine, cider, grape juice, and lemonade. Foods that you would not see at a Medieval Feast would include turkey, tomatoes, peanuts, pineapples, corn, coffee, and bananas. More information on medieval foods can easily be found on the Internet.

I. **A few commonsense tasks to tackle before the feast:**

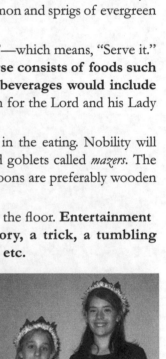

A. Choose a feast director to delegate tasks and coordinate the event.

B. Choose a site.

C. Create a menu.

D. Select a Lord and a Lady.

E. Recruit workers.

F. Invite all guests to participate in costume.

G. Select or assign entertainment.

H. Prepare banners, tablecloths, plates, goblets, saltcellars, etc.

I. Recruit a photographer.

J. Just prior to the arrival of the guests, set bread out on tables.

II. **Suggested outline of events for the feast:**

A. **Processional entrance** of the Lord, the Lady, and immediate party. Horns and/or drums may announce their entrance.

B. **Prayer** and blessing of the food.

C. The Lord gives a **toast** to his guests, shouting, "Wassail!"—which means "Be well." The guests reply, "Drink hale!"

D. Beginning with the head table, a **handwashing bowl** and cloths are passed from table to table by a young page called an *ewerer*. (The bowl holds warm water with thin slices of lemon and sprigs of evergreen or mint. Several bowls can be used to accommodate lots of tables.)

E. A server announces the first course of the meal, shouting, "Messe it Forth!"—which means, "Serve it." The dish is served first to the Lord, the Lady, and their party. **The first course consists of foods such as soup or broth, round loaves of bread, and cheese. Non-alcoholic beverages would include apple cider, grape juice, or lemonade.** A food taster should taste the dish for the Lord and his Lady before they eat to check for freshness, as well as poison!

F. After the Lord and Lady begin their first course, **all are served** and join in the eating. Nobility will eat off of pewter, silver, or gold plates. They will drink from silver or gold goblets called *mazers*. The commoners will eat out of wooden bowls or bread bowls called *trenchers*. Spoons are preferably wooden (forks have not been invented yet).

G. As the first course of the meal is enjoyed, an entertainer takes the middle of the floor. **Entertainment could include any of the following: a juggling act, a dance, a story, a trick, a tumbling demonstration, a song, a sword match, a rare physical feat, a pet trick, etc.**

H. A server announces the second course, shouting, "Messe it Forth!" It again goes to the Lord and his table first. **The second course consists of foods such as green vegetables, pork, or chicken.** (Barbecued wings work nicely for this event.) Beverages are refilled and the food taster samples the Lord's and Lady's food again.

I. In the middle of this course, I suggest an **entremet** (or mini-course), consisting of some special soltety, be served to the head table.

J. Another **entertainer** takes the floor.

K. A server announces the third course, shouting, "Messe it Forth!" This again goes first to the Lord and his table. **The third course consists of foods such as sweet fruits with cream (no ice cream), spicy desserts like cinnamon peaches, pies, tarts, pastries, etc.**

L. Another **entertainer** takes the floor.

(At this point, your group could opt for more courses or other entremets. This would then allow for more entertainment. After the last course is served and entertainment provided, proceed with the following closing.)

M. **Handwashing bowls** and cloths are passed around again by an ewerer.

N. **Grace** is said again in thanks for the meal.

O. The Lord, his Lady, and all the members of his party are escorted first from the feast with great fanfare and the exchange of greetings with the guests.

P. All others are allowed to leave.

Q. The cleanup crew, aided by the dog, tidies up after the guests.

ACTIVITY 61

COAT OF ARMS

The term ***coat of arms*** comes from the long-ago practice of a knight wearing an embroidered emblem on a *surcoat* over his *armor*. The emblem helped to identify a knight among his foes on the battlefield. Over time, a coat of arms was used to identify an entire family on an official document, such as on a deed in the sale of land. This was helpful for those who couldn't read or write. ***Heraldry*** developed as the art of using these emblems. The term came from officials called *heralds*. Heralds supervised the selection of colors and designs to prevent duplication.

In official heraldry, very specific names have been given to the placement of figures and decorations on a coat of arms. I suggest that older students research these names and the meaning behind them. A standard coat of arms would contain at least a main figure known as a ***charge*** along with a motto on the background of a shield. This background is called the ***field***. Extra images such as lions or dragons are called ***supporters*** and often surrounded the main charge as an added artistic touch.

Design an individual or family coat of arms!

Materials: Notebook-sized poster board, pencils, markers, colored pencils, three-hole punch

As you design your individual or family coat of arms, bear in mind emblems, mottoes, or designs that might distinguish you or your family from others. These items might include the shape of your state or country, a favorite Bible verse, physical traits, sports interests, etc. Your coat of arms might be one emblem that covers an entire shield or the combination of four emblems, each in a quadrant of its own. Below are samples of real coats of arms designed by modern-day knights. (There are still those who practice the art of chivalry!)

Make your coat of arms on notebook-sized poster board using pencil first, outlining it with marker, and shading it with colored pencils. Punch three holes in it and place it in your Student Notebook under "Europe: England."

Carey

ACTIVITY 62
JOUSTING TOURNAMENT

Background Information: Though knights were expected to be gentlemen under a high code of conduct, they still had their differences with other knights. In the 1100s, if one knight felt he was dishonored by another, he would challenge his opponent to a duel. In this duel, the knights would charge one another on horseback carrying a long lance. Their aim was to pierce their enemy to death!

However, by the 1200s, these duels became more of a sport than a means to settle a dispute. The new sport was called *jousting*. Rather than fight to the death, a knight aimed to knock his opponent off his horse using a dull lance. Though the knights met in an enclosed field, they wore such heavy armor (up to 80 pounds of it) that they could hardly move or turn their heads.

The knight's lack of mobility led to the sport of *tilting* in the 1400s in which narrow lanes were created for knights and horses to charge down without colliding. This sport is frequently portrayed in the movies. Naturally, jousting and tilting tournaments became great social gatherings.

Here are suggestions for a simple, but fun, "modified" jousting tournament (minus the horses) that you can hold with your friends.

Materials: Empty wrapping-paper tubes, trash-can lids with handles

1. Each jouster has a wrapping-paper tube for a dull lance and a trash-can lid for a shield.
2. Jousters stand 20 to 40 feet apart.
3. Jousters take off toward each other with a lance in one hand and their shield in the other.
4. Without wavering, jousters must aim for one another's shield. (For safety reasons, any jouster who pokes his lance near his opponent's face is automatically disqualified!)
5. Whoever can joust the longest with the least amount of damage to his lance is the tournament winner. Several rounds may be required to determine the winner. Make it fun and fair, and keep it safe!

ACTIVITY 62A

PRINCESS HAT AND GOWN

Make a tall, pointy princess hat (also called a hennin).

Materials: One piece of poster board, stapler, strong tape, scissors, 1 yard strand of ribbon (or less if elastic), ½ yard solid fabric, ¼ yard sheer fabric (tulle), glue, ½ yard braided strand, fur trim (optional), fake jewels

Photo 1

1. Twist a piece of poster board into the shape of a cone that stands about 13 inches tall. Keep a small hole at the top. (Ignore the excess amount of poster board at the bottom. You will trim this later.)

2. Staple the cone in the places you can reach. Tape the inside seam.

3. Now cut the bottom of the cone in a straight-line fashion to give it a flat base.

4. Cover the cone with solid fabric (prints were not yet stylish). I suggest that you wrap the edges of the fabric up under the hat and secure it there with tape. It will give the hat a smoother edge. (Photo 1)

5. Glue braided strand around the bottom edge of the cone.

6. Glue fur trim just above the braid.

7. Attach fake jewels. (Photo 2)

8. Run a width of sheer fabric just far enough through the top of the cone to secure it with strong tape. "Poof" the remaining sheer fabric to allow it to flow elegantly out of the top of the cone.

9. Measure ribbon or an elastic band to fit. Attach it on the inside of the cone with staples.

10. Be sure to take a picture of this activity and file it in your notebook under "Europe: England." (Photo 3)

Photo 2

Make a princess gown.

Materials: Approximately 3 yards of 54-inch-wide fabric (for an average 7 year old), fur trim, braid trim, fake jewels, 1½ to 2 yards of cord for a belt (optional), sewing machine, thread

1. Fold the fabric in half lengthwise (with the outer fabric face to face on the inside).

2. Use a light pencil on your material to "enlarge" the gown sketch on the next page, keeping your dimensions equal on the right and left sides. You are basically creating a simple T-shaped gown with bell sleeves. (Keep the neck open wide enough to avoid the need for a zipper. If the neck proves too tight, cut a simple straight slit in the back opening.)

Photo 3

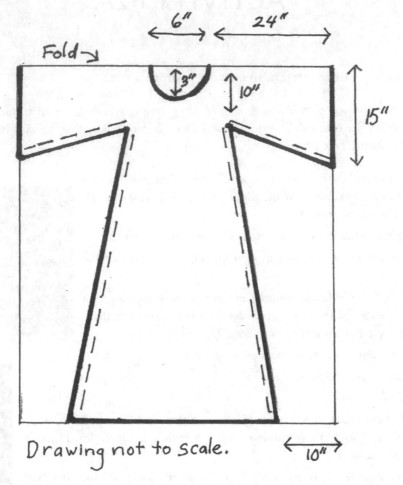

Fold →

6" 24"

3" 10" 15"

Drawing not to scale. 10"

3. Cut out the pattern on the solid lines.

4. Sew the gown at the dotted lines.

5. Rather than hem the rough edges around the neck and sleeves, I suggest you attach fur or braided trim to hide the edges. My personal opinion is that the addition of fur trim makes the garment look very medieval. So, add that option if at all possible! It might be best to hem the bottom of the gown to prevent tripping on any frayed edges.

6. Be sure to photograph the wearer of the gown and file the photo under "Europe: England." (Photo 4)

Photo 4

ACTIVITY 62A
MONEY POUCH

Make a money pouch for your coins.

Materials: One photocopy of the money pouch pattern, scissors, ¼ yard of cloth or felt, three to four straight pins, needle and thread, shoestring, coins (perhaps chocolate ones)

1. Begin by photocopying the pattern of the money (see page 625) pouch.
2. Cut out the pattern on the wide line.
3. Fold the cloth or felt in half, which gives you two layers.
4. Lay the pattern on top of the cloth and pin it in three to four places.
5. Cut the fabric using the pattern as a guide. (Photo 1)

Photo 1

6. Remove the pattern and pins.
7. Use a needle and thread to sew the two edges of the pouch together (except for the top). (Photo 2)

Photo 2

8. Cut four holes in the cloth about 1½ inches from the top. (Allow the holes to go through both layers of cloth, creating eight holes.) (Photo 3)

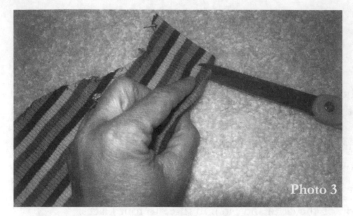

9. Lace the shoestring through the holes to create a drawstring. (Photo 4)

10. Fill the money pouch with coins. Chocolate coins would be the most fun! (Photo 5)

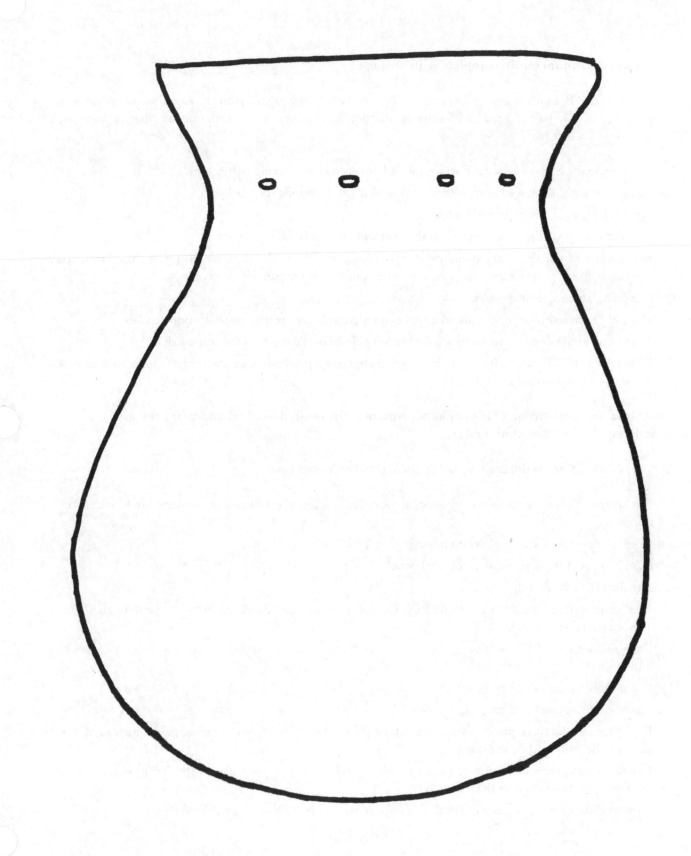

ACTIVITY 63A
SAMURAI OUTFIT

Make a samurai outfit, complete with armor.

Materials: Bath necessities, robe, sash or rope for belt, baggy pajama pants or sweat pants, shoestrings, old pair of tube socks, scissors, flip-flop sandals, one fake sword, one fake dagger, baby oil, hair band

1. Before you dress like a samurai warrior, take a bath, as was the custom before war.
2. After your bath, wrap a large robe around you with a sash or rope for a belt.
3. Slip on baggy pajama pants or sweat pants.
4. Pull the sleeves of the robe up high on the arm and tie it with shoestrings.
5. Pull the bottom of the pants up high above your knee. If there is elastic on the bottom of the pants, allow the elastic to keep the pants up. If not, use shoestrings to tie the pants in place.
6. Put on a pair of old tube socks.
7. Cut a slit between your big toe and the other toes that will allow you to wear flip-flop sandals.
8. Insert one long sword under your belt on the left side. Slide a dagger on the other side.
9. Slick your hair back with baby oil. If it is long enough for a ponytail, place the ponytail high on your head and make a loop with the extra hair.

Make samurai armor. (This could be worn over the outfit described above or used as a "standalone" over other clothing.)

Materials: Cardboard, crayons, hole punch, string or leather laces

1. For an armor skirt, cut out four large rectangular panel pieces of cardboard (approximately 12 inches by 5 inches).
2. Color the pieces of cardboard with horizontal stripes.
3. Punch holes in the top of the cardboard panels.
4. Lay the cardboard on the floor.
5. Lace twine, string, or leather pieces through the holes, leaving enough length in the twine to tie the skirt of armor around your waist.
6. For shoulder armor, cut out three small rectangular panel pieces of cardboard (approximately 8 inches by 4 inches).
7. Color these pieces with stripes as well.
8. Punch holes across the top.
9. Lace together the three pieces just as you did the armor skirt. (There are only three panels instead of four because the front will be left open.)
10. Drape the top pieces of armor over your shoulders and across your back like a cape. Tie loosely so that it does not pull tightly across the throat area.
11. Take a photo of your samurai outfit. File it in your Student Notebook under "Asia: Japan."

ACTIVITY 63C
SAMURAI DEATH POEMS

Read the following samples of samurai death poems. Consider the emptiness and lack of hope within them. Rewrite one of the poems below or make up one yourself about death. Write it from the viewpoint of a Christian who can have joy, peace, and hope knowing there is a place for him or her in heaven through Jesus Christ. File your poem under "Asia: Japan" in your Student Notebook.

(1) *Minamoto Yorimasa   1104–1180*

Like a rotten log
half buried in the ground -
my life, which
has not flowered, comes
to this sad end.

(2) *Hojo Ujimasa   1538–1590*

Autumn wind of eve,
blow away the clouds that mass
over the moon's pure light
and the mists that cloud our mind,
do thou sweep away as well.
Now we disappear,
well, what must we think of it?
From the sky we came.
Now we may go back again.
That's at least one point of view.

(3) *Ouchi Yoshitaka   1507–1551*

Both the victor
and the vanquished are
but drops of dew,
but bolts of lightening -
thus should we view the world.

(4) *Tokugawa Ieyasu   1542–1616*

Whether one passes on or remains is all the same.
That you can take no one with you is the only difference.
Ah, how pleasant! Two awakenings and one sleep.
This dream of a fleeing world! The roseate hues of early dawn!

Poems accessed on the Internet: www.samurai-archives.com/deathq.html. The following is the source information provided at this Web site:
1. Hoffmann *Japanese Death Poems* p. 48.
2. Sadler *The Maker of Modern Japan* p. 160–161.
3. Hoffmann *Japanese Death Poems* p. 53.
4. Sadler *The Maker of Modern Japan* p. 324.

ACTIVITY 66A
THE MAGNA CARTA

The original Magna Carta contains 63 points of detail. For the sake of younger and middle students, this is a scaled-down version of just a few of these points. Photocopy this page and trim it at the line below. Next, proceed to make this document appear "aged" following the directions in Activity 66A in the lesson.

· ·

THE MAGNA CARTA

Know that before God, for the health of our soul and those of our ancestors and heirs, . . .

First, that we have granted to God . . . that the English Church shall be free. . .

The city of London shall enjoy all its ancient liberties and free customs. . .

No man shall be forced to perform more service for a knight's fee or other free holding of land from it.

. . . a free man shall be fined only in proportion to the degree of his offense . . .

No constable or other royal official shall take corn or other movable goods from any man without payment. . .

No constable may compel a knight to pay money for castle-guard . . .

Neither we nor any royal official will take wood for our castle, or for any other purpose, without consent of the owner.

To no one will we sell, to no one deny or delay right or justice.

All merchants may enter or leave England unharmed and without fear, and may stay or travel . . . for purposes of trade . . .

All forests that have been created in our reign shall at once be disafforested.

All evil customs related to forests. . . are at once to be investigated . . . by twelve sworn knights. . .

Given by our hand in the meadow that is called Runnymede, between Windsor and Staines, on the fifteenth day of June in the seventeenth year of our reign. . .

Claire Breay, *Magna Carta: Manuscripts and Myths*, (2002). Accessed on the British Library Web site: www.bl.uk/collections/treasures/magnatranslation.html.

FREDERICK II

ACTIVITY 72C
BANNOCKBURN

At Bannockburn the English lay-
The Scots they were na far away,
But waited for the break o'day
That glinted in the east;

But soon the sun broke through the heath
And lighted up that field o'death,
When Bruce, wi' saul-inspiring breath,
His heralds thus addressed: -

Scot, who hae wi' Wallace bled,
Scots, wham Bruce has aften led;
Welcome to your gory bed,
Or to victorie.

Now's the day, and now's the hour,
See the front o'battle lour;
See approach proud Edward's power –
Chains and slaverie!

Wha will be a traitor knave?
Wha can fill a coward's grave?
Wha sae base as be a slave
Let him turn and flee!

Wha for Scotland's king and law
Freedom's sword will strongly draw,
Freeman stand, or freeman fa'?
Let him follow me!

By Oppression's woes and pains!
By your sons in servile chains!
We will drain our dearest veins
But they shall be free!

Lay the proud usurpers low!
Tyrants fall in every foe!
Liberty's in every blow!
Let us do, or die!

—Written by Robert Burns, 1793

From *The Royal Gallery of Poetry and Art.* New York and St. Louis: N. D. Thompson Publishing Co., 1888; p. 231.

ACTIVITY 74A
AZTEC COLORING PAGE

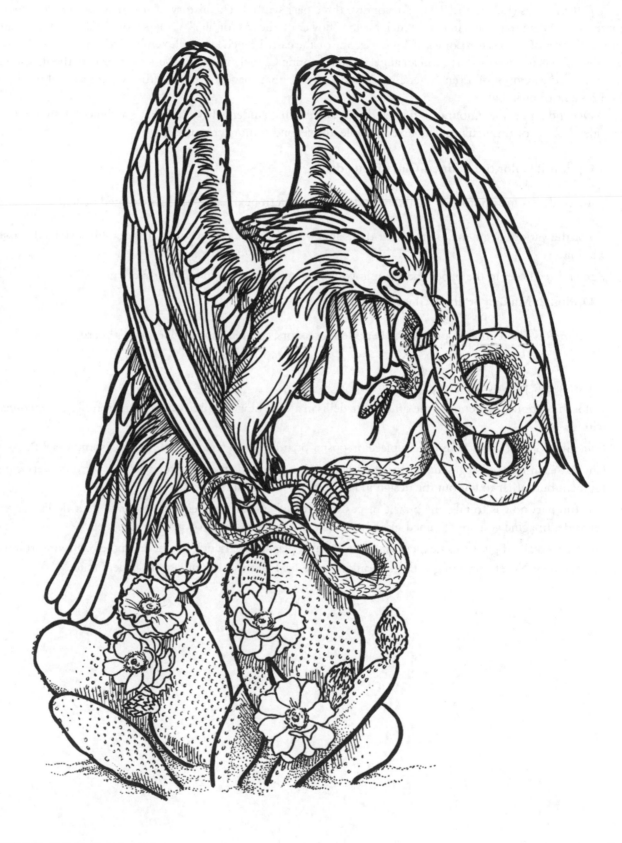

ACTIVITY 81A

THE FLEUR-DE-LIS

A fleur-de-lis (flur duh LEE) is a decorative three-part symbol. The history of it is filled with much legend. Some would claim that the name in French means "flower of the iris (or lily)." Others would claim that the name means "flower of Clovis (or Louis)." Clovis was one of the early French kings who embraced Christianity. Legend says that Clovis received an iris from an angel upon accepting Christianity. Regardless of its origin, the fleur-de-lis has remained a symbol of French heraldry. It is no wonder that Joan of Arc used the symbol as well to inspire the French troops in battle.

Depending on the amount of time and/or patience that students have, you have a choice of two options provided below for this activity. The first is simple, the second is more complicated.

Option 1: Color the Stained-Glass Fleur-de-lis.

Materials: One photocopy of the fleur-de-lis (see pattern next page), scissors, colored pencils

1. Color the various segments of the fleur-de-lis in a wide range of pretty colors to resemble a stained-glassed window.
2. Punch three holes in the paper and file it in your Student Notebook under "Europe: France."

Option 2: Make a Stained-Glass Puzzle.

Materials: Two photocopies of the fleur-de-lis, scissors, colored pencils, glue, poster board, closable plastic bag

1. Set aside one photocopy of the fleur-de-lis.
2. Color the various segments of the other fleur-de-lis in a wide range of pretty colors to resemble a stained-glass window.
3. Glue this colored fleur-de-lis onto a piece of poster board (to give your "puzzle pieces" some weight).
4. Cut out each colored segment on the bold lines. (Younger students may prefer to not cut out every single segment but rather to cut out the design in larger, more manageable pieces.)
5. The fun part now is to take the puzzle pieces you created and match them on the blank fleur-de-lis that you set aside. Imagine you are a stained-glass craftsman laying down pieces of glass in a frame.
6. Store your stained-glass puzzle pieces inside a closable plastic bag. Punch two holes in the bag to insert it into your Student Notebook along with the blank fleur-de-lis. File this work under "Europe: France."

Note to Teacher: All the suggestions in this resources list are optional, to be used for further enrichment and exploration. They are not necessary to complete the course. "Younger Students" refers to those children about kindergarten through about 2nd grade. "Middle Students" would mean 3rd to about 6th grade. "Older Students" refers to 7th grade and up. Many of these would be considered high school level only.

It is difficult to suggest movies according to age because all families have their own set of standards. I sometimes allow my younger children to see older movies for their historical value and significance, with some screening on my part. But I wouldn't do this with all movies. Please use YOUR best judgment on any of the movies listed here.

TOPIC RESOURCES

The following books relate to several chapters, characters, and/or time periods in Volume II.

CASTLES

- **Younger Students:**
(1) *Ms. Frizzle's Adventures: Medieval Castle,* Joanna Cole (Magic School Bus Series, Scholastic, 2003). A favorite of the younger set.
(2) *Coat of Arms,* Catherine Daly-Weir (Grosset and Dunlap, 2000). Well-presented, easy-to-follow activity book.

- **Middle Students:**
(1) *Usborne Internet-Linked Book of Castles,* Lesley Sims (Usborne, 2002).
(2) *The Amazing World of Castles,* Barbara Taylor (Anness Publishing, 2003). Fascinating information plus projects and activities.
(3) *Castle,* David Macaulay (Houghton Mifflin Books, 1982). Beautiful black-and-white detail of castle architecture.
(4) *Castle Life,* Struan Reid (Age of Castles Series, Raintree Steck-Vaughn, 1998). Describes medieval castles and the people who lived in them.
(5) *How Castles Were Built,* Peter Hicks (Raintree Steck-Vaughn, 1999). Colorful and informative.
- **Movie:** *Castle* (1995). Turner Home Entertainment, PBS Home Video. Based on the book by David Macaulay.
Using animation and live-action sequences, this award-winning video explains castle design, cultural, and sociological significance in the Middle Ages.

MIDDLE AGES

- **Younger Students:**
(1) *Days of Knights and Damsels: An Activity Guide,* Laurie Carlson (Chicago Review Press, 1998). More than 100 illustrated crafts, projects, and games to recreate the world of the Middle Ages.
(2) *My First Amazing History Explorer,* CD-ROM (DK Multimedia, 1998).

- **Middle Students:**
(1) *Middle Ages,* Mike Corbishley (Cultural Atlas for Young People Series, Facts on File, 2003). Includes information on ancient burial mounds, the Doomsday book, and the Bayeux Tapestry.

(2) *The Middle Ages,* edited by William Chester Jordan (A Watts Guide for Children, Franklin Watts, Inc., 2000). Encyclopedia format; fantastic resource for middle and upper grades.

(3) *Castle Diary: The Journal of Tobias Burgess, Page,* Richard Platt (Candlewick Press, 1999). Interesting story for 9 to 12 year olds.

(4) *Medieval World* (Usborne World History). Numerous, colorful illustrations.

(5) *The Door in the Wall,* Marguerite de Angeli (Yearling Books, 1990). Newbery Medal winner; fiction set in medieval Europe.

- **Middle and Older Students:**

(1) *The Greenleaf Guide to Famous Men of the Middle Ages,* Rob Shearer (Greenleaf Press, 1992).

(2) *Knights and Armor Coloring Book,* A. G. Smith (Dover Coloring Book). Very detailed.

(3) *Fire, Bed & Bone,* Henrietta Branford (Candlewick Press, 1998). Historical fiction set in 1381 England and told from the viewpoint of a hunting dog.

- **Older Students:** *The New Penguin Atlas of Medieval History,* Colin McEvedy (Penguin USA, 1992).

ROME

- **All Students:**

(1) *What Do We Know About the Romans?* Mike Corbishley (Hodder and Stoughton, 1991). Check for this at your library.

(2) *Ancient Rome,* Avery Hart and Sandra Gallagher (Kaleidoscope Kids Book, Williamson Publishing, 2002). Excellent overview for ages 7 to 12.

- **Younger Students:** *The Ancient Romans,* Jane Shuter (Heineman Library, 1998). Good overview for younger grades.

- **Middle Students:**

(1) *Detectives in Togas,* Henry Winterfeld (Odyssey Classics, 2002). Fun, fictional account of ancient Rome.

(2) *The Roman Empire,* Martyn Whittock (Peter Bedrick Books, 1996). Informative overview now out of print—check your library.

(3) *The Roman News,* Langley and DeSouza (Candlewick Press, 1999). A newspaper-style presentation of ancient Rome.

CHURCH HISTORY AND SAINTS

- **Middle Students:** *Trials and Triumph: Stories from Church History,* Richard M. Hannula (Canon Press, 1999). A collection of brief biographies—very relevant to this study.

- **Middle and Older Students:**
The Story of Christianity, Michael Collins and Matthew Price (DK Books, 1999). Richly illustrated, this book covers 2,000 years of Christianity.

- **Movie:** The Storykeepers video series. Recommended for younger and middle students. These exciting and animated videos portray fictional characters living under Roman persecution in A.D. 62. www.storykeepers.videos.com

CULTURES

- **All Students:** *The Atlas of Legendary Places: A Guide to the World's Most Mystical Locations,* James and Jennifer Westwood (Konecky & Konecky, 1997). This is a beautiful picture book for all and adds text for older students. Breathtaking photos that cover topics in both Vol. I and Vol. II of *The Mystery of History.*

- **Middle and Older Students:**

(1) *Great Civilizations of the East,* Daud Ali, et al. (Lorenz Books, 2003). Covers Mesopotamia, the ancient Chinese empire, ancient India, and ancient Japan; 800 photos, illustrations, and maps. Also includes activities.

(2) *The Medieval World,* Mike Corbishley (Peter Bedrick Books, 1993).

LESSON RESOURCES

(Note that words in all-capital letters in lesson titles are the Volume II key events and dates to be memorized.)

QUARTER 1

LESSON 1 PENTECOST and the First Followers of Jesus (c. A.D. 33 to 476)

- **All Students:** Acts 1–7, the Bible.

- **Younger and Middle Students:** *Art History Coloring Book: New Testament* (KidsArt). For a catalog, call 530-926-5076 or visit www.kidsart.com

- **Middle and Older Students:** *The Church in History,* B.K. Kuiper (Wm. B. Eerdmans Publishing, 1995).

- **Older Students:** *The Early Christians: In Their Own Words,* edited by Eberhard Arnold (Plough Publishing, 1998). A sourcebook of original writings.

LESSON 2 "Saul, Who Also Is Called Paul"

- **All Students:** Acts 13–29, the Bible.

- **Younger Students:** *Adventures in Odyssey Classics #4, Bible Eyewitness: New Testament.* Audiobook on CD (Thomas Nelson).

LESSON 3 Paul's Missionary Journeys

- **All Students:**

(1) Acts 13–29, the Bible.

(2) *Exploring Ancient Cities of the Bible,* Michael Carroll and Caroline Carroll (Chariot Victor Pub., 2001; Cook Communications Ministries). This 44-page reference book is from a young-earth perspective and based on the latest archaeological finds. See finds related to the Coliseum and "Fish in the Sand" (secret symbol for Christ's followers).

- **Younger Students:** *Paul: God's Message Sent Apostle Post,* Mike Thaler (Chariot Victor Pub.; Cook Communications Ministries). A humorous retelling of Bible stories that focus on the character trait of honesty.

- **Movies:**

(1) *I, Paul* (1980). Gateway Films/Vision Video, Box 540, Worcester, PA 19490. This 26-minute video is a re-enactment of Paul transcribing his last letter to Timothy while in a Roman prison. Slow, but very powerful. Have a Bible in hand to read along.

(2) *Paul the Emissary.* Vision Video. Available through Bob Jones ShowForth Videos, 54 minutes. For a catalog, call 1-800-845-5731 or visit showforth.bjup.com

LESSON 4 Nero

- **Middle Students:**

(1) *Nero: Destroyer of Rome,* Julie Morgan (Rosen Publishing Group, 2003).

(2) *Nero,* Elizabeth Powers (World Leaders Past and Present, Chelsea House Publishers, 1988). Out of print but can probably be found at the library.

- **Older Students:**

(1) *The Flames of Rome,* Paul Maier (Kregel Publications, 1996). Historically accurate documentary novel about the early Christian church.

(2) *Quo Vadis,* Henryk K. Sienkiewicz, Joe Wheeler (Focus on the Family Great Stories Series, Tyndale House, 2000). Historical novel originally published in 1896. The story takes place in Rome during the reign of Nero and explores the romance between a young Christian woman and a Roman officer.

- **Movie:** *Quo Vadis* (1951). Recommended for older students. Although this movie (starring Peter Ustinov) is disturbing in content and slow in plot, it does portray the difficult life and times of early Christians under the reign of Nero.

LESSON 5 Martyrs of the Early Church

- **All Students:** *Exploring Ancient Cities of the Bible,* Michael Carroll and Caroline Carroll (Chariot Victor Pub., 2001; Cook Communications Ministries). This 44-page reference book is from a young-earth perspective and based on the latest archaeological finds. See finds related to the Coliseum and "Fish in the Sand" (secret symbol for Christ's followers).

- **Middle and Older Students:**

(1) *Lives and Legends of the Saints,* Carole Armstrong (Simon and Schuster, 1995). Twenty stories of well-known saints, beautifully illustrated; features artwork by the world's greatest artists.

(2) *Jesus Freaks,* dc Talk and The Voice of the Martyrs (Bethany House, 1999).

(3) *Martyr of the Catacombs: A Tale of Ancient Rome* (Kregel Publications, 1991). A 145-page fiction novel based on fact.

(4) *Foxe's Christian Martyrs of the World* (sometimes referred to as Foxe's Book of Martyrs).

- **Older Students:** *Quo Vadis,* Henryk K. Sienkiewicz, Joe Wheeler (Focus on the Family Great Stories Series, Tyndale House, 2000). Historical novel originally published in 1896. The story takes place in Rome during the reign of Nero and explores the romance between a young Christian woman and a Roman officer.

- **Movie:** *Quo Vadis* (1951). Recommended for older students. Although this movie (starring Peter Ustinov) is disturbing in content and slow in plot, it does portray the difficult life and times of early Christians under the reign of Nero.

LESSON 6 Josephus

- **Middle and Older Students:**

(1) *For the Temple,* G. A. Henty (Lost Classics Book Co., 1999).

(2) *The Works of Josephus,* translated by William Whiston, A.M. (Hendrickson Publishers, 1987).

LESSON 7 Masada

- **All Students:** *Exploring Ancient Cities of the Bible,* Michael Carroll and Caroline Carroll (Chariot Victor Pub., 2001; Cook Communications Ministries). This 44-page reference book is from a young-earth perspective and based on the latest archaeological finds. See finds related to the Coliseum and "Fish in the Sand" (secret symbol for Christ's followers).

- **Younger and Middle Students:** *Masada,* Neil Waldman (Boyds Mills Press, 2003).

- **Middle and Older Students:**

(1) *The Story of Masada,* Yigael Yadin; retold for young readers by Gerald Gottlieb (Random House, 2003). A famous archaeologist uncovers the dramatic secrets of an ancient desert.

(2) *Masada: The Last Fortress,* Gloria D. Miklowitz (Wm. B. Eerdmans Publishing, 1998).

- **Older Students:**

(1) *Masada,* Tim McNeese (Chelsea House Publishers, 2003).

(2) The *Jewish War* by Josephus.

LESSON 8 The Dead Sea Scrolls

- **All Students:** *Exploring Ancient Cities of the Bible,* Michael Carroll and Caroline Carroll (Chariot Victor Pub., 2001; Cook Communications Ministries). This 44-page reference book is from a young-earth perspective and based on the latest archaeological finds. See finds related to the Coliseum and "Fish in the Sand" (secret symbol for Christ's followers).

- **Middle and Older Students:** *The Dead Sea Scrolls,* Ilene Cooper (William Morrow, 1997). A dramatic, fast-paced narrative.

LESSON 9 The Buried City of Pompeii

- **All Students:** *Exploring Ancient Cities of the Bible,* Michael Carroll and Caroline Carroll (Chariot Victor Pub., 2001; Cook Communications Ministries). This 44-page reference book is from a young-earth perspective and based on the latest archaeological finds. See finds related to the Coliseum and "Fish in the Sand" (secret symbol for Christ's followers).

- **Younger Students:** *Pompeii...Buried Alive,* Edith Kunhardt (Step Into Reading, Step 3; Random House, 1983).

- **Middle and Older Students:**

(1) *Lost City of Pompeii,* Dorothy Hinshaw Patent (Marshall Cavendish, 2000).

(2) *The Buried City of Pompeii,* Shelley Tanaka (I Was There Books, Hyperion Press, 2000). A narrative history with informative sidebars, highlighted by photographs, paintings, and diagrams.

(3) *Pompeii: Exploring a Roman Ghost Town,* Ron Goor and Nancy Goor (Harper Collins, 1987). A fascinating and thorough account illustrated with many detailed black-and-white photographs.

- **Older Students:** *Pompeii: Nightmare at Midday,* Kathryn Long Humphrey (Franklin Watts, 1990). This book not only details the disaster at Pompeii but also explores the destruction of Herculaneum with the discovery of skeletons on the beach as recently as 1982.

- **Movie:** *Eyewitness: Volcano* (1996). Dorling Kindersley. This 35-minute video shows the ins and outs of volcanic activity and makes considerable mention of Mt. Vesuvius.

LESSON 10 Bar-Kokhba

- **Older Students:**

(1) *Bar Kokhba: The Rediscovery of the Legendary Hero of the Last Jewish Revolt Against Imperial Rome,* Yigael Yadin (Weidenfeld and Nicolson, 1971).

(2) *The Mystery of Bar Kokhba: An Historical and Theological Investigation of the Last King of the Jews,* Rabbi Leibel Reznick (Jason Aronson Publishers, 1996).

LESSON 12 St. Valentine

- **Younger Students:** *St. Valentine's Day,* Clyde Robert Bulla (HarperCollins Juvenile Books, 1987). Out of print—check your library.

- **Younger and Middle Students:** *Saint Valentine,* Robert Sabuda (Simon and Schuster, 1998). Stunning mosaics.

LESSON 14 Constantine I and the EDICT OF MILAN (313)

- **Movie:** *Constantine and the Cross* (1960). Starring Cornel Wilde and Christine Kaufmann. 120 minutes. Caution: Though historically accurate, the portrayal of martyrdom may be disturbing to sensitive students. Otherwise, highly recommended.

LESSON 15 The Golden Age of India

- **Younger and Middle Students:** *India: The Culture, India: The People,* and *India: The Land,* Bobbie Kalman (Crabtree Books, 1990, 2000, 2001, respectively). Series of three books, very colorful.

- **Older Students:**

(1) *Exploration into India,* Anita Garneri (New Discovery, 1994).

(2) *Great Civilizations of the East,* Daud Ali, et al. (Lorenz Books, 2003). Contains several chapters on India.

(3) With parental approval, obtain a copy of the *Mahabharata,* which contains the *Bhagavad Gita* (or "Lord's Song").

LESSON 16 The Maya

- **Younger Students:** *Ancient Civilizations: Maya,* Tami Deedrick (Raintree Steck-Vaughn, 2001).

- **Younger and Middle Students:**

(1) *The Maya,* Jane Shuter (Heinemann Library, 2002).

(2) *The Mystery of the Maya: Uncovering the Lost City of Palenque,* Peter Lourie (Boyds Mills Press, 2004). Visit the site of a real archaeological dig at the lost city of Palenque, which flourished in Mexico for almost 400 years.

- **Middle and Older Students:** *Maya Quest – The Mystery Trail,* CD-ROM (The Learning Co.). Recommended for ages 10 to 16.

- **Older Students:** *Maya Civilization,* Patricia D. Netzley (Lucent Books, 2002).

- **Movie:** From the series titled *Ancient Civilizations for Children* (a library resource), view *Ancient Maya.*

LESSON 17 St. Augustine of Hippo

- **All Students:** *Augustine: The Farmer's Boy of Tagaste,* P. De Zeeuw (Inheritance Publications, 1988).

- **Older Students:**

(1) *Letters of Saint Augustine,* edited by John Leinenweber (Triumph Books, 1993). An abbreviated version of Saint Augustine's letters that gives a good introduction and vision of Augustine the man.

(2) *The Confessions of St. Augustine,* translated by E. B. Pusey (Barnes and Noble Books, 2003). This 356-page book is not an easy read for any student, but it may be valuable for those interested in owning or examining classical original works.

LESSON 18 The Holy Bible and the Vulgate by Jerome

- **Younger Students:** *St. Jerome and the Lion,* Margaret Hodges (Orchard Books, 1991). Interesting retelling of the medieval legend, Androcles and the lion. This book is out of print—check your library.

- **Older Students:** *The Apocrypha.*

- **Movies:** *The Indestructible Book.* (Bueno Distribution). Recommended for older students. Video available through Bob Jones ShowForth This two-video (120 minutes each) commentary on the heritage of the Bible follows the Scriptures from Mt. Sinai to Plymouth Rock. For a catalog, call 1-800-845-5731 or visit showforth.bjup.com

LESSON 19 St. Patrick, Missionary to Ireland

- **All Students:** *KidsArt History: Celtic Ireland.* (KidsArt). Contains art projects, jewelry, illuminations, Irish folk art, and more. Also available: *Art History Coloring Book: Ancient Ireland.* For a catalog, call 530-926-5076 or visit kidsart.com

- **Middle Students:** *Saint Patrick: Pioneer Missionary to Ireland,* Michael J. McHugh (Christian Liberty Press, 1999).

- **Older Students:** For the activity regarding the research of Halloween—see *Handbook of Today's Religions,* Josh McDowell and Don Stewart. (Thomas Nelson Publishers, 1996).

LESSON 20 Attila the Hun

- **Middle and Older Students:**
(1) *The Greenleaf Guide to Famous Men of the Middle Ages,* Rob Shearer (Greenleaf Press, 1992).
(2) *Attila,* Steven Bela Vardy (World Leaders Past and Present, Chelsea House Publishers). This book is out of print—check your library.

LESSON 21 FALL OF THE WESTERN ROMAN EMPIRE (476)

- **Middle and Older Students:**
(1) *The Roman Empire,* Don Nardo (World History Series, Lucent Books, 1994). Chapter 7 of this excellent library book describes the fall of Rome.
(2) *The Fall of the Roman Empire,* Don Nardo (Lucent Books, March, 2004). New book that discusses some of the possible causes leading to the end of the Roman Empire.

QUARTER 2

LESSON 22 Daily Life in the Dark Ages

- **All Students:** *Life in a Medieval Castle and Village Coloring Book,* John Green (Dover, 1991).

- **Younger Students:** *The Middle Ages,* Maria Rius (Journey Through History Series, Barrons Juveniles, 1988).

- **Middle Students:** *The Middle Ages,* Jane Shuter (Heinemann, 2000).

LESSON 23 King Arthur and the Knights of the Round Table

- **All Students:**
(1) Historic model to build: Medieval Castle or Castles (KidsArt). For a catalog, phone 530-926-5076 or visit www.kidsart.com
(2) *King Arthur and His Knights* (Greathall Productions, Inc.). Audiocassettes by master storyteller Jim Weiss. (The two-tape set includes *The Three Musketeers* and *Robin Hood.*)

- **Younger Students:**
(1) *Knight in Armor Sticker Soldier,* A.G. Smith. (Dover Publication). This is a small, fun sticker book for little ones.
(2) *Knights in Armor Paper Dolls,* A.G. Smith.
(3) *Castles* (Kingfisher). Giant, colorful paperback.

- **Younger and Middle Students:**
(1) *The Sword in the Tree,* Clyde Robert Bulla (HarperTrophy, 2000). Great reader for younger kids.
(2) *Favorite Medieval Tales,* Mary Pope Osborne (Hyperion Books for Children, 2002). Some magic themes.
(3) *The Kitchen Knight,* Margaret Hodges (Holiday House 1990). A richly illustrated retelling of the first part of "The Tale of Sir Gareth of Orkney."

(4) *Knights in Shining Armor,* Gail Gibbons (Little, Brown and Co.). Colorful, short, and informative.

(5) *Knights,* Catherine Daly-Weir (All Aboard Reading Series–Level 2, Grosset and Dunlap, 1998). Colorful, 50 pages.

- **Middle and Older Students:**

(1) *King Arthur,* Don Nardo (Heroes and Villains Series, Lucent Books, 2003).

(2) *King Arthur and His Knights in Mythology,* Evelyn Wolfson (Enslow Publishers, 2002). Some magic references.

(3) *A Connecticut Yankee in King Arthur's Court,* Mark Twain (Bantam, 1994).

(4) *The Boy's King Arthur,* edited by Sidney Lanier from Thomas Malory's *King Arthur and the Knights of the Round Table;* illustrated by N.C. Wyeth (Atheneum Books for Young Readers, Simon and Schuster). Very long.

- **Older Students:**

(1) *Seafarer,* an Anglo-Saxon poem.

(2) "Holy Grail," a poem in *Idylls of the King* by Alfred, Lord Tennyson.

(3) "The Lady of Shalott," a poem by Alfred, Lord Tennyson.

- **Movie:** *Camelot* (Rated G, 1967). Stars Richard Harris and Vanessa Redgrave. Though the movie appears to glamorize the unfaithfulness of Guinevere and Lancelot, it concludes with the devastation brought by immorality. Author's all-time personal favorite musical. Exceptional casting, staging, and music. Some would find suitable for the entire family.

LESSON 24 Justinian I and Theodora, Rulers of the Byzantine Empire

- **Middle and Older Students:**

(1) *Anna of Byzantium,* Tracy Barrett (Laurel Leaf, 2000). A historical novel through the eyes of a princess.

(2) *Famous Men of the Middle Ages,* Rob Shearer (Greenleaf Press, 1992).

LESSON 25 Columba, Missionary to Scotland

- **Younger Students:** *Across a Dark & Wild Sea,* Don Brown (Roaring Brook, 2002).

- **Younger and Middle Students:** *Marguerite Makes a Book,* Bruce Robertson (J. Paul Getty Trust Pub., 1999). A lovely story about medieval bookmaking and illumination; gorgeous book; enjoyable for all ages.

LESSON 26 Early Japan and Prince Shotoku

- **All Students:** *Ancient Japanese Art* (KidsArt). Art history coloring book. Also available: *Ancient Japan,* a multicultural and historical coloring book. For a catalog, phone 530-926-5076 or visit www.kidsart.com

- **Older Students:** *Handbook of Today's Religions,* Josh McDowell and Don Stewart (Thoms Nelson Publishers, 1996). See the chapter on Shintoism.

LESSON 28 The Sui and Tang Dynasties of China

- **All Students:**

(1) *Ancient China* (See Through History), Brian Williams, (Viking Books, 1996).

(2) *Ancient Chinese Art* (KidsArt). Art history coloring book. Also available: *Ancient China,* a multicultural and historical coloring book. For a catalog, phone 530-926-5076 or visit www.kidsart.com

- **Middle Students:** *China: A History to 1949,* Valjean McLenighan (Scholastic, 1983). Covers the dynasties; some evolutionary assumptions.

- **Older Students:** *The Ancient Chinese,* Hazel Mary Martell (Silver Burdett, 1993).
- **Movie:** From the series titled *Ancient Civilizations for Children* (a library ressource), view *Ancient China.*

LESSON 29 Mohammad and the BIRTH OF ISLAM (622)
- **Middle and Older Students:** *Famous Men of the Middle Ages,* Rob Shearer (Greenleaf Press, 1992).
- **Older Students:** Due to present world conditions, there are a great number of new books on the life of Mohammed that can be obtained through your local Christian bookstore. I suggest parent and student consider these together.

LESSON 30 The Spread of Islam
- **Younger and Middle Students:** *Saladin,* Diane Stanley (HarperCollins, 2002).
- **Older Students:** Due to present world conditions, there are a great number of new books on understanding Islam that can be obtained through your local Christian bookstore. I suggest parent and student consider these together.

LESSON 31 Wu Zetian, the Empress of China
- **All Ages:** *Empress of China: Wu Ze Tian,* Cheng-an Chiang (Victory Press, 1998). Lavish illustrations.

LESSON 32 The Epic of Beowulf
- **Younger and Middle Students:** *Favorite Medieval Tales,* Mary Pope Osborne (Hyperion Books for Children, 2002). Some magic themes.
- **Middle and Older Students:**
(1) *Beowulf the Warrior,* Ian Serraillier (Bethlehem Books, 1995). Historical fiction.
(2) *Beowulf: A New Verse Translation,* Seamus Heaney (W.W. Norton, 2001). Available in book and audio versions.
- **Older Students:** *After the Flood,* Bill Cooper and B. A. Hons (New Wine Press, 1995). Fascinating text. Can be found online at www.ldolphin.org/cooper

LESSON 33 Al-Andalus: "The Ornament of the World" in Medieval Spain
- **Older Students:**
(1) *The Ornament of the World,* Maria Rosa Menocal (Little Brown and Co., 2002) Available in hardcover and paperback. Though not necessarily Christian in its view, this is a very interesting read about the mixed culture of medieval Spain.
(2) *Moorish Spain,* Richard Fletcher (University of California Press, 1993). A summary of the 700 years of Islamic rule in Moorish Spain.

LESSON 34 St. Boniface, Apostle to Germany
- **Middle and Older Students:**
Trial and Triumph: Stories From Church History, Richard M. Hanula (Canon Press, 1999). See Chapter 9.
- **Older Students:** *The Letters of St. Boniface,* translated by Ephraim Emerton (Columbia University Press, 2000).

LESSON 35 The Iconoclast Movement
- **Middle and Older Students:** *The Story of Christianity,* Michael Collins and Matthew Price (DK Books, 1999).

LESSON 36 Charles Martel and the BATTLE OF TOURS (732)

- **Middle and Older Students:** *Famous Men of the Middle Ages,* Rob Shearer (Greenleaf Press, 1992).

LESSON 37 Charlemagne

- **Younger and Middle Students:** *Favorite Medieval Tales,* Mary Pope Osborne (Hyperion Books for Children, 2002). See the chapter on *The Song of Roland.*

- **Middle and Older Students:**

(1) *Son of Charlemagne,* Barbara Willard (Bethlehem Books, 1998). Historical fiction.
(2) *The Importance of Charlemagne,* Timothy Levi Biel (Greenhaven Press, 1997).
(3) *Famous Men of the Middle Ages,* Rob Shearer (Greenleaf Press, 1992).
(4) *Trial and Triumph: Stories From Church History,* Richard M. Hanula (Canon Press, 1999). See Chapter 10.
(5) *The Song of Roland,* an epic poem.

LESSON 38 The Thousand and One Nights: Tales from Arabia

- **All Students:** *Arabian Nights,* (Greathall Productions, Inc.). Audiocassettes by master storyteller Jim Weiss. (The two-tape set includes *The Jungle Book.*)

- **Middle Students:** *Shadow Spinner,* Susan Fletcher (Aladdin, 1999). Great read-aloud for all ages; a story that will keep you at the edge of your seat.

- **Middle and Older Students:**

(1) *The Arabian Nights,* illustrated (Junior Library Edition).
(2) *The Seven Voyages of Sinbad,* John Yeoman, illustrations by Quentin Blake (Chrysalis Books, 2003). Another great read aloud filled with adventure, shipwrecks, sea monsters, and more.

LESSON 39 INVASION OF THE VIKINGS (793) and

LESSON 40 The Vikings: Their Families, Their Homes, and Their Faith

- **All Students:**

(1) *Vikings* (KidsArt). Art history coloring book. For a catalog, phone 530-926-5076 or visit www.kidsart.com
(2) *Story of the Vikings Coloring Book,* A.G. Smith (Dover Coloring Book). Very detailed.
(3) *Viking,* Susan M. Margeson (Eyewitness Books, DK Publishing). Color pictures.
(4) *Documentary: The Vikings* (Nova, 2000). Two hours.
(5) Historic model to build: Viking Settlement (KidsArt). For a catalog, phone 530-926-5076 or visit www.kidsart.com

- **Younger and Middle Students:**

(1) *If You Were There: Viking Times,* Anthony Mason (Simon and Schuster Children's Publishing, 1997).
(2) *You Wouldn't Want to Be a Viking Explorer,* Andrew Langley (Franklin Watts, 2000).
(3) *Adventures with the Vikings,* Linda Bailey (Kids Can Press, 2001).
(4) *Viking Adventure,* Clyde Robert Bulla. Fiction.
(5) *Who Were the Vikings?* (Usborne Starting Point History, E.D.C. Publishing, 2002).
(6) *The Viking World,* Philippa Wingate and Dr. Anne Millard (Usborne Illustrated World History, E.D.C. Publishing, 1994). Busy pages full of fascinating detail and illustrations.
(7) *Hands-On Heritage: Viking Activity Book* (Edupress).

- **Middle Students:** *Beorn the Proud,* Madeline Polland (1961). The author weaves a Christian theme into a story of captivity and adventure set in Viking times.

- **Middle and Older Students:**

(1) *The Vikings and Jorvik,* Hazel Mary Martel (Silver Burdett Press, 1993).

(2) *The Vikings,* Elizabeth Janeway (Landmark Books). Nonfiction.

(3) *Viking Explorers,* Luigi Pruneti (Peter Bedrick, 2001).

(4) *The Viking News,* Rachel Wright, Richard Hall (Candlewick Press).

(5) *The Story of Rolf and the Viking Bow,* Allen French (Adventure Library Series, Bethlehem Books, 1995).

- **Movie:** *The Vikings* (1958, not rated). Starring Kirk Douglas. Good historical depiction of Viking life. Though not acted out, this film does contain reference to rape and immorality.

LESSON 42 Alfred the Great, King of England

- **Younger and Middle Students:** *Anglo-Saxon Helmet* (British Museum Press, 1993).

- **Middle and Older Students:**

(1) *The Dragon & the Raven: Or the Days of King Arthur,* G. A. Henty (PrestonSpeed Publications, 1995). Historical fiction.

(2) *Famous Men of the Middle Ages,* Rob Shearer (Greenleaf Press, 1992).

(3) *Augustine Came to Kent,* Barbara Willard (Bethlehem Books, 1996).

(4) *Trial and Triumph: Stories From Church History,* Richard M. Hanula (Canon Press, 1999). SeeChapter 11.

QUARTER 3

LESSON 43 Lydveldid Island (Iceland)

- **Middle and Older Students:** *The Story of Rolf and the Viking Bow,* Allen French (Adventure Library Series, Bethlehem Books, 1995). Entertaining historical fiction.

LESSON 44 The Maori of New Zealand

- **Middle Students:**

(1) *The Maoris,* Charles Higham (Cambridge Introduction to World History, Cambridge University Press, 1983).

(2) *New Zealand,* Mary Virginia Fox (Enchantment of the World Series, Chicago Children's Press, 1995).

LESSON 45 The Great Zimbabwe of Africa

- **All Students:** *Art of Africa* (KidsArt). African wildlife, masks, metalwork, textiles, and more. Also available: *African Art,* a multicultural and historical coloring book. For a catalog, phone 530-926-5076 or visit www.kidsart.com

- **Middle Students:**

(1) *Exploration into Africa,* Isimeme Ibazebo (New Discovery Books). Covers African history, including a chapter on the Great Zimbabwe.

(2) *Great African Kingdoms,* Sean Sheehan (Ancient World Series, RSVP Publishers).

- **Middle and Older Students:** *Africa,* Jocelyn Murray (Cultural Atlas for Young People Series, Facts on File, 1990). Some evolution.

- **Movie:** From the series titled *Ancient Civilizations for Children* (a library resource), view *Ancient Africa.*

LESSON 46 "Good King Wenceslas"

- **Younger Students:** *Good King Wenceslas,* John Mason Neale, woodcut illustrations by Christopher Manson (North-South Books, 1994)

LESSON 47 Otto I and the Holy Roman Empire

- **Younger Students:** For Activity 47A: Obtain any version of Grimm's fairy tales.

LESSON 48 Vladimir I of Russia

- **Younger Students:** *Look What Came From Russia,* Miles Harvey (Franklin Watts, 1999).
- **Middle Students:** *Russia,* Kathleen Berton Murrell (Eyewitness Books, DK Publishing, 2000).
- **Older Students:** *War and Peace,* Leo Tolstoy.

LESSON 51 Eric the Red and the Settlement of Greenland

- **Younger Students:** *The Polar Regions–the Arctic–The Antarctic,* Marie Hablitzel and Kim Stitzer (Draw-Write-Now Series, Book 4, Barker Creek Publishing, 1997). Available at www.kingsharvest.com
- **Younger and Middle Students:** *Eric the Red,* Neil Grant (What's Their Story? Series, Oxford University Press, 1998).
- **Middle and Older Students:** *Greenland Mummies,* Janet Buell (Time Traveler Series, 21st Century, 1998).
- **Older Students:**
(1) *The Greenlanders Saga.* (Original work by Jon Tordarsson in 1380; completed by Magnus Torhallsson.)
(2) *The Saga of Eric the Red.* (Original work by Hauk Erlendsson, born in 1265.)
(3) *Land Under the Pole Star,* Helge Ingstad (St. Martin's Press, 1966). This book pulls many excerpts from the original sagas listed above.

LESSON 52 LEIF ERICSSON DISCOVERS AMERICA (c. 1003)

- **Younger and Middle Students:**
(1) *Leif Eriksson Norwegian Explorer,* Cynthia Klingel (Child's World, 2003). A brief introduction to the life and accomplishments of the Norwegian explorer.
(2) *Leif the Lucky,* Ingri and Edgar D'Aulaire (Beautiful Feet Books, 1994). A beautifully illustrated read-aloud for younger students or stands on its own for middle students.
- **Middle and Older Students:** *Leif Eriksson and the Vikings,* Charnan Simon (World's Great Explorers Series, Scholastic Library Pub., 1991).
- **Older Students:**
(1) *The Greenlanders Saga.* (Original work by Jon Tordarsson in 1380; completed by Magnus Torhallsson.)
(2) *The Saga of Eric the Red.* (Original work by Hauk Erlendsson, born in 1265.)
(3) *Land Under the Pole Star,* Helge Ingstad (St. Martin's Press, 1966). This book pulls many excerpts from the original sagas listed above.

LESSON 53 Macbeth, King of Scotland

- **Younger Students:**
(1) *Macbeth: For Kids,* Lois Burdett (Firefly Books, 1996).
(2) *Castle,* David Macaulay (Houghton Mifflin Books, 1982). Beautiful black-and-white detail of castle architecture.
- **Younger and Middle Students:** *Beautiful Stories from Shakespeare for Children,* E. Nesbitt (Smithmark, 1997). A wonderful resource with 20 of Shakespeare's best dramas and comedies written so that children can understand and enjoy them.
- **Older Students:** *Macbeth* by William Shakespeare.

- **Movie:** *Macbeth*. A ShowForth Video, produced by Classic Players. Acted out by Dr. and Mrs. Bob Jones III. 129 minutes. For a catalog, call 1-800-845-5731 or visit showforth.bjup.com

LESSON 54 El Cid, a Spanish Hero

- **Younger and Middle Students:** *Ballad of El Cid*, Vincent Buranelli (Classics for Kids, Silver Burdett Press, 1985).
- **Middle Students:** *El Cid*, Geraldine McCaughrean (Oxford Illustrated Classics, Oxford University Press, 2002).
- **Middle and Older Students:** *Famous Men of the Middle Ages*, Rob Shearer (Greenleaf Press, 1992).
- **Older Students:**
(1) *Classic Spanish Stories and Plays*, Marcel Charles Andrade (McGraw Hill, 2001). Eight classics from 1140 to 1630, including El Cid and Don Quixote.
(2) *The Poem of the Cid: A Bilingual Edition with Parallel Text*, edited by Ian Michael and Rita Hamilton (Penguin Classic, 1985). This received a 4½-star rating on Internet reviews.
- **Opera:** *El Cid* by Jules Massenet. Available from CBS Records Masterworks (Austria, 1989)
- **Movie:** *El Cid* (1961). Allied Artists, Starring Charlton Heston.

LESSON 55 William the Conqueror and the BATTLE OF HASTINGS (1066)

- **All Students:** *Middle Ages*, Mike Corbishley (Cultural Atlas for Young People Series, Facts On File, 2003). Ancient burial mounds, the Doomsday book, and the Bayeux Tapestry.
- **Younger Students:** *Cathedral: The Story of Its Construction*, David Macaulay (Houghton Mifflin/Walter Lorraine Books, 1981). High-quality illustrations!
- **Younger and Middle Students:** *Don't Know Much About the Kings and Queens of England*, Kenneth C. Davis, (HarperCollins, 2002). Interesting read for kids and adults.
- **Middle and Older Students:**
(1) *The King's Shadow*, Elizabeth Alder (Aladdin, 2001). Historical fiction.
(2) *Hastings*, Samuel Willard Crompton (Battles That Changed the World Series, Chelsea House Publications, 2002).
(3) *Striped Ships*, Eloise McGraw (Simon and Schuster, 1991). Historical fiction. Follows the life of a young girl in 1066 who eventually ends up working on the Bayeux Tapestry.
(4) *Famous Men of the Middle Ages*, Rob Shearer (Greenleaf Press, 1992).
- **Older Students:** *1066: The Year of the Conquest*, David Howarth (Penguin, 1981). Includes maps and illustrations.

LESSON 57 THE EARLY CRUSADES (1096)

- **All Students:** *Paper Soldiers of the Middle Ages* (KidsArt). For a catalog, phone 530-926-5076 or visit www.kidsart.com
- **Middle Students:** *The Crusades*, John Child et al. (P. Bedrick, 1996).
- **Middle and Older Students:** *The Ramsay Scallop*, Francis Temple (HarperTrophy, 1995). Historical fiction; 14-year-old Elenor of Ramsay is sent on a religious pilgrimage with her betrothed, a man who has just returned from the Crusades.

LESSON 58 The Petrobrusians and the Waldensians

- **Younger (As a Read-Aloud) and Middle Students:** *Paula the Waldensian*, Eva Lecomte, translated by W. M. Strong (A.B Publishing, Inc., 1940). This book is a pure delight; historical fiction from a strong Christian perspective. (Available through Inheritance Publications, 1-800-563-3594.)

- **Middle and Older Students:** *Trial and Triumph: Stories From Church History,* Richard M. Hanula (Canon Press, 1999). See Chapter 14.
- **Adults:** *The Waldensian Dissent: Persecution and Survival, c. 1170–c. 1570,* Gabriel Audisio (Cambridge University Press, 1999).

LESSON 59 Eleanor of Aquitaine, the Queen of Two Nations

- **Younger and Middle Students:** *Don't Know Much About the Kings and Queens of England,* Kenneth C. Davis, (HarperCollins, 2002). Henry II and Eleanor of Aquitaine (see p. 10).
- **Middle and Older Students:**

(1) *Queen Eleanor: Independent Spirit of the Medieval World,* Polly Schoyer Brooks (Houghton Mifflin, 1999).

(2) *A Proud Taste for Scarlet and Miniver,* E.L. Konigsburg (Yearling, 1985). Fantasy fiction by an award-winning author.

- **Older Students:**

(1) *Eleanor of Aquitaine: A Life,* Alison Weir (Ballantine Books, 2001).

(2) *Eleanor of Aquitaine and the Four Kings,* Amy Ruth Kelly (Harvard Press, 1974).

(3) *If All the Swords in England: A Story of Thomas Becket,* Barbara Willard (Living History Library Series, Bethlehem Books, 2000).

- **Movie:** *The Lion in Winter* (1968. rated PG). Starring Peter O'Toole and Katharine Hepburn. One of author's personal favorites due to the role of Katherine Hepburn, but be cautious of the immoral themes true to the time period.

LESSON 60 The Jews of the Middle Ages

- **Movie:** *Fiddler on the Roof* (1971). Though not the exact time period of the lesson, this touching musical classic depicts the love of a Jewish family.

LESSON 61 Richard the Lionhearted, Saladin, and the Third Crusade

- **All Students:**

(1) *In the Time of Knights,* Shelley Tanaka (I Was There Series, Hyperion Books for Children, 2000). A fictionalized story of the world's greatest knight.

(2) *Coat of Arms,* Catherine Daly-Weir (Grosset and Dunlap, 2000). Well-presented, easy-to-follow activity book.

- **Younger Students:** *The Making of a Knight: How Sir James Earned His Armor,* Patrick O'Brien (Charlesbridge Publishing, 1998).

- **Middle Students:**

(1) *Richard the Lionheart and the Crusades,* Christopher Gibb (Life and Times Series, Bookwright Press, 1986) One of the best summaries of the Crusades I've read.

(2) *The Lost Baron,* Allen French (Bethlehem Books, 2001). Historical fiction set in Cornwall in the year 1200.

(3) *Winning His Spurs: A Story of the Crusades,* G. A. Henty (PrestonSpeed Publications, 2000). Historical fiction full of adventure and excitement. You'll feel like you were there!

LESSON 62 The Classic Tale of Robin Hood

- **All Students:** *The Three Musketeers* and *Robin Hood* (Greathall Productions, Inc.). Audiocassettes by master storyteller Jim Weiss. (The two-tape set includes *King Arthur and His Knights.*)

- **Younger and Middle Students:**

(1) *Robin Hood of Sherwood Forest,* Ann McGovern (Scholastic Junior Classics, 2001) Ten adventures of the legendary hero and his band of loyal men.

(2) *Favorite Medieval Tales,* Mary Pope Osborne (Hyperion Books for Children, 2002) Some magic themes.

(3) *Great Illustrated Classics:Ivanhoe,* Sir Walter Scott, adapted by Malvina G. Vogel (Baronet Books, 1994). This is an "easy reader" with large print and illustrations.

- **Middle Students:**

(1) *Robin Hood,* Neil Philip (Gerstenberg, 1998). Includes both the Robin Hood story and information on life in the Middle Ages.

(2) *Ivanhoe for Children* (Wishbone Classic). A good children's version of the classic by Sir Walter Scott.

- **Older Students:** *Ivanhoe,* Sir Walter Scott.

- **Movies:**

(1) *Robin Hood* (1973, rated G). Walt Disney Home Video.

(2) *Robert and Marian* (1976). Starring Sean Connery and Audrey Hepburn.

LESSON 63 The Shoguns and Samurai of Japan

- **Younger and Middle Students:** *Samurai Warriors,* Jenny Roberts (History Highlights Series, Scholastic Library Pub., 1990). Colorful and informative.

- **Older Students:** *Life Among the Samurai,* Eleanor J. Hall (Greenhaven Press, 1999).

QUARTER 4

NONFICTION

- **Older Students:** *The Story of Liberty,* Charles Coffin, (Maranatha Publications, 1997) First published in 1879; a fascinating portrayal of God's hand at work in establishing human freedom. Strongly Calvinist.

FICTION

- **All Students:** *The Apple and the Arrow,* Conrad Buff (Houghton Mifflin, 2001). A 1952 Newbery Honor Book.

- **Younger Students:** *The Legend of William Tell,* Terry Small (Bantam Little Rooster Book, Random House, 1991). A lavish blend of rhyme and illustrations.

- **Middle Students:** *William Tell,* Leonard Everett Fisher (Farrar, Straus and Giroux, 1996).

- **Middle and Older Students:**

(1) *The Trumpeter of Krakow,* Eric Kelly (Simon and Schuster, 1968). The 1929 Newbery medal winner.

(2) *The Lion of St. Mark,* G. A. Henty (Robinson Books, 2002). This story takes place in 1380 in Venice, Italy.

- **Older Students:** *Men of Iron,* Howard Pyle (Timeless Classics, Dover Publications, 2003).

LESSON 64 St. Francis of Assisi, St. Clara, and St. Dominic

- **Younger Students:** *St. Francis of Assisi,* Nina Bawden (Random House Children's Books, 1983). Out of print—check your library.

- **Younger and Middle Students:** *Saint Francis,* Brian Wildsmith (Wm. B. Eerdmans Publishing, 1996). A beautiful book.

- **Middle and Older Students:** *Trial and Triumph: Stories From Church History*, Richard M. Hanula (Canon Press, 1999). See Chapter 15.

LESSON 65 The Children's Crusade

- **Younger Students:** *The Pied Piper of Hamelin,* Robert Browning and Kate Greenaway (Alfred A. Knopf, 1993).
- **Middle and Older Students:** *A Journey of Souls,* C.D. Baker (PrestonSpeed Publications, 2000). Fictional account of the most tragic of all crusades. A newer version by the same author is called *Crusade of Tears: A Novel of the Children's Crusade* (Chariot Victor Publications, 2004).
- **Older Students:**
(1) *An Army of Children,* Evan H. Rhodes (Bantam Dell Publishing Group, 1978). Out of print—check with your library.
(2) *The Children's Crusade: A History,* George Zabriskie Gray (William Morrow, 1972).
(3) *The Blind Cross: A Novel of the Children's Crusade,* Michael Mott (Delacorte Press, 1969).
(4) *Experiencing God,* Henry Blackaby. Book, devotional and journal, workbook, and related products. Published by Broadman and Holman Publishers and also by Lifeway Christian Resources.

LESSON 66 King John and the Magna Carta

- **Middle Students:** *Adam of the Road,* Elizabeth Janet Gray (Puffin Newbery Library, Puffin Books, 1987). A 1943 Newbery winner. Story of Adam's travels around England in the 1200s.
- **Middle and Older Students:** *The Magna Charta,* James Daugherty (Landmark Books).

LESSON 67 Frederick II, "The Amazement of the World"

- **Middle and Older Students:** *The King's Road,* Cecelia Holland (Simon and Schuster, 1970). An adventure story of what might have happened in Frederigo's unorthodox and unkingly childhood.
- **Older Students:** *The 100 Most Important Events in Christian History,* Curtis, Lang, and Petersen (Fleming H. Revell, 1991).

LESSON 68 St. Thomas Aquinas, Philosopher of the Middle Ages

- **Middle Students:** *St. Thomas Aquinas: The Story of the Dumb Ox,* Mary Fabyan Windeatt (TAN Books and Publishers, 1994).

LESSON 69 Roger Bacon, Scientist of the Middle Ages

- **Middle and Older Students:** *The First Scientist: A Life of Roger Bacon,* Brian Clegg (Carroll and Graf Publishers, 2004).

LESSON 70 The Great Khans and the Mongol Invasion of China

- **All Students:** *The King and His Hawk* A short story retold by James Baldwin in *The Book of Virtues* by William J. Bennett (Simon and Schuster, 1993). See pp. 37–39.
- **Middle Students:** *Genghis Khan and the Mongol Horde,* Harold Lamb (Linnet Books, 1990).
- **Older Students:**
(1) *Storm from the East: From Ghengis Khan to Khubilai Khan,* Robert Marshall, (University of California Press, 1993) Based on the BBC documentary of the same name.
(2) The poem *Xanadu: The Ballad of Kublai Khan* by Samuel Taylor Coleridge. Web source: www.zyra.org.uk/kublai.htm

LESSON 71 MARCO POLO TRAVELS EAST (1271)

- **Younger and Middle Students:**
(1) *Marco Polo,* Charles Parlin Graves (Junior World Explorers Books, Chelsea House, 2002).
(2) *Marco Polo: A Journey Through China,* Fiona MacDonald (Franklin Watts, 1998).
(3) *The Silk Route,* John S. Major (HarperTrophy, 1996).

- **Middle and Older Students:**
(1) *Marco Polo for Kids: His Marvelous Journey to China,* Janis Herbert (Chicago Review Press, 2001). Story of his journey, plus activities.
(2) *Marco Polo and the Medieval Explorers,* Rebecca Stefoff (Chelsea House, 1992).
(3) *Famous Men of the Middle Ages,* Rob Shearer (Greenleaf Press, 1992).

LESSON 72 Sir William Wallace and Robert Bruce: "Bravehearts" of Scotland

- **Middle and Older Students:**
(1) *In Freedom's Cause: A Story of Wallace and Bruce,* G. A. Henty (Dover Publications, 2002). Historical fiction.
(2) *The Scottish Chiefs,* Jane Porter, illustrations by N. C. Wyeth (Athenium, 1991).
(3) *Famous Men of the Middle Ages,* Rob Shearer (Greenleaf Press, 1992).

- **Older Students:**
(1) *The King's Swift Rider,* Mollie Hunter (HarperCollins, 1998). Historical fiction, much battle violence.
(2) The poem *Bruce to His Men at Bannockburn* by Robert Burns.

LESSON 73 Dante Alighieri, Poet of the Middle Ages

- **Older Students:** *The Divine Comedy* by Dante Alighieri.

LESSON 74 The Aztecs (The Mexica)

- **All Students:** *Inca and Aztec* (KidsArt). A multicultural and historical coloring book. For a catalog, phone 530-926-5076 or visit www.kidsart.com

- **Middle and Older Students:**
(1) *Life in the Time of Moctezuma and the Aztecs,* Roy Burrell (Steck-Vaughn, 1993).
(2) *Aztec, Inca and Maya,* Elizabeth Baquedano (Eyewitness Books, DK Publishing, 2000).
(3) *The Aztec Empire,* R. Conrad Stein (Cultures of the Past Series, Benchmark Books, 1996).

LESSON 75 The Hundred Years' War

- **Middle and Older Students:**
(1) *The White Company,* Sir Arthur Conan Doyle (HarperCollins, 1988).
(2) *The Hundred Years' War,* William Lace (Lucent Books, 1994).
(3) *St. George for England: A Tale of Cressy and Poitiers in the Years 1337–1453,* G. A. Henty (PrestonSpeed Publications, 2000). The beginning of the Hundred Years' War.

- **Older Students:**
(1) *Henry V* by Shakespeare.
(2) The poem *Battle of Agincourt* by Michael Drayton.

LESSON 76 The Black Death of Europe

- **Middle and Older Students:**
(1) *The Black Death,* Phyllis Corzine (Gale Group, 1997).
(2) *A Parcel of Patterns,* Jill Paton Walsh (Aerial, 1992). Historical fiction.

- **Older Students:**

(1) *The Black Death,* edited by Don Nardo (Turning Points in World History Series, Gale Group, 1999).

(2) *Decameron* by Giovanni Boccaccio.

LESSON 77 The Ming Dynasty of China and the Forbidden City

- **Older Students:** *The Examination,* Malcolm Bosse (Farrar, Straus and Giroux, 1996). Two brothers face famine, flood, pirates, and rivals as they journey through China. Fiction.s

LESSON 78 JOHN WYCLIFFE, "MORNING STAR OF THE REFORMATION (1377)

- **Middle and Older Students:**

(1) *The Beggars' Bible,* Louise Vernon (Herald Press, 1971).

(2) *Morning Star of the Reformation,* Andy Thomson (Light Line Series, Bob Jones University Press, 1988).

(3) *Trial and Triumph: Stories From Church History,* Richard M. Hanula (Canon Press, 1999). See Chapter 18.

- **Movies:**

(1) *Wycliffe: The Morning Star.* Gateway Films.

(2) *John Wycliffe: The Morning Star.* Vision Videos. Available through Bob Jones ShowForth Videos. 75 minutes. This piece earned "Best Film" from the Christian Film Distributors Association. For a catalog, call 1-800-845-5731 or visit showforth.bjup.com

LESSON 79 Geoffrey Chaucer and The Canterbury Tales

- **Younger Students:**

(1) *Chanticleer and the Fox,* Geoffrey Chaucer, adapted and illustrated by Barbara Cooney (HarperCollins, 1989). A Caldecott Medal winner.

(2) *Favorite Medieval Tales,* Mary Pope Osborne (Hyperion Books for Children, 2002).

- **Middle Students:**

(1) *The Canturbury Tales,* Geoffrey Chaucer, adapted by Geraldine McCaughrean (Puffin Classics, 1997).

(2) *The Canturbury Tales,* Geoffrey Chaucer, adapted by Barbara Cohen, illustrated by Trina Schart Hyman (Lothrop Publications, 1988). Lovely illustrations may make it suffice as a read-aloud for younger students.

- **Middle and Older Students:**

(1) *Life in the Middle Ages: The Church,* Kathryn Hinds (Benchmark Books, 2000). Includes excerpts from The Canterbury *Tales.* Informative and beautifully illustrated.

(2) *Geoffrey Chaucer Selected Canterbury Tales* (Dover Thrift Editions, Unabridged. 1994). This paperback edition makes reading Chaucer much more enjoyable.

(3) Other works by Chaucer include *Troilus and Criseyde* and *The Legend of Good Women.*

- **Movie:** *Black Shield of Falworth* (1954). Starring Tony Curtis and Janet Leigh. This older movie is a great summary of life, love, and politics from this time period.

LESSON 80 John Huss

- **Middle and Older Students:**

(1) *The Trial and Burning of John Huss!* An Eyewitness Account By a Member of the Council of Constance (Wittenburg Publications). This is a riveting and powerful retelling of the event. (Available through Inheritance Publications, 1-800-563-3594.)

(2) *Crushed Yet Conquering,* Deborah Alcock. (Also available through Inheritance Publications, 1-800-563-3594.)

(3) *Trial and Triumph: Stories From Church History,* Richard M. Hanula (Canon Press, 1999). See Chapter 18.

- **Movie:** *John Huss.* Vision Video. Available through Bob Jones ShowForth Videos. 55 minutes. This piece earned "Best Film of the Year" from the Academy of Cinematographic Arts. For a catalog, call 1-800-845-5731 or visit showforth.bjup.com

LESSON 81 The Life and DEATH OF JOAN OF ARC (1431)

- **Younger and Middle Students:** *Joan of Arc,* Diane Stanley (HarperTrophy, 2002). Terrific text and illustrations.
- **Middle Students:** *Joan of Arc,* Nancy Ross (Random Library, 1963).
- **Middle and Older Students:**

(1) *Personal Recollections of Joan of Arc,* Mark Twain (Gramercy Books, 1995). First published in Harpers magazine in 1895. Mark Twain spent 12 years researching this fascinating subject.

(2) *Famous Men of the Middle Ages,* Rob Shearer (Greenleaf Press, 1992).

(3) *St. Joan,* George Bernard Shaw (1923).

- **Movie:** *The Passion of Joan of Arc* (1928, no rating). Internet review stated, "Greatest performance ever to be captured on film. It was initially banned in England for being so powerful. Based on actual trial transcripts." Also, view one of the more modern films on Joan of Arc.

LESSON 82 The Inkas of South America

- **Younger and Middle Students:** *The Incas and Machu Picchu,* Philip Steele (Silver Burdett Press, 1993).
- **Middle Students:** *Machu Picchu: The Story of the Amazing Inkas and Their City in the Clouds,* Elizabeth Mann (Wonders of the World Book, Mikaya Press, 2000). Excellent text.
- **Middle and Older Students:** *Aztec, Inca and Maya,* Elizabeth Baquedano (Eyewitness Books, DK Publishing, 2000).
- **Older Students:** *Atlas of Past Worlds: A Comparative Chronology of Human History 2000 BC–AD 1500,* John Manley (Cassell Books, London; distributed in the U. S. by Sterling Publishers, New York; 1993).
- **Movie:** From the series titled *Ancient Civilizations for Children* (a library resource), view *Ancient Inca.*

LESSON 83 The Ottoman Turks Take Constantinople

- **Middle and Older Students:** *The Ottoman Empire,* Adriane Ruggiero (Cultures of the Past Series, Benchmark Books).

LESSON 84 Johannes Gutenberg Invents the Printing Press

- **Younger and Middle Students:** *Book,* Karen Brookfield (Eyewitness Books, DK Publishing, 1993). Several references to Johannes Gutenberg and the Gutenberg Bible. A fascinating look at bookmaking from the very beginning; includes many photographs.
- **Middle Students:**

(1) *Ink on His Fingers,* Louise A. Vernon (Herald Press, 2002).

(2) *Fine Print: A Story About Johann Gutenberg,* Joann Johansen Burch (Carolrhoda Books, 1992).

- **Middle and Older Students:** *Famous Men of the Middle Ages,* Rob Shearer (Greenleaf, 1992).

Course Recommendations:
Bible
3-ring binder for each student with 8 tab dividers
Bible dictionary
Globe
Rand McNally *Answer Atlas* (ISBN: 0-528-83872-5)
Rand McNally *Historical Atlas of the World* (ISBN: 528-83969-1)
The Student Bible Atlas by Tim Dowley (ISBN: 0-8066-2038-2)
Colored pencils: brown, blue, purple, red, gray, pink, black, green, yellow, orange

Memory Cards:
3″x5″ ruled index cards (with 2 holes punched in the top) Oxford Index Card Binder (item No. 73501)
Light purple marker
Gray marker Yellow
highlighter

Timeline:
Pattern-cutting board (sewing board) or use a notebook
History Through the Ages—Resurrection to Revolution ©2003 by Amy Pak, Homeschooling in the Woods
Poster board or plain index cards if you make your own figures

LESSON ACTIVITIES, REVIEWS, EXERCISES, AND SUPPLEMENTAL ACTIVITIES

Lesson	Younger Students	Middle Students	Older Students
QTR. 1 BEGINS			
1		Bible	Tape recorder or video camera
2	Blindfold		Newspaper
3	Missionary's address	Bible, Bible map	Bible dictionary
Field Trip	Visit a synagogue		
Review 1	OL Map 1, "Mediterranean" OL Map 2, "Eastern Mediterranean" Blue, green, red colored pencils Globe, Bible atlas, modern atlas	OL Map 1, "Mediterranean" OL Map 2, "Eastern Mediterranean" Blue, green, red colored pencils Globe, Bible atlas, modern atlas	OL Map 1, "Mediterranean" OL Map 2, "Eastern Mediterranean" Blue, green, red colored pencils Globe, Bible atlas, modern atlas

Lesson	Younger Students	Middle Students	Older Students
Exercise 1	Bible	Bible	Bible
4	Act. Supp. 4A Medium-weight cardboard Tape, scissors, hole-punch 6 rubber bands Crayons, markers, or fabric paint	Act. Supp. 4C Picture of ruins of the Colosseum Picture of Christian fish symbol from catacombs	Act. Supp. 4C Picture of ruins of the Colosseum Picture of Christian fish symbol from catacombs
5	Spice-scented candle	Foxe's *Christian Martyrs of the World*	*Quo Vadis* movie starring Peter Ustinov
6	Notebook paper, colored pencils	Bible encyclopedia	Bible encyclopedia, original works of Josephus
Review 2	OL Map 1, "Mediterranean" Ruler, paper, scissors Historical atlas, map of Italy, Bible atlas	OL Map 1, "Mediterranean" Ruler, paper, scissors Historical atlas, map of Italy, Bible atlas	OL Map 1, "Mediterranean" Ruler, paper, scissors Historical atlas, map of Italy, Bible atlas
7	Cardboard, ribbon, markers Dehydrated foods such as raisins, soup, prunes, beef jerky, dried apples	Several large plastic bowls Mesh cloth, colored pencils Rubber bands or string Clean rocks or weights Pictures of battering ram and assault tower	*The Jewish War* by Josephus
8	Paper, 4 black tea bags, pot, water Tongs, shoes, matches, pencils 3-hole plastic sleeve for notebook	Epsom salt, scissors, water, camera Black construction paper Small plastic container with a lid Foil pie pan or shallow saucer	Bible dictionary
9	Short plastic bottle (ex: 8-oz. water bottle) Vinegar, funnel, baking soda Red food coloring, dirt, water Liquid dish soap	Short plastic bottle (ex: 8- oz. water bottle) Vinegar, funnel, baking soda Red food coloring, dirt, water Liquid dish soap	Act. Supp. 9C *Pompeii: Nightmare at Midday* by Kathryn Long Humphrey, Franklin Watts, 1990.
Review 3	OL Map 3, "World" Atlas, Bible atlas	OL Map 3, "World" Atlas, Bible atlas	OL Map 3, "World" Atlas, Bible atlas
Exercise 3	Colored pencils: pink, black, green, yellow, orange, red, gray, purple, blue, brown	Colored pencils: pink, black, green, yellow, orange, red, gray, purple, blue, brown	Colored pencils: pink, black, green, yellow, orange, red, gray, purple, blue, brown

Lesson	Younger Students	Middle Students	Older Students
10	3 lbs. mulch, sand, potting soil, or leaves & pine needles Medium-sized box (somewhat larger than a shoebox) Hand/garden shovel, newspaper Large slotted spoon, tongs, and/or tweezers Small paint brush, camera Permanent marker Several sandwich-sized plastic bags Colander and/or strainer		
10	Choose a few relics to hide. Relics: coins (foreign and/or local) Sandal, small mirror, small tool Coffee mug, ball of yarn Scrap pieces of fabric Blank stationery, raffia ribbon Wrinkled documents with the name "Bar-Kokhba" included		
10	Old lipstick or lip balm tube Black spray paint (optional), Bible Small strips of paper, writing pen Hot-glue gun Narrow strip of cloth (1/2" wide and long enough to tie around student's head or wrist)	Old lipstick or lip balm tube Black spray paint (optional), Bible Small strips of paper, writing pen Hot-glue gun Narrow strip of cloth (1/2" wide and long enough to tie around student's head or wrist)	
11	Act. Supp. 11B Water, pot, tongs, shoes, matches 3-hole plastic sleeve for notebook 4 black tea bags, dictionary	Act. Supp. 11B Water, pot, tongs, shoes, matches 3-hole plastic sleeve for notebook 4 black tea bags, dictionary	Act. Supp. 11B
12	Sugar cookie ingredients Paper, markers		*Handbook of Today's Religions* by Josh McDowell and Don Stewart, Thomas Nelson Publishers, 1996.
Field Trip		Visit a chocolate factory	Visit a chocolate factory

Lesson	Younger Students	Middle Students	Older Students
Review 4	OL Map 4, "Israel" OL Map 5, "Review 4 Answer Key" Bible atlas with topographical or relief map of Israel or ancient Palestine Salt, white flour, water, tape, globe Food coloring, toothpicks, paper Cardboard (10" x 13"), camera Soft tape measure	OL Map 4, "Israel" OL Map 5, "Review 4 Answer Key" Bible atlas with topographical or relief map of Israel or ancient Palestine Salt, white flour, water, tape, globe Food coloring, toothpicks, paper Cardboard (10" x 13"), camera Soft tape measure	OL Map 4, "Israel" OL Map 5, "Review 4 Answer Key" Bible atlas with topographical or relief map of Israel or ancient Palestine Salt, white flour, water, tape, globe Food coloring, toothpicks, paper Cardboard (10" x 13"), camera Soft tape measure
13	OL Map 6, "United States" (2 copies) Fine-point pen, scissors, glue Plastic bag that zips closed Crayons or colored pencils Lightweight cardboard or poster board	3"x 5" index cards (50 total)	Encyclopedia
14	Act. Supp. 14A Large white pc. of cardboard Pencil, carbon paper, stapler Tape, 2 pcs. of elastic Black marker Red marker or crayon	Act. Supp. 14A Large white pc. of cardboard Pencil, carbon paper, stapler Tape, 2 pcs. of elastic Black marker Red marker or crayon	
14	Yardstick, pencil, scissors 20" length of muslin-type cloth ½ yd. of gold ribbon or cord 2 empty paper-towel holders Glue, permanent marker	Yardstick, pencil, scissors 20" length of muslin-type cloth ½ yd. of gold ribbon or cord 2 empty paper-towel holders Glue, permanent marker	
14		Act. Supp. 14B	Act. Supp. 14B
15	Silky clothes, toothpick, paper Sample of calico, muslin, and cotton material Paper or camera	Large, medium, and small balls Flashlight, camera, encyclopedia	Copy or summary of *Bhagavad Gita*
Review 5	OL Map 7, "East Asia" Markers or colored pencils Sheet of colored paper (8½» x 11") Ruler, scissors, glue Sheet of notebook paper Globe, atlas, or world map	OL Map 7, "East Asia" Markers or colored pencils Sheet of colored paper (8½" x 11") Ruler, scissors, glue Sheet of notebook paper Globe, atlas, or world map	OL Map 7, "East Asia" Markers or colored pencils Sheet of colored paper (8½» x 11") Ruler, scissors, glue Sheet of notebook paper Globe, atlas, or world map
Exercise 5	Hat or bowl, 13 small pcs. of paper Pen or pencil	Hat or bowl, 13 small pcs. of paper Pen or pencil	Hat or bowl, 13 small pcs. of paper Pen or pencil

Lesson	Younger Students	Middle Students	Older Students
Planning Note for Lesson 22	Trade and Barter Day occupations such as stained-glass maker, baker, shoemaker, tailor, silversmith, rope maker, butcher, candlemaker, illuminator (calligrapher), potter, weaver, tanner, butter maker, wool maker, barber, alchemist, goldsmith, jeweler, embroiderer, dish maker, fast-food cook, armor maker, carpenter, cartographer (mapmaker), cooper (barrel maker), fruit and vegetable seller, florist, soap maker	Trade and Barter Day occupations such as stained-glass maker, baker, shoemaker, tailor, silversmith, rope maker, butcher, candlemaker, illuminator (calligrapher), potter, weaver, tanner, butter maker, wool maker, barber, alchemist, goldsmith, jeweler, embroiderer, dish maker, fast-food cook, armor maker, carpenter, cartographer (mapmaker), cooper (barrel maker), fruit and vegetable seller, florist, soap maker	Trade and Barter Day occupations such as stained-glass maker, baker, shoemaker, tailor, silversmith, rope maker, butcher, candlemaker, illuminator (calligrapher), potter, weaver, tanner, butter maker, wool maker, barber, alchemist, goldsmith, jeweler, embroiderer, dish maker, fast-food cook, armor maker, carpenter, cartographer (mapmaker), cooper (barrel maker), fruit and vegetable seller, florist, soap maker
Planning Note for Lesson 22	Items for masters to prepare for trade such as pieces of rope, beads, stray dishes, nails, flowers, apples, vegetables, scraps of fabric, deli meats, candles, shoelaces, buttons, butter packets, hot corn cobs on a stick, etc.	Items for masters to prepare for trade such as pieces of rope, beads, stray dishes, nails, flowers, apples, vegetables, scraps of fabric, deli meats, candles, shoelaces, buttons, butter packets, hot corn cobs on a stick, etc.	Items for masters to prepare for trade such as pieces of rope, beads, stray dishes, nails, flowers, apples, vegetables, scraps of fabric, deli meats, candles, shoelaces, buttons, butter packets, hot corn cobs on a stick, etc.
16	String, waxed paper, tissue paper Beads, pumpkin or sunflower seeds, or insect wings Colored pencils or markers Rainforest animal book or encyclopedia Pictures of the Maya		
17	Cassette recorder		Act. Supp. 17C *The Confessions of St. Augustine* (modern translation)
18	Bible		

Lesson	Younger Students	Middle Students	Older Students
Review 6	OL Map 8, "Mexico & Central America" OL Map 9, "Northern Africa" Historical atlas with map of Mayan World Modern-day atlas, scissors Colored pencils, stapler Clear transparency, 3-hole punch Globe or atlas, transparency marker	OL Map 8, "Mexico & Central America" OL Map 9, "Northern Africa" Historical atlas with map of MayanWorld Modern-day atlas, scissors Colored pencils, stapler Clear transparency, 3-hole punch Globe or atlas, transparency marker	OL Map 8, "Mexico & Central America" OL Map 9, "Northern Africa" Historical atlas with map of MayanWorld Modern-day atlas, scissors Colored pencils, stapler Clear transparency, 3-hole punch Globe or atlas, transparency marker
Planning Note for Lesson 22	Markers or crayons, poster board	Markers or crayons, poster board	Bowl, paper, pen, list of trades/crafts available at Trade and Barter Day
19	Notebook paper, green crayon		*Handbook of Today's Religions* by Josh McDowell and Don Stewart, Thomas Nelson Publishers, 1996.
19	Hymnal with "I Bind unto Myself Today" and "Christ Be Beside Me"	Hymnal with "I Bind unto Myself Today" and "Christ Be Beside Me"	
20	Broom	Act. Supp. 20C	Act. Supp. 20C
21	A fresh vegetable, a pc. of fruit Loaf of bread, pair of jeans Blanket, bar of soap Roll of toilet paper, 10 dimes Pkg. of gum or candy Small toy, a pc. of jewelry	A fresh vegetable, a pc. of fruit Loaf of bread, pair of jeans Blanket, bar of soap Roll of toilet paper, 10 dimes Pkg. of gum or candy Small toy, a pc. of jewelry	Act. Supp. 21C
Review 7	OL Map 10, "British Isles" OL Map 3, "World" Poster board or light cardboard Glue, scissors, historical atlas 2 plastic sandwich bags Permanent marker Colored pencils: green, red, gold, blue, brown, purple, orange, yellow	OL Map 10, "British Isles" OL Map 3, "World" Poster board or light cardboard Glue, scissors, historical atlas 2 plastic sandwich bags Permanent marker Colored pencils: green, red, gold, blue, brown, purple, orange, yellow	OL Map 10, "British Isles" OL Map 3, "World" Poster board or light cardboard Glue, scissors, historical atlas 2 plastic sandwich bags Permanent marker Colored pencils: green, red, gold, blue, brown, purple, orange, yellow

Lesson	Younger Students	Middle Students	Older Students
QTR. 2 BEGINS			
22	Act. Supp. 22A Vegetable stew and bread Tables, camera, paper bags Chairs or drop cloths	Act. Supp. 22A Vegetable stew and bread Tables, camera, paper bags Chairs or drop cloths	Act. Supp. 22A Vegetable stew and bread Tables, camera, paper bags Chairs or drop cloths
22	Empty paper-towel roll, clear tape Plain sheet of paper Red marker or wide red tape	Tape measure or ruler, matches, timer Pencil, candleholder, camera Slender 8" or 9" candle (approx. ½ " dia.)	Bible concordance Girls: Etiquette book, camera Boys: Checkbook or savings account bankbook
23	Cup or goblet, aluminum foil Rubber bands, string, or silver duct tape Bike or football helmet Black-and-white pictures of English castles Celtic music (e.g., Michael Card, Ceili Rain) Colored pencils, camera, streamers	Book about King Arthur and The Knights of the Round Table Sheet of paper	Book about King Arthur and The Knights of the Round Table, Works by Alfred, Lord Tennyson such as *The Seafarer*, "Holy Grail," a poem in *Idylls of the King*; "The Lady of Shalott" Mark Twain's *A Connecticut Yankee in King Arthur's Court*, *Camelot*, 1967 musical
24	Stuffed bears, robes, jewels, crowns Camera	Girls: Act. Supp. 24B, video camera	
24		Boys: Tape recorder Girls: Paper, 4 black tea bags, pencils pot, water, tongs, shoes, matches 3-hole plastic sleeve for notebook Picture of the cathedral of Saint Sophia in Istanbul Copy of the Justinian Code	Boys: Tape recorder Girls: Paper, 4 black tea bags, pencils pot, water, tongs, shoes, matches 3-hole plastic sleeve for notebook Picture of the cathedral of Saint Sophia in Istanbul Copy of the Justinian Code
Review 8	OL Map 11, "Byzantine Empire, c. 568" Paper, pencil, purple colored pencil 3 different blue colored pencils	OL Map 11, "Byzantine Empire, c. 568" Paper, pencil, purple colored pencil 3 different blue colored pencils	OL Map 11, "Byzantine Empire, c. 568" Paper, pencil, purple colored pencil 3 different blue colored pencils

Lesson	Younger Students	Middle Students	Older Students
25	Act. Supp. 25 Colored pencils, markers, or crayons	Act. Supp. 25 Colored pencils, markers, or crayons	Act. Supp. 25 Colored pencils, markers, or crayons
25	Bagpipe music, picture of bagpipes Nontoxic body paint or food coloring and body or hand lotion Encyclopedia, Bible	Heavy-duty gloves Medium-sized log Tape measure, camera	Bible, paper, calculator, pen, clock Picture of the Lindisfarne Gospels Book of Kells (print from Internet)
26	Sushi, colored pencils, glue, paper Picture of Mount Fuji Pictures of traditional Japanese clothing	Sushi Pictures of earthquake destruction	Act. Supp. 26C Sushi *Handbook of Today's Religions* by Josh McDowell and Don Stewart, Thomas Nelson Publishers, 1996.
27	Hymn "When I Survey the Wondrous Cross" Large brown paper bag for lawn and garden waste (use a self-standing large paper bag, 16" x 12" x35") 2 to 3 ft. cord or pc. of rope Pencil, scissors, camera CD titled "Chant"	Hymn "When I Survey the Wondrous Cross" Pictures of pope and/or monk	Hymn "When I Survey the Wondrous Cross" Pictures of ceiling of Sistine Chapel
Review 9	OL Map 12, "Japan" OL Map 13, "Honshu" OL Map 14, "Hokkaido, Shikoku, and Kyushu" Poster board, glue, scissors, hole punch Colored pencils, bold marking pen Yarn or string, clothes hanger, ruler Camera	OL Map 12, "Japan" OL Map 13, "Honshu" OL Map 14, "Hokkaido, Shikoku, and Kyushu" Poster board, glue, scissors, hole punch Colored pencils, bold marking pen Yarn or string, clothes hanger, ruler Camera	OL Map 12, "Japan" OL Map 13, "Honshu" OL Map 14, "Hokkaido, Shikoku, and Kyushu" Poster board, glue, scissors, hole punch Colored pencils, bold marking pen Yarn or string, clothes hanger, ruler Camera
28	Chinese tea, tea cups without handles Chopsticks, camera	Act. Supp. 28B Bible	Act. Supp. 28B
29	Camera		Newspaper or magazine articles of World Trade Center Towers on Sept. 11, 2001 Map of world that expresses where Christian persecution exists: The Voice of the Martyrs, PO BOX 443, Bartlesville, OK 74005-0443, 918-337-8015, www.persecution.com

Lesson	Younger Students	Middle Students	Older Students
30	Encyclopedia, samples of Arabic art	Act. Supp. 30B	
Review 10	OL Map 7, "East Asia" OL Map 15, "Saudi Arabia" OL Map 16, "Review 10 Answer Key" Atlas or globe, scissors, toothpicks, Colored pencils, mixing bowl, water Blue crayon (or pencil or marker) Spoon, paper, tape, pen or pencil, sand Black marker, small scrap of paper Yarn or string (just a few inches) Large rectangular plastic tub or food container (approx. 8½ " x 11")	OL Map 7, "East Asia" OL Map 15, "Saudi Arabia" OL Map 16, "Review 10 Answer Key" Atlas or globe, scissors, toothpicks Colored pencils, mixing bowl, water Blue crayon (or pencil or marker) Spoon, paper, tape, pen or pencil, sand Black marker, small scrap of paper Yarn or string (just a few inches) Large rectangular plastic tub or food container (approx. 8½ " x 11")	OL Map 7, "East Asia" OL Map 15, "Saudi Arabia" OL Map 16, "Review 10 Answer Key" Atlas or globe, scissors, toothpicks Colored pencils, mixing bowl, water Blue crayon (or pencil or marker) Spoon, paper, tape, pen or pencil, sand Black marker, small scrap of paper Yarn or string (just a few inches) Large rectangular plastic tub or food container (approx. 8½ " x 11")
31	Act. Supp. 31A Dull pencil, clear tape, glue, birdseed Small pc. of duct tape, 7 paper or plastic bowls (the size of a common cereal bowl) Approx. 1 yd. of yarn, a paper or plastic coffee cup 4 paper or plastic dinner plates Books, picture of pagoda	Act. Supp. 31A Dull pencil, clear tape, glue, birdseed Small pc. of duct tape, 7 paper or plastic bowls (the size of a common cereal bowl) Approx. 1 yd. of yarn, a paper or plastic coffee cup 4 paper or plastic dinner plates Books, picture of pagoda Picture of a carved Buddha in Dunhuang caves	

Lesson	Younger Students	Middle Students	Older Students
32	Act. Supp. 32A Cardboard from the side of a large box Hole punch, scissors, carbon paper Crayons or markers 2 pcs. of string or elastic about 2 ft. long each Copy of dragon picture from this activity Stapler, tape, pencil Choose simple or complex sword: **Simple:** Cardboard tubes from paper towels or wrapping paper **Complex:** Sandpaper, nails, hammer, camera Silver and gold paints, permanent marker A pc. of wood 2½ ft. long, 2½" wide, ½" thick (one end trimmed to make a dull point; the other end trimmed to create a narrow handle) 2 blocks of wood approx. 6" long, 1" wide, 1/2" thick	Act. Supp. 32A Cardboard from the side of a large box Hole punch, scissors, carbon paper Crayons or markers 2 pcs. of string or elastic about 2 ft. long each Copy of dragon picture from this activity Stapler, tape, pencil Choose simple or complex sword: **Simple:** Cardboard tubes from paper towels or wrapping paper **Complex:** Sandpaper, nails, hammer, camera Silver and gold paints, permanent marker A pc. of wood 2½ ft. long, 2½" wide, ½" thick (one end trimmed to make a dull point; the other end trimmed to create a narrow handle) 2 blocks of wood approx. 6" long, 1" wide, 1/2" thick	
32	Pictures of monsters, dragons, and dinosaurs	Pictures of monsters, dragons, and dinosaurs	
32		*After the Flood* by Bill Cooper	*After the Flood* by Bill Cooper
33	Act. Supp. 38B Grape juice, olive oil, glass jar Liquid soap, eyedropper Encyclopedia, camera, paper	Act. Supp. 38B Grape juice, olive oil, glass jar Liquid soap, eyedropper	
33		Act. Supp. 33C Prints or photocopies of Islamic art and architecture Colored paper, scissors, dictionary Heavy marker, glue stick, 3-hole punch Pen or pencil *The Ornament of the World* by Maria Rosa Menocal, 2002	Act. Supp. 33C Prints or photocopies of Islamic art and architecture Colored paper, scissors, dictionary Heavy marker, glue stick, 3- hole punch Pen or pencil *The Ornament of the World* by Maria Rosa Menocal, 2002

Lesson	Younger Students	Middle Students	Older Students
Field Trip	Visit mosque or museum to view Islamic art and architecture	Visit mosque or museum to view Islamic art and architecture	Visit mosque or museum to view Islamic art and architecture
Review 11	OL Map 17, "Spain" Act. Supp. Review 11 Globe, colored pencils, scissors, glue	OL Map 17, "Spain" Act. Supp. Review 11 Globe, colored pencils, scissors, glue	OL Map 17, "Spain" Act. Supp. Review 11 Globe, colored pencils, scissors, glue
Quiz 11	Colored pencils	Colored pencils	Colored pencils
34	Pc. of yellow construction paper 20 pcs. of green foil-wrapped chocolate candy 5 pcs. of red foil-wrapped chocolate candy Instead of the green and red candy: Pc. of green construction paper Silver foil-wrapped chocolate candy Colored pencils	3 Sprigs of evergreen Lightbulb, candle, or flashlight Bible, colored pencils	Lightbulb, candle, or flashlight Bible, colored pencils
35	Act. Supp. 35B Choose elegant or rugged cross: **Elegant:** Copy of cross pattern, beads, buttons Small bunches of tiny dried herbs or flowers Decorative ribbon, cardboard, glue Pen or pencil, large paper clip, camera **Rugged:** Cardboard, ruler, pencil, scissors Glue, large paper clip, camera A pkg. of approx. 4"-long dried cinnamon sticks 2 pkgs. of black hemp cord or thick twine or leather lace	Act. Supp. 35B Choose elegant or rugged cross: **Elegant:** Copy of cross pattern, beads, buttons Small bunches of tiny dried herbs or flowers Decorative ribbon, cardboard, glue Pen or pencil, large paper clip, camera **Rugged:** Cardboard, ruler, pencil, scissors Glue, large paper clip, camera A pkg. of approx. 4"-long dried cinnamon sticks 2 pkgs. of black hemp cord or thick twine or leather lace	Act. Supp. 35C
36	Ice-cube tray, 2 dz. plastic Army men	Pencil, 60-70 medium-sized nails 2"x 4" block of wood (approx. 1 ft. in length) Camera	Bible

Lesson	Younger Students	Middle Students	Older Students
Review 12	OL Map 18, "France and Spain" Globe or map Green and orange colored pencils 3-6 ice cubes, camera	OL Map 18, "France and Spain" Globe or map Green and orange colored pencils 3-6 ice cubes, camera	OL Map 18, "France and Spain" Globe or map Green and orange colored pencils 3-6 ice cubes, camera
Exercise 12	Timer	Timer	Timer
37	Bible, notebook paper	Dictionary or encyclopedia	Dictionary or encyclopedia Bible commentary "The Song of Roland" poem
38		Tape recorder	The Thousand and One Nights
39	Act. Supp. 39A Copy of mask pattern, crayons, scissors Paper or plastic plate, glue, hole punch Glittery gold and silver fabric paints A pc. of elastic or a rubber band Camera, animal skins and/or Viking helmet mask	Video copy of the Nova documentary on Vikings	Video copy of the Nova documentary on Vikings
Review 13	OL Map 19, "Charlemagne's Empire" OL Map 20, "Viking Voyages" Tracing paper, tape, pencil, glue Colored pencils: black, orange, yellow, green Globe or map, sunny window Few inches of yarn in 3 colors	OL Map 19, "Charlemagne's Empire" OL Map 20, "Viking Voyages" Tracing paper, tape, pencil, glue Colored pencils: black, orange, yellow, green Globe or map, sunny window Few inches of yarn in 3 colors	OL Map 19, "Charlemagne's Empire" OL Map 20, "Viking Voyages" Tracing paper, tape, pencil, glue Colored pencils: black, orange, yellow, green Globe or map, sunny window Few inches of yarn in 3 colors
40	Shoebox, cardboard, furry fabric, sticks Mud, grass, grass seed (optional) Salt, heavy whipping cream, camera Decorative jeweled pin, comb, keys Leather jacket or fleecy woolen blanket	Act. Supp. 40B Chicken or beef bone, knife, hammer Plaster of Paris, small box, screwdriver Camera	*The Vikings* movie, 1958, starring Kirk Douglas and Tony Curtis Balls or bean bags for juggling
41	Finger paint or watercolors Illustrated children's Bible	Act. Supp. 41 B	Globe or map

Lesson	Younger Students	Middle Students	Older Students
42	*Anglo-Saxon Helmet* ISBN 0714116734 Patriotic songs	*Anglo-Saxon Helmet* ISBN 0714116734 Patriotic songs	One of these works: *Consolation of Philosophy* by Boethius, *Pastoral Care* by Gregory, *Universal History* by Orosius, *Ecclesiastical History of England* by Bede Also, detailed dictionary with etymology Listings
Review 14	OL Map 21, "Slavic Nations and the Byzantine Empire, c.888" Map of England and the United States Yellow, pink, green, blue highlighters Pencil	OL Map 21, "Slavic Nations and the Byzantine Empire, c.888" Map of England and the United States Yellow, pink, green, blue highlighters Pencil	OL Map 21, "Slavic Nations and the Byzantine Empire, c.888" Map of England and the United States Yellow, pink, green, blue highlighters Pencil

Lesson	Younger Students	Middle Students	Older Students
QTR. 3 BEGINS			
43	Any of these meats: mutton, lamb, salmon, cod, trout, halibut, or raw pickled salmon Phonebook	Any of these meats: mutton, lamb, salmon, cod, trout, halibut, or raw pickled salmon	Any of these meats: mutton, lamb, salmon, cod, trout, halibut, or raw pickled salmon
44	Photograph of a kiwi bird, camera Toothpick, pc. of kiwi fruit, scissors Permanent marker, emery board, glue Tape measure	Picture of the Southern Cross	Bible
45	Several nuggets of "fool's gold" or similar material (gold foil- wrapped chocolate coins) Metal lids	Glass beads, picture of Victoria Falls	Maps of Sudan, Nigeria, Zimbabwe
Review 15	Permanent marker, round balloon Globe or atlas, camera	Permanent marker, round balloon Globe or atlas, camera	Permanent marker, round balloon Globe or atlas, camera
Exercise 15	Scissors	Scissors	Scissors
46	Act. Supp. 46A Bible, camera Highlighters or colored pencils	Act. Supp. 46A Bible, camera Highlighters or colored pencils	Act. Supp. 46A Bible, camera Notebook paper
47	Recipes for beef goulash, bockwurst, and/or potato dumplings, and apple strudel Camera, video camera Any of *Grimm's Fairy Tales*	Recipes for beef goulash, bockwurst, and/or potato dumplings, and apple strudel Camera	Recipes for beef goulash, bockwurst, and/or potato dumplings, and apple strudel Camera
48	Sound recording of *Nutcracker Suite* by Peter Ilich Tchaikovsky	Pictures of Russian architecture and famous sites	Encyclopedia or biography of Leo N. Tolstoy *War and Peace* by Leo N. Tolstoy Dictionary
Review 16	Atlas, globe, or a set of encyclopedias	Atlas, globe, or a set of encyclopedias	Atlas, globe, or a set of encyclopedias
49	Quarter, thin cardboard, pencil, scissors Foil, glue, hole punch, string, tape Ruled legal paper (preferably of a pretty color) 10"-12" of fancy cord or string Dozens of small colorful feathers from a craft store	Compass, calligraphy pen Book with Chinese characters Silk-scarf painting kit or light-colored (undecorated) silk scarf and quality fabric paint; or silk scarf, rubber bands, and watery fabric paint	

Lesson	Younger Students	Middle Students	Older Students
Field Trip	Visit a pottery maker, ceramic kiln, or porcelain maker	Visit a pottery maker, ceramic kiln, or porcelain maker	Visit a pottery maker, ceramic kiln, or porcelain maker
50	Bathroom scales 3-4 empty gallon-sized milk containers	Mustard seed, notebook paper	
51	Disposable plastic bowl (dome-shaped like a cereal bowl) Water, ice cubes, plate *Draw-Write-Now: The Polar Regions-The Arctic-The Antarctic* by Marie Hablitzel and Kim Stitzer	Pictures of polar bears	*Greenland Mummies* by Janet Buell, 1998 *The Greenlanders Saga* *The Saga of Eric the Red*
Review 17	Globe or atlas, marker, camera Sturdy paper plate (preferably waterproof) ¼ c. dirt, 3-5 ice cubes, 4-5 toothpicks ½ c. salt	Globe or atlas, marker, camera Sturdy paper plate (preferably waterproof) ¼ c. dirt, 3-5 ice cubes, 4-5 toothpicks ½ c. salt	
Exercise 17	40 self-sticking Post-It notes (3" x 3") or paper (3" x 3") and tape Pen or pencil	40 self-sticking Post-It notes (3" x 3") or paper (3" x 3") and tape Pen or pencil	40 self-sticking Post-It notes (3" x 3") or paper (3" x 3") and tape Pen or pencil
52	Grapes, paper, can of salmon *Leif the Lucky* by Ingri and Edgar Parin D'Aulaire	*Leif the Lucky* by Ingri and Edgar Parin D'Aulaire	*The Saga of Eric the Red*, in *Hauk's Book* by Hauk Erlendsson *Skalholt Book* by Hauk Erlendsson *The Greenlander's Saga* in *Flateyar Book* by Jon Tordarsson *Land Under the Pole Star* by Helge Ingstad, St. Martin's Press, 1966, (Library of Congress Catalog Card Number: 66-21921).
53	Act. Supp. 53A Silver, gold, or blue poster board Copy of crown pattern, pencil, scissors Stapler, tape, glue, camera Markers or crayons 1 yd. (for king) or 2 yds. (for queen) of shimmery cloth cut into 6-8" wide strips A small pkg. of flat-sided fake jewels *Castle* by David Macaulay	*After the Flood* by Bill Cooper	*After the Flood* by Bill Cooper Movie or book *Macbeth* by Shakespeare; or live performance if possible

Lesson	Younger Students	Middle Students	Older Students
54			*The Poem of the Cid: a Bilingual Edition with Parallel Text* (A Penguin Classic), edited by Ian Michael and Rita Hamilton *El Cid* by Jules Massenet, CBS Records Masterworks (Austria, 1989) *El Cid* film starring Charlton Heston, 1961
Review 18	OL Map 22, "Canada" Modern globe or atlas Black and red markers Colored pencils: pink, purple, dark green, dark blue, light green, light blue, brown, red, orange, yellow, white, gold, turquoise, silver or gray	OL Map 22, "Canada" Modern globe or atlas Black and red markers Colored pencils: pink, purple, dark green, dark blue, light green, light blue, brown, red, orange, yellow, white, gold, turquoise, silver or gray	OL Map 22, "Canada" Modern globe or atlas Black and red markers Colored pencils: pink, purple, dark green, dark blue, light green, light blue, brown, red, orange, yellow, white, gold, turquoise, silver or gray
55	Paper, marker, tape, colored pencils Plastic Army men, plastic horses, hill *Cathedral: The Story of Its Construction* by David Macaulay	Paper, marker, tape, colored pencils Plastic Army men, plastic horses, hill *Cathedral: The Story of Its Construction* by David Macaulay	Colored pencils Pictures of Westminster Abbey Pictures of Tower of London
55		Embroidery sample kit from craft store Notebook paper, 3-4 tea bags, water Pot, matches, shoes, concrete outdoor area 3-hole, clear-plastic notebook sleeve	Embroidery sample kit from craft store Notebook paper, 3-4 tea bags, water Pot, matches, shoes, concrete outdoor area 3-hole, clear-plastic notebook sleeve
56	Yardstick, clothespin, at least 2 people Jump rope or long cord	Yardstick, clothespin, at least 2 people Jump rope or long cord Bible concordance	Yardstick, clothespin, at least 2 people Jump rope or long cord Bible concordance
57	Red cloth, pencil, ruler, scissors, safety pins	Pictures of significant holy sites of Jerusalem	Hymn "O Sacred Head Now Wounded" by Bernard of Clairvaux
Review 19	OL Map 10, "The British Isles" OL Map 3, "World" Atlas, colored pencils, globe, scissors 2 different shades of fluorescent highlighters	OL Map 10, "The British Isles" OL Map 3, "World" Atlas, colored pencils, globe, scissors 2 different shades of fluorescent highlighters	OL Map 10, "The British Isles" OL Map 3, "World" Atlas, colored pencils, globe, scissors 2 different shades of fluorescent highlighters

Lesson	Younger Students	Middle Students	Older Students
Exercise 19	Whiteboard with dry-erase markers or chalkboard with chalk	Whiteboard with dry-erase markers or chalkboard with chalk	Whiteboard with dry-erase markers or chalkboard with chalk
58	Jewelry, cloth, Bible	Bible	
59	Act. Supp. 59 Banquet-style tables, one of them elevated Banners, draperies, tablecloths, towels Wooden spoons and bowls Handwashing bowls Saltcellar Pewter, silver, or gold plates Silver or gold goblets Various banquet foods and soltety creations (see descriptions in Act. Supp. 59) Well-behaved dog! For any item not available, substitutions are acceptable!	Act. Supp. 59 Banquet-style tables, one of them elevated Banners, draperies, tablecloths, towels Wooden spoons and bowls Handwashing bowls Saltcellar Pewter, silver, or gold plates Silver or gold goblets Various banquet foods and soltety creations (see descriptions in Act. Supp. 59) Well-behaved dog! For any item not available, substitutions are acceptable!	Act. Supp. 59 Banquet-style tables, one of them elevated Banners, draperies, tablecloths, towels Wooden spoons and bowls Handwashing bowls Saltcellar Pewter, silver, or gold plates Silver or gold goblets Various banquet foods and soltety creations (see descriptions in Act. Supp. 59) Well-behaved dog! For any item not available, substitutions are acceptable!
59	Thumbtacks, camera, suitcase Lightweight decorative blankets or sheets	Thumbtacks, camera, suitcase Lightweight decorative blankets or sheets	The Lion in Winter (1968) starring Katharine Hepburn and Peter O'Toole
60	*Fiddler on the Roof* (1971)	*Fiddler on the Roof* (1971) Bible	*Fiddler on the Roof* (1971) Bible
60	Tape, marker, foot-long cord, camera 2 empty paper-towel rolls 3 sheets of tan parchment-looking paper	Tape, marker, foot-long cord, camera 2 empty paper-towel rolls 3 sheets of tan parchment-looking paper	
Field Trip	Tour a local synagogue	Tour a local synagogue	Tour a local synagogue
Review 20	OL Map 23, "England and France" Atlas, colored pencils	OL Map 23, "England and France" Atlas, colored pencils	OL Map 23, "England and France" Atlas, colored pencils
Quiz 20	Colored pencils	Colored pencils	Colored pencils
61	Act. Supp. 61 Markers, colored pencils, crayons Notebook-sized poster board 3-hole punch	Act. Supp. 61 Markers, colored pencils, crayons Notebook-sized poster board 3-hole punch	Act. Supp. 61 Markers, colored pencils, crayons Notebook-sized poster board 3-hole punch
61	Pears, peaches, rice, blender, scissors Green construction paper, long stick	Pictures of crossbows, encyclopedia	Photos of the Dome of the Rock

Lesson	Younger Students	Middle Students	Older Students
62	Act. Supp. 62 Empty wrapping-paper tubes Trash-can lids with handles	Act. Supp. 62 Empty wrapping-paper tubes Trash-can lids with handles	Act. Supp. 62 Empty wrapping-paper tubes Trash-can lids with handles Invite a trained falconer for Demonstration
62	Act. Supp. 62A: Princess Hat and Gown A pc. of poster board, stapler, scissors Strong tape, fur trim (optional), fake jewels, ½ yd. solid fabric, camera 1 yd. strand of ribbon (or less if elastic) ¼ yd. of sheer fabric (tulle), ½ yd. of braided strand Approx. 3 yds. of 54"-wide fabric (for an average 7 year old), fur trim, thread Braid trim, fake jewels, sewing machine 1½ to 2 yds. of cord for belt (optional)		
62	Act. Supp. 62A: Money Pouch Copy of the money pouch pattern Scissors, needle, thread, shoestring ¼ yd. of cloth or felt, 3-4 straight pins Coins (perhaps chocolate ones) Toy bow-and-arrow set Disney's animated version of Robin Hood	Robin Hood book	Bible Film or book of *Ivanhoe* by Sir Walter Scott *Robert and Marian* (1976) starring Sean Connery and Audrey Hepburn

Lesson	Younger Students	Middle Students	Older Students
63	Act. Supp. 63A Bath necessities, robe, shoestrings Sash or rope for belt, baby oil, hair band Baggy pajama pants or sweat pants Old pair of tube socks, scissors Flip-flop sandals, fake sword, camera Cardboard, crayons, hole punch String or leather laces, fake dagger Crayons, markers, or colored pencils Rice, duct tape, straw, stiff pc. of paper	Paper plates, crayons, elastic	Act. Supp. 63C Notebook paper
Review 21	OL Map 24, "The Crusades" Pencil, pen, or colored pencils 3 shades of highlighters or crayons	OL Map 24, "The Crusades" Pencil, pen, or colored pencils 3 shades of highlighters or crayons	OL Map 24, "The Crusades" Pencil, pen, or colored pencils 3 shades of highlighters or crayons Atlas

Lesson	Younger Students	Middle Students	Older Students
QTR. 4 BEGINS			
64	Hymn "All Creatures of Our God and King" Matches or lighter, candle, rock, camera Peanut butter, pinecone, birdseed	Hymn "All Creatures of Our God and King"	Hymn "All Creatures of Our God and King" Copy of portrait of St. Francis by Francisco de Zurbaran
65	Pied Piper of Hamelin, flute or recorder Paper, inkpad	Paper, inkpad Bible	*Experiencing God* by Henry Blackaby
66	Act. Supp. 66A Paper, coffee, paper towel Rubber stamp, sealing wax, candle wax Gold-foil sticker or markers Hole punch or 3-hole plastic sleeve protector	Act. Supp. 66A Paper, coffee, paper towel Rubber stamp, sealing wax, candle wax Gold-foil sticker or markers Hole punch or 3-hole plastic sleeve protector	Copy of the United States Bill of Rights
Review 22	OL Map 24, "The Crusades" Atlas, globe, or map 2 highlighters or crayons	OL Map 24, "The Crusades" Atlas, globe, or map 2 highlighters or crayons	OL Map 24, "The Crusades" Atlas, globe, or map 2 highlighters or crayons
67	Act. Supp. 67A Crayons, markers, or colored pencils Glue, gold glitter, red yarn, any other color yarn Toothpicks or uncooked spaghetti Loose sequins or small buttons Small feathers, other household items Sturdy paper, 3-hole plastic sleeve protector	Act. Supp. 67A Crayons, markers, or colored pencils Glue, gold glitter, red yarn, any other color yarn Toothpicks or uncooked spaghetti Loose sequins or small buttons Small feathers, other household items Sturdy paper, 3-hole plastic sleeve protector	*The 100 Most Important Events in Christian History* by Curtis, Lang, and Petersen
68	Bible	Woodburning kit, dictionary	
69	Paper, pencil, or pen Mirror, flashlight, magnifying glass Items such as coin, leaf, insect's wing Remote-control airplane Food colors	Paper, pencil, or pen Mirror, flashlight, magnifying glass Items such as coin, leaf, insect's wing Remote-control airplane Food colors	Paper, pencil, or pen Mirror, flashlight, magnifying glass, sun Items such as coin, leaf, insect's wing
Review 23	OL Map 2, "Eastern Mediterranean" Atlas or globe, colored pencils Mustard in squeeze bottle, 2 slices of bread, 1 pc. of salami (or other deli meat)	OL Map 2, "Eastern Mediterranean" Atlas or globe, colored pencils Mustard in squeeze bottle, 2 slices of bread, 1 pc. of salami (or other deli meat)	OL Map 2, "Eastern Mediterranean" Atlas or globe, colored pencils Mustard in squeeze bottle, 2 slices of bread, 1 pc. of salami (or other deli meat)

Lesson	Younger Students	Middle Students	Older Students
70	*The Book of Virtues* by William J. Bennett Scraps of felt, fabric, or old cloth Cord, goat's milk	*The Book of Virtues* by William J. Bennett	*The Book of Virtues* by William J. Bennett
71	Swimming pool (if you have access to one) Spices such as pepper, nutmeg, cloves, ginger, allspice, mace, mustard, cinnamon	Swimming pool (if you have access to one) Spices such as pepper, nutmeg, cloves, ginger, allspice, mace, mustard, cinnamon	
71		Scissors, glue, blank sheet of paper Colored pencils or markers Visit a Chinese restaurant	Scissors, glue, blank sheet of paper Colored pencils or markers Visit a Chinese restaurant
72	Silly String plastic stream material	Pen or pencil, slips of paper, tape	Act. Supp. 72C
Review 24	OL Map 3, "World" OL Map 25, "The Mongol Empire" Clear transparency (8½" by 11") 3-hole punch, clear tape, colored pencils Red, blue, and green wet-erase markers	OL Map 3, "World" OL Map 25, "The Mongol Empire" Clear transparency (8½" by 11") 3-hole punch, clear tape, colored pencils Red, blue, and green wet- erase markers	OL Map 3, "World" OL Map 25, "The Mongol Empire" Clear transparency (8½" by 11") 3-hole punch, clear tape, colored pencils Red, blue, and green wet-erase markers
Exercise 24	5 of each: penny, nickel, dime, quarter, dollar Timer	5 of each: penny, nickel, dime, quarter, dollar Timer	5 of each: penny, nickel, dime, quarter, dollar Timer
73		Italian/English dictionary, Bible	*The Divine Comedy* by Dante Bible, Bible concordance
74	Frog legs, fish or turtle soup, corn tortillas	Frog legs, fish or turtle soup, corn tortillas	Frog legs, fish or turtle soup, corn tortillas
74	Act. Supp. 74A Red construction paper, scissors, glue Colored pencils, markers, or crayons Small horn Girls: Plain pair of inexpensive thong sandals, fake jewels, gems, camera, glue or hot glue, turquoise stones	Copy of the flag of Mexico Bark from tree, large zipper plastic bag Crayons or markers, 3-hole punch Small boxes, spray paint, clay, camera Craft store supplies to make a turquoise jewelry necklace	Small boxes, spray paint, clay, camera Craft store supplies to make a turquoise jewelry necklace

Lesson	Younger Students	Middle Students	Older Students
75	Girls: Dress-up clothes to be a princess Boys: All-black clothing, black cape	Copies of medieval weaponry (including a steel-tipped crossbow) Copies of photos of armor	Movie or book *Henry V* by William Shakespeare *Ballad of Agincourt* by Michael Drayton
Review 25	OL Map 8, "Mexico and Central America" OL Map 26, "Review 25 Answer Key" Colored pencils, modern atlas	OL Map 8, "Mexico and Central America" OL Map 26, "Review 25 Answer Key" Colored pencils, modern atlas	OL Map 8, "Mexico and Central America" OL Map 26, "Review 25 Answer Key" Colored pencils, modern atlas
76	Pen or pencil, paper, small prize Camera, toothpicks Raw and/or dried fruit	Copies of photos of fleas	Bible *Decameron* by Giovanni Boccaccio
77	Copies of photos of the Forbidden City	Copies of photos of the Forbidden City Charcoal, sketch paper	Copies of photos of the Forbidden City
Field Trip	Visit the office of your mayor, governor, or local legislator; visit the White House if possible!	Visit the office of your mayor, governor, or local legislator; visit the White House if possible!	Visit the office of your mayor, governor, or local legislator; visit the White House if possible!
78	Paper, chalkboard, or erasable white board Pointy dress shoes	Paper, chalkboard, or erasable white board Video *Wycliffe: The Morning Star*	Paper, chalkboard, or erasable white board Video *Wycliffe: The Morning Star*
Review 26	OL Map 1, "Mediterranean" Green, red, and black markers Globe or atlas	OL Map 1, "Mediterranean" Green, red, and black markers Globe or atlas	OL Map 1, "Mediterranean" Green, red, and black markers Globe or atlas
Exercise 26	Bag of chocolate chips or carob chips Timer	Bag of chocolate chips or carob chips Timer	Bag of chocolate chips or carob chips Timer
Field Trip	Visit a public historical cemetery	Visit a public historical cemetery	Visit a public historical cemetery
79	Children's version of *The Canterbury Tales*		*Selected Canterbury Tales* by Geoffrey Chaucer (Dover Thrift Editions, Unabridged, ISBN 0-486-28241-4) *Troilus and Criseyde* by Geoffrey Chaucer *The Legend of a Good Woman* by Geoffrey Chaucer

Lesson	Younger Students	Middle Students	Older Students
80		*The Trial and Burning of John Huss! An Eyewitness Account By a Member of The Council of Constance* (ISBN 0-92176-10-9), Inheritance Publications (1-800-563-3594) *Crushed Yet Conquering* by Deborah Alcock (ISBN 1-894666-01-1)	*The Trial and Burning of John Huss! An Eyewitness Account By a Member of The Council of Constance* (ISBN 0-921716-10-9), Inheritance Publications (1-800-563-3594) *Crushed Yet Conquering* by Deborah Alcock (ISBN 1-894666-01-1)
81	Act. Supp. 81A Choose one: Option 1 – Copy of the fleur-de-lis, scissors, colored pencils, 3-hole punch Option 2 – 2 copies of the fleur-de-lis, scissors, glue, colored pencils, poster board, closable plastic bag	Act. Supp. 81A Choose one: Option 1 – Copy of the fleur-de-lis, scissors, colored pencils, 3-hole punch Option 2 – 2 copies of the fleur-de-lis, scissors, glue, colored pencils, poster board, closable plastic bag	
81	Sticks, twine	Copy of any Joan of Arc letter, Bible 4 black tea bags, pot, tongs, water, 3-hole plastic sleeve for notebook *Saint Joan* play by George Bernard Shaw, 1923 *Joan of Arc* by Mark Twain Movie *The Passion of Joan of Arc* (1928) Or a book by any other author about the life and death of Joan of Arc	Copy of any Joan of Arc letter, Bible 4 black tea bags, pot, tongs, water 3-hole plastic sleeve for notebook *Saint Joan* play by George Bernard Shaw, 1923 *Joan of Arc* by Mark Twain Movie *The Passion of Joan of Arc* (1928) Or a book by any other author about the life and death of Joan of Arc
Review 27	Atlas	OL Map 27, "France" Atlas, colored pencils	OL Map 27, "France" Atlas, colored pencils
82	Pencil or marker, popcorn, rope Poster board or large pc. of paper	Popcorn, permanent markers, camera Gourd (or melon or squash), crackers Spicy, hot peppers, water	Popcorn, rope, craft sticks, rocks, paints Camera
83	Strips of paper, stapler	String, brick, 20 pencils	
Field Trip	Visit a print shop	Visit a print shop	Visit a print shop
84	Potato, sharp knife, dull pencil, ink, or paint		
Review 28	OL Map 28, "South America" Colored pencils, modern atlas	OL Map 28, "South America" Colored pencils, modern atlas	OL Map 28, "South America" Colored pencils, modern atlas

Anderson, Madelyn Klein. *Greenland: Island at the Top of the World*. New York: Dodd, Mead & Co., 1983.

Armitage, Ronda. *Countries of the World: New Zealand*. New York: The Bookwright Press, 1988.

Ashbaugh, Brian and Julie Lostroh. *World Geography in Christian Perspective*. Pensacola, FL: A Beka Book.

Augustine. *The Confessions of Saint Augustine*. Translated by E. B. Pusey. New York: Barnes & Noble Books, 2003.

Barnes-Svarney, Patricia. *Major World Nations: Zimbabwe*. Philadelphia: Chelsea House Publishers, 1999.

Beck, Barbara L. *The Aztecs*. New York: Franklin Watts, 1983.

Beliles, Mark A., and Stephen K. McDowell. *America's Providential History*. Charlottesville, VA: The Providence Foundation, 1989.

Berry, Roger L. *God's World: His Story*. Harrisonburg, VA: Christian Light Publications, Inc., 1976.

Bingham, Jane, Fiona Chandler, and Sam Taplin. *The Usborne Internet-Linked Encyclopedia of World History*. London: Usborne Publishing Ltd., 2000.

Brooks, Polly Schoyer. *Queen Eleanor, Independent Spirit of the Medieval World: A Biography of Eleanor of Aquitaine*. New York: J.B. Lippincott, 1983.

Bull, Angela. *Joan of Arc*. New York: Dorling Kindersley, 2000.

Cooke, Jean, Ann Kramer, and Theodore Rowland-Entwistle. *History's Timeline, A 40,000-Year Chronology of Civilization*. New York: Barnes & Noble Books, 1996.

Cooper, Bill, and B. A. Hons. *After the Flood: The Early Post-Flood History of Europe Traced Back to Noah*. Chichester (England): New Wine Press, 1995.

Corrick, James A. *World History Series: The Early Middle Ages*. San Diego: Lucent Books, 1995.

Corrick, James A. *World History Series: The Late Middle Ages*. San Diego: Lucent Books, 1995.

Curtis, A. Kenneth, J. Stephen Lang, and Randy Petersen. *The 100 Most Important Events in Christian History*. Grand Rapids, MI: Fleming H. Revell, 1991.

Day, David. *King Arthur*. New York: Barnes & Noble Books, 1999.

Dead Sea Scrolls. New South Wales: Art Gallery of New South Wales, 2000.

Delort. Robert. *Life in the Middle Ages*. New York: Universe Books, 1972.

Drew, David. *Inca Life*. Hauppauge, NY: Barron's Educational Series, Inc., 2000.

Durant, Will. *Caesar and Christ*. Vol. III of *The Story of Civilization*. New York: Simon and Schuster, 1944.

Durant, Will. *Our Oriental Heritage*. Vol. I of *The Story of Civilization*. New York: Simon and Schuster, 1954.

Durant, Will. *The Age of Faith*. Vol. IV of *The Story of Civilization*. New York: Simon and Schuster, 1950.

Ercelawn, Ayesha. *Countries of the World: New Zealand*. Milwaukee: Gareth Stevens Publishing, 2001.

Everett, Felicity, and Struan Reid. *The Usborne Book of Explorers from Columbus to Armstrong*. London: Usborne Publishing Ltd., 1991.

Foxe's Christian Martyrs of the World. Westwood, NJ: Barbour and Co., Inc., 1985.

Gibb, Christopher. *Richard the Lionheart and the Crusades*. New York: The Bookwright Press, 1986.

Gish, Duane T., Ph.D. *Dinosaurs by Design*. Green Forest, AR: Master Books, 1996.

Goff, Denise. *Early China*. New York: Gloucester Press, 1986.

Grant, Neil. *What's Their Story? Eric the Red*. New York: Oxford University Press, 1997.

Great Leaders of the Christian Church. Edited by John D. Woodbridge. Chicago: Moody Press, 1988.

Harpur, James, and Jennifer Westwood. *The Atlas of Legendary Places*. Old Saybrook, CT: Konecky & Konecky, 1997.

Haskins, James, and Kathleen Benson. *African Beginnings*. New York: Lothrup, Lee and Shepard Books, 1998.

Hobar, Linda. *The Mystery of History–Volume I: Creation to the Resurrecton*. Dover, DE: Bright Ideas Press, 2002.

Holdsworth, Mary. *Images of Asia: The Forbidden City*. Oxford and New York: Oxford University Press, 1988.

Holy Bible, The. New King James Version. Nashville: Thomas Nelson Publishers, 1982.

Honan, Linda. *Picture the Middle Ages*. New York: Golden Owl Publishing Co., Inc., 1994.

Hull, Robert. *The Ancient World: The Aztecs*. Austin: Raintree Steck-Vaughn, 1998.

Inglis, Rewey Belle, Donald A. Stauffer, and Cecil Evva Larsen. *Adventures in English Literature* (Mercury ed.). New York: Harcourt, Brace and Co., 1949.

James, Ian. *Inside China*. New York: Franklin Watts, 1989.

Jianin, Zhu. *Treasures of the Forbidden City*. New York: Viking Penguin, 1986.

Johnston, Reginald F. *Twilight in the Forbidden City*. New York: D. Appleton–Century Co., 1934.

Johnstone, Patrick, and Jason Mandryk. *Operation World*. Waynesboro, GA: Paternoster Publishing, 2001.

Josephus, Flavius. *The Works of Josephus*. Translated by William Whiston, A.M. Peabody, MA: Hendrickson Publishers, 1988.

Kallay, Zelma. *Kings, Queens, Castles, and Crusades: Life in the Middle Ages*. Torrance, CA: Good Apple, 1997.

Kalman, Bobbie. *China: The Culture*. New York: Crabtree Publishing Co., 2001.

Kalman, Bobbie. *China: The People*. New York: Crabtree Publishing Co., 1989.

Kingfisher Illustrated History of the World, The. New York: Kingfisher Books, 1993.

Lepthien, Emilie U. *Enchantment of the World: Greenland*. Chicago: Children's Press, 1989.

Living Bible Encyclopedia in Story and Pictures, The, Art Treasure ed. New York: H. S. Stuttman Co., Inc., 1968.

Macdonald, Fiona. *How Would You Survive in the Middle Ages?* New York: Franklin Watts, 1995.

Macdonald, Fiona. *Metropolis: Inca Town*. New York: Franklin Watts, 1998.

MacFarqular, Roderick. *The Forbidden City: China's Ancient Capital*. New York: Newsweek, 1972.

Manley, John. *The Atlas of Past Worlds: A Comparative Chronology of Human History 2000 BC–AD 1500*. London: Cassell Academic, 1993.

Mann, Elizabeth. *Machu Picchu: The Story of the Amazing Inkas and Their City in the Clouds* (A Wonders of the World Book). New York: Mikaya Press, 2000.

Marks, Geoffrey J. *The Medieval Plague: The Black Death of the Middle Ages*. Garden City, NY: Doubleday & Co., Inc., 1971.

Martell, Hazel Mary. *Everyday Life in Viking Times*. New York: Franklin Watts, 1994.

Matthews, Michael D., Ron Tagliapietra, and Pam Creason. *Geography for Christian Schools* (2nd ed.). Greenville, SC: Bob Jones University Press, 1998.

McDowell, Josh. *The New Evidence That Demands a Verdict*. Nashville: Thomas Nelson Publishers, 1999.

McDowell, Josh, and Don Stewart. *Handbook of Today's Religions*. San Bernardino, CA: Here's Life Publishers, Inc., 1983. (There is also a 1996 edition published by Thomas Nelson Publishers, Nashville.)

McEvedy, Colin. *The New Penguin Atlas of Medieval History*. New York: Penguin Putnam, Inc., 1992.

Menocal, Maria Rosa. *The Ornament of the World: How Muslims, Jews, and Christians Created a Culture of Tolerance in Medieval Spain*. New York: Little, Brown and Co., 2002.

Minks, Louise. *World History Series: Traditional Africa*. San Diego: Lucent Books, 1996.

Nardo, Don. *World History Series: Traditional Japan*. San Diego: Lucent Books, 1947.

Poggius, Fra. *The Trial and Burning of John Huss: An Eyewitness Account By a Member of the Council of Constance*. Toronto: Wittenburg Publications. (Taken from Concilium zu Constenca–1483. Author: Incunabula U. Richental.)

Praying Through the 100 Gateway Cities of the 10/40 Window. Edited by C. Peter Wagner, Stephen Peters, and Mark Wilson). Seattle: YWAM Publishing, 1995.

Roberts, Jenny. *History Highlights: Samurai Warriors*. New York: Gloucester Press, 1990.

Ryrie, Charles C. *A Survey of Bible Doctrine*. Chicago: Moody Press, 1972.

Sabuda, Robert. *Saint Valentine*. New York: Aladdin Paperbacks, 1999.

Sands, Stella. *Kids Discover the Maya*. New York: EdPress, March 1993.

Schaff, David S., *History of the Christian Church (Vol. 5: The Middle Ages, 1049–1294)*. Peabody, MA: Hendrickson Publishers, Inc., 1996.

Sheehan, Scan. *The Ancient World: Great African Kingdoms*. Austin: Raintree Steck-Vaughn, 1999.

Simon, Charnan. *The World's Great Explorers: Leif Eriksson and the Vikings*. Chicago: Children's Press, 1991.

Speed, Peter. *Life in the Time of Harald Hardrada and the Vikings*. Austin: Raintree Steck-Vaughn, 1993.

St. Simon. Mokatm. Cairo, Egypt: Dar Ilias El Asria, April 1996.

Steele, Philip. *Hidden Worlds: The Incas and the Machu Picchu*. New York: Dillon Press, 1993.

Steele, Philip. *Step Into the Chinese Empire*. New York: Lorenz Books, 1998.

Stefoff, Rebecca. *World Explorers: The Viking Explorers*. New York: Chelsea House Publishers, 1993.

Tao, Wang. *Exploration into China*. Philadelphia: Chelsea House Publishers, 2001.

Thompson, George T., and Laurel Elizabeth Hicks. *World History and Cultures in Christian Perspective* (1st ed.). Pensacola, FL: A Beka Book, 1985.

Thompson, George, and Jerry Combee. *World History and Cultures in Christian Perspective* (2nd ed.). Pensacola, FL: A Beka Book, 1997.

Today's Dictionary of the Bible. Compiled by T. A. Bryant. Minneapolis: Bethany House Publishers, 1982.

Unger, Merrill. *Unger's Bible Dictionary*. Chicago: Moody Press, 1979.

Wallbank, T. Walter, and Alastair M. Taylor. *Civilization Past and Present*. Chicago: Scott, Foresman and Co., 1949.

Wells, H. G. *The Outline of History*. Garden City, NY: Garden City Books, 1961.

Wilcox, Jonathan. *Cultures of the World: Iceland*. Tarrytown, NY: Marshall Cavendish, 1997.

Wingate, Philippa, et al. *The Usborne Book of Kings & Queens* (Famous Lives Series). Tulsa: Educational Development Corp., 1995.

Wingate, Philippa, and Dr. Anne Millard. *The Usborne Illustrated World History: The Viking World.* London: Usborne Publishing, 1993.

Wood, Tim. *See-Through History: The Incas.* New York: Viking (Penguin Group), 1996.

World Book Encyclopedia, 50th Anniversary ed. Chicago: Field Enterprises Educational Corp., 1966.

World's Great Letters, The. Edited by M. Lincoln Schuster. New York: Barnes & Noble Books, 2003.

Yadin, Yigael. *Bar-Kokhba: The Rediscovery of the Legendary Hero of the Last Jewish Revolt Against Imperial Rome.* London: Weidenfield and Nicolson, 1978.

QUARTER 1

PRETEST 1

1. Jesus
2. Holy Spirit
3. Stephen
4. Saul (or Paul)
5. Antioch
6. Barnabas
7. Mars Hill
8. Malta

PRETEST 2

1. Roman
2. lyre
3. crime
4. lions
5. blood
6. Pharisee
7. Revolt
8. history

PRETEST 3

1. F
2. T
3. F
4. T
5. T
6. T
7. F
8. T

PRETEST 4

1. Temple
2. finger
3. archaeologist
4. beliefs
5. 100
6. February
7. love
8. arrow

PRETEST 5

1. g
2. a
3. h
4. f
5. c
6. b
7. d
8. e

ACTIVITY 15C

Note: The answers to Week 5: Activity 15C, found on the next page.

PRETEST 6

1. Who are the Maya?
2. What is the Bering Strait?
3. What is a hieroglyph?
4. What is rhetoric?
5. What is Hippo?
6. What is *Confessions*?
7. What are the original languages of the Bible?
8. What is the Vulgate?

PRETEST 7

1. kidnapped
2. shamrock
3. horses
4. scourge
5. tribute
6. "barbarians"
7. burned
8. Dark Ages

WEEK 5: ACTIVITY 15C

Algebra solutions and answers

(a.) We are given the following details about the swarm:

One-fifth did one thing.

One-third did another.

Three times the difference of one-fifth and one-third did something else.

The remainder of the swarm is only one bee, which did something else.

To find out how large the swarm is, we need to find out what fraction of the swarm the remainder is.

Therefore:

$$\text{The swarm} = x$$
$$(1/5)x + (1/3)x + 3(1/3 - 1/5)x + 1 = x$$

Rewriting the fractions using the lowest common denominator (15):

$$(3/15)x + (5/15)x + (6/15)x + 1 = x$$
$$(14/15)x + 1 = x$$
$$x - (14/15)x = 1$$
$$(1/15)x = 1$$
$$x = 15$$

The straggling bee (the one that remained hovering) is 1/15 of the swarm, so the swarm must consist of 15 bees.

(b.) If R stands for rubies, E for emeralds, and P for pearls, then we know that:

$$8R = 10E = 100P$$

Therefore:

$$1E = .8R \quad \text{and} \quad 1P = .08R$$

If:

$$1R + 1E + 1P = 47, \text{ then}$$
$$1R + .8R + .08R = 47$$
$$1.88R = 47$$
$$R = 47/1.88$$
$$R = 25$$

One ruby is worth $25.

One emerald is worth $20 (.8 x 25).

One pearl is worth $2 (.08 x 25).

QUARTER 2

PRETEST 8

1. serf
2. barber
3. a sword
4. Holy Grail
5. Guinevere
6. Justinian
7. Theodora
8. cathedral of Saint Sophia

PRETEST 9

1. dove
2. Scotland
3. Fuji
4. Shinto
5. founder
6. popes
7. monk
8. poor/sick

PRETEST 10

1. T
2. T
3. F
4. F
5. T
6. F
7. T
8. F

WEEK 10, ACTIVITY 29C

a. 40 feet long, 35 feet wide, 50 feet high
b. Hajji
c. Seven
d. During the 10th and 11th months as well as during the first 10 days of the 12th month of the Islamic year
e. Nine times
f. The first was by angels at the beginning of time

   The second was by Adam

   The third by Seth, Adam's son

The fourth by Abraham and Ishmael

The seventh by Qusay, chief of the Quraish tribe

The eighth by other Quraish leaders in Mohammed's time

The ninth by Muslim leaders in 681

The tenth by Muslim leaders in 696—it is the one that stands today

WEEK 10, ACTIVITY 30C

a. Sunnis

b. Shiites

c. Sunnis

d. Shiites

e. Prophet

f. Party of Ali

PRETEST 11

1. empress

2. shrines

3. monster

4. arm

5. dragon

6. Hercules

7. Africa

8. wealth

PRETEST 12

1. f

2. e

3. h

4. b

5. c

6. a

7. d

8. g

WEEK 12, ACTIVITY 35A

? – Question   ♣ – Good luck

™ – Trademark   % – Percentage

♥ – Love   & – And

– Number   ☺ – Smiley face

© – Copyright

PRETEST 13

1. What are the Papal States?
2. What is the meaning of *Charlemagne*?
3. What is the Treaty of Verdun?
4. What is Baghdad?
5. What is *The Thousand and One Nights*?
6. Who is Aladdin?
7. What is Scandinavia?
8. What is a scramasax?

PRETEST 14

1. brooches
2. charcoal chewer
3. Thor
4. Bulgaria
5. alphabet
6. read
7. Ten Commandments
8. *Anglo-Saxon Chronicle*

QUARTER 3

PRETEST 15

1. Arctic Circle
2. Iceland
3. Floki Vilgerdarson
4. Maori
5. kiwi
6. Southern Cross
7. Zimbabwe
8. gold

PRETEST 16

1. Christmas
2. snow
3. brother
4. West
5. Holy
6. Vikings
7. Russia
8. Orthodox

PRETEST 17

1. F
2. T
3. F
4. T
5. F
6. F
7. F
8. T

PRETEST 18

1. Lucky
2. Christianity
3. North America
4. Scotland
5. William Shakespeare
6. star
7. knight
8. Reconquista

PRETEST 19

1. h
2. f
3. g
4. c
5. b
6. d
7. a
8. e

PRETEST 20

1. Who were the Petrobrusians?
2. Who were the Waldensians?
3. Who was Eleanor of Aquitaine?
4. What is a *troubadour*?
5. Who was Richard the Lionhearted?
6. Who was John?
7. Who was Moses ben Maimon?
8. What is an *exilarch*?

PRETEST 21

1. sultan
2. Third
3. horse
4. Robert, Earl of Huntingdon
5. Maid Marian
6. shogun
7. protect
8. swords

QUARTER 4

PRETEST 22

1. St. Francis of Assisi
2. St. Clara
3. St. Dominic
4. Nicholas
5. Stephen of Cloyes
6. Magna Carta
7. King John
8. Isabella

PRETEST 23

1. Sicily
2. world
3. pope
4. Dominicans
5. logic
6. Greek
7. cars
8. secret

PRETEST 24

1. F
2. T
3. T
4. F
5. T
6. T
7. T
8. F

PRETEST 25

1. poet
2. three
3. girl
4. hummingbird
5. conch shell
6. turquoise
7. crossbow
8. 7

PRETEST 26

1. f
2. d
3. a
4. c
5. b
6. h
7. g
8. e

PRETEST 27

1. What was the destination of the pilgrims in *The Canterbury Tales*?
2. Who is called "the father of the English language"?
3. Who is Chanticleer?
4. What was the Great Schism?
5. Who were the followers of John Huss?
6. What is a *dauphin*?
7. What was the nickname of Joan of Arc?
8. Who captured Joan of Arc?

PRETEST 28

1. South America
2. Amazon
3. puma
4. Balkans
5. Istanbul
6. cheese
7. Bible
8. Word

QUARTER 1

WEEK 1: EXERCISE

1. Acts 10:45
2. Acts 9:3–4
3. Acts 2:2–4
4. Acts 1:8
5. Acts 17:16–34
6. Acts 19:11–12
7. Acts 5:38–39
8. Acts 16:25–26

WEEK 2: QUIZ

1. b
2. c
3. b
4. a
5. a
6. c
7. d
8. b

WEEK 3: EXERCISE

(2 answer formats)

By number:

1. c – Pentecost
2. e – Saul
3. j – Priscilla and Aquila
4. i – Nero
5. b – Tertullian
6. a – Josephus
7. h – Eleazar
8. f – Dead
9. d – Vesuvius
10. g – Pompeii

OR

(see next column)

By letter:

a. Josephus – gray jail bars
b. Tertullian – red drop of blood
c. Pentecost – pink "50"
d. Vesuvius – brown mountain
e. Saul – black smiley face
f. Dead – blue waves
g. Pompeii – brown, black and gray shower of ash
h. Eleazar – purple sword
i. Nero – yellow and orange flames
j. Priscilla and Aquila – green tent

WEEK 4: QUIZ

1. Holy Spirit
2. Saul
3. Barnabas
4. Nero
5. Trajan
6. Josephus
7. Masada
8. Essenes
9. Pompeii
10. Bar-Kokhba
11. Apostles' Creed
12. St. Valentine

WEEK 5: EXERCISE

(Answers will vary)

WEEK 6: QUIZ

1. T
2. F
3. F
4. F
5. T
6. F
7. F
8. T
9. F
10. T
11. F
12. T
13. F
14. T
15. F

WORKSHEET 1

I. Copy as directed

II.
   a. 7
   b. 2
   c. 4
   d. 8
   e. 1
   f. 5
   g. 3
   h. 6

III.
   1. d
   2. f
   3. i
   4. b
   5. g
   6. a
   7. j
   8. h
   9. c
   10. e

WEEK 7: SOMEWHERE IN TIME #2

Largest to smallest:

1. U.S. – 3.797 million square miles
2. China – 3.705 million square miles. (Additional territories are in dispute. If counted, China would be larger than the U.S.)
3. Australia – 2.97 million square miles
4. Roman Empire (1st Century) – 2.2 million square miles

IV.

1. 400
2. 20,000
3. 960
4. 1947
5. 800
6. 200–400
7. 1,500
8. 2,000
9. 11

V.

1. First
2. Second
3. Second
4. First
5. First
6. Second
7. Second
8. Second
9. First
10. Second

VI. (Order may vary)

India

1. Diameter of the **moon**
2. **Revolution** of the Earth
3. 12-month **calendar**
4. Use of decimals and **algebra**
5. Position of the earth's **poles**
6. Arrangement of the **stars**

Both

1. Concept of **zero**
2. **Eclipses**

Maya

1. Orbit of **Venus**
2. Days in a **year**

VII.

1. c
2. f
3. a
4. b
5. g

6. d
7. e

VIII.
1. heart
2. clover
3. pen
4. clover
5. lightbulb
6. heart
7. pen
8. lightbulb

IX. Possible answers include:
1. the large size of Rome
2. army made up of barbarians
3. rise of taxes
4. rise of inflation
5. invasion of outside tribes
6. moral decline
7. materialism

QUARTER 2

WEEK 8: EXERCISE

ACROSS
1. sword
4. Lupercalia
5. Three
6. Nero
9. Maya
10. Nika
12. John
13. Clover
15. Masada
16. Saul
19. Josephus
20. Milan

DOWN
1. Scourge
2. Pompeii
3. Diocletian
7. Cotton
8. Bar-Kokhba
11. Hippo
14. Vandals
17. Barber
18. Vulgate
21. Catholic
22. Pentecost
23. Sea

WEEK 9: QUIZ

I.

1. Valentine's
2. provinces
3. cross
4. *Vedas*
5. pyramids
6. rhetoric
7. Apocrypha
8. pig

II.

1. d
2. f
3. a
4. b
5. g
6. e
7. c
8. h

WEEK 10: EXERCISE

1. Replace Jupiter with Maximian.
2. Replace Apostles' with Nicene.
3. Replace Shotoku with Gupta.
4. Replace Gibraltar with Bering.
5. Replace Attila with Ambrose.
6. Replace Pompeii with Hippo.
7. Replace Bar-Kokhba with pirates.
8. Replace elephants with horses.
9. Replace Nero with Romulus Augustus.
10. Replace pie with bread.
11. Replace triangular with round.
12. Replace musical with circus.
13. Replace "duck" with "dove."
14. Replace *Samurai* with *Nippon*.
15. Replace Market with Monastery.
16. Replace Taj Mahal with Grand Canal.
17. Replace Byzantium with Medina.
18. Replace Prophecy with Ignorance.

WEEK 11: QUIZ

I.
1. e
2. h
3. a
4. b
5. f
6. i
7. c
8. g
9. d

II.
1. g
2. f
3. b
4. h
5. i
6. a
7. c
8. d
9. e

WEEK 12: EXERCISE

Group I:
a. 4
b. 5
c. 2
d. 3
e. 1

Group II:
a. 3
b. 1
c. 4
d. 2
e. 5

Group III:
a. 3
b. 1
c. 5
d. 4
e. 2

Group IV:

    a. 2

    b. 5

    c. 3

    d. 4

    e. 1

WEEK 13: QUIZ

1. cross
2. islands
3. monk
4. Tang
5. worship
6. Koran
7. shrines
8. Grendel
9. Hercules
10. tree
11. breaker
12. hammer
13. Great
14. Baghdad
15. Denmark

WORKSHEET 2

I. Copy as directed.

II.

    1. wood, straw, wool

    2. bread, staple

    3. school, rare

    4. serfs, villeins

    5. leeches, blood, blood

    6. faith, baptizing, weddings, burying

III.

    1. Arthur, Guinevere, England

    2. Justinian, Theodora, Byzantine Empire

    3. Li Shi Min, Wu Zetian, China

    4. Mohammed, Khadijah, Mecca

    5. Shahriyar, Scheherazade, Baghdad

    6. Methodius, Cyril, Slavic nations

IV.

    1. d

    2. b

3. f

4. a

5. c

6. e

V.

1. Japan

2. China

3. China

4. China

5. Japan

6. China

7. Japan

8. China

9. Japan

10. Japan

11. China

12. Japan

13. Japan

14. China

VI.

Holy Grail – Arthur's knights

Spider – Mohammed

Monster – Beowulf

Arabian horses – Moors

Christmas tree – Boniface

Statue of Mary – Iconoclast

Magic lamp – Aladdin

Scramasax – Vikings

VII.

Koran

1. suras

2. one author

3. 22-yr. time span

4. no prophecy

5. one language

6. one place

7. Jesus as only a prophet

8. Allah is god

9. Mohammed is a prophet

Bible

    1. Old & New Testament books

    2. 40 authors

    3. 1,000-yr. time span

    4. hundreds of prophecies

    5. three languages

    6. three continents

    7. Jesus as God

    8. Allah not mentioned

    9. Mohammed not mentioned

VIII

    1. five

    2. god, Mohammed

    3. poor

    4. sunrise, Ramadan

    5. Mecca

IX. Answers will vary.

SEMESTER I TEST

I.

    1. c

    2. d

    3. a

    4. b

    5. e

    6. f

II.

    1. F

    2. T

    3. F

    4. F

    5. T

    6. T

III.

    7. b

    8. c

    9. d

    10. d

    11. a

    12. c

IV.

    13. "Our Lord"

    14. cross

    15. Samudragupta

    16. Maya

    17. North Africa

    18. Latin Vulgate

V.

    19. b

    20. f

    21. a

    22. e

    23. d

    24. c

VI.

    25. monasteries

    26. constitution

    27. Gregory

    28. Confucius

    29. Hegira

    30. Kaaba

VII.

    31. d

    32. f

    33. e

    34. a

    35. b

    36. c

VIII.

    37. Charlemagne

    38. Scheherazade

    39. Vikings

    40. Odin

    41. Methodius and Cyril

    42. Alfred the Great

IX. Possible answers include:

The Early Middle Ages have been called the Dark Ages because this was the time period AFTER the fall of the Western Roman Empire when many people in Europe were struggling to survive. This was also considered "Dark" because, with the collapse of society, many lost the ability to read God's Word.

QUARTER 3

WEEK 15: EXERCISE

(Answers may vary slightly in wording.)

2.	c. A.D. 35	—	The conversion of Saul
4.	c. A.D. 64–257	—	Christians martyred
6.	313	—	The Edict of Milan
8.	382–405	—	Jerome translates the Vulgate
10.	563	—	Columba shares Christ in Scotland
12.	863	—	Methodius and Cyril teach the Slavic nations

WEEK 16: QUIZ

Questions and answers will vary.

WEEK 17: EXERCISE

1.	i	8.	j	15.	s
2.	d	9.	a	16.	m
3.	o	10.	f	17.	n
4.	b	11.	g	18.	t
5.	l	12.	e	19.	c
6.	h	13.	p	20.	r
7.	k	14.	q		

WEEK 18: QUIZ

I.

    1. b

    2. c

    3. a

    4. c

    5. d

II.

    6. d

    7. e

    8. c

    9. a

    10. b

III.

    11. F

    12. T

    13. T

    14. F

    15. T

    16. F

    17. T

    18. T

WEEK 19: EXERCISE

Answers will vary.

WEEK 20: QUIZ

I.

1. Creed
2. Latin
3. monk
4. Koran
5. Beowulf
6. Iconoclast

II.

7. e
8. c
9. a
10. b
11. f
12. d

III.

13. E
14. G
15. A
16. F
17. B
18. H
19. C
20. D

WORKSHEET 3

I. Copy as directed.

II. (Order may vary.)

North America: Greenland, Canada

Asia: Israel, Japan, Russia, China

Europe: Spain, Scotland, Bohemia, Holy
Roman Empire, Iceland, England, France

Africa: Egypt, Zimbabwe

III.

1. k
2. c
3. a
4. l
5. i
6. d

7. m

8. h

9. b

10. e

11. j

12. f

13. g

IV.

1. Iceland

2. New Zealand

3. Iceland

4. New Zealand

5. Greenland

6. New Zealand

7. Iceland

8. Greenland

9. Greenland

10. New Zealand

11. Iceland

12. New Zealand

V.

1. Zealand, Great Zimbabwe

2. Otto I, Wenceslas

3. mountain, Red

4. Macbeth, El Cid

5. Conqueror, Gregory, Investiture

6. Waldensians, Eleanor of Aquitaine

7. John, Robin Hood

8. Saladin, shogun

VI.

1. d

2. h

3. e

4. b

5, c

6. a

7. g

8. f

VII.

1. 4

2. 2

3. 5

4. 9
5. 10
6. 1
7. 7
8. 8
9. 6
10. 3

VIII.

1. Example
2. Replace *died of starvation* with *drowned*.
3. Replace *shot by an arrow* with *ill with fever*.
4. Replace *figs* with *falcons*.
5. Replace *in an epic poem* with *on a tombstone*.
6. Replace *Josephus* with *Sir Walter Scott*.
7. Replace *Gupta* with *Fujiwara*.
8. Replace *moko* with *kamishimo*.

IX. Answers will vary. Reasons could include:

1. The Seljuk Turks forbad pilgrimages to the Holy Land.
2. The Seljuk Turks persecuted Christians.
3. The Byzantine Emperor asked for help from the West against the Turks.
4. Pope Urban II recruited help from the masses offering forgiveness of sins.
5. Some crusaders were looking for adventure.
6. Some crusaders were looking for ways to make money and gain land.
7. Some crusaders were sincerely concerned for the Holy Land.
8. Some crusaders were inspired by Bernard of Clairvaux.

QUARTER 4

WEEK 22: EXERCISE

```
+ + P H A R I S E E S + I D E + + + + + A + + +
+ + + + H + + + A G + G + E S + + + + R + + + + +
+ + + + A E + + N L N + + M S + + + T + + + + + +
+ + + + S + N A + A I + + M E + + H + + + + + + +
+ + + + S + T R T + + S + A N + U S + + + + + + +
+ + E + O + + I Y W + + + H E R + U + + + + + + N
O + + C R + U + I I + + + O S K C I R T A P + + I
+ T + + A S + L + + I + + M + + K I N G J O H N D
+ + T + B F L + + + + + + + W + + + + + + + + + A
+ + + O R I I S O N G + + + + A + + + + V + B + L
D E T R A E H N O I L E H T D R A H C I R D A + A
J + + M B T + A O + + + + + + X + + Y + I + R + S
U + + + K + I + B B + + + + + L + R + H + + N + +
S + + + C S + M + M + + N + + C N + S + + + A + +
T + + + I + A + O + U A + + + E + A + + + B + +
I + S + R + + D + T I L + + H + R D E R F L A + +
N + T + E + + + D T H + O + + L + + + + + S + +
+ + C + D + + + E U + Y + C A + + + + + + + + +
+ + L + E + + Z + + C + + N E L E A N O R + + + +
+ + A + R + U + + + + E U + + + + + + + + + + + +
+ + R + F W + + + + + R E + + + + + + + + + + + +
+ + A + + + + + + A + + S + + + + + + + + + + + +
+ + + + + + + + H + + + + + + + + + + + + + + +
+ + + + + + + + + + + + + + + + + + + + + + + +
P R A C Y L O P + + + + + + + + + + + + + + + +
```

WEEK 23: QUIZ

I

1. f
2. d
3. h
4. a
5. b
6. e
7. c
8. g

II.

9. Kaaba
10. Grendel
11. Ornament
12. Christmas
13. Vikings
14. Commandments
15. gold
16. Duke, Eastern

III.

    17. b

    18. c

    19. d

    20. a

    21. c

    22. d

    23. a

    24. c

IV. Answers will vary, but may include any one of the following:

    1. Unique to the culture of New Zealand are the Maori people with their hemp skirts, moko markings, and the game of poi. Also unique to New Zealand are kiwi birds, the moa bird, and "Captain Cookers."

    2. Roger Bacon developed ideas on refraction, reflection, and magnifying glasses. He also thought of guns, cars, airplanes, submarines, and traveling to Asia toward the West. Roger Bacon thought experimentation was important.

WEEK 24: EXERCISE

1.	b	14.	d
2.	d	15.	b
3.	a	16.	a
4.	b	17.	d
5.	a	18.	d
6.	c	19.	c
7.	c	20.	a
8.	b	21.	c
9.	d	22.	b
10.	c	23.	a
11.	a	24.	d
12.	b	25.	b
13.	b		

WEEK 25: QUIZ

I.

    1. Barnabas

    2. Nero

    3. Bar-Kokhba

    4. The Ramayana

    5. St. Patrick

    6. King Arthur

    7. Gregory the Great

    8. Mohammed

    9. Abd al-Rahman

II.

10. T

11. F

12. F

13. T

14. F

15. T

16. F

17. T

18. F

III.

19. Law

20. Richard

21. Robin Hood

22. shogun

23. Bacon

24. Marco Polo

25. spider

26. Divine

27. hearts

IV. Answers will vary, but should resemble the following:

Example: "The Hundred Years' **War** was between **France** and **England**."

1. "The **armies** of **Edward III** beat the armies of **Philip VI** using the **crossbow**."

2. "**Charles VI** and **Richard II** became kings when they were just **children**."

3. "**Richard II** married Princess **Isabelle** when she was just **7**."

4. "**Henry V** beat the French at the **Battle of Agincourt** and later **married Catherine**."

5. "**William Shakespeare** wrote a **play** about **Henry V**."

WEEK 26: EXERCISE

Exact answers will vary, but should be close to the following:

1. Paul: Once Saul, first missionary

2. Nero: Evil Roman emperor, blamed Christians for fire in Rome, persecuted many

3. Polycarp: Christian martyr, fire wouldn't burn him during execution

4. St. Valentine: Roman martyr killed and remembered on February 14

5. Constantine: Roman emperor who gave religious freedom through the Edict of Milan

6. Samudragupta: Founder of ruling family in India during the Golden Age

7. St. Patrick: Born in Great Britain, captured by pirates, became a missionary to Ireland

8. Attila the Hun: Leader of the Huns who swept through eastern Europe

9. Romulus Augustus: Last of the Western Roman Emperors, ousted by German war chief

10. King Arthur: Celtic war chief who supposedly became the greatest of all kings of England, had a round table for his knights, removed the sword in the stone, and had a queen named Guinevere

11. Justinian: Byzantine emperor married to Theodora, wrote an important code

12. Belisarius: Hired by Justinian to put down a riot, had 30,000 killed

13. Columba: Irishman with a temper, vowed to be a missionary to Scotland, set up many monasteries

14. Prince Shotoku: Brought Buddhism to Japan, wrote a constitution, called the founder of Japanese civilization.

15. Li Shi Min: Interesting ruler of the Tang dynasty in China, reinstated Confucianism, married Wu Zetian

16. Mohammed: Arab, founder of the Islamic faith

17. Wu Zetian: Ruthless but successful female ruler of China

18. Wiglaf: Helped Beowulf fight a dragon in Sweden

19. St. Boniface: English missionary to Germany, used evergreen as symbol of God's love

20. Charles Martel: Fought and won the Battle of Tours that stopped the Arab invasion of Europe

21. Pepin: Crowned king of the Franks by the pope, the father of Charlemagne

22. Aladdin: Fictitious character from *The Arabian Nights* who steals a magical lamp

23. Thor: Norse god from whom Thursday is named, usually depicted with a hammer

24. Rostislav: Moravian king who requested missionaries to the Slavic region to help bring peace to warring countries

25. Good King Wenceslas: Kindly duke (king) of Bohemia from whom we get a Christmas carol

26. Vladimir: Grand Duke of Kiev who brought the Eastern Orthodox Church to Russia

27. General Zhao Kuang Yin: Started the Song dynasty in China

28. St. Simon: Said by the Coptic Church to have prayed to move a mountain

29. Eric the Red: Born in Norway, grew up in Iceland, named and settled Greenland

30. Malcolm III: Killed Macbeth in revenge for the death of his father and the throne of Scotland

31. El Cid: Hero to the Spanish for driving the Muslims out of Spain

32. William the Conqueror: Norman who invaded England at the Battle of Hastings

33. Hildebrand: Original name of Pope Gregory VII who was involved in the Investiture Controversy with Henry IV

34. Eleanor of Aquitaine: Queen of France and later of England, the wife of Henry II and mother of Richard the Lionhearted and King John, well known for her romanticism

35. Maimonides: Jewish philosopher who compiled the books of the Law and the Talmud into the Mishneh Torah

36. Frederick Barbarossa: One of three kings who started on the Third Crusade, drowned during the crusade, also started the term for the "Holy" Roman Empire

37. Robin Hood: Outlaw in England during the reigns of Richard the Lionhearted and King John, became a legend for fighting injustice though it may or may not be true

38. Minamoto Yoritomo: Moved the authority of the Japanese emperor to himself, began the position of shogun

39. Stephen of Cloyes: French shepherd boy who led thousands of children in a crusade to the Holy Land; most of the children he led were drowned in sinking ships or taken as slaves to Africa

40. King John: Unpopular son of Eleanor of Aquitaine; sealed the Magna Carta against his will, limiting the rights of kings

41. Frederick II: Holy Roman Emperor, king of Sicily and king of Jerusalem, regarded as brilliant by some and despised by others, especially Pope Gregory IX who found him immoral and ungodly

42. Albert Magnus: Philosopher and the tutor of Thomas Aquinas

43. Roger Bacon: Brilliant scientist who thought of cars, planes, and motorboats before they existed, exiled by the Franciscans

44. Genghis Khan: Feared Mongolian leader who conquered a vast part of the world including China, grandfather of Kublai Khan

45. Rustichello: French cellmate of Marco Polo and writer of *The Book of Marco Polo*

46. Beatrice: Young woman with whom Dante fell in love, used as part of the story line in *The Divine Comedy*

47. Montezuma: Last of the Aztec chiefs, conquered by Cortes

48. Henry V: King of England who won the Battle of Agincourt against the French in the Hundred Years' War

49. Carrier of the bubonic plague: the flea

50. John Wycliffe: Early reformer in England whose works were controversial, helped in process of translating the Bible into English

51. Edward III: King of England who favored the ideas of John Wycliffe and encouraged him to discuss controversial matters with the pope, which led to Wycliffe's being fired from Oxford and his writings burned

WEEK 27: QUIZ

I.

1. h
2. i
3. g
4. b
5. c
6. f
7. a
8. j
9. d
10. e

II.

11. Floki Vilgerdarson
12. The Zimbabweans
13. Wenceslas
14. General Zhao Kuang Yin
15. Eric the Red
16. Leif Ericsson
17. Macbeth
18. William the Conqueror
19. Pope Urban II
20. Saladin

III.

21. e
22. g
23. b
24. f

25. h

26. j

27. d

28. a

29. c

30. i

IV.   Answers will vary but could include the following:

   1.   It was not wise for Nicholas and Stephen to lead children on a crusade because (a) they were unprepared, (b) they were told not to by their parents, (c) they were told not to by church leaders, (d) it was dangerous.

   2.   The Black Death was most commonly spread (a) through fleas that infected rats, (b) through the air by those with infected lungs.

   3.   The Forbidden City was forbidden in order to (a) protect the emperor from outsiders, (b) keep the emperor inside China.

   4.   Joan of Arc was accused of (a) being a witch, (b) heresy, (c) wearing men's clothing, (d) starting a crusade against the Hussites.

WORKSHEET 4

I.   Copy as directed.

II.

   1.   St. Joan of Arc

   2.   St. Dominic

   3.   St. Clara

   4.   St. Thomas Aquinas

   5.   St. Francis

III.

   1.   c

   2.   e

   3.   a

   4.   d

   5.   b

IV.

   1.   a

   2.   b

   3.   c

   4.   d

   5.   e

   6.   f

   7.   g

   8.   h

V.

   1.   Emperor Yongle

   2.   south

   3.   Tiananmen

4. 720,000

5. long life

6. clocks, bonsai

7. invisible, compass

8. 9,999, nine, nine

9. Five, five, five

10. Purple, Gu Gong

VI.

1. Cross – John Huss

2. Flag – William Wallace

3. Cross – John Huss

4. Teardrop – Joan of Arc

5. Flag – William Wallace

6. Flag – William Wallace; & Teardrop – Joan of Arc

7. Teardrop – Joan of Arc

8. Flag – William Wallace

9. Teardrop – Joan of Arc

10. Flag – William Wallace

11. Cross – John Huss

12. Cross – John Huss; & Teardrop – Joan of Arc

13. Cross – John Huss

VII.

1. Inka

2. Inka

3. Aztec

4. Inka

5. Inka

6. Aztec

7. Aztec

8. Aztec

9. Inka

10. Aztec

11. Inka

12. Inka

13. Aztec

14. Aztec

VIII.

1. c

2. g

3. e

4. a

5. i

6. h

7. b

8. d

9. f

IX.

- *The Divine Comedy* – Dante

- Cars, planes, & subs – Roger Bacon

- *The Canterbury Tales* – Chaucer

- *Summa Theologica* – Thomas Aquinas

- Book on falcons – Frederick II

X. Answers may vary, but could include the following:

1. The invention of the printing press was significant because:

- it made books more affordable.

- it helped to produce more books than ever before.

- it helped in the mass production of Bibles.

- it ultimately helped in spreading the Gospel of Christ.

2. Good topics to focus on in answering this question might include: the work of St. Francis and others in meeting the needs of people; the writing of the Magna Carta; the Black Death drawing many to the church; the courage of John Wycliffe and John Huss in trying to reform the church; the inspiration of Joan of Arc; the invention of the printing press.

SEMESTER II TEST

I.

1. b

2. e

3. f

4. a

5. c

6. d

II.

43. F

44. T

45. F

46. F

47. T

48. T

III.

49. d

50. c

51. b

52. a

53. d

54. b

IV.

    55. Hastings

    56. Investiture

    57. Hermit

    58. heresy

    59. England

    60. Mishneh Torah

V.

    61. d

    62. a

    63. f

    64. b

    65. e

    66. c

VI.

    67. pope

    68. Dominicans

    69. Franciscans

    70. Kublai

    71. Millions

    72. Robert Bruce

VII.

    73. c

    74. e

    75. a

    76. f

    77. b

    78. d

VIII.

    79. Geoffrey Chaucer

    80. John Huss

    81. Joan of Arc

    82. Pachacuti

    83. Mohammed II

    84. Johannes Gutenberg

IX. Answers will vary but could include these thoughts:

The main factor that contributed to the spread of the Black Death in Europe was ignorance of the fact that fleas carried the plague germs. Fleas infected rats, which were spread by the trading industry. Another factor contributing to the problem was poor hygiene and treatment of sewage in the Middle Ages. Mongols were guilty of throwing diseased body parts at their enemies in warfare. Though less common, some plague germs were passed through coughing, making it another factor in the spread of the Black Death.

INDEX

-A-

Abbas, al-, 211
Abbasid dynasty, 183, 184, 211
Abbey of Fulda, 195
Abd al-Rahman, 183, 185, 208
Abraham, 166
Abu Bekr, 161, 162, 164, 168, 169
Acre, 351, 393
Adam, 318
Aelia Capitolina, 53
Africa, 65, 83, 99, 100, 166, 169, 182, 183, 201,
    262–264, 305, 381, 484
Agincourt, Battle of, 436, 467
Agrippina, 24, 26
Ainu, 139
Aix-la-Chapelle, 208
Alaska, 292
Albania, 483
Albigensians, 335
Alexander the Great, 409
Alexandria, 201, 287
Alfonsi, Petrus, 188
Alfred the Great, King of Wessex and England,
    228–231, 314
Ali, 161, 169
Alighieri, Dante, *see* Dante Alighieri
Allah, 161–164, 167–169, 185, 186, 197
Allah-Taala, 161
Alps, 97, 380, 381
Alrui, David, 344
Amazon, 477
Ambrose, Bishop of Milan, 83
America, *see* United States
Americans, 300, 355
Andalus, al-, 114, 182–186. *See also* Cordoba; Sefarad
Andalusians, 209
Andes, 477
Angles, 99, 124, 145, 229, 314
Anglo-Saxons, 100, 179, 180, 230, 317
Anna, 277
Antarctica, 257
Antioch, 13, 14
Antonius Pius, 28
Ao-tea-roa, *see* New Zealand
Apocrypha, 42, 88
Apostles' Creed, 57, 58
Aquila, 16
Aquinas, Thomas, Saint, 370, 395–397, 427
Aquino, 395

Aquitaine, 335–338
Arab Empire, 323, 341
Arabia, 160, 164, 166, 183, 197, 201
Arabs, 114, 160, 164, 166, 183, 184, 284, 287, 381, 487
Aragon, 306
Arch of Constantine, 67
Argentina, 334, 478
Aristotle, 396
Armenia, 411
Arnarson, Ingolf, 255
Arthur (grandson of Eleanor of Aquitaine), 339
Arthur, King of England, 123–126, 229, 314, 337
Asia, 4, 14–16, 65, 68, 72, 80, 96, 166, 169, 257, 264,
    410, 413, 443, 477, 482–484
Asoka, King of India, 156
Assisi, 374
Assyrians, 341
Atacama Desert, 477
Athens, 15
Attila the Hun, 96–98, 100, 275
Augustine of Canterbury, Saint, 145, 229
Augustine of Hippo, Saint, 4, 83–85, 87, 314
Augustus Caesar, 23
Augustus, Philip, King of France, 351
Aurelius, Marcus, 29, 65
Australia, 257, 258
Averroës, 396
Aztecs, 370, 429–432
Aztlan, 429

-B-

Babylonia, 181
Babylonians, 166, 341
Bacon, Roger, 370, 399–401
Baffin Island, 301
Baghdad, 211
Balkan Mountains, 483
Balkan Peninsula, 483
Balkans, 483
Baltic Sea, 276
Bangladesh, 169
Bannockburn, 417
Bar-Kokhba, 4, 53–56, 323
Barbarossa, Frederick, 274, 351, 391, 395
Barcelona, 209
Barnabas, 12–15
Bayeux Tapestry, 316
Beatrice, 426–428
Beautiful Gate, 9

Becket, Thomas à, Archbishop of Canterbury, Saint, 337, 338, 459

Bede, 182

Bedouins, 42, 166

Beijing, 445, 446. *See also* Peking

Belisarius, 130

Belize, 82

Ben Maimon, Moses, *see* Maimonides, Moses

Ben Yair, Eleazar, 40, 41

Benedict of Nursia, Saint, 102

Beowulf, 179–181

Berbers, 183, 184

Berengaria, 353

Bering Strait, 80

Berkshire, 229

Bernard of Clairvaux, 325, 428

Berserks, 215

Bethar, 54

Bethlehem, 23

Bi Sheng, 283

Bible (Word of God), 3, 8, 9, 11, 16, 42, 44, 73, 84–88, 101, 121, 125, 126, 130, 137, 140, 168, 180, 181, 186, 197, 202, 226, 227, 230, 382, 400, 428, 433, 450, 451, 462, 465, 486–488

Bill of Rights, 384

Black Death, 370, 435, 442, 444

Black Sea, 68, 226, 275, 443, 483

Blandina, 29

Blondel, 353

Boccaccio, Giovanni, 445

Bohemia, 227, 271–274, 462, 487

Bohemians, 273, 462

Boleslav, 272

Bolivia, 478

Bonaparte, Napoleon, 208

Boniface, Saint, 115, 194–196, 201

Boris, King of Bulgaria, 227

Bors, Sir, 126

Bothnagowan, 304

Bretigny, Treaty of, 435

Britain, *see* Great Britain

Bruce, Robert, King of Scotland, 370, 416, 417, 434

Brude, 137

Bruis, Peter, 333

Buddha, 141, 156, 168, 177

Buddhism, 115, 140, 141, 356

Buddhists, 157, 411

Bulgaria, 227, 483

Bulgarians, 483

Bulgars, 226, 275

Burgos, 307

Burgundians, 469

Burgundy, 274,

Burma, 115, 410, 411

Byzantine Empire, 97, 101, 114, 128, 130, 131, 144, 208, 212, 216, 226, 276, 277, 287, 323, 324, 336, 370, 483, 484

Byzantium, 68, 128, 482. *See also* Constantinople; Istanbul

-C-

Cadiz, 182

Caedmon, 182

Caesar Augustus, *see* Augustus Caesar

Caesarea, 16

Caffa, 443

Calais, 434

Calicut, 72

Calvin, John, 85

Cambodia, 115, 410

Camelot, 123

Canada, 292, 301, 384

Canossa, 321

Canterbury, 459

Canterbury Tales, The, 457, 459, 487

Cape of Good Hope, 415

Carolingian, 207

Carrick, 417

Carthage, 83, 201

Caspian Sea, 276

Castile, 306

Catacombs, 26

Catherine of Alexandria, Saint, 467

Catherine of Siena, Saint, 445, 466

Catherine of Valois, 436

Caxton, William, 487

Celts, 95, 123, 124, 228, 229, 314, 317

Central America, 4, 80, 82, 370

Chalons-sur-Marne, Battle of, 97

Chang'an (Xi'an), 157, 282

Charlemagne, 207–210, 274, 319, 320, 335, 337, 341, 392, 409

Charles VI, 435, 467

Charles VII, 467–470

Charles "Martel," 201, 207

Charles University, 462

Chaucer, Geoffrey, 370, 457, 459, 460, 487

Cheng Ho, 415

Chile, 478

Chin empire, 410

China, 114, 115, 139, 141, 155–158, 176–178, 181, 212, 250, 262, 263, 282–285, 370, 400, 409, 410, 413, 414, 445, 446, 448, 477

Chinese, 114, 140, 155, 176, 283, 284, 410, 411, 413, 414, 445, 446, 448, 486

Christ (Jesus), 3–5, 8, 10–16, 23, 25, 27, 31, 54, 58, 60, 66–69, 73, 83–88, 96, 115, 125, 126, 136, 137, 140, 141, 143, 167, 168, 177, 186, 194, 195, 198, 200, 226, 230, 249, 260, 271, 276, 286, 287, 323, 324, 333, 334, 340, 341, 344, 369, 374–378, 393, 411, 462, 467, 482, 487, 488

Christianity, 27, 29, 30, 57, 68, 73, 83–85, 100, 115, 130, 139, 145, 160, 167, 168, 197, 198, 201, 209, 216, 224, 229, 249, 271, 274, 277, 286, 300, 303, 306, 314, 341, 369, 393, 396, 411

Christians, 3, 4, 9–13, 15, 17, 25, 27–29, 44, 47, 54, 57, 58, 60, 65–69, 98, 114, 120, 121, 126, 137, 143, 157, 164, 167–169, 182, 184, 186, 197–199, 251, 276, 287–289, 305–307, 323, 325, 341–343, 350–352, 380, 396, 411, 482

Cipango, *see* Japan

Clara dei Sciffi, Saint, 369, 374–378

Clement IV, 401

Cleopatra, 23, 178

Clovis, 100, 201

Cologne, 380

Colosseum, 4, 26, 27

Columba, Saint, 115, 136, 137, 194, 215, 303

Columbus, Christopher, 300, 302, 307, 400

Compiegne, 469

Confucius, 156, 177, 282, 283

Conrad III, 325

Constantine I (Constantine the Great), 4, 67–69, 84, 98, 120, 128, 342, 482, 484

Constantine V, 199

Constantine XI, 484

Constantinople, 69, 128–130, 199, 211, 226, 276, 277, 323, 336, 370, 413, 482–484, 488.
    See also Byzantium; Istanbul

Cook, Captain James, 260

Copts, 286, 287

Cordoba, 182, 184, 185, 211. *See also* Andalus, al-; Sefarad

Corinth, 16

Cortes, 432

Council of Constance, 463

Council of Nicaea, 69

Crecy, 434

Crusades, 249, 274, 323–325, 336, 338, 351, 370, 376, 380, 384, 396
    Children's, 380–382
    First, 323, 324
    Second, 323, 325, 336, 350, 428
    Third, 350, 351, 380

Culhuan tribe, 429

Cupid, 60

Cuzco, 478, 479

Cyprian of Carthage, 29

Cyprus, 53, 129

Cyril, 115, 226, 227, 270

Czech Republic, 226, 270, 462

Czechoslovakia, 270

-D-

Daibutsu, 141

Damascus, 13, 183, 185, 211, 325

Damascus (Bishop), 87

Danegeld, 216

Danelaw, 230, 314

Danes, 180, 229–231

Dante Alighieri, 370, 426–428, 460

Danube, 97

Day of Pentecost, 9

Dead Sea, 40, 42, 43, 53, 55

Dead Sea Scrolls, 4, 42, 43, 55

Delhi, 71

Demetrius, 16

Denmark, 179, 181, 214, 216, 222

Diaz, Rodrigo, *see* El Cid

Diocletian, 65, 66, 68, 86, 128

Divine Comedy, The, 426–428

Dome of the Rock, 350, 352, 380

Dominic, Saint, 369, 374–378, 411

Dominicans, 377, 378, 395, 411

Domitian, 27

Domremy, 467

Donar, 194

Donati, Gemma, 427

Dorset (people), 292

Drahomira, 270, 271

Druids, 95

Dublin, 216

Dunbar, Battle of, 416

Duncan I, King of Scotland, 303, 304

Duns Scotus, John, 398

Dunsinane, 304

-E-

Eastern Orthodox Church, 276, 277

Ecuador, 478

Edict of Milan, 68, 482

Edward I, 342, 416

Edward II, 384, 417

Edward III, 417, 434, 435, 450

Edward the Black Prince, of Wales, 435

Edward the Confessor, 314, 315

Egypt, 45, 53, 169, 212, 262, 286, 287, 376

Egyptians, 224, 263, 286

Ed Cid, 250, 305–307

Eleanor of Aquitaine, 250, 335–339, 342, 350, 383

England, 65, 99, 100, 123–126, 136, 145, 179–181,
194, 215, 216, 228, 229–231, 250, 260, 314–316,
319, 337, 355, 370, 377, 383–385, 399, 416, 417,
434–436, 443, 449–451, 462, 463, 469, 477, 487

English, 230, 231, 315–317, 337, 384, 416, 417, 435,
436, 466–470

English Channel, 342, 434

Ephesus, 16

Eric the Red, 290–293, 300

Ericsson, Leif (Leif the Lucky), 249, 291, 300–302

Eskimos, *see* Inuit

Essenes, 31, 43, 44

Eulogius, 186

Euphrates River, 183

Europe, 3-5, 14–16, 65, 68, 87, 96, 98, 99–101, 113–
115, 118–123, 130, 137, 155, 157, 158, 166, 169,
181–184, 186, 197, 198, 201, 202, 208, 214–216,
224, 226, 228, 229, 231, 250, 262, 264, 274, 276,
283, 316, 334, 338, 341, 342, 350, 351, 357, 358,
370, 376, 380, 392, 393, 396, 400, 410, 414, 435,
442, 443, 460, 463, 470, 480, 482–488

Europeans, 114, 115, 158, 201, 209, 224, 260, 283,
293, 380, 414, 443, 448

Eve, 318

-F-

Faeroe Islands, 254

Falkirk, 416

Fatima, 169

Fatimy, Moaz Ladeen Allah El, 287, 288

Faustines, 28

Felicitas, 29

Felix, 16

Ferdinand, King of Spain, 307

Festus, 16

Flagellant Brothers, 442

Flavius, 33

Flora, 186

Florence, 426

Forbidden City, 370, 445–448, 478

France, 95, 100, 121, 182, 201, 207, 208, 210, 216, 250,
274, 314, 316, 319, 333, 335, 339, 342, 351, 370,
381, 384, 434–436, 443, 463, 467, 468, 477

Francis of Assisi, Saint, 369, 374–378, 399, 411

Franciscans, 375, 377, 378, 399, 401, 411

Franks, 100, 201, 207–209

Frederick II (Stupor Mundi), 370, 391–393

Freisland, 194, 195

French, 434, 435, 468–470

Frey, 224

Freydid, 302

Frigg, 224

Froissart, Jean, 436

Fuji, Mount, 139

Fujiwara family, 357

-G-

Gabriel, 161, 162

Galahad, Sir, 126

Galileans, 32

Gamaliel, 10

Gardar, 254, 256

Gardarsholm, *see* Iceland

Gaul, 97, 100

Gelasius, 60

Genghis Khan, 409–411, 445, 482, 483

Genoa, 381, 414, 443

Gentiles, 9, 10, 29, 341

George, Saint, 66, 181

Germans, 97, 98, 196, 274, 339, 393

Germany, 194, 195, 201, 207, 208, 210, 271, 273, 274,
276, 319, 321, 380, 391, 393, 443, 463

Gibraltar, Strait of, 182, 305

Gobi Desert, 409

God, 3, 4, 10, 12, 15–17, 23, 25, 28, 54, 66, 69, 73,
83–88, 95, 115, 120, 136, 137, 140, 160, 164,
167–169, 181, 186, 195, 197, 199, 200–202, 224,
251, 260, 276, 277, 282, 286, 288, 289, 304, 306,
318, 324, 333, 334, 341, 342, 371, 375–377, 381,
395–397, 427, 428, 433, 442–444, 450, 451, 462

Golden Horn, 484

Gospel, 3, 4, 10, 14, 16, 95, 96, 115, 125, 136, 144,
145, 194, 201, 224, 226, 249, 260, 270, 300, 303,
377, 378, 411, 433

Goths, 100, 275

Granada, 307, 341

Grand Canal, 155

Great Britain, 94, 95, 123, 136

Great Schism, 463

Greece, 15, 24, 71, 72, 197, 199, 275, 483

Greeks, 15, 197–199, 224, 447

Greenland, 216, 249, 250, 290–293, 300, 301

Greenlanders, 292, 293, 300

Gregory I (Gregory the Great), 143–146, 229, 341

Gregory VII, 251, 318–322, 392, 427

Gregory IX, 392, 393

Gregory XI, 450

Grimm, Jacob, 275

Grimm, Wilhelm, 275

Groote, Gerhard, 453
Grosseteste, Robert, 400
Gu Gong, *see* Forbidden City
Guatemala, 81, 82
Gudrid, 301
Guinevere, Queen of England, 126, 337
Gupta dynasty, 71, 72
Gutenberg, Johannes, 486, 487
Guthrum, 230

-H-

Hadrada, Harold, King of Norway, 315
Hadrian, 28, 53, 124
Hagar, 166
Han dynasty, 155
Hangchow, 155
Hannibal, 183
Harold of Wessex, 315
Hasdai, 187
Hastings, Battle of, 250, 315, 434
Hawaii, 258
Hebrews, 340
Hebrides, 254
Hegira, 163
Helluland, *see* Baffin Island
Henry II (Henry Plantagenet), 336–339, 383, 459
Henry III, 385
Henry IV, 251, 318–322, 392, 427
Henry V, 436, 467
Henry VII, 427
Henry VIII, 319
Herculaneum, 48
Herjolfsson, Bjarni, 300–302
Herod Agrippa, 16
Herod the Great, 24, 32, 39, 40
Hesse, 194
Hildebrand, *see* Gregory VII
Hindu (Hinduism), 73
Hippo, 87
Hitler, Adolf, 342
Hjorleif, 255
Hokkaido, 139
Holy Spirit, 3, 8–10, 86, 115, 195, 378
Honduras, 81
Honshu, 139
Hood, Robin (Robert), 250, 353–355, 383
Horiuji Temple, 141
Hroswitha, 185
Hsi Hsia empire, 410
Hugh the Iron, 381
Huitzilopochtli, 429

Hundred Years' War, 370, 434–436, 467
Hungarians, 273
Hungary, 227
Hungwu (Zhu Yuanzhang), 445, 446
Huns, 96–99, 275
Huss, John, 369, 462–465, 470, 487
Hussites, 465, 469, 470

-I-

Iberian Peninsula, 182, 183
Iberians, 182
Ibn al-Arabi, 208
Ibn Battuta, 415
Ibn Hazm, 186
Ibn Nagrila, Samuel, 187
Iceland, 216, 249, 254–257, 290–292, 300–302, 477
Icelanders, 254
Iconoclast Controversy, 197, 198
Ignatius, 27
Independence (people), 292
India, 4, 71–73, 80, 169, 212, 400, 411, 413, 477
Indians, 4, 72, 73
Indonesia, 169
Indonesians, 140
Inkas, 370, 477–481, 484
Innocent III, 375, 381, 383, 384, 391
Interamna, 60
Inti, 479
Intihuatana, 478, 479
Inuit, 293, 302
Investiture Controversy, 251, 318, 319
Iona, 136, 137
Iran, 169, 275
Iranians, 275
Ireland, 95, 96, 136, 137, 194, 216, 255, 417
Irene, 199, 209
Irish, 94–96, 136
Isabella, 383
Isabella, Queen of Spain, 307
Isabelle, Princess, 435
Ishmael, 166
Islam, 115, 160–162, 164, 166–169, 182, 201, 287, 323
Isle of Avalon, 126
Isle of Patmos, 27
Israel, 28, 32, 39, 41, 54–56, 169, 323
Israelites, 56, 197, 340, 380
Istanbul, 68, 484. *See also* Byzantium; Constantinople
Italians, 273, 443, 487
Italy, 45, 100, 199, 208, 258, 273, 274, 391, 395, 396, 427, 443, 463, 483
Itil, 276

-J-

Jaffa, 351, 352

James, 305

Janissaries, 484

Japan, 114, 115, 139–141, 181, 250, 356–358, 410, 477

Japanese, 139–141, 356, 357, 410, 414

Jerome, Saint, 4, 86–88, 451

Jerusalem, 4, 12, 16, 17, 32, 40, 53–56, 100, 121, 162, 169, 306, 323–325, 342, 350–352, 380, 392, 393

Jesus, *see* Christ

Jewish Revolt
First, 32, 39, 53, 54
Second, 53–56

Jews, 4, 9, 10–12, 15, 16, 25, 27, 29, 32, 33, 39–41, 43, 44, 47, 53–56, 87, 88, 100, 114, 162–164, 166, 168, 169, 182, 184, 185, 197, 251, 276, 287–289, 323, 325, 340–344, 350, 351, 383, 393, 396, 442, 443

Jimmu Tenno, 140

Joan of Arc, Saint, 370, 436, 466–470

Job, 145

John (apostle), 4, 9, 10, 27

John of Montecorvino, 411

John, King of England, 339, 342, 353, 355, 370, 383–385

John XII, 274

Jomsvikings, 215

Joseph, 23

Joseph of Arimathea, 125

Josephus, 31–33, 39–41, 43, 53, 55

Jovita, 28

Judaism, 12, 31, 73, 160

Judea, 13

Julius Caesar, 23, 97, 123, 228, 229, 314, 479

Juno, 60

Jupiter (Zeus), 53, 54, 66

Justinian I, 128–131, 276, 482–484

Jutes, 100, 123, 145, 229, 314

-K-

Kaaba, 160, 161, 163, 164, 166

Kaifeng, 282

Kallaallit Nunaat, *see* Greenland

Kami, 140

Kara Kitai empire, 410

Khadijah, 161

Kharaz, Simaan El, *see* Simon, Saint

Khazars, 275

Kiev, 216, 276, 377

Koran, 161, 164, 168

Korea, 115, 139, 410

Koreans, 140, 486

Kublai Khan, 370, 409–411, 413, 414, 445, 446

Kukulcan, 81

Kupe, 257

Kush, 262

Kushites, 262, 263

Kyushu, 139

-L-

Labrador, 301

Lancelot, Sir, 126

Langland, William, 354

Lech River, 273

Leo III, 198, 199, 209

Leon, 306

Lesbos, 199

Li Shi Min, 156, 157, 176

Li Yuan, 156

Li Zhi, 176, 177

Lindisfarne, 215

Lollards, 451, 465, 487

Lombards, 144, 208

Lombardy, 145

London, 230, 337, 350, 443, 460

Louis VII, 325, 335, 336

Lucius III, 334

Ludmilla, 270, 271

Lully, Raymond, 398

Lumhanan, 304

Lupercalia, 60

Luther, Martin, 85, 452

Lydveldid Island, *see* Iceland

Lyon, 333

-M-

Macbeth, 250, 303, 304

Maccabees, 43

Machu Picchu, 479, 480

Magna Carta, 383–385

Magnus, Albert(us), 396, 427

Magyars, 273, 275

Mahabharata, 72

Maimonides, Moses, 342–343, 396

Mainz, 195, 486

Malcolm III, 304

Malory, Sir Thomas, 436

Malta, 17

Maori, 250, 257–260

Margaret, Saint, 467

Mark (apostle), 286

Mark-land, *see* Labrador

Mars Hill, 15

Marseille, 381

Martin V, 451, 463

Martyr, Justin, 29
Martyr(s), 10, 27, 29
Mary (Jesus' mother), 23, 198, 450
Masada, 3, 39-41, 53
Massenet, Jules, 307
Matilda, Queen, 315, 316
Mauri, 183
Maxentius, 67
Maximian, 65, 66
Maya, 4, 80–82, 431
Mecca, 160–163, 166, 185
Medina, 162–164, 169
Mediterranean Sea, 16, 99, 100, 182, 263, 380,
    413, 483
Melanesia, 257
Merlin, 124, 126
Meroe, 263
Merovingians, 207
Mesopotamia, 53, 201, 212, 350
Methodius, 115, 226, 227, 270
Mexica, see Aztecs
Mexico, 4, 80–82, 429, 430
Mexico City, 429, 430
Mi Feng, 284
Michael the Archangel, 467
Michelangelo, 158, 428
Micronesia, 258
Middle East, 99, 169
Milan, 183
Milvian Bridge, Battle of, 67, 68
Minamoto Yoritomo, 357
Ming dynasty, 370, 445, 446
Ming Huang, 159
Mishneh Torah, 343
Mohammed, 114, 115, 161–164, 166–169, 183, 186,
    197, 211, 323, 393
Mohammed II, 484, 485
Mokattam Mountain, 289
Mongolia, 409, 410, 445, 446
Mongolian empire, 409, 411
Mongols, 275, 409–411, 443–446
Monica, 83
Montezuma, 432
Moors, 114, 182, 183, 185, 201, 305
Moravia, 227
Moravians, 226
Mordred, 126
Moses, 288
Moses (from the Old Testament), 168, 197, 393
Mount Badon, Battle of, 125
Mozarabs, 184, 186
Mozart, 428

Muallqat, 166
Muslims, 114, 157, 160, 163, 164, 166–169, 182, 184,
    185, 197, 201, 202, 208, 209, 251, 276, 287, 289,
    305–307, 323–325, 341, 351, 352, 376, 380, 393,
    396, 411

-N-
Naddod, 254
Nahal Hever, 55
Naples, University of, 392, 395
Nara, 141
Native Americans, 293, 302
Navarre, 305
Nebuchadnezzar, 181
Nero, 3, 17, 23–27, 31, 32, 66
Netherlands, 260
New Zealand, 250, 257–260, 477
New Zealanders, 259
Newfoundland, 301
Nicene Creed, 69
Nicholas, 380, 381
Nicholas, Saint, 61
Nieuw Zeeland, see New Zealand
Nigeria, 169, 263
Nile River, 263
Nippon, see Japan
Noah, 254, 477
Nok, 263
Normandy, 216, 314, 316
Normans, 231, 314–317, 434
North Africa, 83, 201
North America, 80, 216, 257, 292, 300–302, 355, 477
North Americans, 400
North Atlantic Sea, 291
North Island (of New Zealand), 258
Norway, 214, 216, 222, 255, 290, 291, 300
Norwegians, 255
Notre Dame, 121
Nova Scotia, 301
Novgorod, 276
Nubians, see Kushites
Nunavut, 301

-O-
Obadiah, 343
Oceania, 257, 258
Octavia, 24
Octavian, 23
Odin (Woden), 224
Odoacer, 100
Olbia, 275
Orleans, 469

Osman, 483
Ostrogoths, 100
Otto I (Otto the Great), 249, 273, 274, 277
Ottoman Empire, 482, 485
Ottoman Turks, 370, 482–485, 488
Oxford University, 399, 443, 449, 450, 462

-P-

Pachacuti, 478, 479, 481, 484
Pakistan, 169
Palestine, 201, 323–325, 381, 392, 413
Pan, 60
Panticapaeum, 275
Paris, 216, 336, 395, 396, 399, 443
Parthians, 39
Patricius, 83
Patrick, Saint, 4, 94–96, 164
Paul (Saul of Tarsus; apostle), 3, 4, 11–17, 25, 27, 31, 197, 341, 482
Peking, 155, 410, 413. *See also* Beijing
Pelagius, 186
Pelagius II, 144
Pentecost, 18
Pepin the Short, 207, 320, 392
Percivale, Sir, 126
Perfectus, 186
Perpetua, 29
Persia, 212, 275, 410, 443
Persians, 166, 275
Peru, 478
Peter (apostle), 4, 8–10, 25, 27, 143, 195
Peter the Hermit, 324, 325
Petrarch, Francesco, 429
Petrobrusians, 249, 333, 334
Pharisee, 11, 12, 15, 31, 43
Philip VI, 434
Phoenicians, 182
Phrygia, 66
Picts, 136, 137
Pied Piper of Hamelin, 380
Pilate, 125
Pillars of Hercules, 183
Pliny the Younger, 48
Poggius, Fra, 463, 464
Poitiers, 201
  Battle of, 201, 435
Poland, 227, 273
Poles, 273
Polo, Marco, 139, 370, 411–414, 445
Polycarp, 28
Polynesia, 258

Polynesian Islands, 257, 258
Polynesians, 258
Pompeii, 45–47
Poppaea, 24
Portugal, 182, 306
Portuguese, 448
Porziuncola, 375, 377
Prague, 272, 462
Priscilla, 16
Procopius, 129
Protestants, 143, 451
Punic Wars, 183
Pyrenees Mountains, 182, 208, 209, 305

-Q-

Qin dynasty, 155
Qumran, 43
Quraish, 162

-R-

Rachel, 197
Radbod, 194, 195
Ramayana, 72
Rashid, Harun al-, 211, 212
Reconquista, 306, 307
Red Sea, 137, 160, 381
Reims, 468, 469
Renoir, 428
Reykjavik, 255
Rhine River, 380
Richard I (the Lionhearted), 250, 338, 339, 350–353, 355, 380, 383, 384
Richard II, 384, 435
Roland, 209
Rollo, 216
Roman Catholic Church, 143, 378, 397, 452, 470
Roman Empire, 23, 27, 65, 68, 84, 87, 96, 98–100, 120, 128, 144, 155, 208, 209, 274, 409
  Eastern, *see* Byzantine Empire
  Holy, 209, 273, 274, 321, 322, 391, 427
  Western, 4, 67, 97, 100, 101, 113, 123, 128, 143, 183, 184, 201, 208, 229, 482
Romania, 483
Romans, 4, 16, 24, 25, 27, 31–33, 39, 47, 53, 72, 80, 84, 85, 97–99, 114, 123, 124, 128, 136, 166, 183, 184, 197, 198, 224, 228, 229, 273, 314, 317, 323, 341, 447
Rome, 4, 16, 17, 23–27, 31–33, 41, 42, 44, 47, 54, 60, 65, 71, 81, 85, 97, 100, 114, 121, 128, 143–145. 195, 197, 209, 229, 273, 287, 321–323, 373, 377, 463, 485

Romulus Augustus, 100
Rostislav, King of Moravia, 226
Rouen, 466, 469
Rudolf, 321
Runnymede, 384
Rurik, 276
Rus, 276
Rusafa, 185
Russia, 216, 224, 226, 227, 250, 275–277, 292, 410,
    411, 443, 484
Rustichello, 414

-S-
Sacsahuaman, 478
Sadducees, 31, 43
Sahara, 262, 263
Saint Andrew, Monastery of, 144
Saint Damian, chapel of, 374
Saint Helens, Mount, 46
Saint Peter's Cathedral, 209
Saladin, 350–352, 380
Salerno, University of, 392
Salisbury Castle, 338
Samudragupta, 71
Santiago de Compostela, 308
Saracens, 209
Saragossa, 209, 306
Sardinia, 145
Sarmatians, 275
Sarqaq (people), 292
Saudi Arabia, 287
Sawiras, 287, 288
Saxons, 100, 124, 125, 145, 208, 209, 229, 314
Scandinavia, 115, 214, 254, 443
Scheherazade, 212
Scotland, 136, 137, 194, 216, 303, 304, 416, 417
Scots (Scottish), 124, 137, 304, 416, 417
Scott, Sir Walter, 355
Scythians, see Persians
Second Order of Saint Francis (Poor Clares), 376, 378
Sefarad, 114, 182. See also Andalus, al-; Cordoba
Seine River, 216, 470
Seljuk Turks, 323–325, 351, 483
Seneca, 24
Serbia, 227
Serbs (Yugoslavians), 483
Serene, 343
Sergius Paulus, 13
Shah Jahan, 411
Shahriyar, 212
Shakespeare, William, 303, 304, 436

Shang dynasty, 155
Sheng Kuo, 283
Shikoku, 139
Shinto, 140
Shotoku Taishi, Prince, 114, 140, 141, 356, 357
Siberia, 292
Sicilians, 393
Sicily, 145, 391, 393, 395
Silas, 15
Simon, Saint, 249, 288, 289
Siward of Northumberland, 304
Skerries, 291. See also Greenland
Skraelings, 302
Slavs, 226, 227, 273, 275
Slovakia, 227
Sluys, 434
Smyrna, 28
Snorri, 301
Snowland (Snaeland), 254. See also Iceland
Song dynasty, 282–285, 410
Sophia, Saint, 129, 130, 276, 277, 483
South America, 258, 370, 477, 481
South Americans, 477
South Island (of New Zealand), 258, 259
Spain, 45, 100, 114, 182–184, 186, 201, 207–209, 211,
    216, 305–307, 341, 343, 376, 377, 477, 487
Spanish, 186, 305–307, 432, 479–481
Stafford, Robert, 355
Stephen (apostle), 4, 10, 11
Stephen of Cloyes, 381
Stewart Island (of New Zealand), 258
Stilicho, 102
Stirling Bridge, Battle of, 416
Stonehenge, 228, 229, 314, 317
Stuart, David, 82
Stylites, Simeon, 85
Sudan, 169, 263
Sui dynasty, 155, 156
Sweden, 179, 181, 214–216, 222, 254
Swedes, 180
Swift, River, 451
Switzerland, 208, 463
Symphorosa, 28
Synod of Worms, 320
Syria, 183, 185, 201, 326

-T-
Taj Mahal, 411
Tajikistan, 169
Talmud, 343
Tamerlane, 411

Tanais, 275
Tang dynasty, 156–158, 282
Tariq, 183
Tarsus, 11, 12
Tasman, Abel, 260
Tawantinsuyo, 477, 479
Tchaikovsky, Peter Ilich, 277
Temple (Jewish), 9, 32, 39, 53, 54, 100, 323, 343, 350, 380
Tenochtitlan, 430
Tertullian, 30
Texcoco, Lake, 430
Thailand, 115, 411
Thames River, 384
Theodora, 128–131, 482, 483
Theodosia, 275
Theodosius II, 97
Thessalonica, 226
Thjodhild, 291, 300
Thor, 194, 224, 255
Thorfinn, 301
Thorvald, 301
Thulte (people), 292, 293
Tiananmen Square, 447
Tiber River, 100
Tigris River, 350
Timothy, 15
Titicaca, Lake, 479
Titus, 32, 33, 100
Tiw, 224
Toledo, 184
Tolstoy, Leo Nikolaevich, 278
Torah, *see* Mishneh Torah
Tours, 201, 207, 468
  Battle of, 201, 202
Tower of London, 316
Trajan, 27, 28
Troyes, Treaty of, 436
Tryggvason, Olaf, 300
Tunisia, 169, 212
Turkey, 11, 413, 483
Turkistan, 323, 411

-U-
Umayyad dynasty, 114, 183, 184, 186, 208, 211, 305, 341
United States, 46, 80, 94, 169, 201, 258, 260, 262, 334, 355, 370, 384, 429
Unity of the Brethren, 465, 487
Urban II, 323, 324, 325
Uruguay, 334

-V-
Valencia, 306, 307
Valentine, Saint, 4, 60
Valentinian III, 121
Valerian, 29
Vandals, 100, 183
Varangians (Swedish Vikings), 216
Vedas, 73
Venetians, 414
Venice, 413, 414
Venus, 60
Vercingetorix, 127
Verdun, Treaty of, 210
Vespasian, 32
Vesuvius, Mount, 45–47
Vietnam, 411
Vikings, 115, 214–216, 222–224, 229, 230, 255, 276, 293, 302, 304, 314, 317, 409
Vilgerdarson, Floki, 254, 255
Vinland, 216, 301, 302
Virgil, 427
Visigoths, 97, 100, 183
Vitus, Saint, 272
Vladimir I of Russia, Grand Duke of Kiev, 250, 275–277
Volga River, 276
Voltaire, 231
Vulgate, 87, 88

-W-
Wailing Wall, 162
Waitangi, Treaty of, 260
Waldensians, 249, 333, 334
Waldo, Peter, 333, 334
Wales, 136
Wallace, William, 370, 416, 417
Walter the Penniless, 324, 325
Wang, Empress, 176
Wenceslas, Duke of Bohemia, 249, 270–272
Wessex, 194, 229, 230
Western Roman Church, 276
Westminster Abbey, 315
William the Conqueror, 216, 250, 314–317, 319, 322, 336, 434
William the Pig, 381
Wiltshire, 228
Winfrid, *see* Boniface, Saint
Wu Tao-tze, 158
Wu Zetian (Wu Zhao, Mei-Niang), 157, 176–178, 282
Wycliffe, John, 369, 449–452, 462, 464, 487

-X-

Xia dynasty, 155
Xi'an (Chang'an), 157, 282

-Y-

Yadin, Yigael, 55
Yamato clan, 140
Yang Guang, 155, 156
Yang Jian, 155
Yang Kwei-fei, 159 Yangtze River, 155
Yaroslav the Wise, 277
Yellow Sea, 410
Yemen, 169
Yongle, Emperor, 446
York, 216, 315

Yorkshire, 353
Yuan dynasty, 410
Yugoslavia, 483

-Z-

Zaid, 161
Zealots (Sicarii), 39, 40
Zeeland province (in the Netherlands), 260
Zenobia, Queen, 59
Zhao Kuang Yin, 282
Zhejiang province (in China), 284
Zhongguo, *see* China
Zhou dynasty, 155
Zhu Yuanzhang, *see* Hungwu
Zimbabwe, 250, 262–264, 477

PHOTO AND ILLUSTRATION CREDITS CONTINUED:

PHOTO CREDITS

Also, **Linda Lacour Hobar:** pp. 4, 24, 28, 68, 69, 99, 101, 113 (2), 114 (knight), 115 (window), 118, 120 (sign), 121 (Vatican), 122, 125, 126, 143, 166, 167, 168, 178, 181, 185, 195 (tree), 198, 215 (ship), 223 (horn), 250 (flying buttresses), 251, 287 (archway), 321, 324, 352, 369, 371 (Christ with Cross), 378, 417, 435, 451, 457, 488. **Ron Hobar:** pp. 121 (Notre Dame), 124, 129, 215 (sunset), 226, 227 (Western church), 250 (cathedral), 257, 258 (two), 260, 270, 272, 276, 278, 292, 302, 342, 381, 400, 413, 414 (Venice), 444, 450, 463, 465, 467.

Also, **Maggie Hogan:** 228. **Ray Lacour:** pp. 230, 314, 371 (author with broken arm), 430. **Mark Lyons:** p. 84 (2). **Kathleen D. Mitchell:** pp. 9, 53, 162. **Jim Rumelhart:** pp. 370, 477, 478, 479, 480 (2), 483. **Herman and Clare Rumpke:** pp. 139, 141, 357, 359. **Carol Topp:** pp. 370, 447 (2). **David B. Smith:** pp. 80, 81, 115 (statue), 169 (2). **Scott Sheets:** pp. 16, 17, 484. **Noha Zaki:** p. 287 (papyrus painting). **Lěng Yù** on zh.wikipedia: 283 (Chinese coins) licensed CC-by-SA 3.0, original file available at http://commons.wikimedia.org/wiki/File:China_coin1.JPG; full license text available at http://creativecommons.org/licenses/by-sa/3.0/deed.en.

All photos in the Activity Supplement are by **Linda Lacour Hobar** and **Ron Hobar.**

ILLUSTRATION CREDITS

Amy Pak continued:

Quarter 2: pp. 123, 124, 128 (2), 137, 138, 140, 144, 145, 155, 156, 161 (2), 163, 164, 176, 180, 184, 194, 198, 199, 202, 207, 208, 209, 211, 212, 222, 227, 229, 231.

Quarter 3: pp. 249, 254, 259, 264, 271, 274, 276, 282, 289, 291, 301, 304, 307, 314, 316, 320, 321, 324, 325 (2), 334, 336, 337 (2), 343, 350 (2), 351, 354, 357.

Quarter 4: pp. 376, 377, 381, 383, 384, 391, 392, 396 (2), 398, 399, 410, 411, 413, 416, 427, 428, 429, 435, 442, 445, 446, 450, 459, 462, 463, 468, 477, 484, 487.

Activity Supplement: pp. 578, 591, 619, 621.

Also, **Noha Zaki:** p. 588. **Linda Lacour Hobar:** pp. 566, 570, 585, 586, 592, 599, 605, 612, 615, 623

Author cover photo by Lyons Photography, Inc., Cincinnati, Ohio.

TRADEMARKS

The following trademarks were referred to in the lessons and activities:

Jeopardy® television series game show is a registered trademark of Jeopardy Productions, Inc.

Pictionary® board game is a registered trademark of Pictionary Incorporated.

Monopoly® board game is a registered trademark of Tonka Corporation.

Post-it® stationery notes is a registered trademark of the 3M Company.

Silly String® plastic stream material and toy dispenser of this material is a registered trademark of Wham-O Manufacturing Company.

THE MYSTERY OF HISTORY

Christ-centered world history for all ages

THE MYSTERY OF HISTORY unfolds vibrant stories of heroes and heroines, victories and defeats, discovery and invention around the world through the ages. Each lesson illuminates the tapestry of mankind and helps students identify the unifying threads which run from era to era—from the beginning of the world to modern times, one side of the globe to the other.

The Mystery of History series provides a historically accurate, Christ-centered approach to world history for all ages. By incorporating hands-on activities along with reading, writing, and research projects, *The Mystery of History* offers something for all learning styles and supports all methods of education.

CHRONOLOGICAL

Beginning with Creation, *The Mystery of History* four-volume series presents world history in chronological order, covering every corner of the globe.

- Volume I: Creation to the Resurrection (c. 4004 B.C. – c. A.D. 33)
- Volume II: The Early Church and the Middle Ages (c. A.D. 33 – 1456)
- Volume III: The Renaissance, Reformation, and Growth of Nations (1455 –1707)
- Volume IV: Wars of Independence to Modern Times (1708 – 2014)

CHRISTIAN

The Mystery of History is distinctively written from a Christian worldview. Creation-based and standing on the authoritative Word of God, lessons in *The Mystery of History* are like pieces of a mosaic that reveal a much bigger picture and tell a much larger story. Together, they point toward God's redemptive plan for mankind through the Gospel of Jesus Christ.

COMPLETE

The Mystery of History Student Readers can stand alone for all ages to enjoy. For those who wish to delve deeper, the user-friendly Companion Guides bring lessons to life with multi-age activities, timeline directions, mapping exercises, Memory Card ideas, pretests, quizzes, games, worksheets, tests, film and literature suggestions, and more. It's easy to use for one student at home, ten in a co-op, or hundreds in a school.

GEOGRAPHY
Everything happens somewhere . . .

EVERYTHING HAPPENS SOME*WHERE.*
Geography is more than just place
names and gross domestic product—it's
understanding the world around us, how it
works, and how it impacts lives. Geographers ask
the questions: "Where? Why there? Why care?"
Developing a deep understanding of geography has
real-life applications beyond academics, impacting
your student's career, citizenship, and ministry. At
Bright Ideas Press, we help you show your students
how fascinating and useful geography is.

NORTH STAR GEOGRAPHY

North Star Geography is our flagship geography program
for 7th–12th grades. It is designed to give students a wide
knowledge of the world and a deep understanding of how
geography impacts all of us every day, all while fulfilling a
full high school credit. Written from a distinctly Christian
perspective by Tyler Hogan (a homeschool grad, and now
a homeschool dad), *North Star Geography* covers:

- Geography skills (such as reading maps and
  navigating)
- Physical geography (the lithosphere, hydrosphere,
  atmosphere, and biosphere)
- Human geography (social structures, culture
  and heritage, and how people interact with the
  environment)

In addition to the Student Reader, the Companion Guide
(digital copy included) contains:

- Hands-on activities and projects
- Map work, memorization, and geographic research
  questions (with answers!)
- Quizzes, a final exam, answer keys, and a convenient grading rubric

- Reproducible outline and reference maps,  ak-
  ing pages, and graphic organizers
- Detailed—yet flexible—schedules

WONDERMAPS

WonderMaps is a customizable collection of over
300 different maps. With nearly endless possibilities,
WonderMaps makes it easy to regularly integrate map
study into a variety of lessons and make the most of
every learning opportunity. Whether it's history, literature, science, current events, or Bible, maps play an
integral role in thoroughly understanding the topic at
hand.

WonderMaps is designed with easy-to-use layers that
let you customize each map. And now, you can also edit
and annotate your maps before printing!

WonderMaps includes:

- 75 maps of the world
- 60+ maps of the USA
- 150+ historical maps, including 30 biblical maps
- Map sets from *The Mystery of History Vᵢ...es
  I–IV* and *All American History Volumes I and II*

HUMANITIES

Understand the world and your God-given place in it

TRUE KNOWLEDGE REQUIRES interaction with the world around us through inquiring, thinking, and pondering. Studying the humanities gives us the opportunity to do just that—to engage with the world around us. The humanities require us to ask questions like "What was the author thinking? Why did the author write this? How does this make me feel?" or "What emotion was the composer expressing?" It is through this type of analysis and evaluation that we grow as humans—understanding the human condition, evaluating our world and our God-given place in it.

The *Young Scholar's Guide* series introduces students to the humanities through engaging lessons that include biographies, exposure to the arts, and application of students' learning. Biographies are sure to mention other artists who influenced the composers (*A Young Scholar's Guide to Composers*) or poets (*A Young Scholar's Guide to Poetry*), to help students understand that artists don't create in a vacuum but draw on the work of their contemporaries and those who came before. With activities for every learning style, our *Young Scholar's Guide* series includes timelines, note-taking pages, coloring pages, and notecard activities to cement learning. Each book encourages students to apply what they learn. *A Young Scholar's Guide to Composers* provides a YouTube playlist of suggested pieces and guides students to listen for specific musical elements. *A Young Scholar's Guide to Poetry* encourages students as they write their own poems to incorporate the poetic elements learned. Best of all, the clear information in these books guides and enables even those parents who aren't knowledgeable about these subjects to teach them with confidence.